for Jon

and in memory of Great Aunt Myra Snow

INTRODUCTION

Natural Food Feasts from the Eastern World is a natural foods cookbook using common easy-to-obtain ingredients in the cuisines of China, Japan, Indonesia, India and the Middle East. More, *Feasts* is an illustrated manual telling exactly how to cook these foods. It contains over 800 illustrated recipes of which more than half are vegetarian. Every section covers basic techniques and has recipes for every course, including meat, chicken and fish dishes. To help find and use all these recipes and ingredients, menus are provided and the book is fully indexed.

The origins of *Feasts* go back many years. My great aunt Myra spent several years in China as a missionary and sent our family several fascinating gifts from there. Some of my first memories are of a pewter cup etched with small animals, and a set of beautifully carved chopsticks. A culture which produced such unusual objects intrigued me. My family's curiosity about and reverence for the East led to my early enjoyment of Chinese cooking. Since then, numerous meals in Chinese and Japanese restaurants have bolstered my interest. After moving to Canada I added Indonesian and Indian cooking to my experience, and broadened my knowledge of Chinese and Japanese cooking. Later I was able to use this knowledge of the world's cuisines in exchange with friends who knew Middle Eastern and Indian food.

Like many people at the beginning of the '70s I became interested in natural foods, and found that Eastern food already conformed to the cardinal principle: not to cook out the vitality. As well as nutrition, Eastern menus traditionally offer good taste and beautiful colors. No grits-and-brown-rice meals here; Eastern food is a feast for the eye and the palate as well as the body. Importantly for busy people, short cooking time and inexpensive ingredients make Eastern cooking a quick, economical alternative to prepackaged, denatured foods.

Feasts resulted from the urging of friends and neighbors who kept asking for recipes and finally talked me into teaching them for a year of Thursday nights. The class became "the Thursday Night Feast" because each meeting we prepared fifteen to twenty dishes and then feasted on them. In the six years since then, Russian Hill gourmets and natural food freaks have worked side-by-side in my kitchen, testing and criticizing each recipe in *Feasts*. Recipes have been tried repeatedly so that they are easy to follow and produce a uniform result no matter how inexperienced the cook.

In this book, Margaret Putnam's illustrations have taken the place of my demonstrations: each step that would have been demonstrated in class has been illustrated in sequence in *Feasts*. Every process—how to sautée onions, how to soak mushrooms, how to deep fry—is fully explained where it is used, each time it is used. Variations are always directly opposite the main recipe on a two-page spread. The only nonvariable is method. When you are out of this or low on that, you may choose a suggestion from among many alternative ingredients that are

NATURAL FOOD FEASTS

From the Eastern World

China
Japan
India
Indonesia
The Middle East

Sigrid M. Shepard

Illustrated by Margaret V. Putman

Arco Publishing, Inc.

New York

Published 1979 by Arco Publishing, Inc.
219 Park Avenue South, New York, N. Y. 10003

Copyright © 1976, 1977 by Sigrid M. Shepard

Illustrations copyright © 1976 by Margaret V. Putman

Library of Congress Cataloging in Publication Data

Shepard, Sigrid M
  Natural food feasts from the Eastern World.

    Published in 1976 under title: The Thursday night
feast and good plain meals cookbook.
    Includes index.
    1. Cookery, Oriental.   2. Cookery (Natural foods)
I. Title.
TX724.5.A1S44 1979   641.5'95   78-15773
ISBN 0-668-04699-6

Printed in the United States of America

easy to find in North America. Nor are elaborate kitchen equipment and appliances necessary for preparing Eastern dishes. *Feasts* shows that old-fashioned cast iron pots and frying pans and improvised steamers work as well as woks, karhais and bamboo steamers; many of the feasts-or-just-plain-meals have been prepared over Yukon campfires as well as in fancy urban kitchens.

For centuries, both philosophical and economic reasons have determined that the countries covered in this book have practised low-meat or vegetarian cuisine. Protein sources such as beans, bean curd, sprouts, lentils, nuts and seeds are used in place of, or to enhance the small use of, expensive meat. The appeal of eastern food is that proteins are naturally balanced after centuries of experience with vegetarian and low-meat diets. Eat the way the people of these countries do and you will have a wholesome natural foods diet. If you wish further information on balancing vegetarian proteins, Francis Lappe's *Diet for a Small Planet* covers the subject extensively.

Feasts is designed for both vegetarians and meat eaters. It calls for a sparing use of both eggs and diary products. The major ingredient substitutions that make it a natural foods cookbook are honey for sugar, brown rice and whole wheat for white processed varieties, and cold-pressed unsaturated vegetable oils for animal fat. Sea salt is always used; monosodium glutamate (MSG), never. Herbs and spices are essential in *Feasts'* recipes, as are beans, grains, fruits, vegetables and nuts, but prepackaged and prepared foods are never used. Most of the dishes can be served hot or cold the next day for lunch or dinner, so nothing need be wasted. In fact, one of the beauties of eastern food is that a leftover dinner can turn into a feast with the addition of one or two dishes.

Sautee, steaming, stir-frying, deep frying and grilling are the main methods of cooking. The East's low fuel supplies and small stoves with no ovens have dictated these methods; they translate to Western kitchens with good results for energy conservation. Much kitchen time is spent in grating, slicing, julienning, chopping, and marinating—all preparatory steps which others can speed up by lending a hand. Although many dishes in *Feasts*, by being short on cooking time, are long on preparation time, there are also many quick meals. You can put together many of them in 20 to 30 minutes—cashew fried rice and cabbage with sesame dressing is a quick Chinese supper; noodles steamed with egg custard and vegetables (Odamaki Mushi) is a quick one-pot Japanese meal, and the Indonesians cook fish, soy sauce, peppers and onions together and serve it with coconut cooked rice and a shrimp-peanut-pepper tossed salad for yet another quick meal.

North Americans have accomplished the strange feat of habitually turning one of the richest harvests the world has ever enjoyed into a nutritional wasteland of tasteless food. *Feasts* was put together to help you discover the simple methods and fine foods which millions of people for thousands of years have used to provide themselves with a delicious and wholesome diet. Whether you eat to live or live to eat, make it a Feast.

ACKNOWLEDGMENTS

Without the aid of many good friends this book would not have been possible. I am particularly grateful to my Great Aunt Myra, a missionary in China, who brought the Orient to my attention when I was very young. Six people have generously shared their knowledge of eastern food with me, and many of their recipes occur in *Natural Food Feasts*. After eating Chinese feasts at our home, Yeshwant Bakshi gave me most of my Indian recipes, saying "If you can prepare Chinese food, you can do Indian too." Jan and Claire Scheffer and Wilhelmina Scheffer introduced me to hot Indonesian food and over the years have contributed many recipes to my files. In Berkeley my neighbor Diana Nash showed me how to prepare many of the Middle Eastern dishes in *Feasts* in trade for my knowledge of other cuisines, and started me on the road to my cooking classes. Mr. Sato generously gave of his time to teach me how to make tofu after I had struggled to perfect the technique for five years.

A large group—namely my cooking classes—have had a hand in helping me form this book, and I wish to thank all of them for their assistance and helpful criticism. Together with them I have tried out and corrected all the recipes in *Feasts*. Barbara Wilson has been invaluable in helping me test my recipes and bolstering my morale when it has been down—plus adding a few recipes herself to make the collection more complete. McCarthy Coyle has provided much needed assistance in writing introductions. Most of all I wish to thank my patient husband, Jon, who has served as guinea pig, assistant, copy editor, and critic throughout this long project. My typists, Shirley Newberry and Arel Manchester, have proved invaluable; they not only typed the bulky, difficult manuscript but also helped immensely by editing it as they typed.

TABLE OF CONTENTS

CHAPTER ONE
CHINESE

INTRODUCTION

The Confucian quest for beauty and art, even in food, has been balanced by the Taoist concern for simplicity and nutrition so that Chinese cuisine, humble or elaborate, strives for an exquisite blend of aroma, texture, flavor and appearance. Low-cost, nutrition and variety is the natural result.

It is not necessary to be a super-chef to master the simple methods of Chinese food preparation. Most dishes are prepared in the wok and the steamer rack which fits inside it. However, these are not a necessity; any large heavy pot will do. The major rule in steaming is to have your water boiling before the vegetables go in; this assures quick uniform cooking. If you're stir-frying in a wok the heat source should first be red-hot so the ingredients cook almost instantly. Again, when deep-frying have your oil hot enough so the food doesn't sink to the bottom and absorb too much oil. The point of these techniques is to save natural flavor and vitamin goodness. Simmering is usually reserved for meats and firm vegetables.

Green onions, fresh ginger root, wine, soy sauce, sesame oil, hot peppers and stock are some condiments used to enhance the flavors of bok choy, snowpeas and shui choy, as well as our western vegetables tomatoes, corn, broccoli, carrots and yellow onions. Chinese cooks use mung and soy bean sprouts as well as soy bean curd, which is one of the major sources of vegetable protein in China. Any meat can substitute for bean curd; I suggest chicken, fish or beef but the Chinese often cook with pork. Ingredients are always chopped and sliced in uniform size so as to cook evenly and condiments are minced and blended to enhance but not conceal the food flavors. Almonds, cashews, walnuts and sesame seeds also enrich the Chinese diet.

A Chinese dinner usually consists of one dish per person as well as soup and rice. Everyday dinners can include one stir-fry and a cold vegetable dish plus soup and rice or noodles. Very simple dinners for two can consist of a main dish with a vegetable and protein source and rice or noodles. Westerners may want to follow the soup to sweet routine. Or you can do as the Chinese traditionally do and enjoy your soup in the middle of dinner, alternate a hot dish or course with a cold one and sample sweets to clear the palate after an especially spicey or heavy course.

MEAL SUGGESTIONS

1 TO 2 PERSONS
Egg Fu Yung (will keep well for another day)
Rice

Sweet and Sour Eggs
Rice
Sesame Cabbage Salad

Noodles with Shrimp and Stock
Soy Dressed Vegetables

Stir-Fry Vegetable with meat, nuts or bean curd
Rice
Soup (optional)

Lunches: Leftovers or Bean Curd with Syrup
Breakfast: Congee

3 TO 5 PERSONS
Light Chicken Soup
Curry Beef Vegetables
Cashew Chicken
Rice
Steamed Buns
Sesame Cabbage
Almond Curd

Bean Curd, Mushroom and Green Soup
Egg Roll
Tomato and Onion Salad
Steamed Bean Curd
Sweet and Sour Eggs
Broccoli and Onion Stir-Fry with Cashews
Rice
Sweet Fried Apples or Bean Curd with Syrup

Egg Drop Soup
Egg Fu Yung
Sesame Celery Salad
Savory Bean Curd with Clouds-Ear Mushrooms
   and Vegetables
Rice
Almond Cookies or Fruit

Large Stir-Fry with Meat and Vegetables
Rice
Soup
Cold Vegetable Dish (optional)

Large Savory Main Dish with Vegetables
Rice
Soup
Cold Vegetable Dish (optional)

FEASTS

Feast I Mixed [10 to 12 people]
Cold Course:
   Sweet Savory Mushrooms
   Deep Fried Chicken Balls
   Sweet and Sour Cucumbers
Soup:
   Bean Curd and Green Soup

Cold Course:
   Egg Roll
   Tomato and Onion Salad
   Soy Dressed Chicken
Hot Course:
   Steamed Buns
   Rice
   Savory Soy Chicken
   Bok Choy and Mushroom Stir-Fry
Cold Course:
   Almond Curd
   Almond Cookies

Feast II Vegetarian [10 to 12 people]
Cold Course:
   Egg Rolls
   Tomato and Onion Salad
   Sesame Celery Salad
Soup:
   Egg Drop Soup
Cold Course:
   Crushed Radishes
   Sweet and Sour Cucumbers
Hot Course:
   Savory Bean Curd with Clouds-Ear Mushrooms
      and Vegetables
   Broccoli and Onion Stir-Fry with Cashews
   Steamed Buns with Cashew Filling
   Fried Noodles
Cold Course:
   Precious Rice Pudding

Feast III Vegetarian [8 to 10 people]
Cold Course:
   Savory Mushrooms
   Sweet and Sour Chinese Cabbage
   Fried Egg Rolls
Soup:
   Winter Melon Soup
Hot Course:
   Sweet Savory Eggs
   Bean Curd in Black Bean Sauce with Tomatoes
   Steamed Buns with Cashew Filling
   Rice
Cold Course:
   Almond Curd with Mandarin Oranges

Feast IV Meat [12 to 14 people]
Cold Course:
   Sweet Savory Mushrooms
   Savory Chicken Livers
   Deep Fried Chicken Balls
Soup:
   Sizzling Rice Soup
Cold Course:
   Soy Dressed Chicken
   Crab Meat Egg Rolls
   Tomato and Onion Salad with Beef
Hot Course:
   Snowpeas or Green Beans and Meat with Tomatoes
   Steamed Buns with Chicken and Mushroom Filling
   Sweet and Sour Pork
   Rice
Cold Course:
   Almond Curd or Sweet Fried Bananas
   Almond Cookies

BASIC INGREDIENTS

FIVE SPICES MIX

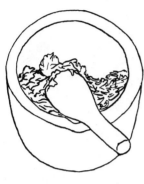

1 part star aniseed
1 part licorice root
1 part cardamom
1 part dried orange peel
1 part cinnamon

When whole spices are used grind each separately in a blender or mortar and pestle. Measure after grinding. Mix well. If ground spices are used, mix well. Store in tightly covered container away from light and heat.

TEN SPICES MIX

1 part star aniseed
1 part dried orange peel
1 part cinnamon
1 part ginger
1 part licorice root
1 part cardamom
1 part nutmeg
1 part cumin
1 part red pepper
1 part black pepper

When whole spices are used grind each separately in a blender or mortar and pestle. Measure after grinding. Mix well. If ground spices are used, mix well. Store in tightly covered container away from light and heat.

PLUM SAUCE   [Makes 1½ cups]

1 cup fresh plums
  OR 1½ cups canned plums
½ cup green tomato chutney, pureed in blender [See Basic Indian section]
½ cup mild honey
1 Tbsp. rice vinegar
3 thin slices fresh ginger root, minced
½ to 1 tsp. Ten spices mix

Chop and pit plums. Place in heavy saucepan with other ingredients. Bring to boil over high heat. Stir constantly. Reduce heat to low. Simmer 1 hour. Stir often to prevent burning. Puree through a foodmill. Place in a jar. Chill. Do not double recipe as it will not thicken. Plum sauce keeps indefinitely in refrigerator. Use for a side dish with rice at a main meal. Also used in cooking fowl.

HOT MUSTARD SAUCE   [Makes 1 cup]

1 cup boiling water
2 Tbsp. rice vinegar
½ tsp. sea salt
½ cup powdered mustard

Mix mustard and salt. Slowly add boiling water to mustard. Mix constantly to prevent lumpy sauce. Add vinegar. Mix well. Place in a tightly covered container. Chill 1 hour or overnight before using. Keeps indefinitely in refrigerator. Use for meat dipping sauce.

SPROUTS   [Makes about 1 quart]

½ cup mung beans
  OR soybeans
  OR lentils

Soak beans overnight in warm water. Drain. Place in a covered container. I use a canning jar with a sprout lid (can be purchased at any natural foods store). If no sprout lid is available cover top of jar with double layer of cheesecloth held on with a thick rubber band or canning jar ring. Sit jar on side in a warm dark place — or cover jar with towel and set in warm place. Rinse sprouts with water (not ice cold since this retards sprouting). Rinse 1 to 2 times a day. Soybeans should be rinsed 4 or 5 times a day. Be sure to rinse completely each time or beans will ferment. Takes 2 to 3 days to fill jar with sprouts. Store in refrigerator up to 1 week.

The secret of good Chinese food is a good stock. Many Chinese dishes have a stock base. No monosodium glutamate (MSG) is necessary if a rich stock is used. For vegetarians, soybean stock and bean sprout stock are included. These can be used in place of meat stock in any recipe.

CHICKEN STOCK   [Makes 6 cups]

1 chicken, cut into 8 to 10 pieces
  OR bones and skin from 2
  filleted chickens
½ inch cube fresh ginger root
1 green onion, cut in half
  lengthwise
8 cups water

Place ingredients in large saucepan. Cover. Bring to boil over high heat. Remove cover. Skim top of liquid 3 to 5 minutes to remove foam and excess fat. Cover. Reduce heat to medium low. Simmer 50 minutes to 1 hour until chicken meat easily comes off bones. Line a colander or sieve with a damp cloth (old sheet or well boiled old diaper). Place over a large bowl. Pour chicken and stock into sieve or colander. Remove chicken from bones. Reserve for other dishes. Chill stock overnight and remove fat. Stock keeps up to 1 week in refrigerator. Keeps well frozen. Freeze in ice cube trays. Store cubes in plastic sacks for easy use.

BEAN SPROUT STOCK   [Makes 6 cups]

1 lb. bean sprouts
¼ inch fresh ginger root
1 green onion, cut in half
  lengthwise
6 cups water

Place ingredients in large saucepan. Cover. Bring to boil over high heat. Reduce heat to medium low. Simmer 30 minutes. Do not overcook (stock will become bitter). Line a colander or sieve with a damp cloth (old sheet or well boiled old diaper). Place over a large bowl. Pour stock into sieve or colander. Discard pulp. Stock does not keep well unfrozen. For easy use, freeze in ice cube trays and store cubes in plastic bags.

MUSHROOM STOCK   [Makes 1 cup]

4 to 6 dried mushrooms
1½ cups boiling water

Place mushrooms in bowl. Pour boiling water over them. Place weight on mushrooms to keep under water. Soak 15 minutes to 1 hour. Remove mushrooms from water. Squeeze dry. Remove tough stems. Reserve mushrooms for other use. Stock keeps up to 1 week. Keeps well frozen. For easy use, freeze in ice cube trays and store cubes in plastic bags.

FISH STOCK   [Makes 6 cups]

1 lb. white fish
½ inch fresh ginger root
1 green onion, cut in half
  lengthwise
6 cups water

Place ingredients in a large saucepan. Cover. Bring to boil over high heat. Reduce heat to low. Simmer 30 minutes. Strain stock through a muslin cloth. Reserve fish for Congee. Stock keeps well frozen. Freeze stock in ice cube trays. Store cubes in plastic sacks for easy use.

SOYBEAN STOCK   [Makes 6 cups]

2 cups soybeans
½ inch fresh ginger root
2 green onions, cut in half
  lengthwise
12 cups water

Place ingredients in a large saucepan. Cover. Bring to boil over high heat. Reduce heat to medium low. Simmer 2 to 3 hours until soybeans are tender. Strain stock. Reserve soybeans for other dishes. Stock keeps well frozen. Freeze stock in ice cube trays. Store cubes in plastic sacks for easy use.

BASIC INGREDIENTS

MEAT STOCK [Makes 6 cups]

3 to 4 lbs. soup bones [beef, pork, etc.]
½ inch fresh ginger root
2 green onions, cut in half lengthwise
8 cups water

Place ingredients in a large saucepan. Cover. Bring to boil over high heat. Remove cover. Skim top of liquid 3 to 5 minutes to remove foam and excess fat. Cover. Reduce heat to medium low. Simmer 1 to 2 hours until meat easily comes off bones. Line a colander or sieve with a damp cloth (old sheet or well boiled old diaper). Place over a large bowl. Pour soup bones and stock into sieve or colander. Remove meat from bones. Reserve for other dishes. Chill stock overnight. Remove fat. Stock keeps up to 1 week in refrigerator. Freeze in ice cube trays. Store cubes in plastic sacks for easy use.

BEAN CURD BOX [Make 2]

A box out of wood (do not use cedar as bean curd will taste like cedar) 4 inches by 5 inches and 6 inches high. It should have a bottom and a lid. The bottom of the box should be inset 1 inch. Sides and bottom should have small holes drilled in them to allow liquid to drain from bean curd. A lid which fits just inside and is quite snug should be made. It is put on the bean curd after pouring the curded liquid into the box. A weight is placed on top of the lid so it will force most of the water from the curd so the lid should just fit within the inside dimensions of the box.

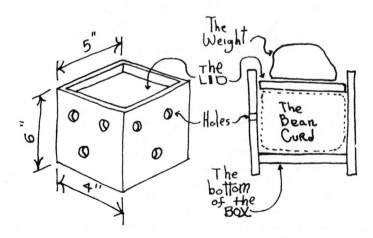

TOFU [Bean Curd—Soy Cheese—Bean Cake]
WHOLE SOYBEAN METHOD [Makes 2 large cakes]

2 cups soybeans
6 cups water

Place soybeans in a large bowl. Cover with water. Soak 6 to 8 hours or overnight. Drain. Soybeans will swell to approximately 5 cups.

MAKING PUREE:

12 cups water   BLENDER :

Place 1 cup soaked soybeans in blender with a little over 1 cup water. Blend 30 seconds to 1 minute until soybeans are a fine puree. Pour puree into a very large heavy saucepan. Blend next cup of soybeans and water. Continue until all soybeans are ground. Do not blend more than 1 cup at a time because soybeans will not be sufficiently ground. Add rest of water left over from grinding to soybean puree.

CORONA HANDMILL OR MEAT GRINDER:

Place soaked soybeans on an absorbent towel. Pat dry. Put soybeans through a handmill or meat grinder 1 cup at a time. Use fine grind. Place ground soybeans in a very large heavy saucepan. Grind next cup of soybeans. Grind until all soybeans are ground. Slowly add water to soybeans. Mix constantly so no lumps form.

COOKING:

Bring soybean puree to boil over medium heat. Stir constantly. Have cold water handy to add to soybean puree as it comes to a boil so it does not boil over (it does this very easily). Reduce heat to medium low or pull back from hot part of stove. Cook 30 to 40 minutes until foam goes down, bubbles get small and remaining foam turns light gray. Stir often to prevent burning. Remove from heat.

MAKING SOYMILK:

Place a colander over a large bowl. Line colander with a damp cloth (cotton tea towel, old sheet, or well boiled old diaper). Pour cooked soybean puree into colander. Drain 10 minutes. Wash saucepan at once as soybean puree is hard to remove when it gets cold. After puree has drained, form cloth into a bag and squeeze excess liquid from puree. Make sure not to get any pulp into bowl as this will make bean curd grainy. Pulp can be used for soybean casseroles, added to bread or omelets, or fed to the chickens — they love it.

CURDING:

1 Tbsp. epsom salts
¼ cup boiling water

OR IN PLACE OF ABOVE:
¾ cup strained lemon juice
**   OR ¾ cup rice vinegar**
**   OR ¾ cup cider vinegar**
**   OR 2 tsp. nigiri**
**   and**
**   1 cup cold water**

Mix salts with water. Dissolve. Pour one of curding agents (epsom salts water, lemon juice or vinegar) into warm soymilk. Pour in a circular motion to distribute curding agent well. Circle wooden spoon gently through soymilk 2 or 3 times. Let sit 10 minutes. Line bean curd boxes, colander or sieve with a damp cloth. Make sure cloth fits well because any wrinkle will show up on bean curd later. Pour curded soymilk into boxes, colander or sieve. Fold cloth over top of bean curd. Place lid (plate that just fits colander or

sieve or box lid) on top of bean curd. Place weight on lid. Too heavy a weight will force some of the curd through the cloth. A jar filled with water is a good weight. I have a couple of favorite rocks that are just right so they sit on my shelf and are designated bean curd rocks. Press 1 to 3 hours depending on how firm you like your bean curd. Remove from bean curd mold. Remove cloth at once. Wash cloth well, otherwise curd will stick to it. To store, place curd in a bowl of cold water. Keeps 1 to 2 weeks if water is changed daily.

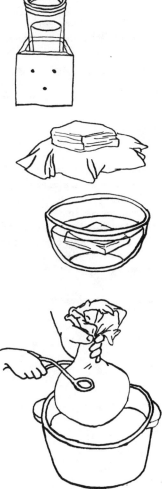

SOYMILK POWDER METHOD

1 cup soymilk powder
4 cups water

[Makes 1 small cake]

Mix soymilk powder with water slowly so no lumps are formed. If a blender is available, blend 2 cups water with soymilk powder and then add rest of water and blend well. Pour soymilk into top of double boiler. Cook 30 to 40 minutes until foam goes down, bubbles get small and remaining foam turns light gray. Stir often to prevent burning.

MAKING SOYMILK:

Place a large sieve over a bowl. Line with a damp cloth (cotton tea towel, old sheet, or well boiled old diaper). Pour cooked soymilk into sieve. Drain 10 minutes. Wash double boiler at once as soymilk is hard to remove when it gets cold. After soymilk has drained, form cloth into a bag and squeeze excess liquid from puree. Make sure not to get any pulp into bowl as this will make bean curd grainy. Pulp can be used for soybean casseroles, added to bread or omelets, or fed to the chickens.

1 tsp. epsom salts
2 Tbsp. boiling water

OR IN PLACE OF ABOVE:
3 to 4 Tbsp. strained lemon juice
  OR 3 to 4 Tbsp. rice vinegar
  OR 3 to 4 Tbsp. cider vinegar
  OR ½ to ¾ tsp. nigiri
  and
  ½ cup cold water

CURDING:

Mix salts with water. Dissolve. Pour one of curding agents (epsom salts water, lemon juice or vinegar) into warm soymilk. Pour in a circular motion to distribute curding agent well. Circle wooden spoon gently through soymilk 2 or 3 times. Let sit 10 minutes. Line bean curd box or sieve with a damp cloth. Make sure cloth fits well because any wrinkle will show up on bean curd later. Pour curded soymilk into cloth-lined bean curd box or sieve. Fold cloth over top of curd. Place lid (plate that just fits sieve or box lid) on top of bean curd. Place weight on lid. Too heavy a weight will force some of curd through the cloth. Press bean curd 1 to 3 hours depending on how firm you like your bean curd. Remove from bean curd mold. Remove cloth at once. Wash cloth well, otherwise curd will stick to it. To store, place curd in a bowl of cold water. Keeps 1 to 2 weeks if water is changed daily.

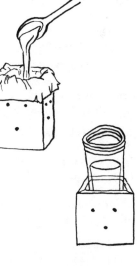

SOUPS

Chinese soups can be served with any dinner meal. The rich hearty ones make excellent lunches. Soups like Fish Ball or Bean Curd, Mushroom and Green Soup can be used as main dishes for simple meals. At feasts, soups can be served at the beginning, as a contrast in the middle, or to clear the palate after a rich course.

EGG DROP SOUP   [Serves 4 to 6]

4 cups chicken stock
OR soybean stock

Bring stock to boil in a large saucepan.

2 green onions, julienned
3 thin slices fresh ginger root,
julienned
2 Tbsp. soy sauce
1 cup fresh or frozen green peas
OR green beans, cut into pea-
sized pieces, presteamed 3 to 5
minutes

Add ingredients to stock and mix well. Bring stock to full rolling boil again.

3 eggs, slightly beaten

If eggs are too well mixed will not form threads. Pour eggs into boiling stock in a fine thread. Stir stock with chopsticks while pouring. Stir with circular motion in same direction so long threads form. Speed of stirring determines whether eggs are globular (slow stirring), threads (medium stirring, or fine bits (brisk stirring). Thin threads are the desired result. When stock clears after addition of eggs, soup is done. Remove from heat and serve hot. Good, quick dinner soup. Good hot or cold for lunch the next day.

FISH SOUP   [Serves 4 to 6]

4 dried mushrooms
1 cup boiling water

OR IN PLACE OF ABOVE:
4 to 6 fresh mushrooms
[wild ones best], cut into 1/8
inch slices. Do not soak.

Place mushrooms in bowl. Pour boiling water over them. Place weight on mushrooms to keep under water. Soak 15 minutes to 1 hour. Remove from water and squeeze dry. Remove tough stem. Cut mushrooms into ¼ inch strips. Reserve stock for other use.

½ lb white fish fillet, cut into
½ inch cubes
1 Tbsp. arrowroot starch
1 Tbsp. soy sauce
1 Tbsp. sake
OR dry sherry
OR rice vinegar

Mix fish cubes with other ingredients until well coated. Marinate 15 to 30 minutes.

5 cups fish stock
1 cup mushroom stock
OR vegetable stock

Bring stock to boil in a large saucepan. Add fish. Mix to separate the pieces of fish (gently to prevent fish from breaking up). Add mushrooms. Bring to a boil again. Reduce heat to low. simmer 1 to 2 minutes.

2 green onions, julienned
3 thin slices of fresh ginger root,
  julienned
1½ Tbsp. soy sauce
1 tsp. sea salt
1 thin slice citrus peel
  [lemon, tangerine or orange],
  julienned

Increase heat to high. Add ingredients to stock. Mix gently. Bring to a boil. Remove from heat. Serve hot. A good dinner soup. Good cold for lunch next day.

LIGHT CHICKEN SOUP   [Serves 4 to 6]

4 dried mushrooms
1 cup boiling water

OR IN PLACE OF ABOVE:
4 to 6 fresh mushrooms, cut into
  1/8 inch slices. Do not soak.

Place mushrooms in bowl. Pour boiling water over them. Place weight on mushrooms to keep under water. Soak 15 minutes to 1 hour. Remove from water and squeeze dry. Remove tough stem. Cut mushrooms into ¼ inch strips. Reserve stock for later use.

4 to 5 cups chicken stock

Place stock in large saucepan. Bring to boil over high heat.

2 green onions, julienned
2 thin slices fresh ginger root,
  julienned
2 Tbsp. soy sauce
½ to 1 tsp. sea salt
½ chicken breast, cut
  into ¼ inch strips
¼ cup small shrimp, washed
  [optional]
5 to 6 snowpeas, snipped and
  strings removed, cut into thirds
  OR 4 green beans, cut into thin
  diagonal slices
1 Tbsp. sake
  OR dry sherry
  OR rice vinegar

Add to stock. Mix well so chicken is separated into individual pieces. Bring to a boil again. Remove from heat. Serve at once. Good dinner soup. An excellent feast soup. I like it cold for lunch the next day if there is any left over.

VARIATION:

LIGHT MEAT SOUP   [Serves 4 to 6]

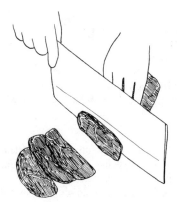

¼ lb boneless meat
  [pork or beef],
  cut into thin strips
4 to 6 cups meat stock

Follow recipe for Light Chicken Soup. Use meat in place of chicken. Use meat stock in place of chicken stock. Cook as directed. Mix well so meat strips are well separated. Good dinner soup. An excellent feast soup. I like it cold for lunch the next day if there is any left over.

CHICKEN BALL SOUP   [Serves 4 to 6]

1 chicken breast, bones removed

Pound chicken with back of meat cleaver until well flattened. Cut into thin strips. Mince. Place in bowl.

2 green onions, minced
2 thin slices fresh ginger root, minced
1 egg white, slightly beaten
½ tsp. sesame oil [optional]
1 Tbsp. arrowroot starch
2 tsp. soy sauce
1 tsp sea salt
¼ tsp. white pepper

Add to chicken. Mix well. Marinate 30 minutes to 1 hour. Form into ½ inch balls.

5 cups chicken stock

Place stock in large saucepan. Bring to boil over high heat. Drop balls into soup one by one. Skim off foam. Reduce heat to medium and simmer 3 to 5 minutes until chicken balls cooked.

2 green onions, julienned
3 thin slices fresh ginger root, julienned
2 Tbsp. soy sauce
5 to 6 snowpeas, cut into
   3 diagonal slices
   OR green beans, cut into thin diagonal slices
   OR 1 small carrot, cut into thin diagonal slices
4 fresh mushrooms, cut into
   1/8 inch slices
1 tsp. sea salt
1 Tbsp. sake
   OR dry sherry
   OR rice vinegar

Increase heat to high. Add ingredients to stock and chicken balls. Bring to boil. Serve at once. A good dinner soup. Can be a main dish for a simple meal. Good cold for lunch the next day.

VARIATION:

MEAT BALL SOUP
[Serves 4 to 6]
½ lb. ground meat [beef or pork]
2 green onions, minced
3 thin slices fresh ginger root, minced
1 Tbsp. soy sauce
1 tsp. sesame oil
1 Tbsp. arrowroot starch
1 egg white, slightly beaten
1 tsp. sea salt
¼ tsp. black pepper

Mix ingredients well. Marinate 30 minutes to 1 hour. Form into ½ inch ball.

5 cups meat stock

Place stock in large saucepan. Bring to boil over high heat. Drop balls into soup one at a time. Skim off foam. Cook 3 to 5 minutes until meat balls done. Follow remainder of recipe for Chicken Ball Soup. Cook as directed. A good dinner soup. Can be a main dish for a simple meal. Good cold next day for lunch.

VARIATION:

FISH OR SHRIMP BALL SOUP
[Serves 4 to 6]
½ lb. raw shrimp, shelled and
   deveined
   OR fish fillet [red snapper, bass, carp, salmon, butterfish, etc.]

Pound fish or shrimp to flatten. Cut into thin strips. Mince. Follow recipe for Chicken Ball Soup. Use fish or shrimp in place of chicken. A good dinner soup. Can be a main dish for a simple meal. Good cold for lunch the next day.

SIZZLING RICE SOUP   [Serves 4 to 6]

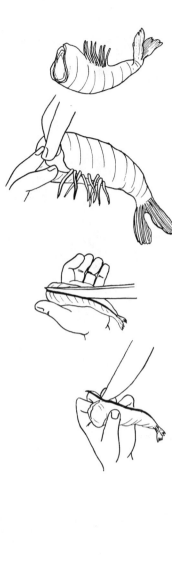

4 to 6 dried mushrooms
1 cup boiling water

Place mushrooms in bowl. Pour boiling water over them. Place weight on mushrooms to keep under water. Soak 15 minutes to 1 hour. Remove from water. Squeeze dry. Remove tough stems. Cut mushrooms into ¼ inch strips. Reserve stock for other dishes.

6 cups chicken stock

Place in large saucepan. Bring to boil over high heat.

½ lb. raw shrimp, shelled and
** deveined**
4 to 5 water chestnuts, peeled
** and cut in thin slices**
** OR 1 jerusalem artichoke, cut**
** into thin slices**
2 to 3 bamboo shoots, cut into
** thin slices [optional]**
½ head Chinese green [bok choy,
** sou choy, etc.], stalks cut into**
** long diagonals and greens**
** shredded**
** OR ½ lb. North American**
** cooking greens [spinach, swiss**
** chard, etc.], shredded**
2 thin slices fresh ginger root,
** julienned**
2 green onions, julienned
1 small red or green chili pepper,
** julienned**
** OR ¼ to ½ tsp. chili pepper**
** minced**

Add to soup. Bring to boil. Reduce heat to medium. Simmer 3 to 5 minutes until shrimp are pink and tender.

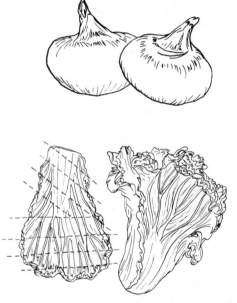

1½ cups rice crusts saved from
** bottom of rice cooking pan,**
** broken into 1 inch pieces**
** OR 1½ cups cooked rice,**
** pressed flat on greased**
** cookie sheet and dried out at**
** 200° in an oven for 10 to 15**
** minutes [do not brown],**
** break into 1 inch cubes**
2½ cups peanut oil
** OR vegetable oil**
2 Tbsp. to ¼ cup sesame oil

Heat a wok. Add oil. Heat over high heat until a piece of rice crust added sizzles. Add rice crusts. Fry 2 to 3 minutes until golden brown. Drain. While still very hot place in a serving bowl. Pour hot soup over rice crusts - which will sizzle - hence sizzling rice soup. A great feast dish. Good meal-in-a-bowl dish. Do not serve cold. Rice crusts can be made ahead and stored in a tight container. Fry when soup is made.

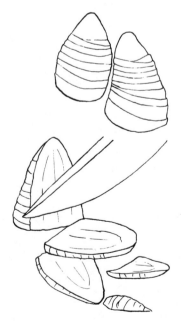

Too Cold   Too Hot   Correct Temperature

HOT AND SOUR FISH SOUP [Serves 4 to 6]

¼ **cup dried shrimp**
1 cup boiling water

Wash shrimp well. Place in a small bowl. Pour boiling water over them. Place weight on shrimp to keep under water. Soak 30 to 60 minutes until soft and bendable. Remove from water. Reserve stock for later use. Cut shrimp in halves if large variety.

4 to 6 dried mushrooms [optional]
1 cup boiling water

Place mushrooms in small bowl. Pour boiling water over them. Place weight on mushrooms to keep under water. Soak 15 minutes to 1 hour. Remove from water. Reserve stock for other use. Remove tough stems. Cut mushrooms into thirds.

2 thin slices fresh ginger root,
   julienned
1 lb. white fish fillet
   [red snapper, butterfish, carp,
   turbot, sole, cod, etc.], cut into
   1 by 3 inch pieces
5 cups fish stock
1 cup shrimp stock

Place stock in large saucepan. Add fish, shrimp and ginger to stock. Bring to boil over medium heat. Skim any foam. Simmer 5 to 10 minutes until fish is flaky.

2 stalks celery, cut in to thin
   diagonal slices
   OR 2 stalks bok choy, stalks cut
into thin diagonals and greens
into 1 inch slices
2 Tbsp. rice vinegar
   OR dry sherry
   OR sake
½ **tsp. white pepper**
1 to 4 dried chili peppers,
   minced
1 tsp. soy sauce
½ **tsp. sea salt**
1 green onion, cut into thin
   diagonal slices

Add to stock and fish along with mushrooms. Cook over medium heat 3 to 5 minutes until celery is just tender. Serve hot. A good dinner soup. Good cold for lunch the next day.

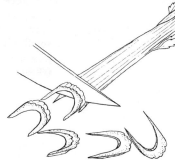

VARIATION:

HOT AND SOUR MEAT SOUP [Serves 4 to 6]

¼ **lb boneless meat**
   [beef or pork],
     cut into thin strips
1 to 2 cakes bean curd [optional],
   cut into 1 inch cubes
½ **tsp. black pepper**
5 cups meat stock
1 cup mushroom stock

Follow recipe for Hot and Sour Fish Soup. Use meat and bean curd in place of fish and dried shrimp. Use meat and mushroom stock in place of shrimp and fish stock. Use black pepper in place of white pepper. Add meat when fish is added. Add bean curd with last ingredients. Cook as directed. Serve hot. A good dinner soup. Served with vegetables and rice it can be used as a main dish for a simple dinner. Good cold for lunch the next day.

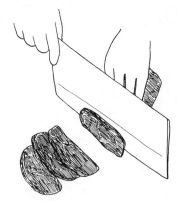

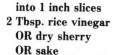

VELVET CHICKEN WITH SWEET CORN SOUP [Serves 4 to 6]

½ **chicken breast, bones removed** 1 **Tbsp. arrowroot starch**	Dust meat with arrowroot starch. Pound meat with back of meat cleaver to flatten. Cut into thin strips and then cut into small pieces crosswise of the strips.

2 **tsp. sake**
   OR dry sherry
   OR rice vinegar
1 **egg white, well beaten**
	Add to minced chicken. Mix well. Marinate 15 to 30 minutes.

1½ **cups whole kernel corn**
   OR whole kernel canned corn
   OR ¾ cup canned cream corn
	Drain canned corn. Place whole corn kernels in blender. Blend until smooth and creamy. Do not blend cream corn. If no blender is available, mince corn well and then place in a bowl and crush well.

5 **cups chicken stock**	Place stock in a large saucepan. Bring stock to boil over high heat.

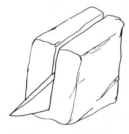

1 **tsp. sea salt** 1 **tsp. soy sauce** 2 **thin slices fresh ginger root, minced** ¼ **tsp. freshly ground black pepper**	Add ingredients to stock with corn and chicken. Mix well so each piece of chicken separates. Bring to boil. Simmer 2 to 3 minutes if using raw corn. Stir soup until thickened. Remove from heat.
2 **green onions, cut into thin diagonal slices**	Add green onions. Mix. Serve hot. Good dinner soup. Excellent for lunch, hot or cold.

BEAN CURD SOUP [Serves 6 to 8]

6 **cups bean sprout stock**	Bring stock to boil in a large saucepan.

2 **thin slices fresh ginger root, julienned**
3 **Tbsp. soy sauce**
1 **Tbsp. sake**
   OR dry sherry
   OR rice vinegar
1 **tsp. sea salt**
	Add to stock and simmer for 1 minute

1 **cup chinese cabbage, cut into 1 inch sections** ½ **cup fresh mushrooms, slices thin**	Add to stock and simmer for 1 minute.
½ **cup bean sprouts**	Add to stock and simmer for 1 minute

1 **lb. bean curd, cut into ½ inch cubes**	Add to stock and simmer for 2 minutes. Serve at once. Good dinner soup. Does not reheat well.

BEAN CURD, MUSHROOM AND GREEN SOUP [Serves 4 to 6]

4 dried mushrooms
1 cup boiling water
OR IN PLACE OF ABOVE:
4 to 6 fresh mushrooms, cut into
  1/8 inch slices. Do not soak.

4 cups soybean stock
  OR bean sprout stock
1 cup mushroom stock

2 green onions, julienned
2 thin slices fresh ginger root,
  julienned
5 stalks bok choy, stalks cut into
  long thin diagonals and greens
  cut into 1 inch strips
  OR any other Chinese green,
  stalks cut into long diagonals
  and greens cut into 1 inch strips
  OR any North American cooking
  green, cut into 1 inch strips
  [spinach, swiss chard, etc.]
1 to 2 cakes bean curd, cut into
  ½ by 1 inch pieces
3 Tbsp. soy sauce
1 tsp. sea salt
1 Tbsp. sake
  OR dry sherry
  OR rice vinegar

Place mushrooms in bowl. Pour boiling water over them. Place weight on mushrooms to keep under water. Soak 15 minutes to 1 hour. Remove from water. Remove tough stem. Cut mushrooms into ¼ inch strips. Reserve stock for later use.

Place stock in large saucepan. Bring to boil over high heat.

Add to stock. Mix gently so bean curd does not break into smaller pieces. Bring to boil again. Remove from heat. Serve at once. Good dinner soup. An excellent feast soup. I like it cold for lunch the next day if there is any left over.

VARIATION:
BEAN CURD, MUSHROOM AND GREEN SOUP WITH MEAT [Serves 4 to 6]

¼ lb. boneless meat
  [pork or beef],
  cut into thin strips
4 cups meat stock
1 cup mushroom stock

Follow recipe for Bean Curd, Mushroom and Green Soup. Use meat stock in place of soybean stock. Add meat strips before bean curd. Mix well so meat strips are well separated. Add rest of ingredients and cook as directed. An excellent dinner soup. Can serve as a main dish for a simple meal. Excellent cold for lunch the next day.

VARIATION:
CHICKEN AND GREEN SOUP [Serves 4 to 6]

½ chicken breast, cut into
  ¼ inch strips
4 cups chicken stock
1 cup mushroom stock

Follow recipe for Bean Curd, Mushroom and Green Soup. Use chicken stock in place of soybean stock. Use chicken in place of bean curd. Mix well so chicken is separated into individual pieces. Cook as directed. An excellent dinner soup. A good feast soup. Good cold for lunch the next day.

VARIATION:
BEAN CURD, MUSHROOM AND GREEN SOUP WITH CHICKEN [Serves 4 to 6]

½ chicken breast, cut into
  ¼ inch strips
4 cups chicken stock
1 cup mushroom stock

Follow recipe for Bean Curd, Mushroom and Green Soup. Use chicken stock in place of soybean stock. Add chicken before bean curd. Mix well so chicken is separated into individual pieces. Add rest of ingredients and cook as directed. An excellent dinner soup. Can serve as a main dish for a simple meal. Excellent cold for lunch the next day.

VARIATION:
MEAT AND GREEN SOUP [Serves 4 to 6]

¼ lb. boneless meat
  [pork or beef],
  cut into thin strips
4 cups meat stock
1 cup mushroom stock

Follow recipe for Bean Curd, Mushroom and Green Soup. Use meat stock in place of soybean stock. Use meat in place of bean curd. Cook as directed. Mix well so meat strips are well separated. An excellent dinner soup. A good feast soup. Good cold for lunch the next day.

WINTER MELON OR WINTER SQUASH SOUP [Serves 4 to 6]

1 inch square dried tangerine peel [optional]
¼ cup boiling water

Place peel in small bowl. Pour boiling water over it. Weight to keep under water. Soak 30 minutes until soft. Remove white inner membrane. Mince.

6 cups chicken stock
1 chicken breast, cut into ¼ inch strips
OR 1 cup cooked chicken meat, shredded
1 green onion, julienned
1 slice fresh ginger root, julienned
1 tsp. sea salt

Place stock and tangerine peel in a large pot. Bring to boil over high heat. Add chicken. Mix well to keep pieces separated. If cooked meat is used, add later. Simmer over medium heat 5 minutes.

1 to 2 lbs. winter melon, peeled, seeded and cut into ½ by 1 inch pieces
OR winter squash, peeled, seeded and cut into ½ x 1 inch pieces

Add winter melon. Bring to a boil over high heat. Cover. Reduce heat to medium. Simmer 20 to 30 minutes until melon is tender. Add cooked meat at this time. Simmer 1 minute to heat meat. A good dinner soup for a cold winter evening. Good for lunch also. Can be easily reheated.

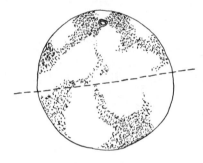  

VARIATION:
WINTER MELON OR WINTER SQUASH SOUP WITH MEAT [Serves 4 to 6]

¼ lb. boneless meat [pork or beef], cut into thin strips
OR 1 cup cooked meat [pork or beef], cut into thin strips
6 cups meat stock

Follow recipe for Winter Melon Soup. Use meat in place of chicken. Use meat stock in place of chicken stock. If cooked meat is used add at last minute and just heat. Cook soup as directed. Serve hot for dinner. Can easily be reheated for a hearty winter lunch.

COLD DISHES

The cold dishes are divided into appetizers and salads and can be served Western style. However, in a traditional Chinese meal cold courses alternate with hot.

EGG ROLL [Serves 6 to 8]

Egg skins:

5 eggs and 3 egg yolks, beaten
   until well mixed but not frothy
1/2 tsp. soy sauce
1/4 tsp. sea salt
1 Tbsp. peanut oil
   OR vegetable oil

Add soy sauce and salt to eggs. Mix well. Heat a medium size cast iron skillet over medium heat. Oil skillet with a pastry brush. When a small drop of egg sets well, add 3 Tbsp. egg mixture. Roll pan to evenly distribute egg mixture. Fry 1 to 2 minutes until edge is brown and easily pulls away from sides of skillet. Loosen edges with a knife and flip egg skin. Fry 30 seconds. Remove from pan. Oil pan again. Repeat process until all the egg mixture is used. Set egg skins aside for later use.

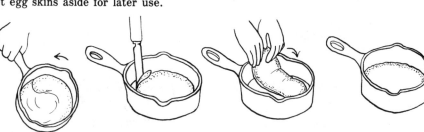

Filling: Prepare after egg skins are made.

1 egg white
1 Tbsp. arrowroot starch
1 tsp. mild honey
1 tsp. sea salt

Beat egg white slightly. Add starch. Mix well. Add salt and honey. Mix well.

2 green onions, minced
3 thin slices fresh ginger root,
   minced
4 hard-boiled eggs, chopped
2 cups bok choy, stalks minced
   and greens shredded
1 small carrot, grated

Mix vegetables and eggs. Add above starch paste and mix well.

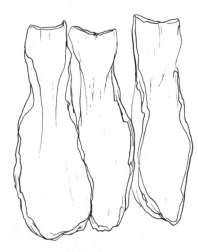

Paste:

2 egg whites
1 Tbsp. arrowroot starch

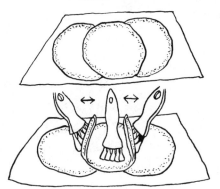

Beat egg whites slightly. Add starch. Mix well.

ASSEMBLING AND STEAMING EGG ROLL: Place 3 egg skins on moist cloth. Set middle skin on top of 2 side ones so that it overlaps them 1/3 on each side. Brush upper sides and overlaps of egg skins well with paste. Place 2 Tbsp. bok choy filling on each side skin. Place 1 Tbsp. bok choy filling on center skin. Spread mix evenly and thinly over skins. Tightly roll left side of roll towards the center. Bunch up towel to hold side and tightly roll other side to center also. Seal center of scroll with paste. Wrap tightly in moist cloth. (Rolls can be made with individual skins. Paste skin with egg first. Place 3 Tbsp. filling on skin — leave 1 inch free on right side. Spread filling thinly over skin leaving free strip. Roll tightly from left. Paste edge with egg paste. Wrap in cloth.) Continue process until all skins are used. Steam rolls 20 minutes. Unwrap at once — if chilled in cloth, rolls will stick to cloth. If serving hot cut at once into 1 inch slices. If cold, chill whole and then cut into 1 inch slices when ready to serve. Served cold as an appetizer or snack. Hot as a main dish. Good served as one of dishes in cold course at a feast.

VARIATION:

CRAB OR CHICKEN EGG ROLL [Serves 6 to 8]

1 cup crab meat, drained
  OR 1 cup cooked chicken meat,
  shredded

Follow recipe for Egg Roll. Use crab or chicken in place of hard-boiled eggs in filling. Cook as directed. Serve cold as an appetizer or hot as a main dish. Good served as one of dishes in cold course at a feast.

DEEP-FRIED SHRIMP OR CRAB EGG ROLLS
[Serves 6 to 8]
Egg skins:

4 eggs and 3 egg yolks, beaten
  until well mixed but not frothy
½ tsp. sea salt
1 Tbsp. peanut oil
  OR vegetable oil

Add salt to eggs. Mix well. Heat a medium cast iron skillet over medium heat. Oil skillet with a pastry brush. When a small drop of egg sets, add 3 Tbsp. egg mixture. Roll pan to evenly distribute egg mixture. Fry 1 to 2 minutes until edge is brown and easily pulls away from sides of skillet. Loosen edges with a knife and flip egg skin. Fry 30 seconds. Remove from pan. Oil pan again. Repeat process until all egg mixture is used. Set egg skins aside for later use.

Filling: Prepare after egg skins are made.

1 Tbsp. peanut oil
  OR vegetable oil
2 thin slices fresh ginger root,
  minced
2 green onions, cut into
  thin diagonal slices

Heat a wok over high heat. Add oil Heat until a piece of onion added sizzles. Add ginger and onion. Stir and fry 30 seconds.

½ cup fresh or frozen peas
  OR green beans, cut into
  long thin diagonals

Add to wok. Stir and fry 1 minute to heat.

½ cup small fresh or canned
  shrimp
  OR crab meat

Add to wok. Stir and fry 1 minute to heat.

2 cups cabbage, shredded
  OR bean sprouts
½ tsp. sea salt
½ tsp. mild honey

Add cabbage or bean sprouts. Sprinkle salt and honey over vegetables. Mix well. Cook 30 seconds. Remove from heat. Place in a bowl. Cool.

1 egg white
1 Tbsp. arrowroot starch
1 tsp. mild honey
1 tsp. sea salt
½ tsp. soy sauce

Beat egg white slightly. Add starch. Mix well. Add salt and honey. Mix well. Pour over filling mixture. Mix well.

Paste:

2 egg whites
1 Tbsp. arrowroot starch

Beat egg whites slightly. Add starch. Mix well.

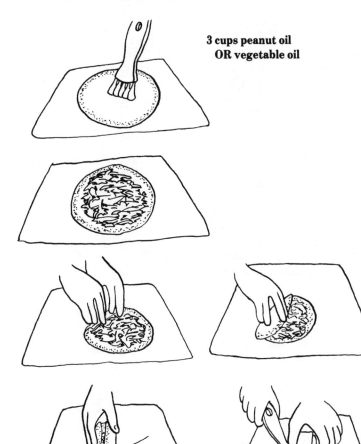

3 cups peanut oil
OR vegetable oil

ASSEMBLING AND FRYING EGG ROLL:
Place egg skin on bread board sprinkled lightly with arrowroot starch. Paste inside of egg skin. Place 3 Tbsp. filling on skin. Spread filling evenly over egg skin. Leave 1 inch free on right, left and top sides of egg skin. Fold right side over filling. Fold left side over filling. Roll toward unfilled top. Seal edge of roll with paste. Continue process until all skins are used. Heat a wok over high heat. Add oil and heat until a piece of egg skin added sizzles. Place 1 egg roll on a large wire spoon or tempura spoon. Lower into hot oil Fry over medium high heat 3 to 5 minutes until golden brown. Remove from oil. Fry until all egg rolls are cooked. Cut into 1 inch slices. Best served warm. Serve with mustard sauce or plum sauce to dip egg rolls in. Excellent snack or appetizer. Good served as one of dishes in cold course at a feast.

VARIATION:

VEGETARIAN DEEP-FRIED EGG ROLLS [Serves 6 to 8]

Leave out shrimp in filling

Follow recipe for Deep-Fried Shrimp or Crab Egg Rolls. Cook as directed. Leave out shrimp in filling. Excellent snack or appetizer. Good served as one of dishes in cold course at a feast.

VARIATION:

DEEP-FRIED MEAT EGG ROLLS [Serves 6 to 8]

**1 cup cooked meat
[pork or beef],
cut into small thin strips**

Follow recipe for Deep-Fried Shrimp or Crab Egg Rolls. Cook as directed. Use meat in place of shrimp or crab. Excellent snack or appetizer. served as one of dishes in cold course at a feast.

VARIATION:
DEEP-FRIED CHICKEN EGG ROLLS [Serves 4 to 6]

**1 cup cooked chicken,
cut into thin strips**

Follow recipe for Deep-Fried Shrimp or Crab Egg Rolls. Cook as directed. Use chicken in place of shrimp or crab. Excellent snack or appetizer. Good served as one of dishes in cold course at a feast.

SWEET SAVORY MUSHROOMS [Serves 4]

4 large dried mushrooms
1 cup boiling water

Place mushrooms in a small bowl. Pour boiling water over them. Place weight on mushrooms to keep under water. Soak 15 minutes to 1 hour. Remove from water. Squeeze dry. Remove tough stems. Reserve stock for use in soups and savory dishes.

2 Tbsp. peanut oil
  OR vegetable oil
2 thin slices fresh ginger root, minced
1 Tbsp. soy sauce
1 Tbsp. mild honey

Heat a small cast iron skillet over medium heat. Add oil and heat slightly. Add ginger and mix well. Add honey and then soy sauce. Bring to a boil. Reduce heat to low. Add mushrooms. Simmer 5 to 10 minutes until all liquid is absorbed. Turn mushrooms often to prevent scorching. Chill. Cut into ¼ inch slivers before serving. Excellent snack. Great feast dish served with deep-fried chicken, fish or meat balls and egg rolls as a cold course.

SAVORY CHICKEN LIVERS [Serves 4 to 6]

1 lb chicken livers
3 cups water

Wash livers. Place in a shallow saucepan. Add water. Bring to a boil over medium heat. Simmer 10 minutes. Drain liquid.

3 Tbsp. soy sauce
1 Tbsp. sake
  OR dry sherry
  OR rice vinegar
1 Tbsp. mild honey
1 tsp. five spices

Mix ingredients well. Pour over liver in saucepan. Bring to boil. Reduce heat to medium low. Simmer 15 to 20 minutes uncovered until most of the liquid is absorbed. Turn livers occasionally. Remove livers from pan and chill. Cut into ¼ inch strips. Serve with mustard sauce or plum sauce and sesame seeds as a dip for the liver. Excellent snack. Good served as appetizer or one of dishes in cold course at a feast.

VARIATION:

SAVORY MEAT LIVER [Serves 4 to 6]

1 lb meat liver
  [pork, calf or beef]

Follow recipe for Savory Chicken Liver. Use meat liver in place of chicken liver. Cook as directed. Excellent snack. Good served as appetizer or one of dishes in cold course at a feast.

PAN FRIED PEANUTS [Serves 6]

½ Tbsp. peanut oil
  OR vegetable oil
½ Tbsp. sesame oil
2 cups raw peanuts

Heat a cast iron skillet over medium high heat. Add oil. Heat until a drop of water added sputters. Add peanuts. Reduce heat to medium. Stir and fry 5 to 10 minutes until peanuts are golden brown. Remove from heat.

1 tsp. soy sauce
½ tsp. sea salt
1 chili pepper, minced [optional]

Sprinkle over warm peanuts. Mix well. Serve hot. An excellent snack.

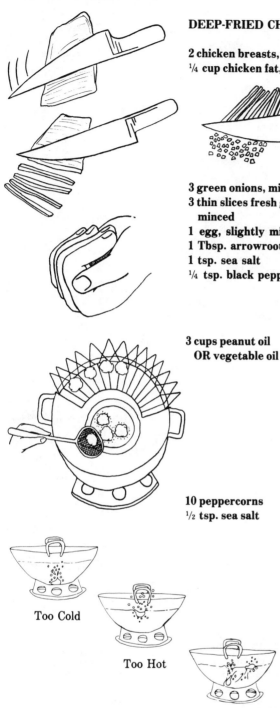

DEEP-FRIED CHICKEN BALLS   [Serves 6]

2 chicken breasts, bones removed
¼ cup chicken fat, minced

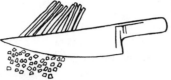
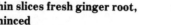

Pound chicken with the back of a meat cleaver until well flattened. Cut into thin strips and mince. Place in a bowl. Add fat to chicken and mix well.

3 green onions, minced
3 thin slices fresh ginger root, minced
1 egg, slightly mixed
1 Tbsp. arrowroot starch
1 tsp. sea salt
¼ tsp. black pepper

Add ingredients to chicken. Mix well. Marinate 30 minutes to 1 hour. Form into balls.

3 cups peanut oil
** OR vegetable oil**

Heat a wok over high heat. Add oil. Heat until a small piece of chicken added sinks to the bottom and then rises almost at once. Reduce heat to medium high. Slowly lower 5 balls one at a time into the oil. Fry 5 to 10 minutes until golden brown. Do not remove too quickly or center will not be done. Keep oil on medium high heat so it does not get too hot. When balls are brown remove from oil and drain. Repeat process until all chicken is fried. Place chicken balls in a bowl.

10 peppercorns
½ tsp. sea salt

Heat a small cast iron skillet over high heat. Add peppercorns. Parch 1 minute. Remove from pan. Crush in a mortar and pestle. Sprinkle crushed pepper and salt over chicken balls. Mix well. Serve warm. Can be made ahead and reheated in 200° oven. Excellent snack. Good served as appetizer or one of dishes in cold course for a feast.

Too Cold

Too Hot

Correct Temperature

VARIATION:
DEEP-FRIED SHRIMP BALLS   [Serves 6]

1 lb. shrimp, shelled and deveined
** OR canned shrimp**

Pound shrimp with back of meat cleaver until well flattened. Cut into thin strips and mince. Place in a bowl. Follow recipe for Deep-Fried Chicken Balls. Use shrimp in place of chicken. Cook as directed. Excellent snack. Good served as appetizer or one of dishes in cold course at a feast.

VARIATION:
DEEP-FRIED FISH BALLS   [Serves 6]

1 lb. white fish fillet
** [carp, red snapper, cod, sole, etc.]**

Pound fish with back of meat cleaver until well flattened. Cut into thin strips and mince. Place in bowl. Follow recipe for Deep-Fried Chicken Balls. Use fish in place of chicken. cook as directed. Excellent snack. Good served as appetizer or one of dishes in cold course at a feast.

VARIATION:
DEEP-FRIED MEAT BALLS   [Serves 6]

1 lb. ground meat

Follow recipe for Deep-Fried Chicken Balls. Use meat in place of chicken. Cook as directed. Excellent snack. Good served as appetizer or one of dishes in cold course at a feast.

MIXED PICKLED VEGETABLES [Makes about 2 quarts]

6 cups water 1½ cups sea salt	Place in a saucepan. Bring to boil over high heat. Stir to dissolve salt. Remove from heat. Cool until just warm to finger.
2 lbs. Chinese Cabbage, cut into 3 inch cubes 4 medium carrots, cut in half lengthwise and then cut into 2 inch pieces ½ lb. green beans OR bean sprouts	Place vegetables in a large glass casserole or a crock. Place in alternate layers - cabbage, carrot, green bean and then repeat.
2 to 6 dried chili peppers, minced	Add peppers to brine. Mix well. Pour over vegetables in crock. Cover. Let stand for 1 week. Take out amount of pickle to be used for each meal. Shred vegetables. Place in small bowl.
½ to 1 tsp. sesame oil ¼ tsp. soy sauce drop of honey	Mix ingredients well. Add to each cup of chopped pickles. Mix. Serve cold. A must at lunches and dinner. Good served at feasts.

TOMATO AND ONION SALAD [Serves 4 to 6]

1 lb. tomatoes [3 medium sized] cut in half, seeded, washed and drained, cut halves into thin strips
1 yellow onion, cut in half lengthwise then julienned paper thin

Gently mix onions and tomatoes.

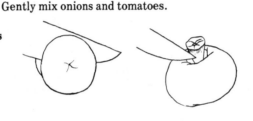

2 Tbsp. soy sauce
1½ tsp. rice vinegar OR apple cider vinegar
1 tsp. mild honey
1 tsp. sesame oil

Mix ingredients well. Pour over tomatoes and onions in a shallow dish. Marinate 20 minutes. Leave dish covered. Stir gently a few times to mix dressing with vegetables. Serve cold. An excel-dinner salad. Good served as one of dishes in cold course at a large feast.

VARIATION:

TOMATO AND ONION SALAD WITH COOKED MEAT [Serves 4 to 6]

1 cup cooked meat [pork or beef], cut into thin small strips

Follow recipe for Tomato and Onion Salad. Add meat along with onion. Cook as directed. A good dinner salad. Excellent as one of dishes in cold course at a large feast.

VARIATION:

TOMATO AND ONION SALAD WITH COOKED CHICKEN [Serves 4 to 6]

1 cup cooked chicken meat, cut into thin small strips

Follow recipe for Tomato and Onion Salad. Add chicken along with onion. cook as directed. A good dinner salad. Excellent as one of dishes in cold course at a large feast.

SESAME CELERY SALAD [Serves 4 to 6]

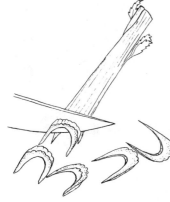

**4 large stalks celery, cut
diagonally into thin slices**

Place in shallow bowl.

**2 Tbsp. soy sauce
1½ Tbsp. rice vinegar
1 tsp. mild honey
1 Tbsp. sesame seeds
OR 1 tsp. sesame oil**

Parch sesame seeds in small heavy skillet or seed popper for 1 minute. Remove from heat and mince with knife or blend 15 seconds. If sesame oil is used the preceding steps are not necessary. Add oil to other ingredients. Mix well. Pour over celery. Marinate 20 minutes. Serve cold. Stir few times to mix dressing with celery. A good dinner salad. An excellent salad for camping as celery keeps well without refrigeration.

VARIATION:
SESAME CABBAGE SALAD [Serves 4 to 6]

**½ head green cabbage, shredded
OR ½ head Chinese cabbage,
shredded**

Follow recipe for Sesame Celery Salad. Use cabbage in place of celery. A good dinner salad. An excellent salad for camping as cabbage keeps well without refrigeration.

CRUSHED RADISHES [Serves 4]

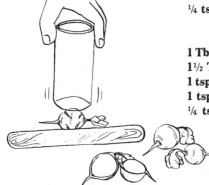

**20 radishes, washed, trimmed,
leaving a few leaves at the top
¼ tsp. sea salt**

Crack each radish with a sharp blow from the bottom of a glass. Use only crisp radishes or they will not crack well. Sprinkle with salt and chill for 15 minutes.

**1 Tbsp. soy sauce
1½ Tbsp. rice vinegar
1 tsp. mild honey
1 tsp. sesame oil
¼ tsp. sea salt**

Mix ingredients well. Pour over radishes just before serving. Mix well and serve at once. A good snack or dinner salad.

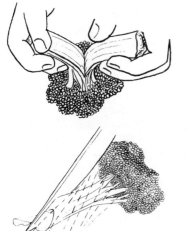

SOY DRESSED VEGETABLES [Serves 4]

**1 lb bean sprouts, steamed
1 minute
OR 4 stalks celery, cut in thin
diagonals
OR 2 medium cucumbers,
sliced thin
OR ½ lb. broccoli, sliced thin
and steamed 5 minutes
OR ½ head cabbage, shredded**

Use any one or a combination of these vegetables. Arrange them on a shallow dish. Chill.

**3 Tbsp. soy sauce
1½ Tbsp. rice vinegar
½ tsp. mild honey
1 tsp. sesame oil**

Mix honey and vinegar well. Add oil and soy sauce and mix well. Pour over vegetables. Marinate 20 minutes. Mix occasionally. Good dinner salad.

SOY DRESSED CHICKEN WITH VEGETABLES [Serves 4 to 6]

1 to 2 cups chicken reserved
  from making stock

Shred chicken with fingers into thin slivers. Do not cut with a knife. Place on a small platter.

2 medium turnips, cut in half
  lengthwise and then cut into
  thin slices
  OR 1 daikon radish, cut into
  thin round slices

Arrange on platter along with chicken.

3 Tbsp. soy sauce
1½ Tbsp. rice vinegar
  OR apple cider vinegar
½ tsp. mild honey
1 Tbsp. sesame oil

Mix ingredients well. Pour over chicken and vegetables. Marinate 30 minutes. Serve cold. Good dinner or feast salad.

VARIATION:
SOY DRESSED MEAT WITH VEGETABLES [Serves 4 to 6]

1 to 2 cups meat
  [pork or beef],
  reserved from making stock

Follow recipe for Soy Dressed Chicken with Vegetables. Use meat in place of chicken. Shred meat with fingers into thin slivers. Do not cut with a knife. Cook as directed. Good dinner or feast salad.

SWEET AND SOUR CUCUMBERS [Serves 4 to 6]

2 Tbsp. vegetable oil
5 to 10 peppercorns

Heat a medium cast iron skillet over medium high heat. Add oil. Heat until a drop of water added sputters. Add peppercorns. Fry 1 minute. Remove from heat. Crack peppercorns with a pestle or back of a spoon.

4 green onions, julienned

Place skillet with pepper oil over medium high heat. Add green onions. Stir and fry 1 minute until just tender.

3 Tbsp. soy sauce
3 Tbsp. rice vinegar
2 Tbsp. mild honey

Add honey, vinegar and soy sauce. Simmer over medium high heat 2 minutes to heat well.

1 tsp. arrowroot starch
2 tsp. water

Mix starch and water. Add to sauce, stir 1 minute until sauce thickens. Remove from heat.

2 cucumbers, cut into 2 inch
  pieces and steam 1 minute

Add cucumbers to sauce. Mix well and chill. Serve cold. Good dinner salad. Excellent as one of dishes in cold course at a large feast.

SWEET AND SOUR CHINESE CABBAGE [Serves 4 to 6]

20 leaves Chinese cabbage

Separate each leaf from stalk and wash well. Steam 3 minutes or until just limp. Steam no more than 5 leaves at a time. Trim stalk ends. Starting from top of the stem gently press out excess moisture. Roll leaves from stem end of leaf to top of leaf in a tight roll. Slice rolls into 1 inch slices. Arrange on a plate with rolls on their sides or on end. Chill 15 to 30 minutes. Press cabbage lightly and drain well. Save stock for soups.

1 Tbsp. sesame oil
  OR vegetable oil
1 to 3 dried chili peppers, minced

Heat a small cast iron skillet over medium heat. Add oil. Heat until a small piece of pepper added sizzles. Add pepper. Cook for 1 to 2 minutes until just lightly browned.

1 Tbsp. soy sauce
2 Tbsp. rice vinegar
1 Tbsp mild honey
1/2 tsp. sea salt

Add ingredients to oil. Reduce heat to medium. Stir and cook for 3 minutes until sauce is well blended. Pour over cabbage. Chill. Serve cold. Good dinner salad. Excellent dish in cold course at a large feast.

VARIATION:

SWEET AND SOUR GREENS [Serves 4 to 6]

1 lb spinach
  OR swiss chard
  OR 20 leaves green cabbage

Follow recipe for Sweet and Sour Chinese Cabbage. Use spinach, swiss chard or green cabbage in place of Chinese cabbage. Good dinner salad. Excellent dish in cold course at a large feast.

RICE, BREAD AND NOODLES

Rice or noodles are a must with every meal in China. Plain rice accompanies pungent dishes to balance the flavors. Fried rice, noodle dishes, and congee (thick rice soup) can serve as simple main dishes.

PLAIN COOKED RICE [Serves 4 to 6]

2 cups long-grain [preferred]
  brown rice
4 cups water

Place water and rice in a large heavy saucepan. Cover. Bring to a boil over high heat. As soon as the pan is steaming well reduce heat to medium low. Simmer 30 minutes. Remove from heat. Let stand 10 minutes. Do not double water when doubling recipe. Add enough water so level is 1 inch above rice.

FRIED RICE WITH NUTS [Serves 4 to 6]

2 Tbsp. vegetable oil
1 cup cashew pieces
  OR other nuts

Heat a wok over high heat. Add oil. Add nuts. Stir and fry ½ to 1 minute until nuts are lightly golden brown. Remove from pan. Set aside to add later.

¼ cup peanut oil
  OR vegetable oil
6 green onions, chopped
3 thin slices fresh ginger root,
  minced

Add oil to wok. Heat until a haze forms. Add green onions and ginger. Stir and fry 1 minute until just brown.

2 cups mixed vegetables
  [peas, sliced mushrooms, thinly
  sliced carrots, thinly sliced
  beans, etc.]

Add to wok. Stir and fry 3 to 4 minutes until vegetables just tender.

3 to 4 cups cooked long grain
  [preferred] brown rice, chilled

Add rice 1 cup at a time. Break up each cup of rice with a spoon before adding another cup. Stir and fry 4 to 6 minutes over high heat until rice begins to brown.

¼ cup soy sauce
2 tsp. mild honey
1 tsp. sea salt
1 to 2 cups bean sprouts [optional]

Add to rice and mix well. Add nuts and mix well. Serve hot. A meal-in-a-bowl for a simple vegetarian meal. Good served with a simple main dish or at a feast. Good cold for lunch the next day.

VARIATION:

MEAT STRIPS FRIED RICE [Serves 4 to 6]

1 cup cooked meat
  [pork or beef],
  cut into thin strips

Follow recipe for Fried Rice with Nuts. Use meat in place of nuts. Add meat strips just before serving rice. Mix well. Cook 1 minute to heat meat. Serve hot. A meal-in-a-bowl for a simple meal. Good cold for lunch the next day.

VARIATION:

CHICKEN STRIP FRIED RICE [Serves 4 to 6]

1 cup cooked chicken meat;
  cut into thin strips

Follow recipe for Fried Rice with Nuts. Use chicken in place of nuts. Add chicken strips just before serving rice. Mix well. Cook 1 minute to heat chicken. Serve hot. A meal-in-a-bowl for a simple meal. Good cold for lunch the next day.

VARIATION:

EGG STRIP FRIED RICE
[Serves 4 to 6]
2 to 3 eggs, beaten until well
  mixed but not frothy
½ tsp. sea salt
½ tsp. soy sauce
½ tsp. mild honey

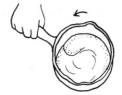

Add other ingredients to eggs. Mix well. Heat a
medium cast iron skillet over medium heat. Oil
skillet with a pastry brush. When a small drop
of egg sets, add 3 Tbsp. egg mixture. Roll pan
to evenly distribute egg mixture. Fry 1 to 2
minutes until edge is brown and easily pulls
away from sides of skillet. Loosen edges with a
knife and flip egg skin. Fry 30 seconds. Remove
from pan. Oil pan again. Repeat process until all
egg mixture is used. Cut egg skins in half. Cut
into thin strips. Set aside for later use.

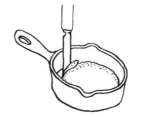

Follow recipe for Fried Rice with Nuts. Use egg
strips in place of nuts. Add egg strips just
before serving rice. Mix well. Serve hot. A
meal-in-a-bowl for a simple vegetarian meal.
Good served with a simple main dish or at a
feast. Good cold for lunch the next day.

VARIATION:

MEAT, EGG AND CHICKEN STRIP FRIED RICE
[Serves 4 to 6]

½ cup cooked meat [beef or
  pork], cut into thin strips
½ cup cooked chicken, cut into
  thin strips
½ cup egg strips

Follow recipe for Fried Rice with Nuts. Use
meat, chicken and egg strips in place of nuts.
Add meat and chicken strips just before
serving. Mix well. Cook 1 minute to heat. Place
on serving platter. Top with egg strips. Serve
hot. A good meal-in-a-bowl dish. An excellent
feast dish.

SHRIMP FRIED RICE [Serves 4 to 6]

2 Tbsp. vegetable oil
1 to 2 cups small shrimp

Heat a wok over high heat. Add oil. Heat until a haze forms. Add shrimp. Stir and fry 1 to 2 minutes until shrimp are lightly browned. Remove from wok. Set aside to add later.

3 Tbsp. peanut oil
  OR vegetable oil
6 green onions, chopped
3 thin slices fresh ginger root,
  minced

Add oil to wok. Heat over high heat until a haze forms. Add green onions and ginger. Stir and fry 30 seconds to 1 minute until just brown.

1 cup mixed vegetables [peas,
  sliced mushrooms, thinly sliced
  carrots, thinly sliced green
  beans, etc.]
  OR ½ head cabbage, cut in
  ¼ inch slices

Add to wok. Stir and fry 3 to 4 minutes until vegetables are just tender.

3 to 4 cups cooked long grain
  [preferred] brown rice, chilled

Add rice 1 cup at a time. Break up each cup of rice with a spoon before adding another cup. Stir and fry 4 to 6 minutes over high heat until rice begins to brown.

¼ cup soy sauce
2 tsp. mild honey
1 tsp. sea salt
1 cup bean sprouts [optional]

Add to rice. Mix well. Stir and fry 1 minute. Add shrimp. Mix well. Serve hot. A good dinner side dish. Can be a main dish at a simple meal. Good cold for lunch the next day. An excellent feast dish.

VARIATION:

CHICKEN FRIED RICE [Serves 4 to 6]

2 Tbsp. peanut oil
  OR vegetable oil
1 chicken breast, cut into
  thin strips

Follow recipe for Shrimp Fried Rice. Use chicken in place of shrimp. Cook as directed. Serve hot. A good dinner side dish. Can be a main dish at a simple meal. Good cold for lunch the next day. An excellent feast dish.

VARIATION:

MEAT FRIED RICE [Serves 4 to 6]

2 Tbsp. peanut oil
  OR vegetable oil
¼ lb. boneless meat [pork or
  beef], cut into thin strips

Follow recipe for Shrimp Fried Rice. Use meat in place of shrimp. Cook as directed. Serve hot. A good dinner side dish. Can be a main dish at a simple meal. Good cold for lunch the next day. An excellent feast dish.

Congee is a rice soup that is served for breakfasts or lunches but not as a soup course. Served with fish, chicken or meat and a vegetable, it makes a good simple meal.

VEGETABLE CONGEE [Serves 4 to 6]

½ **cup brown rice**
7 **cups soybean stock**
  OR water
½ **to 1 tsp. sea salt**
1 **slice fresh ginger root, minced**
dash white or black pepper

Place ingredients in a large heavy saucepan. Cover. Bring to boil over high heat. Reduce heat to medium low. Simmer 1 to 2 hours until rice becomes paste-like. Stir to prevent sticking. Remove from heat. Beat with egg beater until porridge is smooth and creamy.

1 **turnip, cut into ¼ inch cubes**
  OR 1 carrot, cut into pea-sized
     pieces
  OR 1 parsnip, cut into pea-sized
     pieces
  OR ¼ lb. green beans, cut into
     pea-sized pieces

Add one of vegetables to rice mixture. Place over medium low heat. Cook 15 to 20 minutes until vegetables just tender.

Garnish:
¼ **cup green onions, cut into**
   thin diagonal slices
   OR parsley, minced
   OR Chinese parsley, minced
   OR watercress, minced

Serve congee with one of garnishes. Place congee in individual bowls and top with sprinkle of garnish. Good lunch or breakfast.

VARIATION:

PLAIN CONGEE [Serves 4 to 6]

½ **cup brown rice**
7 **cups water**
½ **to 2 tsp. sea salt**

Follow recipe for Vegetable Congee. Leave out ginger, pepper and vegetables. Do not have to use garnish. An excellent dish when not feeling well. Good for lunch or breakfast.

VARIATION:

CHICKEN OR MEAT CONGEE [Serves 4 to 6]

7 **cups chicken or meat stock**

Follow recipe for Vegetable Congee. Use chicken or meat stock in place of soybean stock.

1 **cup cooked chicken or meat,**
  cut into thin strips

Add to congee when it has finished cooking. Heat 1 minute. Serve hot for lunch. Place in individual bowls and top with garnish. Can be a main dish for a simple dinner meal.

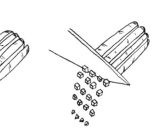

VARIATION:

FISH CONGEE [Serves 4 to 6]

7 **cups fish stock**

Follow recipe for Vegetable Congee. Use fish stock in place of soybean stock.

½ **to 1 cup fish reserved from**
   making fish stock
1 **Tbsp. soy sauce**
2 **tsp. sake**
   OR dry sherry
   OR rice vinegar
½ **tsp. mild honey**
1 **tsp. sesame oil**
1 **thin slice fresh ginger root,**
  minced

Mix ingredients with fish. Marinate 30 minutes. Place in bowl. Pour congee over fish mixture. Mix well. Place congee in individual bowls. Top with garnish. Good lunch dish. Can be a main dish at a simple meal.

STEAMED BUNS [Serves 6 to 8]
Makes about 2 to 3 dozen

Dough:

5 cups whole-wheat flour
2¼ cups lukewarm water
4 tsp. yeast

OR IN PLACE OF ABOVE:
use your favorite whole-wheat
bread dough

Place flour in a large bowl. Make indentation in top of flour. Place yeast in indentation. Pour ¾ cup lukewarm water over it. Let dissolve 5 minutes. Add remainder of ingredients to flour. Mix well. Turn dough on lightly floured board. Knead 10 to 15 minutes. Work dough with moist hands so no flour is worked into dough. Knead until dough is elastic and forms blisters on outside. Place dough in oiled bowl. Cover with moist cloth. Set aside to double, about 2 hours.

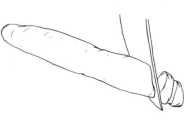

ASSEMBLING AND STEAMING:

Punch dough down. Divide in half. Form into long ropes 2 inches in diameter. Cut dough into 1 to 1½ inch slices and shape into round smooth balls. With a circular motion of fingers form into 1/8 inch thick rounds. Place 1½ to 2 Tbsp. filling in center of each round. Make sure to keep oil from filling off edge of dough or bun won't seal. Pinch two opposite sides together. Bring other two sides together in center and pinch. Seal top well. Twist top of bun to seal well and remove excess dough. Place buns on lightly floured board and let rise 20 to 30 minutes until dough springs back when touched. Invert buns on a steam rack covered with moist cloth. Allow room for buns to expand while steaming. Steam 15 to 20 minutes until dough is no longer sticky. A good feast dish. An excellent snack. Serve hot or cold with soy sauce. A good one-day pack trip meal since it is a sealed sandwich that doesn't need wrapping. Keeps well 2 to 3 days.

Fillings:

CASHEW AND GREEN ONION FILLING

3 cups cashew pieces, well
chopped
2 cups green onions, chopped
4 thin slices fresh ginger root,
minced
2 Tbsp. soy sauce
3 Tbsp. sesame oil
½ tsp. sea salt

Mix ingredients well. Cover and marinate for 20 minutes.

MEAT AND GREEN ONION FILLING

¼ lb. beef or pork [pot roast,
flank steak, etc.]
OR ground meat

2 cups green onions, chopped
4 thin slices fresh ginger root,
minced
1 Tbsp. soy sauce
1 Tbsp. sake
2 Tbsp. sesame oil
½ tsp. sea salt

Pound meat with the back of a meat cleaver until well flattened. Cut into thin strips and mince.

Mix ingredients together with beef. Cover and marinate for 20 minutes.

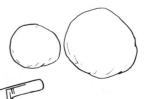

FILLINGS:

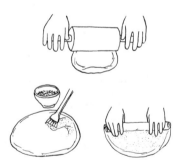

CHICKEN AND MUSHROOM FILLING

3 to 4 dried mushrooms
1 cup boiling water

Place mushrooms in a bowl. Pour boiling water over them. Place weight on mushrooms to keep under water. Soak 15 minutes to 1 hour. Remove from water. Squeeze dry. Remove tough stems. Cut mushrooms into thin slivers and then chop.

1 to 2 chicken breasts

Pound meat with the back of a meat cleaver until well flattened. Cut into thin strips and mince.

6 green onions, chopped
4 thin slices fresh ginger root, minced
2 Tbsp. soy sauce
1½ Tbsp. sesame oil
½ tsp. sea salt
½ tsp. mild honey

Mix ingredients together with chicken and mushrooms. Cover and marinate for 20 minutes.

VARIATION:

SHRIMP OR CRAB AND MUSHROOM FILLING

½ lb. cooked shrimp
 OR crab meat

Pound shrimp with back of meat cleaver. Mince. Follow recipe for Chicken and Mushroom filling. Use shrimp or crab in place of chicken.

SESAME-FLAVORED FLOWER ROLLS   MAKES 2 DOZEN

½ batch steamed bun dough
 OR dough left over from
making steamed buns

OR IN PLACE OF ABOVE:
 Use your favorite whole wheat bread dough

Cut dough in half. Place half of dough on well floured bread board. Roll into 12 by 20" rectangle. Roll second half also.

4 Tbsp. sesame seeds

Heat a small cast iron skillet over high heat. Add seeds. Parch 30 seconds to 1 minute until seeds are just lightly browned. Remove from heat. Crush slightly with a mortar and pestle or blend for 20 seconds.

2 Tbsp. sesame oil
1 tsp. sea salt
1½ tsp. mild honey

Mix ingredients well. Spread over dough rectangles. Sprinkle toasted sesame seeds evenly over dough. Roll dough like cinnamon rolls, starting from the long side. Cut each roll into 12 slices. Firmly press center of each roll with chopsticks. Pull ends of cut sides away from center of roll. Press ends of extended sides together. Bring under roll and press together. Place on floured board with pinched side down. Let rise 30 minutes until dough springs back when touched. Place buns on a steam rack covered with moist cloth. Allow room for buns to expand while steaming. Steam 15 to 20 minutes until dough is no longer sticky. Remove from heat. Serve with savory main dishes. Good served as regular rolls.

Wheat Noodle dishes are one of the staples in the Northern Chinese diet. They are easy and quick to prepare and can be a meal-in-a-bowl.

FRIED NOODLES WITH VEGETABLES [Serves 4 to 6]

1 lb. whole wheat spaghetti
  OR whole wheat vermicelli
  OR soy noodles
6 cups water

Place water in a large saucepan. Bring to boil over high heat. Add noodles. Reduce heat to medium low. Mix to separate noodles. Cover. Simmer 5 to 10 minutes until noodles are tender. Drain. Rinse well. Chill.

2 to 4 dried mushrooms
1 cup boiling water

OR IN PLACE OF ABOVE:
  4 fresh mushrooms, cut into thin slices

Place mushrooms in bowl. Pour boiling water over them. Place weight on mushrooms to keep under water. Soak 15 minutes to 1 hour. Remove from water. Squeeze dry. Remove tough stems. Cut mushrooms into ¼ inch strips. Reserve stock for later use.

3 to 6 green onions, chopped
3 thin slices fresh ginger root, minced
3 Tbsp. sesame oil
  OR peanut oil
  OR vegetable oil

Heat a wok over high heat. Add oil. Heat until a haze forms. Add ginger and green onions. Stir and fry 1 minute until lightly browned.

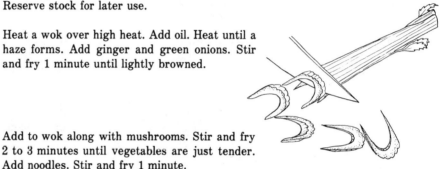

1 cup celery, cut into thin diagonal slices
  OR 2 carrots, cut into thin diagonal slices
  OR 1 cup green beans, cut into thin diagonal slices
  OR 1 cup asparagus, cut into thin diagonal slices
  OR 1 cup green peas
  OR ½ head green cabbage, cut into 1 inch cubes
  OR any other firm uncooked vegetable cut into thin diagonal slices

Add to wok along with mushrooms. Stir and fry 2 to 3 minutes until vegetables are just tender. Add noodles. Stir and fry 1 minute.

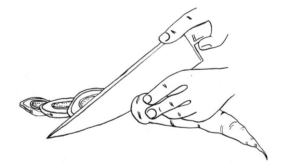

Sauce:

3 Tbsp. soy sauce
1 Tbsp. sake
  OR dry sherry
  OR rice vinegar
1 tsp. mild honey
½ to 1 tsp. sea salt
1 cup mushroom stock

Add to noodles and vegetables. Bring to boil. Mix well. Reduce heat to medium. Cover. Simmer 5 to 10 minutes until all liquid is absorbed. Remove from heat. Serve hot. This dish is also good cold for lunches or breakfast the next day.

VARIATION:

FRIED NOODLES WITH VEGETABLES AND CASHEWS
[Serves 4 to 6]

1 cup cashew pieces
3 Tbsp. vegetable oil

Heat a wok over high heat. Add oil. Immediately add nuts. Cook 1 to 2 minutes until light brown. Remove from oil. Reserve for later use.

Follow recipe for Fried Noodles with Vegetables. Cook cashews first. Add cashews just before serving. Serve hot. A good meal-in-a-bowl dish. Good cold for lunch or breakfast the next day.

VARIATION:

FRIED NOODLES WITH VEGETABLES AND CHICKEN
[Serves 4 to 6]

1 chicken breast, cut into
  ¼ inch strips
3 Tbsp. peanut oil
  OR vegetable oil

OR IN PLACE OF ABOVE:
1 cup cooked chicken, cut into
  ¼ inch slices [Do not fry]

Heat a wok over high heat. Add oil. Heat until a haze forms. Add chicken. Stir and fry 2 to 3 minutes until lightly browned. Remove from pan. Reserve for later use.

1 cup chicken stock

Follow recipe for Fried Noodles. Cook chicken first. Use chicken stock in place of mushroom stock in sauce. Add chicken with sauce. Cook as directed. Serve hot. A good meal-in-a-bowl dish. Good cold for lunch or breakfast the next day.

VARIATION:

FRIED NOODLES WITH VEGETABLES AND BEAN CURD [Serves 4 to 6]

1 to 2 cakes bean curd, cut into
  into ½ by 1 inch pieces

Follow recipe for Fried Noodles with Vegetables. Add bean curd with sauce. Cook as directed. Serve hot. A good meal-in-a-bowl dish. Good cold for lunch or breakfast the next day.

VARIATION:

FRIED NOODLES WITH VEGETABLES AND MEAT [Serves 4 to 6]

¼ lb. boneless meat [beef or
  pork], cut into thin strips
3 Tbsp. peanut oil
  OR vegetable oil

OR IN PLACE OF ABOVE:
1 cup cooked meat, cut into
  ¼ inch slices [Do not fry]

Heat a wok over high heat. Add oil. Heat until a haze forms. Add meat. Stir and fry 2 to 3 minutes until no longer pink. Remove from pan. Reserve for later use.

1 cup meat stock

Follow recipe for Fried Noodles with Vegetables. Cook meat first. Use meat stock in place of mushroom stock in sauce. Add meat with sauce. Cook as directed. Serve hot. A good meal-in-a-bowl dish. Good cold for lunch or breakfast the next day.

VARIATION:

FRIED NOODLES WITH VEGETABLES AND SHRIMP [Serves 4 to 6]

¼ lb. fresh small shrimp
  OR 1 can canned shrimp,
  drained

Follow recipe for Fried Noodles with Vegetables. Add shrimp with sauce. Cook as directed. Serve hot. A good meal-in-a-bowl dish. Good cold for lunch or breakfast the next day.

FRIED NOODLES WITH MUSHROOMS AND CABBAGE [Serves 4 to 6]

½ **to 1 lb. whole wheat spaghetti**
  OR whole wheat vermicelli
  OR soy noodles
6 **cups water**

Place water in a large saucepan. Bring to boil over high heat. Add noodles. Reduce heat to medium low. Mix to separate noodles. Cover. Simmer 5 to 10 minutes until noodles are tender. Drain. Rinse well. Chill.

4 **to 6 dried mushrooms**
1 **cup boiling water**

OR IN PLACE OF ABOVE:
  4 **fresh mushrooms, cut into**
    thin slices

Place mushrooms in a bowl. Pour boiling water over them. Place weight on mushrooms to keep under water. Soak 15 minutes to 1 hour. Remove from water. Squeeze dry. Remove tough stems. Cut mushrooms into ¼ inch strips. Reserve stock for later use.

4 **green onions, julienned**
1 **clove garlic, crushed and minced**
2 **thin slices fresh ginger root,**
  minced
4 **Tbsp. peanut oil**
  OR vegetable oil

Heat a wok over high heat. Add oil. Heat until a haze forms. Add ginger, garlic and green onions. Stir and fry 1 minute until lightly browned.

½ **head green cabbage, cut into**
  1 **inch cubes**

Add cabbage along with mushrooms. Stir and fry 2 to 3 minutes until cabbage and mushrooms are just tender. Add noodles. Stir and fry an additional 2 to 3 minutes to heat well and mix with other ingredients.

Sauce:
1 **cup mushroom stock**
1 **Tbsp. sake**
  OR dry sherry
  OR rice vinegar
1 **Tbsp. soy sauce**
1 **tsp. sea salt**
¼ **tsp. black pepper**
1 **tsp. mild honey**

Add to noodles. Mix well. Bring to boil. Reduce heat to medium. Cover. Simmer 5 to 10 minutes until all liquid is absorbed. Remove from heat. Serve hot. This dish good cold for lunch or breakfast.

VARIATIONS:

Use the same variations as for Fried Noodles with Vegetables.

NOODLES AND CHICKEN WITH STOCK [Serves 4 to 6]

1 lb. whole wheat spaghetti
  OR whole wheat vermicelli
  OR soy noodles
6 cups water

Place water in a large saucepan. Bring to boil over high heat. Add noodles. Reduce heat to medium low. Mix to separate noodles. Cover. Simmer 5 to 10 minutes until noodles are tender. Drain. Rinse in hot water. Place in 4 to 6 individual serving bowls.

1 to 2 cups cooked chicken,
  cut small
3 green onions, julienned

Place chicken and onions on top of noodles in bowls.

5 cups chicken stock
1 tsp. sea salt
1 Tbsp. soy sauce
½ tsp. mild honey

Place in a large saucepan. Bring to a boil over high heat.

2 stalks bok choy, stems cut into long thin diagonals and greens cut into 1 inch slices
  OR 2 large leaves Chinese cabbage, stems cut into long thin diagonals and greens cut into 1 inch slices
  OR ¼ lb. spinach, cut into 1 inch strips
  OR 2 large leaves swiss chard, cut into 1 inch strips
  OR any other cooking green cut into 1 inch strips
4 or 5 mushrooms, sliced thin

Add vegetables to stock. Bring to boil. Cover. Reduce heat to medium. Simmer 1 minute. Mix well. Ladle stock and vegetables over noodles in individual bowls. Mix. Serve hot. A good lunch dish. Makes a good dinner side dish or a simple meal-in-a-bowl.

VARIATION:

NOODLES WITH SHRIMP AND STOCK [Serves 4 to 6]

¼ lb. fresh small shrimp
  OR 1 can canned shrimp, drained
Follow recipe for Noodles and Chicken with Stock. Use shrimp in place of chicken. Cook as directed. Serve hot. A good lunch. A meal-in-a-bowl for a simple dinner.

VARIATION:

NOODLES WITH BEAN CURD AND STOCK

1 to 2 cakes bean curd, cut into ½ by 1 inch cubes
5 cups soybean stock
  OR chicken stock

Follow recipe for Noodles and Chicken with Stock. Use bean curd in place of chicken. Use soybean stock in place of chicken stock. Cook bean curd with stock. When mixing stock and vegetables with noodles make sure to mix gently so bean curd is not broken into small pieces. Serve hot. A good lunch. A meal-in-a-bowl for a simple dinner.

VARIATION:

NOODLES WITH FISH AND STOCK [Serves 4 to 6]

1 to 2 cups cooked fish, cut into thin strips
5 cups fish stock
Follow recipe for Noodles and Chicken with Stock. Use fish in place of chicken. Use fish stock in place of chicken stock. Cook as directed. Serve hot. A good lunch. A meal-in-a-bowl for a simple dinner.

VARIATION:

NOODLES WITH MEAT AND STOCK [Serves 4 to 6]

1 to 2 cups cooked meat [beef or pork], cut into thin strips
5 cups meat stock

Follow recipe for Noodles and Chicken with Stock. Use meat in place of chicken. Use meat stock in place of chicken stock. Cook as directed. Serve hot. A good lunch. A meal-in-a-bowl for a simple dinner.

STIR-FRYS AND HOT VEGETABLES

TECHNIQUE

Stir-fry literally translated from the Chinese means "air-tossed." This is the secret of a good stir-fry, to use a searing heat and keep the ingredients moving so they cook as quickly as possible. The Chinese use a wok and a special wok spoon, but a heavy cast iron frying pan or dutch oven and a wooden spoon can be substituted. Have all preparations done before cooking, i.e., cut all vegetables, soak and prepare mushrooms, mix sauce, cut up onions, etc., and mix the thickener. Have ingredients arranged in the order they go into the pan. Have the burner red hot if an electric stove, on full heat if a gas stove or remove the plate and cook right on the fire if using a wood stove. Place the wok or pan directly on the heat. Do not use the wok stand, this is for holding the wok steady when frying, stewing or steaming. Heat the wok and then add the oil. Fry nuts at medium heat just after the oil is added so they will not burn. Remove nuts after 1 or 2 minutes when they are lightly browned. Heat the oil until a haze forms and then start cooking. Cook your meat or chicken first and remove from the pan when browned since these do not cook at the same speed as vegetables and also would inhibit the vegetables' cooking quickly and flavor them too strongly. Next cook the oil flavorings, ginger, green onions or garlic. The vegetables should be cooked in order of the hardest first, i.e., broccoli, carrots, beans before onions, mushrooms, celery before bok choy or shui choy. Many of the harder vegetables such as broccoli, carrots or beans are par-steamed, otherwise they would have to be fried too long before they became sufficiently tender. After stirring and frying the vegetables a few minutes pour the sauce over them. Mix well. Add bean curd at this time and mix gently so it does not break into small pieces. Put meat back into the stir-fry at this time. Cover the pot with a lid and simmer 1 to 2 minutes. Remove the lid and then push the vegetables aside and add the thickener to the sauce. When the sauce thickens add the nuts, and mix the dish with the sauce. Cook no more than a total of 5 to 7 minutes, otherwise the dish will be overdone and limp. Serve while hot. Many of these dishes can be one-pot meals if served with rice and are the quickest Chinese dishes to prepare and cook.

37

Here are approximately one hundred variations on the theme of stir-frys. Do not be held to them specifically, but come up with your own combinations. The method is the only invariable part of these recipes. These dishes can be simple meal-in-a-bowl dishes when served with rice or noodles or can be featured as one of the dishes in hot courses at feasts. The vegetables-in-sauce dishes are used at dinner meals to accompany rice and a main dish. All of these dishes are excellent cold for lunch the next day.

CURRY VEGETABLES WITH BEAN CURD [Serves 4 to 6]

1 to 2 cakes bean curd, cut into 1 inch cubes
¼ tsp. sea salt

Sprinkle bean curd with salt. Set aside to add later.

3 Tbsp. peanut oil
OR vegetable oil
2 green peppers, cut into 2 inch squares
   OR 2 carrots, cut into thin diagonals and steamed 2 to 3 minutes
   OR ¼ lb. mushrooms, sliced thin
   OR 2 stalks celery, cut into thin diagonal pieces
   OR any other vegetable that contrasts in color and texture from the tomatoes and onions
2 to 3 medium yellow onions, quartered and quarters cut in half, then separated into individual layers

Heat a wok over high heat. Add oil. Heat until a haze forms. Add onions and green peppers or vegetables in place of green peppers. Stir and fry 2 to 3 minutes until vegetables are just beginning to get tender.

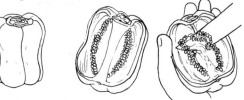

Sauce:
¾ to 1 cup soybean stock
1 inch fresh ginger root, grated
1 tsp. garam-masala [see Basic Indian section]
1 tsp. mild honey
½ to 1 tsp. sea salt

Mix ingredients well. Add to vegetables. Cover. Simmer 1 to 2 minutes.

Thickening:
1 Tbsp. arrowroot starch
2 Tbsp. water

Mix starch and water well. Push vegetables aside. Add thickening to sauce. Stir 1 minute until sauce thickens.

4 tomatoes, cut into bite-sized pieces

Add bean curd and tomatoes. Mix gently. Heat 30 seconds to 1 minute to heat tomatoes and bean curd but do not cook them to pieces. Serve hot. An excellent main dish. A meal-in-a-bowl served with rice or noodles. A good pungent-course feast dish. Good cold for lunch the next day.

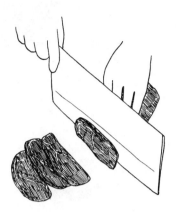

VARIATION:

CURRY VEGETABLES WITH BEEF [Serves 4 to 6]

¼ to ½ lb. boneless beef, cut into paper-thin strips [easier to cut thin if meat is partly frozen. Thaw before frying.]
3 Tbsp. peanut oil
  OR vegetable oil

Heat a wok over high heat. Add oil. Heat until a haze forms. Add beef. Stir and fry 2 to 3 minutes until beef is just seared but still slightly pink. Remove from pan. Set aside to add later.

¾ to 1 cup meat stock

Follow recipe for Curry Vegetables with Bean Curd. Use beef in place of bean curd. Use meat stock in place of soybean stock. Add meat after sauce. Mix well. Cook as directed. An excellent main dish. A meal-in-a-bowl served with rice or noodles. Good cold for lunch. A good hot pungent-course feast dish.

VARIATION:

CURRY VEGETABLES WITH PORK [Serves 4 to 6]

¼ to ½ lb. boneless pork, cut into paper-thin strips [easier to cut thin if meat is partly frozen. Thaw before frying.]
3 Tbsp. peanut oil
  OR vegetable oil

Heat a wok over high heat. Add oil. Heat until a haze forms. Add pork. Stir and fry 2 to 3 minutes until pork is just seared but still slightly pink. Remove from pan. Set aside to use later.

¾ to 1 cup meat stock

Follow recipe for Curry Vegetables with Bean Curd. Use pork in place of bean curd. Use meat stock in place of soybean stock. Add meat after sauce. Mix well. Cook as directed. An excellent main dish. A meal-in-a-bowl served with rice or noodles. Good cold for lunch. A good hot pungent-course feast dish.

VARIATION:

CURRY VEGETABLES WITH CHICKEN [Serves 4 to 6]

1 chicken breast, cut into ¼ inch cubes
3 Tbsp. peanut oil
  OR vegetable oil

Heat a wok over high heat. Add oil. Heat until a haze forms. Add chicken. Stir and fry 3 to 5 minutes until chicken lightly browned. Remove from pan. Set aside to use later.

¾ to 1 cup chicken stock

Follow recipe for Curry Vegetables with Bean Curd. Use chicken in place of bean curd. Use chicken in place of bean curd. Use chicken stock in place of soybean stock. Add chicken after sauce. Mix well. Cook as directed. An excellent main dish. A meal-in-a-bowl served with rice or noodles. Good cold for lunch the next day. A good hot pungent-course feast dish.

BROCCOLI AND ONIONS WITH NUTS [Serves 4 to 6]

1 lb. broccoli, cut into long thin diagonals. [See opposite directions]

3 to 4 water chestnuts, peeled and sliced thin [optional]

OR 1 to 2 jerusalem artichokes, peeled and cut into thin slices [optional]

Cut off lower tough part of broccoli stem. Save for soup stocks. Cut broccoli stalks in half and then into long thin diagonals. Start from the bottom of the stalk and pull apart when the flower is reached because the flowers fall apart when cut with a knife. Steam 3 to 5 minutes until just beginning to get tender and still bright green. Set aside for later use.

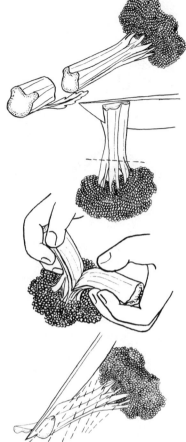

3 Tbsp. peanut oil

OR vegetable oil

1 cup almonds

OR cashew pieces

OR other nuts

OR ½ cup sunflower seeds

Heat a wok over high heat. Add oil. Add nuts immediately. Cook 1 to 2 minutes until just brown. Remove from pan. Set aside for later use.

1 Tbsp. peanut oil

OR vegetable oil

2 thin slices fresh ginger root, minced

2 to 3 medium yellow onions, quartered and quarters cut in half, then separated into individual layers

Add oil to wok. Heat until a haze forms. Add ginger and stir and fry 30 seconds. Add onions and stir and fry 2 minutes. Add steamed broccoli and water chestnuts. Stir and fry an additional 1 to 2 minutes.

Sauce:

¾ to 1 cup soybean stock

3 Tbsp. soy sauce

1 Tbsp. sake

OR dry sherry

OR rice vinegar

1 tsp. mild honey

½ to 1 tsp. sea salt

Mix ingredients well. Add to vegetables. Cover. Simmer 1 to 2 minutes. Uncover.

Thickening:

1 Tbsp. arrowroot starch

2 Tbsp. water

Mix starch and water well. Push vegetables aside. Add thickening to sauce. Stir 1 minute until sauce thickens. Add nuts and mix well. Serve hot. A good meal-in-a-bowl served with rice or noodles. An excellent feast dish. Good cold for lunch the next day.

VARIATION:

BROCCOLI AND ONIONS WITH BEAN CURD [Serves 4 to 6]

1 to 2 cakes bean curd, cut into 1 inch pieces

Follow recipe for Broccoli and Onions with Nuts. Use bean curd in place of nuts. Do not fry bean curd. Add bean curd to dish after the sauce. Mix gently so bean curd does not break into smaller pieces. Cook as directed. A good meal-in-a-bowl served with rice or noodles. An excellent feast dish. Good cold for lunch the next day.

VARIATION

BROCCOLI AND ONIONS WITH MEAT [Serves 4 to 6]

¼ to ½ lb. boneless meat [pork or beef], cut into paperthin strips [easier to cut thin if meat is partly frozen. Thaw before frying]

Heat a wok over high heat. Add oil. Heat until a haze forms. Add meat. Stir and fry 2 to 3 minutes until meat is just seared but still slightly pink. Remove from pan. Set aside to add later.

¾ to 1 cup meat stock

Follow recipe for Broccoli and Onions with Nuts. Use meat in place of nuts. Add meat after sauce. Mix well. Use meat stock in place of soybean stock. Cook as directed. Serve hot. A meal-in-a-bowl served with rice or noodles. An excellent feast dish. Good cold for lunch.

VARIATION—

BROCCOLI AND ONIONS WITH CHICKEN [Serves 4 to 6]

**1 chicken breast, cut into ¼ inch
  cubes**
**3 Tbsp. peanut oil
  OR vegetable oil**

Heat a wok over high heat. Add oil. Heat until a haze forms. Add chicken. Stir and fry 3 to 5 minutes until chicken is just brown. Remove from pan. Set aside to add later.

¾ to 1 cup chicken stock

Follow recipe for Broccoli and Onions with Nuts. Use chicken in place of nuts. Add chicken after sauce. Mix well. Use chicken stock in place of soybean stock. Cook as directed. Serve hot. A meal-in-a-bowl served with rice or noodles. An excellent feast dish. Good cold for lunch.

VARIATION—

GREEN BEANS AND ONIONS WITH BEAN CURD [Serves 4 to 6]

1 lb. green beans, cut into long thin diagonals

Steam beans 2 to 3 minutes until starting to get tender but still bright green. Remove from heat. Set aside for later use.

1 to 2 cakes bean curd, cut into 1 inch pieces

Follow recipe for Broccoli and Onions with Nuts. Use bean curd in place of nuts. Do not fry bean curd. Use green beans in place of brocolli. Add bean curd to dish after sauce. Mix gently so bean curd does not break into smaller pieces. Cook as directed. A good meal-in-a-bowl served with rice or noodles. An excellent feast dish. Good cold for lunch the next day.

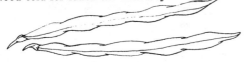

VARIATION—

GREEN BEANS AND ONIONS WITH CHICKEN [Serves 4 to 6]

1 chicken breast, cut into ¼ inch cubes
**3 Tbsp. peanut oil
  OR vegetable oil**

Heat a wok over high heat. Add oil. Heat until a haze forms. Add chicken. Stir and fry 3 to 5 minutes until chicken is just brown. Remove from pan. Set aside to add later.

1 lb. green beans, cut into long thin diagonals

Steam beans 2 to 3 minutes until starting to get tender but still bright green. Remove from heat. Set aside for later use.

VARIATION—

GREEN BEANS AND ONIONS WITH NUTS
[Serves 4 to 6]

**1 lb. green beans, cut into long
  thin diagonals**

Steam beans 2 to 3 minutes until starting to get tender but still bright green. Remove from heat. Set aside for later use.
Follow recipe for Broccoli and Onions with Nuts. Use green beans in place of broccoli. Cook as directed. A good meal-in-a-bowl served with rice or noodles. An excellent feast dish. Good cold for lunch.

VARIATION—

GREEN BEANS AND ONIONS WITH MEAT
[Serves 4 to 6]

**¼ to ½ lb. boneless meat [pork or beef], cut
  into paper-thin strips [easier to cut thin if
  meat is partly frozen. Thaw before frying]**
**3 Tbsp. peanut oil
  OR vegetable oil**

Heat a wok over high heat. Add oil. Heat until a haze forms. Add meat. Stir and fry 2 to 3 minutes until meat is just seared but still slightly pink. Remove from pan. Set aside to add later.

1 lb. green beans, cut into long thin diagonals

Steam beans 2 to 3 minutes until starting to get tender but still bright green. Remove from heat. Set aside for later use.

¾ to 1 cup meat stock

Follow recipe for Broccoli and Onions with Nuts. Use meat in place of nuts. Use green beans in place of broccoli. Use meat stock in place of soybean stock. Add meat after sauce. Mix well. Cook as directed. Serve hot. A meal-in-a-bowl served with rice or noodles. A good hot-course feast dish. Good cold for lunch.

¾ to 1 cup chicken stock

Follow recipe for Broccoli and Onions with Nuts. Use chicken in place of nuts. Use green beans in place of broccoli. Use chicken stock in place of soybean stock. Add chicken after sauce. Mix well. Cook as directed. Serve hot. A meal-in-a-bowl served with rice or noodles. A good hot-course feast dish. Good cold for lunch.

BOK CHOY [OR OTHER GREENS] AND CASHEWS [Serves 4 to 6]

3 Tbsp. peanut oil
  OR vegetable oil
½ to 1 cup cashew pieces
  OR other nuts
  OR ½ cup sunflower seeds

Heat wok over high heat. Add oil. Add nuts immediately. Cook 1 to 2 minutes until just brown. Remove from pan. Set aside for later use.

2 thin slices fresh ginger root, julienned
2 green onions, cut into thin diagonal slices
1 to 2 cloves garlic, crushed and minced [optional]

Add to hot oil. Stir and fry 30 seconds to 1 minute until just tender.

10 to 15 stalks bok choy, stalks cut into long thin diagonals and leaves cut into 1 inch strips
  OR Chinese cabbage cut into 1 inch strips
  OR any cooking greens cut into 1 inch strips
3 to 4 water chestnuts, peeled and sliced thin [optional]
  OR 1 to 2 jerusalem artichokes, peeled and sliced thin [optional]

Add bok choy stalks and water chestnuts to wok. Stir and fry 2 to 3 minutes until just tender. Add leaves. Mix well.

Sauce:
¾ to 1 cup soybean stock
2 Tbsp. soy sauce
1 to 2 Tbsp. sake
  OR dry sherry
  OR rice vinegar
½ to 1 tsp. sea salt
1 to 2 tsp. mild honey

Mix ingredients well. Add to vegetables. Cover Simmer 1 minute.

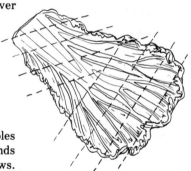

Thickening:
1 Tbsp. arrowroot starch
2 Tbsp. water

Mix starch and water well. Push vegetables aside. Add thickening to sauce. Stir 30 seconds to 1 minute until sauce thickens. Add cashews. Mix well. Serve hot. An excellent meal-in-a-bowl served with rice or noodles. A good mild-course feast dish. Good cold for lunch the next day.

VARIATION:

BOK CHOY WITH BEAN CURD [Serves 4 to 6]

1 to 2 cakes bean curd, cut into 1 inch pieces

Follow recipe for Bok Choy and Cashews. Use bean curd in place of cashews. Do not fry bean curd. Cook as directed. Add bean curd after sauce is added. Mix gently so bean curd does not break into small pieces. Cover. Cook as directed. Serve hot. A meal-in-a-bowl served with rice or noodles. A good mild-course dish for a feast. Good cold for lunch the next day.

VARIATION:

BOK CHOY IN SAUCE [Serves 4 to 6]

Follow recipe for Bok Choy and Cashews. Do not use cashews. Cook as directed. Serve hot. A good hot vegetable dish served with a main dish and rice or noodles for a simple dinner meal. Good cold for lunch the next day with rice or noodles and a main dish left-over. A good mild-course feast dish.

VARIATION:
FIRM VEGETABLES WITH CASHEWS [Serves 4 to 6]

1 lb. asparagus, cut into thin
  diagonal slices
  OR 1 lb. green beans, cut into
      thin diagonal slices
  OR 1 lb. broccoli, stalks cut
      into long thin diagonal
      slices and heads broken
      into small pieces
  OR 2 medium carrots, cut into
      long thin slices and
      2 green peppers, seeded and
      cut into bite-sized pieces
  OR 2 cups snowpeas, ends
      snipped and strings removed
  OR any firm vegetable or
      combination of firm
      vegetables, cut into thin
      diagonal slices

Do not steam green peppers or snowpeas. Steam other vegetables 2 to 3 minutes until just beginning to get tender but still bright colored.

Follow recipe for Bok Choy and Cashews. Use firm steamed vegetable, green peppers or snowpeas in place of bok choy. Cook as directed. Serve hot. A meal-in-a-bowl served with rice or noodles. A good mild-course feast dish. Excellent cold for lunch the next day.

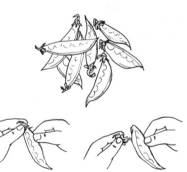

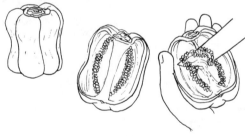

VARIATION:

FIRM VEGETABLES WITH BEAN CURD
[Serves 4 to 6]

1 to 2 cakes bean curd, cut in
  1 inch cubes

Follow recipe for Bok Choy and Cashews. Use firm steamed vegetable, green peppers or snowpeas in place of bok choy. Use bean curd in in place of cashews. Do not fry bean curd. Cook as directed. Add bean curd after sauce is added. Mix gently so bean curd does not break into small pieces. Cover. Cook as directed. Serve hot. A meal-in-a-bowl served with rice or noodles. A good mild-course feast dish. Good cold next day for lunch.

VARIATION:

FIRM VEGETABLES IN SAUCE [Serves 4 to 6]

Follow recipe for Bok Choy and Cashews. Do not use cashews. Use firm steamed vegetables, green peppers or snowpeas in place of bok choy. Cook as directed. Serve hot. A good hot vegetable dish served with a main dish and rice or noodles for a simple meal. A good mild-course feast dish. Excellent cold for lunch the next day served with rice or noodles and a leftover main dish.

BOK CHOY [OR OTHER GREENS] AND CHICKEN [Serves 4 to 6]

1 chicken breast, cut into
   1/4 inch cubes
1 tsp. soy sauce
1 tsp. sake
   OR dry sherry
   OR rice vinegar
1/2 tsp. mild honey
1/4 tsp. sea salt
1 Tbsp. arrowroot starch

Mix chicken, soy, sake, honey, salt and starch. Marinate 20 to 30 minutes.

3 Tbsp. peanut oil
   OR vegetable oil

Heat a wok over high heat. Add oil. Heat until a haze forms. Add chicken. Stir and fry 3 to 5 minutes until lightly browned. Remove from pan. Set aside to add later.

2 Tbsp. peanut oil
   OR vegetable oil
2 green onions, julienned
3 thin slices fresh ginger root, minced
1 to 2 cloves garlic, crushed and minced [optional]

Add oil to wok. Heat until a haze forms. Add ginger and green onions. Stir and fry 30 seconds until just tender.

1 head bok choy, stalks cut into long thin diagonals and leaves cut into wide strips
   OR any cooking green, cut into
      1 inch strips

Add stalks to wok. Stir and fry 2 to 3 minutes. Add leaves. Mix well.

Sauce:
2/3 cup chicken stock
2 Tbsp. soy sauce
1 Tbsp. sake
   OR dry sherry
   OR rice vinegar
1 Tbsp. mild honey
1/2 to 1 tsp. sea salt

Mix ingredients well. Add to bok choy. Cover and simmer 1 minute. Remove lid. Add chicken. Mix well.

Thickening:
1 Tbsp. arrowroot starch
2 Tbsp. water

Mix starch and water well. Push vegetables and chicken aside. Add thickening to sauce. Stir 1 minute until sauce thickens. Serve hot. A good meal-in-a-bowl served with rice or noodles. An excellent mild-course feast dish. Good cold for lunch.

VARIATION:

BOK CHOY AND MEAT [Serves 4 to 6]

1/4 to 1/2 lb. boneless meat [pork or beef], cut into paper-thin slices [easier to cut thin if meat is partly frozen. Thaw before frying]
3 Tbsp. peanut oil
   OR vegetable oil

2/3 cup meat stock

Follow recipe for Bok Choy and Chicken. Use meat in place of chicken. Use meat stock in place of chicken stock. Cook as directed. Serve hot. A good meal-in-a-bowl served with rice or noodles. An excellent mild-course feast dish. Good cold for lunch.

Heat a wok over high heat. Add oil. Heat until a haze forms. Add meat. Stir and fry 2 to 3 minutes until meat is just seared but still slightly pink. Remove from pan. Set aside to add later.

VARIATION:
BOK CHOY AND SHRIMP [Serves 4 to 6]

¼ to ½ lb. large shrimp,
  shelled and deveined,
  cut into ½ inch pieces
3 Tbsp. peanut oil
  OR vegetable oil

Heat a wok over high heat. Add oil. Heat until a haze forms. Add shrimp. Stir and fry 2 to 3 minutes until shrimp pink. Remove from pan. Set aside to add later.
Follow recipe for Bok Choy and Chicken. Use shrimp in place of chicken. Cook as directed. Serve hot. A good meal-in-a-bowl served with rice or noodles. Good cold for lunch. An excellent mild-course feast dish.

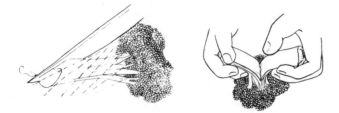

VARIATION:

FIRM VEGETABLES WITH SHRIMP
[Serves 4 to 6]

¼ to ½ lb. large shrimp,
  shelled and deveined,
  cut in ½ inch pieces
3 Tbsp. peanut oil
  OR vegetable oil

Do not steam green pepper or snowpeas. Steam other vegetables 2 to 3 minutes until just beginning to get tender but still bright colored. Remove from steam. Set aside to add later.
Follow recipe for Bok Choy and Chicken. Use shrimp in place of chicken. Use firm steamed vegetables, green peppers or snowpeas in place of bok choy. Cook as directed. Serve hot. A meal-in-a-bowl served with rice or noodles. A good hot-mild-course feast dish. Good cold for lunch the next day.

VARIATION:

FIRM VEGETABLES WITH CHICKEN
[Serves 4 to 6]

Follow recipe for Bok Choy and Chicken. Use firm steamed vegetables, green peppers or snowpeas in place of bok choy. Cook as directed. Serve hot. A good meal-in-a-bowl served with rice or noodles. An excellent hot-mild-course feast dish. Good cold for lunch.

VARIATION:
FIRM VEGETABLES WITH MEAT [Serves 4 to 6]

¼ to ½ lb. boneless meat [pork
  or beef], cut into paper-thin
  slices [easier to cut thin if
  meat is partly frozen. Thaw
  before frying]
3 Tbsp. peanut oil
  OR vegetable oil

Heat a wok over high heat. Add oil. Heat until a haze forms. Add meat. Stir and fry 2 to 3 minutes until meat is just seared but still slightly pink. Remove from pan. Set aside to add later.

1 lb. asparagus, cut into thin
  diagonal slices
  OR 1 lb. green beans, cut into
    thin diagonal slices
  OR 1 lb. broccoli, stalks cut
    into long thin diagonals and
    heads broken into small
    flowerlets
  OR 2 medium carrots, cut into
    long thin diagonal slices and
    2 green peppers, seeded and
    cut into bite-sized pieces
    OR any other firm vegetable,
      cut into thin diagonal
      slices
  OR 2 cups snowpeas, ends
    snipped and strings removed
  OR any other firm vegetable or
    combination of firm
    vegetables, cut into thin
    diagonal slices

Do not steam green pepper or snowpeas. Steam other vegetables 2 to 3 minutes until just beginning to get tender but still bright colored. Remove from steam. Set aside to add later.

⅔ cup meat stock

Follow recipe for Bok Choy and Chicken. Use meat in place of chicken. Use firm steamed vegetables, green peppers or snowpeas in place of bok choy. Use meat stock in place of chicken stock in sauce. Cook as directed. Serve hot. A good meal-in-a-bowl served with rice or noodles. An excellent hot-mild-course feast dish. Good cold for lunch the next day.

BEAN CURD IN BLACK BEAN SAUCE WITH TOMATOES [Serves 4 to 6]

1 to 2 cloves garlic, crushed and minced

2 Tbsp. salted black beans, coarsely chopped

3 Tbsp. peanut oil
OR vegetable oil

Heat a wok over high heat. Add oil. Heat until a haze forms. Add garlic and black beans. Stir and fry 30 seconds.

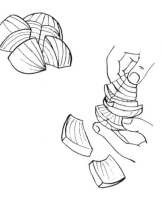

2 to 3 medium yellow onions, quartered and quarters cut in half then separated into individual layers

Add to wok. Stir and fry 2 to 3 minutes until onions just beginning to get tender.

Sauce:
¾ to 1 cup soybean stock
½ inch fresh ginger root, grated
2 Tbsp. soy sauce
1 tsp. mild honey

Mix ingredients well. Add to onions. Cover. Simmer 1 to 2 minutes.

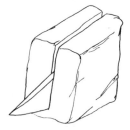  

1 to 2 cakes bean curd, cut into 1 inch pieces

Add bean curd. Simmer 1 minute, uncovered.

Thickening:
1 Tbsp. arrowroot starch
2 Tbsp. water

Mix starch and water well. Push vegetables aside. Add thickening to sauce. Stir 1 minute until sauce thickens.

4 tomatoes, cut into bite-sized pieces

Add tomatoes. Mix gently. Heat 30 seconds to 1 minute to heat tomatoes but not cook them to pieces. Serve hot. An excellent main dish. A meal-in-a-bowl served with rice or noodles and a cold vegetable dish. A good hot course feast dish. Good cold for lunch the next day.

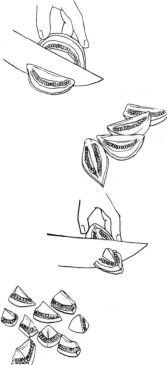

VARIATION:

MEAT IN BLACK BEAN SAUCE WITH TOMATOES [Serves 4 to 6]

¼ to ½ **lb. boneless meat [pork or beef], cut into paper-thin strips [easier to cut thin if meat is partly frozen. Thaw before frying]**
3 **Tbsp. peanut oil OR vegetable oil**

Heat a wok over high heat. Add oil. Heat until a haze forms. Add meat. Stir and fry 2 to 3 minutes until meat is just seared but still slightly pink. Remove from pan. Set aside to add later.

¾ **to 1 cup meat stock**

Follow recipe for Bean Curd in Black Bean Sauce with Tomatoes. Use meat in place of bean curd. Use meat stock in place of soybean stock. Add meat after sauce. Mix well. Cook as directed. Serve hot. A meal-in-a-bowl served with rice or noodles. An excellent hot-pungent feast dish. Good cold for lunch.

VARIATION:

SHRIMP IN BLACK BEAN SAUCE WITH TOMATOES [Serves 4 to 6]

¼ to ½ **lb. large shrimp, shelled and deveined, cut in ½ inch pieces**
3 **Tbsp. peanut oil OR vegetable oil**

Heat a wok over high heat. Add oil. Heat until a haze forms. Add shrimp. Stir and fry 2 to 3 minutes until pink. Remove from pan. Set aside to add later.

¾ **to 1 cup chicken stock**

Follow recipe for Bean Curd in Black Bean Sauce with Tomatoes. Use shrimp in place of bean curd. Use chicken stock in place of soybean stock. Add shrimp after sauce. Mix well. Cook as directed. Serve hot. A meal-in-a-bowl served with rice or noodles. An excellent hot-pungent feast dish. Good cold for lunch.

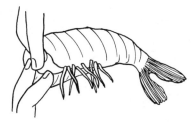

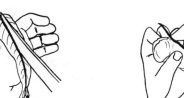

BEAN CURD IN BLACK BEAN SAUCE WITH BROCCOLI AND ONIONS
[Serves 4 to 6]

$^{1}/_{2}$ to 1 lb. broccoli, cut into long thin diagonals [See opposite directions]

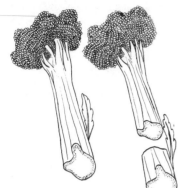

Cut off lower tough part of broccoli stem. Save for soup stocks. Cut broccoli stalks in half and then into long thin diagonals. Start from the bottom of the stalk and pull apart when the flower is reach because the flowers fall apart when cut with a knife. Steam 3 to 5 minutes until just beginning to get tender and still bright green. Set broccoli aside for later use.

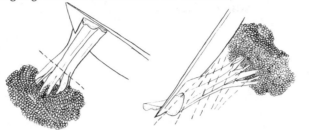

1 to 2 cloves garlic, crushed and minced

2 Tbsp. salted black beans coarsely chopped

3 Tbsp. peanut oil OR vegetable oil

Heat a wok over high heat. Add oil. Heat until a haze forms. Add garlic and black beans. Stir and fry 30 seconds.

2 to 3 medium yellow onions, quartered and quarters cut in half then separated into individual layers

Add to wok. Stir and fry 2 to 3 minutes until onions just beginning to get tender.

Sauce:

$^{3}/_{4}$ to 1 cup soybean stock

$^{1}/_{2}$ inch fresh ginger root, grated

2 Tbsp. soy sauce

1 tsp. mild honey

Mix ingredients well. Add to onions and broccoli. Cover. Simmer 1 to 2 minutes. Uncover.

1 to 2 cakes bean curd, cut into 1 inch pieces

Add to wok. Mix gently so bean curd does not break into pieces. Simmer 1 minute, uncovered.

Thickening:

1 Tbsp. arrowroot starch

2 Tbsp. water

Mix starch and water well. Push vegetables aside. Add thickening to sauce. Stir 1 minute until sauce thickens. An excellent main dish. A meal-in-a-bowl served with rice or noodles and a cold vegetable dish. A good pungent-course feast dish. Good cold for lunch the next day.

VARIATION:

MEAT IN BLACK BEAN SAUCE WITH BROCCOLI AND ONIONS [Serves 4 to 6]

$^{1}/_{4}$ to $^{1}/_{2}$ lb. boneless meat [pork or beef], cut into paper-thin strips [easier to cut thin if meat is partly frozen. Thaw before frying]

3 Tbsp. peanut oil OR vegetable oil

Heat a wok over high heat. Add oil. Heat until a haze forms. Add meat. Stir and fry 2 to 3 minutes until meat is just seared but still slightly pink. Remove from pan. Set aside to add later.

¾ **to 1 cup meat stock**

Follow recipe for Bean Curd in Black Bean Sauce with Broccoli and Onions. Use meat in place of bean curd. Use meat stock in place of soybean stock. Add meat just after sauce. Mix well. Cook as directed. Serve hot. A meal-in-a-bowl served with rice or noodles. An excellent hot-pungent feast dish. Good cold for lunch.

VARIATION:

SHRIMP IN BLACK BEAN SAUCE WITH BROCCOLI AND ONIONS [Serves 4 to 6]

¼ **to** ½ **lb. large shrimp, shelled and deveined, cut in** ½ **inch pieces**

Heat a wok over high heat. Add oil. Heat until a haze forms. Add shrimp. Stir and fry 2 to 3 minutes until pink. Remove from pan. Set aside to add later.

¾ **to 1 cup chicken stock**

Follow recipe for Bean Curd in Black Bean Sauce with Broccoli and Onions. Use shrimp in place of bean curd. Use chicken stock in place of soybean stock. Add shrimp after sauce. Mix well. Cook as directed. Serve hot. A meal-in-a-bowl served with rice or noodles. An excellent hot-pungent feast dish. Good cold for lunch.

VARIATION:

SHRIMP IN BLACK BEAN SAUCE WITH GREEN BEANS [Serves 4 to 6]

¼ **to** ½ **lb. large shrimp, shelled and deveined, cut in** ½ **inch pieces**
3 **Tbsp. peanut oil OR vegetable oil**

Heat a wok over high heat. Add oil. Heat until a haze forms. Add shrimp. Stir and fry 2 to 3 minutes until pink. Remove from pan. Set aside to add later.

¾ **to 1 cup chicken stock**

Follow recipe for Bean Curd in Black Bean Sauce with Broccoli and Onions. Use shrimp in place of Broccoli. Use chicken stock in place of soybean stock. Add shrimp just after sauce. Mix well. Cook as directed. Serve hot. A meal-in-a-bowl served with rice or noodles. An excellent hot-pungent feast dish. Good for lunch.

VARIATION:

BEAN CURD IN BLACK BEAN SAUCE WITH GREEN BEANS [Serves 4 to 6]

½ **to 1 lb. green beans, cut into long thin diagonals**

Steam beans 2 to 3 minutes until starting to get tender but still bright green. Remove from heat. Set aside for later use.

Follow recipe for Bean Curd in Black Bean Sauce with Broccoli and Onions. Add green beans with onions. Use in place of broccoli. Cook as directed. Serve hot. An excellent main dish. A meal-in-a-bowl served with rice or noodles. A good pungent-course feast dish. Good cold for lunch the next day.

VARIATION:

MEAT IN BLACK BEAN SAUCE WITH GREEN BEANS [Serves 4 to 6]

¼ **to** ½ **lb. boneless meat [pork or beef], cut into paper-thin strips [easier to cut thin if meat is partly frozen. Thaw before frying]**
3 **Tbsp. peanut oil OR vegetable oil**

Heat a wok over high heat. Add oil. Heat until a haze forms. Add meat. Stir and fry 2 to 3 minutes until meat is just seared but still slightly pink. Remove from pan. Set aside to add later.

¾ **to 1 cup meat stock**

Follow recipe for Bean Curd in Black Bean Sauce with Broccoli and Onions. Use meat in place of bean curd. Use meat stock in place of soybean stock. Use green beans in place of broccoli. Add meat just after sauce. Mix well. Cook as directed. Serve hot. A meal-in-a-bowl served with rice or noodles. An excellent hot-pungent feast dish. Good cold for lunch.

BOK CHOY, [OR OTHER GREENS] MUSHROOMS AND CASHEWS   [Serves 4 to 6]

6 to 8 dried mushrooms
1 cup boiling water

Place mushrooms in a bowl. Pour boiling water over them. Place weight on mushrooms to keep under water. Soak 15 minutes to 1 hour. Remove from water. Squeeze dry. Reserve liquid. Remove tough stems. Cut each mushroom into 3 to 4 pieces. Set aside for later use.

3 Tbsp. peanut oil
    OR vegetable oil
½ to 1 cup cashew pieces
    OR other nuts
    OR ½ cup sunflower seeds

Heat a wok over high heat. Add oil. Add nuts immediately. Cook 1 to 2 minutes until just brown. Remove from pan. Set aside for later use.

2 thin slices fresh ginger root, julienned
2 green onions, cut into thin diagonal slices

Add to hot oil. Stir and fry 30 seconds to 1 minute until ginger and onions are just tender.

10 to 15 stalks bok choy, stalks cut into long thin diagonals and leaves cut into 2 inch strips
    OR any cooking green, cut into 1 inch strips
3 to 4 water chestnuts, peeled and sliced thin [optional]
    OR 1 to 2 jerusalem artichokes, peeled and sliced thin [optional]

Add bok choy stalks, mushrooms and water chestnuts. Stir and fry 2 to 3 minutes until stalks just tender. Add leaves. Mix well.

Sauce:
¾ to 1 cup mushroom stock
2 Tbsp. soy sauce
2 Tbsp. sake
    OR dry sherry
    OR rice vinegar
½ to 1 tsp. sea salt
1 to 2 tsp. mild honey

Mix ingredients well. Add to bok choy and vegetables. Cover. Simmer 1 minute. Remove lid.

Thickening:
1 Tbsp. arrowroot starch
2 Tbsp. water

Mix starch and water well. Push vegetables aside. Add thickening to sauce. Stir 30 seconds to 1 minute until sauce thickens. Add nuts. Mix well. Serve hot. An excellent meal-in-a-bowl served with rice or noodles. A good mild-course feast dish. Good cold for lunch the next day.

VARIATION:

BOK CHOY, [OR OTHER GREENS] MUSHROOMS AND BEAN CURD
[Serves 4 to 6]

1 to 2 cakes bean curd, cut into 1 inch pieces

Follow recipe for Bok Choy, mushrooms and Cashews. Use bean curd in place of cashews. Do not fry bean curd. Cook as directed. Add bean curd after sauce is added. Mix gently so bean curd does not break up into small pieces. Cover. Cook as directed. Serve hot. A meal-in-a-bowl served with rice or noodles. A good mild-course dish for a feast. Good cold for lunch the next day.

VARIATION:

BOK CHOY, [OR OTHER GREENS] AND MUSHROOMS IN SAUCE [Serves 4 to 6]

Follow recipe for Bok Choy, Mushrooms and Cashews. Do not use cashews. Cook as directed. Serve hot. A good hot-vegetable dish served with a main dish and rice or noodles for a simple meal. Good mild-course feast dish. Excellent cold for lunch the next day.

VARIATION:

BOK CHOY, [OR OTHER GREENS]
MUSHROOMS AND MEAT [Serves 4 to 6]

¼ to ½ lb. boneless meat [pork
  or beef], cut into paper-thin
  strips [easier to cut thin if
  meat is partly frozen. Thaw
  before frying]
3 Tbsp. peanut oil
  OR vegetable oil

½ cup meat stock
½ cup mushroom stock

Heat a wok over high heat. Add oil. Heat until a
haze forms. Add meat. Stir and fry 2 to 3
minutes until meat is seared but still slightly
pink. Remove from pan. Set aside to use later.
Follow recipe for Bok Choy, Mushrooms and
Cashews. Use meat in place of cashews. Use
meat stock with mushroom stock. Add meat just
after sauce. Mix well. Cook as directed. Serve
hot . An excellent meal-in-a-bowl served with
rice or noodles. An excellent hot-mild feast
dish. Good cold for lunch.

VARIATION:

BOK CHOY, [OR OTHER GREENS]
MUSHROOMS AND CHICKEN [Serves 4 to 6]

1 chicken breast, cut into
  ¼ inch slices
½ tsp. sea salt
3 Tbsp. peanut oil
  OR vegetable oil

Heat a wok over high heat. Add oil. Heat until a
haze forms. Add chicken. Sprinkle over salt.
Stir and fry 3 to 5 minutes until light golden
brown. Remove from pan. Set aside to add
later.
½ cup chicken stock
½ cup mushroom stock

Follow recipe for Bok Choy, Mushrooms and
Cashews. Use chicken in place of cashews. Use
chicken stock with mushroom stock. Add
chicken just after sauce. Mix well. Cook as
directed. Serve hot. An excellent meal-in-a-bowl
served with rice or noodles. An excellent hot-
mild feast dish. Good cold for lunch.

VARIATION:

BOK CHOY, [OR OTHER GREENS]
MUSHROOMS AND SHRIMP [Serves 4 to 6]

¼ to ½ lb. large shrimp, shelled
  and deveined, cut in
  ½ inch pieces
3 Tbsp. peanut oil
  OR vegetable oil

Heat a wok over high heat. Add oil. Heat until a
haze forms. Add shrimp. Stir and fry 2 to 3
minutes until shrimp pink. Remove from pan.
Set aside to add later.

Follow recipe for Bok Choy, Mushrooms and
Cashews. Use shrimp in place of cashews. Add
shrimp just after sauce. Mix well. Cook as
directed. Serve hot. An excellent meal-in-a-bowl
served with rice or noodles. A good hot-mild
feast dish. Good cold for lunch.

51

FIRM VEGETABLES, MUSHROOMS AND CASHEWS [Serves 4 to 6]

6 to 8 dried mushrooms
1 cup boiling water

Place mushrooms in a bowl. Pour boiling water over them. Place weight on mushrooms to keep under water. Soak 15 minutes to 1 hour. Remove from water. Squeeze dry. Reserve liquid. Remove tough stems. Cut each mushroom into 3 to 4 pieces. Set aside for later use.

3 Tbsp. peanut oil
  OR vegetable oil
½ to 1 cup cashew pieces
  OR other nuts
  OR ½ cup sunflower seeds

Heat a wok over high heat. Add oil. Add nuts immediately. Cook 1 to 2 minutes until just brown. Remove from pan. Set aside for later use.

2 thin slices fresh ginger root, julienned
2 green onions, cut into thin diagonal slices

Add to hot oil. Stir and fry 30 seconds to 1 minute until ginger and onions are just tender.

1 lb. asparagus, cut into
  thin diagonal slices
  OR 1 lb. green beans, cut into
    thin diagonal slices
  OR 1 lb. broccoli, stalks cut
    into long thin diagonals
    and heads broken into
    small flowerlets
  OR 2 medium carrots, cut into
    long thin diagonal slices and
    2 green peppers, seeded
    and cut into bite-sized pieces
    OR any other firm vegetable
      cut into thin diagonal
      slices
  OR 2 cups snowpeas, ends
    snipped and strings removed
  OR any firm vegetable or
    combination of firm
    vegetables, cut into thin
    diagonal slices

Do not steam green peppers or snowpeas. Steam other vegetables 2 to 3 minutes until just beginning to get tender but still bright colored. Add one of vegetables or a combination to wok. Stir and fry 2 to 3 minutes until just tender.

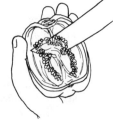

Sauce:
¾ to 1 cup mushroom stock
2 Tbsp. soy sauce
2 Tbsp. sake
  OR dry sherry
  OR rice vinegar
½ to 1 tsp. sea salt
1 to 2 tsp. mild honey

Mix ingredients well. Add to vegetables. Cover. Simmer 1 minute. Remove lid.

Thickening:
1 Tbsp. arrowroot starch
2 Tbsp. water

Mix starch and water well. Push vegetables aside. Add thickening to sauce. Stir 30 seconds to 1 minute until sauce thickens. Add nuts. Mix well. Serve hot. An excellent meal-in-a-bowl served with rice or noodles. A good mild-course feast dish. Good cold for lunch the next day.

VARIATION:
FIRM VEGETABLES, MUSHROOMS AND BEAN CURD [Serves 4 to 6]

1 to 2 cakes bean curd, cut into
  1 inch cubes

Follow recipe for Firm Vegetables, Mushrooms and Cashews. Use bean curd in place of cashews. Do not fry bean curd. Cook as directed. Add bean curd after sauce is added. Mix gently so bean curd does not break into small pieces. Cover. Cook as directed. Serve hot. A meal-in-a-bowl served with rice or noodles. A good mild-course feast dish. Good cold for lunch the next day.

VARIATION:
FIRM VEGETABLES AND MUSHROOMS IN SAUCE [Serves 4 to 6]

Follow recipe for Firm Vegetables, Mushrooms and Cashews. Do not use cashews. Cook as directed. Serve hot. A good hot vegetable dish served with a main dish and rice or noodles for a simple meal. A good mild-course feast dish. Good cold for lunch the next day served with rice or noodles and a left-over main dish.

VARIATION:
FIRM VEGETABLES, MUSHROOMS AND CHICKEN [Serves 4 to 6]

1 chicken breast, cut into ¼ inch
  slices
½ tsp. sea salt
3 Tbsp. peanut oil
  OR vegetable oil

Heat a wok over high heat. Add oil. Heat until a haze forms. Add chicken. Sprinkle over salt. Stir and fry 3 to 5 minutes until light golden brown. Remove from pan. Set aside to add later.

½ cup chicken stock
½ cup mushroom stock

Follow recipe for Firm Vegetables, Mushrooms and Cashews. Use chicken in place of cashews. Use chicken stock with mushroom stock in sauce. Add chicken just after sauce. Mix well. Cook as directed. Serve hot. A meal-in-a-bowl served with rice or noodles. A good mild-course feast dish. Good cold for lunch.

VARIATION:
FIRM VEGETABLES, MUSHROOMS AND MEAT [Serves 4 to 6]

¼ to ½ lb. boneless meat [pork
  or beef], cut into paper-thin
  strips [easier to cut thin if
  meat is partly frozen. Thaw
  before frying]
3 Tbsp. peanut oil
  OR vegetable oil

Heat a wok over high heat. Add oil. Heat until a haze forms. Add meat. Stir and fry 2 to 3 minutes until meat is seared but still slightly pink. Remove from pan. Set aside to use later.

½ cup meat stock
½ cup mushroom stock

Follow recipe for Firm Vegetables, Mushrooms and Cashews. Use meat in place of cashews. Use meat stock with mushroom stock in sauce. Add meat just after sauce. Mix well. Cook as directed. Serve hot. A meal-in-a-bowl served with rice or noodles. A good mild-course feast dish. Good cold for lunch.

VARIATION:
FIRM VEGETABLES, MUSHROOMS AND SHRIMP [Serves 4 to 6]

¼ to ½ lb. large shrimp, shelled
  and deveined, cut
  in ½ inch pieces
3 Tbsp. peanut oil
  OR vegetable oil

Heat a wok over high heat. Add oil. Heat until a haze forms. Add shrimp. Stir and fry 2 to 3 minutes until shrimp pink. Remove from pan. Set aside to add later.

Follow recipe for Firm Vegetables, Mushrooms and Cashews. Use shrimp in place of cashews. Add shrimp just after sauce. Cook as directed. Serve hot. A meal-in-a-bowl served with rice or noodles. A good mild course feast dish. Good cold for lunch.

SNOWPEAS OR GREEN BEANS AND BEAN CURD WITH TOMATOES [Serves 4 to 6]

3 Tbsp. peanut oil
  OR vegetable oil
2 thin slices fresh ginger root,
  julienned

Heat a wok. Add oil. Heat until a haze forms. Add ginger. Stir and fry 30 seconds until just tender.

2 medium yellow onions,
  quartered and quarters cut in
  half then separated into
  individual layers

Add to wok. Stir and fry 2 to 3 minutes until just tender and slightly browned.

2 cups snowpeas, snipped and
  strings removed
  OR green beans, cut into long
    thin diagonals

Add to onions. Stir and fry 1 to 2 minutes.

Sauce:
¾ to 1 cup soybean stock
1 Tbsp. sake
  OR dry sherry
  OR rice vinegar
2 Tbsp. soy sauce
1 tsp. mild honey
½ to 1 tsp. sea salt

Mix ingredients well. Add to vegetables. Cover. Simmer 1 minute. Remove cover.

Thickening:
1 Tbsp. arrowroot starch
2 Tbsp. water

Mix water and starch well. Push vegetables aside. Add thickening to sauce. Stir 1 minute until sauce thickens.

2 to 3 tomatoes, cut into bite-
  sized pieces
1 to 2 cakes bean curd, cut into
  1 inch pieces

Add tomatoes and bean curd. Mix gently so bean curd does not break into smaller pieces. Serve hot. A meal-in-a-bowl served with rice or noodles. A good mild-course feast dish. Good cold for lunch the next day.

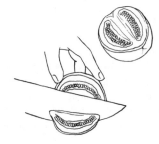   

VARIATION:
SNOWPEAS OR GREEN BEANS AND CHASHEWS WITH TOMATOES [Serves 4 to 6]

2 Tbsp. peanut oil
  OR vegetable oil
½ to 1 cup cashew pieces
  OR other nuts
  OR ½ cup sunflower seeds

Heat a wok over high heat. Add oil. Add nuts immediately. Cook 1 to 2 minutes until just brown. Remove from pan. Set aside for later use.

Follow recipe for Snowpeas or Green Beans and Bean Curd with Tomatoes. Use nuts in place of bean curd. Cook as directed. Add nuts with tomatoes. Serve hot. A meal-in-a-bowl served with rice or noodles. A good mild-course feast dish. Good cold for lunch the next day.

VARIATION:
SNOWPEAS OR GREEN BEANS WITH TOMATOES IN SAUCE [Serves 4 to 6]

Follow recipe for Snowpeas or Green Beans and Bean Curd with Tomatoes. Do not use bean curd. Cook as directed. Serve hot. A good hot vegetable dish served with a main dish and rice or noodles for a simple meal. An excellent mild-course feast dish. Good cold for lunch the next day with rice or noodles and a main dish leftover.

VARIATION:
SNOWPEAS OR GREEN BEANS, MUSHROOMS WITH TOMATOES IN SAUCE [Serves 4 to 6]

6 to 8 dried mushrooms
1 cup boiling water

Place mushrooms in a bowl. Pour boiling water over them. Place weight on mushrooms to keep under water. Soak 15 minutes to 1 hour. Remove from water. Squeeze dry. Reserve stock. Remove tough stems. Cut each mushroom into 3 to 4 pieces.

1 cup mushroom stock

Follow recipe for Snowpeas or Green Beans and Bean Curd with Tomatoes. Do not use bean curd. Use mushroom stock in place of soybean stock in sauce. Add mushrooms with snowpeas. Cook as directed. Serve hot. A good hot vegetable dish served with a main dish and rice or noodles for a simple meal. An excellent mild-course feast dish. Good cold for lunch the next day with rice or noodles and a main dish leftover.

VARIATION:
SNOWPEAS OR GREEN BEANS, MUSHROOMS AND BEAN CURD WITH TOMATOES [Serves 4 to 6]

6 to 8 dried mushrooms
1 cup boiling water

Place mushrooms in a bowl. Pour boiling water over them. Place weight on mushrooms to keep under water. Soak 15 minutes to 1 hour. Remove from water. Squeeze dry. Reserve stock. Remove tough stems. Cut each mushroom into 3 to 4 pieces.

¾ to 1 cup mushroom stock

Follow recipe for Snowpeas or Green Beans and Bean Curd with Tomatoes. Add mushrooms with snowpeas. Use mushroom stock in place of soybean stock in sauce. Cook as directed. Serve hot. A meal-in-a-bowl served with rice or noodles. A good mild-course feast dish. Good cold for lunch the next day.

VARIATION:
SNOWPEAS OR GREEN BEANS, MUSHROOMS AND CASHEWS WITH TOMATOES [Serves 4 to 6]

6 to 8 dried mushrooms
1 cup boiling water

Place mushrooms in a bowl. Pour boiling water over them. Place weight on mushrooms to keep under water. Soak 15 minutes to 1 hour. Reserve stock. Remove tough stems. Cut each mushroom into 3 to 4 pieces.

2 Tbsp. peanut oil
  OR vegetable oil
½ to 1 cup cashew pieces
  OR other nuts
  OR ½ cup sunflower seeds

Heat a wok over high heat. Add oil. Add nuts immediately. Cook 1 to 2 minutes until just brown. Remvoe from pan. Set aside for later use.

¾ to 1 cup mushroom stock

Follow recipe for Snowpeas or Green Beans and Bean Curd with Tomatoes. Use nuts in place of bean curd. Use mushroom stock in place of soybean stock in sauce. Add mushrooms with snowpeas. Add nuts with tomatoes. Cook as directed. Serve hot. A meal-in-a-bowl served with rice and noodles. A good mild-course feast dish. Good cold for lunch the next day.

SNOWPEAS OR GREEN BEANS AND CHICKEN WITH TOMATOES [Serves 4 to 6]

1 chicken breast,
  cut into ¼ inch cubes
¼ tsp. sea salt
1 tsp. sake
  OR dry sherry
  OR rice vinegar
pinch of black pepper

Mix chicken with other ingredients. Marinate 15 to 30 minutes.

3 Tbsp. peanut oil
  OR vegetable oil

Heat a wok over high heat. Add oil. Heat until a haze forms. Add chicken. Stir and fry 3 to 5 minutes until chicken is light golden brown. Remove from pan. Set aside to add later.

1 Tbsp. peanut oil
  OR vegetable oil
1 green onion, julienned
2 thin slices fresh ginger root,
  julienned

Add oil to wok. Heat until a haze forms. Add ginger and onions. Stir and fry 30 seconds until just tender.

6 water chestnuts, peeled and
  sliced thin [optional]
  OR 2 jerusalem artichokes,
    peeled and sliced thin
    [optional]
4 fresh mushrooms, sliced thin

Add to wok. Stir and fry 2 to 3 minutes until vegetables are just tender.

2 cups snowpeas, snipped and
  strings removed
  OR green beans, cut into long
    thin diagonals

Add to vegetables. Stir and fry 1 to 2 minutes until just heated but still crisp and bright green.

Sauce:
¾ to 1 cup chicken stock
1 Tbsp. sake
  OR dry sherry
  OR rice vinegar
2 Tbsp. soy sauce
1 tsp. mild honey
½ to 1 tsp. sea salt

Mix ingredients well. Add to vegetables. Cover. Simmer 1 to 2 minutes. Remove lid. Add chicken. Mix well.

Thickening:
1 Tbsp. arrowroot starch
2 Tbsp. water

Mix starch and water well. Push vegetables and chicken aside. Add thickening to sauce. Stir 1 minute until sauce thickens.

4 tomatoes, cut into bite-sized
  pieces

Add tomatoes. Mix gently so tomatoes do not break up. Cook 1 minute to heat. Serve hot. A meal-in-a-bowl served with rice or noodles. An excellent feast dish. Good cold for lunch.

VARIATION:
SNOWPEAS OR GREEN BEANS AND MEAT WITH TOMATOES [Serves 4 to 6]

¼ to ½ lb. boneless meat [pork
  or beef], cut into paper-thin
  strips [easier to cut thin if
  meat is partly frozen. Thaw
  before frying]
3 Tbsp. peanut oil
  OR vegetable oil

Heat a wok over high heat. Add oil. Heat until a haze forms. Add meat. Stir and fry 2 to 3 minutes until meat is seared but still slightly pink. Remove from pan. Set aside to add later.

1 cup meat stock

Follow recipe for Snowpeas or Green Beans and Chicken with Tomatoes. Use meat in place of chicken. Use meat stock in place of chicken stock in sauce. Cook as directed. Serve hot. A meal-in-a-bowl served with rice or noodles. An excellent hot mild-course feast dish. Good cold for lunch.

VARIATION:
SNOWPEAS OR GREEN BEANS AND SHRIMP WITH TOMATOES [Serves 4 to 6]

¼ to ½ lb. large shrimp,
  shelled and deveined,
  cut into ½ inch pieces
3 Tbsp. peanut oil
  OR vegetable oil

Heat a wok over high heat. Add oil. Heat until a haze forms. Add shrimp. Stir and fry 2 to 3 minutes until shrimp pink. Remove from pan. Set aside to add later.
Follow recipe for Snowpeas or Green Beans and Chicken with Tomatoes. Use shrimp in place of chicken. Cook as directed. Serve hot. A meal-in-a-bowl served with rice or noodles. An excellent hot mild-course feast dish. Good cold for lunch.

VARIATION:
SNOWPEAS OR GREEN BEANS, MUSHROOMS AND CHICKEN WITH TOMATOES [Serves 4 to 6]

6 to 8 dried mushrooms
1 cup boiling water

Place mushrooms in a bowl. Pour boiling water over them. Place weight on mushrooms to keep under water. Soak 15 minutes to 1 hour. Remove from water. Squeeze dry. Reserve stock. Remove tough stems. Cut each mushroom into 3 to 4 pieces.

½ cup mushroom stock
½ cup chicken stock

Follow recipe for Snowpeas or Green Beans and Chicken with Tomatoes. Add mushrooms with snowpeas. Use mushroom stock in place of half of chicken stock. Cook as directed. Serve hot. A meal-in-a-bowl served with rice or noodles. An excellent feast dish. Good cold for lunch.

VARIATION:
SNOWPEAS OR GREEN BEANS, MUSHROOMS AND MEAT WITH TOMATOES [Serves 4 to 6]

6 to 8 dried mushrooms
1 cup boiling water

Place mushrooms in a bowl. Pour boiling water over them. Place weight on mushrooms to keep under water. Soak 15 minutes to 1 hour. Remove from water. Squeeze dry. Reserve stock. Remove tough stems. Cut each mushroom into 3 to 4 pieces.

¼ to ½ lb. boneless meat [pork or beef], cut into
  paper-thin slices [easier to cut thin if meat is
  partly frozen. Thaw before frying]
3 Tbsp. peanut oil
  OR vegetable oil

Heat a wok over high heat. Add oil. Heat until a haze forms. Add meat. Stir and fry 2 to 3 minutes until meat is just seared but still slightly pink. Remove from pan. Set aside to add later.

½ cup mushroom stock
½ cup meat stock

Follow recipe for Snowpeas or Green Beans and Chicken with Tomatoes. Add mushrooms with snowpeas. Use meat in place of chicken. Use meat stock and mushroom stock in place of chicken stock. Cook as directed. Serve hot. A meal-in-a-bowl served with rice or noodles. An excellent feast dish. Good cold for lunch.

VARIATION:
SNOWPEAS OR GREEN BEANS, MUSHROOMS AND SHRIMP WITH TOMATOES [Serves 4 to 6]

6 to 8 dried mushrooms
1 cup boiling water

Place mushrooms in a bowl. Pour boiling water over them. Place weight on mushrooms to keep under water. Soak 15 minutes to 1 hour. Remove from water. Squeeze dry. Reserve Stock. Remove tough stems. Cut each mushroom into 3 to 4 pieces.

¼ to ½ lb. large shrimp,
  shelled and deveined,
  cut into ½ inch pieces
3 Tbsp. peanut oil
  OR vegetable oil

Heat a wok over high heat. Add oil. Heat until a haze forms. Add shrimp. Stir and fry 2 to 3 minutes until shrimp pink. Remove from pan. Set aside to add later.

½ cup mushroom stock
½ cup chicken stock

Follow recipe for Snowpeas or Green Beans and Chicken with Tomatoes. Use shrimp in place of chicken. Use mushroom stock in place of half of chicken stock. Cook as directed. Serve hot. A meal-in-a-bowl served with rice or noodles. An excellent feast dish. Good cold for lunch.

PEAS AND MUSHROOMS WITH CHICKEN [Serves 4 to 6]

1 chicken breast,
  cut into ¼ inch cubes
¼ tsp. sea salt
1 tsp. sake
  OR dry sherry
  OR rice vinegar
pinch black pepper

Mix chicken with other ingredients. Marinate 15 to 30 minutes.

3 Tbsp. peanut oil
  OR vegetable oil

Heat a wok over high heat. Add oil. Heat until a haze forms. Add chicken. Stir and fry 3 to 5 minutes until chicken is light brown. Remove from pan. Set aside to add later.

3 cups fresh peas
  OR frozen peas [need not be steamed]

Steam fresh peas 2 to 3 minutes until just tender but still bright green. Set aside for later use.

2 Tbsp. peanut oil
  OR vegetable oil
2 green onions, cut into thin diagonal slices
2 thin slices fresh ginger root, julienned

Heat a wok over high heat. Add oil. Heat until a haze forms. Add green onions and ginger. Stir and fry 30 seconds until just tender.

4 to 8 fresh mushrooms, cut into thin slices

Add mushrooms to wok. Stir and fry 2 minutes until just beginning to get tender. Add peas. Stir and fry 1 more minute.

Sauce:
¾ to 1 cup chicken stock
2 Tbsp. soy sauce
1 Tbsp. sake
  OR dry sherry
  OR rice vinegar
1 tsp. mild honey
½ to 1 tsp. sea salt

Mix ingredients well. Add to vegetables. Cover. Simmer 1 minute. Remove cover. Add chicken. Mix well.

Thickening:
1 Tbsp. arrowroot starch
2 Tbsp. water

Mix starch and water well. Push vegetables aside. Add thickening to sauce. Stir 1 minute until sauce thickens. Serve hot. A good meal-in-a-bowl served with rice or noodles. A good hot mild-course dish at a feast. Good cold for lunch.

VARIATION:

PEAS AND MUSHROOMS WITH SHRIMP
[Serves 4 to 6]

¼ to ½ lb. large shrimp,
   shelled and deveined,
   cut into ½ inch pieces
3 Tbsp. peanut oil
  OR vegetable oil

Heat a wok over high heat. Add oil. Heat until a haze forms. Add shrimp. Stir and fry 2 to 3 minutes until pink. Remove from pan. Set aside for later use.

Follow recipe for Peas and Mushrooms with Chicken. Use shrimp in place of chicken. Cook as directed. Serve hot. A good meal-in-a-bowl served with rice or noodles. A good hot mild-course dish at a feast. Good cold for lunch.

VARIATION:

PEAS AND MUSHROOMS IN SAUCE
[Serves 4 to 6]

¾ to 1 cup stock [chicken or
   soybean]

Follow recipe for Peas and Mushrooms with Chicken. Do not use chicken. Use soybean stock if vegetarian. Cook as directed. A good hot vegetable dish served with a main dish and rice or noodles for a simple meal. An excellent hot mild-course feast dish. Good cold for lunch the next day with rice and noodles and a leftover main dish.

VARIATION:

PEAS AND MUSHROOMS WITH BEAN CURD
[Serves 4 to 6]

1 to 2 cakes bean curd, cut into
  1 inch pieces

¾ to 1 cup soybean stock
  OR chicken stock

Follow recipe for Peas and Mushrooms with Chicken. Use bean curd in place of chicken. Add bean curd after sauce is added. Mix gently so bean curd does not break into smaller pieces. Cook as directed. A meal-in-a-bowl served with rice or noodles. A good hot mild-course feast dish. Good cold for lunch the next day.

VARIATION:

PEAS AND MUSHROOMS WITH CASHEWS
[Serves 4 to 6]

2 Tbsp. peanut oil
  OR vegetable oil
½ to 1 cup cashew pieces
  OR other nuts
  OR ½ cup sunflower seeds

Heat a wok over high heat. Add oil. Add nuts immediately. Cook 1 to 2 minutes until just brown. Remove from pan. Set aside for later use.

¾ to 1 cup soybean stock
  OR chicken stock

Follow recipe for Peas and Mushrooms with Chicken. Use cashews in place of chicken. Use soybean stock if vegetarian. Add nuts after sauce thickens. Cook as directed. Serve hot. A meal-in-a-bowl served with rice or noodles. A good hot mild-course feast dish. Good cold for lunch the next day.

BEAN SPROUTS AND CASHEWS [Serves 4 to 6]

2 Tbsp. peanut oil
  OR vegetable oil
½ cup cashew pieces
  OR other nuts
  OR sunflower seeds

Heat a wok over high heat. Add oil. Add nuts immediately. Cook 1 to 2 minutes until just brown. Remove from pan. Set aside for later use. Remove oil from pan.

2 Tbsp. sesame oil
  OR peanut oil
  OR vegetable oil
3 green onions, cut into thin
  diagonal slices
2 thin slices fresh ginger root,
  julienned
1 clove garlic, crushed and minced
  [optional]

Add oil to wok. Heat until a haze forms. Add ginger and onions. Stir and fry 30 seconds to 1 minute until just tender.

1 lb. bean sprouts
  OR other sprouts
½ to 1 tsp. sea salt

Add to wok. Stir and fry 15 to 30 seconds until just warm and still crisp. Remove from heat. Sprinkle over salt. Place on platter. Sprinkle over cashews. Serve hot. Good main dish served with rice or noodles.

VARIATION:
BEAN SPROUTS AND BEAN CURD [Serves 4 to 6]

1 cake bean curd cut into
  ½ inch cubes

Follow recipe for Bean Sprouts with Cashews. Use bean curd in place of cashews. Do not fry bean curd. Add bean curd after onions and before sprouts. Mix gently with onions, ginger and oil so bean curd does not break into smaller pieces. Add sprouts. Cook as directed. Serve hot. Good main dish served with rice or noodles.

VARIATION:
STIR-FRIED BEAN SPROUTS [Serves 4 to 6]

Follow recipe for Bean Sprouts and Cashews. Do not use cashews. Cook as directed. Serve hot. A good hot vegetable dish served with a main dish and rice or noodles for a simple meal.

VARIATION:
BEAN SPROUTS AND CHICKEN [Serves 4 to 6]

1 cup cooked chicken meat,
  cut into thin strips

Follow recipe for Bean Sprouts and Cashews. Use chicken in place of cashews. Add chicken meat to wok before bean sprouts. Stir and fry 1 minute to heat. Cook as directed. Serve hot. Good main dish served with rice or noodles.

VARIATION:
BEAN SPROUTS AND MEAT [Serves 4 to 6]

1 cup cooked meat [beef or
  pork], cut into thin strips

Follow recipe for Bean Sprouts and Cashews. Use meat in place of cashews. Add meat to wok before bean sprouts. Stir and fry 1 minute to heat. Cook as directed. Serve hot. Good main dish served with rice or noodles.

VARIATION:
BEAN SPROUTS AND SHRIMP [Serves 4 to 6]

1 cup cooked small shrimp

Follow recipe for Bean Sprouts and Cashews. Use shrimp in place of cashews. Add shrimp before bean sprouts. Stir and fry 1 minute to heat. Cook as directed. Serve hot. Good main dish served with rice or noodles.

CHICKEN AND PEANUTS [Serves 4 to 6]

1 cup raw peanuts

Roast at 300° 5 to 10 minutes until golden brown. Remove from oven. Chop slightly. Set aside to use later.

2 Tbsp. peanut oil
  OR vegetable oil
1 to 2 chicken breasts, cut into
  ½ inch cubes
1 Tbsp. arrowroot starch
1 egg white, slightly beaten
¼ tsp. sea salt

Mix chicken, starch, egg white and salt well. Heat a wok over high heat. Add oil. Heat until a haze forms. Add chicken. Stir and fry 3 to 5 minutes until golden brown. Remove from pan. Set aside to add later.

2 Tbsp. peanut oil
  OR vegetable oil
1 clove garlic, crushed
  and minced
2 to 3 chili peppers, minced
4 green onions, cut into thin
  diagonal slices
2 thin slices fresh ginger root,
  julienned

Add oil to wok. Heat over high heat until a haze forms. Add ingredients. Stir and fry 1 minute until just browned.

Sauce:
¼ cup chicken stock
3 Tbsp. soy sauce
1 Tbsp. sake
  OR dry sherry
  OR rice vinegar
1 tsp. mild honey
½ to 1 tsp. sea salt

Mix ingredients well. Add to wok. Add chicken and peanuts. Stir and mix for 1 minute until chicken is well coated with sauce.

Thickening:
1 tsp. arrowroot starch
2 tsp. water

Mix starch and water well. Add thickening to chicken and peanuts. Stir 1 minute until sauce thickens and coats the chicken well. Serve hot. A spicy main dish served with rice and noodles and a vegetable side dish. An excellent hot-pungent course feast dish. Good cold for lunch.

VARIATION:

MEAT AND PEANUTS [Serves 4 to 6]

¼ to ½ lb. boneless meat [beef
  or pork] cut into ¼ inch strips

¼ cup meat stock

Follow recipe for Chicken and Peanuts. Use meat in place of chicken. Use meat stock in place of chicken stock in sauce. Cook as directed. Serve hot. A spicy main dish served with rice or noodles and a vegetable side dish. An excellent hot-pungent course feast dish. Good cold for lunch.

VARIATION:

FISH AND PEANUTS [Serves 4 to 6]

1 lb. white fish fillet, cut into
  ½ inch cubes

Follow recipe for Chicken and Peanuts. Use fish in place of chicken. Cook as directed. Serve hot. A spicy main dish served with rice or noodles and a vegetable side dish. An excellent hot-pungent course feast dish. Good cold for lunch.

VARIATION:

SHRIMP AND PEANUTS [Serves 4 to 6]

½ to 1 lb. large shrimp,
  shelled and deveined,
  cut into ¼ inch pieces

Follow recipe for Chicken and Peanuts. Use shrimp in place of chicken. Cook as directed. Serve hot. A spicy main dish served with rice or noodles and a vegetable side dish. An excellent hot-pungent course feast dish. Good cold for lunch.

SAVORY SIMMERED DISHES

TECHNIQUE

Savory dishes resemble most closely the North American stew, but with a great flavor difference. Meat is sear-cooked and then flavored with various sauces and simmered until tender. For vegetarian savory dishes, bean curd, eggs, and vegetables are simmered in pungent sauces. The method of cooking these dishes is very similar to stew cooking in North America so the technique needs no explanation. The only admonition is again to have all ingredients prepared ahead so the dish can go together quickly in the initial stages and then simmer slowly until done.

Simmered and savory dishes are a meal-in-a-bowl dishes when served with rice and vegetables. Many of them have their own vegetables in the dish so they can be served just with rice for a simple meal. Savory dishes are excellent hot-course dishes at a feast. Cold, they make a great lunch.

EGG FU YUNG [Serves 4 to 6]

¼ **lb. bean sprouts**
3 **thin slices fresh ginger root,**
 minced
1 **Tbsp. sake**
 OR dry sherry
 OR rice vinegar

Mix ingredients together well.

5 **eggs**
1 **tsp. sea salt**

Add to bean sprouts and beat with chopsticks 2 to 3 minutes until light and frothy.

2 **Tbsp. peanut oil**
 OR vegetable oil

Heat a medium or large cast iron skillet over medium heat. Add oil. Heat until a small amount of egg added sets well. Add egg and bean sprout mixture to center of pan so it follows oil to edges. Cover pan. Reduce heat to medium low. Leave 10 minutes. Remove lid. Loosen edges with a knife. Invert egg mixture onto a plate. Slide back into the skillet. Cook 2 to 4 more minutes until well set. Remove from heat. Invert onto a deep serving platter.

2 **Tbsp. peanut oil**
 OR vegetable oil
2 **green onions, julienned**
2 **thin slices fresh ginger root,**
 julienned

While the eggs are cooking heat a cast iron skillet or wok over high heat. Add oil. Heat until a haze forms. Add ginger and onions. Stir and fry 30 seconds until just tender.

4 **to 5 fresh mushrooms,**
 sliced thin
 OR ¼ cup clouds-ear
 mushrooms soaked 5 minutes
 in 1 cup hot water, then
 drained
1 **stalk celery, cut into thin**
 diagonal slices
 OR 1 medium carrot, cut into
 thin diagonals
 OR ¼ lb. snowpeas, snipped
 and strings removed, cut
 into 3 to 4 diagonal slices
¼ **cup fresh peas, par-steamed 2 to**
 3 minutes

Add mushrooms to wok. Stir and fry 2 to 3 minutes until just lightly browned. Add celery and peas. Stir and fry an additional 2 to 3 minutes.

Sauce:
1½ cups stock
2 Tbsp. soy sauce
1 Tbsp. sake
  OR dry sherry
  OR rice vinegar
1 tsp. mild honey
1 tsp. sea salt

Add to vegetables. Mix well. Bring to a boil. Reduce heat to medium. Simmer 1 ro 2 minutes.

Thickening:
1 Tbsp. arrowroot starch
2 Tbsp. water

Mix starch and water well. Add to vegetable sauce. Stir and mix 1 minute until sauce thickens. Remove from heat and pour over egg omelet on platter. Serve hot. An excellent meal-in-a-bowl served with rice or noodles. A good hot mild-course feast dish. Good cold for lunch the next day.

VARIATION:

CRAB OR SHRIMP EGG FU YUNG [Serves 4 to 6]

¼ lb. crab meat
  OR ¼ lb. small cooked shrimp
1½ cups chicken stock

Follow recipe for Egg Fu Yung. Add crab or shrimp to bean sprouts. Use chicken stock in place of vegetarian stock in sauce. Cook as directed. Serve hot. An excellent meal-in-a-bowl served with rice or noodles. A good hot mild-course feast dish. Good cold for lunch.

VARIATION:

CHICKEN EGG FU YUNG [Serves 4 to 6]

½ to 1 cup cooked chicken meat,
  cut into thin strips
1½ cups chicken stock

Follow recipe for Egg Fu Yung. Add chicken to bean sprouts. Use chicken stock in place of vegetarian stock in sauce. Cook as directed. Serve hot. A meal-in-a-bowl served with rice or noodles. A good hot mild-course feast dish. Good cold for lunch.

VARIATION:

MEAT EGG FU YUNG [Serves 4 to 6]

½ to 1 cup cooked meat [beef
  or pork], cut into thin strips

1½ cups meat stock

Follow recipe for Egg Fu Yung. Add meat to bean sprouts. Use meat stock in place of vegetarian stock in sauce. Cook as directed. Serve hot. A meal-in-a-bowl served with rice or noodles. A good hot mild-course feast dish. Good cold for lunch.

BEAN CURD WITH CARROT AND GREEN BEANS [Serves 4 to 6]

2 cakes bean curd
2 Tbsp. soy sauce
1 Tbsp. rice vinegar
   OR sake
   OR dry sherry
1 cup water

Cut 2 cakes of bean curd into 1 inch cubes. Place in a bowl. Pour mixture of soy sauce, vinegar and water over bean curd. Marinate 1 hour or overnight. Drain well. Dry 1 hour. Set aside for later use.

2 cakes bean curd

Tightly wrap 2 cakes of bean curd in a muslin cloth (old sheet good). Place on drain board. Cover with a plate. Place weight on top to press out excess moisture. Press 1 hour or overnight. Cut into ½ inch cubes. Set aside for later use.

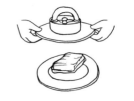

¼ cup peanut oil
   OR vegetable oil
2 Tbsp. sesame oil [optional]

Heat a large cast iron skillet over medium high heat. Add oil. Heat until a small piece of marinated bean curd added sizzles. Add marinated bean curd. Reduce heat to medium. Fry 3 to 5 minutes until light golden brown. Turn once to brown evenly. Remove from pan. Drain. Set aside to add later.

2 Tbsp. above oil
3 thin slices fresh ginger root, julienned
6 green onions, julienned

Heat a wok over high heat. Add oil. Heat until a haze forms. Add ginger and onions. Stir and fry 30 seconds until just tender.

2 carrots, cut into thin diagonal slices

Add to ginger and onions. Stir and fry 2 to 3 minutes.

¼ cup soy sauce
2 Tbsp. sake
   OR dry sherry
   OR rice vinegar
2 tsp. mild honey

Add to carrots. Mix well. Bring to boil. Boil 30 seconds.

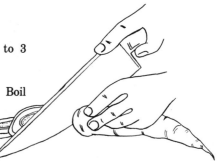

2 cups stock

Add to carrots. Bring to boil. Mix well. Cover. Reduce heat to medium low. Simmer 10 minutes until carrots are just tender.
Add pressed bean curd cubes. Mix gently so bean curd does not break into smaller pieces. Cover. Cook 2 to 3 minutes until well heated.

½ cup green beans, cut into long thin diagonals
   OR snowpeas, snipped and strings removed, cut into 3 to 4 diagonal slices
   OR fresh peas
   OR frozen peas [need not be steamed]

Steam 3 to 5 minutes until just tender and still bright green. When carrots are tender and bean curd is heated add green beans and fried bean curd. Gently fold into dish so bean curd does not break into smaller pieces. Simmer 1 minute. Serve hot. An excellent meal-in-a-bowl served with rice or noodles. Good feast dish. Good cold for lunch the next day.

VARIATION:

MEAT WITH BEAN CURD, CARROTS AND GREEN BEANS [Serves 4 to 6]

½ lb. boneless meat [beef or
   pork], cut into ½ inch cubes
2 Tbsp. peanut oil
   OR vegetable oil

Heat a wok over high heat. Add oil. Heat until a haze forms. Add meat cubes. Stir and fry 2 to 3 minutes until meat is just seared but still slightly pink.

2 cups meat stock

Follow recipe for Bean Curd with Carrots and Green Beans, Use meat in place of pressed bean curd. Use meat stock. Cook marinated bean curd as directed. After meat is fried add ginger and onions. Follow remainder of recipe. Serve hot. An excellent meal-in-a-bowl served with rice or noodles. Good feast dish. Good cold for lunch.

SAVORY BEAN CURD WITH CLOUDS-EAR MUSHROOMS AND VEGETABLES [Serves 4 to 6]

2 cakes bean curd, cut into
   1 by 2 inch pieces

Set on a plate for later use.

¼ to ½ cup clouds-ear
   mushrooms
1 cup boiling water

Place mushrooms in bowl. Pour boiling water over them. Place weight on mushrooms to keep under water. Soak 15 minutes to 1 hour. Remove from water. Squeeze dry. Reserve stock for later use.

2 green onions, cut into thin
   diagonal slices
2 slices fresh ginger root,
   julienned
2 Tbsp. sesame oil
   OR peanut oil
   OR vegetable oil

Heat a heavy skillet over high heat. Add oil. Heat until onion added sizzles. Add onions and ginger. Stir and fry 30 seconds until just tender.

1 to 2 medium carrots, cut into
   thin diagonal slices
   OR ½ lb. green beans, cut
      into thin diagonal slices
   OR ½ lb. snowpeas, snipped and
      strings removed

Add to onions and ginger. Stir and fry 3 to 5 minutes. Add clouds-ear. Stir and fry 1 minute.

¼ cup soy sauce
1 Tbsp. mild honey
1 Tbsp. sake
   OR dry sherry
   OR rice vinegar
½ tsp. sea salt

Add to carrots. Mix well. Bring to boil. Simmer 1 minute.

½ cup soybean stock
½ cup mushroom stock

Add to carrots. Mix well. Bring to boil. Cover. Simmer 5 to 10 minutes until carrots just beginning to get tender. Add bean curd. Simmer 1 to 2 minutes to heat.

1 Tbsp. arrowroot starch
2 Tbsp. water

Mix starch and water well. Add to sauce. Mix gently so bean curd does not break. Cook 1 minute until sauce thickens. Serve hot. A simple meal-in-a-bowl when served with rice. Good feast dish. Good cold for lunch the next day.

FISH WITH BEAN CURD IN SAVORY SAUCE [Serves 4 to 6]

1 lb. white fish fillet, cut into
   3 inch pieces
1 Tbsp. sake
   OR dry sherry
   OR rice vinegar
½ tsp. sea salt
¼ inch fresh ginger root,
   grated

Mix sake, salt and ginger well. Pour over fish. Marinate 30 minutes to 1 hour. Drain over wire rack. Save sauce to add later.

⅓ cup peanut oil
   OR vegetable oil

Heat a cast iron skillet over high heat. Add oil. Heat until a small piece of fish added sizzles. Reduce heat to medium. Add fish. Fry 3 to 5 minutes until golden brown. Turn once to brown both sides. Turn gently so fish does not break into smaller pieces. Remove from pan. Drain. Set aside for later use.

2 green onions, julienned
3 slices fresh ginger root,
   julienned
2 Tbsp. peanut oil
   OR vegetable oil

Heat a wok over high heat. Add oil. Heat until a small piece of onion added sizzles. Add onion and ginger. Stir and fry 30 seconds to 1 minute until just tender.

Sauce:
Reserved marinade sauce
3 Tbsp. soy sauce
2 tsp. mild honey
1 Tbsp. sake
   OR dry sherry
   OR rice vinegar
1 tsp. sea salt
¼ cup chicken stock

Add to ginger and onions. Add fish. Baste well with sauce. Cook 3 to 4 minutes until fish well coated with sauce.

Thickening:
2 tsp. arrowroot starch
2 Tbsp. water

Mix starch and water well. Push fish to side of wok. Add thickening to sauce. Stir 1 minute until sauce thickens.

1 to 2 cakes bean curd, cut into
   2 inch cubes

Add to fish and sauce. Mix gently so bean curd does not break into smaller pieces. Cook 1 to 2 minutes to heat bean curd and cover well with sauce. Serve hot. A good main dish. Serve with rice or noodles and a vegetable side dish. A good hot-pungent feast dish. Good cold for lunch the next day.

SHRIMP IN BLACK BEAN SAUCE [Serves 4 to 6]

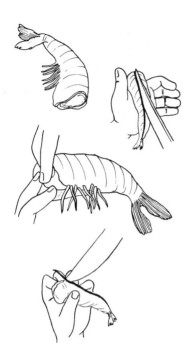

1 lb. large shrimp,
  shelled and deveined
3 Tbsp. peanut oil
  OR vegetable oil

Heat a wok over high heat. Add oil. Heat until a haze forms. Add shrimp. Stir and fry 2 to 3 minutes until pink.

1 to 2 cloves garlic, crushed and
  minced
2 Tbsp. salted black beans,
  coarsely chopped
1 thin slice ginger root,
  julienned
2 green onions, minced

Add to shrimp. Stir and fry 30 seconds to 1 minute until garlic and ginger are tender.

Sauce:
¼ cup chicken stock
1 Tbsp. sake
  OR dry sherry
  OR rice vinegar
3 Tbsp. soy sauce
1 tsp. mild honey
½ to 1 tsp. sea salt
½ tsp. arrowroot starch

Mix ingredients well. Add to shrimp. Bring to a boil. Reduce heat to medium. Simmer 5 to 10 minutes until most of liquid is absorbed and sauce thickens. Serve hot. An excellent main dish. Serve with rice or noodles and a vegetable side dish for a simple meal. A good hot-pungent-course feast dish. Good cold for lunch the next day.

SIMMERED CHICKEN WITH BEAN CURD [Serves 4 to 6]

½ chicken,
  cut into medium sized
  pieces
2 green onions, cut in half
  lengthwise
1 inch cube fresh ginger root,
  crushed
4 cups water

Place ingredients in a large heavy saucepan. Bring to boil over high heat. Cover. Reduce heat to medium low. Simmer 1 hour until chicken is tender. Remove from heat. Strain chicken stock. Drain well. Remove chicken from bones. Julienne chicken meat. Reserve stock and chicken for laster use.

1 to 2 cakes bean curd, cut
  into ½ inch cubes
¼ cup peanut oil
  OR vegetable oil
2 Tbsp. sesame oil [optional]

Heat a large cast iron skillet over medium high heat. Add oil. Heat until a small piece of bean curd added sizzles. Add bean curd. Reduce heat to medium. Fry 3 to 5 minutes until light golden brown. Turn once to brown evenly. Remove from pan. Drain. Set aside to add later.

½ to 1 tsp. sea salt

Sprinkle over fried bean curd.

2 Tbsp. peanut oil
  OR vegetable oil
  OR oil reserved from frying
    bean curd
2 green onions, minced
2 thin slices fresh ginger root,
  minced

Heat a wok over high heat. Add oil. Heat until a haze forms. Add ginger and green onions. Stir and fry 30 seconds until just tender.

Sauce:
1 cup chicken stock
3 Tbsp. soy sauce
1 tsp. mild honey
½ tsp. sea salt

Add to ginger and green onions. Bring to boil. Add chicken and bean curd. Mix well with sauce. Reduce heat to medium. Simmer 15 to 20 minutes until liquid is almost all absorbed by meat and bean curd. Serve hot. An excellent main dish. Serve with rice or noodles and a vegetable side dish. Good hot mild feast dish. Good cold for lunch.

SAVORY CASHEW CHICKEN [Serves 4 to 6]

½ to 1 cup cashew pieces
   OR other nuts
3 Tbsp. peanut oil
   OR vegetable oil

Heat a cast iron saucepan over high heat. Add oil. Add nuts immediately. Stir and fry 1 to 2 minutes until nuts just brown. Remove from pan. Set aside for later use.

½ to 1 chicken,
   skinned and cut into
   bite-sized pieces
1 Tbsp. peanut oil
   OR vegetable oil

Add to saucepan. Stir and fry 3 to 5 minutes until light brown.

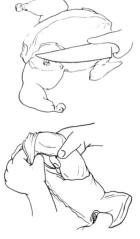

2 green onions, minced
3 slices fresh ginger root,
   minced

Add to chicken. Stir and fry 1 to 2 minutes until ginger and onions tender.

Sauce:
¼ cup soy sauce
2 Tbsp. sake
   OR dry sherry
   OR rice vinegar
1½ Tbsp. mild honey
½ cup chicken stock
½ to 1 tsp. sea salt

Add to chicken. Bring to boil. Reduce heat to medium. Cover. Simmer 20 to 30 minutes until chicken is tender.

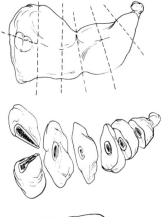

Thickening:
2 tsp. arrowroot starch
2 Tbsp. water

Mix starch and water well. Add to chicken. Stir 1 minute until sauce thickens. Add cashews. Cook 1 minute until well coated with sauce. A good main dish. Serve with rice or noodles and a vegetable side dish for a simple meal. An excellent hot-pungent-course feast dish. Good cold for lunch.

SAVORY SOY CHICKEN [Serves 4 to 6]

½ to 1 chicken,
   skinned and cut into
   bite-sized pieces
3 Tbsp. vegetable oil

Heat a heavy cast iron saucepan over high heat. Add oil. Heat until a haze forms. Add chicken. Stir and fry 5 minutes until chicken is lightly browned.

3 green onions, chopped
2 thin slices fresh ginger root,
   minced
1 small clove garlic, crushed and
   minced

Add to chicken. Stir and fry 2 to 3 minutes until soft and well mixed with chicken.

Sauce:
⅓ cup soy sauce
2 Tbsp. mild honey
2 Tbsp. sake
   OR dry sherry
   OR rice vinegar
½ to 1 tsp. sea salt

Add to chicken. Bring to a boil. Baste chicken with sauce 1 to 2 minutes until well coated.

1 cup water
   OR stock

Add to chicken and sauce. Bring to a boil over high heat. Reduce heat to medium low. Cover. Simmer 20 to 30 minutes until chicken is tender.

Thickening:
1 Tbsp. arrowroot starch
2 Tbsp. water

Mix starch and water well. Add to chicken. Stir 1 minute until sauce thickens. Serve hot. A good main dish. Serve with rice or noodles and a vegetable side dish for a simple meal. An excellent hot pungent-course feast dish. Good cold for lunch.

VARIATION:

SAVORY SOY CHICKEN WITH VEGETABLES [Serves 4 to 6]

6 to 8 dried mushrooms
  [optional]
1 cup boiling water

Place mushrooms in a bowl. Pour boiling water over them. Place weight on mushrooms to keep under water. Soak 15 minutes to 1 hour. Remove from water. Squeeze dry. Reserve stock. Remove tough stems. Cut each mushroom into 3 to 4 pieces.

½ cup mushroom stock
½ cup chicken stock

Follow recipe for Savory Soy Chicken. Use in place of water.

2 to 3 carrots, cut into thin
  diagonal slices
  OR ½ lb. green beans, cut into
    thin diagonal slices
  OR ¼ lb. snowpeas, snipped
    and strings removed
  OR any other hard vegetable,
    cut into thin diagonals

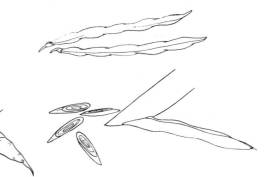

Add to chicken along with mushrooms 10 minutes after it has begun to simmer. Simmer 10 to 15 minutes until vegetables and meat are tender. Cook as directed. Serve hot. A meal-in-a-bowl served with rice or noodles. An excellent hot pungent-course feast dish. Good cold for lunch.

SAVORY WALNUT CHICKEN [Serves 4 to 6]

3 Tbsp. vegetable oil
½ cup walnut halves
   OR walnut pieces

Heat a wok over high heat. Add oil. Immediately add walnuts. Stir and fry 1 to 2 minutes until light golden brown. Remove from wok. Set aside for later use.

½ chicken,
   cut into bite-sized
   pieces
2 Tbsp. arrowroot starch

Mix chicken and starch well. Add to wok. Stir and fry 3 to 5 minutes until golden brown.

1 green onion, chopped
2 thin slices fresh ginger root,
   minced

Add to chicken. Stir and fry 1 minute until well mixed with chicken and green onions and ginger are tender.

Sauce:
½ cup chicken stock
2 Tbsp. soy sauce
1 Tbsp. sake
   OR dry sherry
   OR rice vinegar
2 tsp. mild honey
½ tsp. sea salt

Add to chicken. Bring to a boil. Reduce heat to medium. Cover. Simmer 20 to 30 minutes until chicken is tender and sauce thickens. Add fried walnuts. Mix well. Heat 1 to 2 minutes. Serve hot. An excellent hot-pungent course feast dish. Good cold for lunch.

SWEET AND SOUR CHICKEN [Serves 4 to 6]

½ to 1 chicken,
   skinned and cut into
   bite-sized pieces
2 Tbsp. soy sauce
1 Tbsp. mild honey
1 tsp. sea salt
3 Tbsp. arrowroot starch
1 inch fresh ginger root,
   grated
1 tsp. thick red soy
   OR molasses

Mix ingredients well. Marinate 30 minutes. Mix often. Drain chicken. Reserve sauce to add later.

Sauce:
3 Tbsp. sake
   OR dry sherry
   OR rice vinegar
2 Tbsp. mild honey
1 tsp. molasses
⅓ cup water

Combine with remainder of marinade sauce. Mix well. Set aside to add later.

3 Tbsp. peanut oil
   OR vegetable oil

Heat a heavy cast iron skillet over medium high heat. Add oil. Heat until a haze forms. Add chicken. Stir and fry 3 to 5 minutes until lightly browned. Drain excess oil. Add combined sauce. Stir well. Cover. Bring to a boil. Reduce heat to medium low. Simmer 20 to 30 minutes until chicken is tender and sauce thickens. Serve hot. An excellent main dish. Serve hot with rice or noodles and a vegetable side dish. A good hot-pungent-course feast dish. Good cold for lunch the next day.

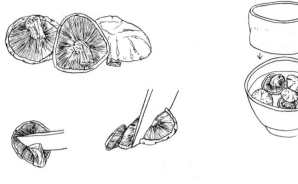

VARIATION:
SWEET AND SOUR CHICKEN WITH VEGETABLES [Serves 4 to 6]

6 to 8 dried mushrooms
[optional]
1 cup boiling water

Place mushrooms in a bowl. Pour boiling water over them. Place weight on mushrooms to keep under water. Soak 15 minutes to 1 hour. Remove from water. Squeeze dry. Reserve stock. Remove tough stems. Cut each mushroom into 3 to 4 pieces.

2 to 3 carrots, cut into thin
diagonal slices
OR ¹⁄₂ lb. green beans, cut
into thin diagonal slices
OR ¹⁄₄ lb. snowpeas, snipped
and strings removed
OR any other hard vegetable,
cut into thin diagonals

Follow recipe for Sweet and Sour Chicken. Add to chicken along with mushrooms 10 minutes after it has begun to simmer. Simmer 10 to 15 minutes until vegetables and meat are tender. Cook as directed. Serve hot. A meal-in-a-bowl served with rice or noodles. An excellent hot-pungent-course feast dish. Good cold for lunch the next day.

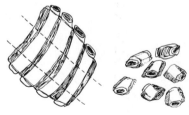

VARIATION:

SWEET AND SOUR MEAT [Serves 4 to 6]

1 to 2 lbs. beef shortribs,
cut in half lengthwise [ask
your butcher to do this]
OR 1 lb. other meat cut into
1 inch cubes
OR 1 to 2 lbs. pork spareribs,
cut in half lengthwise [ask
your butcher to do this]

Follow recipe for Sweet and Sour Chicken. Use meat in place of chicken. Cook as directed. Serve hot. An excellent main dish. Serve with rice or noodles and a vegetable side dish. Good hot-pungent-course feast dish. Good cold for lunch the next day.

SWEET AND SOUR FISH [Serves 4 to 6]

1 to 2 lbs. firm white fish
    fillet, cut into 3 to 4 inch
    pieces
  OR 2 to 3 lbs. whole fish
      scored three times on
      each side
2 Tbsp. soy sauce
1 Tbsp. sake
  OR dry sherry
  OR rice vinegar
1 tsp. mild honey

Mix soy, sake and honey well. Pour over fish. Marinate 15 to 20 minutes. Turn often. Remove fish from sauce. Drain on wire racks for 5 minutes. Reserve sauce to add later.

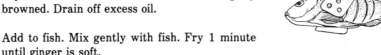

¹/₃ cup peanut oil
  OR vegetable oil

Heat a heavy cast iron skillet over medium high heat. Add oil. Heat until a small piece of fish added sizzles. Add fish. Reduce heat to medium. Fry 2 to 3 minutes on each side until lightly browned. Drain off excess oil.

3 thin slices ginger, minced

Add to fish. Mix gently with fish. Fry 1 minute until ginger is soft.

Sauce:
1 Tbsp. soy sauce
1 tsp. mild honey
1 Tbsp. sake
  OR dry sherry
1 Tbsp. rice vinegar
3 Tbsp. water

Mix with remaider of marinade sauce. Add sauce to fish. Bring to a boil over medium heat. Reduce heat to medium low. Simmer 15 to 25 minutes until most of liquid is absorbed. Baste often. Serve hot. An excellent main dish. Serve with rice or noodles and a vegetable side dish. A good hot-pungent-course feast dish. Good cold for lunch the next day.

VARIATION:

SWEET AND SOUR FISH WITH VEGETABLES [Serves 4 to 6]

6 to 8 dried mushrooms
  [optional]
1 cup boiling water

Place mushrooms in a bowl. Pour boiling water over them. Place weight on mushrooms to keep under water. Soak 15 minutes to 1 hour. Remove from water. Squeeze dry. Reserve stock. Remove tough stems. Cut each mushroom into 3 to 4 pieces.

3 Tbsp. mushroom stock

Follow recipe for Sweet and Sour Fish. Use mushroom stock in place of water in stock.

2 to 3 carrots, cut into thin
  diagonal slices
  OR ¹/₂ lb. green beans, cut
    into thin diagonal slices
  OR ¹/₄ lb. snowpeas, snipped
    and strings removed
  OR any other hard vegetable,
    cut into thin diagonals

Add to fish along with mushrooms 10 minutes after it has begun to simmer. Simmer 10 to 15 more minutes until vegetables are tender. Cook as directed. Serve hot. A meal-in-a-bowl served with rice or noodles. An excellent hot-pungent-course feast dish. Good cold for lunch the next day.

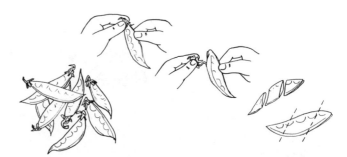

SAVORY SIMMERED DISHES

SWEET AND SOUR PRAWNS [Serves 4 to 6]

1 to 1½ lbs. raw prawns
  with shells

Make a shallow slit just to one side down the center back. Remove the intestine with the tip of the knife. Remove the legs but leave the shell on the prawns.

1 Tbsp. soy sauce
2 tsp. mild honey
½ tsp. sea salt
1½ Tbsp. arrowroot starch
½ inch fresh ginger root,
  grated
½ tsp. thick red soy
  OR molasses

Mix ingredients well. Pour over prawns. Mix well. Marinate 20 to 30 minutes. Mix often. Drain well. Reserve sauce to add later.

Sauce:
2 Tbsp. rice vinegar
  OR sake
  OR dry sherry
1 Tbsp. mild honey
½ tsp. molasses
¼ to ½ tsp. red pepper
¼ to ½ tsp. 5-spice mix
2 tsp. tomato sauce
2 Tbsp. water

Combine with marinade sauce. Mix well. Set aside to add later.

2 Tbsp. peanut oil
  OR vegetable oil

Heat a heavy cast iron skillet over medium heat. Add oil. Heat slightly. Add prawns. Stir and fry over medium heat 5 to 8 minutes until pink. Drain excess oil. Add combined sauce. Stir well. Cover and bring to a boil. Reduce heat to medium low. Simmer 10 to 15 minutes. Stir occasionally. Serve hot. An excellent hot-pungent-course feast dish. Good cold for lunch the next day.

VARIATION:
SWEET AND SOUR PRAWNS WITH VEGETABLES [Serves 4 to 6]

1 to 2 green peppers, seeded
  and cut into bite-sized pieces
  OR ¼ lb. green beans, cut
    into long thin diagonal
    slices
  OR ½ cup peas
    [frozen or fresh]

Follow recipe for Sweet and Sour Prawns. Add peppers 5 minutes after prawns are simmering.

2 to 4 tomatoes, cut into
  bite-sized pieces [optional]

Add tomatoes 2 minutes before serving. Stir gently so tomatoes do not break into small pieces. Serve hot. An excellent hot-pungent-course feast dish. Good cold for lunch the next day.

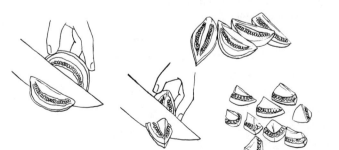

SWEET AND SOUR EGGS [Serves 4 to 6]

2 Tbsp. peanut oil
  OR vegetable oil
3 green onions, minced
2 thin slices fresh ginger root,
  minced

Heat a medium cast iron saucepan over high heat. Add oil. Heat until a small piece of onion added sizzles. Add onion and ginger. Stir and fry 30 seconds until just tender.

Sauce:
2 Tbsp. sake
  OR dry sherry
  OR rice vinegar
1/3 cup soy sauce
1 1/2 Tbsp. mild honey
1/2 to 1 tsp. sea salt

Add to saucepan. Bring to boil. Reduce heat to medium low.

8 hard-boiled eggs, cut in half
  lengthwise

Add to sauce yolkside up. Cook 2 to 3 minutes. Baste eggs often with sauce.

1 cup water
  OR stock

Add to saucepan. Mix well. Cover. Simmer 10 minutes.

Thickening:
1 Tbsp. arrowroot starch
2 Tbsp. water

Mix starch and water well. Add to sauce. Mix well. Stir gently 1 to 2 minutes until suace thickens. These can be served hot as a main dish or cold as an appetizer. Good cold for lunch the next day. An excellent savory-course feast dish.

VARIATION:
SWEET AND SOUR EGGS WITH MUSHROOMS [Serves 4 to 6]

6 to 8 dried mushrooms
1 cup boiling water

Place mushrooms in a bowl. Pour boiling water over them. Place weight on mushrooms to keep under water. Soak 15 minutes to 1 hour. Remove from water. Squeeze dry. Reserve stock. Remove tough stems. Cut each mushroom into 3 to 4 pieces.

1 cup mushroom stock

Follow recipe for Sweet and Sour Eggs. Use mushroom stock in place of water in sauce. Add mushrooms with eggs. Cook as directed. A good main-course dish. An excellent savory feast dish. Good cold for lunch.

VARIATION:
SWEET AND SOUR EGGS WITH VEGETABLES [Serves 4 to 6]

2 carrots, cut into thin diagonal
  slices
OR 1/4 lb. green beans, cut into
    thin diagonal slices
  OR 1/4 lb. snowpeas, snipped
    and strings removed
  OR any other hard vegetable
    cut into thin diagonals

Follow recipe for Sweet and Sour Eggs. Add vegetables just after ginger and onions. Stir and fry 2 to 3 minutes. Cook as directed. Serve hot. A good meal-in-a-bowl served with rice or noodles. An excellent hot savory-course feast dish. Good cold for lunch.

SAVORY BANBOO SHOOTS WITH MUSHROOMS [Serves 4 to 6]

4 Tbsp. peanut oil
  OR vegetable oil
8 medium bamboo shoots, cut
  into thin slices

Heat a wok over high heat. Add oil. Heat until a haze forms. Add banboo shoots. Stir and fry 2 to 3 minutes until just lightly browned. Remove from pan. Drain. Remove oil from wok.

8 dried mushrooms
1 cup boiling water

Place mushrooms in a bowl. Pour boiling water over them. Place weight on mushrooms to keep under water. Soak 15 minutes to 1 hour. Remove from water. Squeeze dry. Reserve stock. Remove tough stems. Cut mushrooms into thin slivers.

1 large clove garlic, crushed
  and minced
2 thin slices fresh ginger root,
  julienned
1 Tbsp. peanut oil
  OR vegetable oil

Heat a wok over high heat. Add oil. Heat until a haze forms. Add ginger and garlic. Stir and fry 30 seconds until just tender. Add bamboo shoots and mushrooms. Stir and fry an additional 1 to 2 minutes.

Sauce:
3 Tbsp. soy sauce
1 tsp. mild honey
½ cup mushroom stock

Add to wok. Mix well. Bring to a boil. Reduce heat to medium low. Simmer 15 to 20 minutes until bamboo shoots are tender and most of liquid is absorbed. Serve hot. An excellent vegetable dish served with rice and noodles and a main dish for a simple meal. An excellent savory-course feast dish.

VARIATION:
SAVORY BAMBOO SHOOTS WITH MUSHROOMS AND BEAN CURD [Serves 4 to 6]

1 to 2 cakes bean curd, cut
  into 1 inch pieces

Follow recipe for Savory Bamboo Shoots with Mushrooms. Cook as directed. Add bean curd in the last 5 minutes of cooking. Mix gently so bean curd does not break up into small pieces. A meal-in-a-bowl served with rice or noodles. A good savory-course feast dish. Good cold for lunch the next day.

CHINESE BARBEQUE MEAT [Serves 6 to 8]

2 lbs. boneless meat [beef,
    lamb or pork], cut paper-thin
    [easier to do if meat is partly
    frozen. Thaw before
    marinating]
1 cup soy sauce
1 cup sake
    OR dry sherry
    OR rice vinegar
1 tsp. sesame oil
1 tsp. sea salt
dash to ½ tsp. black pepper
2 cloves garlic, crushed and
    minced
6 green onions, julienned
2 Tbsp. mild honey

Mix meat with other ingredients. Marinate 15 minutes to 1 hour. Heat a small griddle or solid grill at a table or heat griddle over medium high heat on a stove. Each person grills meat as they want it. Serve hot with rice or noodles and a cold vegetable side dish. A good feast dish. Good cold for lunch the next day.

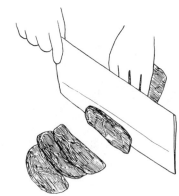

PLUM SAUCE CHICKEN OR DUCK [Serves 4 to 6]

1 roasting chicken
    OR duck
2 tsp. sea salt
½ to 1 tsp. 10-spice mix

Wash chicken or duck well. Pat dry. Allow to sit 1 to 2 hours to dry well. Rub with salt and spice mix. Place in a 350° oven for 40 minutes.

Sauce:
½ cup plum sauce
1 Tbsp. sake
    OR dry sherry
    OR rice vinegar
1 Tbsp. soy sauce
2 Tbsp. chicken stock

Place ingredients in small saucepan. Cook over medium heat 2 to 3 minutes until well mixed. Remove from heat. Keep warm. Slide chicken from oven. Using a pastry brush baste chicken or duck with sauce. Bake another 5 minutes. Baste again. Continue until chicken or duck is tender. Serve hot or cold. An excellent feast dish. Good cold for lunch the next day.

GREEN BEANS SIMMERED WITH GROUND MEAT [Serves 4 to 6]

½ lb. ground meat [beef or pork]
2 Tbsp. vegetable oil
½ tsp. sesame oil

Heat a wok over high heat. Add oil. Heat until a piece of meat added sizzles. Add meat. Stir and fry 3 to 5 minutes until no longer pink but not brown.

4 to 6 green onions,
    cut into thin diagonals
½ inch fresh ginger root, minced

Add to meat. Stir and fry 2 to 3 minutes.

1 lb. green beans, cut into long,
    thin diagonals

Add to meat. Stir and fry 1 to 2 minutes.

Sauce:
1 Tbsp. soy sauce
1 tsp. mild honey
1 Tbsp. sake
    OR dry sherry
1 tsp. sea salt

Add to meat and beans. Bring to a boil.

1 cup water
    OR meat stock
    [pork or beef]

Add to meat and beans. Cover. Bring to a boil. Reduce heat to medium. Simmer 15 to 20 minutes until all water is absorbed and beans are tender. A meal-in-a-bowl served with rice. An excellent feast dish. Good cold for lunch the next day.

STEAMED DISHES

TECHNIQUE

Steaming is another essential method in Chinese cooking. Many of the dishes are mild in flavor and range from breads to casseroles. Also, steaming is used to par-cook many ingredients to be used in other cooking methods. The Chinese use a wok with bamboo steaming trays or special steamers, but these are not necessary. The following illustrations will show some improvised steamers that work as well and that are far less expensive. Steaming is a quick cooking method which insures vitamin and color retention, both important factors in Chinese cooking. It also is a substitute for an oven, which is not a common thing in many Chinese homes. When steaming, it is necessary to have the water at a full boil before placing anything in the steamer. If the water is brought to a boil after ingredients are added they will be limp and over-cooked by the time they have steamed the required time. Once ingredients are added the heat can be reduced but make sure steam keeps rising. When par-steaming do not cook to desired doneness since the vegetables will continue to cook while they are cooling, and dipping them in cold water after steaming to cool them causes vitamin loss.

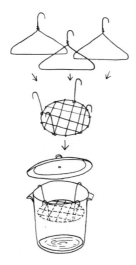

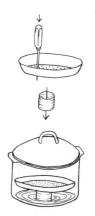

These steamed dishes are mild-flavored main dishes that make a complete meal when served with rice or noodles.

STEAMED BEAN CURD [Serves 4 to 6]

4 to 6 dried mushrooms 1 cup boiling water	Place mushrooms in a bowl. Pour boiling water over them. Place weight on mushrooms to keep under water. Soak 15 minutes to 1 hour. Remove from water. Squeeze dry. Reserve stock. Remove tough stems. Cut mushrooms into ¼ inch strips.
1 to 2 cakes bean curd, cut into 2 inch cubes	Place in a shallow casserole that fits inside your steamer.

4 green onions, cut into
   thin diagonal slices
2 thin slices fresh ginger root,
   julienned
4 water chestnuts, peeled
  and cut into thin slices
  OR 2 jerusalem artichokes,
    peeled and cut into thin
    slices
10 almonds, cut in half
  [optional]
	Arrange around bean curd in casserole. Arrange mushrooms around bean curd also.

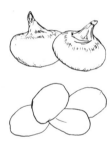

Sauce:

1 cup soybean stock
1 cup mushroom stock
2 Tbsp. sake
  OR dry sherry
  OR rice vinegar
2 tsp. soy sauce
1½ tsp. sea salt
1 tsp. honey
2 tsp. arrowroot starch
	Mix starch and stock well. Place in a small saucepan with other ingredients. Bring to a boil over medium heat. Pour over bean curd and vegetables in casserole. Cover casserole. Steam 15 to 20 minutes until vegetables are tender Serve hot. A good meal-in-a-bowl served with rice or noodles. An excellent mild-hot-course feast dish.

VARIATION:
SOYBEAN CURD AND CLOUDS-EAR MUSHROOM STEAMED CASSEROLE [Serves 4 to 6]

¼ to ½ cup clouds-ear
   mushrooms
1 cup boiling water

Place mushrooms in a bowl. Pour boiling water over them. Place weight on mushrooms to keep under water. Soak 15 minutes to 1 hour. Remove from water. Squeeze dry. Reserve stock for later use.

Reserved mushroom stock
Soybean stock to make 2 cups

Follow recipe for Steamed Bean Curd. Use clouds-ear mushrooms in place of dried mushrooms. Use mushroom stock from clouds-ear and enough soybean stock to make 2 cups liquid. Cook as directed. Serve hot. A good meal-in-a-bowl served with rice or noodles. Good mild-hot-course feast dish.

STEAMED EGGS [Serves 4 to 6]

2 cups soybean stock
  OR chicken stock

Bring to a boil over high heat. Remove from heat. Pour into a shallow casserole. Cool 10 to 15 minutes until lukewarm to touch.

4 eggs, beaten until well mixed
  but not frothy
2 green onions, julienned
1 Tbsp. sake
  OR dry sherry
  OR rice vinegar
½ to 1 tsp. sea salt
½ tsp. mild honey
1 tsp. soy sauce
1 tsp. sesame oil
  OR peanut oil
  OR vegetable oil
1 cup chinese cabbage, shredded
  OR green cabbage, shredded
  OR bok choy, shredded

Combine all ingredients with eggs. Mix well but do not beat until frothy. Slowly pour mixture into warm stock. Mix well. Steam 20 to 30 minutes over medium heat until a knife inserted in the middle comes out clean. Serve hot.

PUNGENT STEAMED FISH [Serves 4 to 6]

4 dried mushrooms
1 cup boiling water

Place mushrooms in bowl. Pour boiling water over them. Place weight on mushrooms to keep under water. Soak 15 minutes to 1 hour. Remove from water. Squeeze dry. Reserve stock. Remove tough stems. Cut each mushroom into 3 to 4 pieces.

1½ lbs. firm white fish fillet,
  scored on each side
  OR 2 to 3 lbs. whole fish
    scored three times on
    each side
2 tsp. sesame oil

Rub fish with sesame oil. Place in a casserole which will fit in your steamer.

6 green onions, cut into thin
  diagonal slices
4 thin slices fresh ginger root,
  julienned

Arrange around fish along with mushrooms.

Sauce:
¼ cup fish stock
¼ cup mushroom stock
2 Tbsp. sake
  OR dry sherry
1 Tbsp. rice vinegar
1 Tbsp. mild honey
1 tsp. sea salt
1½ tsp. arrowroot starch

Place ingredients in a small saucepan. Mix well. Bring to boil over medium heat. Remove from heat. Pour over fish. Cover casserole. Steam 30 minutes until fish is just done. Do not oversteam or fish will break into small pieces. Serve hot. An excellent feast dish. Good cold for lunch the next day.

SWEETS

Sweets in China are not necessarily served at the end of the meal. Often they occur within the meal as a contrast to the other courses. They are also a favorite Chinese snack.

ALMOND COOKIES [Makes 3 dozen]

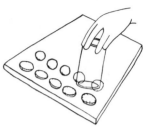

1 cup butter 6 Tbsp. mild honey	Beat together well.

1 tsp. almond extract	Add to butter and honey. Mix well.

2 cups sifted whole-wheat pastry flour ½ tsp. baking powder ½ cup ground almonds ¼ tsp. sea salt	Mix ingredients well. Mix gradually into butter and honey. Form into balls using a rounded tablespoon of dough. Place on a cookie sheet. Flatten with the end of a glass dipped in flour.

36 whole almonds 1 cup boiling water	Place almonds in a small bowl. Pour water over them and allow to soak 5 to 10 minutes. Remove skins. Top each cookie with a whole almond. Bake 10 to 12 minutes at 350°. Excellent snack or dessert.

ALMOND CURD [Serves 4 to 6]

20 almonds, blanched ½ cup boiling water	Place almonds in a blender. Blend to powder. Add liquid. Blend 1 minute. Strain almond milk through a muslin cloth. Press almond paste to remove all liquid. Discard pulp. Set aside almond milk to use later.

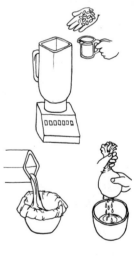

1½ cups water 6 inches agar-agar, shredded 2 Tbsp. mild honey	Place ingredients in a deep saucepan. Add almond milk and mix well. Bring to a boil over medium heat. Stir constantly. Reduce heat to low and stir until agar-agar dissolves.

¼ tsp. almond extract	Add to almond mixture. Stir well. Pour into flat bowl or pan. Skim top to remove foam. Chill 1 to 2 hours until well set. Cut into 1 inch cubes.

1 to 2 Tbsp. honey 1 cup hot water	Mix ingredients well. Pour over almond curd. Chill for 1 hour. Drain and place 4 to 5 pieces in individual serving bowls.

2 Tbsp. arrowroot starch
2 Tbsp. water
2 to 3 oranges, peeled and
  sectioned
½ cup water
½ cup orange juice
3 to 4 Tbsp. mild honey
  [depends on sweetness of
  oranges]
	Mix starch and water well. Place in a saucepan with other ingredients. Mix well. Bring to boil over medium heat. Stir until sauce thickens. Remove from heat. Chill. Pour over almond curd. Serve cold. An excellent way to end a feast. A good snack.

SWEET STEAMED BUNS WITH BEAN AND DATE FILLING [Makes about 2 to 3 dozen]

Filling:
3 Tbsp. butter
1 cup red bean paste [See Basic Japanese section]
½ lb. pitted dates, minced

Mix ingredients well. Wet hands. Knead and mix until a paste forms. Place in a double boiler. Heat 5 to 10 minutes until butter melts and filling is well mixed. Stir often to prevent sticking. Remove from heat. Cool. With moist hands form filling into 1 inch balls. Set aside for later use.

Dough:
5 cups whole-wheat flour
2¼ cups lukewarm water
4 tsp. yeast
3 Tbsp. mild honey
½ tsp. sea salt

Place flour in a large bowl. Make indentation in top of flour. Place yeast in indentation. Pour ¼ cup lukewarm water over it. Let dissolve 5 minutes. Add remaining ingredients to flour. Mix well. Turn dough on lightly floured board. Knead 10 to 15 minutes. Work dough with moist hands so no flour is worked into dough. Knead until dough is elastic and forms blisters on outside. Place dough in oiled bowl. Cover with moist cloth. Set aside to double, about 2 hours. Punch dough down. Divide in half. Form into long ropes 2 inches in diameter. Cut dough into 1 to 1½ inch slices and shape into round smooth balls. With a circular motion of fingers form into 1/8 inch thick rounds. Place ball of filling in center of round. Pinch two opposite sides together. Bring other two sides together in center and pinch. Seal top well. Twist top of bun to seal well and remove excess dough. Place buns on lightly floured board and let rise 20 to 30 minutes until dough springs back when touched. Invert buns on a steam rack covered with moist cloth. Allow room for buns to expand while steaming. Steam 15 to 20 minutes until dough is no longer sticky. A good snack or feast dish. Serve hot or cold. A good one-day pack-trip sweet as it is all sealed and is a good protein balance. Keeps well 2 to 3 days.

SWEET BEAN CURD WITH SYRUP [Serves 4]

2 to 3 cakes bean curd
½ to 1 cup pears
   OR peaches
   OR other canned fruit
   OR soft fresh fruit in season [strawberries, raspberries, melons, etc.]

Place in a blender. Blend until smooth. If no blender is available, mince and mash fruit and beat bean curd with an egg beater until smooth. Mix fruit and bean curd. Place in individual serving bowls. Indent center with a spoon.

¼ cup raw block sugar
   OR ¼ cup mild honey and 1 Tbsp. molasses
2 Tbsp. water

Place in a saucepan over medium high heat. Melt sugar 2 to 3 minutes. Cook until just begins to thicken. Pour hot syrup into indentation in center of bean curd. Serve cold. An excellent and quick dessert.

PRECIOUS RICE PUDDING [Serves 6]

2 cups sweet brown rice
  OR short-grain brown rice
3 cups water

Wash rice well. Allow to dry 1 hour. (optional step) Place rice in a heavy iron saucepan with water. Cover and bring to a boil over high heat. Reduce heat to low and simmer 35 minutes. Remove from heat and set aside covered for 10 minutes. Allow to cool uncovered for 1 hour or overnight. Mix occasionally to dry rice. Turn chilled rice onto large wet chopping board. Chop with a wet knife for 2 to 3 minutes until well chopped and begins to stick together.

5 Tbsp. mild honey
2 Tbsp. butter

Add to rice. Knead and mix rice with moist hands for 5 to 10 minutes until well mixed and sticky. Keep hands moist otherwise rice will stick to them.

Filling:
½ cup nuts, [almonds, walnuts,
  or cashews], chopped
½ cup dates, chopped
½ cup raisins, chopped
½ cup figs, chopped [optional]
1 Tbsp. butter
2 Tbsp. hot water

Mix ingredients well. Wet hands and knead and mix until paste forms. Set aside.

Decoration:
1 cup dried fruit [prunes,
  apricots, peaches, apples or
  pears, etc.]
2 cups boiling water
OR IN PLACE OF ABOVE:
  5 to 6 pieces of non-sugared
    canned fruit [pears, apricots,
    peaches, apple slices, etc.]
  OR ½ to 1 cup fresh fruit in
    season [strawberries, pears
    peaches, apricots, etc.] and
    1½ cups water

Place dried fruit in a bowl. Pour boiling water over fruit. Cover and allow to soak 1 to 2 hours or overnight. Drain. Reserve fruit stock for later use. If canned fruit is used save the juice for later use. If fresh fruit is used, crush or blend some with water and reserve for later use.

¼ cup of 2 of the following
  [raisins, blanched almonds,
  walnut halves, figs cut in half,
  pitted dates]
2 Tbsp. butter

Butter the inside of a medium-sized casserole well. Line the inside of the casserole with an attractive arrangement of fruit and nuts (like an upside-down cake). Set 1 cup of the rice mixture aside. Press the remaining rice evenly over the fruit-and-nut arrangement. Leave a 2 cup depression in the center of the pudding. Add filling to the center. Press firmly and spread out evenly. Cover top of filling with remaining cup of rice. Smooth top with a wet knife. (At this time the dessert can be stored in the refrigerator for up to 3 days or it can be frozen). Steam pudding for 1 to 1½ hours until firm. Run a knife around the edge to loosen and invert pudding onto a deep serving platter.

Glace Sauce:

1½ cups fruit stock
⅓ cup mild honey
2 Tbsp. arrowroot starch

Place ingredients in a small saucepan. Mix well. Bring to a boil over medium heat. Simmer 2 to 3 minutes until sauce thickens. Pour over hot pudding. Serve hot. An excellent feast course. Good cold as a snack.

SWEET FRIED BANANAS [Serves 4 to 6]

1 to 2 Tbsp. sesame seeds

Heat a small cast iron skillet over high heat. Add sesame seeds. Parch 1 minute until lightly toasted and popping. Shake pan often to prevent burning. Set aside for later use.

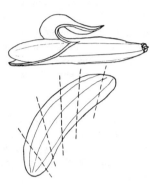

2 egg whites
3 tsp. liquid mild honey

Beat egg whites until partly stiff. While still beating, drizzle honey 1 tsp. at a time over egg whites. Continue to beat until egg whites are stiff.

6 Tbsp. whole-wheat pastry
flour, sifted
6 Tbsp. arrowroot starch
½ cup ice water

Mix starch and flour well. Add water and mix well. Fold into egg whites. Chill batter 15 to 30 minutes.

5 or 6 firm ripe bananas
2 to 3 cups peanut oil
OR vegetable oil

Cut bananas diagonally into 1 inch pieces. Place wok on stand over hot burner. Heat oil in wok until a small piece of batter added sinks to the bottom and then rises almost at once. Dip banana in batter and fry 5 or 6 pieces at a time. Fry 3 to 4 minutes until brown but banana still firm. Remove from oil and drain on a rack over a bowl of cold water. Repeat process until all bananas are fried.

Too Cold

1 cup mild honey

Place in a small saucepan. Bring to a boil over heat. Simmer 3 to 5 minutes until slightly thickened. Remove from heat. Dip fried drained bananas in honey. Allow to soak 1 minute. Place on a deep serving platter. When all bananas are honeyed pour remaining honey over bananas. Sprinkle toasted sesame seeds over bananas. Serve warm. Excellent snack or dessert. Very sweet so do not eat too many of them.

Too Hot

Correct Temperature

VARIATION:
SWEET FRIED APPLES [Serves 4 to 6]

4 to 5 firm ripe apples

Halve and core apples. Slice halves into ½ inch slices.

Follow recipe for Sweet Fried Bananas. Cook as directed. Excellent snack or dessert. Very sweet so do not eat too many of them.

CHAPTER TWO
MIDDLE EASTERN

INTRODUCTION

The food of the Middle East is a very old and traditional cuisine. It varies from the simple food of the desert, milk, sheep and dates to elaborate Persian feasts with numerous dishes prepared from the many varieties of foods grown in the fertile Mediterranean region. The Persians were so taken with food that they had poetry contests to laud it. A friend, who resided in Morocco for several years, gave me my first taste of Middle Eastern food and taught me many dishes. Since being introduced to this delicious cuisine I have added a number of dishes from other areas so this section covers the cuisines from Morocco to Turkey.

The ingredients in Middle Eastern food are many and varied. The more exotic items can be purchased or ordered from Greek or Arab stores. The Middle East has used a wide variety of spices for many centuries in a rich, pungent yet mild cuisine. The food is characterized by the use of large amounts of and many different types of oils. The most common are olive oil and a form of clarified butter. Olive oil is used in cold dishes and to flavor hot dishes while butter is only used in hot dishes to add richness and flavor.

A base for many dishes is an onion-garlic mixture or just onions. Garlic is also used to flavor cold dishes. A wide selection of vegetables and fruits are used in the Middle East. Those used in Feast are easily obtained in North America or common substitutes are suggested. Dairy products are most often encountered in the form of yoghurt or yoghurt cheese and like the flat Arab bread accompany almost every meal. Arab cuisine though not mainly vegetarian uses many grains, lentils, nuts and seeds to augment a sparse use of expensive meats. Traditionally honey, whole grains, cold pressed oils and other natural ingredients are used in Middle Eastern food making for easy adaption to natural foods.

Middle Eastern food with its combination of fresh salads, yoghurt, and wheat bread at every meal makes a highly nutritious cuisine. With an emphasis on vegetarian dishes and the sparse use of meat Middle Eastern food is also very economical. Many of the main dishes included are vegetarian. Through many centuries the Middle Eastern peoples have worked out the needed combinations of vegetable protein so they have a well balanced protein diet with the use of small amounts of meat. Vegetables are served raw or sauteed in oil and then simmered slowly in their own juices. Consequently, few vitamins are lost. All of these aspects combine to make Middle Eastern food a highly nutritous, inexpensive, vitamin rich cuisine.

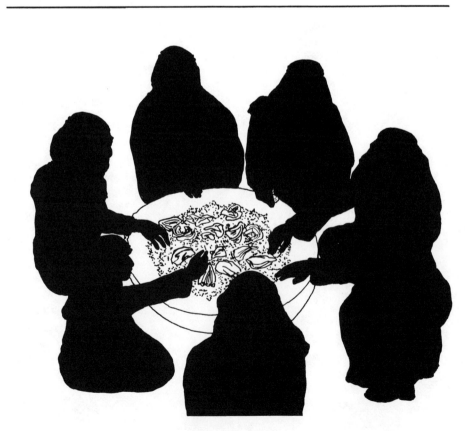

MEAL SUGGESTIONS

1 TO 2 PERSON MEALS
Kukue Sabzy
Pilaf
Cucumber and Tomato Salad
Pita and Yoghurt (optional)

Borek
Yoghurt
Salatet Moroccan

Majadarra
Salatet Malfoof

Kabab
Pita
Salatet Loubiah

3 TO 5 PERSON MEALS
Yaknit el Kousa
Pilaf
Tabbouleh
Havij bi Zayt

Kukue Sabzy
Pilaf
Mussak'a
Karnabeet bi Lamoun
Khyaar bi Leban
Baklava

Kousa Mashi
Shouabat' Adas
Pita
Kousa bi Zayt
Parsley Salad
Fruit in Quatir Dressing

Seflan
Pilaf
Tabbouleh
Pickles
Khosaf

Kabab
Pita
Bayd B'Lamoun
Havij bi Zayt

Yakhnit Lahm bi Kousa
Pilaf
Salatet Moroccan
Havij bi Zayt
Fruit

FEASTS

Vegetarian Feast
Borek
Bayd B'Lamoun
Salatet Hummus
Salatet Tahini
Tamia
Salatet Khyaar bi Leban
Kousa bi Zayt
Batingaan Mashi
Lentils with Noodles
Balouza
Kukue Sabzy

Meat Feast
Hummus b'Tahini
Pita
Shourabat' Adas
Tabbouleh
Mussaka
Dajaj Kabab
Havij bi Zayt
Karnabeet bi Lamoun
Bulgur Pilaf
Kukue Sabzy
Quatir Dressed Fruit
Morrocan Mint Tea

Small Feast
Dajaj Mashi
Parsley Salad
Salatet Moroccan
Pita
Khyaar bi Leban
Baklava

BASIC INGREDIENTS

FILO

3 cups whole wheat pastry flour **3 cups whole wheat flour** **1½ tsp. sea salt**	Mix well and place in a large bowl.
2 eggs, beaten until well mixed **but not frothy** **1 to 1½ cups water** **OR no eggs and 2 cups water**	Mix water and eggs well. Pour into bowl with flour. Mix and knead to a soft, sticky dough for 15 to 20 minutes. Kneading develops the dough so the gluten stretches well and the dough then stretches without breaking. Add water to bowl and not flour as you are kneading. Dough should be moist, not dry.
3 Tbsp. olive oil **OR vegetable oil**	Add slowly to dough while continuing to knead 10 to 15 more minutes. Cover dough and let sit two to three hours to let dough rest. Place on counter. Beat dough with rolling pin or wooden bar until it blisters. Let sit 30 minutes. Divide into 30 to 40 pieces. Roll each piece of dough between sheets of wax paper into 9 by 13-inch rectangles, very thin.
½ cup arrowroot starch	Sprinkle each sheet of dough with arrowroot starch and let dry 30 minutes to 1 hour, until slightly stiff. When dried can be frozen for later use if each sheet is separated by wax paper and then batches are wrapped in foil to exclude air. Used in Baklava, Sfihan and other Middle Eastern main dishes. To make strudel with filo, use half as many sheets as commercial filo, since homemade filo is not as thin.

RAS EL HANOUT [HEAD OF THE HOUSE SPICE MIX] [Makes 6 Tbsp.]

½ tsp. each of the following spices and herbs:
cardamom
mace
ginger
nutmeg
cinnamon
paprika
black pepper
red pepper
lavender
allspice
turmeric or saffron
rosewater

When whole spices are used grind each separately in a blender or mortar and pestle. Measure after grinding. Mix well. If ground spices are used, mix well. Store in tightly covered container away from light and heat. Keeps up to 1 month.

TAHINI [SESAME SEED PASTE] [Makes 1½ Cups]

1 cup sesame seeds [hulled or unhulled]

Place in a shallow baking pan in a 200° oven. Roast 3 to 5 minutes until hot but not browned. Remove from heat. Grind in a blender, Corona handmill or Japanese mortar and pestle (shirabashi). Grind ⅓ cup at a time to a fine powder or paste.

⅓ to ⅔ cup vegetable oil

Place in a bowl. Add enough oil to make medium gravy consistency. The finer the grind on the seeds the more oil is needed. Keeps indefinitely in refrigerator.

CHICKEN STOCK [Makes 6 cups]

1 chicken cut into 8 pieces OR bones and skin from 2 filleted chickens
1 green onion, sliced lengthwise
3 to 4 celery leaves OR sprigs of parsley
8 cups water

Place ingredients in a large heavy saucepan. Cover. Bring to a boil over high heat. Reduce heat to low. Simmer 1 hour. Strain through a colander. Reserve chicken for pilafs or soups. Chill stock and remove most of the fat. Stock keeps well frozen. Freeze in ice-cube trays. Store cubes in plastic bags for easy use.

GARBANZO BEAN STOCK [Makes 4 to 6 cups]

2 cups garbanzo beans
8 to 12 cups water

Soak garbanzoes in cold water overnight (optional step). Place in a heavy saucepan. Cover and bring to boil over high heat. Reduce heat to low. Simmer 3 to 4 hours until tender. To pressure cook: use 8 cups water and bring to full pressure for 1 hour. Strain. Reserve garbanzoes for many dishes. Stock keeps well frozen. Freeze in ice-cube trays. Store cubes in plastic bags for easy use.

MEAT STOCK [Makes 6 to 8 cups]

2 lbs. soup bones [beef, lamb or veal]
2 Tbsp. celery leaves
1 green onion, sliced lengthwise OR 2 to 3 sprigs parsley
8 to 12 cups water

Place ingredients in a large heavy saucepan. Cover. Bring to a boil over high heat. Reduce heat to low. Simmer 1 hour. Strain through a colander. Reserve meat for pilafs. Chill stock. Remove most of the fat. Stock keeps well frozen. Freeze in ice-cube trays. Store cubes in plastic bags for easy use. Freeze some of fat also since this should be added in small amounts to some dishes.

MACROBURGER [Makes 1 gallon]

5 cups soybeans
1/2 to 1 tsp. chili pepper
1 tsp. thyme
1 tsp. oregano
2 cloves garlic, crushed and
   minced
1 yellow onion, cut into eighths
1 1/2 tsp. sea salt
1/2 tsp. cumin
8 to 12 cups water

Soak soybeans overnight in water (optional step). Place soybeans and other ingredients in a large heavy saucepan. Cover. Bring to boil over high heat. Reduce heat to medium low. Simmer 3 to 4 hours until soybeans are very tender. To pressure cook place soybeans and 8 cups of water in a pressure cooker with other ingredients. Bring to full pressure. Cook at full pressure for 1 hour. However cooked, drain soybeans and mash well. Reserve stock for soups or bread.

1 cup soy sauce
3/4 cup safflower oil
1 tsp. chili pepper
1 1/2 tsp. Mexican chili powder
2 tsp. dry mustard
7 cloves garlic, crushed and
   minced
1 1/2 tsp. ground cumin
3 tsp. dill weed
3 tsp. celery seed
3 tsp. ground thyme

Add to soybeans. Mix well.

3 cups millet
1 tsp. sea salt
6 cups water

Place in a large heavy saucepan. Cover. Bring to boil over high heat. Reduce heat to medium low. Simmer 25 to 30 minutes until well done. Remove from heat. Place in a large bowl.

3 cups rolled oats, toasted at
   300° for 5 minutes
3 yellow onions, minced
1 large carrot, grated fine
2 stalks celery, minced

Add to millet. Mix well. Add millet and oat mixture to soybean mixture. Mix well. Keeps 2 to 3 weeks in refrigerator. Freezes well. Add water to moisten when unfreezing so mix will not be too dry to hold shape when formed into meat balls. Use in any recipe that calls for ground meat.

LEBAN [YOGHURT] [Makes 1 quart]

WHOLE MILK METHOD:

1 quart whole milk
2 Tbsp. unflavored commercial
   yoghurt
   OR homemade yoghurt

Place milk in a heavy enamel or stainless steel saucepan. Heat over medium heat until bubbles start to form around the edge of the pan (110°). Remove from heat. Beat yoghurt until liquid. Stir into hot milk (now 108°). Mix well. Let stand covered in a warm place 6 to 8 hours until yoghurt is thick. Keeps in refrigerator for about 2 weeks. The longer it keeps the sourer it gets.

POWDERED MILK METHOD:

1 cup whole milk
1 Tbsp. unflavored commercial yoghurt
  OR homemade yoghurt
1 cup warm water [110°]

Place in blender. Blend 10 to 15 seconds until smooth. If no blender is available place in jar with tight fitting lid and shake until smooth.

1 cup non-instant powdered milk

Add to blender ¼ cup at a time. Blend until smooth. If no blender is available add to jar of milk and yoghurt and shake until smooth.

2 cups warm water [110°]

Add to blender. Blend until smooth. If no blender is available add to jar of milk and yoghurt and shake until smooth. Pour into a large canning jar with a loose fitting lid, a crock, or glass casserole. Cover and keep warm (108°) for 6 to 8 hours until thickened. Keeps in refrigerator for about 2 weeks. The longer it keeps the sourer it is.

WAYS OF KEEPING YOGHURT WARM:

1. Put in cold oven and turn to 150° for 5 minutes only. Turn off heat. Let sit undisturbed for 6 to 8 hours until thickened.

2. Wrap with an electric heating pad set at 108° for 6 to 8 hours until thickened.

3. Place in a pan of warm water (108°) and keep warm by putting over gas pilot light — check to make sure heat of water is maintained.

4. Place in a pan of warm water (108°) and keep warm in electric oven turned to about 100° — check to make sure heat of water is maintained.

5. Place in pan of warm water (108°) and keep warm in a gas oven with the pilot light on — check to make sure heat of water is maintained.

6. Any warm place you can think of that will maintain the yoghurt in an undisturbed manner at 108° for 6 to 8 hours.

BREADS

Pita accompanies every meal. It is used to pick up food and is excellent stuffed as a sandwich. The stuffed turnovers are good with a meal but make excellent lunches or snacks also. Griddle bread can be used in place of pita when no oven is available.

BOREK [TURNOVERS WITH STUFFING] [Serves 5 to 6]

Dough:

2 Tbsp. dry yeast
1 cup lukewarm water
1 tsp. mild honey

Mix ingredients well in a large bowl. Allow to sit 10 minutes until soft and foamy.

2¼ to 2½ cups whole wheat
    flour
½ tsp. sea salt
1 Tbsp. vegetable oil

Add flour, oil and salt to water and yeast. Mix well. Knead 10 minutes until dough is soft and elastic. Place in an oiled bowl and allow to rise 1 hour until double in bulk.

Method of filling and baking:

Punch dough down when it has raised to double its bulk. Pull out into a long rope 2 inches in diameter. Cut off 2 inch pieces. Form into balls. Roll out to 1/8 inch thick rounds. Place 2 Tbsp. of filling on one half of circle. Dot edges with water. Fold in half and seal edges well. Place on a greased cookie sheet and allow to rise 30 minutes in a warm place. Bake at 450° for 10 minutes. Makes about 20 turnovers. Serve hot or cold. Good snack or appetizer for feast. Excellent lunch. Cheese or meat-filled turnovers can be used as a main dish. Good 1 day backpack meal.

Filling: [Spinach]

3 cups spinach, shredded
   OR any cooking green [Swiss
      chard, collards, etc.]
¼ cup olive oil
   OR vegetable oil
1 large yellow onion, minced
1 cup nuts, [walnuts, cashews,
   pinenuts, almonds, sunflower
   seeds, peanuts, or pistachios],
   chopped
½ cup currants
¼ cup lemon juice
1 tsp. sea salt
¼ tsp. black pepper
1 to 2 tsp. ras el hanout
   OR 1 tsp. cinnamon and
      1 tsp. allspice

Mix all ingredients well. Marinate 10 minutes to 1 hour. Use as much lemon as you like for tartness. If filling is left over add to ½ head lettuce that has been torn into bite-sized pieces and toss for a salad.

Filling: [Cheese]

1 lb. feta cheese
OR 1 lb. dry cottage cheese
OR 1 lb. dry ricotta cheese

To dry cottage cheese or ricotta cheese place in a double-layered cheesecloth bag for a day. Suspend over sink or bowl and allow to drip for a day or overnight.

3 large sprigs parsley, minced
3 small sprigs dill, minced
OR ½ tsp. dried dill
OR ¼ tsp. dill seed, crushed
1 large spring mint, minced
OR ¼ tsp. dried mint
2 Tbsp. olive oil
OR vegetable oil

Mix with cheese and allow to marinate 30 minutes to 1 hour.

Filling: [Meat]

1 lb. meat, ground or chopped
fine [lamb, veal, or beef]
OR Macroburger
1 yellow onion, minced
1 clove garlic, crushed and
minced
2 Tbsp. olive oil
OR vegetable oil

Heat a medium cast iron skillet over medium heat. Add oil. Heat until a piece of onion added sizzles. Add onions, meat and garlic. Stir and fry 5 to 10 minutes until onions are soft and transparent but not brown.

2 Tbsp. nuts, chopped slightly
[pinenuts, almonds, walnuts,
cashews or pistachios, etc.]
1 tsp. sea salt
1 tsp. ras el hanout
OR ½ tsp. cinnamon and
½ tsp. allspice
1 tsp. mild honey

Add to meat and onions and mix well. Stir and fry an additional 2 to 3 minutes.

¼ cup water

Add to meat and nut mixture. Mix well. Simmer 3 to 5 minutes over medium heat until water is absorbed.

PITA [ARAB BREAD] [Makes 20 to 30]

6 cups whole-wheat flour
1 Tbsp. yeast
½ cup lukewarm water

Place flour in a large bowl. Make an indentation in the top of the flour. Place yeast in hole. Pour water over yeast. Let yeast dissolve 5 to 10 minutes.

1 Tbsp. sea salt
¼ cup olive oil
OR vegetable oil
2 cups lukewarm water

Add to flour. Mix well. Turn dough out on lightly floured board. Knead 5 to 10 minutes until dough is elastic and forms blisters on outside. Place dough in oiled bowl. Oil top and cover with damp cloth. Place in warm corner. Allow to rise until double, about 1 hour. Punch dough down. Form dough into long, 2 inch diameter rope. Cut into 2 inch slices. Shape into smooth balls. Dip in flour and squash slightly. Cover with moist cloth. Let rise 30 minutes. Heat oven to 500°. Must be this temperature to puff. Press balls into flat ¼ inch thick cakes. Place on lightly floured board. Roll out lightly into slightly thinner rounds. Cover. Allow to rise 30 minutes until light. Place on large cookie sheet so they are not touching. Bake 2 to 3 minutes until just starting to brown and they are well puffed out. Cut in half while still hot. Store in tight container after they are cool. They will keep unfrozen for 1 week. Frozen they will keep well up to 6 months. To reheat, place in a steamer for a few minutes or in the oven at 350° for a few minutes.

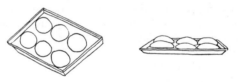

GRIDDLE BREAD [Makes 12 to 15 Large Thin Breads]

6 cups whole wheat flour
1 Tbsp. yeast
2 Tbsp. sourdough starter
[optional]
½ cup lukewarm water

Place flour in large bowl. Make an indentation in top of flour. Place yeast in hole. Pour water over yeast. Add sourdough starter. Let sit for 5 to 10 minutes for yeast to dissolve.

1 Tbsp. sea salt
2 to 2½ cups lukewarm water

Add to flour. Mix well. Turn dough out on lightly floured board. Knead 10 to 15 minutes until dough is velvet textured and elastic. Place in oiled bowl and let rise 1 hour to double its size. Punch down dough and let rise to double its size again. Form dough into long, 2 inch diameter rope. Cut into 3 inch slices. Form into round balls. Roll out on lightly floured board into large, round, paper-thin sheet. Bake on a hot griddle 1 to 2 minutes until lightly browned. Turn once. Press with wide spatula to make air bubble rise. Place on cloth-covered plate. Cover to keep warm and moist. Repeat process until all dough is grilled. Good hot or cold. Serve in place of pita. A good camp bread since it needs no baking.

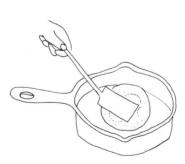

APPETIZERS AND SNACKS

Many Middle Eastern appetizers are served as between-meal snacks as well as the beginning of a meal. Salad snacks are also common. Both appetizers and salads are served with the Arab bread pita. (Optional)

HUMMUS B'TAHINI [GARBANZO SESAME PASTE DIP] [Serves 4 to 6]

1 cup garbanzos
4 cups water [more water as
    needed to keep garbanzos
    covered]

Cover garbanzos with water. Soak overnight (optional step). Place garbanzos in a heavy saucepan. Bring to boil over high heat. Cover. Reduce heat to medium low. Simmer 3 to 4 hours until tender (easily mashed with a fork). To pressure cook: place garbanzos in pressure cooker with water. Cover. Bring to full pressure. Cook at full pressure 1 hour. Remove from heat. Cool. However cooked, drain and reserve stock for later use. Mash garbanzos with a foodmill, fork, or your fingers ½ cup at a time. Do not use a blender - it will burn out at this task.

⅓ cup lemon juice
2 to 3 large cloves garlic,
    crushed and minced
⅓ cup tahini [sesame paste]
1 to 1½ cups garbanzo stock
    OR water
1 tsp. sea salt

Add to garbanzo paste. Mix until a smooth paste is formed. Add more stock or water to the mixture as needed to make it diplike in consistency. Place in a bowl. Chill 2 to 3 hours or overnight.

2 Tbsp. olive oil
    OR vegetable oil

Pour over top of dip.

¼ to ½ tsp. chili pepper,
    ground
1 large sprig parsley

Sprinkle red pepper around edge of bowl and in a cross pattern across the center. Place 1 sprig of parsley on side. Serve with pita (Arab bread), carrots, radishes, celery, cabbage, cauliflower, or other crisp vegetables. Excellent snack or appetizer for a party. Good served with vegetables, a main dish and pilaf for dinner.

BABA GHANNOUJ [EGGPLANT SESAME PASTE DIP] [Serves 4 to 6]

1 large eggplant or
    OR 2 small eggplant

Cut off tip of eggplant. Bake at 350°, 20 to 30 minutes, until soft all over and partly collapsed. Cool. Remove from peel. Place in bowl. Mash with fork, foodmill or electric egg beater until a smooth paste. Place in a mixing bowl.

⅓ cup lemon juice
2 to 3 large cloves garlic,
    crushed and minced
3 to 4 Tbsp. garbanzo stock
    OR water
6 Tbsp. tahini [sesame paste]
1 tsp. sea salt

Mix until a smooth paste is formed. Add more liquid to mixture as needed to make it dip-like in consistency. Chill at least 2 to 3 hours or overnight.

2 Tbsp. olive oil
    OR vegetable oil

Pour over top of dip.

¼ tsp. chili pepper, ground
1 sprig parsley

Sprinkle pepper around the edge of the bowl and in a cross pattern in the center. Place the sprig of parsley on the side. Serve with pita (Arab bread), carrots, radishes, celery, cauliflower, or other crisp vegetables. Excellent snack or appetizer for a party. Good served with vegetables, main dish and pilaf for a dinner.

TAMIA [VEGETABLE AND FAVA BEAN FRITTERS] [Serves 4 to 6]

2 large dry onions,
  minced
3 cloves garlic,
  crushed and minced
5 large sprigs parsley,
  minced
½ to ¾ cup green beans,
  minced
  OR snowpeas, minced
  OR celery, minced
2 small carrots,
  grated fine
1 cup fava bean flour
  OR garbanzo bean flour
1 to 2 tsp. ground cumin
½ to 1 tsp. ground coriander
½ to 1 tsp. ground chili pepper
1½ tsp. sea salt

½ cup fava bean flour
  OR garbanzo bean flour

2 to 3 cups vegetable oil
½ cup olive oil

Mix ingredients well. Form into ½ inch balls. Do not press too hard or the mixture will just squeeze through your fingers. Use firm pressure. Form into oblong balls not perfectly round. Keep hands moist so dough does not stick to them.

As balls are formed roll them in flour and set on a board sprinkled with bean flour.

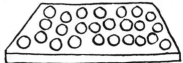

Heat a wok over high heat. Add oil. Heat oil until a small piece of mixture added falls to the bottom and then rises almost at once. Fry 6 to 8 tamia at a time. Fry 3 to 5 minutes over medium high heat until well browned. Do not have oil too hot or tamia will not be cooked inside. Remove from pan. Drain on rack or absorbent paper. Keep warm. Continue until all tamia are fried.

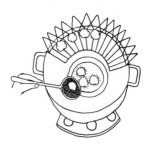

Optional step:
1 to 2 cups lettuce, shredded
  OR cabbage, shredded
3 to 4 sprigs parsley,
  minced
12 pita [Arab bread]

Mix lettuce and parsley. Split pita in half. Place some of lettuce mixture in each half and top with tamia. Pour over any of the following sauces. Tamia may also be served by themselves along with one of the sauces or tahini salad for a dip. Good served this way as an appetizer for a large Arab meal. Good lunch with pita, tahini sauce, and/or Tabbouleh.

Too Cold

Too Hot

Correct Temperature

TAHINI SAUCE [Makes 1 cup]

²/₃ cup tahini
　[sesame paste]
¹/₃ cup lemon juice
1 small clove garlic,
　crushed and minced
¹/₂ tsp. sea salt
2 to 3 Tbsp. garbanzo stock
　OR water

Mix ingredients well. Sauce should be the consistency of medium gravy. Cut with water or garbanzo stock to reach the right consistency. Chill. Beat to liquify. Serve with tamia as a dipping sauce or to pour over tamia in stuffed pitas. Also good dipping sauce for crisp vegetables or bread.

SAM'S SECRET SAUCE [Makes 1 cup]

²/₃ cup tahini
　[sesame paste]
¹/₃ to ¹/₂ cup yoghurt
¹/₂ tsp. sea salt
¹/₄ to ¹/₂ tsp. ground chili pepper

Mix ingredients well. Sauce should be the consistency of medium gravy. Cut with more yoghurt to reach right consistency. Chill. Beat to liquify. Serve with tamia as a dipping sauce or to pour over tamia in stuffed pitas. Also good dipping sauce for crisp vegetables or bread.

PARSLEY SAUCE [Makes 1 cup]

¹/₂ cup tahini
　[sesame paste]
3 cloves garlic,
　crushed and minced
¹/₃ cup lemon juice
¹/₃ cup yoghurt
　OR garbanzo stock
　OR water
20 large sprigs parsley,
　minced
¹/₂ tsp. cumin
¹/₂ tsp. sea salt
dash of red or black pepper

If blender is used leave all ingredients in large pieces. Place in a blender. Blend to a smooth creamy gravy-like consistency. If no blender is available mince all ingredients well. Mix to a creamy smooth gravy consistency. Chill. Beat to liquify. Serve with tamia as a dipping sauce or to pour over tamia in stuffed pitas. Also good dipping sauce for crisp vegetables or bread.

DUKKAH [SESAME, NUT, SPICE SNACK] [Serves 6 to 8]

1 cup sesame seeds	Roast 10 to 15 minutes at 300° until lightly browned. Grind ⅓ cup at a time in a blender, Corona handmill, meat grinder or Japanese mortar and pestle. Want seeds coarsely ground.

1 cup nuts
  [peanuts, almonds, cashews,
  filberts, pistachio nuts,
  pine nuts, etc.]
	Roast 5 to 10 minutes at 300° until light brown. brown. Grind ⅓ cup at a time in a blender, Corona handmill, meat grinder or Japanese mortar and pestle. Want nuts well chopped.

¼ cup cumin seeds **1 Tbsp. coriander seeds** **8 to 10 peppercorns** **1½ cups dried shredded coconut**	Roast 5 to 10 minutes at 300° until brown. Grind seeds and peppercorns ⅓ cup at a time in a blender, Corona handmill, meat grinder or Japanese mortar and pestle. Want seeds coarsely ground.
½ tsp. sea salt	Mix all ingredients in bowl. Add salt and mix well.

½ cup olive oil
  OR vegetable oil
bread, cut into 1 inch by 2 inch
  pieces
  OR 12 pita
    [Arab pocket bread]
	Serve with olive oil and pita (Arab bread) or other bread. Dip bread in oil and then in Dukkah. Good lunch served with a vegetable dish. An excellent snack.

VARIATION:

DUKKAH MADE WITH HUMMUS [SESAME, NUT, GARBANZO AND SPICE SNACK]
[Serves 6 to 8]

1 cup garbanzos
8 to 12 cups water

Soak garbanzos in cold water overnight (optional step). Place in a heavy saucepan. Cover and bring to a boil. Reduce heat and simmer 2 to 3 hours until just tender. To pressure cook: cook with 8 cups of water. Bring to full pressure and cook 50 minutes. Remove from heat and cool. Drain. Cool. Chop coarsely. Roast 15 to 20 minutes at 300° until just dry. Stir often.

2 Tbsp. dry mint
1 tsp. cinnamon

Mix with garbanzos. Follow recipe for Dukkah and add remaining ingredients. Serve as directed. Good appetizer or snack. Good for lunch served with a vegetable dish.

DOLMEH [STUFFED VINE LEAVES] [Serves 6]

1 lb. jar grape leaves
   OR 1 lb. fresh grape leaves
   OR 1 lb. swiss chard
   OR 1 head green cabbage

Canned grape leaves: wash in cold water. Drain well. Fresh grape leaves, cabbage leaves and swiss chard: wash; steam 30 seconds to 1 minute until just limp but still bright colored. Cool. Remove stems.

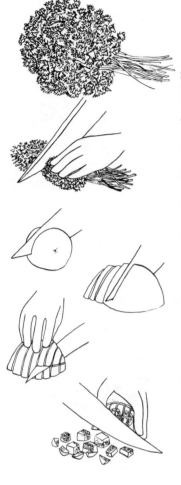

Stuffing:
1 cup brown rice
½ cup garbanzos
4 cups water

Soak overnight in water. Drain and dry for 1 hour. Place in a meat grinder and grind with medium blades.

½ cup parsley,
   minced
½ cup green onions,
   minced
2 Tbsp. mint,
   minced
1 large tomato,
   cut into 1/8 inch cubes
1 cup olive oil
   OR vegetable oil
1 tsp. sea salt
1 tsp. ras el hanout
   [spice mix]
   OR ½ tsp. cinnamon and
      ½ tsp. allspice
¼ tsp. black pepper
3 Tbsp. lemon juice
1 tsp. mild honey

Mix well with garbanzos and rice. Marinate 30 minutes to 1 hour. Place 1 to 2 tsp. stuffing in center of the vein side of leaf. (More for cabbage). Fold bottom of leaf over stuffing. Fold each side towards middle. Roll towards tip into a firm roll. Roll one at a time.

1 large tomato,
   cut into 1/8 inch slices
2 cloves garlic,
   crushed and minced
3 Tbsp. lemon juice
½ tsp. sea salt
2 cups water

Place sliced tomato and garlic in the bottom of a deep saucepan. Add ½ tsp. sea salt and 3 Tbsp. lemon juice. Place one layer of rolls folded-side down in bottom of the pan. Place all the rolls in each layer in the same direction. Place the next layer of rolls in the opposite direction. Place a stainless steel rack or glass plate over the rolls and weight with a rock to keep rolls from floating. Cover the rolls with 2 cups water. Bring to a boil over low heat. Cover and simmer 50 minutes. Remove from heat. Cool. Drain sauce when cool. Lift rolls onto a serving plate. Chill. Serve cold. Simmer sauce until thick. Taste and add more lemon or salt as needed. Chill and serve separately with the rolls. Good as appetizer for large meal or as a snack. Good lunch or simple meal main dish.

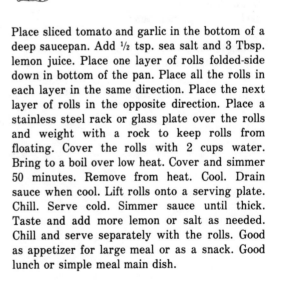

SOUPS

Many Middle Eastern soups are a meal-in-a-bowl. When served with pita (Arab bread), a salad and yoghurt these soups make a complete meal. The lentil soups served cold with salad and bread are very good for a quick lunch. Soups are also served at the beginning of a meal in Middle Eastern households.

'ADAS BI HAAMUD [LENTIL AND SWISS CHARD SOUP] [Serves 4 to 6]

1½ cups lentils 6 cups water	Wash lentils well. Place in a large heavy saucepan. Add water. Cover. Bring to a boil over high heat. Reduce heat to low. Simmer 45 minutes.
2 medium yellow onions, chopped ½ cup olive oil OR vegetable oil	Heat a small cast iron skillet over medium heat. Add oil. Heat until a small piece of onion added sizzles. Add onion. Stir and fry 5 to 10 minutes until onions are soft and transparent.
3 cloves garlic, crushed and minced 1½ tsp. sea salt	Crush garlic with salt and then mince. Add to onions. Fry 1 minute.

1½ lbs. swiss chard leaves,
  shredded
   OR any cooking green,
    shredded
    [spinach, mustard greens,
    etc.]
12 to 15 sprigs parsley,
  minced
¼ tsp. black pepper
dash to ¼ tsp. chili pepper
	Add to lentils along with fried onions and garlic. Mix well. Simmer 3 to 5 minutes until greens just cooked.

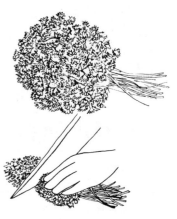

½ cup lemon juice 2 tsp. whole wheat flour	Mix flour with 2 Tbsp. of lemon juice. Add remaining lemon juice. Mix well. Add to soup. Simmer until soup thickens. Serve hot. Good dinner soup. Good cold for lunch next day served with pita (Arab bread). Serve with bread and a vegetable dish for a simple meal.

'ADAS BI SABAANIKH [LENTIL AND SPINACH SOUP] [Serves 4 to 6]

1½ cups lentils
6 cups water

Wash lentils well. Place in a large heavy saucepan. Add water. Cover and bring to a boil over high heat. Reduce heat to low. Simmer 45 minutes.

2 medium yellow onions,
   minced
½ cup olive oil
   OR vegetable oil

Heat a small cast iron skillet over medium heat. Add oil. Heat until a small piece of onion added sizzles. Add onion. Stir and fry 5 to 10 minutes until onions are soft and transparent.

3 cloves garlic,
   crushed and minced
1 tsp. sea salt

Crush garlic with salt and then chop well. Add to onions. Fry 1 minute.

1½ lbs. spinach, shredded
   OR any cooking green,
      shredded [swiss chard,
      collards, etc.]
10 to 12 sprigs parsley,
   minced
1/8 to ½ tsp. chili pepper

Add to lentils along with fried onions and garlic. Mix well. Simmer 3 to 5 minutes until spinach just tender.

2 Tbsp. tomato paste

Add to soup. Mix well. Serve hot. Good dinner soup. Serve with bread and a vegetable dish for a simple meal. Good cold for lunch.

KHYAAR BI LEBAN [CUCUMBER AND YOGHURT SOUP] [Serves 4 to 6]

4 cups yoghurt
1 cup water
2 Tbsp. lemon juice
1 cucumber,
   grated coarsely
1 tsp. sea salt
1 tsp. mild honey

Mix lemon and honey well. Add other ingredients. Mix well. Allow to chill 30 minutes.

½ cup raisins
½ cup hot water

Wash raisins well. Place in bowl with hot water. Soak 10 to 15 minutes until soft.

3 large sprigs mint,
   coarsely chopped
   OR 1 tsp. dried mint,
      crumbled

Sprinkle mint and raisins over the top of each bowl of soup. Serve cold. Excellent on a hot day for lunch. Good dinner soup.

SHOUABAT 'ADAS [LENTIL SOUP] [Serves 4 to 6]

2 cups red lentils
  [other lentils can be used]
8 cups water
½ cup drained stewed tomatoes
  OR 1 large tomato, quartered
2 large cloves garlic,
  crushed
1 large yellow onion,
  cut in eighths

Wash, sort and drain lentils. Bring water to boil in heavy saucepan. Add lentils, tomatoes, yellow onion, and garlic. Bring to boil again over high heat. Cover. Reduce heat to medium low. Simmer 30 to 45 minutes until lentils are soft. Remove from heat. Puree lentils through a foodmill, large sieve, or in a blender. Place pureed soup back in saucepan. Slowly bring to boil over medium heat.

1 yellow onion, minced
1 Tbsp. butter
  OR vegetable oil
¼ tsp. black pepper
2 tsp. cumin
1½ tsp. sea salt

While lentils are cooking, heat a cast iron skillet over medium heat. Add butter. Heat until a small piece of onion added sizzles. Add onions. Fry 5 to 10 minutes until onions are soft and transparent but not brown. Set aside to add to soup. When soup is pureed add fried onions, pepper, cumin, and salt. Simmer over low heat 3 minutes.

4 Tbsp. butter

Add to soup. Mix well. Remove from heat and serve hot.

8 lemon wedges [optional]

Serve soup with lemon wedges. They can be individually squeezed into soup depending on personal taste. Serve hot for dinner. Good cold for lunch. Serve with bread and a vegetable dish for a simple meal.

BAYD B'LAMOUN [EGG AND LEMON SOUP] [Serves 4 to 6]

4 cups chicken
  OR garbanzo stock
¼ cup long-grain brown rice
  [preferred]
1 tsp. sea salt
dash of black pepper
1 Tbsp. celery leaves
  OR 2 sprigs parsley

Place ingredients in a large heavy saucepan. Cover. Bring to a boil over high heat. Reduce heat to low. Simmer 30 to 40 minutes until rice is tender. Remove celery leaves or parsley.

2 eggs
¼ cup lemon juice

Beat or blend eggs until yellow and thick. Slowly add lemon juice to egg, stirring constantly. When rice is cooked add ½ cup hot soup slowly to egg and lemon mixture, stirring constantly. Add lemon/egg mixture slowly to remaining soup, stir slowly but constantly to mix well. Reduce heat to low. Simmer 5 to 10 minutes until soup thickens. Stir frequently and do not cook fast or eggs will curdle.

¼ to ½ tsp. allspice
  OR cinnamon
½ cup cooked chicken,
  shredded
  [optional]

Slowly add spice and chicken to soup. Mix gently but well. Pour into individual soup bowls.

2 large sprigs parsley,
  minced
  OR 2 Tbsp. chives,
    minced

Sprinkle over soup bowls. Serve hot for dinner. Good cold for lunch.

CHICKEN BALL SOUP [Serves 4 to 6]

½ lb. raw chicken meat,
  minced
1 tsp. ras el hanout
  [spice mix]
  OR combination of cinnamon,
    allspice and nutmeg
4 sprigs parsley, minced
2 sprigs mint, minced
  OR ½ tsp. dried mint,
    crumbled
1 small yellow onion, minced
1 tsp. sea salt
1/8 to ½ tsp. chili pepper,
  ground
2 Tbsp. olive oil
  OR vegetable oil

Mix chicken, spices and herbs together. Marinate 30 minutes. Form ½ inch balls. Heat a cast iron skillet over medium high heat. Add oil. Heat until a meat ball added sizzles. Add meat balls and fry 2 to 3 minutes until lightly browned. Turn once or twice to brown evenly. Remove from pan and drain.

4 cups chicken stock
¼ cup long-grain [preferred]
  brown rice

While meat balls are marinating, place stock and rice in a large heavy saucepan. Cover. Bring to boil over high heat. Reduce heat to low. Simmer 10 minutes. Add meat balls. Cook 20 to 25 minutes until rice tender. Serve hot for dinner. Good cold for lunch. Makes a simple meal served with bread and a vegetable dish.

MEAT BALL SOUP [Serves 4 to 6]

1 lb. ground meat
  [beef, lamb or veal]
  OR Macroburger
1 small yellow onion, grated
3 sprigs parsley, minced
2 sprigs mint, minced
  OR 1 tsp. dried mint,
    crumbled
1 tsp. cumin, ground
½ tsp. coriander, ground
2 tsp. paprika
1 tsp. sea salt
1/8 to ½ tsp. chili pepper,
  ground
1 tsp. mild honey
2 Tbsp. olive oil
  OR vegetable oil

Mix meat, spices and herbs well. Marinate 30 minutes. Form into ½ inch balls. Heat a cast iron skillet over medium high heat. Add oil. Heat until a meat ball added sizzles. Add meat balls. Fry 3 to 5 minutes until just brown. Turn once or twice to brown evenly. Remove from pan. Drain.

4 cups meat stock
  OR garbanzo stock
¼ cup long-grain [preferred]
  brown rice
2 Tbsp. tomato paste

While meat balls are marinating, place ingredients in a large heavy saucepan. Cover. Bring to boil over high heat. Reduce heat to medium low. Simmer 10 minutes. Add meat balls. Cook 20 to 25 minutes until rice is tender and meat balls are done. Serve hot for dinner. Good cold for lunch. Makes a simple meal served with bread and a vegetable dish.

RICE AND PILAFS

A pilaf or rice dish accompanies most meals. For dishes like rice pottage, chicken pilaf, and stuffed chicken which contain rice or bulgur wheat, grain dishes are not necessary.

RICE PILAF I [FRIED RICE AND NOODLES] [Serves 6]

1 cup whole wheat noodles broken into small pieces

Place the noodles on a towel. Wrap tightly. Break them on edge of a table or counter into 1/8 inch pieces. Or wrap tightly in a towel and stomp on them with feet. Or place in a sack and crush with a rolling pin.

2 cups long-grain [preferred] brown rice
3 Tbsp. butter
  OR olive oil
  OR vegetable oil

Heat a heavy saucepan over medium heat. Add butter. Melt. Add noodles and rice. Increase heat to medium high. Stir and fry 3 to 5 minutes until the rice and noodles become opaque, crackle and turn golden.

5½ cups water
  OR garbanzo bean stock
  OR chicken stock
1½ tsp. sea salt
1 tsp. cumin
½ tsp. oregano

Add ingredients to rice and noodles. Mix well. Cover saucepan tightly. Bring to a boil over high heat. Reduce the heat to medium low. Cook 30 to 40 minutes until all water is absorbed. Remove from heat and let stand 10 minutes. Serve hot with salads or vegetable dishes and a main dish for dinner. Do not serve with main dishes already containing rice or other grain. A must at feasts.

VARIATION:

BULGAR PILAF I
[FRIED BULGUR WITH NOODLES]
[Serves 4 to 6]

2 cups bulgur wheat
3 Tbsp. butter
  OR olive oil
  OR vegetable oil

Follow recipe for Rice Pilaf I but use Bulgur in place of rice. Use **3 cups of liquid**. Cook only 20 minutes until water is absorbed. Serve hot with salads or vegetable dishes and a main dish for dinner. Do not serve with main dishes already containing rice or other grain. A must at feasts.

BULGUR PILAF II [FRIED BULGUR] [Serves 4 to 6]

1 medium onion, cut in half lengthwise and sliced paper-thin
2 Tbsp. butter
  OR olive oil
  OR vegetable oil

Heat a cast iron saucepan. Add butter. Melt over medium heat. Heat until a piece of onion added sizzles. Add onions. Stir and fry 5 to 10 minutes until onions are soft and transparent.

2 cups bulgur wheat
2 Tbsp. butter
  OR olive oil
  OR vegetable oil

Add to onions. Stir and fry 3 to 5 minutes until bulgur begins to crackle and turn brown.

3 cups water
  OR garbanzo bean stock
  OR chicken stock
1½ tsp. sea salt
¼ tsp. black pepper
1 tsp. oregano
½ tsp. cumin, ground

Add to bulgur. Mix well. Cover pan tightly. Bring to a boil. Reduce heat to medium low. Simmer 20 minutes until all water is absorbed. Remove from heat and allow to cool 10 minutes. Serve hot. Serve with salad and main dishes for dinner except those main dishes already containing rice or another grain.

VARIATION:

RICE PILAF II
[Serves 4 to 6]

2 cups long-grain [preferred]
  brown rice
4 cups liquid

Follow recipe for Bulgur Pilaf II. Use rice in place of bulgur wheat. Cook 30 to 40 minutes until water is absorbed. Serve hot with salads or vegetable dishes and a main dish for dinner. Do not serve with main dishes already containing rice or other grain. A must at feasts.

SAFFRON RICE [Serves 4 to 6]

2 cups rice
¼ cup butter

Heat a heavy saucepan over medium heat. Add butter. Melt. Add rice. Stir and fry 4 to 5 minutes until rice crackles and turns opaque.

4 cups water
1 tsp. sea salt
6 to 10 threads saffron
  OR ¼ to ½ tsp. saffron
¼ tsp. black pepper

Add water and spices. Mix well. Cover and bring to a boil over high heat. Reduce heat to medium low. Simmer 20 minutes.

1 cup dried fruit
  [raisins, currants, dates],
  chopped

Add to rice. Mix well. Cover. Cook another 10 to 20 minutes until all water is absorbed. Let sit 10 minutes. Place on a platter. Serve hot with salads or vegetable dishes and a main dish for dinner. Generally reserved for feasts.

BULGUR PILAF III [BULGUR PILAF WITH RAISINS AND NUTS]
[Serves 4 to 6]

1 medium yellow onion,
  cut in half lengthwise and
  sliced paper thin
2 Tbsp. butter
  OR olive oil
  OR vegetable oil

Heat a heavy cast iron saucepan over medium heat. Add butter. Melt. Add onion. Stir and fry 5 to 10 minutes until onions are soft and transparent.

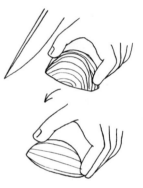

2 cups bulgur wheat
3 Tbsp. butter
  OR olive oil
  OR vegetable oil

Add butter to onions. Melt. Add bulgur. Stir and fry 3 to 5 minutes until bulgur begins to crackle and brown.

3 cups water
  OR garbanzo bean stock
  OR chicken stock
1 tsp. oregano
½ tsp. cumin
1½ tsp. sea salt
¼ tsp. black pepper

Add to bulgur. Mix well. Cover pan. Bring to a boil over high heat. Reduce heat to medium low. Simmer 10 minutes.

1 cup dried fruit
  [raisins, currants, dates],
  chopped

Add raisins, currants or chopped dates to bulgur. Mix well. Cover. Simmer another 10 minutes. Remove from heat and let sit 10 minutes.

1 cup mixed nuts or seeds,
  use 1, 2 or 3 combined
  [sesame seeds, sunflower seeds,
  peanuts, almonds, walnuts,
  pistachios or cashews],
  chopped slightly
⅓ cup butter
  OR 3 Tbsp. butter and
    3 Tbsp. olive oil
      OR vegetable oil

While bulgur is cooking, heat a cast iron skillet over medium heat. Add butter. Melt. Add nuts. Stir and fry over medium heat 3 to 5 minutes until nuts and seeds are browned. When bulgur is done pour fried nuts into pan with bulgur and mix well or arrange bulgur on platter and pour nuts over top. Serve hot with salads or vegetable dishes and a main dish for dinner. Do not serve with main dishes already containing rice or other grain. A must at feasts. Can act as a vegetarian main dish served with vegetables or a salad. Good camp dish.

VARIATION:

RICE PILAF III
[RICE PILAF WITH RAISINS AND NUTS]
[Serves 4 to 6]

2 cups long-grain [preferred]
  brown rice
4 cups of liquid

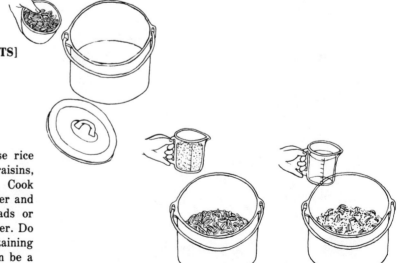

Follow recipe for Bulgur Pilaf III but use rice instead. Cook 20 minutes and then add raisins, currants or chopped dates. Mix well. Cook another 10 to 20 minutes. Place on a platter and pour nuts over top. Serve hot with salads or vegetable dishes and a main dish for dinner. Do not serve with main dishes already containing rice or other grain. A must at feasts. Can be a vegetarian main dish served with vegetables.

SALADS

Salads are used as snacks in the Middle East as well as appearing at most meals. Middle Eastern salads are very piquant with lemon which helps offset oily foods.

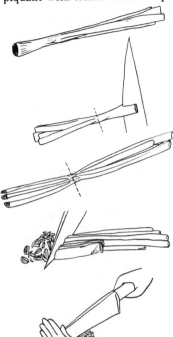

TABBOULEH [PARSLEY AND BULGUR WHEAT SALAD] [Serves 6 to 8]
[Easy to cut in half]

1 cup bulgur wheat
1 cup hot water

Wash bulgur. Drain. Place in bowl. Pour hot water over it. Allow to soak 15 to 30 minutes. Drain. Place in large salad bowl.

5 to 6 green onions, minced
3 large sprigs mint, minced
  OR 1 tsp. dried mint, crumbled
1 cucumber, chopped
  OR 3 stalks celery, minced
3 to 4 large tomatoes, chopped and drained [optional with season]
4 cups minced parsley [2 large bunches]
juice of 4 lemons
½ cup olive oil
  OR vegetable oil
1 tsp. sea salt
¼ tsp. freshly ground black pepper
1 tsp. allspice

Toss ingredients together with bulgur. Chill 30 minutes.

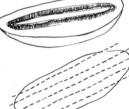

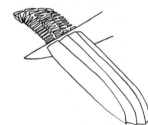

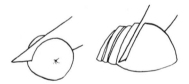

Optional step:

1 head Romaine lettuce, separated into individual leaves
10 to 15 pita [Arab bread]

Line salad bowl with Romaine leaves. Place salad in bowl. Use Romaine as scoops for salad. Tabbouleh is also served with pita as a snack or appetizer. The salad is stuffed into the pocket of the bread. An excellent dinner salad and a must for potlucks.

LEVANT POTATO SALAD [Serves 4 to 6]

5 to 6 small new potatoes
   OR 4 medium potatoes
4 cups water

Place in a large suacepan. Bring to a boil over high heat. Cover. Reduce heat to medium low and simmer 15 to 20 minutes until potatoes are tender. Remove from heat. Drian. Peel while hot — easiest to do this by spearing potato with a fork and then peeling it. Cut into ½ to 1 inch chunks and place in a glass bowl.

⅓ cup olive oil
   OR vegetable oil
⅓ cup lemon juice
   [2 large lemons]
1 to 2 cloves garlic,
   crushed and minced
5 to 6 green onions,
   minced
6 to 8 large sprigs parsley,
   minced
5 to 6 small sprigs fresh
   dillweed, minced
   OR 1 tsp. dried dillweed,
      crumbled
2 sprigs mint,
   minced
   OR 1 tsp. dried mint,
      crumbled
1 tsp. sea salt
½ tsp. white pepper,
   ground
   OR black pepper
dash chili pepper,
   ground

Mix ingredients well. Pour over hot potatoes. Mix. Chill 1 to 2 hours or overnight.

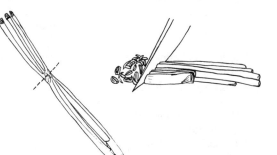

1 cup Greek olives
   OR black olives

Mix with salad. Serve cold. Good on a hot summer day with Kababs and pita (Arab bread). Serve any time potato salad would be served. Good snack.

CUCUMBER AND TOMATO SALAD [Serves 4 to 6]

1½ cucumber,
   grated
1 tomato,
   cut into 1/8 inch cubes
2 green onions,
   minced
¼ cup lemon juice
¼ cup olive oil
   OR vegetable oil
1 tsp. mild honey
½ tsp. sea salt
½ tsp. cumin,
   ground
¼ tsp. coriander,
   ground
½ tsp. paprika

Combine all ingredients and mix well. Chill 20 minutes. Mix again. Serve cold. Good with any main dish and pilaf. Expecially good with mussak'a (Garbanzo Eggplant casserole).

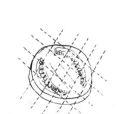

SALATET MALFOOF [CABBAGE SALAD] [Serves 4 to 6]

3 sprigs mint,
  minced
  OR 1 tsp. dried mint,
    crumbled
1 medium head cabbage,
  shredded
1 tsp. sea salt
¼ tsp. fresh ground
  black pepper

Place cabbage and mint in a bowl. Sprinkle with salt and pepper. Crush the cabbage slightly with your hands. Let stand 10 minutes.

¼ cup lemon juice
  [1 lemon]
1 large clove garlic,
  crushed and minced
¼ cup olive oil
  OR vegetable oil

Toss with cabbage and serve immediately. Good served with Majadarra or Lentils with Noodles. Keeps well. Good for lunch with other leftovers. Good camp salad as cabbage keeps well without refrigeration.

SALATET TAHINI [SESAME PASTE SALAD] [Serves 4 to 6]

3 cloves garlic,
  crushed and minced
⅓ cup lemon juice
½ cup tahini
  [sesame paste]
10 to 15 large sprigs parsley,
  minced
½ tsp. cumin
½ tsp. sea salt
dash of pepper

If a blender is used leave all ingredients in large pieces. Place in a blender. Blend 30 seconds to 1 minute until well mixed and sauce is a smooth green color. If a blender is not available, mince ingredients well and mix until smooth. Serve with pita (Arab bread) or tamia as a dip sauce. Good dip for crisp vegetables also. Excellent snack dish.

SALATET KHYAAR BI LEBAN [CUCUMBER AND YOGHURT SALAD]
[Serves 4 to 6]

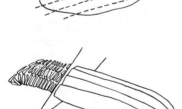

2 cups yoghurt

Place in a bowl. Mix with a spoon until smooth and slightly liquid.

1 large cucumber,
  chopped fine
1 to 2 cloves garlic,
  crushed and minced
¼ tsp. white pepper
1 tsp. sea salt

Mix ingredients well with yoghurt. Marinate 20 minutes. Mix again.

3 sprigs mint,
  minced
  OR 1 tsp. dried mint,
    crumbled

Sprinkle over top of salad. Serve cold. This salad is good with mussakk'a, a pilaf, or a meat dish.

VARIATION:

LETTUCE AND YOGHURT SALAD [Serves 4]

¼ head lettuce,
  shredded
  OR ¼ head green cabbage,
    shredded

Follow recipe for Cucumber and Yoghurt Salad. Substitute lettuce for cucumber when cucumbers are out of season.

SALATET MOROCCAN [MOROCCAN TOMATO SALAD] [Serves 4]

2 large tomatoes,
    cut in half along the side,
    seeded, washed, drained
    and julienned into 1/8 inch
    slivers
2 medium cucumbers,
    seeded and julienned into
    2 inch by 1/16 inch slivers
1 small green pepper,
    seeded and julienned
1 clove of garlic,
    crushed and minced
½ medium yellow onion,
    grated

juice of 1 lemon
1 tsp. rice vinegar
    OR apple cider vinegar
3 Tbsp. olive oil
1 tsp. cumin
1 tsp. paprika
dash of chili pepper
1 tsp. mild honey

Place ingredients in a bowl.

Mix ingredients well. Add to salad vegetables. Marinate in dressing 30 minutes. Serve cold. Excellent served with Kabab and pita (Arab bread). Good dinner salad. Keeps well for several days. A good camping salad.

SALATET BAYD [EGG SALAD] [Serves 4 to 6]

½ head lettuce,
    shredded
    OR cabbage,
    shredded
3 sprigs fresh mint,
    shredded
    OR 1 tsp. dried mint,
    crumbled

6 to 8 hard-boiled eggs,
    cut into ¼ inch slices
2 tomatoes,
    sliced thin
    [optional with season]
2 boiled potatoes,
    cut into 1/8 inch slices
6 green onions,
    julienned
1 large cucumber,
    sliced thin

⅓ cup olive oil
    OR vegetable oil
⅓ cup lemon juice
1 clove garlic,
    crushed and minced
½ tsp. sea salt
¼ tsp. fresh ground
    black pepper

Mix well. Spread an even layer of mixture on a large platter.

Arrange vegetables and eggs on the lettuce and mint leaves.

Mix well. Pour over vegetable platter. Serve immediately. Good served with bread for a summer lunch. Can be used as a vegetarian main dish served with pilaf and soup. An excellent potluck dish.

SALATET LOUBIAH [GREEN BEAN SALAD[[Serves 4 to 6]

1 lb. green beans,
  snipped and strings removed,
  cut into long thin diagonal
  slices
  OR 1 lb. broccoli,
    stems cut into long thin
    diagonal slices with
    heads broken into small
    pieces
¼ tsp. sea salt

Sprinkle beans with salt. Steam beans 5 to 10 minutes until just tender and still bright green. Same for broccoli. Remove from heat. Place in a glass bowl.

½ cup olive oil
  OR vegetable oil
½ cup lemon juice
  [2 large lemons]
1 clove garlic,
  crushed and minced
4 to 5 sprigs parsley,
  minced
2 sprigs mint,
  minced
  OR 1 tsp. dried mint,
    crumbled
1 yellow onion,
  cut in half lengthwise and
  sliced paper-thin
5 to 6 small sprigs
  fresh dillweed,
  minced
  OR 1 tsp. dried dillweed,
    crumbled
1 tsp. sea salt
¼ to ½ tsp. black pepper
  ground
dash chili pepper,
  ground

Mix ingredients well. Add to hot beans. Mix well. Chill 2 to 3 hours or overnight.

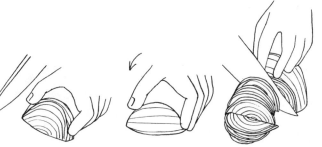

Optional step:

1 to 2 large tomatoes,
  cut in half lengthwise and
  then cut into thin slices

Mix with salad. Serve cold. Good on a hot summer day with Kababs and pita (Arab bread), Good dinner or lunch salad. Keeps well for several days. Good snack.

SALATET HUMMUS [GARBANZO SALAD] [Serves 4 to 6]

1½ cups dried **garbanzo beans**
8 to 12 cups water

Soak garbanzos in cold water overnight (optional step). Place in a heavy saucepan. Cover. Bring to a boil over high heat. Reduce heat. Simmer 3 to 4 hours until tender. To pressure cook use 8 cups water. Bring to full pressure 1 hour. When cooked drain. Reserve stock for pilafs and soups.

1 to 3 cloves **garlic**,
    crushed and minced
juice of 2 lemons
⅓ cup **olive oil**
    OR vegetable oil
1 tsp. **sea salt**
¼ tsp. **fresh ground**
    black pepper

Mix ingredients well with warm beans in a large bowl. Cover. Marinate 1 hour or overnight. Mix several times to distribute flavors well.

2 sprigs **fresh mint**, minced
    OR 1 tsp. dried mint,
    crumbled
5 to 6 sprigs **fresh green herbs**,
    minced [oregano,
    winter savory, thyme, etc.]
    [optional]
    OR 1 tsp. dried crumbled
        green herbs
1 cup **parsley**,
    minced
½ head **cabbage**,
    shredded [optional]
    OR lettuce,
        shredded [optional]
6 to 8 **green onions**,
    minced
½ cup **Greek or Arab olives**
    [optional]
    OR Black olives
        [optional]

Mix with garbanzos. Serve salad cold. Good for lunch with bread. Good summer vegetarian main dish served with pilaf or bread and soup.

VARIATION:

FAVA BEAN SALAD
[DRIED BROAD BEAN SALAD]
[Serves 4 to 6]

1½ cups dried **fava beans**
8 to 12 cups water

Cook beans like garbanzos. Follow recipe for Garbanzo Salad. Serve cold. Good for lunch with bread. Good summer vegetarian main dish served with pilaf or bread and soup.

VARIATION:

SALATET 'ADAS
[LENTIL SALAD]
[Serves 4 to 6]

3 cups cooked **green lentils**

Mix lentils with marinade ingredients. Follow recipe for Garbanzo Salad. Serve cold. Good for lunch with bread. Good summer vegetarian main dish served with pilaf or bread and soup.

VARIATION:

WHITE BEAN SALAD
[Serves 4 to 6]

1½ cups dried white beans
8 to 12 cups water

Cook like garbanzos.

1 to 3 cloves garlic,
 crushed and minced
¼ cup lemon juice
3 Tbsp. rice vinegar
 OR apple cider vinegar
⅓ cup olive oil
 OR vegetable oil
1 tsp. sea salt
¼ tsp. fresh ground
 black pepper

Mix ingredients well with warm beans in a large
bowl. Cover. Marinate 1 hour or overnight. Mix
several times to distribute flavors. Follow
remainder of recipe for Garbanzo Salad. Good
for lunch with bread. Good summer vegetarian
main dish served with pilaf or bread and soup.

PARSLEY SALAD [Serves 4 to 6]

12 to 15 large sprigs parsley,
 minced [1 bunch]
2 green onions,
 minced
pulp of 1 lemon
juice of 1 lemon
2 Tbsp. olive oil
 OR vegetable oil
½ tsp. sea salt
¼ tsp. fresh ground
 black pepper

Just before serving combine all ingredients. Mix
well. Serve cold. This salad is good with rich
foods such as Daja Mashi or Mussaka.

LEVANT TOSSED GREEN SALAD [Serves 4 to 6]

1 head lettuce,
   torn into bite-sized pieces
1 green pepper,
   julienned
1 to 2 large tomatoes,
   cut into 1/8 inch cubes
   [optional with season]
1 cucumber,
   cut into thin slices
3 to 4 green onions,
   minced
4 to 5 sprigs parsley,
   minced
4 to 5 sprigs fresh mint,
   minced
   OR 2 tsp. dried mint,
   crumbled

OR IN PLACE OF ABOVE:
your favorite tossed green salad
   and
4 to 5 sprigs fresh mint,
   minced
   OR 2 tsp. dried mint,
      crumbled

Place in a salad bowl. Toss. Chill.

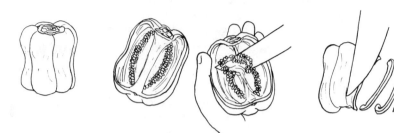

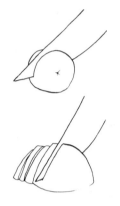

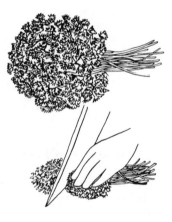

Dressing:

¼ cup lemon juice
¼ cup olive oil
   OR vegetable oil
1 clove garlic,
   crushed and minced
½ tsp. sea salt
¼ tsp. fresh ground
   black pepper

Pour dressing over salad. Serve at once. A good
dinner salad.

PICKLES

Pickles are served as snacks or in place of salads at lunch or dinner.

MARINATED SUMMER SQUASH [Makes 1 to 2 quarts]

2 large zucchini,
   cut into ¼ inch slices
1 Tbsp. sea salt

Place squash in large colander. Sprinkle with salt. Let sit 2 hours. Stir occasionally.

1 cup rice vinegar
   OR apple cider vinegar
2 cups water

Place squash in a saucepan with water and vinegar. Bring to a boil over medium high heat. Simmer 5 minutes over medium low heat. Remove from heat. Drain well.

6 large cloves garlic,
   crushed and minced
1 Tbsp. oregano
¼ tsp. black pepper
2 cups olive oil

Arrange one layer of squash in the bottom of a large glass crock or casserole. Sprinkle with garlic, oregano and pepper. Place another layer of squash over the first and sprinkle with seasonings again. Repeat until all squash is used. Cover with oil and allow to sit for 7 days covered. This pickle will keep indefinitely. When squash is low just add more vinegared squash and spices to oil. Refrigerate. Good as snack with bread. Good served at lunch with leftovers. Should be served at large feasts.

VARIATION:

MARINATED EGGPLANT
[Makes 1 to 2 quarts]

2 large eggplant,
   cut in half lengthwise and
   then cut into ¼ inch slices

Follow recipe for Marinated Summer Squash. Good as snack with bread. Good served at lunch with leftovers. Should be served at large feasts.

COOKED VEGETABLES

Cooked vegetable dishes can be served hot or cold. Vegetables cooked in oil should be served to balance a sour dish. Vegetables cooked in lemon are best served with oily dishes such as Mussaka or Dajaj Mashi.

KOUSA BI ZAYT [SQUASH COOKED IN OLIVE OIL] [Serves 4 to 6]

1 clove garlic,
  crushed and minced
1 large yellow onion,
  chopped
½ cup olive oil
  OR vegetable oil

Heat a cast iron skillet over medium heat. Add oil. Heat until a small piece of onion added sizzles. Add onions and garlic. Fry 5 to 10 minutes until onions are soft and transparent.

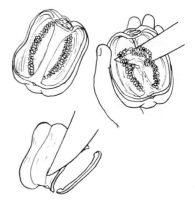

1 green pepper,
  seeded and julienned
  [optional]
4 cups zucchini squash,
  cut into ¼ inch even slices
  OR other summer squash,
    cut into ¼ inch even slices
  OR 4 cups winter squash
  [hubbard or butternut]
    cut into 1/8 inch even slices,
    steamed 5 minutes

Make sure to cut squash slices evenly or they will cook unevenly and the dish will not taste as good. Add green peppers and squash to onions. Stir and fry 5 to 10 minutes until just tender.

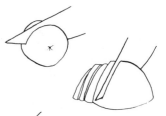

4 tomatoes,
  cubed
  OR 1½ cups stewed tomatoes,
  drained and chopped
1 tsp. paprika
½ tsp. cumin
¼ tsp. black pepper
1 tsp. sea salt

Add tomatoes and spices. Cover and simmer 10 minutes. Remove lid and simmer another 5 to 10 minutes until almost all liquid is absorbed and squash is tender (winter squash will take longest to cook). Good served hot at dinner or cold for lunch. Good cold as a dinner salad. Keeps 1 to 2 weeks in refrigerator. Good camp dish since it keeps well.

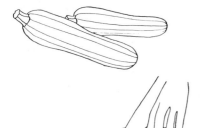

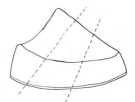

COOKED VEGETABLES

VARIATION:

LOUBIAH BI ZAYT
[GREEN BEANS COOKED IN OLIVE OIL]
[Serves 4 to 6]

3 cups green beans,
cut into long thin diagonal
slices, steamed 5 minutes

Follow recipe for Kousa Bi Zayt. Use green beans instead of squash. Good served hot at dinner or cold for lunch. Good cold as a dinner salad. Keeps 1 to 2 weeks in refrigerator. Good camp dish since it keeps well.

VARIATION:

HAVIJ BI ZAYT
[CARROTS COOKED IN OLIVE OIL]
[Serves 4 to 6]

3 cups carrots,
cut into thin even diagonal
slices, steamed 5 minutes

Follow recipe for Kousa Bi Zayt. Use carrots instead of squash. Good served hot at dinner or cold for lunch. Good cold as a dinner salad. Keeps 1 to 2 weeks in refrigerator. Good camp dish since it keeps well.

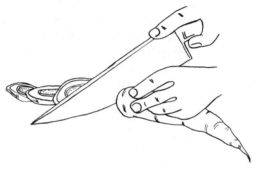

VARIATION:

BROCCOLI COOKED IN OLIVE OIL
[Serves 4 to 6]

1 lb. broccoli,
stems cut into long thin
diagonals with heads broken
into small pieces, steamed
5 minutes

Follow recipe for Kousa bi Zayt. Use broccoli in place of squash. Cook as directed. Good served hot at a dinner or cold for lunch. Good cold as a dinner salad. Keeps 1 to 2 weeks in refrigerator. Good camp dish since it keeps well.

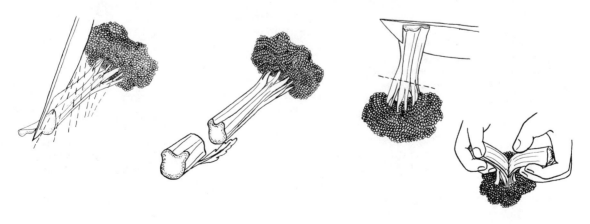

BATINGANN BI ZAYT [EGGPLANT COOKED IN OLIVE OIL] [Serves 4 to 6]

3 cloves garlic,
   crushed and minced
1 yellow onion,
   cut in half lengthwise
   and sliced thin
½ cup olive oil
   OR vegetable oil

Heat a cast iron skillet over medium heat. Add oil. Heat until a small piece of onion added sizzles. Add onion and garlic. Stir and fry 5 to 10 minutes until onions are soft and transparent.

2 eggplant,
   cut in half lengthwise
   and sliced into 1/8 inch slices

Add to onions. Stir and fry 5 to 10 minutes until just browned.

4 large tomatoes,
   cubed
   OR 1½ cups stewed tomatoes,
      drained and chopped
1 tsp. ras el hanout
   [spice mix]
   OR ½ tsp. cinnamon and
      ½ tsp. allspice
1 tsp. sea salt
¼ tsp. black pepper

Add tomatoes and spices to eggplant. Cover and simmer 10 minutes. Uncover and cook 5 to 10 minutes until liquid is absorbed. Good served hot at dinner or cold for lunch. Good cold as a dinner salad. Keeps 1 to 2 weeks in refrigerator. Good camp dish as it keeps well.

VARIATION:

KOUSA BI ZAYT II
[SQUASH COOKED IN OLIVE OIL]
[Serves 4 to 6]

4 cups zucchini squash,
   cut into ¼ inch even slices
   OR other summer squash,
      cut into ¼ inch even slices
   OR 4 cups winter squash,
      [hubbard or butternut]
      cut into 1/8 inch even slices,
      steamed 5 minutes

Follow recipe for Batingaan bi Zayt. Cook as directed. Use squash in place of eggplant. Good served hot at dinner or cold for lunch. Good cold as a dinner salad. Keeps 1 to 2 weeks in refrigerator. Good camp dish as it keeps well.

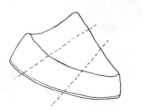

HAVIJ BI ZAYT II [CARROTS IN OLIVE OIL] [Serves 4 to 6]

1 large yellow onion, chopped
2 cloves garlic,
  crushed and minced
½ cup olive oil
  OR vegetable oil

Heat a heavy saucepan over medium high heat. Add oil. Heat until a small piece of onion added sizzles. Add onions and garlic. Stir and fry 5 to 10 minutes until soft and transparent.

1 tsp. sea salt
¼ tsp. black pepper
1 tsp. allspice
3 cups carrots,
  cut into thin diagonal
  even slices

If carrots are not sliced the same thickness they will cook unevenly. Add carrots and spices to onions. Mix well. Stir and fry 10 minutes until just tender.

1½ cups stewed tomatoes,
  drained
  OR 2 tomatoes,
  chopped

Add tomatoes to carrot mixture. Mix well. Bring to boil. Cover. Reduce heat to medium low. Simmer 5 to 10 minutes. Remove cover and simmer another 5 minutes until liquid is absorbed and carrots are tender. Good served hot at dinner or cold for lunch. Good cold as a dinner salad. Keeps 1 to 2 weeks in refrigerator. Good camp dish as it keeps well.

VARIATION:

LOUBIAH BI ZAYT II
[GREEN BEANS COOKED IN OLIVE OIL]
[Serves 4 to 6]

3 cups green beans,
  cut into thin diagonal slices

Follow recipe for Carrots Cooked in Olive Oil. Use green beans instead of carrots. Good served hot at dinner or cold for lunch. Good cold as a dinner salad. Keeps 1 to 2 weeks in refrigerator. Good camp dish as it keeps well.

VARIATION:

BROCCOLI COOKED IN OLIVE OIL II
[Serves 4 to 6]

1 lb. broccoli,
  stems cut into long thin
  diagonals with heads
  broken into small pieces

Follow recipe for Carrots Cooked in Olive Oil. Use broccoli in place of carrots. Good served hot at a dinner or cold for lunch. Good cold as a dinner salad. Keeps 1 to 2 weeks in refrigerator. Good camp dish as it keeps well.

KARNABEET BI LAMOUN [CAULIFLOWER WITH LEMON] [Serves 4 to 6]

1 medium head cauliflower

Steam 10 to 15 minutes until just tender. Drain. Break into 1 inch flowerlets.

2 Tbsp. olive oil
  OR vegetable oil
2 Tbsp. butter
¼ cup lemon juice
1 large clove garlic,
  crushed and minced
1 tsp. sea salt
¼ tsp. or dash black pepper

Heat a heavy skillet over medium heat. Add oil. Heat. Add butter and melt. Add lemon juice, salt, pepper and garlic. Mix well. Add cauliflower. Roll well in oil. Stir gently for 5 minutes until all lemon juice absorbed by cauliflower. Good vegetable side dish for dinner. Good cold for lunch or as a salad. Best served with oily dishes such as Mussakka or Dajaj Mashi.

VARIATION:

BROCCOLI WITH LEMON
[Serves 4 to 6]

1 lb. broccoli,
  cut into ¼ inch diagonal
  slices with heads broken
  into 1 inch pieces

Follow recipe for Karnabeet bi Lamoun. Use broccoli in place of cauliflower. Steam broccoli 5 to 10 minutes only. Good vegetable side dish for dinner. Good cold for lunch or as a salad. Best served with oily dishes such as Mussakka or Dajaj Mashi.

STUFFED VEGETABLES

Stuffed vegetables may be used as main dishes or chilled and served cold as appetizers or salads. As a main course they are served along with a pilaf, salad and yoghurt for a full meal.

MASHI [STUFFING]

VEGETARIAN:

½ **cup garbanzos**
3 cups water

Soak garbanzos overnight. Drain. Add to saucepan with water. Bring to a boil over high heat. Cover. Reduce heat to medium low. Simmer 2 to 3 hours until just tender. Drain. Reserve stock for other use. To pressure cook bring to full pressure and cook at full pressure 45 minutes. Cool. Drain. Chop garbanzos coarsely.

½ **cup brown rice**
2 cups water

Soak rice overnight. Drain well. Allow to dry 10 to 15 minutes (optional). Chop coarsely. Add to garbanzos.

1 large yellow onion,
  minced
1 clove garlic,
  crushed and minced
2 Tbsp. olive oil
  OR vegetable oil

Heat a medium cast iron skillet over medium heat. Add oil. Heat until a piece of onion added sizzles. Add onion and garlic. Stir and fry 5 minutes until just beginning to get transparent and still not too tender. Remove from heat and add to garbanzos and rice mixture.

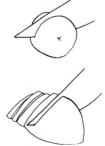

1 large tomato,
  chopped
  OR ¾ cup stewed tomatoes,
    drained and chopped
2 Tbsp. tomato paste
1 tsp. sea salt
¼ **tsp. black pepper**
1 tsp. ras el hanout
  [spice mix]
  OR ½ tsp. allspice
        and
    ½ **tsp. cinnamon**

Add to garbanzos and rice. Mix well. Knead well with your hands. Allow to soak 30 minutes to 1 hour.

Optional:

¼ **cup nuts**
  [pinenuts, peanuts, cashews,
  almonds, walnuts, or
  pistachio nuts]
  OR seeds
2 Tbsp. butter
  OR olive oil
  OR vegetable oil

Heat a small cast iron skillet. Add butter or oil. Heat over low heat. Add nuts. Stir and fry 3 to 5 minutes until browned. Remove from heat. Chop coarsely. Add to filling. Mix well. Stuff vegetables loosely to allow rice to expand.

MASHI [STUFFING]

MEAT:

½ cup brown rice
2 cups water

Soak rice overnight. Drain well. Allow to dry 10 to 15 minutes (optional). Chop coarsely. Add after tomatoes cooked.

½ lb. ground meat
  [lamb, veal or beef]
  OR Macro Burger
2 Tbsp. olive oil
  OR vegetable oil

Heat a heavy saucepan over medium heat. Add oil and heat until a small piece of meat added sizzles. Add meat. Stir and fry 3 to 5 minutes until just browned.

1 large onion,
  minced
2 cloves garlic,
  crushed and minced

Add to meat. Stir and fry 5 to 10 minutes until just tender.

1 large tomato,
  chopped
  OR ¾ cup stewed tomatoes,
    drained and chopped
1 tsp. sea salt
¼ tsp. black pepper
1 tsp ras el hanout
  [spice mix]
  OR 1 tsp. cinnamon
    and
    1 tsp. allspice

Add to onions and meat. Stir and fry 3 to 5 minutes until mixture begins to get dry. Remove from heat. Add rice. Mix well.

Optional step:

¼ cup nuts
  [cashews, peanuts, pinenuts, almonds, walnuts
  or pistachio nuts]
  OR seeds
2 Tbsp. butter
  OR olive oil
  OR vegetable oil

Heat a small cast iron skillet. Add butter. Melt over medium low heat. Add nuts. Stir and fry 3 to 5 minutes until browned. Remove from heat. Chop nuts coarsely. Add to filling with rice. Mix well. Allow to marinate 30 minutes to hour. Stuff vegetables loosely to allow rice to expand.

KOUSA MASHI [STUFFED SQUASH] [Serves 4 to 6]

6 to 8 medium sized zucchini
   OR other summer squash
      at least 2 to 3 inches
      in diameter and 6 to 8
      inches long

Cut off one end of squash. Save ends. Hallow out centers with a small spoon.

FILLING:

Use either:
   vegetarian stuffing
   OR meat stuffing

Stuff squash loosely to allow room for rice to expand. Place ends back on squash and secure with toothpicks.

COOKING:

¼ cup butter
   OR olive oil
   OR vegetable oil

Heat a large skillet over medium high heat. Add butter or oil. Heat 30 seconds. Add stuffed squash. Fry over medium heat 3 minutes to a side. Remove from pan and drain.

2 tomatoes,
   cut into ¼ inch slices
   OR 1 cup stewed tomatoes,
      drained and chopped

Place tomato slices or drained tomatoes in bottom of a large heavy saucepan. Place squash on top of tomatoes.

¼ cup tomato paste
¼ cup lemon juice
1 clove garlic,
   crushed and minced
½ cup tomato juice
   [from drained tomatoes]
1 tsp. sea salt
¼ tsp. black pepper

Mix well. Blend 15 seconds. If no blender is available mix well. Pour sauce over squash. Cover. Bring to boil over medium heat. Reduce heat to low and simmer 30 to 45 minutes until rice is done. Remove cover. Simmer 5 to 10 minutes until most of liquid is absorbed. Serve hot as a main dish or as a vegetable side dish for dinner. Good cold as a salad or appetizer. Excellent cold lunch.

STUFFED VEGETABLES

VARIATION:

STUFFED WINTER SQUASH
[Serves 4 to 6]

6 acorn squash,
  cut in half lengthwise
  and seeds removed

Follow recipe for Kousa Mashi. Fry squash halves before stuffing. Stuff and then cook as directed for Kousa Mashi. Serve hot as a main dish or as a vegetable side dish for dinner. Good cold as a salad or cut into slices it is good as an appetizer. Excellent cold lunch.

VARIATION:

BATINGANN MASHI
[STUFFED EGGPLANT]
[Serves 4 to 6]

4 to 6 long thin eggplant
  OR 2 large eggplant
1 tsp. sea salt

Cut off tops of eggplant. Save tops. Hollow out centers with a spoon. Sprinkle with salt. Invert and drain 30 minutes. Follow recipe for Kousa Mashi. Cook as directed. Serve hot as a main dish or as a vegetable side dish for dinner. Good cold as a salad or cut into slices it is a good appetizer. Excellent cold for lunch.

VARIATION:

STUFFED PUMPKIN
[Serves 4 to 6]

1 small pumpkin,
  cut lengthwise in quarters
  and seeds removed

Follow recipe for Kousa Mashi. Fry pumpkin quarters before stuffing. Stuff and then cook as directed for Kousa Mashi. Serve hot as a main dish or as a vegetable side dish for dinner. Good cold as a salad or cut into slices it is good as an appetizer. Excellent cold lunch.

BATINGANN MASHI II [STUFFED EGGPLANT] [Serves 4 to 6]

4 to 6 long thin eggplant
OR 2 large eggplant
1 tsp. sea salt

Cut off tops of eggplant. Save tops. Hollow out centers with a spoon. Sprinkle with salt. Invert and drain 30 minutes.

FILLING:

Use either:
vegetarian stuffing
OR meat stuffing

Stuff eggplant loosely to allow room for rice to expand. Place ends back on eggplant and secure with toothpicks.

COOKING:

⅓ cup olive oil
OR vegetable oil
2 Tbsp. butter

Heat a large cast iron skillet. Add oil. Heat slightly. Add butter and melt over medium heat. Add stuffed eggplant. Fry 5 to 10 minutes on each side. Remove from pan and drain.

OR IN PLACE OF ABOVE:

½ cup vegetable oil

2 tomatoes,
chopped
OR 1 cup stewed tomatoes,
drained and chopped
2 tsp. mild honey
2 cloves garlic,
crushed and minced
½ cup tomato juice
1 tsp. sea salt
¼ tsp. black pepper

Place ingredients in a large heavy saucepan. Add stuffed fried eggplant. Cover and bring to a boil over high heat. Reduce heat to medium low. Simmer 30 to 45 minutes until rice is done. Turn eggplant once. Remove cover. Simmer 5 to 10 minutes until most of liquid is absorbed. Serve hot as a main dish or as a vegetable side dish for dinner. Good cold as a salad or appetizer. Excellent cold lunch.

VARIATION:

KOUSA MASHI II [STUFFED SQUASH] [Serves 4 to 6]

6 to 8 medium sized zucchini
OR other summer squash
at least 2 to 3 inches in
diameter and 6 to 8 inches
long

Cut off one end of squash. Save ends. Hollow out centers with a small spoon. Follow recipe for Batingann Mashi II. Cook as directed. Use squash in place of eggplant. Serve hot as a main dish or as a vegetable side dish for dinner. Good cold as a salad or appetizer. Excellent cold for lunch.

VARIATION:

STUFFED WINTER SQUASH II
[Serves 4 to 6]

6 acorn squash,
cut in half lengthwise and
seeds removed

Follow recipe for Batingann Mashi II. Fry squash halves before stuffing. Cook as directed. Use squash in place of eggplant. Serve hot as a main dish or as a vegetable side dish for dinner. Good cold as a salad or appetizer. Excellent cold for lunch.

VARIATION:

STUFFED PUMPKIN II
[Serves 4 to 6]

1 small pumpkin,
cut in quarters and
seeds removed

Follow recipe for Batingann Mashi II. Fry pumpkin quarters before stuffing. Use pumpkin instead of eggplant. Cook as directed. Serve hot as a main dish or as a vegetable side dish for dinner. Good cold as a salad or appetizer. Excellent cold for lunch.

TAMATEM MASHI [STUFFED TOMATOES] [Serves 4 to 6]

6 large firm ripe tomatoes

Slice off top. Save tops. Scoop out centers. Reserve pulp. Invert tomatoes and drain.

FILLING:

Use either:
   vegetarian stuffing
   OR meat stuffing

Stuff tomatoes loosely to allow room for rice to expand. Place tops back on tomatoes. Secure with toothpicks.

COOKING:

¼ cup olive oil
   OR vegetable oil

Place tomatoes in a casserole. Pour olive oil over tomatoes.

pulp from tomatoes
2 Tbsp. tomato paste
¼ cup water
1 tsp. sea salt
1 tsp. mild honey
¼ tsp. black pepper

Blend ingredients well. If no blender is available, mix well. Pour over tomatoes. Cover casserole. Bake at 350° for 20 to 30 minutes until rice is done. Uncover and bake 5 to 10 minutes until most of liquid is absorbed. Serve hot as a main dish or as a vegetable side dish for dinner. Good cold as a salad or appetizer. Excellent cold lunch.

FEIFEL MASHI [STUFFED GREEN PEPPERS] [Serves 4 to 6]

6 green peppers

Cut off tops. Remove seeds. Save tops.

FILLING:

Use either:
   vegetarian stuffing
   OR meat stuffing

Stuff peppers loosely to allow room for rice to expand. Place tops on peppers. Secure with toothpicks.

COOKING:

3 Tbsp. olive oil
   OR vegetable oil

Place stuffed peppers in an oiled casserole. Pour oil over peppers.

2 tomatoes,
  chopped
  OR 1½ cups stewed tomatoes,
    drained and chopped
3 Tbsp. tomato paste
¼ cup tomato juice
  OR water
1 tsp. sea salt
¼ tsp. black pepper
½ tsp. ras el hanout
  [spice mix]
  OR ¼ tsp. cinnamon and
    ¼ tsp. allspice

Blend ingredients well. If no blender is available mix well. Pour over peppers. Cover casserole and bake for 20 to 30 minutes at 350° until rice is done. Remove lid and cook 5 to 10 minutes until liquid is absorbed. Serve hot as a main dish or a vegetable side dish for dinner. Good cold as a salad or appetizer. Excellent cold lunch.

VEGETARIAN MAIN DISHES

Vegetarian main dishes make a complete meal when served with rice or wheat dishes, salad and a yoghurt dish. Those which contain both grain and beans or lentils need not be accompanied by a grain dish for a complete protein meal. See also stuffed vegetables and salads for vegetarian main dishes.

YAKNIT EL KOUSA [SQUASH STEW WITH GARBANZOS] [Serves 4 to 6]

2 cups garbanzos
6 cups water

Cover garbanzos with water. Soak overnight. Drain (optional step). Place garbanzos in a heavy saucepan. Add water. Bring to a boil over high heat. Cook covered 3 to 4 hours over medium heat until beans are tender. To pressure cook: place in pressure cooker with 4 cups water. Cover and bring to full pressure. Cook at full pressure 50 minutes. Remove from heat and cool. However cooked, drain and reserve stock for later use.

2 medium potatoes,
   cut into 1 inch cubes
1 large zucchini
   OR any other summer squash,
      cut into 1 inch slices
   OR 1 lb. winter squash,
      cut into ¼ inch slices
1 cup garbanzo stock
2 leeks,
   chopped
   OR 4 green onions,
      chopped

Place in large heavy saucepan. Cover. Bring to a boil over high heat. Reduce heat to medium low and simmer 15 to 20 minutes until potatoes are just tender. Add garbanzos.

1 large yellow onion, minced
2 cloves garlic,
   crushed and minced
¼ cup olive oil
   OR vegetable oil

While potatoes and squash are cooking, heat a cast iron skillet over medium heat. Add oil. Heat until a small piece of onion added sizzles. Add onions and garlic. Stir and fry 5 to 10 minutes until onions are soft and transparent but not brown.

5 to 8 sprigs parsley,
   minced
1½ tsp. sea salt
¼ tsp. black pepper
1 cup stewed tomatoes
¼ cup tomato paste

Add to garbanzos along with onions. Mix well. Cover. Simmer on low heat 3 to 5 minutes. Just enough to heat added ingredients and mix well with other flavors.

¼ cup lemon juice

Add to stew. Mix well. Serve at once with pilaf and salad. Good cold for lunch.

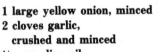

VARIATION:

YAKNIT EL KOUSA II
[SQUASH STEW WITH DRIED BEANS]
[Serves 4 to 6]

2 cups dried beans
  [fava, red, pinto, small white]
6 cups water

Cook beans like garbanzos in Yaknit el Kousa. Use any one of these beans in place of garbanzos. Follow recipe for Yaknit el Kousa. Cook as directed. Serve hot with pilaf and salad. Good cold for lunch.

VARIATION:

YAKNIT EL LOUBIAH
[GREEN BEAN STEW WITH GARBANZOS]
[Serves 4 to 6]

1 lb. green beans,
  cut into 1 inch pieces

Follow recipe for Yaknit el Kousa. Use green beans in place of squash. Cook as directed. Serve hot with pilaf, yoghurt and salad. Good cold for lunch.

VARIATION:

YAKNIT EL LOUBIAH II
[GREEN BEAN STEW WITH DRIED BEANS]
[Serves 4 to 6]

2 cups dried beans
  [fava, red, pinto, small white]
1 lb. green beans,
  cut into 1 inch pieces

Cook beans like garbanzos in Yaknit el Kousa. Use any of these beans in place of garbanzos. Use green beans in place of squash. Follow recipe for Yaknit el Kousa otherwise. Cook as directed. Serve hot with pilaf and salad. Good cold for lunch.

VARIATION:

YAKNIT EL LOUBIAH III
[GREEN BEAN STEW WITH LENTILS]
[Serves 4 to 6]

2 cups green lentils
  OR other large lentils
4 cups water

Place lentils and water in a large heavy saucepan. Cover. Bring to a boil over high heat. Reduce heat to low. Simmer 35 to 40 minutes until lentils are tender.

1 cup water
1 lb. green beans,
  cut into 1 inch pieces

Follow recipe for Yaknit el Kousa but use lentils in place of garbanzos and water in place of garbanzo stock. Use beans in place of squash. Add ingredients to lentils in saucepan along with water. Cook as directed. Serve hot with pilaf, salad and yoghurt. Good cold for lunch.

VARIATION:

YAKNIT EL KOUSA III [SQUASH STEW WITH LENTILS]   [Serves 4 to 6]

2 cups green lentils
  OR other large lentils
4 cups water

Place lentils and water in a large heavy saucepan. Cover. Bring to a boil over high heat. Reduce heat to low. Simmer 35 to 40 minutes until lentils are tender.

1 cup water

Follow recipe for Yaknit el Kousa but use lentils in place of garbanzos and water in place of garbanzo stock. Add ingredients to lentils in saucepan along with water. Cook as directed. Serve hot with pilaf, salad and yoghurt. Good cold for lunch.

YAKNIT EL BATINGANN [EGGPLANT STEW WITH GARBANZOS]
[Serves 4 to 6]

2 cups garbanzos
6 cups water

Cover garbanzos with water. Soak overnight. Drain (optional step). Place garbanzos in a heavy saucepan. Add water. Bring to a boil over high heat. Cook covered 3 to 4 hours over medium heat until beans are tender. To pressure cook: place in pressure cooker with 4 cups water. Cover and bring to full pressure. Cook at full pressure 50 minutes. Remove from heat and cool. However cooked, drain and reserve stock for later use.

1 large eggplant, cut in
  half lengthwise and cut
  into 1 inch cubes
¼ cup olive oil
  OR vegetable oil

Heat a heavy cast iron skillet over medium high heat. Add oil. Heat until a piece of eggplant added sizzles. Add eggplant. Fry 3 to 5 minutes to a side until lightly browned. Remove from pan. Drain.

2 medium potatoes,
  cut into 1 inch cubes
1 cup garbanzo stock
2 leeks, chopped
  OR 4 green onions, chopped

Place in large heavy saucepan with fried eggplant. Cover. Bring to a boil over high heat. Reduce heat to medium low. Simmer 15 to 20 minutes until potatoes are just tender. Add garbanzos.

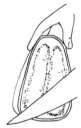

1 large yellow onion, minced
2 cloves garlic,
  crushed and minced
¼ cup olive oil
  OR vegetable oil

While potatoes and eggplant are cooking, heat a cast iron skillet over medium heat. Add oil. Heat until a small piece of onion added sizzles. Add onions and garlic. Stir and fry 5 to 10 minutes until onions are soft and transparent but not brown.

5 to 8 sprigs parsley,
  minced
1½ tsp. sea salt
¼ tsp. black pepper
1 cup stewed tomatoes
¼ cup tomato paste

Add to garbanzos along with onions. Mix well. Cover. Simmer on low heat 3 to 5 minutes. Just enough to heat added ingredients and mix well with other flavors.

¼ cup lemon juice

Add to stew. Mix well. Serve at once with pilaf and salad. Good cold for lunch.

VARIATION:

YAKNIT EL BATINGANN II [EGGPLANT STEW WITH DRIED BEANS] [Serves 4 to 6]

2 cups dried beans
  [fava, red, pinto, small white]
6 cups water

Cook beans like garbanzos in Yaknit el Batingann Use any of these beans in place of garbanzos. Follow recipe for Yaknit el Batingann. Use beans in place of garbanzos. Cook as directed. Serve hot with pilaf, yoghurt and salad. Good cold for lunch.

VARIATION:

YAKNIT EL BATINGANN III [EGGPLANT STEW WITH LENTILS] [Serves 4 to 6]

2 cups green lentils
  OR other large lentils
4 cups water

Place lentils and water in a large heavy saucepan. Cover. Bring to a boil over high heat. Reduce heat to low. Simmer 35 to 40 minutes until lentils are tender. Follow recipe for Yaknit el Batingann but use lentils in place of garbanzos and water in place of garbanzo stock. Cook as directed. Serve hot with pilaf, salad and yoghurt. Cood cold for lunch.

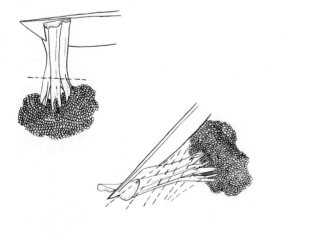

VARIATION:

BROCCOLI STEW WITH GARBANZOS [Serves 4 to 6]

1 lb. broccoli,
  stems cut into long thin
  diagonals with heads broken
  into small pieces

Follow recipe for Yaknit el Batingann. Use broccoli in place of eggplant. Do not fry broccoli. Cook as directed. Serve hot with pilaf, yoghurt and salad. Good cold for lunch.

VARIATION:

BROCCOLI STEW WITH LENTILS [Serves 4 to 6]

2 cups green lentils
  OR other large lentils
4 cups water

Place lentils and water in a large heavy saucepan. Cover. Bring to a boil over high heat. Reduce heat to low. Simmer 35 to 40 minutes until lentils are tender. Follow recipe for Yaknit el Batingann but use lentils in place of garbanzos and water in place of garbanzo stock. Use broccoli in place of eggplant. Do not fry broccoli. Add ingredients to lentils in saucepan along with water. Cook as directed. Serve hot with pilaf, salad and yoghurt. Good cold for lunch.

VARIATION:

BROCCOLI STEW WITH DRIED BEANS [Serves 4 to 6]

2 cups dried beans
  [fava, red, pinto, small white]
1 lb. broccoli,
  stems cut into long thin
  diagonals with heads broken
  into small pieces

Cook beans like garbanzos in Yaknit el Batingann. Use any one of these beans in place of garbanzos. Use broccoli in place of eggplant. Do not fry broccoli. Follow recipe for Yaknit el Batingann otherwise. Cook as directed. Serve hot with pilaf and salad. Good cold for lunch.

LENTILS WITH NOODLES [Serves 4 to 6]

2 cups green lentils
½ lb. noodles
[whole wheat, spinach
or soy] broken into
¼ to 1/8 inch pieces
5 cups water

To break noodles wrap tightly in a towel and break evenly ¼ inch along the edge of a table or counter; or place in a bag and roll with a rolling pin; or wrap tightly in a towel and stomp on them with your feet. Place with lentils in a heavy cast iron saucepan. Add water. Cover. Bring to a boil over high heat. Reduce heat to medium low and simmer 30 to 35 minutes.

1 large yellow onion,
minced
2 cloves garlic,
crushed and minced
2 Tbsp. butter
2 Tbsp. olive oil
OR vegetable oil

While lentils are cooking heat a small cast iron skillet. Add oil and butter and melt over medium heat. Add onions and garlic. Stir and fry 5 to 10 minutes over medium heat until onions are soft and transparent.

½ to 1 tsp. coriander
½ to 1 tsp. cumin
1 tsp. sea salt
¼ tsp. black pepper

Add to onions. Remove from heat. When lentils and noodles are done add onions and spices to lentils. Mix well. Let sit 10 minutes. Serve with yoghurt, ½ lemon per serving, crisp salad vegetables such as radishes, or 2 tomatoes cut in eighths. Good with Salatet Malfoof. Good cold for lunch with pickles and bread.

BAYD BI TAMATEM [EGGS COOKED WITH TOMATOES] [Serves 4 to 6]

1 large yellow onion,
minced
1 clove garlic,
crushed and minced
3 Tbsp. olive oil
OR vegetable oil

Heat a stainless steel skillet over medium heat. Add oil. Heat until a small piece of onion added sizzles. Add onion and garlic. Stir and fry 5 to 10 minutes until onions are soft and transparent.

4 to 5 tomatoes,
chopped
OR 2 cups stewed tomatoes,
drained and chopped

Add to onions. Mix well. Stir and fry 2 to 3 minutes.

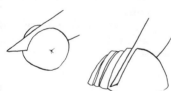

2 Tbsp. tomato paste
2 Tbsp. water
OR tomato juice from
drained tomatoes
1 tsp. ras el hanout
OR ½ tsp. allspice
and
½ tsp. cinnamon
1 tsp. sea salt
¼ tsp. black pepper

Add to tomatoes and onions. Mix well.

8 to 10 hard-boiled eggs,
cut in half lengthwise

Add to tomato mixture with yolk side up. Baste with sauce. Cover. Simmer 5 to 10 minutes. Baste often. Serve hot. Good served with pilaf. Excellent cold for lunch.

MAJADARRA [LENTIL AND RICE POTTAGE] [Serves 4 to 6]

2 cups green lentils
1 cup long-grain [preferred]
  brown rice
2 tsp. sea salt
¼ tsp. black pepper
6 cups water

Place ingredients in a heavy saucepan. Cover. Bring to boil over high heat. Reduce heat to medium low. Simmer 35 minutes until rice is done.

2 cups yellow onions,
  minced
½ cup olive oil
  OR vegetable oil
⅓ cup water

While lentils are cooking fry onions. Heat a medium cast iron skillet over medium heat. Add oil. Heat until a small piece of onion added sizzles. Add onions. Stir and fry 5 to 10 minutes until onions are soft and transparent. Add water. Simmer 10 to 15 minutes until all water is absorbed. When lentils are done, add to lentils and rice. Mix well. Cover and let sit 10 minutes. Serve with yoghurt, ½ lemon per serving, crisp salad vegetables such as radishes, cucumbers, green peppers, carrots, cabbage or 2 tomatoes cut in eighths. Good with Salatet Malfoof. Good cold for lunch with pickles and bread.

LENTILS IN BUTTER [Serves 4 to 6]

2 cups green lentils
2 cups water

Soak lentils overnight in water. Drain well. Allow to dry 5 to 10 minutes.

1 large yellow onion,
  chopped
1 to 2 cloves garlic,
  crushed and minced
1 Tbsp. olive oil
  OR vegetable oil
3 Tbsp. butter

Heat a heavy cast iron saucepan. Add oil. Heat slightly. Add butter and melt over medium low heat. Add onions, garlic and lentils. Increase heat to medium. Stir and fry 5 to 10 minutes until lentils begin to make a crackling sound.

3 cups water
1 tsp. sea salt
¼ tsp. black pepper

Add to lentils and onions. Mix well. Cover. Bring to a boil over high heat. Reduce heat to medium low. Simmer 30 to 35 minutes until all liquid is absorbed. Remove from heat. Let sit 10 minutes.

2 Tbsp. lemon juice

Add to lentils and serve at once. Serve with rice and vegetables, or with yoghurt, crisp vegetables, bread and an egg omelet. Good cold for lunch with bread and pickles or a salad.

KUKUE SABZY [HERB AND VEGETABLE OMELET] [Serves 4]

½ cup parsley,
   minced
4 green onions,
   minced
2 leeks,
   chopped [optional]
3 leaves romaine,
   shredded
   OR sorrel,
      shredded
1 tsp. dillseed,
   roughly ground
3 sprigs mint,
   minced
1 tsp. oregano
¼ tsp. turmeric
1 tsp. sea salt
¼ tsp. black pepper
6 eggs

Combine all ingredients. Beat with a fork 2 to 3 minutes until well mixed and eggs frothy.

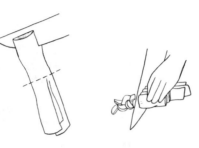

2 Tbsp. olive oil
   OR vegetable oil

Heat a 9 inch cast iron skillet. Add olive oil. Heat until a small drop of egg mixture just sets. Reduce heat to medium and pour in ingredients. Cover and cook 5 minutes. Uncover and loosen the edges of the omelet with a knife. Fold omelet in half using a broad spatula. Half of brown bottom should now be on top. Cover and let cook an additional 3 to 4 minutes until omelet is set but still moist. Remove from pan. Place on a platter. Cut into 2 inch strips. Serve hot with pilaf and a salad. Good cold for lunch the next day.

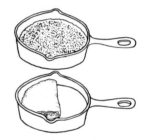

CAULIFLOWER OMELET [Serves 4]

½ cauliflower

Bring steamer to full rolling boil. Place cauliflower in steamer. Steam 10 to 15 minutes. Cut into small pieces. Chop coarsely. Cool.

5 eggs
4 green onions,
   chopped
1 clove garlic,
   crushed and minced
1 tsp. sea salt
¼ tsp. black pepper

Combine eggs with cauliflower and other ingredients. Beat with a fork 2 to 3 minutes until well mixed and eggs are frothy.

2 Tbsp. olive oil
   OR vegetable oil

Heat a 9 inch cast iron skillet. Add olive oil. Heat until a small drop of egg mixture just sets. Reduce heat to medium and pour in ingredients. Cover and cook 5 minutes. Uncover and loosen edges of omelet with a knife. Fold omelet in half using a broad spatula. Half of brown bottom should now be on top. Cover and let cook an additional 3 to 4 minutes until omelet is set but still moist. Remove from pan. Place on a platter. Cut into 2 inch strips. Serve hot with pilaf and a salad. Good cold for lunch the next day.

MUSSAKK'A [GARBANZO CASSEROLE WITH EGGPLANT AND OLIVE OIL]
[Serves 6 to 8] [Easy to cut in half]

2 cups garbanzos
6 to 8 cups water
  [more water as needed to
  keep garbanzos covered]

Cover garbanzos with water. Soak overnight. Drain. (optional step). Place garbanzos in a heavy saucepan. Add water. Cover. Bring to a boil over high heat. Reduce heat to medium. Simmer 3 to 4 hours until tender (easily mashed with a fork). To pressure cook: place garbanzos in pressure cooker with water. Cover and bring to full pressure. Cook 50 minutes at full pressure. Remove from heat. Cool. However cooked, drain garbanzos. Reserve stock for other use.

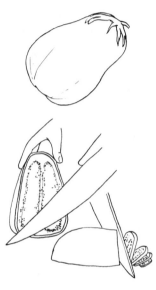

1 cup olive oil
  OR vegetable oil
2 large eggplants,
  cut into 1 inch slices and
  then each slice halved

Heat a heavy skillet over medium heat. Add oil. Heat until a small piece of eggplant added sizzles. Add eggplant. Cover and fry 5 minutes. Uncover and turn eggplant. Cover and fry 3 to 5 more minutes until soft and brown. Remove from pan. Place on bottom of large casserole. Fry remaining eggplant and place in casserole when done.

3 large yellow onions,
  chopped
2 Tbsp. olive oil
  OR vegetable oil

After eggplant is fried add olive oil to oil in pan. Heat until small piece of onion added sizzles. Add onion. Stir and fry over medium heat 5 to 10 minutes until lightly browned and soft. Spread evenly over top of eggplant in casserole. Place cooked garbanzos on top of onions, spread evenly.

3 cups stewed tomatoes
½ cup tomato paste
1½ cups water
2 tsp. sea salt
½ tsp. black pepper
1 tsp. cinnamon
1 tsp. allspice
1 tsp. nutmeg
OR IN PLACE OF ABOVE
SPICES:
3½ tsp. ras el hanout
  [head of the household
  spice mix]

Place ingredients together. Mix well. If a blender is available blend 15 seconds. Pour sauce over ingredients in casserole. Bake 1 to 2 hours at 350° until all liquid is absorbed. Serve hot. Good if cooked a day ahead and then reheated. Serve with a pilaf and a sour salad and yoghurt. Good cold for lunch. Excellent feast dish.

VARIATION:

GARBANZO CASSEROLE WITH ZUCCHINI AND OLIVE OIL [Serves 6 to 8]
[Easy to cut in half]

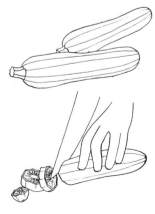

2 large zucchini,
  cut into 1 inch slices
  OR 4 small zucchini,
  cut into 1 inch slices

Follow recipe for Mussakk'a. Use zucchini in place of eggplant. Use only ½ cup oil. Do not use extra oil with onions. Dish is not as rich using zucchini in place of eggplant since it does not need as much oil to cook. Good if cooked a day ahead and then reheated. Serve with a pilaf and sour salad and yoghurt. Good cold for lunch. Excellent feast dish.

MEAT MAIN DISHES

Meat main dishes are served with a salad, pilaf and bread. The Kababs are placed in the pockets of pita (Arab bread). In the Middle East meat dishes are most frequently served on special occasions because meat is too expensive for everyday use.

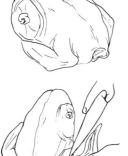

DAJAJ KABAB [CHICKEN KABOB] [Serves 4 to 6]

½ to 1 skinned chicken,
    deboned [optional] and
    cut into 1 inch pieces
juice of 1 lemon
2 medium yellow onions,
    minced
5 to 8 large sprigs parsley,
    minced
1 tsp. sea salt
¼ tsp. black pepper

Mix ingredients well in a large bowl. Place a plate on top and weight meat down with rocks or some other heavy object. Marinate 2 to 3 hours. Place chicken on skewers. Oil grill or broiler pan before using. Grill over charcoal or broil in oven. Turn several times. Baste with marinade. Cook 10 to 15 minutes until well browned. Serve hot.

1 tsp. cumin

Sprinkle cumin over hot grilled chicken before serving. Serve with salad or vegetable dish and pita (Arab bread) cut in half. To eat, each person stuffs meat from skewer in pita. Good served with pilaf also. An excellent cold lunch. A must at feasts.

VARIATION:

SHISH KABAB
[LAMB OR BEEF KABOB]
[Serves 4 to 6]

1½ lbs. meat
    [lamb or beef],
    cut into 1 inch cubes

Follow recipe for Dajaj Kabab. Use meat in place of chicken. Serve hot with salad or vegetable dish and pita (Arab bread) cut in half. To eat, each person stuffs meat from skewer in pita. Good served with pilaf also. An excellent cold lunch. A must for feasts.

DAJAJ KABAB II [CHICKEN ON SKEWERS] [serves 4 to 6]

½ to 1 skinned chicken,
   deboned [optional]
   and cut into 1 inch
   pieces
¼ cup olive oil
   OR vegetable oil
¼ cup vinegar
   OR dry white wine
5 to 6 large sprigs parsley,
   minced
1 small yellow onion, grated
3 sprigs mint, minced
   OR 1 tsp. dried mint,
     crumbled
2 to 3 cloves garlic,
   crushed and minced
3 sprigs oregano, minced
   OR 1½ tsp. dried oregano,
     crumbled

Mix ingredients well in a large bowl. Place a plate on top and weight meat down with rocks or some other heavy object. Marinate 1 to 2 hours. Place chicken on skewers. Oil grill or broiler pan before using. Grill over charcoal or broil in oven. Turn several times. Baste with marinade sauce. Cook 10 to 15 minutes until browned. Serve hot. Serve with salad or vegetable dish and pita (Arab bread) cut in half. To eat, each person stiffs meat from skewer in pita. Good served with pilaf also. An excellent cold lunch. A must for feasts.

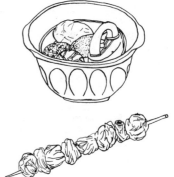

VARIATION:

SHISH KABAB II [LAMB OR BEEF KABAB] [Serves 4 to 6]

1½ lbs. meat [lamb or beef],
   cut into 1 inch cubes
Use red wine instead of white

Follow recipe for Dajaj Kabab II. Use meat in place of chicken. Serve hot with salad or vegetable dish and pita (Arab bread) cut in half. To eat, each person stuffs meat from skewer in pita. Good served with pilaf also. An excellent cold lunch. A must for feasts.

SAMAK KABAB [SKEWERED FISH] [Serves 4 to 6]

1 to 2 lbs. firm fish
   [swordfish, red snapper, cod,
    etc.], cut into 1 inch cubes
¼ cup olive oil
¼ cup vinegar
   OR dry white wine
1 tsp. sea salt
¼ tsp. black pepper
½ tsp. oregano, ground

Mix ingredients well in a large bowl. Marinate 1 hour to overnight.

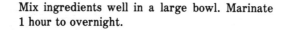

2 large yellow onions,
   cut into eight wedges and
   the wedges cut in half
2 large firm tomatoes,
   cut into eight wedges and
   the wedges cut in half

Place onions and tomatoes on skewers alternately with fish. Oil grill or broiler pan before using. Grill over charcoal or broil in oven. Baste often with marinade sauce. Turn several times. Grill 10 to 15 minutes until fish is flaky and browned.

juice of 2 lemons

Remove fish from skewers and sprinkle with lemon juice. Serve with salad, pilaf and a vegetable dish. May also be served with pita (Arab bread) cut in half. To eat, each person stuffs fish from skewer in pita. An excellent cold lunch. A must for a feast.

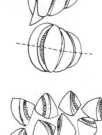

VARIATION:
LAMB, BEEF OR CHICKEN KABAB
[SKEWERED MEAT] [Serves 4 to 6]

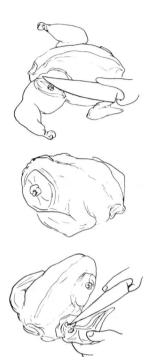

1½ to 2 lbs. meat
    [lamb or beef], cut into
    1 inch cubes
    OR ½ to 1 skinned chicken,
      deboned [optional] and
      cut into 1 inch pieces
For meat use dry red wine
  in place of white wine

Follow recipe for Samak Kabab. Use meat or chicken in place of fish. Serve hot with salad, pilaf and a vegetable dish. May also be served with pita (Arab bread) cut in half. To eat, each person stuffs meat or chicken from skewer in pita. An excellent cold lunch. A must for feasts.

KABAB [MEAT ON SKEWERS] [Serves 4 to 6]

1½ lbs. beef
    [chuck steak, pot roast],
    cut into ¼ inch cubes
¼ lb. beef fat,
    cut into 1/8 inch cubes
    [smaller than the meat]
2 medium onions, minced
5 sprigs parsley, minced
1 tsp. sea salt
¼ tsp. black pepper

15 to 20 pita [Arab bread]
  OR french bread
1 small plate of salt
1 small plate of cumin

Mix ingredients well in a large bowl. Place a plate on top of the meat and weight it down with rocks or some other heavy object. Marinate 2 to 3 hours. Place 3 to 3½ inches of meat and fat morsels on individual skewers. Alternate pieces of meat and fat. Oil grill or broiler pan before using. Grill over charcoal or broil in oven. Turn four or five times while grilling. Cook 10 to 15 minutes until well browned.

Each person removes the meat form the skewers and sprinkles it with salt and cumin to taste. The pita is torn in half and the seasoned, grilled meat is placed in the pocket and eaten with the bread. Serve with Morrocan Tomato Salad or other salad and pilaf. Also good served cold for lunch. A must at feasts.

VARIATION:
CHICKEN OR LAMB KABAB
[MEAT ON SKEWERS]
[Serves 4 to 6]

1½ lb. lamb,
    OR ½ to 1 skinned chicken, cut
      from bones and then cut
      into ¼ inch pieces
¼ lb. lamb or chicken fat
    depending on meat used, cut
    into 1/8 inch pieces
    [smaller than meat]

Follow recipe for Meat Kabab. Serve with Arab bread, a salad and pilaf. Also good served cold for lunch. A must at feasts.

KOFTA MOROCCAN [MOROCCAN MEAT BALLS] [Serves 4 to 6]

1½ lbs. ground meat
   [beef or lamb, 30% fat]
   OR Macroburger
1 small yellow onion, grated
3 sprigs parsley, minced
2 sprigs mint, minced
  OR 1 tsp. dried mint,
    crumbled
1 tsp. cumin
1 tsp. paprika
¼ tsp. coriander
¼ tsp. allspice
dash to ½ tsp. chili pepper
1 tsp. sea salt

Mix ingredients well. Knead together for several minutes. Marinate several hours. Form into small ½ inch balls with wet hands. Place meat balls on skewers. Press meat balls onto skewers well. Oil grill or broiler pan before using. Grill over charcoal or broil in oven. Cook 10 to 15 minutes until well browned. Turn four or five times while grilling. Serve with pita (Arab bread) or pilaf and a salad. To eat, each person stuffs meat balls into pita (Arab bread) cut in half. Good cold for lunch. A must at feasts.

VARIATION:

KOFTA MOROCCAN WITH EGGPLANT [MOROCCAN MEAT BALLS GRILLED WITH EGGPLANT] [Serves 4 to 6]

1 large eggplant,
   cut into 1 inch cubes

Follow recipe for Kofta Moroccan. Alternate cubes of eggplant with meat balls on skewers. Brush eggplant with oil as it cooks. Cook as directed. Serve with pita (Arab bread) cut in half and a salad. Also good served with pilaf and a salad. Good cold for lunch the next day. A must for feasts.

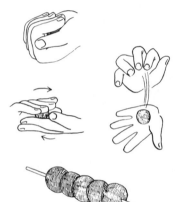

SEFLAN [MOROCCAN MEAT BALLS IN SAUCE] [Serves 4 to 6]

Make meat balls
  OR Macroburger balls as
   directed in Kofta Moroccan
2 Tbsp. butter
  OR vegetable oil

Heat a heavy cast iron skillet. Add butter. Melt over medium heat. Add meat balls. Fry 3 to 5 minutes until just browned. Turn several times to brown evenly. Remove from pan and drain.

Sauce:

2 cloves garlic,
   crushed and minced
2 large yellow onions,
   minced
¼ cup olive oil
  OR vegetable oil

Heat a heavy saucepan over medium heat. Add oil. Heat until a piece of onion added sizzles. Add onions and garlic. Stir and fry 5 to 10 minutes until soft and transparent.

½ cup tomato paste
1 cup water
  OR tomato juice
1 Tbsp. paprika
1 Tbsp. cumin
1/8 to 1 tsp. chili pepper
1 tsp. sea salt
3 large sprigs parsley,
   whole, tied together
   with string

Add to onions and garlic. Keep parsley to one side. Mix well. Cover and bring to a boil over high heat. Uncover, reduce heat to medium low and simmer 45 minutes to 1 hour. Remove parsley. Add fried meat balls. Boil quickly 5 to 10 minutes until meat balls are done. Serve with Arab bread, or French bread and a salad. Good cold for lunch. An excellent feast dish.

DAJAJ MASHI [STUFFED CHICKEN] [Serves 4 to 6]

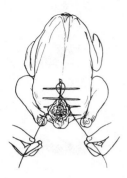

1 whole large roasting chicken

Remove giblets and neck. Wash and drain.

Filling:

¼ lb. almonds
  OR other nuts
    [walnuts, cashews, pine-nuts, pistachio nuts, etc.]
4 Tbsp. butter
  OR vegetable oil

Heat a medium-sized cast iron skillet over medium heat. Add butter. Melt. Add almonds. Stir and fry 3 to 5 minutes until lightly browned. Remove from heat. Chop fine.

2 to 3 cups cooked long-grain [preferred] brown rice
2 Tbsp. butter
1 cup raisins, washed and drained
1 tsp. ras el hanout
  OR ¼ tsp. cinnamon and
    ¼ tsp. allspice and
    ¼ tsp. nutmeg and
    ¼ tsp. lavender
1 tsp. sea salt

Mix rice and butter well. Add spices, raisins and almonds. Mix well. Stuff chicken. Sew up body cavity with heavy thread. Stuff neck opening also and sew up skin. Tie legs and wings securely to body.

Cooking:

½ tsp. dried ginger
1½ large yellow onions, cut lengthwise into eighths
1½ tsp. sea salt
¼ tsp. powdered saffron
  OR 8 to 10 threads
2 to 3 cups water

Put stuffed chicken in a large deep heavy saucepan. Pour water to half height of chicken in pan. Add other ingredients. Cover and bring to a boil over high heat.

¼ cup butter

Add to boiling chicken. Reduce heat to medium and simmer for 35 to 45 minutes covered. Gently turn chicken after 20 minutes. Remove lid and cook for another 15 to 20 minutes until most of liquid has evaporated. Baste chicken often. After the chicken is tender and the stock boiled down remove the chicken and place on a platter.

1 Tbsp. mild honey
¼ tsp. cinnamon

Add honey and cinnamon to sauce. Mix well. Bring to a boil over high heat. Simmer 2 to 3 minutes. Pour sauce over chicken. The stuffed chicken is usually eaten with the fingers and can be served with pita (Arab bread) or French bread and a sour salad. A good feast dish. Excellent cold for lunch the next day.

DAJAJ M'QALIA [CHICKEN WITH MINT] [Serves 4 to 6]

3 to 4 lb. whole chicken
1 to 2 tsp. sea salt
¼ tsp. black pepper

Wash chicken well. Drain. Dry. Rub with salt and pepper inside and out. Tie legs and wings securely to body.

1 tsp. coriander seed,
  ground
½ tsp. cumin seed,
  ground
10 to 15 saffron threads,
  ground
1 clove garlic,
  crushed and minced
¼ cup fresh mint leaves,
  minced
  OR 2 Tbsp. dried mint,
    crumbled
2 Tbsp. fresh parsley,
  minced
3 Tbsp. olive oil
  OR vegetable oil

Mix ingredients well. If blender is used leave ingredients in large pieces. Blend to smooth sauce. Pat sauce all over chicken. Place in a large saucepan.

1 large yellow onion,
  cut in half lengthwise and
  then cut into paper-thin
  slices
2 cups chicken stock
  OR water

Surround chicken with onions. Pour chicken stock down sides of saucepan so it will not wash paste off chicken. Bring to boil over high heat. Cover. Reduce heat to medium. Simmer 45 to 50 minutes until chicken is tender. Remove chicken from saucepan. Carve into 4 to 6 serving pieces. Place on a broiler pan skin side up. Broil 5 to 10 minutes until chicken is golden brown. While chicken is being carved and broiled heat sauce over medium high heat. Cook 10 to 15 minutes until sauce is reduced by half.

½ tsp. sea salt
dash of pepper

Add to sauce. Mix. Strain sauce. Serve in a bowl with chicken. Dip chicken in sauce as it is being eaten. Serve hot with pita (Arab bread) or pilaf and a salad or vegetable dish. Good cold next day for lunch. An excellent feast dish.

BATINGANN MASHI [STUFFED BAKED EGGPLANT] [Serves 4 to 6]

2 eggplants,
  cut lengthwise into quarters
¼ cup olive oil
  OR vegetable oil
¼ cup butter

Heat a heavy skillet. Add oil and butter. Melt over medium heat. Add eggplant and fry over medium heat 5 to 10 minutes until lightly browned on all sides. Remove from pan as done and place in a casserole. Slit each quarter eggplant down the center. Place slit side up in a casserole.

Filling:

1 lb. ground meat
  [lamb, beef or veal]
  OR Macroburger
¼ cup butter
  OR vegetable oil
1 onion, chopped

Add butter to pan in which eggplant was cooked. Melt over medium heat. Add ground meat. Cook 3 to 4 minutes. Add onions. Stir and fry 5 to 10 minutes until soft and transparent but not browned. Remove from pan and place in a bowl.

¼ cup butter
  OR vegetable oil
½ cup nuts
  [pinenuts, almonds, cashews
    or pistachio nuts]

Add butter to pan in which meat was cooked. Melt over medium heat. Add nuts. Stir and fry 3 to 5 minutes until lightly browned. Chop slightly and add to meat in bowl.

3 tsp. ras el hanout
  [spice mix]
  OR 1 tsp. allspice and
       1 tsp. nutmeg and
       1 tsp. cinnamon
1 tsp. sea salt
¼ tsp. black pepper

Add to meat and nuts. Mix well. Place stuffing in slits in eggplant and excess around sides.

Cooking:

1½ cups tomato sauce
½ cup water

Mix water and tomato sauce well. Pour over stuffed eggplant. Bake at 350°, 35 to 40 minutes. Serve hot. Serve with pilaf, yoghurt, and a sour salad or vegetable dish. Good cold for lunch. An excellent feast dish.

VARIATION:
STUFFED ACORN SQUASH
[Serves 4 to 6]

4 medium acorn squash,
  cut in half and seeded
¼ cup olive oil
  OR vegetable oil

Heat a heavy skillet. Add oil. Heat over medium heat 1 minute. Add squash yellow side down. Fry 3 to 5 minutes on each side. Remove from pan. Drain. Place in a casserole. Follow recipe for Batingaan Mashi filling. Stuff squash hollows. Cook as directed for eggplant. Serve with pilaf, yoghurt and a sour salad or vegetable dish. Good cold for lunch. An excellent feast dish.

VARIATION:

FEIFEL MASHI
[STUFFED GREEN PEPPERS]
[Serves 4 to 6]

6 to 8 green peppers,
  tops cut off, seeded

Save tops. Do not fry green peppers. Place in a casserole. Follow recipe for Batingaan Mashi filling. Stuff green peppers. Place tops on peppers. Secure with toothpicks. Cook as directed for eggplant. Serve with pilaf, yoghurt and a sour salad or vegetable dish. Good cold for lunch. An excellent feast dish.

VARIATION:
STUFFED PUMPKIN
[Serves 4 to 6]

1 small pumpkin,
  cut lengthwise in quarters
  and seeds removed
¼ cup olive oil
  OR vegetable oil

Heat a heavy akillet. Add oil. Heat over medium heat 1 minute. Add pumpkin slices. Fry 3 to 5 minutes on each side. Remove from pan. Drain. Place in a casserole skin side down. Follow recipe for Batingann Mashi filling. Stuff pumpkin hollows. Cook as directed for eggplant. Serve with pilaf, yoghurt and a sour salad or vegetable dish. Good cold for lunch. An excellent feast dish.

SFIHAN [MEAT, YOGHURT AND BAKLAVA DOUGH CASSEROLE]
[Serves 6 to 8] [Easy to cut in half]

2 lbs. ground meat
  [lamb, veal, beef]
  OR Macroburger
4 yellow onions,
  minced
2 Tbsp. butter
2 Tbsp. olive oil
  OR vegetable oil

Heat a cast iron skillet. Add oil and butter. Melt over medium heat. Add meat and onions. Stir and fry 5 to 10 minutes until onions are soft and transparent. Remove from heat.

½ cup nuts
  [pinenuts, almonds, walnuts,
  cashews or pistachio nuts]
¼ cup butter

Heat a small cast iron skillet. Add butter and melt over medium heat. Add nuts. Stir and fry 3 to 5 minutes until golden brown. Remove from heat and chop slightly. Add to meat and onions.

½ cup yoghurt
⅓ cup lemon juice
1 tsp. sea salt
¼ tsp. black pepper
1½ tsp. ras el hanout
    OR 1 tsp. cinnamon and
      ½ tsp. allspice

Add to meat, onions and nuts. Mix well.

14 to 20 sheets
  of filo dough
½ to ¾ cup butter,
  melted

Butter a 9 x 13" cake pan. Place a sheet of dough in pan and brush well with butter. Continue to layer and butter sheets until 7 to 10 sheets are in bottom of pan. Spread meat, onions and nuts and yoghurt mixture evenly over dough. Top with 7 to 10 more layers of buttered filo dough. Butter top well. If possible refrigerate 3 to 4 hours before baking. Bake at 350°, 30 to 40 minutes until lightly browned. Cut into 2 to 3 inch squares. Serve hot with a salad or vegetable dish. Good cold for lunch. An excellent feast dish.

SAMAK B'CAMOUN [FISH BAKED WITH CUMIN SAUCE] [Serves 4 to 6]

3 to 4 lbs. fish with head
  if possible [striped bass,
  red snapper or cod], cleaned,
  scaled, washed and scored
  on both sides
  OR 2 lbs. fish fillet
    [red snapper, cod, sole,
    etc.]

Place fish on large piece of foil.

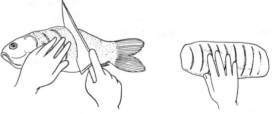

Sauce:

1 tsp. sea salt
¼ tsp. black pepper
1 Tbsp. cumin seeds, ground
1 Tbsp. paprika
1 to 2 cloves garlic,
  crushed and minced
½ cup parsley, minced
½ cup olive oil
  OR vegetable oil
1 Tbsp. lemon juice

Mix ingredients well. If blender is used leave ingredients in large pieces. Blend to smooth sauce. Spread sauce evenly over fish. Wrap in foil. Bake 30 to 40 minutes at 400° until fish is flaky. Turn fish onto platter.

2 lemons,
  cut into 8 wedges each

Surround fish with lemon wedges. Serve hot with pilaf and a salad or vegetable dish. Good cold next day for lunch. An excellent feast dish.

SAMAKA TAJIN [FISH WITH SESAME SAUCE] [Serves 6]

2 lbs. fish fillet
  OR one whole fish,
    scored on both sides
1 tsp. sea salt
¼ tsp. black pepper

Rub fish with salt and pepper. Let sit 1 hour.

2 Tbsp. olive oil
  OR vegetable oil

Rub oil into fish and place in a shallow baking dish. Bake at 350°, 10 to 15 minutes.

½ cup olive oil
  OR vegetable oil
2 medium yellow onions,
  minced

While fish is baking heat a cast iron skillet. Add oil. Heat until a small piece of onion added sizzles. Add onions and reduce heat to medium. Fry 5 to 10 minutes until the onions are soft and transparent.

½ cup lemon juice
1 cup tahini
  [sesame paste]
½ cup water
1 clove garlic,
  crushed and chopped

Place lemon juice, tahini, water and garlic in a blender. Blend 30 seconds. If no blender is available mix well. Add onions and olive oil. Mix well. Pour over fish and bake another 15 to 20 minutes until fish is flaky. Serve hot with pilaf and a salad or vegetable dish. Good cold for lunch the next day. An excellent feast dish.

MEAT AND SPINACH STEW [Serves 4 to 6]

1 yellow onion,
  chopped
3 Tbsp. olive oil
  OR vegetable oil
  OR butter

Heat a large cast iron skillet over medium heat. Add oil. Heat until a piece of onion added sizzles. Add onions. Stir and fry 5 to 10 minutes until onions are soft and transparent.

1 lb. meat
  [lamb, beef or veal], cut
  into ¼ inch cubes
1 tsp. sea salt
¼ tsp. black pepper
½ tsp. ras el hanout
  [spice mix]
  OR ¼ tsp. cinnamon and
    ¼ tsp. allspice

Add meat to onions. Stir and fry 1 to 2 minutes until meat changes color.

1 cup meat stock
  OR water

Add to meat and onions. Cover. Bring to boil over high heat. Reduce heat to medium low. Simmer 15 to 20 minutes until meat is tender.

1 lb. spinach,
  shredded
  OR 1 lb. any cooking green
    [swiss chard, collards,
    etc.], shredded

Add spinach to meat. Simmer 5 to 10 minutes until spinach is just tender but still bright green.

juice of 1 lemon

Add to spinach and meat dish. Mix. Serve hot with pilaf and a rich vegetable dish. Good simple-meal dish.

YAKNIT LAHM BI KOUSA   [MEAT STEW WITH SQUASH] [Serves 4 to 6]

1 to 1½ lbs. stew meat
   [lamb, veal or beef],
   cut into ½ inch cubes
3 Tbsp. olive oil
   OR vegetable oil
2 cups water
1 tsp. oregano

Heat a heavy saucepan over medium heat. Add oil. Heat until a piece of meat added sizzles. Add meat. Stir and fry 5 to 10 minutes until golden brown. Add water and oregano. Cover and bring to a boil. Reduce heat to medium low. Simmer 40 to 50 minutes until meat slightly tender.

2 medium potatoes,
   cut into 1 inch cubes
1 large zucchini
   OR any other summer squash,
      cut into 1 inch slices
   OR 1 lb. winter squash,
      cut into ¼ inch even slices
2 leeks, chopped
   OR 4 green onions, chopped

Add to meat in saucepan. Bring to a boil over high heat. Cover and reduce heat to medium low. Simmer 15 to 20 minutes until potatoes are just tender.

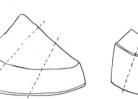 

1 large yellow onion,
   minced
2 cloves garlic,
   crushed and minced
3 Tbsp. olive oil
   OR vegetable oil

Heat a cast iron skillet over medium heat. Add oil. Heat until a small piece of onion added sizzles. Add onion and garlic. Stir and fry 5 to 10 minutes until onions are soft and transparent.

5 large sprigs parsley,
   chopped
1½ tsp. sea salt
¼ tsp. black pepper
1 cup stewed tomatoes
   OR 2 tomatoes,
      cubed
¼ cup tomato paste

Add along with fried onions to stew when potatoes are done. Mix well. Simmer on low 3 to 5 minutes.

¼ cup lemon juice

Add to stew. Mix well. Serve hot. A one-pot-meal. Also good served with pilaf and a salad. Good cold for lunch.

YAKNIT DAJAJ BI KOUSA
[CHICKEN STEW WITH SQUASH]
[Serves 4 to 6]

1 small chicken,
  cut into 1 inch pieces
  OR 2 chicken breasts,
    cut into 1 inch pieces

Follow recipe for Yakhnit Lahm bi Kousa. Use chicken in place of meat. Cook as directed. Serve hot. A one-pot meal. Also good served with pilaf and a salad. Good cold for lunch.

VARIATION:

YAKNIT LAHM BI LOUBIAH
[MEAT STEW WITH GREEN BEANS]
[Serves 4 to 6]

1 lb. green beans,
  cut into 1 inch pieces

Follow recipe for Yakhnit Lahm bi Kousa. Use green beans in place of squash. Cook as directed. Serve hot. A one-pot-meal. Also good served with pilaf and a salad. Good cold for lunch.

VARIATION:

MEAT STEW WITH BROCCOLI
[Serves 4 to 6]

1 lb. broccoli,
  stems cut into long thin
  diagonals with heads broken
  into small pieces

Follow recipe for Yakhnit Lahm bi Kousa. Use broccoli in place of squash. Cook as directed. Serve hot. A one-pot-meal. Also good served with pilaf and a salad. Good cold for lunch.

VARIATION:

YAKNIT DAJAJ BI BATINGANN
[CHICKEN STEW WITH EGGPLANT]
[Serves 4 to 6]

1 small chicken,
  cut into 1 inch pieces
  OR 2 chicken breasts,
    cut into 1 inch pieces

Follow recipe for Yakhnit Lahm bi Batinjan. Use chicken in place of meat. Cook as directed. Serve hot. Also good served with pilaf and a salad. Good cold for lunch.

VARIATION:

YAKNIT DAJAJ BI LOUBIAH
[CHICKEN STEW WITH GREEN BEANS]
[Serves 4 to 6]

1 small chicken,
  cut into 1 inch pieces
  OR 2 chicken breasts,
    cut into 1 inch pieces
1 lb. green beans,
  cut into 1 inch pieces

Follow recipe for Yakhnit Lahm bi Kousa. Use chicken in place of meat. Use green beans in place of squash. A one-pot meal. Also good served with pilaf and a salad. Good cold for lunch.

VARIATION:

CHICKEN STEW WITH BROCCOLI
[Serves 4 to 6]

1 small chicken,
  cut into 1 inch pieces
  OR 2 chicken breasts,
    cut into 1 inch pieces
1 lb. broccoli,
  stems cut into long thin
  diagonals with heads broken
  into small pieces

Follow recipe for Yakhnit Lahm bi Kousa. Use chicken in place of meat. Use broccoli in place of squash. Cook as directed. Serve hot. A one-pot meal. Also good served with pilaf and a salad. Good cold for lunch.

VARIATION:

YAKNIT LAHM BI BATINGANN
[MEAT STEW WITH EGGPLANT]
[Serves 4 to 6]

2 large eggplant,
  cut into 2 inch cubes
½ cup olive oil

Heat a heavy skillet. Add oil and heat until a piece of eggplant added sizzles. Add eggplant. Cover and fry 5 minutes over medium heat. Remove cover. Turn eggplant. Cover and fry another 3 to 5 minutes until eggplant is golden brown on both sides. Remove from pan. Follow recipe for Yakhnit Lahm bi Kousa. Add fried eggplant in place of squash. Cook as directed. Serve hot. A one-pot-meal. Also good served with pilaf and salad. Good cold for lunch.

DAJAJ PILAF [CHICKEN PILAF] [Serves 6 to 8] [Easy to cut in half]

3 lbs. chicken,
  cut into 6 to 8 pieces
  OR bones and skin from
    2 filleted chickens
8 cups water
1 tsp. sea salt
½ tsp. black pepper
1 to 2 large cinnamon sticks

Place chicken, water and spices in a large heavy saucepan. Bring to a boil over high heat. Skim fat 5 minutes while at a full rolling boil. Reduce heat to medium. Cover. Cook for 1 hour until meat pulls away from the bone. Drain chicken. Reserve stock. Remove chicken from bone. Discard skin and bones.

2 cups long-grain [preferred]
  brown rice
2 cups hot water
  [optional]
¼ cup butter

Soak rice in hot water 30 minutes. Drain well. (optional step). Heat a large heavy saucepan. Add butter and melt over low heat. Raise heat to medium high. Add rice. Stir and fry 3 to 5 minutes until the rice crackles and starts to brown.

3½ to 4 cups chicken stock
  from cooking chicken

Add chicken stock to rice. Cover. Bring to a boil over high heat. Reduce heat to medium low and simmer 20 minutes.

1 cup dried fruit
  [raisins, currants or dates],
  chopped

Add dried fruit to rice. Mix well. Place chicken on top of rice. Cover. Continue to cook 10 to 15 minutes until rice is tender and dry. Let sit 10 minutes so rice will absorb excess moisture. Oil or butter a large casserole. Pack cooked rice into casserole. Unmold rice onto large platter. surround with chicken meat.

½ cup nuts or seeds
  [sunflower, sesame, peanuts
  combined]
  OR almonds and pinenuts
  OR walnuts and cashews
¼ cup butter
2 Tbsp. olive oil

Heat a small cast iron skillet. Add oil. Heat 10 seconds. Add butter. Melt over medium heat. Add nuts. Stir and fry 3 to 5 minutes until lightly browned. Chop slightly. Pour over molded rice. Serve hot with a sour salad or vegetable dish. Good feast dish. Excellent cold lunch dish.

LAHM PILAF [LAMB OR MEAT PILAF] [Serves 6 to 8] [Easy to cut in half]

**2 to 3 lbs. lamb,
  cut into 1 inch cubes
  OR beef, cut into 1 inch cubes
8 cups water
1 tsp. sea salt
¼ tsp. black pepper
1 to 2 large cinnamon sticks**

Place ingredients in a large saucepan. Bring to a boil over high heat. Skim fat for 5 minutes while at a full rolling boil. Cover. Reduce heat to medium and cook 1 hour until meat is tender. Drain meat. Reserve stock.

**3 cups long-grain [preferred]
  brown rice
¼ cup butter
  OR olive oil
  OR vegetable oil**

Heat a large, heavy saucepan. Add butter. Melt over medium heat. Add rice. Increase heat to medium high. Stir and fry 3 to 5 minutes until rice crackles and starts to brown.

**5½ cup meat stock from
  cooking meat**

Add stock to rice. Cover. Bring to boil over high heat. Reduce heat to medium low. Simmer 20 minutes. Place meat on top of rice. Continue to simmer 10 to 15 minutes until rice is tender and dry. Let sit 10 minutes so rice will absorb excess water. Turn rice out onto a large platter. Place meat in center of rice.

**2 Tbsp. olive oil
  OR vegetable oil
½ cup butter
½ tsp. cumin seeds,
  ground coarsely
½ tsp. coriander seed,
  ground coarsely**

Heat a medium cast iron skillet. Add oil. Heat 10 seconds over medium heat. Add butter. Melt over medium heat. Add herbs. Fry 1 minute. Pour sauce over lamb and rice. Serve hot with a sour salad or vegetable dish. Traditionally served by itself as a one-dish feast with coffee served for dessert. Good cold for lunch. An excellent feast dish.

SWEET DISHES

Sweet dishes are served as snacks or desserts. Quite often a dish of fresh fruit ends the meal and pastries are used more as snacks. Mint tea is served at snack time but is also served to clear the palate at the end of a meal.

BAKLAVA [HONEY NUT PASTRY] [Serves 10 to 20]

Filling:
2 cups nuts
   [almonds, pistachios or
   walnuts], chopped
1 Tbsp. honey
½ tsp. cardamom

Mix ingredients well.

Syrup:
1 cup honey
¼ cup water

Place in a small saucepan. Bring to a boil over medium heat. Simmer 8 to 10 minutes until syrup thickens slightly.

1 Tbsp. orange-blossom water
   OR 1 Tbsp. rosewater
1 Tbsp. lemon juice

Add to syrup. Mix well. Remove from heat. Chill.

Assembly and baking:
24 sheets of filo dough
1 cup melted butter

Place 1 filo sheet in bottom of a 9 x 13" sheet-cake pan. Brush well with melted butter. Layer in six sheets of filo dough, brushing each sheet well with butter. Spread sixth sheet with ⅓ nut mixture. Layer in six more sheets of filo dough, liberally brushing each sheet with butter. Spread ⅓ nut mixture on top of sixth sheet. Layer in six more sheets, each spread with butter. Place last of nut mixture on top of sixth sheet. Layer in six more sheets filo spread with butter. Bake at 350°, 30 minutes until light golden brown. Cut into 2 to 3 inch diamonds. Pour cold syrup over Baklava. Cool. Cut again and serve cold. Excellent snack. May be served at a feast but best for simple snacks or dinners.

FRUIT WITH QUATIR DRESSING [FRUIT WITH ROSEWATER SYRUP DRESSING]
[Serves 6 to 10]

1 cup mild honey
1½ cups water
   OR fruit juice

Place in a saucepan. Bring to a boil over high heat. Reduce heat to medium. Simmer 5 to 10 minutes until slightly thickened.

2 Tbsp. lemon juice
1 Tbsp. rosewater
1/8 tsp. orange essence
   [optional]

Add to honey syrup. Simmer a few additional seconds. Remove from heat and chill 1 to 2 hours until cold.

2 to 3 quart mixture of fresh
   or home-canned fruit
   [apples, strawberries, bananas,
   melons, grapes, peaches,
   pears, or any combination,
   or fruits in season], cut
   into bite sized pieces

Mix well with rosewater syrup. Chill 1 hour or overnight. Serve cold. An excellent feast dessert. Good as a snack any time.

BALOUZA [ALMOND PUDDING] [Serves 6 to 8]

1 cup plus 20 almonds
2 cups boiling water

Blanch and remove almond skins. Dry almonds in oven at 200°, 15 minutes until dried but not brown. Grind 20 almonds in blender until a fine powder. Set aside. Grind remaining almonds in blender ⅓ cup at a time until fine. Set aside for later use. Now take almond powder from 20 almonds and add ¼ cup boiling water. Place in blender and blend 15 seconds. Add another ¼ cup water to blender. Blend another 30 seconds. Continue until 2 cups of water are added to almond powder. If no blender is available, chop almonds or grind very fine, then crush in mortar with pestle. Add water slowly to make a paste and crush well. Add remaining water and mix well. Strain resulting liquid through a muslin cloth. Squeeze almond pulp to get all liquid removed. Discard pulp (bitter).

2 cups almond milk [approx.]
  from above
½ cup water — enough to
  make 2½ cups fluid
½ cup mild honey
⅓ cup arrowroot starch

Place all ingredients except arrowroot in a saucepan. Mix arrowroot starch with ¼ cup of above liquid and then add to saucepan. Mix well. Bring to boil over medium heat. Reduce heat to medium low. Simmer 3 to 5 minutes until starch thickens. Stir constantly to prevent burning.

1 cup ground almonds
¼ tsp. almond extract

Add to pudding. Mix well. Bring to boil again. Cook over medium low heat 5 to 10 minutes. Stir frequently to prevent burning. Add almond extract and stir well. Cook 1 more minute.

1 tsp. rosewater
  OR ½ tsp. vanilla

Add to pudding. Mix well. Remove from heat. Place in individual bowls to serve. Chill.

10 almonds, slivered
  OR pistachio nuts, slivered
seeds of 1 pommegranate
  [optional]

Sprinkle nuts and seeds over top of each bowl before serving. Serve cold. An excellent feast dessert. Good for simple meals also. An excellent snack.

IRMIK HELVASI [BULGUR WHEAT PUDDING] [Serves 6 to 8]

½ cup butter
½ cup nuts, chopped slightly
  [almonds, pinenuts, walnuts,
  cashews or filberts]

Heat a heavy skillet over medium heat. Add butter. Melt. Add nuts. Stir and fry 3 to 5 minutes until nuts are golden brown.

1 cup fine bulgur wheat
  OR 1 cup coarse bulgur wheat,
  rolled with a rolling pin
  to break up

Add bulgur. Mix well. Cook 5 to 10 minutes until mixture begins to brown and follow spoon around pan.

1½ cups boiling water
½ cup honey

Slowly add water and honey to wheat and nut mixture. Continue to stir while adding liquid. Cook over medium heat 10 to 15 minutes until mixture is thick enough so spoon stands up in it. Remove from heat. Cover and allow to sit 10 minutes. Place in individual bowls. Chill.

1 tsp. cinnamon
  OR cardamom, ground

Sprinkle spice over pudding and serve.

MOROCCAN MINT TEA [Serves 4 to 6]

1 to 2 tsp. green tea
½ cup boiling water

Heat a teapot with boiling water. Pour out water and place tea in bottom. Pour ½ cup boiling water over tea. Allow to sit 2 minutes. Pour off water.

¼ cup dried mint leaves
  OR 6 sprigs fresh mint
    [do not use peppermint]
¼ cup mild honey
boiling water to fill pot

Place mint in pot with tea. Pour boiling water over mint and tea. Mix well. Allow to steep 3 to 5 minutes. Remove mint floating on top of tea. Add honey. Mix well. Serve hot in small glasses.

KHOSHAF [DRIED FRUIT STEW] [Serves 6 to 8]

½ cup almonds, blanched
  OR other nuts
  OR seeds

To blanch almonds pour boiling water over them. Cover. Soak 15 minutes. The skins will come off the nuts with just a slight pressure after soaking.

2 cups dried apricots,
  cut in half
  OR 2 cups dried peaches,
    cut in half
2 cups dried figs,
  cut in half lengthwise
½ cup raisins
2 cups water
½ cup honey
1 Tbsp. rosewater
1 cup cooked rice, barley or
  bulgur wheat

Place all ingredients in a bowl. Mix. Allow to soak 48 hours. Add almonds. Serve cold. To shorten preparation time place all ingredients except rosewater, almonds and cooked grain in a heavy saucepan. Bring to a boil over high heat. Cover and reduce heat to low. Simmer 1 hour. Remove from heat. Add rosewater, almonds and grain. Mix well. Chill and serve cold. Excellent for breakfast with yoghurt.

AWAM IN SYRUP [DOUGHNUTS IN SYRUP] [Makes 3 dozen]

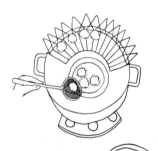

2 Tbsp. vegetable oil
½ cup orange juice
2 eggs
1 Tbsp. mild honey

Beat or blend ingredients until well mixed.

1¾ to 2 cups whole-wheat flour
1 tsp. soda
½ tsp. sea salt

Mix in a bowl. Add liquid ingredients. Mix well. Let rest 15 minutes to 1 hour.

1 cup mild honey
¼ cup lemon juice

Bring honey to a boil. Reduce heat to low and simmer for 5 minutes. Add lemon juice and remove from heat. Do not add to batter.

2 to 3 cups vegetable oil

Heat a large saucepan or wok over high heat. Add oil. Heat until a small piece of batter added sinks to the bottom of oil and then rises almost at once. Drop a spoonful of batter into oil. Cook 5 to 6 doughnuts at a time. Cook over medium high heat 3 to 4 minutes until golden brown. Do not cook at too high a temperature or doughnuts will not cook in center. Remove from oil. Drain. Drop in warm syrup. Let soak 2 to 3 minutes. Remove from syrup and place on a plate. When all doughnuts are cooked pour remaining syrup over doughnuts. Best served warm. Good snack. Can be served at a feast but make sure that people do not eat too many since a few go a long way.

CHAPTER THREE
INDONESIAN

INTRODUCTION

Indonesia is a nation of over 3,000 islands and has almost as many cuisines. The people use a common group of ingredients and similar methods of cooking but each area has its own regional specialities and variations of the basic dishes. Some areas of Indonesia have a sweet cuisine, some hot, and others spicy and rich but with little heat and no heaviness. The recipies I have included are mainly Javanese as the people who introduced me to the delights of Indonesian food were originally from the island of Java.

Indonesian food has been influenced in part by Arab, Indian, Chinese, and Dutch cultures. The Dutch influence is mainly shown in the use of many common western vegetables. The recipies I have included use these vegetables and therefore are easily prepared anywhere in North America. Indonesia is a rice culture and does not use hard grains. The people of Indonesia use a wide variety of vegetables, fruits, nuts, fish, and spices along with some meat and eggs. From numerous ingredients I have chosen those which are easily obtained throughout North America or suggested substitutes for the more exotic items. If one wants to be totally authentic some of the more exotic spices can be ordered from speciality shops whose addresses I have included.

Some of the distinctive ingredients used in Indonesian food are coconut, peanuts, sweet soy and a spicy shrimp paste. Coconut either shredded or made into coconut milk is included in many dishes. I use dry unsweetened coconut which is widely available. Indonesians use peanuts deliciously and imaginatively as meat marinades, in dressings for cooked and uncooked vegetables, and as condiments. I use peanut butter in many of these sauces as it is universally available. I suggest using raw peanuts in some recipies but roasted unsalted peanuts can be substituted. Trassi, the spicy shrimp paste, forms a base for many Indonesian foods. It can be obtained from speciality shops but I have included a recipe for a spicy shrimp paste that can be substituted for it. Ketjap manis, sweet Indonesian soy sauce contains sugar so I have included a recipe to make it with tamari soy sauce, honey and molasses. Garlic, yellow onions, chilies, and fresh ginger are also commonly used and readily available items.

Indonesian cooking is essentially a natural foods cuisine. Vegetables are sauteed in small amounts of oil to help retain their vitamins and then simmered in a little liquid, some are steamed until just tender, those that are cooked in liquid are simmered slowly and the liquid is always served with the vegetables. Another nutritional plus to Indonesian food is the low fat content. The spices and fish pastes have no preservatives or additives so can be readily used in a natural foods diet in moderate amounts. The only changes I have made in ingredients are the use of brown rice and honey. In Indonesia palm sugar is used quite often but this is unavailable in North America.

MEAL SUGGESTIONS

1 TO 2 PERSON MEAL
Nasi or Bahmie Goreng
Atjar Tjampur Kuning

Omelette
Nasi Kuning
Sambal Kalapa
Atjar Tjampur Kuning
Fresh fruit

Sop Telor Sajur
   OR
Sop Ajam Sajur
Nasi Putah
Fresh fruit

Ajam Ketjap (will keep for several
  days so makes several meals)
Atjar Ketimun
Nasi Putah

3 TO 5 PERSONS
Sop Tahu Sajur
Nasi Putah
Bumbu Goreng Ikan
Asinan
Sambal Kalapa
Atjar Tjampur Kuning
Pisang Goreng

Sambal Kalapa
Nasi Kuning
Urab
Petjel
Telor Opor
Fruit

Tahu Dadar
Tahu Goreng Ketjap
Sambal Goreng Sajur
Nasi Kuning

Nasi Kuning
Babi Ketjap
Asinan
Sambal Kalapa
Atjar Tjampur Kuning
Fruit

FEASTS

Vegetarian Feast
Rempah
Krupuck
Sambal Tomat
Sambal Kalapa
Nasi Kuning
Gado Gado
Sajur I
Telor Ketjap
Perkadel Dagang
Pisang Goreng
Tahu Dadar
Sajur Tahu Kerrie

Meat Feast
Serundeng
Rampah
Krupuck
Nasi Kuning
Sajur Labuh
Asinan
Gado Gado
Sambal Goreng Sajur
Ajam Ketjap
Telor Opor
Sate Ikan
Tahu Dadar
Atjar Tjampur Kuning
Radjang Ajam
Sambal Pangang Ikan
Dadar Gulung

Mixed Feast
Rempah
Serundeng
Telor Opor
Tahu Goreng Ketjap
Radjang Ajam
Sate Ikan
Nasi Kuning
Gado Gado
Sajur Tahu Goreng
Asinan
Pisang Goreng
Atjar Ketimun

BASIC INGREDIENTS

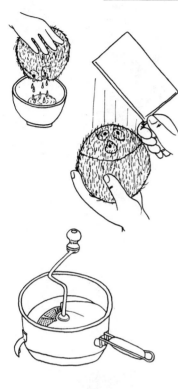

SANTEN [COCONUT MILK] [Makes 2½ cups]

BLENDER METHOD:
1 cup fresh or dry shredded
  coconut
3 cups boiling water

Place in a blender. Blend 1 minute. Pour mixture into a foodmill or sieve which has been placed over a bowl. Squeeze coconut until dry. Reserve coconut for use in Serundeng or Rempah. Repeat process until enough coconut milk is obtained. Do not use more than 1 cup of coconut at a time in the blender. Coconut milk will keep only a few days. Frozen it keeps 3 to 6 months. Freeze in ice-cube trays. Store cubes in plastic bags for easy use.

NON-BLENDER METHOD:
1 cup fresh or dry shredded
  coconut
3 cups boiling water

Place coconut and hot water in a large bowl. Soak for 15 minutes. Knead and squeeze coconut with your hands for another 5 minutes. Place a large sieve over another bowl. Take a handful of coconut and squeeze over the sieve. Throw coconut back into the unstrained bowl of coconut. Mix well. Remove another handful and squeeze. Repeat process until coconut in the first bowl is dry. Reserve coconut for use in Serundeng or Rempah. The advantage of this method is any amount of coconut milk can be made at one time. Coconut milk will keep only a few days but keeps well frozen. Freeze in ice-cube tray. Store cubes in plastic bag for easy use.

THICK COCONUT MILK

1 cup fresh or dry shredded
  coconut
2 cups boiling water

Follow directions for regular coconut milk using either the blender or non-blender method.

COCONUT BUTTER [Makes ¼ cup]

2 cups boiling water
1 cup fresh or dry shredded
  coconut

Follow directions for regular coconut milk using either blender or non-blender method. Place coconut milk in a container with a large opening. Chill overnight in refrigerator. Remove congealed coconut butter from top of milk. Drain. Keeps in refrigerator for about 1 week. Keeps indefinitely if frozen.

KETJAP MANIS [INDONESIAN SWEET SOY SAUCE] [Makes 1 cup]

1 cup soy sauce
¼ cup dark molasses
¼ cup mild honey

Combine in a saucepan. Bring to a boil over medium heat. Reduce heat to medium low. Simmer 5 minutes. Remove from heat. Cool. Do not double recipe because the honey will not thicken. Keep in covered container. Indonesian soy sauce will keep indefinitely.

VEGETARIAN SPICE CAKE

¼ cup mashed cooked soybeans
1 Tbsp. light or dark miso

1 Tbsp. coconut oil
  OR peanut oil
  OR vegetable oil
1 Tbsp. coriander, ground
3 Tbsp. nut meal [cashew,
  almond or macadamia]
½ tsp. cumin, ground
1 tsp. laos
1 tsp. sea salt
1 large clove garlic,
  grated fine
1 tsp. paprika
dash chili pepper, ground

Puree soybeans and miso through a sieve or foodmill. Set aside for later use.

Heat a small cast iron skillet over medium high heat. Add oil. Heat until a small amount of nuts added sizzles. Reduce heat to medium. Add nuts. Stir and fry 30 seconds until just brown. Add other ingredients. Mix well. Stir and fry 1 to 2 minutes until a paste is formed. Add soybean puree and mix well. Reduce heat to low. Cook 5 minutes until beans are well mixed with spices and getting dry. Cool. Pack into a small round mold and press overnight with a weight. (A small juice can works well for a mold.) Remove from mold and store in airtight container in refrigerator. Keeps indefinitely. Use in place of fish paste - trassi - for vegetarian dishes.

FISH PASTE [TO BE USED IF NO TRASSI OR BLANCHAN IS AVAILABLE]
[Makes 1 cup]

1 cup small dried fish or shrimp
3 Tbsp. peanut oil
  OR vegetable oil

Blend, chop or break up fish or shrimp into a powder. Add oil slowly and mix until a paste is formed. Pack into a small round mold and press overnight with a weight. (A small juice can works well for mold.) Remove from mold and store in airtight container in refrigerator. Keeps indefinitely.

SHRIMP STOCK [Makes 4 cups]

¼ lb. dried shrimp
4 cups boiling water

Wash shrimp in cold water. Place in bowl and pour boiling water over them. Allow to soak 30 minutes. Strain. Save shrimp for Sambal Goreng Udang (hot fried dried shrimp). Keeps well frozen. Freeze in ice-cube trays. Store cubes in plastic bags for easy use.

BEEF STOCK [Makes 1 quart]

2 to 3 large soup bones
  OR ¼ lb. beef stew meat
5 cups water
1 leek, cut in half lengthwise
  OR 2 green onions, cut in half
    lengthwise
1 small cube fresh ginger root,
crushed

Place ingredients in a large saucepan. Cover. Bring to boil over high heat. Reduce heat to medium low. Simmer 1 hour. Strain. Save meat for fried rice or noodles. Stock keeps well frozen. Freeze in ice cube trays. Store cubes in plastic bags for easy use.

RICE FLOUR [Makes 1 to 2 cups]

BLENDER METHOD:
1 cup brown rice

Place in shallow baking pan. Roast at 300° for 5 to 10 minutes until just lightly browned. Remove from pan. Blend ¼ cup of rice at a time until well powdered. Cool and store in a tight container.

FOODMILL METHOD:
1 cup brown rice

Place in foodmill and grind on fine setting. Put through twice for fine flour. Store in tight container.

ASSAM [TAMARIND WATER] [Makes 1 cup]

2 Tbsp. dried tamarind pulp
1 cup boiling water

Place tamarind in a heavy bowl. Pour boiling water over tamarind. Break up with a fork. Stir and mash occasionally. Soak for 1 hour. Press hard through a fine sieve or blend and then sieve. If blender is available soak only 15 minutes, then blend and sieve. Discard pulp and seeds. Keeps in refrigerator up to 1 week.

CONDIMENTS AND PICKLES

Condiments and pickles are served with all meals in Indonesia. Most are very peppery but the Serundeng Katjang is mild and goes well with most Indonesian dishes. The dry condiments are sprinkled on top of dishes; the wet ones and pickles are served on the side. Only small amounts of the hot condiments and pickles are needed for one serving.

SAMBAL KELAPA [HOT COCONUT CONDIMENT] [Makes 1 cup]

2 Tbsp. peanut oil
  OR vegetable oil
6 to 8 dried chili peppers,
  ground or blended fine
1 tsp. trassi [shrimp paste],
  minced
  OR fish paste, minced
  OR spice cake, minced
  OR anchovy paste
¼ yellow onion, minced
1 citrus leaf, minced
  OR 1 tsp. lemon juice
1 clove garlic,
  crushed and minced

Heat a medium cast iron skillet over medium heat. Add oil. Heat until a small piece of onion added sizzles. Add ingredients. Stir and fry 5 to 10 minutes until onions are soft and transparent. Mince chilies and onions together so chilies don't scatter.

1 tsp. dark palm sugar
  OR 1 tsp. mild honey and
    ¼ tsp. molasses

Add to onions and spices. Mix well.

1 cup dry or fresh shredded
  coconut

Add to onions and spices. Mix well. Place in oven and bake at 300°, 5 to 10 minutes until coconut is browned. Stir often. Place in a tightly covered jar. Keeps indefinitely in refrigerator. Serve at room temperature. Good served with vegetable, rice or main dishes.

SAMBAL KATJANG [HOT PEANUT CONDIMENT] [Makes 1 cup]

2 cups raw peanuts
1 Tbsp. peanut oil
  OR vegetable oil

Mix oil and peanuts. Bake at 300°, 5 to 10 minutes until peanuts are golden brown. Remove from oven. Chop fine or blend until chopped fine. Do not blend to powder.

OR IN PLACE OF ABOVE:
2 cups unsalted roasted peanuts

Chop fine or blend until chopped fine. Do not blend to powder.

8 small dried chili peppers,
  minced
2 tsp. mild honey

Mix well and then add to peanuts.

2 tsp. to 1½ Tbsp. trassi
  [shrimp paste], minced
  OR fish paste, minced
  OR spice cake, minced
  OR anchovy paste

Bake at 300°, 3 to 5 minutes until lightly toasted. Remove from oven. Add to peanuts. Mix well. Cool. Store in tight container. Sambal Katjang keeps indefinitely in refrigerator. Good served with vegetable, rice, or main dishes.

VARIATION:
HOT NUT OR SEED CONDIMENT [Makes 1 cup]

2 cups nuts [cashews, almonds, or
macadamia]
OR seeds [sesame or sunflower]

Follow recipe for Sambal Katjang. Store in a
tight container. Sambals keep indefinitely in the
refrigerator. Good served with vegetable, rice
or main dishes.

SERUNDENG KATJANG [PEANUT-COCONUT CONDIMENT] [Makes 4 cups]

2 Tbsp. peanut oil
OR vegetable oil
1 medium yellow onion, minced
1 clove garlic, crushed and
minced
½ inch fresh ginger root,
crushed and minced

Heat a large heavy cast iron skillet over
medium high. Add oil. Heat until a small piece
of onion added sizzles. Add ingredients. Stir and
fry 2 to 3 minutes.

1 tsp. cumin, ground
1 tsp. coriander, ground
1 tsp. sea salt
1 tsp. turmeric

Mix well with onions. Fry 2 to 3 minutes until
onions are soft.

1 Tbsp. tamarind water
OR lemon juice
1 tsp. mild honey
½ tsp. dark molasses

Mix well with spices and onions. Fry 2 to 3
minutes until almost dry and paste is formed.

2 to 3 cups fresh or dry
shredded coconut left over
from making coconut milk
OR unused fresh or dry
shredded coconut

Add to spices. Mix well 1 to 2 minutes until
coconut is uniformly colored with turmeric.
Remove from heat. Place in a 300° oven. Bake
30 minutes to 1 hour until coconut is dry and
slightly browned. Stir often.

1½ cups raw peanuts,
chopped
OR other nuts
OR seeds

Bake at 300°, 5 to 10 minutes until just golden
brown. Remove from oven. Add to coconut
mixture when it has finished baking. Mix well.
Serundeng is used as a condiment to sprinkle
over many Indonesian dishes (i.e., sajurs, rice
dishes, main dishes, etc.). It can be stored for
several months in tightly covered container in
the refrigerator. Heat slightly to freshen before
serving.

SAMBAL AMANDEL [HOT ALMOND CONDIMENT WITH COCONUT MILK]
[Makes 1 cup]

1 tsp. water
  [for blender method only]
¼ cup dried chili peppers,
  minced
1 Tbsp. trassi [shrimp paste],
  minced
  OR fish paste, minced
  OR spice cake, minced
  OR 1 tsp. anchovy paste
1 medium yellow onion, minced
4 cloves garlic, crushed and
  minced
½ cup almonds, minced
½ tsp. sea salt

If a blender is used leave ingredients in large pieces. Blend peppers, water and trassi 15 to 30 seconds. Add onions and garlic. Blend until a paste forms. Add salt and almonds. Blend until almonds are chopped fine and well mixed with other ingredients. If no blender is available finely chop and crush each ingredient and mix into a paste. Mince chilies and onions together so chilies don't scatter.

½ cup coconut milk
1 Tbsp. mild honey

Add to almond mixture. Blend 15 seconds until well mixed. If no blender is available mix until well combined.

3 Tbsp. peanut oil
  OR vegetable oil

Heat a medium cast iron skillet over medium heat. Add oil. Heat until a drop of sauce added sizzles. Add sauce. Reduce heat to medium low. Stir and fry 5 to 10 minutes until sauce begins to separate and follows the spoon around the pan and is almost dry. Store in tightly covered jar. Serve cool. Sambal Amandel keeps indefinitely. Used to sprinkle over other dishes when they are served.

VARIATION:
HOT NUT CONDIMENT WITH COCONUT MILK [Makes 1 cup]

½ cup nuts [cashews or
  macadamia], minced

Follow recipe for Sambal Amandel. Use cashews or macadamia nuts in place of almonds. Cook as directed. Store in a tightly covered jar. Serve cool. Keeps indefinitely. Sprinkle over other dishes when they are served.

ATJAR KETIMUN [CUCUMBER PICKLE] [Makes 2 cups]

3 cucumbers, seeded and cut
 into ½ inch cubes
2 to 3 fresh red chili peppers,
 minced
 OR dried chili peppers, minced

Mix cucumbers and peppers. Place in small deep bowl.

½ cup rice vinegar
 OR apple cider vinegar
1½ Tbsp. mild honey
½ tsp. sea salt

Place in a stainless steel saucepan. Bring to boil over medium heat. Remove from heat. Pour over cucumbers. Chill. Serve cold. To preserve pickles, place cucumbers in vinegar when it boils. Bring to boil again and then place in canning jar and seal. Serve at any meal. Good at feasts. Serve as one of dishes around bottom of the rice cone platter.

VARIATION:

RADISH, DAIKON OR TURNIP PICKLE

2 cups daikon radish, cut into ¼
 inch slices
 OR 1 dozen large red radishes,
  cut in half
 OR 2 cups turnip, cut in half
  lengthwise and then into ¼
  inch slices

Follow recipe for Cucumber Pickle. Cook as directed. Serve cold. Served at any meal. Good at feasts. Serve as one of dishes around bottom of the rice cone platter.

SAMBAL TOMAT [HOT TOMATO SAUCE] [Makes ¼ to ½ cup]

1 small ripe tomato
2 to 4 fresh red chili peppers
 OR dried chili peppers
½ tsp. sea salt
1 small clove garlic, crushed

Place in a blender. Blend ingredients 30 seconds to 1 minute until well mixed and sauce forms a paste. If no blender is available, mince all ingredients well. Crush together in bowl or with mortar and pestle until ingredients form a paste. Good with fritters, meat, egg or rice dishes. Keeps 1 to 2 weeks in refrigerator.

ATJAR TJAMPUR KUNING 1 [YELLOW PICKLED MIXED VEGETABLES]
[Makes 2 quarts]

2 to 3 Tbsp. peanut oil
  OR vegetable oil
2 tsp. turmeric
¼ cup ground almonds
  OR cashews
  OR macadamia nuts
  OR sesame seeds
3 cloves garlic, crushed
  and minced

Heat a large saucepan over medium heat. Add oil. Heat until a small piece of garlic added sizzles. Add almonds, turmeric and garlic. Reduce heat to low. Stir and fry 2 to 3 minutes until almonds are golden brown.

1 tsp. coriander, ground
½ tsp. cumin, ground
¼ tsp. black pepper
½ tsp. sea salt
1 to 4 dried chili peppers, minced
1 medium yellow onion, cut in half
  lengthwise and thinly sliced

Add to almond mixture. Stir and fry over low heat 2 to 3 minutes.

2 cups rice vinegar
  OR apple cider vinegar
2 Tbsp. mild honey

Slowly add to spice mixture. Mix well. Bring to boil. Reduce heat. Simmer 5 minutes. Remove from heat.

1 to 2 cups bean sprouts
  OR lentil sprouts
1 cup carrots, julienned
½ head cabbage, shredded

Mix well with vinegar and spices. Marinate in sauce overnight. Serve cold. The pickles will keep indefinitely in the refrigerator in a tightly covered container. Can be processed 30 minutes in hot water bath, sealed, and stored on shelf. Served at any meal. Especially good for lunch with cold rice and left over vegetable or main dishes. A must at feasts.

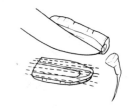

VARIATION:
ATJAR TJAMPUR KUNING II [YELLOW PICKLED MIXED VEGETABLES]
[Makes 2 quarts]

¼ head cabbage, shredded
1 cup green beans, cut in long, thin
  diagonal slices
¼ head cauliflower, cut in small
  flowerlets [cut stem up to
  flower, then pull apart so flower
  does not break]
5 to 6 carrots, julienned
1 to 2 fresh red peppers, julienned
1 cucumber, seeded and julienned

Follow recipe for Atjar Tjampur Kuning. Use the following vegetables in place of sprouts, carrots and cabbage. Steam cauliflower, beans and carrots 2 to 3 minutes until vegetables are hot but not limp. Add to vinegar and spices along with other vegetables. Mix well. Marinate in sauce overnight. Serve cold. Pickle will keep indefinitely in refrigerator in a tightly covered container. Can be processed 30 minutes in hot water bath, sealed, and stored on shelf. Served at any meal. Especially good for lunch with cold rice and leftover vegetable or main dishes. A must at feasts.

APPETIZERS AND SNACKS

Appetizers and snacks are very popular in Indonesia. All of these are deep fried and very quick to prepare. Traditionally most of these are also used as part of the food around the base of the yellow rice cone platter served at a feast.

KRUPUK [SHRIMP PUFFS] [Serves 4 to 6]

1 cup peanut oil
  OR vegetable oil
2 dozen shrimp puffs

Heat a medium cast iron skillet over medium high heat. Add oil. Heat until a small piece of puff added expands. Add 2 puffs. Immerse in oil. Allow to puff to twice normal size. Fry quickly. Remove from oil. Drain. Do not brown. Serve warm. Good as snack or appetizer. Excellent for a feast.

REMPAH [COCONUT FRITTERS] [Makes 12 to 14 / Serves 4]

1 to 1¼ cup fresh or dried
  shredded coconut
¼ tsp. sea salt
½ tsp. coriander, ground
dash of cumin, ground [optional]
1 small clove garlic, crushed
  and minced
2 large eggs, beaten until well
  mixed but not frothy

Mix all ingredients well. Soak 1 to 3 hours. Dough should be just moist enough to form balls when squeezed lightly but firmly in palm of hand. Press about 1 to 2 tsp. dough in hands lightly to compact it. Toss from hand to hand to shape into ½ inch balls.

3 cups peanut oil
  OR vegetable oil

Place oil in a wok. Leave plenty of room as oil froths a lot when coconut balls are added. Heat on high heat until small piece of fritter added sinks to bottom and then rises to top almost at once. Reduce heat to medium high. Add 5 fritters. Do not add too many fritters because oil will froth too much. Turn often. Fry 3 to 5 minutes until golden brown and crisp. Drain. Continue to cook until all fritters are done. Serve warm. Rempah will store well frozen. To reheat, place in 300° oven 5 to 10 minutes until hot. Good as snack, appetizer, or as one of the ingredients around base of yellow rice cone at feast.

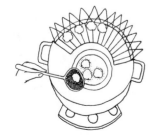

Too Cold   Too Hot   Correct Temperature

KETELLA RAMBAT [SWEET POTATO CHIPS] [Serves 4 to 6]

2 sweet potatoes, cut into 1/8 inch slices - use potato peeler
  OR yams, cut into 1/8 inch slices
1 cup peanut oil
  OR vegetable oil

Heat a wok over high heat. Add oil. Heat until a slice of potato added sizzles well. Add one quarter sliced potatoes. Reduce heat slightly. Stir and fry 5 to 10 minutes until golden brown. Remove from oil. Drain. Repeat until all potatoes fried.

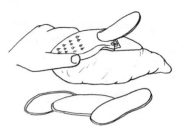

1 to 4 dried chili peppers, minced
1 tsp. sea salt

Sprinkle over hot potatoes. Mix well. Serve hot as a snack or with a salad or Gado Gado Sauce. Excellent for a feast.

REMPEJEK [PEANUT STRIPS] [Makes 2 dozen]

3 to 4 black peppercorns
½ tsp. cumin seed
1 tsp. coriander seed

Heat a small cast iron skillet over medium high heat. Add seeds and pepper. Parch 1 minute until spices are hot. Grind in mortar and pestle or blend 15 to 30 seconds until well broken.

1 to 2 cloves garlic, crushed and minced
¼ small yellow onion, minced
1 tsp. turmeric [optional]

Add to spices. Crush with mortar and pestle into a paste.

¾ cup sifted brown rice flour
3 to 4 Tbsp. whole wheat pastry flour
  OR sifted whole wheat flour
½ tsp. sea salt

Place in a bowl. Mix flour well. Add onion and spices. Mix well.

¾ cup thick coconut milk
¼ to ⅓ cup water

Add coconut milk and water to flour and spices in bowl. Mix until well blended and smooth. Batter should be like pancake batter.

¾ cup raw peanuts, slightly chopped
  OR other nuts
  OR seeds

Add peanuts. Mix well.

½ cup peanut oil
  OR vegetable oil

Heat a medium cast iron skillet. Add oil. Heat over medium high heat until 1 drop of batter sets well. Spoon 2 to 3 Tbsp. batter into pan in long thin strip so batter will not be thick and doughy. If batter breaks apart add more rice flour. Cook 30 seconds to 1 minute, turn and cook until crisp and golden brown. Remove from pan. Drain. Cook one at a time until all the batter is cooked. Serve at room temperature as snack, with Gado Gado sauce, or as one of ingredients around base of yellow rice cone at a feast.

RICE AND NOODLES

Indonesia is a rice-based culture and a rice dish traditionally accompanies every meal. The fried rices, served with a vegetable, make a complete meal. Served cold with pickles they make an excellent lunch. Noodle dishes were introduced to Indonisia by the Chinese but have been changed considerable by the Indonesians. They are served like rice dishes.

NASI PUTAH [DRY COOKED RICE] [Serves 4 to 6]

2 cups long-grain [preferred] brown rice
4 cups water

Place water and rice in a heavy saucepan. Bring to boil over high heat. Stir well. Cover and reduce heat to medium low. Simmer 30 to 35 minutes. Remove from heat and allow to sit 10 minutes. Break up with a fork. Rice is served at most main meals or cold for lunch with leftovers and pickles.

NASI KUNING [YELLOW RICE COOKED IN COCONUT MILK] [Serves 4 to 6]

2 cups long-grain [preferred] brown rice
4 cups coconut milk
1 tsp. turmeric
1 tsp. lemon grass pd.
  OR 2 lime leaves
  OR 2 lemon grass leaves
  OR 1 tsp. lemon juice
1 tsp. sea salt

Place ingredients in heavy pot. Mix well. Cover and bring to boil over high heat. Reduce heat to low and simmer 30 to 35 minutes until all liquid absorbed. Remove from heat. Allow to sit for 10 minutes. Serve hot with main meal or cold with leftovers and pickles for lunch. Also leftover rice good to use in Indonesian fried rice.

Place in a cone shape mold and invert onto a large platter. Decorate with sliced chilies. Surround the bottom with main dishes, fritters, and cold vegetables for a beautiful feast dish.

TUMPEUNG [YELLOW RICE WITH CHICKEN] [Serves 4 to 6]

1 to 3 lb. chicken,
  skinned and cut into
  8 to 10 pieces
  OR bones and skin from 2
    filleted chickens
1½ tsp. sea salt
¼ tsp. black pepper
1 to 2 Tbsp. garam masala
  [See Basic Indian section]
1 tsp. turmeric
dash of cumin, ground
¼ tsp. cardamom, crushed in
  mortar and pestle
2 Indonesian laurel leaves
  OR curry leaves
  OR bay leaves
3 to 4 cloves garlic, crushed and
  minced
1 to 4 chili peppers, minced
2 cups coconut milk

2 cups long-grain [preferred]
  brown rice
stock from cooking chicken
3 cups water [enough to make
  4 cups of liquid]
2 Tbsp. peanut oil
  OR vegetable oil
  OR coconut butter

Place chicken, spices and coconut milk in a large heavy saucepan. Mix well. Cover and bring to boil. Reduce heat to medium low. Simmer 50 minutes to 1 hour until chicken is tender and liquid is reduced. Stir occasionally. Remove chicken. Strain liquid. Reserve to add to rice. Remove chicken from bones. Set aside to use later.

Heat a heavy saucepan. Add oil. Heat slightly. Add rice. Stir and fry 2 to 3 minutes over medium high heat until rice crackles. Add water and stock. Cover and bring to boil. Reduce heat to low. Simmer 30 to 35 minutes. Remove lid. Add chicken meat. Mix well. Cover and allow to sit 10 minutes. Serve hot. Good main dish at a dinner served with a vegetable dish and pickles. Excellent feast dish. Good cold for lunch.

NASI GORENG I WITH NUTS OR MEAT [FRIED RICE] [Serves 4 to 6]

2 medium yellow onions,
  chopped
2 cloves garlic, crushed and
  minced
¼ to 2 tsp. chili pepper, minced
¼ tsp. to 1 Tbsp. trassi
  [shrimp paste], minced
  OR fish paste, minced
  OR spice cake, minced
  OR 1 tsp. anchovy paste
3 Tbsp. peanut oil
  OR vegetable oil

Heat a large cast iron skillet or wok over medium heat. Add oil. Heat until a small piece of onion added sizzles. Add ingredients. Stir and fry 5 to 10 minutes until onions are soft and lightly browned. Mince chilies and onions together so chilies don't scatter.

½ cup cashews, coarsely chopped
  OR peanuts, coarsely chopped
  OR ½ to 1 cup cooked meat
    [chicken, turkey, beef, pork,
    etc.] coarsely chopped

Add cashews or meat to onion mixture, but not both. Stir and fry 2 to 3 minutes over medium heat until just browned.

3 to 4 cups cooked long-grain
  [preferred] brown rice
2 Tbsp. peanut oil
  OR vegetable oil

Add oil. Increase heat to medium high. Mix oil well with nuts and spices. Heat 1 minute. Add rice in small amounts to the onion mixture. Mix well between additions of rice. Stir and fry 5 to 10 minutes until rice is well mixed and hot. Serve hot. Good served with a hot vegetable dish as a meal-in-a-bowl or with a salad and a main dish. Also good cold with pickles and leftovers for lunch. Serve with garnish (optional).

GARNISH: [optional]

1 large yellow onion, cut in half
  lengthwise and sliced paper thin
1 large clove garlic, julienned
3 Tbsp. peanut oil
  OR vegetable oil

Heat a medium cast iron skillet over high heat. Add oil. Heat until a small piece of onion added sizzles. Reduce heat to medium high. Add onion and garlic. Stir and fry 8 to 12 minutes until onions are brown and crisp. Remove from pan with a slotted spoon. Drain. Keep warm in oven.

1 large fresh red chili pepper,
  julienned
  OR dried chili pepper, minced
1 stalk celery, julienned

Use combination of all garnishes or just one separately. Sprinkle over fried rice just before serving.

NASI GORENG II WITH NUTS OR MEAT [FRIED RICE] [Serves 4 to 6]

2 medium yellow onions, minced
2 cloves garlic, crushed and
    minced
¼ to 2 tsp. dried chili peppers,
    minced
1 tsp. to 1 Tbsp. trassi
    [shrimp paste], minced
    OR fish paste, minced
    OR spice cake, minced
    OR 1 tsp. anchovy paste
3 Tbsp. peanut oil
    OR vegetable oil

Heat a large cast iron skillet over medium high heat. Add oil. Heat until a small piece of onion added sizzles. Add ingredients. Stir and fry 5 to 10 minutes until onions are light brown and soft. Mince chilies and onions together so chilies don't scatter.

¼ cup cashews, ground or grated
    OR macadamia nuts, ground
    OR almonds, ground
    OR peanuts, ground

Add to onion mixture. Stir and fry ½ to 1 minute until light brown.

½ cup dried or fresh shredded
    coconut
1 to 2 tsp. coriander, ground

Add to onion mixture. Mix well. Stir and fry 1 to 2 minutes until coconut is light brown.

½ cup cashews, coarsely chopped
    OR raw peanuts, coarsely
      chopped
    OR ½ to 1 cup cooked meat
      [beef, pork, chicken,
      turkey, etc.]
      coarsely chopped

Add cashews or meat but not both. Stir and fry 3 to 5 minutes until just browned.

3 to 4 cups cooked long-grain
    [preferred] brown rice
2 Tbsp. peanut oil
    OR vegetable oil

Add oil. Mix well with nuts and spices. Heat 1 minute. Add rice in small amounts to the onion mixture. Mix well between additions of rice. Stir and fry 5 to 10 minutes until rice is well mixed. Serve hot. Good served with hot vegetable dish as meal-in-a-bowl or with salad and main dish. Also good cold next day with pickles and leftovers. Serve with garnish (optional).

BAHMIE GORENG I WITH NUTS [FRIED NOODLES] [Serves 4 to 6]

½ lb. whole wheat
   OR soy noodles
   OR combination of both
4 cups water

Bring water to boil in a large saucepan. Add noodles. Mix well. If noodles start to boil over add small amount of cold water. Cover and reduce heat to medium low. Simmer 5 to 10 minutes until tender. Stir once or twice to separate noodles. Remove from heat. Drain in a colander or large sieve. Wash well with hot water. Set aside to add later.

1 cup cashews, coarsely chopped
   OR raw peanuts, coarsely
      chopped
   OR ½ cup almonds, coarsely
      chopped
3 Tbsp. peanut oil
   OR vegetable oil

Heat a wok or large cast iron pan. Add oil. Heat 1 to 2 minutes over medium heat. Add nuts. Stir and fry 3 to 5 minutes until lightly browned. Remove from oil with a slotted spoon. Drain. Set aside for later use.

1 to 2 cloves garlic, crushed
   and minced
1 to 2 slices fresh ginger root,
   minced
3 large leeks, chopped
   OR 4 to 6 green onions, chopped

Increase heat to medium high. Add to hot oil. Stir and fry 3 to 5 minutes until leeks are slightly soft.

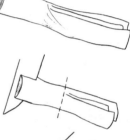

¼ to ½ head cabbage, shredded
1 to 2 cups snow peas, snipped
   and strings removed
   OR 1 to 2 stalks celery, cut
      into thin diagonal slices

Add to leeks. Stir and fry 3 to 5 minutes until just beginning to get soft. Add noodles. Mix well with vegetables and oil. Stir and fry 2 to 3 more minutes.

2 to 4 Tbsp. Indonesian
   soy sauce
½ tsp. sea salt

Add to noodles and vegetables. Mix well. Add nuts. Stir and fry 2 to 3 minutes over medium heat. Serve hot. Good meal-in-a-bowl when served with vegetable dish or hot soup. Also good grain side dish at vegetarian meal. Good cold for lunch next day with pickles and leftovers. Serve with garnish (optional).

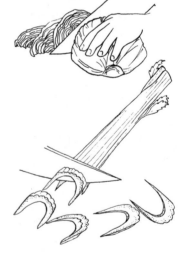

VARIATION I

**BAHMIE GORENG I TAHU
[FRIED NOODLES WITH BEAN
CURD] [Serves 4 to 6]**

½ lb. whole wheat noodles —
  not soy noodles
1 to 2 blocks bean curd, cut into
  ¼ to ½ inch cubes

Follow recipe for Bahmie Goreng I with Nuts
but use bean curd in place of nuts. Do not fry
bean curd. Add with soy sauce. Gently mix with
noodles so bean curd cubes do not break. Heat 3
to 5 minutes until bean curd heated through.
Serve hot. Use any one or all suggested
garnishes. Good vegetarian meal-in-a-bowl or
main dish served with a vegetable dish or soup.
Good cold for lunch.

VARIATION II

**BAHMIE GORENG I WITH MEAT
[FRIED NOODLES WITH MEAT]
[Serves 4 to 6]**

½ to 1 lb. meat [pork, beef, lamb],
  cut into ¼ to 1/8 inch cubes
  OR 1 chicken breast, cut into
    small pieces
  OR ¼ lb. small cooked shrimp
  OR 1 to 2 cups cooked meat
    [chicken, turkey, beef, etc.]
    shredded into small pieces
3 Tbsp. peanut oil
  OR vegetable oil

Heat a wok or large cast iron pan. Add oil. Heat
over medium high heat 1 to 2 minutes. Add
meat. Stir 5 to 10 minutes until light brown.
Leave meat in pan and add leeks, garlic, and
ginger. Follow recipe for Bahmie Goreng I with
Nuts but leave out nuts. Serve hot. Use any one
or all suggested garnishes. Good meal-in-a-bowl
or grain side dish served with a soup or
vegetable dish for dinner. Good cold for lunch.

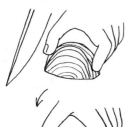

GARNISH: [optional]

1 large yellow onion, cut
  in half lengthwise and sliced
  paper thin
1 large clove garlic,
  julienned
3 Tbsp. peanut oil
  OR vegetable oil

1 large fresh red chili pepper,
  julienned
  OR dried chili pepper, minced
1 stalk celery, julienned

Heat a medium cast iron skillet over high heat.
Add oil. Heat until a small piece of onion added
sizzles. Reduce heat to medium high. Add onion
and garlic. Stir and fry 8 to 12 minutes until
onions are brown and crisp. Remove from pan
with slotted spoon. Drain. Keep warm in oven.

Use combination of all garnishes or just one
separately. Sprinkle over fried rice just before
serving.

BAHMIE GORENG II WITH NUTS [FRIED NOODLES WITH NUTS]
[Serves 4 to 6]

½ lb. whole-wheat
   OR soy noodles
   OR combination of both
4 cups water

Bring water to boil in a large saucepan. Add noodles. Mix well. If noodles start to boil over add small amount of cold water. Cover and reduce heat to medium low. Simmer 5 to 10 minutes until tender. Stir once or twice to separate noodles. Remove from heat. Drain in a colander or large sieve. Wash well with hot water. Set aside to add later.

1 cup cashews, coarsely
   chopped
   OR raw peanuts, coarsely
     chopped
   OR ½ cup almonds, coarsely
     chopped
3 Tbsp. peanut oil
   OR vegetable oil

Heat a wok or large cast iron pan. Add oil. Heat 1 to 2 minutes over medium heat. Add nuts. Stir and fry 3 to 5 minutes until lightly browned. Remove from oil with a slotted spoon. Drain. Set aside for later use.

1 to 2 cloves garlic, crushed
   and minced
1 tsp. coriander seeds,
   crushed
3 large leeks, chopped
   OR 4 to 5 green onions,
     chopped

Increase heat to medium high. Add to hot oil. Stir and fry 3 to 5 minutes until leeks are slightly soft.

¼ to ½ head cabbage,
   shredded
1 to 2 cups snow peas, snipped
   and strings removed
   OR 1 to 2 stalks celery, cut
     into thin diagonal slices

Add to leeks. Stir and fry 3 to 5 minutes until just beginning to get soft. Add noodles. Mix well with vegetables and oil. Stir and fry 2 to 3 more minutes.

4 Tbsp. Indonesian soy sauce
½ cup stock [See Basic
   Chinese section]
½ tsp. sea salt

Add to noodles and vegetables. Mix well. Cover and simmer 2 to 3 minutes until noodles absorb liquid. Uncover and add nuts. Serve hot. Good meal-in-a-bowl when served with a vegetable dish or hot soup. Also good grain side dish at a vegetarian meal. Good served cold for lunch next day with pickles and leftovers. Serve with garnish (optional).

VARIATION I
BAHMIE GORENG II TAHU
[FRIED NOODLES WITH BEAN
CURD] [Serves 4 to 6]

½ lb. whole-wheat noodles, not soy
   noodles
1 to 2 blocks bean curd cut into
   ¼ to ½ inch cubes

Follow recipe for Bahmie Goreng II with Nuts
but use bean curd in place of nuts. Do not fry
bean curd. Add with soy sauce and stock.
Gently mix with noodles so bean curd cubes do
not break. Cover and simmer 3 to 5 minutes
until bean curd is heated through. Serve hot.
Use any one or all suggested garnishes. Good
vegetarian meal-in-a-bowl or main dish served
with a vegetable dish or soup. Good cold for
lunch.

VARIATION II
BAHMIE GORENG II WITH MEAT
[FRIED NOODLES WITH MEAT]
[Serves 4 to 6]

½ to 1 lb. meat [pork, beef, lamb],
   cut into ¼ to 1/8 inch cubes
   OR 1 chicken breast, cut into
      small pieces
   OR ¼ lb. small cooked shrimp
   OR 1 to 2 cups cooked meat
      [chicken, turkey, beef, etc.]
      shredded into small pieces
3 Tbsp. peanut oil
   OR vegetable oil

Heat a wok or large cast iron pan. Add oil. Heat
over medium high heat 1 to 2 minutes. Add
meat. Stir 5 to 10 minutes until light brown.
Leave meat in pan and add garlic, coriander and
leeks. Follow recipe for Bahmie Goreng II with
Nuts but leave out nuts. Use meat stock for
stock. Serve hot. Use any one or all suggested
garnishes. Good meal-in-a-bowl or grain side
dish served with soup or vegetable dish for
dinner. Good cold for lunch.

COLD DRESSED VEGETABLES AND FRUITS

Cold dressed vegetables and fruits can be served as salads, snacks, desserts or as part of a feast. The bean curd dish, Tahu Goreng Ketjap, served with a rice dish, can double as the main course in a simple meal.

URAB [VEGETABLE SALAD WITH SPICY COCONUT DRESSING]
[Serves 4 to 6]

Dressing:

1 cup dried shredded coconut
¼ cup boiling water

Place dried coconut in a shallow bowl. Pour boiling water over it. Soak for 30 minutes.

OR IN PLACE OF ABOVE:
1 cup fresh coconut, grated fine

4 Tbsp. tamarind water
  OR lemon juice
1 Tbsp. lime juice
¼ to 2 dried chili peppers,
  minced
  OR ½ to 2 tsp. sambal olek
    [canned chili peppers]
½ to 1 tsp. trassi
  [shrimp paste], minced
  OR fish cake, minced
  OR spice cake, minced
  OR anchovy paste
1 tsp. mild honey

Combine in a blender. Blend 30 seconds until well mixed. If no blender is available, mix ingredients well. Combine moist coconut (fresh or soaked) with dressing. Allow to soak 5 to 10 minutes. Mince trassi and chilies together so chilies don't scatter.

¼ lb. bean sprouts
2 cups Chinese cabbage,
  shredded
  OR 2 cups cabbage,
    shredded
¼ lb. green beans, cut into
  long, thin diagonal slices

Steam sprouts and cabbage 30 seconds. Steam beans 1 minute. Place on rack to cool.

6 to 8 large leaves Romaine
  lettuce, cut into ¼ inch
  slices
  OR sorrel, cut into ¼ inch
    slices

Place in a large salad bowl with cooled steamed vegetables. Pour dressing over vegetables. Mix well. Serve at once. Serve like any salad. Good feast dish.

VARIATION:

Use favorite tossed salad without tomatoes and above dressing.

ASINAN [RAW VEGETABLE SALAD WITH SPICY SHRIMP DRESSING]
[Serves 4 to 6]

4 to 5 water chestnuts, peeled
  and sliced thin, steamed ½
  minute and cooled
OR 3 jerusalem artichokes,
  sliced thin
OR 1 large firm pear, cored
  and sliced thin
OR 1 firm apple, cored and
  sliced thin
¼ large head cabbage,
  shredded
1 large cucumber,
  sliced thin

Place vegetables in a large salad bowl.

½ cup raw peanuts,
  coarsely chopped

OR IN PLACE OF ABOVE:
½ cup roasted unsalted peanuts,
  coarsely chopped

Bake raw peanuts at 300°, 5 to 10 minutes until lightly browned. Remove from oven. Sprinkle over salad vegetables.

Dressing:

3 to 4 dried shrimp, minced
¼ to 2 dried chili peppers,
  minced
  OR ¼ to 2 tsp. sambal olek
  [canned chili peppers]
2 Tbsp. peanut oil
  OR vegetable oil

Mince chilies and shrimp together. Heat a small cast iron skillet over medium high heat. Add oil. Heat for a few seconds. Add chili and shrimp. Stir and fry 15 to 30 seconds until just brown. Remove from heat.

½ tsp. sea salt
1 tsp. mild honey
2 Tbsp. rice vinegar
  OR apple cider vinegar

Add to oil and shrimp mixture. Mix well. Pour over salad vegetables and peanuts. Mix well. Serve at once. Serve like western salad. Good feast dish.

VARIATION:

Use favorite tossed salad with above dressing.

171

GADO GADO [COLD VEGETABLES WITH PEANUT SAUCE] [Serves 6]

Sauce:

1 large yellow onion, minced
1 to 2 large cloves garlic,
   crushed and minced or grated
½ to 1 inch ginger, crushed
   and minced or grated
1 to 3 dried chili peppers,
   minced
   OR ½ to 2 tsp. sambal olek
     [canned chili peppers]
2 Tbsp. peanut oil
   OR vegetable oil

Mince onion and chilies together so chilies don't scatter. Heat a heavy saucepan over medium high heat. Add oil. Heat until a small piece of onion added sizzles. Reduce heat. Add onions, garlic, ginger and sambal or chili. Stir and fry over medium heat 5 to 10 minutes until onions are soft and transparent but not brown.

2 cups coconut milk
1 to 3 tsp. Indonesian soy sauce
2 tsp. mild honey
½ tsp. sea salt
2 Tbsp. tamarind water
   OR lemon juice
1 cup peanut butter

Blend ingredients well in blender starting with coconut milk and ending with peanut butter. If no blender is available just mix well. Slowly add to onion mixture. Reduce heat to medium and simmer 5 to 10 minutes until sauce thickens. Stir constantly as sauce burns easily. Serve at room temperature with a few or all of these vegetables.

¼ head firm cabbage, cut into
   1 inch slices
¼ head iceburg lettuce, cut
   into 1 inch slices
2 medium cucumbers, cut in
   thick slices
4 hard-cooked eggs, cut in
   thick slices

Place on a large platter in an attractive pattern.

1 lb. spinach
¼ lb. bean sprouts

Steam 1 minute. Cool on a rack. Place on platter.

¼ lb. green beans
1 head cauliflower, broken
   into small flowerlets
2 carrots, cut into thin slices

Steam 5 minutes. Cool on a rack. Place on platter.

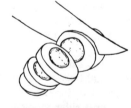

4 new potatoes
   OR 2 medium potatoes

Steam 15 to 20 minutes until done. Cool. Slice into thick slices. Place on platter with other vegetables. All vegetables except potatoes and beans can be served raw with gado gado sauce if you prefer. Arrange all or any 3 to 5 vegetables on a platter with sauce in center. Dip vegetables in sauce to eat. Good for a salad dish for a main meal. Very good for lunch next day with vegetables to dip in sauce and cold rice. Excellent feast dish. Sauce keeps 2 to 3 weeks in refrigerator.

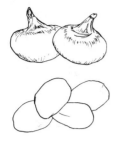

ROEDJAK MANIS [COLD VEGETABLES OR FRUIT WITH SWEET SAUCE]
[Serves 4 to 6]

4 to 5 water chestnuts, peeled
   and sliced thin, steamed
   ¹/₂ minute and cooled
   OR 2 to 3 jerusalem artichokes,
     sliced thin
   OR 1 large firm ripe pear,
     cored and sliced thin
¹/₂ head cabbage, shredded
1 large cucumber,
   sliced thin

Place vegetable fruit mixture in a salad bowl.

OR IN PLACE OF ABOVE:
4 cups mixed raw fruit, sliced
   thin [use any two or combination
   of apples, firm pears, oranges,
   pineapple, firm melons, green
   mangoes, cucumbers]

¹/₂ to 3 dried chili peppers,
   minced
   OR ¹/₂ to 1 tsp. sambal olek
     [canned chili peppers]
1 tsp. trassi
   [shrimp paste], minced
   OR fish paste, minced
   OR spice cake, minced
   OR anchovy paste
2 Tbsp. peanut oil
   OR vegetable oil

Mince chilies and trassi together so chilies don't scatter. Heat a small cast iron frying pan. Add oil. Heat 1 minute. Add trassi and chili. Stir and fry over medium heat 1 minute.

2 Tbsp. mild honey
¹/₂ tsp. molasses
2 Tbsp. tamarind water
   OR lemon juice
2 Tbsp. water

Add to chili and trassi. Stir and fry 3 to 5 minutes until slightly thickened. Remove from heat. Pour over vegetables or fruit. Serve as a salad, as part of a feast, or as a dessert. Good for lunch next day.

TAHU GORENG KETJAP [FRIED BEAN CURD AND VEGETABLES WITH SOY DRESSING] [Serves 4 to 6]

2 to 3 cakes bean curd, cut into 1 by 2 inch pieces
½ cup peanut oil
   OR vegetable oil

   OR IN PLACE OF ABOVE:
4 to 5 cakes age [deep fried bean curd], cut into ½ by ¼ inch slices

Drain bean curd well. Heat a large cast iron frying pan. Add oil. Heat until a piece of bean curd added sizzles. Add half of bean curd. Fry 3 to 5 minutes until lightly browned. Turn once. Remove from oil and drain well. Continue until all bean curd fried. Do not fry age.

2 cups bean sprouts
1 large cucumber, sliced thin

Steam sprouts 30 seconds. Place on a rack to cool. Arrange with cucumbers on a platter. Place fried bean curd on top of vegetables.

2 cloves garlic, crushed and minced
¼ yellow onion, minced
¼ to 1 fresh chili pepper, minced
   OR ¼ to 2 dried chili peppers, minced
   OR ¼ to 1 tsp. sambal olek [canned chili pepper]
½ tsp. sea salt
2 Tbsp. peanut oil
   OR vegetable oil

Mince chilies and onions together so chilies don't scatter. Heat medium cast iron skillet. Add oil. Heat until a small piece of onion added sizzles. Add ingredients. Stir and fry 5 to 10 minutes over medium heat until onions are soft and transparent.

4 Tbsp. Indonesian soy sauce
1 Tbsp. mild honey

Add to onion mixture. Bring to boil. Simmer over low heat 2 to 3 minutes until mixture just begins to thicken.

2 Tbsp. lemon juice
   OR tamarind water

Add to sauce and mix well. Pour over vegetables and bean curd. Serve at once. Good as a salad or can serve as a vegetarian main dish served with rice. Good on a hot summer day. Good cold for lunch the next day. Also served at a feast.

SOUPS AND HOT VEGETABLES

Many soups and hot vegetables are served as main dishes as well as being merely dishes acocmpanying a meal. If they contain a protein source such as eggs, bean curd, prawns or meat they combine well with rice or noodle dishes and pickles or sambals for a nutritious meal. These dishes are also included in feasts.

PETJEL [PEANUT SAUCE WITH HOT COOKED VEGETABLES]
[Serves 4 to 6]

⅓ cup crunchy peanut butter
1 to 2 chili peppers, minced
   OR ½ to 1 tsp. sambal olek
    [canned chili peppers]
1 clove garlic, crushed and
  minced
½ yellow onion, minced
1 tsp. trassi
  [shrimp paste], minced
  OR fish paste, minced
  OR spice cake, minced
  OR anchovy paste
1 Tbsp. mild honey
1 tsp. molasses
½ tsp. sea salt
½ cup thick coconut milk

Mince onions and chilies together so chilies don't scatter. Mix ingredients well. If a blender is used leave onions and garlic in large chunks. Blend with coconut milk and then add other ingredients. If no blender is available mince all ingredients well. Mix sauce well. Place in saucepan. Heat over medium heat 2 to 3 minutes.

½ head cabbage, shredded
  OR 1 lb. spinach, sliced
    thin
  OR 1 lb. broccoli, stems
    cut into thin diagonals
    and heads broken into
    small pieces
  OR 1 lb. green beans, cut
    into thin diagonal slices
  OR 2 to 3 carrots, cut into
    thin diagonal slices

Steam cabbage or spinach 3 minutes. Steam other vegetables 5 to 8 minutes until bright colored and just tender. Serve one or several vegetables hot with warm sauce on side or poured over them. Good vegetable side dish for main meal.

SOP TAHU SAJUR [VEGETABLE AND COCONUT MILK SOUP WITH BEAN CURD] [Serves 6]

2 Tbsp. peanut oil
  OR vegetable oil
1 large yellow onion, cut in
  half lengthwise and thinly
  sliced
1 clove garlic, crushed and
  minced

Heat a large saucepan over medium heat. Add oil. Heat until a small piece of onion added sizzles. Add onion and garlic. Stir and fry 5 to 10 minutes until onions are soft and transparent but not brown.

½ tsp. sea salt
½ to 1 tsp. trassi
  [shrimp paste], minced
  OR fish paste, minced
  OR spice cake, minced
  OR anchovy paste
3 Indonesian laurel leaves
  OR curry leaves
  OR bay leaves
¼ tsp. black pepper
2 tsp. coriander, ground
½ tsp. cumin, ground
1 to 2 dried chili peppers,
  minced
  OR fresh chili peppers,
    minced

Mince chilies and trassi together so chilies don't scatter. Add to onions and mix well. Stir and fry 1 to 2 minutes until a paste forms.

2½ cups chicken stock
  [See Basic Chinese section]
  OR soybean stock
    [See Basic Chinese
    section]
4 cups coconut milk

Add to onions and spice paste. Mix well. Cover and bring to boil over medium heat.

¼ head cabbage, shredded
¼ lb. green beans, cut into
  long thin diagonals
1 medium carrot, cut into long
  thin diagonals
1 green pepper, seeded and
  julienned

Add vegetables. Cover pot and quickly bring to boil. Reduce heat to low and simmer 5 to 8 minutes until vegetables are just tender.

OR IN PLACE OF ABOVE:
If only cabbage and carrots
are available use:
¼ head large cabbage, shredded
  and
2 to 3 carrots, cut into thin
  diagonal slices

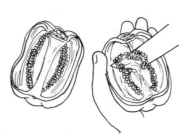

1 cake bean curd, cut into
  ½ inch cubes

Add bean curd and simmer 2 minutes. Serve at once. Good main dish served with rice or noodles. Excellent feast dish.

VARIATION:

SOP TELOR SAJUR [VEGETABLE AND COCONUT MILK SOUP WITH EGGS] [Serves 6]

6 to 8 hard-boiled eggs, cut in half lengthwise

Follow recipe for Sop Tahu Sajur but replace bean curd with eggs. Cook as directed. Good main dish served with rice or noodles. Excellent lunch soup. Good feast dish.

VARIATION:

SOP AJAM SAJUR [VEGETABLE AND COCONUT MILK SOUP WITH CHICKEN] [Serves 6]

1 to 2 chicken breasts, cut into ½ inch cubes
2 Tbsp. peanut oil OR vegetable oil

Heat a large saucepan over medium heat. Add oil. Heat until a small piece of chicken added sizzles. Add chicken. Stir and fry 5 to 10 minutes until lightly browned. Remove from pan. Drain. Set aside to add later.

Follow recipe for Sop Tahu Sajur. Use chicken stock. Add chicken to dish in place of bean curd. Simmer 2 to 3 more minutes and serve at once. Good main dish served with rice or noodles. Excellent feast dish.

VARIATION:

SOP SAJUR [VEGETABLE COCONUT MILK SOUP WITH BEEF, CHICKEN, SHRIMP, ETC.] [Serves 4 to 6]

1 cup cooked beef, cut into thin strips
OR cooked meat [chicken, turkey, duck, pork, lamb, rabbit] cut into thin strips
OR ¼ lb. cooked shrimp
OR ½ lb. cooked fish, cut into 1 by 3 inch pieces

2½ cups meat stock
OR 2½ cups fish stock [See Basic Chinese section]
OR 2½ cups shrimp stock

Follow recipe for Sop Tahu Sajur but replace bean curd with meat or fish and use meat or fish stock. Cook as directed. Good main dish served with rice or noodles. Excellent lunch soup. Good feast dish.

SOP HATI AJAM [CHICKEN LIVER SOUP] [Serves 4 to 6]

1 yellow onion, minced
¼ inch fresh ginger root, grated
½ cup green beans, cut into thin diagonal slices
3 Tbsp. peanut oil OR vegetable oil

Heat a heavy cast iron saucepan over medium heat. Add oil. Heat until a small piece of onion added sizzles. Add onions, ginger and beans. Stir and fry 5 to 10 minutes until onions are soft and transparent but not brown.

½ to 1 tsp. trassi [shrimp paste], minced
OR fish paste, minced
OR spice cake, minced
OR anchovy paste

Add to onions and beans. Mix well. Fry 1 minute.

¼ lb. chicken livers, cut into long thin slices
1 Tbsp. Indonesian soy sauce
½ tsp. sea salt
¼ tsp. black pepper

Add to onions and beans. Mix gently. Stir and fry 3 to 5 minutes until liver is cooked.

5 cups chicken stock [See Basic Chinese section]

Add stock to onion, beans and liver. Mix gently. Bring to boil over medium high heat.

¼ head cabbage, shredded
OR ½ lb. bean sprouts

Add vegetables to soup. Cover. Simmer 5 to 10 minutes until just tender but still bright in color. If using bean sprouts add to soup, mix and serve at once.

1 Tbsp. lemon juice
OR tamarind water

Add to soup just before serving. Mix well. Serve hot. Good main dish as well as soup. Serve with rice or noodle dish. Good lunch soup. Excellent feast dish.

SAJUR KERRIE [CURRIED VEGETABLES IN COCONUT MILK] [Serves 4 to 6]

1 large yellow onion, cut in half
    lengthwise and sliced thin
1 to 2 cloves garlic, crushed
    and minced
2 Tbsp. peanut oil
    OR vegetable oil

Heat a large saucepan over medium heat. Add oil. Heat until a small piece of onion added sizzles. Add onions and garlic. Stir and fry 5 to 10 minutes until onions are soft and transparent but not brown.

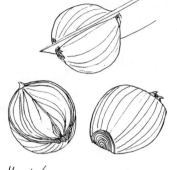

½ tsp. turmeric
3 Indonesian laurel leaves
    OR curry leaves
    OR bay leaves
½ tsp. lemon grass powder
    OR 1 citrus leaf
    OR 1 tsp. lemon juice
1 tsp. laos
1 tsp. sea salt
½ to 1 chili pepper, minced
    OR ½ to 1 tsp. sambal olek
    [canned chili pepper]

Add to onions and mix well. Stir and fry 1 to 2 minutes until a paste is formed.

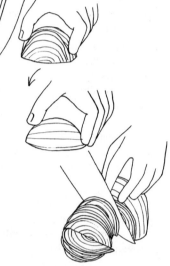

1 cup coconut milk

Slowly add to spice and onion mixture. Cover. Bring to boil over medium heat. Simmer 5 minutes.

2 cups summer squash [yellow
    crookneck, zucchini, etc.], cut
    into thin slices

Add to coconut milk. Mix well. Cover and simmer 5 to 10 minutes until squash just tender. Serve at once. Good with rice and main dish. Good cold for lunch. Excellent feast dish.

VARIATION:

SAJUR AJAM KERRIE [CURRIED CHICKEN AND VEGETABLES IN COCONUT MILK] [Serves 4 to 6]

1 to 2 chicken breasts, cut into
    ½ inch cubes
2 Tbsp. peanut oil
    OR vegetable oil

Heat a large saucepan over meidum heat. Add oil. Heat until a small piece of chicken added sizzles. Add chicken. Stir and fry 5 to 10 minutes until lightly browned. Remove from pan. Drain. Set aside to add later. Follow recipe for Sajur Kerrie. Add chicken after squash has cooked 5 minutes. Simmer until squash in tender. Good main dish served with rice or noodles. Good cold for lunch. Excellent feast dish.

VARIATION:

SAJUR TAHU KERRIE [CURRIED BEAN CURD WITH VEGETABLES IN COCONUT MILK] [Serves 4 to 6]

1 to 2 blocks bean curd, cut into
    ½ by 2 inch slices

Follow recipe for Sajur Kerrie. Add bean curd after squash has cooked 5 minutes. Simmer until squash is tender. Mix gently so bean curd does not break apart. Good vegetarian main dish when served with rice or noodles. Excellent cold for lunch. Good feast dish.

VARIATION:

SAJUR TELOR KERRIE [CURRIED EGGS AND VEGETABLES IN COCONUT MILK] [Serves 4 to 6]

6 to 8 hard-boiled eggs, cut in half
    lengthwise

Follow recipe for Sajur Kerrie. Add eggs yolkside up after squash has cooked 5 minutes. Simmer until squash is tender. Serve at once. Good as main dish when served with rice or noodles. Good cold for lunch. Excellent feast dish.

GULAI PARKIE [VEGETABLE AND COCONUT MILK STEW] [Serves 4 to 6]

2 Tbsp. peanut oil
  OR vegetable oil
2 to 3 small dried fish, crushed
  OR 2 tsp. trassi [shrimp paste], minced
  OR fish paste, minced
  OR spice cake, minced
  OR 1 tsp. anchovy paste
5 to 6 almonds, minced or blended fine
  OR 6 to 10 cashews, minced or blended fine
  OR 2 to 3 macadamia nuts, grated
1 slice fresh ginger root, minced
1 tsp. turmeric
1 to 2 chili peppers, minced
  OR ½ to 1 tsp. sambal olek [canned chili peppers]
1 yellow onion, minced
1 to 2 cloves garlic, crushed and minced

Mince chilies and onions together so chilies won't scatter all over. Heat a large heavy saucepan. Add oil. Heat until a small piece of onion added sizzles. Add ingredients. Stir and fry over medium heat 5 to 10 minutes until onions are soft and transparent and paste forms with spices.

2 cups thick coconut milk
1 tsp. sea salt
¼ cup tamarind water
  OR lemon juice
1 stalk lemon grass
  OR 2 citrus leaves
  OR ½ tsp. lemon grass powder

Add to above paste slowly. Mix well. Bring to a boil. Cook 5 to 10 minutes at medium high heat until liquid is reduced. Stir occasionally.

1 lb. broccoli, stems cut into long thin diagonals and heads broken into small pieces
  OR 2 to 3 large carrots, cut into long thin diagonal slices
  OR 1 lb. green beans, cut into long thin diagonal slices
  OR ½ large head green cabbage, cut into 1 inch cubes

Steam vegetables 5 minutes but do not steam cabbage. Use only one kind of vegetable. Add to coconut milk. Cover. Simmer 3 to 5 minutes until vegetable is just tender. Mix occasionally. Serve at once. If chilled can be reheated once. Good served with rice and a main dish for dinner. Good cold for lunch. Excellent feast dish.

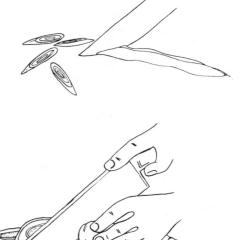

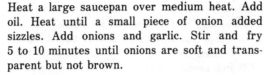

SAJUR LODEH TJAMPUR [VEGETABLES COOKED IN BEEF BROTH AND COCONUT MILK] [Serves 4 to 6]

1 yellow onion, cut in half
  lengthwise and sliced thin
1 small clove garlic, crushed
  and minced
2 Tbsp. peanut oil
  OR vegetable oil

Heat a large saucepan over medium heat. Add oil. Heat until a small piece of onion added sizzles. Add onions and garlic. Stir and fry 5 to 10 minutes until onions are soft and transparent but not brown.

1 tsp. laos
½ to 2 tsp. sambal olek
  [canned chili peppers]
  OR ½ to 2 chili peppers, minced
1 tsp. koenjit [optional]
1 tsp. coriander, ground
2 Indonesian laurel leaves, minced
  OR curry leaves, minced
  OR bay leaves, minced
½ tsp. trassi
  [shrimp paste], minced
  OR fish paste, minced
  OR spice cake, minced
  OR anchovy paste.
½ tsp. sea salt

Mince trassi and chilies together so chilies don't scatter. Add to onions and mix well. Stir and fry 1 to 2 minutes until a paste forms.

2 cups beef broth
2 cups coconut milk

Slowly add to spice and onion mix. Bring to a boil over medium high heat.

½ head cabbage, shredded
  OR Chinese cabbage, shredded
2 carrots, cut into thin diagonals
¼ lb. green beans, cut into thin
  diagonals
¼ head cauliflower,
  cut into flowerlets

Steam carrots, green beans and cauliflower 2 to 3 minutes, but do not steam cabbage. Add steamed vegetables and cabbage to broth. Mix and simmer 5 to 10 minutes until vegetables just tender. Do not overcook.

1 cup bean sprouts

Add to vegetables and broth. Mix well. Serve at once. Good main dish served with rice or noodles. Good soup also. Excellent lunch soup. Excellent feast dish.

SAJUR [VEGETABLES COOKED IN COCONUT MILK] [Serves 6]

3 Tbsp. peanut oil
  OR vegetable oil
2 medium yellow onions, cut
  in half lengthwise and then
  cut into paper-thin slices
½ tsp. trassi
  [shrimp paste], minced
  OR fish paste, minced
  OR spice cake, minced
  OR anchovy paste

Heat a large saucepan over medium heat. Add oil. Heat until a small piece of onion added sizzles. Add onions and trassi. Stir and fry 5 to 10 minutes until onions are soft and lightly browned.

1 clove garlic, crushed and
  minced
2 tsp. laos
1 tsp. paprika
¼ to 1 tsp. chili pepper,
  minced
  OR sambal olek
    [canned chili pepper]
3 Indonesian laurel leaves,
  minced
  OR curry leaves, minced
  OR bay leaves, minced
2 tsp. cumin, ground
1 tsp. tamarind water
  OR lemon juice
1 tsp. mild honey

Add to onions. Mix well. Fry 1 to 2 minutes until a paste is formed.

3 cups coconut milk

Slowly add to spice paste. Cover and bring to boil over medium heat.

½ head cabbage, shredded

Add cabbage. Cover and bring to boil again. Reduce heat. Simmer 5 minutes.

½ lb. small shrimp
  OR 6 to 8 hard-boiled eggs,
    cut in half lengthwise

Add to vegetables. Simmer an additional 5 minutes. Serve immediately. Good soup or main dish. Serve with rice or noodles. Excellent lunch soup. Good feast dish.

VARIATION:

Sajur is also good with carrots, squash, or green beans added to the cabbage or used in place of it. Reduce the amount of cabbage if other vegetables are added and adjust the cooking time so that the vegetables are still slightly crisp when the dish is served. Good main dish with rice or noodles. Excellent lunch soup. Good feast dish.

VARIATION:

SAJUR AJAM [VEGETABLES COOKED IN COCONUT MILK WITH CHICKEN]
[Serves 4 to 6]
1 to 2 chicken breasts, meat
  removed and cut into ½ to 1 inch
  strips
2 Tbsp. peanut oil
  OR vegetable oil

OR IN PLACE OF ABOVE:
1 to 2 cups cooked chicken meat,
  shredded

Heat a large saucepan over medium heat until a piece of chicken added sizzles. Add chicken. Stir and fry 5 to 10 minutes until golden brown. Remove from pan. Drain. Set aside to add when eggs or shrimp are added to Sajur I. Follow recipe for Sajur I but add cooked chicken in place of shrimp or eggs. Good soup or main dish. Serve with rice or noodles. Excellent lunch soup. Good feast dish.

SAJUR LABUH [SQUASH COOKED IN COCONUT MILK] [Serves 4 to 6]

1 large yellow onion, minced
1 clove garlic, crushed and
  minced
1 tsp. to 1 Tbsp. trassi
  [shrimp paste], minced
  OR fish paste, minced
  OR spice cake, minced
  OR 1 tsp. anchovy paste
3 Tbsp. peanut oil
  OR vegetable oil

Heat a heavy saucepan over medium heat. Add oil. Heat until a small piece of onion added sizzles. Add ingredients. Stir and fry 5 to 10 minutes until onions are soft and transparent but not brown.

4 to 5 macadamia nuts, grated
  OR ¼ cup cashews, grated

Nuts can be processed in blender for 15 seconds or grate until quite fine. Add to onions. Fry over low heat 2 to 3 minutes until just brown.

¼ cup coconut milk
¼ cup chicken stock
  [See Basic Chinese section]
  OR ½ cup coconut milk and
    no stock

Add to onions and nuts. Mix well. Increase heat to medium high. Simmer 2 to 3 minutes.

3 to 4 cups zucchini or other
  summer squash, cut into
  1 inch cubes

Add to onions and coconut milk. Mix well with sauce. Cover. Simmer 5 to 10 minutes until just tender. Serve hot. Good served with a main dish and rice for a dinner meal. Good cold for lunch. Excellent feast dish.

VARIATION:

HARD VEGETABLE SAJUR [HARD VEGETABLES COOKED IN COCONUT MILK] [Serves 4 to 6]
1 lb. green beans, cut into thin
  diagonal slices
  OR 3 to 4 carrots, cut into thin
    diagonal slices

Steam vegetables 3 to 5 minutes until just tender. Add to stock and spices in place of zucchini in Sajur Labuh. Cook as directed. Serve at once. Good served with main dish and rice for dinner. Good cold next day for lunch. Excellent feast dish.

VARIATION:

CABBAGE AND VEGETABLES COOKED IN COCONUT MILK [Serves 4 to 6]
½ head cabbage, shredded
  OR a combination of green bean
    slices, carrot slices, cabbage
    slices, and 1 cup bean sprouts

Steam hard vegetables 3 to 5 minutes. Add cabbage to stock and spices in place of zucchini in Sajur Labuh. Simmer 3 to 8 minutes until just tender. If sprouts are used add just before serving dish. Serve at once. Good served with main dish and rice for dinner. Good cold for lunch next day. Excellent feast dish.

SAJUR LODEH BETAWI [VEGETABLES AND SHRIMP COOKED IN COCONUT MILK] [Serves 4 to 6]

2 medium yellow onions, cut in
  half lengthwise and sliced thin
1 clove garlic, crushed and
  minced
½ to 1 tsp. trassi
  [shrimp paste], minced
  OR fish paste, minced
  OR spice cake, minced
  OR anchovy paste
2 Tbsp. peanut oil
  OR vegetable oil

Heat a heavy saucepan over medium heat. Add oil. Heat until a piece of onion added sizzles. Add onions, garlic and trassi. Stir and fry 5 to 10 minutes until onions are soft and transparent.

2 tsp. laos
1 tsp. paprika
½ to 1 dried chili pepper,
   minced
3 Indonesian laurel leaves
   OR curry leaves
   OR bay leaves
2 tsp. cumin, ground
¼ tsp. black pepper
1 tsp. mild honey
drop of molasses
1 tsp. sea salt

Add to onion mixture. Mix well. Stir and fry 2 to 3 minutes until a paste forms.

3 cups coconut milk
1 tsp. tamarind water
   OR lemon juice

Slowly add coconut milk to spice paste. Add tamarind or lemon juice. Mix well. Bring to boil over high heat.

½ head cabbage, shredded
   OR 1 lb. green beans, cut into
     thin diagonal slices,
     steam 3 minutes
   OR 1 lb. broccoli, stems cut
     into thin diagonal slices and
     heads broken into small
     pieces, steam 3 minutes
   OR combination of beans and
     cabbage

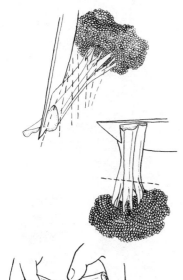

Add vegetables to coconut milk. Cook over medium high heat 5 to 10 minutes until vegetables just tender. Stir occasionally.

½ lb. shrimp

Add to vegetables and coconut milk. Mix well. Simmer 3 more minutes. Serve at once. Good with rice as a main dish for one-pot meal. Also good for lunch. Use as soup for large meal. Excellent feast dish.

VARIATION:

VEGETABLES AND MEAT BALLS COOKED IN COCONUT MILK [Serves 4 to 6]
6 to 8 oz. ground meat [beef, pork
   or lamb or combination of meat]
   OR Macroburger
1 small yellow onion, grated
1 small clove garlic, crushed and
   minced
½ tsp. cumin, ground
1 tsp. coriander, ground
½ tsp. sea salt
1/8 to 1 tsp. chili pepper

3 Tbsp. vegetable oil

Heat heavy cast iron skillet over medium heat. Add oil. Heat until meat ball added sizzles. Add meat balls. Stir and fry 3 to 5 minutes until lightly browned. Remove from pan. Drain. Set aside for later use. Follow recipe for Sajur Lodeh Betawi. Substitute meat balls for shrimp. After meat balls are added, simmer 10 to 15 minutes. Serve hot. Good meal-in-a-bowl when served with rice. Good for lunch or at a feast.

VARIATION:

SAJUR TELOR LODEH [VEGETABLES AND EGGS COOKED IN COCONUT MILK] [Serves 4 to 6]
6 to 8 hard-boiled eggs, cut in half
   lengthwise

Follow recipe for Sajur Lodeh Betawi. Substitute eggs for shrimp. Simmer 3 minutes. Serve at once. Good meal-in-a-bowl when served with rice. Good for lunch or at a feast.

VARIATION:

SAJUR TAHU LODEH [VEGETABLES AND BEAN CURD COOKED IN COCONUT MILK] [Serves 4 to 6]
1 to 2 blocks bean curd, cut into
   ½ by 2 inch slices

Follow recipe for Sajur Lodeh Betawi. Substitute bean curd for shrimp. Simmer 3 minutes. Serve at once. Mix gently so bean curd does not break into pieces. Good meal-in-a-bowl when served with rice. Good lunch or feast dish.

SAMBAL GORENG SAJUR [HOT FRIED VEGETABLES IN COCONUT MILK]
[Serves 4 to 6]

3 to 4 carrots, cut into thin
  diagonal slices
  OR 1 lb. green beans, cut into
    long thin diagonal slices
  OR 1 small head cauliflower,
    broken into 1 inch flowerlets
  OR 1 lb. broccoli, stems cut into
    thin diagonals and heads
    broken into 1 inch flowerlets

  OR ½ head medium cabbage,
    cut into ¼ inch slices

Steam 3 to 5 minutes until just beginning to get tender and still bright colored.

Steam 30 seconds.

2 Tbsp. peanut oil
  OR vegetable oil
1 tsp. cumin, ground
1 tsp. coriander, ground
2 tsp. trassi
  [shrimp paste], minced
  OR fish paste, minced
  OR spice cake, minced
  OR 1 tsp. anchovy paste
1 clove garlic, crushed and
  minced
⅓ yellow onion, minced
1 to 2 chili peppers, minced
  OR 1 to 2 tsp. sambal olek
  [canned chili peppers]

Mince chilies and onions together so chilies don't scatter. Heat a large saucepan over medium heat. Add oil. Heat until a small piece of garlic added sizzles. Add garlic, onion and spices. Fry 3 to 5 minutes until onions are soft. Add vegetables. Stir and fry 3 to 5 minutes until well mixed with spices.

1 cup coconut milk

Slowly add coconut milk to vegetables. Bring to boil over medium high heat. Reduce heat and simmer 5 minutes until liquid reduced but vegetables still slightly crisp. Serve hot. Good main meal side dish. Excellent feast dish.

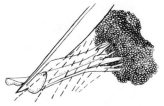

VARIATION:

SAMBAL GORENG UDANG SAJUR [HOT FRIED VEGETABLES WITH PRAWNS IN COCONUT MILK] [Serves 4 to 6]

1 lb. large prawns, shelled and
  deveined
3 cups water

Bring water to boil in a large saucepan. Add prawns. Reduce heat. Simmer 3 to 5 minutes until flesh turns pinkish white. Remove from water. Drain. Save stock for use in soups. Follow recipe for Sambal Goreng Sajur. Add to vegetables after coconut milk. Cook as directed. Serve hot. Good one-pot meal served with rice. Good lunch. Excellent feast dish.

VARIATION:

SAMBAL GORENG BABI SAJUR [HOT FRIED VEGETABLES WITH PORK IN COCONUT MILK[[Serves 4 to 6]

½ lb. pork, cut into thin slices
2 to 3 Tbsp. peanut oil
  OR vegetable oil
½ tsp. sea salt
dash of chili pepper

Heat a wok over high heat. Add oil and heat until a haze forms. Add pork. Stir and fry 5 to 8 minutes until browned. Sprinkle meat with salt and chili pepper. Mix well. Remove from pan to add later. Follow recipe for Sambal Goreng Sajur. Add meat after coconut milk. Cook as directed. Serve hot. Good one-pot meal served with rice. Good lunch. Excellent feast dish.

VARIATION:

SAMBAL GORENG TAHU SAJUR [HOT FRIED VEGETABLES IN COCONUT MILK] [serves 4 to 6]

1 lb. bean curd,
  cut into 1 inch cubes
¼ cup tamarind water
  OR lemon juice
½ tsp. sea salt

½ cup peanut oil
  OR vegetable oil

Soak bean curd in liquid for 1 hour. Mix gently. Drain well and pat dry.

Heat a large heavy frying pan. Add oil. Heat until a small piece of tofu added sizzles. Add half of bean curd. Fry 3 to 5 minutes over medium high heat until lightly browned. Turn once. Remove from oil and drain well. Fry rest of bean curd. Set aside to add to sauce later. Follow recipe for Sambal Goreng Sajur. Add bean curd with coconut milk. Mix well. Cook as directed. Serve hot. Good one-pot-meal dish when served with rice. Good lunch dish. Excellent feast dish.

VARIATION:

SAMBAL GORENG TELOR SAJUR [HOT FRIED VEGETABLES WITH EGGS IN COCONUT MILK] [Serves 4 to 6]

6 to 8 hard-boiled eggs, cut in half
  lengthwise

Follow recipe for Sambal Goreng Sajur. Add eggs yolkside up to vegetables and coconut milk. Baste eggs with coconut milk. Cook as directed. Serve hot. Good one-pot meal served with rice. Good lunch dish or rice table feast dish.

VARIATION:

SAMBAL GORENG IKAN SAJUR [HOT FRIED VEGETABLES WITH FISH IN COCONUT MILK] [Serves 4 to 6]

1 lb. white fish, cut into 1 inch
  by 3 inch pieces
2 to 3 Tbsp. peanut oil
  OR vegetable oil

Heat a castiron frying pan over medium heat. Add oil. Heat until a piece of fish added sizzles. Fry fish 5 to 10 minutes until golden brown on each side. Remove from oil. Drain. Add to vegetables after coconut milk. Cook as directed. Serve hot. Good one-pot meal dish when served with rice. Good lunch dish. Excellent feast dish.

VARIATION:

SAMBAL GORENG AJAM SAJUR [HOT FRIED VEGETABLES WITH CHICKEN IN COCONUT MILK] [Serves 4 to 6]

1 to 2 chicken breasts, cut into
  1 inch slices
2 to 3 Tbsp. peanut oil
  OR vegetable oil

Heat a cast iron skillet over medium heat. Add oil. Heat until piece of chicken added sizzles. Add chicken. Stir and fry 5 to 10 minutes until golden brown. Remove from pan with slotted spoon. Drain.

½ tsp. sea salt
dash chili pepper

Sprinkle sea salt and chili pepper over chicken. Mix well. Follow recipe for Sambal Goreng Sajur. Add chicken to vegetables after coconut milk. Cook as directed. Serve hot. Good one-pot meal served with rice. Good lunch. Excellent feast dish.

VARIATION:

HOT FRIED VEGETABLES WITH PRAWNS AND FISH COOKED IN COCONUT MILK [Serves 4 to 6]

½ lb. white fish, cooked as in
  Sambal Goreng Ikan Sajur and
½ lb. large prawns, cooked as in
  Sambal Goreng Udang Sajur

Follow recipe for Sambal Goreng Sajur. Add to vegetables after coconut milk. Cook as directed. Served hot. Good one-pot meal served with rice. Good lunch. Good feast dish.

VARIATION:

SAMBAL GORENG DENGENG SAJUR [HOT FRIED VEGETABLES WITH BEEF IN COCONUT MILK] [Serves 4 to 6]

½ lb. beef [stew meat, round
  steak, chuck steak, etc.] cut into
  thin slices - if cut very thin, pot
  roast may be used
2 to 3 Tbsp. peanut oil
  OR vegetable oil
½ tsp. sea salt
dash of ground chili pepper

Heat a wok over high heat. Add oil. Heat until oil forms a haze. Add beef. Stir and fry quickly 3 to 5 minutes until meat turns brown. Sprinkle salt and chili over meat. Mix well. Remove from pan to add later. Follow recipe for Sambal Goreng Sajur. Add meat after coconut milk. Cook as directed. Serve hot. Good one-pot meal served with rice. Good lunch. Excellent feast dish.

VEGETARIAN MAIN DISHES

These dishes may be served as a main course, with rice and a vegetable dish in a simple meal, or as part of the elaborate Indonesian feast. For other vegetarian main dishes see the Rice and Noodle, Soups and Hot Vegetables, and Cold Dressed Vegetable and Fruit sections.

SAMBAL GORENG TAHU [HOT FRIED BEAN CURD] [Serves 4 to 6]

2 to 3 cakes bean curd

Wrap each cake tightly in muslin cloth (old sheet good). Place in sink on a board with a pan of water or rock or some heavy weight on it. Press for 2 to 3 hours or overnight. Cut into 1 inch cubes.

½ cup peanut oil
  OR vegetable oil

Heak a wok. Add oil. Heat until a small piece of bean curd added sizzles. Add half of bean curd. Simmer on one side for 3 to 5 minutes until lightly browned then turn and fry on other side. Remove from oil and drain. Cook remainder. Set aside to use later.

2 Tbsp. peanut oil
  OR vegetable oil
1 large yellow onion, chopped
1 large clove garlic, crushed
  and minced
1 tsp. trassi
  [shrimp paste], minced
  OR fish paste, minced
  OR spice cake, minced
  OR anchovy paste
1 Tbsp. fresh chili pepper,
  cut into thin strips
  OR 1 to 2 tsp. dried chili
    pepper, minced
  OR 1 to 2 tsp. sambal olek
    [canned chili peppers]

Mince onion and chilies together so chilies don't scatter. Heat a heavy cast iron skillet over medium heat. Add oil. Heat until a small piece of onion added sizzles. Add ingredients. Mix well. Stir and fry 5 to 10 minutes until onions are soft and transparent.

1 cup thick coconut milk
1 to 2 Indonesian laurel leaves
  OR curry leaves
  OR bay leaves
1 tsp. sea salt

Add ingredients to onion and spice mixture. Mix well. Bring to boil over medium high heat. Simmer 3 to 5 minutes until slightly thickened. Add fried bean curd. Mix well. Simmer 1 to 2 minutes.

1 Tbsp. tamarind water
  OR lemon juice

Add to sauce and bean curd. Mix well. Serve at once. Good with rice or noodle dish and cold vegetable salad or Gado Gado platter. Good cold for lunch with rice and pickles. Excellent feast dish.

TAHU DADAR [BEAN CURD OMELET WITH PEANUT SAUCE] [Serves 4 to 6]

1 Tbsp. Indonesian soy sauce
2 Tbsp. peanut butter
6 Tbsp. coconut milk
2 tsp. honey
½ tsp. coriander, ground
pinch of cumin, ground

Mix ingredients well. Place in a small saucepan or double boiler. Heat 2 to 3 minutes until hot but not boiling. Stir constantly to prevent sticking. Keep warm in double boiler to pour over omelette.

1 to 2 cakes bean curd

Break into small pieces and break up slightly with a fork. Place in a colander and drain well.

4 eggs
½ tsp. sea salt
¼ tsp. trassi
  [shrimp paste], minced
  OR fish cake, minced
  OR spice cake, minced

Mix in a blender. Blend 10 to 15 seconds until eggs are light and frothy. If no blender is available beat eggs until light and frothy. Fold in bean curd. Mix well.

2 Tbsp. peanut oil
  OR vegetable oil

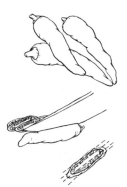

Heat a medium-size cast iron skillet over medium heat. Add oil. Heat until a small drop of egg mixture sets on bottom of the pan. Pour egg mixture into center of skillet. Let it follow oil out to edges. Allow to set 1 to 2 minutes until bottom set. Push egg mixture to center of pan with spoon. Continue until mixture still moist and slightly runny. Reduce heat to medium low. Cover and cook 10 minutes. Do not disturb. Remove cover and loosen edges of omlette with a knife. Place plate over top of skillet and invert skillet so omelette falls on plate. Slip back into skillet and cook 1 to 2 more minutes. Place plate over top and invert again onto plate. Pour peanut butter sauce over. Serve at once. Good served with rice and vegetable dish. Good cold for lunch with rice and pickles. Excellent feast dish, cut into 1 inch diamonds. Serve as one of dishes around bottom of the rice cone platter.

TELOR DADAR BUMBU [HOT OMELET WITH COCONUT MILK] [Serves 4]

6 eggs
2 Tbsp. coconut milk
½ tsp. trassi
  [shrimp paste], minced
  OR fish paste, minced
  OR spice cake, minced
1 small clove garlic,
  crushed and minced

Mix in a blender. Blend 10 to 15 seconds until eggs are light and frothy. If no blender is available beat eggs and other ingredients until light and frothy.

¼ to 1 large fresh red chili
  pepper, julienned
  OR ¼ to 2 dried chili
    peppers, minced
2 Tbsp. peanut oil
  OR vegetable oil

Heat a medium-size cast iron skillet over medium heat. Add oil. Heat until a small piece of pepper added sizzles. Add pepper and fry for 1 minute over medium heat.

6 green onions, cut into
  thin diagonal slices

Pour egg mixture into center of skillet. Let it follow oil out to the edges. Allow to sit for 1 to 2 minutes until bottom has set. Add onions. Mix well. Push egg mixture towards the center with a spoon until eggs moist and still slightly runny. Reduce heat to medium low. Cover and cook for 10 minutes. Do not disturb. Remove cover and loosen edges of omelet with a knife. Place plate over the top of skillet and invert so omelet falls on plate. Slip omelet back into pan and cook 1 to 2 more minutes. Place plate over top again and invert pan. Serve at once. Good for lunch. Also good served with rice and vegetables for a main meal. Excellent feast dish, cut into 1 inch diamonds. Serve as one of dishes around the bottom of the rice cone platter.

TELOR OPOR [EGGS COOKED IN COCONUT MILK] [Serves 4 to 6]

1 Tbsp. water
  [use in blender only]
½ yellow onion, minced
1 tsp. cumin, ground
2 tsp. coriander, ground
¼ to ½ tsp. chili pepper,
  ground
½ inch fresh ginger root,
  crushed and minced
1 clove garlic, crushed and
  minced
3 Indonesian laurel leaves
  OR curry leaves
  OR bay leaves

If blender is used leave all ingredients in large pieces. Add onion and water to blender. Process until well blended. Add garlic and ginger. Process 5 seconds until well blended. Add remaining ingredients and process 10 seconds until well mixed and paste is formed. Mince chilies and onion together so chilies don't scatter. If no blender is available mince and crush everything well and mix together into a paste. (A mortar and pestle is good for this.)

2 Tbsp. peanut oil
  OR vegetable oil

Heat a heavy saucepan over medium heat. Add oil. Heat until a small piece of paste added sizzles. Add spice paste. Stir and fry 3 to 5 minutes until paste is browned.

1 tsp. tamarind water
  OR lemon juice
1 Tbsp. mild honey
½ tsp. Indonesian soy sauce
½ tsp. sea salt

Add to spice paste and mix well. Simmer 2 to 3 minutes.

1½ cups coconut milk

Slowly add to spice paste. Bring to boil over medium high heat.

6 to 8 hard-boiled eggs, cut
  in half lengthwise

Cut eggs in half lengthwise. Set eggs in coconut milk yolkside up. Baste eggs and simmer 10 minutes. Serve hot. Good served with rice and vegetables. Good cold for lunch with rice or noodles and pickles. Excellent feast dish.

VARIATION:

EGGS COOKED IN COCONUT MILK WITH VEGETABLES [Serves 4 to 6]

2 cups green beans, cut into thin
  diagonal slices
  OR 2 cups broccoli, cut into thin
      diagonal slices with heads
      broken into small pieces
  OR 2 cups carrots, cut into thin
      diagonal slices
  OR 2 cups cabbage, cut into
      ¼ inch slices

Follow recipe for Telor Opor. Add vegetables after coconut milk and before eggs. Mix well. Add eggs. Cook as directed. Simmer 5 to 10 minutes until vegetables are just tender. Baste eggs occasionally. Good one-dish meal served with rice. Good cold for lunch with rice. Excellent feast dish.

TELOR KETJAP [EGGS COOKED IN SOY SAUCE] [Serves 4 to 6]

8 to 12 eggs, hard boiled

Peel and prick eggs with fork. Cut in half length wise.

1 small yellow onion, grated
1 clove garlic, grated
2 Tbsp. peanut oil
  OR vegetable oil

Heat a saucepan over medium heat. Add oil. Heat until a piece of onion added sizzles. Add onions and garlic. Stir and fry 2 to 3 minutes until lightly browned.

3 Tbsp. Indonesian soy sauce
1 tsp. cinnamon
½ tsp. sea salt
¼ tsp. black pepper

Add to onion mixture. Stir. Add eggs. Let mixture boil up around eggs and baste eggs well 1 to 2 minutes.

½ cup coconut milk
  OR water

Add to eggs and sauce. Reduce heat to medium low. Mix well. Baste eggs. Allow to simmer 5 to 10 minutes until most of liquid is absorbed. Serve hot. Good with rice and vegetable dish for main meal. Good cold for lunch. Excellent feast dish.

PERKADEL DJAGUNG [CORN FRITTERS] [Serves 4 to 6]

2 cups kernel corn
2 to 4 Tbsp. water
1 clove garlic,
  crushed and minced

Reserve ¼ cup kernel corn. Blend ingredients 15 to 20 seconds until well broken up but still a few kernels showing. If no blender is available chop corn well and crush some of corn in mortar and pestle. Mix blended and unblended corn.

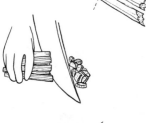

½ stalk celery, minced
  OR 1 cup cabbage, shredded
  OR ½ cup green peas
4 green onions, minced
1 to 3 chili peppers, minced
2 eggs, slightly beaten
4 Tbsp. whole wheat flour
2 Tbsp. arrowroot starch
2 tsp. coriander, ground
½ tsp. cumin, ground
1 tsp. sea salt

Mince chilies and onion together so chilies don't scatter. Add ingredients to corn mixture. Mix well. Allow to sit for 10 minutes to an hour.

⅓ cup peanut oil
  OR vegetable oil

Heat a heavy cast iron skillet over heat just above medium. Add one third of oil. Heat until a small bit of batter added sets. Add 2 Tbsp. of batter at a time and fry three fritters at a time. Make small pancake-type fritters. Fry 3 to 5 minutes. Turn and brown on other side. When oil is low add more oil to pan before frying more fritters. They should be crispy. Keep warm in oven until all fritters are fried. Serve hot. Good cold for lunch the next day. Good main dish served with rice and pickles. Excellent feast dish. Serve as one of dishes around bottom of the rice cone platter.

FISH, CHICKEN AND MEAT MAIN DISHES

SATE IKAN [GRILLED FISH MARINATED IN PEANUT SAUCE] [Serves 4 to 6]

1 large yellow onion, minced
2 cloves garlic, crushed and
  minced
¼ cup tamarind water
  OR lemon juice
2 Tbsp. mild honey
¼ cup Indonesian soy sauce
½ tsp. sea salt
½ tsp. black pepper
2 Tbsp. coriander, ground
½ to 2 tsp. chili peppers,
  minced
  OR sambal olek
    [canned chili peppers]
1 cup peanut butter

Leave ingredients in large pieces if blender is used. Blend all ingredients well in order in which they are given. Add peanut butter in small amounts at end. If no blender is available mince everything fine and then mix well. Mince chilies and onions together so chilies don't scatter. Place mixture in a saucepan and bring to boil over medium heat. Stir frequently as sauce tends to burn easily. Cook 5 to 10 minutes until sauce thickens.

½ cup melted butter
  OR coconut butter
½ cup chicken stock
  [See Basic Chinese ingredients]
  OR fish stock
  [See Basic Chinese
  ingredients]

Add to sauce and mix well. Remove from heat. Cool to room temperature.

1 to 2 lbs. firm white fish
[swordfish, red snapper, sole,
cod, etc.], cut into ½ inch
cubes

Marinate in sauce for 3 hours or overnight. Thread fish on long skewers. Oil grill or broiler pan. Grill or broil slowly 15 minutes until fish is golden brown and done. Turn often so peanut sauce does not burn. Heat remaining sauce over low heat 5 minutes until changes to darker sauce. Stir frequently to prevent burning. Serve with sauce. An excellent main dish served with a rice and vegetable dish. A must at a feast. Good cold next day for lunch with rice and pickles.

VARIATION:

SATE UDANG [GRILLED PRAWNS IN PEANUT SAUCE] [Serves 4 to 6]

1½ to 2 lbs. raw prawns,
  shelled and deveined,
  threaded on long skewers

Use recipe for Sate Ikan Sauce. Use raw prawns in place of fish. Cook as directed. Serve with sauce. An excellent main dish served with rice and a vegetable dish. A must at a feast. Good cold for lunch with rice and pickles.

IKAN KETJAP [FISH COOKED IN SOY SAUCE] [Serves 4 to 6]

1 large yellow onion,
  chopped
1 clove garlic,
  crushed and minced
¼ to 2 tsp. chili pepper,
  minced
    OR sambal olek
      [canned chili peppers]
2 Indonesian laurel leaves,
  minced
    OR curry leaves, minced
    OR bay leaves, minced
1 lb. fish, cut into ½ inch
  cubes
2 Tbsp. peanut oil
    OR vegetable oil

Mince onions and chilies together so chilies don't scatter. Heat a heavy cast iron skillet over medium high heat. Add oil. Heat until a small piece of onion added sizzles. Add ingredients. Stir and fry 10 minutes until fish is cooked and onions are soft and transparent.

¼ cup Indonesian soy sauce
1 Tbsp. mild honey
1 tsp. dark molasses
1 tsp. coriander, ground
¼ cup tamarind water
    OR lemon juice
½ tsp. sea salt

Add to fish and mix well. Allow to simmer 10 more minutes or until sauce thickens. Serve hot. Good quick dinner served with rice and shrimp dressed salad, Asinan. Good cold for lunch with rice and pickles. Excellent feast dish.

VARIATION:

UDANG KETJAP
[PRAWNS COOKED IN SOY SAUCE]
[Serves 4 to 6]

½ to 1 lb. prawns,
  shelled and deveined,
  chopped
    OR ½ to 1 lb. small shrimp,
      chopped
1 Tbsp. tomato paste

Use prawns in place of fish. Follow recipe for Ikan Ketjap. Do not use cumin. Cook as directed. Serve hot or cold. Good quick dinner served with rice and shrimp dressed salad, Asinan. Good cold next day for lunch. Excellent feast dish.

SAMBAL GORENG UDANG [SPICY FRIED PRAWNS IN COCONUT SAUCE]
[Serves 4 to 6]

3 to 4 chili peppers,
  minced or blended fine
1 yellow onion, minced
2 cloves garlic,
  crushed and minced
½ tsp. loas
1 Tbsp. coconut oil
  OR vegetable oil

Place in a blender. Blend to a smooth paste. If no blender is available mix ingredients well.

1 tsp. vegetable oil

Heat a heavy saucepan over medium heat. Add oil. Heat until a small drop of paste added sizzles. Add paste. Stir and fry 3 to 5 minutes until just brown.

¾ to 1 lb. raw prawns,
  shelled and deveined

Add prawns to sauce. Stir and fry 2 to 3 minutes until prawns well coated with sauce and just turned pink.

¼ cup thick coconut milk
1 Tbsp. tamarind water
  OR lime juice
2 Indonesian laurel leaves
  OR curry leaves
  OR bay leaves
½ tsp. sea salt
1 tsp. Indonesian soy sauce

Add to prawns. Mix well. Cover. Simmer 5 minutes. Serve hot with rice and a vegetable dish. Excellent feast dish.

SATE UDANG [GRILLED PRAWNS MARINATED IN SPICY COCONUT MILK]
[Serves 4 to 6]

¼ to ½ tsp. trassi
  OR fish paste
  OR spice cake
1 clove garlic,
  crushed and minced
1 stalk lemon grass, powdered
  OR 1 tsp. lemon grass powder
  OR 1 Tbsp. lemon juice
1 to 2 chili peppers, minced
¼ tsp. sea salt
⅓ cup thick coconut milk
1 Tbsp. lime juice
1 tsp. mild honey
1 tsp. Indonesian soy sauce
1 Tbsp. vegetable oil
¼ cup peanut butter

Blend ingredients well until a smooth paste is formed. If no blender is available mix until a smooth paste is formed.

1 lb. raw prawns,
  shelled and deveined

Place prawns and sauce together in a bowl. Marinate 1 to 2 hours. Place on skewers. Grill 8 to 10 minutes until prawns are pink. Serve hot or cold with rice and a vegetable dish.

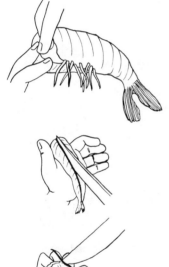

SAMBAL PANGANG IKAN [BAKED FISH IN RED PEPPER SAUCE] [Serves 4 to 6]

1 whole fish with head if possible,
  scored on both sides
   OR 2 large fillets, scored on
    both sides
¼ cup peanut oil
  OR vegetable oil

Heat a large cast iron skillet over medium heat. Add oil. Heat until a small piece of fish added sizzles. Add fish. Fry 5 to 8 minutes until browned on both sides. Turn once. Remove from pan and drain.

2 fresh red chili peppers, minced
  OR green chili peppers, minced
  OR 2 tsp. sambal olek
    [canned chili peppers]
  OR 2 large dried chili peppers,
    minced
2 cloves garlic, crushed and minced
2 medium yellow onions, minced
½ inch fresh ginger root, crushed
  and minced

Mince chilies and onions together so chilies don't scatter. Add to oil fish fried in. Stir and fry over medium heat 5 to 10 minutes until onions are soft and transparent.

½ cup yellow bean sauce
  OR light miso
  OR pureed cooked soybeans
1 Tbsp. mild honey

Add to onion mixture. Mix well. Simmer 2 to 3 minutes.

1½ cups coconut milk

Add to sauce slowly. Mix well. Add fish and baste well with sauce. Bake in a 350° oven 20 minutes. Baste fish frequently. Serve hot. Good served with rice and vegetable dish for dinner. Excellent feast dish. Good cold for lunch with rice and pickles.

BUMBU PANGANG IKAN [BAKED SPICY FISH] [Serves 4 to 6]

1 whole fish with head if possible,
  scored on both sides
   OR 2 large fillets, scored
    on both sides
1 tsp. sea salt
¼ to 1 tsp. chili pepper, minced
2 cloves garlic, crushed and minced

Mix garlic, salt and chili together. Rub fish well with garlic, pepper and salt. Place in a buttered casserole. Bake at 350°, 10 minutes.

½ cup melted coconut butter
  OR butter
3 Tbsp. tamarind water
  OR lemon juice
2 Indonesian laurel leaves,
  minced
  OR curry leaves, minced
  OR bay leaves, minced
1 tsp. laos
¼ to 1 tsp. chili peppers,
  minced
  OR sambal olek
    [canned chili peppers]
1 tsp. mild honey
¼ cup Indonesian soy sauce

Mix ingredients. Blend. If no blender is available, mix well. Baste fish with ⅓ of sauce after it has baked first 10 minutes. Baste again in 5 minutes with another ⅓ of sauce. Repeat in another 5 minutes. Allow to bake 5 more minutes. Place fish on serving platter and pour sauce over fish. Good main meal dish served with rice and vegetables. Excellent feast dish. Good cold for lunch with rice and pickles.

IKAN OPOR [FISH COOKED IN COCONUT MILK] [Serves 6]

1 Tbsp. water
  [for blender only]
1 tsp. laos
½ tsp. sambal olek
  [canned chili peppers]
  OR ½ to 1 chili pepper,
    minced
1 yellow onion, minced
1 clove garlic, crushed and minced
2 Indonesian laurel leaves, minced
  OR curry leaves, minced
  OR bay leaves, minced

Add onion and water to blender. Process until well blended. Add garlic. Process another 5 seconds until well blended. Add remaining ingredients. Process 10 seconds until well mixed and a paste is formed. If no blender is available mince and crush everything well and mix into a paste. Mince onion and chilies together so chilies don't scatter.

2 Tbsp. peanut oil
  OR vegetable oil

Heat a heavy saucepan over low heat. Add oil. Heat until a small piece of paste added sizzles. Add paste. Stir and fry 5 to 8 minutes until a brown paste is formed.

1 Tbsp. tamarind water
  OR lemon juice

Add to spice mix. Mix well. Stir and fry 2 to 3 minutes.

1½ cups coconut milk

Slowly add to spice paste. Bring to boil over medium heat.

2 lbs. white fish fillet,
  cut in 2 inch slices
3 Tbsp. peanut oil
  OR vegetable oil

Heat a heavy cast iron skillet over medium heat. Add oil. Heat until a small piece of fish added sizzles. Add fish. Fry 5 to 8 minutes until just brown. Turn once. Remove from pan. Drain. Add to spices and coconut milk. Simmer 5 to 10 minutes over low heat until fish flaky. Baste often. Serve hot. Good with rice and a cold vegetable dish. Good served cold for lunch next day. Good feast dish.

VARIATION:

FISH COOKED IN COCONUT MILK WITH VEGETABLES [Serves 6]

½ lb. green beans, cut into long
  thin diagonals
  OR ½ lb. broccoli, stems cut
    into long thin diagonals,
    with heads broken into
    small pieces
  OR 2 to 3 carrots, cut into thin
    diagonal slices

Steam vegetables 5 minutes. Follow recipe for Ikan Opor but add vegetables with fish. Simmer 5 to 10 minutes until fish is flaky and vegetables are just tender. A good meal-in-a-bowl served with rice or noodles. Good feast dish.

BUMBU GORENG IKAN [SPICY FRIED FISH] [Serves 4 to 6]

Sauce:

2 Tbsp. peanut oil
  OR vegetable oil
1 medium yellow onion,
  minced
1/2 to 2 tsp. chili pepper,
  minced
  OR sambal olek
    [canned chili pepper]

Heat a medium cast iron skillet over medium heat. Heat until a small piece of onion added sizzles. Add onions and chili. Stir and fry 5 to 10 minutes until onions are soft and transparent.

1/2 cup tamarind water
  OR lemon juice
1 tsp. Indonesian soy sauce
1/4 tsp. laos
1/2 tsp. trassi
  [shrimp paste], minced
  OR fish paste, minced
1 tsp. mild honey
1/2 tsp. molasses
1/2 tsp. lemon grass powder
  OR 1 to 2 crushed lime
    leaves
  OR 1 Tbsp. lime juice
2 thin slices fresh ginger root,
  minced
1 tsp. sea salt

Add ingredients to onions. Increase heat to medium high. Simmer 3 to 5 minutes until sauce thickens. Stir often.

1 Tbsp. tomato paste

Add to sauce. Mix well. Simmer 30 seconds. Remove from heat and keep hot to pour over fried fish.

1/2 to 1 lb. white fish fillet
3 Tbsp. peanut oil
  OR vegetable oil

Heat large cast iron skillet over medium heat. Heat slightly. Add fish and fry 5 to 8 minutes on one side. Turn and brown other side 5 to 10 minutes until fish is flaky. Remove from pan and place on serving platter. Pour sauce over fish. Serve hot. Good main dish with rice and vegetables. Excellent cold for lunch the next day. Good dish to serve at a feast.

SAMBAL GORENG UDANG [HOT FRIED DRIED SHRIMP] [Serves 4 to 6]

1/4 lb. dried shrimp
4 cups boiling water

Place shrimp and boiling water in a bowl. Cover. Allow to soak 30 minutes to 1 hour. Remove from water and wash well. Drain. Save shrimp water to use as fish stock.

2 Tbsp. peanut oil
OR vegetable oil
½ yellow onion, minced
1 clove garlic, crushed and
minced
1 tsp. lemon grass powder
OR 1 Tbsp. lemon juice
OR 1 to 2 citrus leaves,
crushed
1 tsp. laos
½ to 1 tsp. sambal olek
[canned chili peppers]
OR ½ to 2 chili peppers,
minced
¼ to 1 tsp. trassi
[shrimp paste], minced
OR fish paste [minced]
OR anchovy paste
1 tsp. mild honey

Mince onion and chilies together so chilies don't scatter. Heat a medium cast iron skillet over medium heat. Add oil. Heat until a small piece of onion added sizzles. Add ingredients. Stir and fry 5 to 10 minutes until a paste forms with the onions and spices.

1 Tbsp. tamarind water
OR lemon juice
2 Indonesian laurel leaves,
minced
OR curry leaves, minced
OR bay leaves, minced
½ tsp. sea salt
1 Tbsp. tomato paste

Add to onions. Mix well. Add shrimp. Mix well. Simmer 2 to 5 minutes until shrimp well coated with sauce.

1 cup thick coconut milk

Add to mixture slowly. Mix well. Bring to boil over medium heat. Stir often. Cook 5 to 10 minutes until sauce thickens and shrimp are tender. Good main dish with rice and Sajur. Good side dish for a feast. Excellent cold for lunch with rice and pickles.

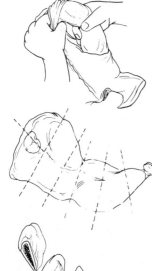

AJAM KETJAP [CHICKEN COOKED IN SOY SAUCE] [Serves 4 to 6]

1 tsp. sambal olek
[canned chili peppers]
OR ½ to 2 chili peppers,
minced
1 yellow onion, chopped
1 clove garlic, crushed and
minced
½ tsp. sea salt
½ to 1 skinned chicken cut into
1 inch pieces
1 tsp. laos [optional]
3 Tbsp. peanut oil
OR vegetable oil

Mince chilies with onion so chilies don't scatter. Heat a heavy cast iron skillet over medium high heat. Add oil. Heat until a small piece of onion added sizzles. Add all ingredients. Stir and fry 10 minutes until chicken is just brown and onions are soft and transparent.

⅓ cup Indonesian soy sauce
1 tsp. mild honey
1 tsp. dark molasses
1 Tbsp. rice vinegar

Add to chicken. Mix well. Cover. Simmer 20 minutes. Remove cover. Simmer 5 to 10 minutes until liquid is almost all absorbed and sauce thickens. Serve hot. Good main dish with rice and vegetable dish. Good cold for lunch the next day. Excellent feast dish.

SATE AJAM [GRILLED CHICKEN IN PEANUT SAUCE] [Serves 4 to 6]

1 large yellow onion, minced
2 cloves garlic, crushed and
   minced
¼ cup tamarind water
   OR lemon juice
¼ to 1 chili pepper, minced
   OR ¼ to 1 tsp. sambal olek
     [canned chili pepper]
¼ cup Indonesian soy sauce
½ tsp. sea salt
½ tsp. black pepper
2 Tbsp. coriander, ground
1 cup peanut butter

Blend all ingredients together well in the order in which they are given. Add peanut butter in small amounts at end. Blend well. If no blender is available mince everything fine. Mince onions and chilies together so chilies don't scatter. Mix well. Place mixture in a saucepan. Bring to boil over low heat. Stir often. Cook 5 to 10 minutes until sauce thickens.

¼ cup coconut milk
½ cup chicken stock
   [See Basic Chinese section]

Add to sauce. Mix well. Remove from heat. Allow to cool to room temperature.

1½ lbs. skinned filleted chicken,
   cut into ¼ inch cubes

   OR 1 chicken cut into
     1 inch cubes

Marinate in sauce 3 hours or overnight. Thread chicken on long skewers. Oil grill or broiler pan. Grill or broil slowly for 20 to 25 minutes until chicken is done. Turn often so peanut sauce does not burn. Heat remainder of sauce 5 minutes over low heat until the sauce turns darker brown. Stir often to prevent burning. Serve with grilled chicken. Serve hot. A must at a feast. Good main dish with rice and cold vegetable dish. Good cold for lunch next day.

RADJANG AJAM [CHICKEN WITH SPICES AND TOMATOES] [Serves 4 to 6]

2 tsp. water [for blender only]
2 cloves garlic,
   minced
3 to 5 red chili peppers, minced
½ tsp. turmeric
½ inch fresh ginger root,
   crushed and minced
1 Tbsp. mild honey
½ tsp. sea salt
3 Tbsp. peanut oil
   OR vegetable oil

If a blender is used leave ingredients in large pieces and use water. Grind all ingredients except oil in a blender for 30 seconds until well mixed and a paste is formed. Mince onion and chilies together so chilies don't scatter. If no blender is available crush and mince all ingredients and then mix well. Heat a cast iron skillet. Add oil. Heat until a small amount of spice mix added sizzles. Stir and fry 2 to 3 minutes over medium heat until a brown paste is formed.

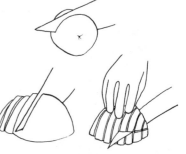

3 Indonesian laurel leaves,
   minced
   OR curry leaves, minced
   OR bay leaves, minced
3 tomatoes, cubed
   OR 1 cup stewed tomatoes
1 large yellow onion, minced
½ tsp. laos

Add to spice paste. Stir and fry over medium heat for 5 to 10 minutes until onions are soft and tomatoes well mixed.

½ to 1 skinned chicken, cut
   into small pieces

Add to tomato sauce and stir and fry 10 to 15 minutes until meat turns white and browns slightly.

½ cup chicken stock
   [See Basic Chinese section]

Add to chicken. Mix well. Cover. Bring to boil. Reduce heat to low. Simmer 30 to 40 minutes until chicken is done. Remove lid. Allow liquid to reduce for 5 to 10 minutes. Stir often. Serve hot. Good served with rice and a vegetable dish. Excellent next day cold for lunch or heated for dinner. Good feast dish.

SATE BUMBU AJAM [MARINATED GRILLED CHICKEN WITH PEANUT SAUCE] [Serves 4 to 6]

½ to 1 skinned chicken cut into 1 inch pieces
1 tsp. sea salt
¼ tsp. black pepper

Sprinkle chicken with salt and pepper. Mix well.

3 cloves garlic, crushed and minced
¼ yellow onion, minced
1 Tbsp. coriander, ground
1 tsp. cumin, ground
½ cup coconut milk
2 Tbsp. Indonesian soy sauce
¼ tsp. white pepper

Combine in a bowl. Mix well. Add chicken. Marinate 1 hour or overnight. Thread chicken on long skewers. Grill or broil slowly for 15 to 20 minutes until soft and brown. Serve hot with the following sauce.

Sauce:

½ medium yellow onion, minced
1 clove garlic, crushed and minced
½ inch fresh ginger root, crushed and minced
¼ to 2 tsp. sambal olek [canned chili peppers]
   OR ¼ to 2 chili peppers, minced
½ tsp. trassi [shrimp paste], minced
   OR fish paste, minced
   OR anchovy paste

Combine in a blender. Blend until paste is formed. If no blender is available mince everything fine and mix well. Mince chilies and onion together so chilies don't scatter.

2 Tbsp. peanut oil
   OR vegetable oil

Heat a heavy saucepan over medium heat. Add oil. Heat until a small amount of spice paste added sizzles. Stir and fry 3 to 5 minutes or until onions are limp and transparent or paste is just brown.

¼ cup tamarind water
   OR lemon juice
1 Tbsp. mild honey
2 Tbsp. Indonesian soy sauce
1½ cups chicken stock [See Basic Chinese section]
½ cup peanut butter

Add to spice mix. Mix well. Stir and fry over medium heat for 2 minutes.

Slowly add to spice mixture. Mix well. Reduce heat to medium low. Slowly bring to boil. Simmer 5 to 8 minutes. Stir frequently to prevent sauce from burning. The sauce is done when it coats the spoon like gravy. Serve hot to dip the chicken in. The sauce can be made ahead and stored. It should be reheated before serving. If it has thickened add water when heating to make it the consistency of medium gravy. Good feast dish. For a simple dinner serve with rice and a vegetable dish. Excellent cold for lunch.

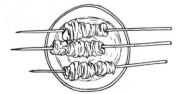

AJAM OPOR [CHICKEN COOKED IN COCONUT MILK WITH SPICES]
[Serves 4 to 6]

⅓ to 1 skinned chicken,
   cut into small pieces
3 Tbsp. peanut oil
  OR vegetable oil

Heat a heavy cast iron skillet over medium high heat. Add oil. Heat until a small piece of chicken added sizzles. Add chicken. Fry over medium high heat 5 to 10 minutes until just golden brown. Remove from oil. Drain.

1 tsp. cumin, ground
2 tsp. coriander, ground
¼ to 1 tsp. sambal olek
   [canned chili peppers]
   OR ¼ to 2 chili peppers,
     minced
pinch cloves
pinch cinnamon
pinch laos [optional]
½ inch fresh ginger root,
   grated
1 clove garlic, grated
1 yellow onion, minced
3 Indonesian laurel leaves,
   minced
  OR curry leaves, minced
  OR bay leaves, minced

Add onion to blender. Process until well blended. Add garlic and ginger. Process another 5 seconds until well blended. Add remaining ingredients. Process 10 seconds until well mixed and a paste is formed. Mince chilies and onions together so chilies don't scatter. If no blender is available mince and crush everything well. Mix into a paste. Add to oil in which chicken was cooked. Stir and fry over medium heat for 3 to 5 minutes until paste is brown.

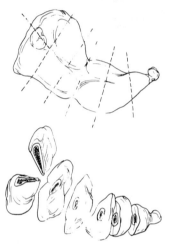

1 Tbsp. mild honey
1 tsp. tamarind water
  OR lemon juice
½ tsp. Indonesian soy sauce
½ tsp. sea salt

Add to spice mix. Mix well. Stir and fry for 2 minutes.

1½ cups coconut milk

Slowly add to spice paste. Bring to boil over medium heat. Add cooked chicken. Reduce heat to medium low. Cook for 30 to 40 minutes or until chicken is soft. Serve hot. Good main dish with rice and cold vegetables. Excellent feast dish. Good cold for lunch.

VARIATION:
CHICKEN COOKED IN COCONUT MILK WITH SPICES AND VEGETABLES [Serves 4 to 6]

½ lb. green beans, cut into long
   thin diagonals
  OR ½ lb. broccoli, stems cut
     into long thin diagonals,
     with heads broken into
     small pieces
  OR 2 to 3 carrots, cut into thin
     diagonal slices

Steam vegetables 5 minutes. Follow recipe for Ajam Opor but add vegetables 10 minutes before chicken is done. Cook until vegetables are just tender and chicken is done. A good meal-in-a-bowl served with rice or noodles. Good feast dish. Excellent cold for lunch.

HATI—HATI [CHICKEN GIBLETS FRIED WITH VEGETABLES AND COCONUT MILK] [Serves 4]

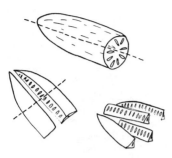

1 medium cucumber, cut into
  1 inch by 3 inch pieces
¼ lb. green beans, cut into thin
  diagonal slices
1 vegetable pear, cut into
  ¼ inch slices
  OR 1 small yellow crookneck
    squash, cut into ¼ inch
    diagonal slices
  OR 2 summer squash, cut into
    ¼ inch diagonal slices
  OR 2 firm winter pears, cut
    into ¼ inch slices
1 tsp. sea salt

Sprinkle vegetables with sea salt. Crush slightly with hands. Mix well. Allow to sit 15 minutes. Pour off liquid.

2 Tbsp. rice vinegar
  OR apple cider vinegar
1 Tbsp. mild honey

Mix well with vegetables. Set aside. Marinate 20 minutes.

1 small yellow onion, minced
1 clove garlic, crushed and
  minced
3 thin slices fresh ginger root,
  crushed and minced
½ tsp. sea salt
½ to 2 tsp. sambal olek
  [canned chili peppers]
  OR ½ to 2 chili peppers,
    minced
½ to 1 tsp. trassi
  [shrimp paste], minced
  OR fish paste, minced
  OR anchovy paste
2 to 3 Tbsp. peanut oil
  OR vegetable oil

Mince onion and chilies together so chilies don't scatter. Heat a cast iron skillet over medium heat. Add oil. Heat until a small piece of onion added sizzles. Add all ingredients. Stir and fry 5 to 10 minutes until onions are soft and transparent.

1 lb. chicken giblets, cut into
  ¼ slices [Pressure cook
  gizzards 2 to 3 minutes first]

Add to onions. Stir and fry gently 5 to 10 minutes until brown.

3 Tbsp. Indonesian soy sauce

Add to onion, giblet mixture. Stir well and cook for 2 to 3 minutes until paste is formed.

1 cup coconut milk

Add to giblet, onion mixture. Bring to boil. Reduce heat to low. Simmer 10 to 15 minutes over low heat uncovered. Add vegetables and vinegar sauce. Simmer 5 minutes until sauce thickens slightly and vegetables are just done. Serve hot. Good meal-in-a-bowl served with rice. Good feast dish.

SATE BUMBU DENGENG [GRILLED SPICY BEEF] [Serves 4 to 6]

3 cloves garlic, crushed and
  minced
½ small yellow onion,
  minced
1 Tbsp. coriander seeds,
  ground
1 tsp. cumin seed, ground
½ cup thick coconut milk
1 Tbsp. Indonesian soy sauce

Mix ingredients well. If a blender is available blend 15 to 30 seconds.

1 to 1½ lbs. beef, cut into
  ½ inch cubes
sea salt
black pepper

Marinate beef in sauce 1 hour or overnight. Place 5 to 6 pieces of meat on each skewer. Sprinkle with salt and pepper. Oil grill or broiler pan. Grill or broil 10 to 15 minutes until well browned. Turn 2 to 3 times. Serve hot with following sauce.

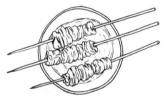

Sauce:

½ medium yellow onion,
  minced
1 clove garlic, crushed and
  minced
½ inch fresh ginger root,
  crushed and minced
¼ to 1 tsp. sambal olek
  [canned chili peppers]
  OR ¼ to 2 chili peppers,
    minced
½ tsp. trassi
  [shrimp paste], minced
  OR fish paste, minced
  OR anchovy paste

Combine in a blender. Blend until paste is formed. If no blender is available mince everything fine and mix well. Mince chilies and onions together so chilies don't scatter.

2 Tbsp. peanut oil
  OR vegetable oil

Heat a heavy saucepan over medium heat. Add oil. Heat until a small amount of spice paste added sizzles. Stir and fry 5 to 8 minutes until onions are limp and transparent or paste is just brown.

¼ cup tamarind water
  OR lemon juice
1 Tbsp. mild honey
2 Tbsp. Indonesian soy sauce

Add to spice mix. Mix well. Stir and fry 2 to 3 minutes.

1½ cups beef stock
½ cup peanut butter

Slowly add to spice mixture. Mix well. Reduce heat to medium low. Slowly bring to boil. Simmer 5 to 8 minutes. Stir frequently to prevent sauce from burning. The sauce is done when it coats the spoon like gravy. Serve hot to dip the beef in. The sauce can be made ahead and stored. It should be reheated before serving. If it has thickened add water when heating to make it the consistency of medium gravy. Good feast dish. For a simple dinner meal serve with rice and a vegetable dish. Good cold for lunch.

VARIATION:

SATE BUMBU BABI [GRILLED SPICY PORK] [Serves 4 to 6]

1 to 1½ lbs. pork, cut into
 ½ inch cubes

Follow recipe for Sate Bumbu Dengeng. Use
pork in place of beef. Cook as directed. Good
feast dish. Serve with rice and vegetables for a
simple meal. Good cold for lunch.

DENGENG MADURA [BEEF MADURA] [Serves 4 to 6]

1 large yellow onion,
 minced
3 cloves garlic, crushed and
 minced
2 thin slices fresh ginger root,
 minced
1 tsp. to 1½ Tbsp. trassi
 [shrimp paste], minced
 OR fish paste, minced
 OR 1 tsp. anchovy paste
1 to 8 chili peppers,
 minced
 OR 1½ tsp. to 2 Tbsp. sambal
  olek [canned chili peppers]
½ tsp. turmeric
¼ tsp. black pepper
3 Tbsp. peanut oil
 OR vegetable oil

Mince chilies and onion together so chilies don't
scatter. Heat a large cast iron skillet over
medium heat. Add oil. Heat until a piece of
onion added sizzles. Add ingredients. Mix well.
Stir and fry 5 to 10 minutes until onions are soft
and transparent.

1 to 2 lbs. beef, cut into
 ½ inch cubes [round, flank
 or chuck steak, stew meat,
 etc.]
1½ tsp. sea salt

Add to onion mixture. Stir and fry 3 to 5
minutes over medium high heat until beef
browns lightly.

½ cup beef stock
 OR water
1 Tbsp. Indonesian soy sauce

Add to beef. Mix well. Cover pan. Simmer
15 to 20 minutes over medium heat until beef is
tender. Good main dish served with rice and
vegetables. Good cold for lunch with rice and
pickles. Excellent feast dish.

VARIATION:

BABI MADURA [PORK MADURA] [Serves 4 to 6]

1 to 2 lbs. pork, cut into
 ½ inch cubes

Use pork in place of beef. Follow recipe for
Dengeng Madura. Cook as directed. Good main
dish served with rice and vegetables. Good cold
for lunch with rice and pickles. Excellent feast
dish.

SATE DENGENG [GRILLED BEEF WITH PEANUT SAUCE] [Serves 4 to 6]

1 large yellow onion, cut in half
   lengthwise, sliced paper thin
2 cloves garlic, crushed and
   minced
¼ cup tamarind water
   OR lemon juice
2 Tbsp. mild honey
¼ cup Indonesian soy sauce
2 Tbsp. coriander, ground
½ to 1 chili pepper, minced
   OR ½ to 1 tsp. sambal olek
     [canned chili pepper]
½ tsp. sea salt
½ tsp. black pepper
1 cup peanut butter

Leave ingredients in large pieces if blender is used. Blend ingredients well in order in which they are given. Add peanut butter in small amounts at end. If no blender is available mince everything fine and then mix well. Place mixture in a saucepan and bring to boil over medium heat. Stir frequently as sauce tends to burn easily. Remove from heat.

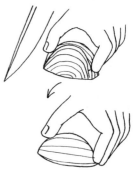

½ cup melted coconut butter
   OR butter
½ cup beef stock

Add to sauce. Mix well. Cool to room temperature.

1 to 2 lbs. beef, cut into
   ½ inch cubes

Add to sauce. Marinate 3 hours to overnight. Thread on long skewers. Grill or broil slowly 15 to 20 minutes until beef is done. Turn often so sauce does not burn. Heat remaining sauce on medium low heat 5 to 10 minutes until sauce turns darker brown. Stir frequently to prevent burning. Serve with hot grilled meat. A must at a feast. Good served with rice and a salad. Good cold for lunch.

VARIATION:

SATE BABI [GRILLED PORK WITH PEANUT SAUCE] [Serves 4 to 6]
1 to 2 lbs. pork, cut into
   ½ inch cubes

Follow recipe for Sate Dengeng. Use pork instead of beef. A must at a feast. Good served with rice and a salad for a simple meal. Good cold for lunch.

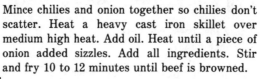

DENGENG KETJAP [BEEF COOKED IN INDONESIAN SOY] [Serves 4 to 6]

½ to 1½ lbs. beef, cut into
   ¼ inch cubes
1½ large yellow onions, chopped
2 cloves garlic, crushed and
   minced
½ to 2 dried chili peppers, minced
   OR ½ to 1 tsp. sambal olek
     [canned chili peppers]
3 Tbsp. peanut oil
   OR vegetable oil

Mince chilies and onion together so chilies don't scatter. Heat a heavy cast iron skillet over medium high heat. Add oil. Heat until a piece of onion added sizzles. Add all ingredients. Stir and fry 10 to 12 minutes until beef is browned.

⅓ cup Indonesian soy sauce
3 Tbsp. mild honey
1 Tbsp. molasses
2 tsp. tamarind water
   OR lemon juice

Add to beef. Mix well. Reduce heat to medium low. Cover and simmer 10 minutes. Mix occasionally. Serve hot with rice and a vegetable dish. Good cold next day for lunch. Excellent feast dish. A fast dinner main dish.

VARIATION:

BABI KETJAP [PORK COOKED IN INDONESIAN SOY] [Serves 4 to 6]

½ to 1½ lbs. pork, cut into
   ¼ inch cubes

Follow recipe for Dengeng Ketjap. Use pork instead of beef. Cook as directed. Serve hot with rice and a vegetable dish. Good cold next day for lunch. A fast dinner main dish. Excellent feast dish.

BABI KETJAP II [BRAISED PORK IN INDONESIAN SOY] [Serves 4 to 6]

1½ to 2 lbs. pork, cut into
   ¼ inch cubes
3 large yellow onions, chopped
2 large cloves garlic, crushed
   and minced
3 thin slices fresh ginger root,
   crushed and minced
1 tsp. coriander
pinch of cumin
2 Indonesian laurel leaves, minced
   OR curry leaves, minced
   OR bay leaves, minced
1 Tbsp. laos
1 to 3 chili peppers, minced
   OR 1 to 3 tsp. sambal olek
      [canned chili peppers]
3 Tbsp. peanut oil
   OR vegetable oil

Mince onion and chilies together so chilies don't scatter. Heat a heavy cast iron skillet over meidum high heat. Add oil. Heat until a piece of onion added sizzles. Add all ingredients. Stir and fry 10 to 12 minutes until pork browned.

2 Tbsp. coconut butter
   OR butter
¼ cup Indonesian soy sauce
2 Tbsp. tamarind water
   OR lemon juice
3 lime leaves, crushed
   OR 1 Tbsp. lime juice
½ tsp. black pepper
1 tsp. sea salt
2 tsp. mild honey
1 tsp. molasses

Add to pork mixture. Reduce heat to medium low. Cover and simmer 10 to 15 minutes. Stir occasionally. Serve hot with rice and a vegetable dish. Good cold the next day for lunch. Excellent feast dish.

VARIATION:

DENGENG KETJAP II [BRAISED BEEF IN INDONESIAN SOY] [Serves 4 to 6]

1½ to 2 lbs. beef, cut into
   ¼ inch cubes

Follow recipe for Babi Ketjap II. Use beef instead of pork. Cook as directed. Serve hot with rice and a vegetable dish. Good the next day cold for lunch. Excellent feast dish.

DENGENG OPOR [BEEF COOKED IN SPICY COCONUT MILK] [Serves 4 to 6]

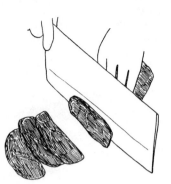

½ to 1 lb. beef, cut into thin slices [partly frozen meat slices easiest]

½ tsp. sea salt

dash ground chili pepper

3 Tbsp. peanut oil
  OR vegetable oil

Heat a heavy cast iron skillet over high heat. Add oil and heat until a haze forms. Add meat. Stir and fry 3 to 5 minutes until lightly browned. Remove from pan. Set aside to use later.

½ large yellow onion, minced

1 large clove garlic, crushed and minced

½ to 1 chili pepper, minced
  OR ½ to 1 tsp. sambal olek [canned chili peppers]

4 thin slices fresh ginger root, minced

2 tsp. coriander, ground

1 tsp. cumin, ground

3 Indonesian laurel leaves, minced
  OR curry leaves, minced

2 tsp. Indonesian soy sauce

Mince chilies and onion together so chilies don't scatter. Reduce heat to medium. Add ingredients. Stir and fry 5 to 10 minutes until onions are soft and a paste forms with spices.

2 Tbsp. tamarind water
  OR lemon juice

Add to spice mix. Mix well.

1 to 1½ cups thick coconut milk

Add coconut milk slowly. Mix well. Bring to boil. Simmer 5 minutes to reduce liquid. Add meat. Cover and simmer 15 to 20 minutes. Serve hot. Good dinner main dish served with rice and a cold vegetable dish. Excellent feast dish.

VARIATION:

DENGENG OPOR II [BEEF COOKED IN SPICY COCONUT MILK WITH VEGETABLES] [Serves 4 to 6]

½ lb. green beans, cut into long thin diagonals
  OR ½ lb. broccoli, stems cut into long thin diagonals, with heads broken into small pieces
  OR 2 to 3 carrots, cut into thin diagonal slices

Steam vegetables 5 minutes. Follow recipe for Dengeng Opor but add vegetables 10 minutes before beef is done. Cook until vegetables are just tender and beef is done. A good meal-in-a-bowl served with rice or noodles. Excellent feast dish.

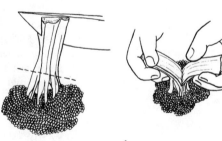

VARIATION:

BABI OPOR [PORK COOKED IN SPICY COCONUT MILK] [Serves 4 to 6]

½ to 1 lb. pork, cut into thin
slices [partly frozen meat
slices easiest]

Follow recipe for Dengeng Opor. Use pork instead of beef. Cook as directed. Serve hot with rice and a cold vegetable dish. Excellent feast dish.

VARIATION

BABI OPOR II [PORK COOKED IN SPICY COCONUT MILK WITH VEGETABLES] [Serves 4 to 6]

½ to 1 lb. pork, cut into thin
slices [partly frozen meat
slices easiest]

½ lb. green beans, cut into
long thin diagonals
OR ½ lb. broccoli, stems cut
into long thin diagonals,
with heads broken into
small pieces
OR 2 to 3 carrots, cut into
thin diagonal slices

Steam vegetables 5 minutes. Follow recipe for Dengeng Opor but use pork in place of beef and add vegetables 10 minutes before pork is done. Cook until vegetables are just tender and pork is done. A good meal-in-a-bowl served with rice or noodles. Good feast dish.

SWEETS

Sweets are usually served as snacks in Indonesia or as part of a feast. The syrups are served as cooling drinks at or between meals. Fresh fruit is the dessert most often served at simple meals.

SARIKAJA [EGG CUSTARD WITH COCONUT MILK] [Serves 6 to 8]

5 eggs	Blend or beat eggs until well mixed but not frothy.
2 Tbsp. dark molasses **¼ cup mild honey** **½ tsp. cinnamon** **¾ cup thick coconut milk**	Add to eggs slowly. Mix well. Pour into a tall pan or deep casserole. Cover. Steam 1 hour or until knife inserted comes out clean. Sarikaja can also be baked at 350° for 45 minutes to 1 hour until a knife inserted comes out clean. Place casserole in a pan of water when baking to prevent curdling. Chill. Serve with fresh fruit. Good snack or dessert. Can be served at a feast.

VARIATION:

CUSTARD WITH FRUIT [Serves 6 to 8]
2 to 3 bananas, sliced
  OR 1 cup fruit [pears,
     strawberries, peaches,
     papayas, etc.], sliced

Add to custard. Mix well. Bake as directed.
Good snack or dessert. Excellent feast dish.

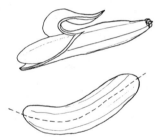

PISANG GORENG [FRIED BANANAS] [Serves 4 to 6]

4 firm ripe bananas	Peel. Cut in half and slice halves lengthwise.
¼ cup peanut oil **OR vegetable oil**	Heat a heavy cast iron skillet over medium high high heat. Add oil. Heat until a small piece of banana added sizzles. Add bananas. Cook 3 to 5 minutes until brown. Turn.
¼ tsp. fresh ground nutmeg **¼ cup lime juice** **1½ Tbsp. mild honey**	Reduce heat to medium. Sprinkle over frying bananas. Cook bananas 5 to 10 minutes until browned. Serve hot. An excellent snack or dessert. Good cold for lunch the next day. Good feast dish.

NANAS GORENG [FRIED PINEAPPLE] [Serves 4 to 6]

1 egg, beaten until well mixed **but not frothy** **2 Tbsp. whole-wheat flour** **1 Tbsp. arrowroot starch** **1 tsp. pineapple juice** **½ tsp. mild honey** **¼ tsp. sea salt**	Mix pineapple juice and honey well. Add to eggs. Mix well. Add other ingredients. Mix until bubbles form in batter. Set aside to chill for 1 hour.

6 to 8 slices fresh pineapple,
  cut into ½ inch slices
  OR 6 to 8 slices unsweetened
    canned pineapple
4 Tbsp. peanut oil
  OR vegetable oil
	Heat a cast iron skillet over medium heat. Add oil. Heat until a small amount of batter added sizzles. Dip pineapple in chilled batter. Fry 5 to 10 minutes until golden brown on both sides. Drain. Place in a deep dish.

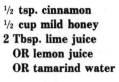

½ tsp. cinnamon
½ cup mild honey
2 Tbsp. lime juice
  OR lemon juice
  OR tamarind water

Combine in a saucepan. Heat until well melted but not boiling. Remove from heat. Pour over pineapple. Serve warm. An excellent snack or dessert. Good cold for lunch the next day. An excellent feast dish.

VARIATION:
APPLES FRIED IN BATTER WITH SWEET SYRUP [Serves 4 to 6]

2 to 3 apples, cut into
  ¼ inch slices
1 tsp. apple juice

Follow recipe for Nanas Goreng. Use apples in place of pineapple and apple juice in place of pineapple juice. Cook as directed. Serve warm. An excellent snack or dessert. Good cold for lunch the next day. An excellent feast dish.

DADAR GULUNG [OMELET ROLLS] [Serves 6 to 8]

4 Tbsp. whole wheat
  pastry flour
4 Tbsp. arrowroot starch
1 Tbsp. mild honey
pinch sea salt
3 eggs
⅔ cup thick coconut milk

Combine ingredients. Beat or blend until a smooth batter is formed. Let sit 1 hour.

1 Tbsp. peanut oil
  OR vegetable oil

Heat a medium sized cast iron skillet over heat just above medium. Oil with a pastry brush dipped in oil or with a piece of paper toweling. Heat until a small amount of batter dripped in pan sets. Pour in about 3 Tbsp. batter (enough to just cover the bottom). Roll pan to distribute batter evenly over bottom. Cook 1 to 2 minutes until edges are browned and curl from sides. Turn and cook 30 seconds to 1 minute on other side. Remove from pan. Re-oil pan. Repeat until all batter is used. Beat batter occasionally while cooking crepes so all flour does not settle to bottom of bowl.

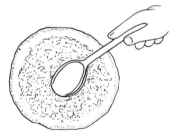

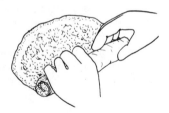

1 cup mild honey
2 Tbsp. lemon juice
  [about ½ lemon]
½ tsp. nutmeg

Combine in a saucepan. Heat until well melted but not boiling. Remove from stove.

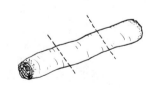

2 cups fresh or dried shredded
  coconut

When pancakes are done, sprinkle each one with 2 to 3 Tbsp. coconut and drizzle 1 to 2 tsp. honey mixture over coconut. Leave 1 inch on crepe free of coconut so it will stay together when rolled. Roll crepe toward unfilled side. Cut into 1 inch slices. Place on tray. When all done pour remaining honey over tray of rolls. Serve hot or cold. An excellent snack or dessert. Also good served at a feast.

SETRUP ASSAM [TAMARIND SYRUP] [Makes 3 cups syrup]

1 cup mild honey 1½ cups water	Place in a saucepan. Bring to boil over high heat. Reduce heat to low and simmer 15 minutes.
½ cup tamarind water	Add to honey syrup and simmer until mixture coats a spoon well. Cool and store in refrigerator. Place 1½ Tbsp. in an 8 oz. glass with ½ cup crushed ice. Add water to fill. Good for summer cooler or served with any Indonesian meal.

VARIATION:

FRUIT SYRUP [Makes 3 cups syrup]

½ cup fruit juice or fruit puree
 [strawberry, raspberry, apple,
 pineapple, papaya, etc.]

Follow recipe for Setrup Assam. Use fruit juice in place of tamarind water. Cook as directed. Good summer cooler or serve with any Indonesian meal.

KOLAK UBI [SWEET POTATO PUDDING] [Serves 4 to 6]

3 Tbsp. coconut butter
  OR dairy butter
2 cups sweet potato, cut in
  ¼ inch pieces
  OR 2 cups carrots, cut into
    pea-sized pieces
	Heat a heavy saucepan over medium high heat. Add butter and melt. Add potatoes. Stir and fry 3 to 5 minutes until potatoes slightly soft.

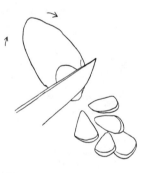

2¾ cups thick coconut milk
½ cup palm sugar
  OR ⅓ cup mild honey
    and
    2 tsp. molasses
1 cinnamon stick
2 to 3 cloves
¼ tsp. sea salt
	Add ½ to ¾ coconut milk to potatoes. Mash potatoes well. Add remaining milk and other ingredients. Mix well. Bring to a boil over medium high heat. Reduce heat to medium low. Simmer 45 minutes to 1 hour until pudding thickens. Stir often to prevent sticking. Pour into individual bowls.

¼ cup nuts [almonds, cashews,
  unsalted macadamia, or
  walnuts], chopped fine
	Sprinkle chopped nuts over bowls of pudding before serving. Serve hot or cold. Good dessert or snack. Good feast dish.

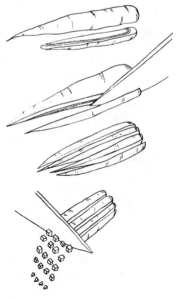

CHAPTER FOUR
INDIAN

INTRODUCTION

Logically the vast sub-continent of India has a varied cuisine. Southern Indians use rice, coconut and lots of spices and chilies. The Punjab in Northern India where most of these recipes are from uses wheat, tomatoes, and spices but not nearly so many chilies. Yeshwant Bakshi, a former Punjabee who gave me many of my recipes, uses chilies with a light hand so these recipes need no adjustment for Western taste. Indian food is always pungent and spicy but does not have to be chili hot.

Most of the ingredients used in Indian cooking are readily available in North America. Many of the vegetables such as peas, beans, cabbage, potatoes, onions and cauliflower are common Western varieties which make the dishes easy to prepare here. For authenticity, a must is the spice mix garam-masala, a mixture of spices and herbs which the West knows as curry powder. Every Indian cook mixes up her own mix and I have included one. Mix your own in small amounts for freshness and flavor as spices deteriorate with age. Tumeric, chilies, cinnamon stick, mustard seed, cumin seed, garlic and fresh ginger root are the other spices and herbs used. Cardamom is used in sweets and can be added to garam-masala. The use of wheat breads which accompany every meal makes Indian cuisine familiar to the western palate.

Indian cooking combines many vegetarian proteins for a well-balanced diet. The food is nutritious and can be easily cooked with little oil making it a low fat cuisine. Vegetables are sauteed in oil, covered and cooked in their own juices or served raw in salads so there is very little vitamin loss. Wheat, rice and numerous types of lentils and beans are cooked in delicious and uncountable styles. Included are the most common methods with suggestions of Indian combinations to get the full use of the proteins. Yoghurt is eaten with almost every meal in a cooling salad or dessert. Most desserts in India are very sweet and made with sugar syrups for which I have substituted honey - small servings are the rule. The other changes I have made are to use brown rice and a raw unsaturated vegetable oil instead of white rice and ghee.

Small, ovenless charcoal stoves are used in India. Breads are grilled over these on dry skillets or fried in small amounts of oil. Breads may also be deep fried. Most other foods are sauteed or deep fried in a wok-like pan called a karhai made of iron or tin-lined brass. A heavy cast iron pan or wok can substitute for this pan. The meat, fish and egg curries are begun with a savory masala of onions, ginger, garlic and other herbs fried in a little oil until tender. Tomato or coconut milk is added and simmered until a thick paste is formed before the spices and other ingredients are added. The dish is then covered and simmered until most of the liquid has evaporated and the main ingredients are tender. Vegetables are sauteed in oil and then simmered until just cooked, dipped in batter and deep fried, or featured cold in salads, or pickled in hot oil and spices. Rice is generally fried with onions and spices and then simmered with tumeric, vegetables and/or raisins for an eye-appealing dish. Most of the desserts included are also cooked on top of the stove. Chutney is ground in a meat grinder or mortar and pestle to add heat or sweetness to Indian meals.

Indian meals are served with all the dishes together on a round tray called a thali. The bread is placed in the center of the thali and small dishes of the various foods being served surround it. The food is then eaten with small pieces of bread. Indian food is not served in courses so can be served easily in a buffet. An Indian cook tries to choose dishes so hot dishes are balanced by cool ones and also takes into consideration the combined appearance of the dishes. I am including simple menus which are easy and fast to prepare. Several elaborate feasts are also described.

MEAL SUGGESTIONS

1 TO 2 PERSONS
Kishmish Pulao/Chapatis
Kima

Egg and Potato Curry
Rice/Chapatis
Peanut Salad

Green Tomato Chutney
Sprout Curry
Pulao/Chapatis
Fruit

Mint Chutney
Dahl
Alu Pulao
Cabbage and Carrot Curry

Upma/Roti
Rhyta
Fruit

3 TO 5 PERSONS
Chutney
Papadums
Channa Curry
Cabbage and Carrot Curry
Pulao/Millet Chapatis
Burphee

Chutney
Kema
Dahl
Pulao/Puree
Green Pepper Curry
Shira

Chutney
Chicken Liver Curry
Pulao/Chapatis
Vegetable Curry
Fruit Salad

Chutney
Pakoras
Dahl
Pulao/Chapatis
Cauliflower Curry
Fruit

Chutney
Curry Tomatoes
Moong Dahl
Pulao/Chapatis
Lado Besan

FEASTS

Vegetarian Feast
Chutney
Papadums
Pulao/Corn flour Chapatis
Dosa, stuffed
Varhya Curry
Carrot Rhyta
Channa Curry
Spinach Balls
Egg Curry
Cabbage and Carrot Curry
Cauliflower Curry with Yoghurt
Galob Jamin

Meat Feast
Mint Chutney
Papadums
Spinach Balls
Deep Fried Channa Dahl
Tamarind Fish
Melon Curry
Kabab
Samosa
Carrot Pickle
Pulao/Chapatis
Chicken Baked with Whole Spices
Vegetable Curry
Rhyta
Burphee

Small Vegetarian Feast
Green Tomato Chutney
Pakoras
Papadums
Pulao/Chapatis
Peanut Salad
Channa Curry
Urd Dahl
Vegetable Curry
Burphee

Small Meat Feast
Chutney
Papadums
Chicken Curry
Kema with Mushrooms
Pulao/Puree
Rhyta
Cabbage and Green Bean Curry
Fruit Salad

BASIC INGREDIENTS

GARAM-MASALA I [STANDARD SPICE MIX]

2 parts coriander
½ to 1 part black pepper
  [½ mild, 1 hot]
1 part cumin
½ part cloves
½ part cinnamon
1 part roasted coconut
  [optional]

Mix spices and herbs together well. Store in a tight container. If whole spices are used blend or grind each one separately and then combine them in the given amounts. Do not mix too much, as spices tend to lose flavor with age. Best with vegetable dishes.

GARAM-MASALA II

2 parts coriander
½ to 1 part black pepper
  [½ mild, 1 hot]
1 part cumin
½ part cloves
½ part cinnamon
¼ to ½ part cardamom

Mix spices and herbs together well. Store in a tight containeer. If whole spices are used blend or grind each one separately and then combine them in the given amounts. Do not mix too much, as spices tend to lose flavor with age. Best with meat dishes.

TAMARIND WATER [Makes 1 cup]

2 Tbsp. dried tamarind,
  chopped
1¼ cup boiling water

Place tamarind in a bowl or blender bottle. Pour boiling water over it. Cover and blend if blender is used. Allow to soak 30 minutes and blend again. If no blender is available allow to soak for 30 minutes to 1 hour. Mash with a fork occasionally. Remove any seeds. Puree pulp and water through a food mill. Keeps refrigerated up to 1 week. Keeps well frozen. Freeze in ice cube trays. Store cubes in plastic bags for easy use.

CHANNA FLOUR [GARBANZO FLOUR]

1 lb. garbanzos

Roast 20 to 30 minutes at 350°. Cool. Grind to a fine powder with a flour mill or ¼ cup at a time in a blender. Sift flour to remove coarse particles. Store in tightly covered container. Keeps about 3 months if kept cool.

MEAT STOCK [Makes 2 quarts]

3 to 4 lbs. meat bones
  [chicken, beef, lamb or
  mutton]
1 inch fresh ginger root,
  crushed
¼ yellow onion,
  cubed
3 quarts water

Place ingredients in a large saucepan. Bring to boil over high heat. Reduce heat to medium. Simmer uncovered for 1 hour. Skim foam from top when first boiling. Remove from heat after 1 hour. Strain stock. Chill to congeal fat. Remove most of fat. Keeps for 1 week in refrigerator. Keeps well frozen. Freeze in ice cube trays. Store cubes in plastic sacks for easy use.

VARHYA [SPICY DRIED LENTIL CAKES] [Makes 40 to 50]

1 cup urad dahl
[see lentil explanation in
Indian Vegetarian Main Dish
section]
1 cup red lentils

Soak 6 hours or overnight in lukewarm water. Drain. Allow to dry 30 minutes to 1 hour. Makes 5 cups soaked lentils.

OR IN PLACE OF ABOVE:
2 cups of either urad dahl
or red lentils

15 Tbsp. water

Place 1 cup soaked lentils in a blender. Add 3 Tbsp. water to lentils. Blend and mix until all lentils are ground and a paste is formed. Place paste in a bowl. Repeat until all lentils are ground. OR grind soaked lentils with a flour mill and add water to flour to make paste.

¾ cup channa
[garbanzo] flour
2 tsp. cumin seed,
coarsely ground
1 Tbsp. garam-masala I
1 Tbsp. sea salt
¼ to ½ tsp. chili pepper,
minced

Add to lentil paste. Mix well. Stir 2 to 3 minutes. Should be thick enough for spoon to stand by itself in pan. Cover. Allow to sit 2 to 3 hours to overnight. Oil 2 large cookie sheets. To form Varhyas: oil the left palm and use it as a platform. Oil a spoon and place 1 heaping tsp. of batter on oiled palm. Shape batter with inside of oiled spoon. Invert hand and drop Varhya onto cookie sheet. Repeat until all batter is used. Dry in sun until light and dry or in a 100° oven for 2 to 3 hours. Turn several times. Dry until Varhyas are very light in weight and bone dry to touch. Store in a tightly covered container. Keep indefinitely in a cool place. Use in vegetarian main dishes.

SPROUTS [Makes about 1 quart]

½ cup mung beans
OR whole urad
OR green lentils

Soak beans overnight in warm water. Drain. Place in covered container. I use a canning jar with holes in the lid or covered with a double layer of cheese cloth held on with a rubber band or canning jar ring. Special lids for sprouting can be purchased at most natural foods stores. Sit jar on side in warm dark place. Rinse sprouts with warm water 2 to 3 times a day. Be sure to rinse completely each time or beans will ferment. Harvest for sprout curry on second or third day; for salads on third or fourth day. Keep in refrigerator up to 1 week.

CHUTNEYS AND PICKLES

Small amounts of chutneys and pickles are used as flavor additive to meals. The pickles eaten with bread and yoghurt dishes make an appetizing lunch. Nut, mint, parsley or coriander chutneys make refreshing vegetable dips for parties.

MINT CHUTNEY [Makes 1½ cups]

1 yellow onion
2 Tbsp. dry shredded coconut
   OR fresh coconut,
      finely grated
1 cup fresh mint,
   tightly packed
1 small green hot pepper
   OR ½ sweet green pepper and
      ¼ to ½ tsp. chili pepper
½ tsp. sea salt

Cut onion in 4 pieces. Place all ingredients in blender. Blend to a paste. If no blender is available grind all ingredients on the finest grind of a meat grinder or mince all ingredients very fine. Mix well. Serve chilled. Excellent with meat or vegetable curries and bread or rice. Good with bread and leftovers for lunch.

VARIATION:

PARSLEY CHUTNEY
[Makes 1½ cups]

1 cup parsley,
   tightly packed

Follow recipe for Mint Chutney. Use parsley in place of mint. Serve chilled. Excellent with meat or vegetable curries and bread or rice. Good with bread and leftovers for lunch.

VARIATION:

CORIANDER CHUTNEY
[Makes 1½ cups]

1 cup coriander leaves,
   tightly packed
1 tsp. cumin seed,
   coarsely ground

Follow recipe for Mint Chutney. Use coriander leaved in place of mint and add cumin seed. Serve chilled. Excellent with meat or vegetable curries and bread or rice. Good with bread and leftovers for lunch.

COCONUT CHUTNEY [Makes 1 cup]

¼ cup fresh grated coconut
   OR ¼ cup dried coconut
      soaked in 2 Tbsp. boiling
      water for 30 minutes
½ large sweet red pepper,
   seeded

¼ cup yoghurt
½ tsp. sea salt
¼ to ½ tsp. chili pepper
   [optional]

Place coconut and sweet pepper in blender. Blend to paste. If no blender is available grind on the finest grind of a meat grinder or mince very fine.

Place in bowl. Add pepper and coconut paste. Fold in gently but well. Chill. Serve cold. Excellent with meat or vegetable curries and bread or rice. Good with bread and leftovers for lunch.

GREEN PEPPER CHUTNEY [Makes 1 cup]

1 yellow onion
½ large sweet green pepper,
   seeded
1 small whole hot green pepper
   OR 1 dried hot green pepper
2 Tbsp. dried coconut
   soaked in 2 Tbsp. boiling
   water for 30 minutes
   OR 2 Tbsp. fresh grated
      coconut
¼ tsp. sea salt

Cut onion into 4 pieces. Place all ingredients in blender. Blend to a paste. If no blender is available grate onion fine and grind pepper on the finest grind of a meat grinder or mince very fine. Add other ingredients and mix well. Chill. Serve cold. Excellent with meat or vegetable curries and bread or rice. Good with bread and leftovers for lunch.

CASHEW CHUTNEY [Makes 1½ cups]

1 cup raw cashews	Blend or grind cashews ¼ cup at a time until finely ground.
1 small hot green pepper **1 inch fresh ginger root,** **crushed and minced** **8 to 10 sprigs parsley** **OR coriander leaves** **1 tsp. sea salt** **1 tsp. garam-masala I** **[optional]** **3 Tbsp. lemon juice**	Add to nuts in blender. Blend to a paste. If no blender is available grind all ingredients well and then mix with lemon juice.
2 Tbsp. yoghurt	Fold into nut and spice mixture. Chill. Serve cold. Good served with fresh vegetables as a dip Excellent with meat or vegetable curries and bread and leftovers for lunch.

VARIATION:

SESAME SEED CHUTNEY
[Makes 1½ cups]

1 cup sesame seeds
½ tsp. cumin seeds,
coarsely ground

Roast sesame seeds 5 to 10 minutes at 300° until just brown. Blend ¼ cup at a time. Follow recipe for Cashew Chutney but use sesame seeds and cumin seeds in place of cashews and garam masala. Chill. Serve cold. Good served with fresh vegetables as a dip. Excellent with meat or vegetable curries and bread or rice. Good with bread and leftovers for lunch.

VARIATION:

ALMOND CHUTNEY
[Makes 1½ cups]

1 cup almonds

Follow recipe for Cashew Chutney. Use almonds in place of cashews. Chill. Serve cold. Good served with fresh vegetables as a dip. Excellent with meat or vegetable curries and bread or rice. Good with bread and leftovers for lunch.

VARIATION:

PEANUT CHUTNEY
[Makes 1½ cups]

1 cup raw peanuts

Roast peanuts 5 to 10 minutes at 300° until just brown. Follow recipe for Cashew Chutney. Use peanuts in place of cashews. Chill. Serve cold. Good served with fresh vegetables as a dip. Excellent with meat or vegetable curries and bread or rice. Good with bread and leftovers for lunch.

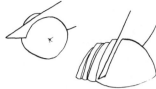

GREEN TOMATO CHUTNEY [Makes 1 quart] One of my favorites!

2 lbs. firm green tomatoes,
  cubed
1 Tbsp. sea salt
2 tsp. cumin seed
½ to 1 tsp. chili pepper
1 inch fresh ginger root,
  minced
1 cup mild honey
¼ cup dark molasses
2 tsp. garam-masala I
1 to 2 whole heads of garlic,
  each clove crushed and minced
1½ cups apple cider vinegar

Place all ingredients in a heavy saucepan. Bring to boil over high heat. Reduce heat to medium low. Simmer uncovered 1 to 2 hours until mixture thickens. Stir frequently to prevent sticking. Just before removing from heat take out 2 cups of mixture and puree through a food mill or blender. Add back to mixture in saucepan. Mix well. Remove from heat. Cool. Keeps in refrigerator indefinitely. Do not double recipe since it will not thicken. To can: process 10 minutes in a hot-water bath after filling jars with hot chutney. Good served with any snack or at a main meal.

TOMATO AND DATE CHUTNEY [Makes 1 quart]

2 lbs. fresh ripe tomatoes,
  cubed
1 cup apple cider vinegar
3 whole heads garlic,
  each clove crushed and minced
2 inches fresh ginger root,
  minced
½ lb. dates,
  chopped small
1 cup raisins,
  chopped
½ to 2 tsp. chili pepper
2 tsp. sea salt
2 to 3 tsp. garam-masala I
1 tsp. coriander seed,
  ground

Place all ingredients in a heavy saucepan. Bring to boil over high heat. Reduce heat to medium low. Simmer uncovered 1 to 2 hours until mixture thickens. Stir frequently to prevent sticking. Just before removing from heat take out 2 cups of mixture and puree through a food mill or blender. Add back to mixture in saucepan. Mix well. Remove from heat. Cool. Keeps in refrigerator indefinitely. Do not double recipe since it will not thicken. To can: process 10 minutes in a hot water bath after filling jars with hot chutney. Good served with snacks, lunch or at a main meal.

CARROT PICKLE [Makes 1 quart]

4 large carrots,
  cut into 1 inch by ¼ inch
  strips
1 small beet,
  cut into 1 inch by ¼ inch
  strips [optional]

Steam 3 to 5 minutes until just tender.

2 Tbsp. garam-masala I
1 Tbsp. whole cumin seed
1 tsp. coriander seed,
  coarsely ground
1 tsp. sea salt
1 to 4 red chili peppers,
  minced
1 cup vegetable oil,
  heated

Place hot steamed carrots in a wide jar or crock. Pour oil and spices over them. Mix well. Allow to soak overnight before using. Keeps indefinitely in refrigerator. Good with main meal. Serve at room temperature. Serve with bread and leftovers for an excellent snack or lunch.

CAULIFLOWER PICKLE [Makes 1½ to 2 quarts]

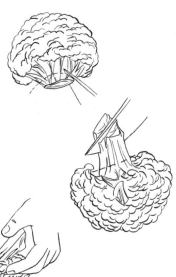

1 large head cauliflower,
   separated into ½ to 1 inch
   flowerlets with stems

Steam 3 to 5 minutes until just tender. Place in a wide jar or crock.

2 Tbsp. garam-masala I
2 Tbsp. mild honey
1 tsp. dark molasses
3 Tbsp. apple cider vinegar
1 tsp. sea salt
1 inch fresh ginger root,
   crushed and minced or
   grated
1 to 4 red chili peppers,
   minced
1 cup vegetable oil

Place in small saucepan. Heat 1 to 2 minutes until honey and oil well mixed. Do not bring to boil. Pour over steamed cauliflower. Mix well. Allow to soak overnight before using. Keep indefinitely in refrigerator. Good with main meal. Serve at room temperature. Serve with bread and leftovers for an excellent snack or lunch.

BREADS

Bread accompanies almost every meal in India. With a yoghurt dish it makes a simple lunch. Breads are used to pick up other foods. Traditionally the bread is placed in the center of a large tray called a thali or more informally in the center of a large plate or banana leaf. The other foods, set in small dishes, surround the bread.

CHAPATIS [WHOLE WHEAT GRIDDLE BREAD] [Makes approximately 2 dozen]

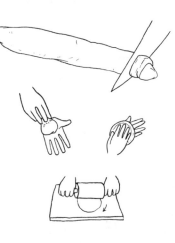

2 to 2¼ cup whole wheat flour
½ tsp. black pepper
   [optional]
1 tsp. sea salt
1 to 1¼ cups water

Mix flour, salt, and pepper well. Add water. Mix well. Have a fairly moist dough. Knead 5 to 10 minutes until dough is soft and elastic. Cover. Let rest 10 to 20 minutes. Pull dough into 2 inch diameter rope. Cut into 2 inch slices. Form into round buns. Flatten with fingers into ¼ inch thick circles. Roll out on lightly floured board into 1/8 to 1/16 inch thick rounds. Turn rounds clockwise while rolling to keep chapatis round. Do not press hard with rolling pin so air is not forced out of bread. Let round rest for 30 seconds. Do not stack on top of each other or you will get a sticky mess.

COOKING METHOD:

2 Tbsp. to ¼ cup butter,
   melted [optional]

Heat a cast iron skillet or griddle over medium high heat. Make sure it is hot before adding chapatis or air bubbles which make the chapatis light will not form. Cook on hot dry griddle. Turn several times during cooking. After first time chapatis is turned press it with a spatula to encourage air bubbles to form and spread out in the bread so it will be light. Cook 1 minute until barely browned but not dry. Place on a dish covered with a dish towel. Brush one side with melted butter if desired. Keep covered between additions of cooked bread. Serve warm. Keeps up to 1 week. Served at all Indian dinner meals. Steam to reheat or place in hot oven for a few minutes. Good camping bread since no oven is needed to cook chapatis.

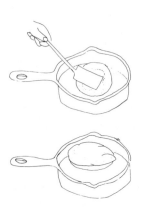

VARIATION:

CORNFLOUR CHAPATIS
[CORNFLOUR GRIDDLE BREAD]
[Makes approximately 2 dozen]

2 cups yellow corn flour
  [do not use corn meal]
¾ cup whole wheat flour
1½ tsp. sea salt
¼ tsp. black pepper
  [optional]
2 Tbsp. vegetable oil

Mix flour, salt and pepper well. Add oil. Mix until flour is mealy.

1 to 1½ cups cold water

Add to dough. Mix well. Follow directions for Chapatis. Mix and roll as directed. Cook as directed. Good main meal bread. Excellent with lentils or yoghurt dishes for lunch. Keep up to 1 week. Steam to reheat or place in hot oven for a few minutes. Good camping bread since no oven is needed to cook chapatis.

VARIATION:

CORNFLOUR CHAPATIS WITH HERBS
[CORN FLOUR GRIDDLE BREAD WITH HERBS] [Makes approximately 2 dozen]

2 green onions,
  minced
6 to 10 sprigs parsley,
  minced
½ to 1 tsp. cumin seed,
  coarsely ground

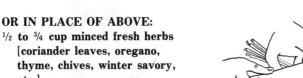

OR IN PLACE OF ABOVE:
½ to ¾ cup minced fresh herbs
  [coriander leaves, oregano,
  thyme, chives, winter savory,
  etc.]
      OR ¼ cup dried herbs,
      crumbled

Follow recipe for Cornflour Chapatis. Add herbs to flour. Mix and roll as directed for Chapatis. Cook as directed. Good main meal bread. Excellent with lentils or yoghurt dishes for lunch. Keep up to 1 week. Steam to reheat or place in hot oven for a few minutes. Good camping bread since no oven is needed to cook chapatis.

VARIATION:

MILLET CHAPATIS
[MILLET GRIDDLE BREAD]
[Makes approximately 2 dozen]

2 cups millet flour
  [make by grinding millet
  in blender or with flour
  mill. Sift flour to remove
  coarse meal. Use coarse
  meal in breads or other
  dishes.]

Follow recipe for Cornflour Chapatis. Use millet flour in place of cornflour. Mix and roll as directed for Chapatis. Cook as directed. Good main meal bread. Excellent with lentils or yoghurt dishes for lunch. Keep up to 1 week. Steam to reheat or place in hot oven for a few minutes. Good camping bread since no oven is needed to cook chapatis.

VARIATION:

MILLET CHAPATIS WITH HERBS
[MILLET GRIDDLE BREAD WITH HERBS]
[Makes approximately 2 dozen]

2 cups millet flour
  [make by grinding millet
  in blender or with flour
  mill. Sift flour to remove
  coarse meal. Use coarse
  meal in breads or other
  dishes.]
2 green onions,
  minced
6 to 8 sprigs parsely,
  minced
½ to 1 tsp. cumin seed,
  coarsely ground

OR IN PLACE OF ABOVE:
½ to ¾ cup minced fresh herbs
  [coriander leaves, oregano,
  thyme, chives, winter
  savory, etc.]
  OR ¼ cup dried herbs,
  crumbled

Follow recipe for Cornflour Chapatis.

PURI [DEEP FRIED BREAD] [Makes approximately 30]

3 cups whole wheat flour
1½ tsp. sea salt
⅓ cup vegetable oil

Mix flour and salt. Add oil. Mix until flour is mealy.

1 to 1¼ cup water

Add water to dough. Mix well. Have a fairly moist dough. Knead 5 to 10 minutes until dough is soft and velvety. Cover. Let rest 10 to 20 minutes. Knead dough another 5 minutes until smooth and elastic. If covered with a damp towel at this stage the dough can be kept for several hours. Form dough into a long, 1½ inch diameter rope. Cut into 1½ inch slices. Form each slice into small round buns. Place on floured board and cover with a moist towel. Flatten with fingers into ¼ inch thick round. Place on lightly floured board. Roll into circles about 1/8 to 1/16 inch thick and 3 inches in diameter. Make Puris up as you fry them as they will dry out and not puff if allowed to sit.

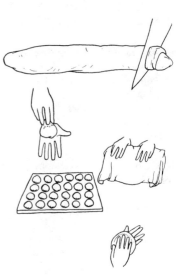

COOKING METHOD:

Heat a deep saucepan or wok over high heat. Add oil. Heat until a small piece of dough added drops to the bottom of the pan and then rises almost at once. Reduce heat to medium high. Fry one puri at a time. Allow to sink into the oil. Hold it down with a slotted spoon until it begins to puff and looks like a blow fish. If one area does not rise keep it under the oil. When it puffs flip after 10 seconds. Do not brown or puri will be too dry and brittle. Remove from oil 10 to 20 seconds after puri is turned. Drain on absorbent paper. Keep warm in 200° oven until ready to serve. Good main meal bread. Very toasted-nutty flavor. Good cold with lentil or yoghurt dishes for lunch.

3 cups vegetable oil

Too Cold Too Hot

Correct Temperature

SAMOSAS [STUFFED BREAD] [Makes approximately 30]

Vegetarian Potato Filling:
4 green onions, minced
2 thin slices fresh ginger root, minced
1 tsp. sea salt
¼ tsp. black pepper
1 to 2 tsp. garam-masala I
2 potatoes, boiled and mashed but still lumpy - I use my hands to mash
½ cup green peas
 OR ¼ cup carrots, cut into pea sized pieces and
  ¼ cup mushrooms, minced
 OR ½ cup green beans, cut into pea sized pieces
 OR ½ cup corn
 OR ½ cup carrots, cut into pea sized pieces
 OR ½ cup mushrooms, minced

Mix ingredients well. Let sit 30 minutes to 1 hour.

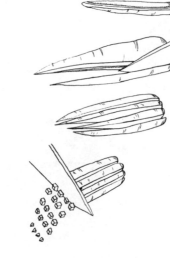

¼ cup fresh parsley, minced
  OR coriander leaves, minced
1 tsp. mango powder
  OR 1 Tbsp. lemon juice
½ cup nuts [cashews, peanuts,
  sunflower seeds, sesame seeds,
  etc.], chopped [optional]

Meat Filling:
4 green onions, minced
2 thin slices fresh ginger root,
  minced
1 clove garlic,
  crushed and minced
1 to 1½ tsp. sea salt
¼ tsp. black pepper
1 to 2 tsp. garam-masala II
⅓ lb. ground meat
  [beef or lamb]
1 large potato,
  boiled and mashed but still
  lumpy - I use my hands to
mash
8 to 10 sprigs parsley,
  minced
  OR coriander leaves,
  minced

Mix ingredients well. Let sit 30 minutes to 1 hour.

1 batch Puri dough

Form dough into long 1½ inch diameter rope. Cut into 1½ inch slices. Form each slice into small round bun. Place on floured board and cover with a moist towel. Flatten one round at a time with fingers into ¼ inch thick round. Place on lightly floured board. Roll into circles about 1/8 inch thick and 3 inches in diameter. Roll out as needed.

ASSEMBLING AND COOKING METHOD:
Place 2 Tbsp. filling on one-half dough round. Moisten edge of round with water. Fold round in half. Seal edges well. Place on oiled cookie sheet. Cover with moist towel. Fill all rounds. When all filled begin to heat oil. Place wok or heavy saucepan over high heat. Add oil. Heat until a small piece of dough added drops to the bottom and then rises almost at once. Add 3 to 5 Samosas. Reduce heat to medium high. Fry 3 to 5 minutes until golden brown. Turn once to brown evenly. Remove from oil. Drain well. Meat filled Samosas fry 5 minutes. If deep frying is not possible brush bread with oil or butter and then bake at 425° for 8 to 10 minutes until golden brown. Serve warm. Keep warm in 200° oven. Reheat in a 350° oven 3 to 5 minutes. Excellent main meal dish. Good cold for lunch the next day. I like them for short backpacking trips since they are a meal in a bun. Great served with any chutney.

3 cups vegetable oil

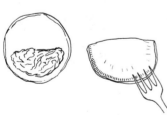

PARATHAS [WHOLE WHEAT GRIDDLE BREAD FRIED IN BUTTER]
[Makes approximately 8 to 12]

2 cups whole wheat flour
1 tsp. sea salt
¼ tsp. black pepper
  [optional]
2 Tbsp. butter,
  melted
  OR vegetable oil

Mix flour, salt and pepper well. Add oil. Mix until flour is mealy.

1 to 1¼ cup water

Add water to flour. Mix well. Have a fairly moist dough. Knead 5 to 10 minutes until dough is soft and velvety. Cover. Let rest 10 to 20 minutes. Pull dough into 2 inch diameter rope. Cut into 3 inch slices. Form slices into round buns. Place on a floured board and cover with a moist towel. Flatten with fingers into ¼ inch thick rounds. Roll on lightly floured board into 1/8 inch thick rounds. Turn rounds clockwise while rolling to keep paratha round.

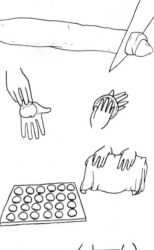

¼ to ⅓ cup butter,
  melted
  OR vegetable oil

When paratha is rolled to desired thinness, brush liberally with melted butter. Fold in half. Roll out again into 1/8 inch thick round. Brush with butter again; fold in half again; roll into a round again. Repeat 2 to 3 times for each paratha. End with a 1/8 inch thick round. Repeat for all parathas. Do not stack on top of each other or you will get a sticky mess.

¼ to ⅓ cup butter
  melted
  OR vegetable oil

COOKING METHOD:
Heat a cast iron skillet over medium high heat. Lightly oil pan with pastry brush or paper towel. Place paratha on griddle. Oil upper side with pastry brush. Turn several times during cooking. Brush with butter each time it is turned. Press cooking bread with spatula during cooking to encourage air bubbles to form and spread out in bread so it becomes lighter. Cook 1 to 2 minutes until lightly browned but not dry. Place on a dish covered with a heavy towel. Keep covered between additions of cooked parathas. Serve warm. Parathas are a very rich tasting bread. Good main meal bread. Good with lentil or yoghurt dishes for lunch. Keeps up to 1 week under refrigeration. To reheat, warm in a 350° oven for 3 to 5 minutes.

APPETIZERS AND SNACKS

These dishes may be served as between-meal snacks, as appetizers for a party, with yoghurt dishes for a tasty lunch, or as part of a large Indian feast.

SPICY INDIAN CASHEWS [Makes 2 cups]

2 cups raw chashew pieces
3 Tbsp. butter
  OR vegetable oil

Heat a medium-sized cast iron skillet over medium heat. Add butter or oil. Heat until a cashew added sizzles. Add nuts. Stir and fry 3 to 5 minutes until golden brown. Remove from pan with a slotted spoon. Drain well on absorbent paper.

1 tsp. sea salt
1 to 2 tsp. garam-masala I
¼ to 1 tsp. ground chili pepper

Sprinkle over hot nuts. Mix well. Serve warm. Keep in refrigerator in tightly covered container To reheat, place in 300° oven for 3 to 5 minutes. Excellent snack. Good appetizer for party or feast.

VARIATION:

**SPICY INDIAN ALMONDS
[Makes 2 cups]**

2 cups almonds

Follow recipe for Spicy Indian Cashews. Use almonds in place of cashews. Cook as directed. Serve warm. Keep in refrigerator in tightly covered container. To reheat, place in 300° oven for 3 to 5 minutes. Excellent snack. Good appetizer for party or feast.

VARIATION:

**SPICY INDIAN MIXED NUTS
[Makes 2 cups]**

**2 cups unsalted mixed nuts
  and seeds [cashews, almonds,
  pecans, walnuts, brazil nuts,
  sunflower seeds, etc.]**

Follow recipe for Spicy Indian Cashews. Use 2 cups mixed nuts in place of cashews. Cook as directed. Serve warm. Keep in refrigerator in tightly covered conatiner. To reheat, place in 300° oven for 3 to 5 minutes. Excellent snack. Good appetizer for party or feast.

VARIATION:

**SPICY INDIAN PEANUTS
[Makes 2 cups]**

2 cups raw peanuts
3 Tbsp. peanut oil
  OR vegetable oil
  OR butter

Heat a medium cast iron skillet over high heat. Add oil. Heat until a peanut added sizzles. Reduce heat to medium. Add peanuts. Stir and fry 5 to 10 minutes until peanuts are golden brown. Remove from pan. Drain well.

1 tsp. sea salt
1 to 2 tsp. garam-masala I
¼ to 1 tsp. ground chili pepper

Sprinkle over hot nuts. Mix well. Serve warm. Keep in refrigerator in tightly covered container. To reheat, place in 300° oven for 3 to 5 minutes. Excellent snack. Good appetizer for party or feast.

PAKORAS I [GARBANZO BATTER POTATO FRITTERS] [Serves 6 to 8]

Batter:
1½ cups channa
     [garbanzo] flour
1 tsp. sea salt
½ tsp. black pepper
1½ cups water

Mix flour, salt and pepper well. Add water. Mix well. Let stand 15 to 30 minutes. Place bowl of batter in larger bowl of ice cubes or in refrigerator.

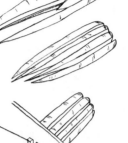

Filling:
1 large baking potato,
     boiled until soft

Peel potato. Mash with hands. It should still have lumps in it but be mashed enough to form a paste to hold other ingredients. Place in a large bowl.

½ to 1 cup fresh vegetables
     [peas or green beans or
     carrots cut into pea-sized
     pieces, or corn or mushrooms
     coarsely chopped, etc.]

Steam fresh vegetables 3 to 5 minutes until just beginning to get tender and still bright colored. Do not steam mushrooms. Cool. Add to potatoes

3 to 4 large sprigs parsley,
     minced
     OR 3 to 4 sprigs coriander,
     minced
2 to 3 green onions,
     minced
1 to 1½ tsp. sea salt
1 to 2 tsp. garam-masala II
¼ tsp. black pepper

Add to potatoes. Mix well. Form potato dough into ½ inch balls. Squeeze gently but firmly so balls are compact and filling does not extrude between fingers. Roll balls between palms so they are round. Place balls on a plate as they rolled.

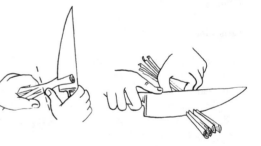

3 cups vegetable oil

COOKING METHOD:
Heat a wok over high heat. Add oil. Heat until a small piece of batter added sinks to bottom and then rises almost at once. Reduce heat to medium high. Dip potato balls in batter and cover well. Place batter coated balls one at a time into oil. Fry 5 to 8 balls at a time. Fry 3 to 5 minutes until golden brown. Remove from oil with slotted spoon or tempura spoon. Drain. Test oil temperature before frying more pakoras. Repeat process until all are fried. Keep warm in 200° oven. Serve warm. May be reheated in 350° oven for 5 to 8 minutes until warmed through. Good snack. Excellent for lunch. Good appetizer for a party or feast. Keep refrigerated 1 to 2 weeks. Leftover batter bits can be saved for soup croutons or put in Rhyta salad (see Indian Salad and Cold Fruits section).

Too Cold

Too Hot

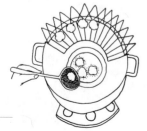

Correct Temperature

PAKORAS II [GARBANZO BATTER VEGETABLE FRITTERS] [Serves 6 to 8]

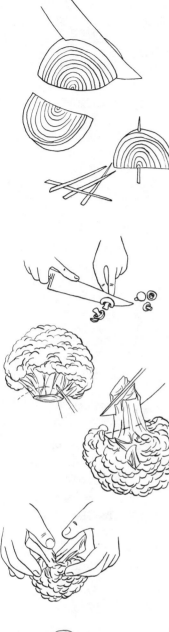

Batter:
1½ cup channa
   [garbanzo] flour
1 tsp. sea salt
½ tsp. black pepper
1 to 2 tsp. garam-masala II
1½ cups water

1 yellow onion,
   cut in half lengthwise and
   then into ¼ inch slices and
   secured with a toothpick
   down the center of each slice
1 carrot,
   cut into 1 inch by ¼ inch
   slices and steamed 3 minutes
1 small eggplant,
   cut in half lengthwise and
   then cut into ¼ by 2 inch
   slices, sprinkled with salt
   and allowed to stand for
   30 minutes. Squeeze off
   excess water
3 large mushrooms,
   cut into 5 thick slices
½ head cauliflower,
   cut into ½ to 1 inch
   flowerlets
½ lb. green beans,
   steamed 3 minutes
OR any firm vegetable,
   cut into pieces that
   cook quickly

3 cups vegetable oil

Mix ingredients well. Let stand 15 to 30 minutes. Place bowl of batter in larger bowl of ice cubes or in refrigerator.

Use 3 or 4 different kinds of vegetables. Place on a plate ready to dip in batter.

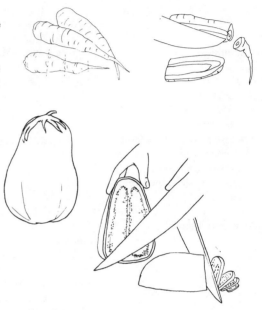

COOKING METHOD:

Heat a wok over high heat. Add oil. Heat until a small piece of batter added sinks to bottom and then rises almost at once. Reduce heat to medium high. Dip vegetables in batter one at a time. Cover well. Place batter-coated vegetables one at a time into hot oil. Fry 5 to 8 vegetables at a time. Fry 3 to 5 minutes until dark golden brown. Turn several times. Remove from oil with slotted spoon or tempura spoon. Drain. Test oil temperature before frying more pakoras. Repeat process until all are fried. Keep warm in a 200° oven. Serve warm. These can be frozen and then reheated by thawing them for 30 minutes and then frying them. Keep refrigerated 1 to 2 weeks. Good snack. Excellent for lunch. Good appetizer for party or feast. Leftover batter bits can be saved for soup croutons or put in Rhyta salad (see Indian Salad and Cold Fruits section).

Too Cold   Too Hot   Correct Temperature

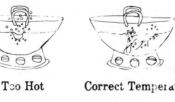

MONGORHIS [DEEP FRIED LENTIL BALLS] [Serves 6 to 12]

1 cup urad dahl
  [see lentil explanation in
  Indian Vegetarian Main
  Dish section]
  OR red lentils
	Soak 6 hours or overnight in lukewarm water. Drain.

2 to 4 Tbsp. water	Place soaked lentils in blender or food mill. Grind to a paste. If necessary, use extra liquid to get dahl ground into a paste.
2 to 3 Tbsp. channa [garbanzo] flour	Add enough channa flour to ground dahl to make into a muffin-like dough. Mix well. Make stiff enough so spoon stands by itself.
3 green onions, minced	Add to dough. Mix well.

½ tsp. turmeric
1 tsp. sea salt
1 tsp. garam-masala I
1 tsp. cumin seed,
  coarsely ground
¼ to 1 tsp. ground chili pepper
  OR 1 small fresh hot green
      pepper, minced
2 to 4 slices fresh ginger root,
  minced

Too Cold

3 cups vegetable oil

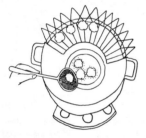

Heat a wok over high heat. Add oil. Heat until a small piece of dough added drops to the bottom and then rises to the surface almost at once. Reduce heat to medium high. Add 5 separate tsp. of mongorhis dough. Fry 5 to 8 minutes until golden brown. Drain. Repeat process until all mongorhis are fried. Serve hot. Can be kept warm in oven. Can be frozen and then reheated in a 350° oven. Keep up to 1 month in refrigerator. Used as a base for many main dishes. An excellent snack. Good appetizer for feast or party.

Too Hot

Correct Temperature

PAPADUMS [DEEP FRIED LENTIL CHIPS] [Serves 6 to 12]
[Purchase at any Indian speciality shop]

6 to 12 assorted papadums,
  broken into quarters
½ to 1 cup vegetable oil

Heat oil in medium-sized cast iron skillet over high heat. Drop small piece of papadum in oil to test temperature. When papadum expands at once but does not brown oil is hot. Reduce heat to medium high. Grasp papadum piece in tongs or chopsticks and dip in oil. Keep holding it while frying. Dip completely under oil and hold for 2 to 3 seconds until it expands completely. Turn once. Lift out of oil before it browns. Watch oil heat closely since papadums will not expand if too cold and burn easily if too hot. Drain. Serve warm. Good served with a main meal. Good appetizer for a party or feast. Excellent dipped in vegetable or nut chutneys.

SPINACH BALLS [Serves 6 to 8]

1 lb. spinach, stems removed,
   shredded
½ cup channa [garbanzo] flour
½ cup whole wheat flour
1 tsp. sea salt
1 green onion, minced
½ tsp. turmeric
¼ tsp. black pepper
1 to 2 tsp. garam-masala I
2 Tbsp. vegetable oil

Mix ingredients well.

¼ to ½ cup water

Add just enough water to spinach mixture so dough forms into firm balls. Form into balls. Squeeze gently but firmly so balls are compact and filling does not extrude between fingers. Roll balls between palms so they are round. Place on a plate.

3 cups vegetable oil

COOKING METHOD:
Heat a wok over high heat. Add oil. Heat until a small piece of dough added sinks to bottom and then rises almost at once. Reduce heat to medium high. Add 5 to 8 balls. Fry 3 to 5 minutes until golden brown. Turn often. Remove from oil with slotted spoon or tempura spoon. Drain. Test oil temperature before frying more spinach balls. Add more and repeat process until all are fried. Keep warm or reheat in a 200° oven. Serve warm. Keep refrigerated 1 week. Good snack. Excellent lunch with bread and yoghurt dish. Good appetizer for feast or party.

VARIATION:

DEEP FRIED SPINACH BALLS WITH BATTER
[Serves 6 to 8]

Batter:
1½ cups channa [garbanzo] flour
1 to 1½ tsp. sea salt
½ tsp. black pepper

Mix ingredients well. Let stand 15 to 30 minutes.

Filling:
1 batch of spinach balls

Place on a plate.

3 cups vegetable oil

COOKING METHOD:
Follow recipe for Spinach Balls but dip balls into batter before putting in oil. Serve warm. Keep warm or reheat in a 200° oven. Keep refrigerated 1 week. Good snack. Excellent lunch with bread and yoghurt dish. Good appetizer for feast or party.

Too Cold

Too Hot

Correct Temperature

DEEP FRIED CHANNA DAHL [DEEP FRIED SPLIT GARBANZOS]
[Makes 2 cups]

1 cup split channa
  [garbanzo] dahl
3 cups water

Soak dahl in water overnight. Drain. Spread on an absorbent cloth to dry for 1 hour.

2 cups vegetable oil

Heat a deep saucepan or wok over high heat. Add oil. Heat until a piece of channa dropped sinks to the bottom and then rises almost at once. Reduce heat to medium high. Add ⅓ cup channa and fry 3 to 5 minutes until channa is lightly browned. Remove from oil with slotted spoon or tempura spoon. Place on absorbent paper to drain. Test oil temperature again before adding more channa. Repeat process until all channa is fried. When it is all fried rub with paper towels to remove excess oil.

1 to 1½ tsp. sea salt
1 to 2 tsp. garam-masala II
½ tsp. ground mango powder
  [optional]
¼ to 1 tsp. ground chili powder

Sprinkle over fried channa. Mix well. Serve warm. The beer nuts of India! To reheat, place in 300° oven for 2 to 5 minutes until warm. Keep 2 to 3 weeks in refrigerator. Excellent snack. Good party or feast appetizer.

VARIATION:

**DEEP FRIED URAD DAHL
[DEEP FRIED LENTILS]
[Makes 2 cups**

1 cup urad dahl
  [see lentil explanation in
  Indian Vegetarian Main
  Dish section]
  OR green lentils

Follow recipe for Deep Fried Channa Dahl. Use urad dahl or green lentils in place of channa dahl. Cook as directed. Serve warm. Keep 2 to 3 weeks in refrigerator. To reheat, place in 300° oven for 3 to 5 minutes. Excellent snack. Good party or feast appetizer.

RICE

Rice dishes, an Indian mainstay, are served at the main meal along with vegetable curries and a vegetarian or a meat main dish. Chutneys and salads make such a meal almost a feast. Several of the rice dishes are one-pot meals with vegetables, rice and a protein source all in one.

PLAIN BROWN RICE [Serves 4 to 6]

¼ cup vegetable oil
1 medium yellow onion,
   cut in half lengthwise and
   then sliced paper thin

Heat a heavy cast iron saucepan over high heat. Add oil. Heat until a small piece of onion added sizzles. Reduce heat to medium high. Add onion. Stir and fry 5 to 10 minutes until onion is soft and transparent and lightly browned.

2 cups long-grain [preferred]
   brown rice

Add rice. Mix well. Stir and fry 3 to 5 minutes until lightly browned and crackling.

4 cups water
1 tsp. sea salt
¼ tsp. black pepper

Add water to rice. Mix well. Add other ingredients. Cover. Bring to boil over high heat. Reduce heat to medium low. Simmer 35 to 40 minutes. Remove from heat. Allow to sit 10 minutes so rice absorbs excess water. Serve hot. Good with any main dish and a vegetable dish for a dinner meal.

FRIED RICE WITH COOKED RICE [Serves 4 to 6]

1 cup nuts
   [cashews, peanuts,
   sunflower seeds, or
   almonds], slightly chopped
4 Tbsp. vegetable oil

Heat a wok over high heat. Add oil. Add nuts. Stir and fry 2 to 3 minutes until nuts are slightly browned. Remove from wok. Set aside for later use.

½ yellow onion,
   chopped
2 to 3 slices fresh
   ginger root,
   minced
1 tsp. cumin seed

Add to oil in wok. Reduce heat to medium high. Stir and fry 3 to 5 minutes until onions are soft and transparent.

1 to 2 medium sized carrots,
   cut into thin diagonal
   slices and steamed
   2 to 3 minutes
   OR any other firm vegetable,
   cut into thin diagonal
   slices and steamed
   2 to 3 minutes

Add to onions. Mix well. Cvoer and cook over medium heat 5 to 6 minutes until carrots are tender.

4 cups cooked long-grain
   [preferred] brown rice

Add rice to carrots and onions 1 cup at a time. Mix well before adding next cup.

1½ tsp. sea salt
½ head cabbage,
   shredded
¼ to ½ tsp. ground chili pepper
   [optional]

Add to rice. Mix well. Stir and fry 5 to 10 minutes until cabbage is just tender. Add nuts. Mix well. Serve hot. Good with any main dish and a vegetable dish for a dinner meal. Good lunch.

PULAO [FRIED RICE] [Serves 4 to 6]

1 tsp. cumin seed
2 [1 inch pieces] dal chini
  [thick cinnamon stick]
2 Tbsp. vegetable oil

Heat a large cast iron saucepan over medium high heat. Add oil. Heat until a piece of cinnamon added sizzles. Add spices. Fry 1 to 2 minutes until cumin seeds pop.

2 Tbsp. butter
  OR vegetable oil
½ yellow onion,
  cut in half lengthwise
  and then sliced paper-thin

Add butter to pan. Melt butter. Add onion. Stir and fry 5 to 10 minutes until onion is soft and transparent and lightly browned.

2 cups long-grain [preferred]
  brown rice

Add to pan. Stir and fry 3 to 5 minutes until lightly browned and crackling.

4 cups water
1 tsp. turmeric
1 tsp. sea salt
¼ to ½ tsp. black pepper

Add to rice. Mix well. Cover. Bring to boil over high heat. Reduce heat to medium low. Simmer 20 minutes.

1 to 2 cups fresh vegetables
  [peas, corn, mushrooms
  cut into ¼ inch slices,
  carrots cut into pea sized
  pieces, cauliflower broken
  into ½ inch flowerlets,
  beans cut into thin diagonals
  etc.]
4 to 5 hard boiled eggs,
  cut in half lengthwise
  [optional]

Add one or a combination of vegetables to rice when water has boiled even with the rice. Mix well. If eggs are used place on top of rice after vegetables are mixed with rice. Cover. Continue to cook 15 to 20 minutes. Remove from heat. Let sit 10 minutes so excess water is absorbed. Turn onto a platter.

optional step:
6 to 12 almonds,
  slivered
  OR ½ to 1 cup raw cashews,
    chopped
  OR ½ to 1 cup raw peanuts,
    chopped
  OR ½ to 2 cups raw sunflower
    seeds, chopped

While rice is cooking roast raw nuts in 300° oven 5 to 10 minutes until golden brown. Sprinkle over rice before serving.

Optional step:
¼ cup fresh parsley,
  chopped
  OR coriander leaves,
    chopped

Sprinkle over rice before serving. A dish to feast the eyes upon with the yellow rice, colored vegetables, nuts and parsley. Excellent served with a main dish for dinner. Keeps up to 1 week in refrigerator. Steam to reheat.

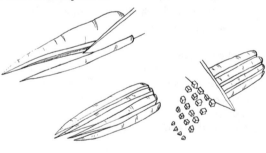

KISHMISH PULAO [FRIED RICE WITH RAISINS] [Serves 4 to 6]

5 to 10 cloves
1 tsp. cumin seed
2 Tbsp. vegetable oil

Heat a large cast iron saucepan over medium high heat. Add oil. Heat until a piece of cinnamon added sizzles. Add spices. Fry 1 to 2 minutes.

¼ cup butter
 OR vegetable oil
½ yellow onion,
 cut in half lengthwise and
 then sliced paper thin

Add butter to pan. Melt butter. Add onion. Stir and fry 5 to 10 minutes until onion is soft and transparent and lightly browned.

2 cups long grain [preferred]
 brown rice

Add to pan. Stir and fry 3 to 5 minutes until lightly browned and crackling.

4 cups water
1 tsp. turmeric
 OR ¼ tsp. saffron
1 tsp. sea salt
¼ tsp. black pepper

Add to rice. Mix well. Cover. Bring to boil over high heat. Reduce heat to medium low. Simmer 20 minutes.

1 cup raisins, washed

Add to rice. Mix well. Cover. Continue to cook 15 to 20 minutes. Remove from heat. Let sit 10 minutes so excess water is absorbed. Turn out on platter.

optional step:
6 to 12 almonds, slivered
 OR ½ to 1 cup raw cashews,
  chopped
 OR ½ to 1 cup raw peanuts,
  chopped
 OR ½ to 1 cup raw sunflower
  seeds, chopped

While rice is cooking roast raw nuts in 300° oven 5 to 10 minutes until golden brown. Sprinkle over rice before serving.

optional step:
¼ cup coriander leaves,
 chopped
 OR fresh parsley,
  chopped

Sprinkle over rice before serving. A dish to feast the eyes upon with yellow rice, black raisins, green parsley and white nuts. Excellent served with a main dish and vegetable dish for dinner. Keeps up to 1 week in refrigerator. Steam to reheat.

VARIATION:

KISHMISH PULAO WITH VEGETABLES
[FRIED RICE WITH RAISINS AND
VEGETABLES]
[Serves 4 to 6]

1 to 2 cups fresh vegetables,
 [peas, corn, mushrooms
 cut into ¼ inch slices, carrots
 cut into pea sized pieces,
 cauliflower broken into ½ inch
 flowerlets, beans cut into thin
 diagonals, etc.]

Follow recipe for Kishmish Pulao. Add one or a combination of vegetables with raisins. Cook as directed. Serve hot. Good served with a main dish for a simple dinner. Keeps up to 1 week in refrigerator. Steam to reheat.

ALU PULAO [POTATO FRIED RICE] [Serves 4 to 6]

5 cloves
1 tsp. cumin seed
2 tsp. coriander seed
2 Tbsp. vegetable oil

2 Tbsp. butter
    OR vegetable oil
1 yellow onion,
    cut in half lengthwise and
    then sliced paper thin

2 medium potatoes,
    cut into ¼ inch cubes
2 cups long-grain [preferred]
    brown rice

4 cups water
1 tsp. turmeric
1 tsp. sea salt
¼ to ½ tsp. black pepper

Optional step:
6 to 12 almonds, slivered
    OR ½ to 1 cup raw cashews,
        chopped
    OR ½ to 1 cup raw peanuts,
        chopped
    OR ½ to 1 cup raw sunflower
        seeds, chopped

Optional step:
¼ cup fresh parsley,
    chopped
    OR coriander leaves,
        chopped

Heat a large cast iron saucepan over medium heat. Add oil. Heat until a clove added sizzles. Add spices. Fry 1 to 2 minutes until cumin seeds pop.

Add butter to pan. Melt butter. Add onion. Stir and fry 5 to 10 minutes until onion is soft and transparent and lightly browned.

Add potatoes. Stir and fry 3 to 4 minutes until partly cooked. Add rice. Stir and fry an an additional 3 to 5 minutes until rice is lightly browned and crackling.

Add to rice. Mix well. Cover. Bring to boil over high heat. Reduce heat to medium low. Simmer 35 minutes. Remove from heat. Allow to sit 10 minutes so rice absorbs excess water. Turn onto a platter.

While rice is cooking roast raw nuts in 300° oven 5 to 10 minutes until golden brown. Sprinkle over rice before serving.

Sprinkle over rice before serving. Serve hot. Excellent served with a main dish and vegetable dish for dinner. Keeps up to 1 week in refrigerator. Steam to reheat.

VARIATION:

**ALU PULAO WITH PEAS
[POTATO AND PEA FRIED RICE]
[Serves 4 to 6]**

1 cup green peas
    OR 1 cup fresh vegetables
    [corn, mushrooms cut into
    ¼ inch slices, carrots cut into
    pea sized pieces, cauliflower
    broken into ½ inch flowerlets,
    beans cut into pea sized
    pieces, etc.]

Follow recipe for Alu Pulao. After rice has simmered 20 minutes add peas. Mix well. Cook an additional 15 minutes over medium low heat. Finish as directed. Serve hot. Excellent served with a main dish for dinner. Keeps up to 1 week in refrigerator. Steam to reheat.

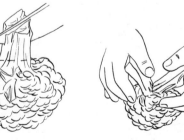

VARHYA PULAO [LENTIL CAKE FRIED RICE] [Serves 4 to 6]

5 cloves
5 peppercorns
2 [1 inch] pieces
  dal chini
  [thick cinnamon stick]
2 tsp. cumin seed
2 Tbsp. vegetable oil
	Heat a large cast iron saucepan over medium high heat. Add oil. Heat until a piece of cinnamon added sizzles. Add spices. Fry 1 to 2 minutes until cumin seeds pop.

3 Tbsp. butter
  OR vegetable oil
1 large yellow onion,
  chopped
10 to 12 **varhya**
  [spicy dried lentil cakes]
  see Indian Basic Ingredients
	Add butter to pan. Melt butter. Add onion and varhya. Stir and fry 5 to 10 minutes until onion is soft and transparent and lightly browned.

2 cups long-grain [preferred] brown rice	Add to pan. Stir and fry 3 to 5 minutes until lightly browned and crackling.
4 cups water 1 tsp. turmeric 1 tsp. sea salt	Add to rice. Mix well. Cover. Bring to boil over high heat. Reduce heat to medium low. Simmer 35 minutes. Remove from heat. Let sit 10 minutes so excess water is absorbed. Turn onto a platter.

Optional step:
¼ cup fresh parsley,
  chopped
  OR coriander leaves,
  chopped
	Sprinkle over rice before serving. Serve hot. Excellent served with a vegetable dish for a simple meal. Steam to reheat.

VARIATION:

**VARHYA PULAO WITH VEGETABLES
[LENTIL CAKE FRIED RICE WITH
VEGETABLES]
[Serves 4 to 6]
A meal in a bowl!**

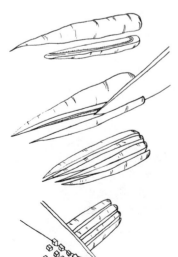

1 to 2 cups fresh vegetables
  [peas, corn mushrooms cut
  into ¼ inch slices, carrots
  cut into pea-sized pieces,
  cauliflower broken into ½ inch
  flowerlets, beans cut into
  thin diagonals, etc.]

Follow recipe for Varhya Pulao. After rice has simmered 20 minutes add one or a combination of vegetables. Mix well. Cover. Simmer an additional 15 minutes over medium low heat. Finish as directed. A quick meal-in-a-bowl. Good served with chutneys or pickles. Steam to reheat.

SHRIMP PULAO [SHRIMP FRIED RICE] [Serves 4 to 6]

1 tsp. cumin seed
2 tsp. coriander seed
2 [1 inch] pieces
   dal chini
   [thick cinnamon stick]
2 Tbsp. vegetable oil

Heat a large cast iron saucepan over medium high heat. Add oil. Heat until a piece of cinnamon added sizzles. Add spices. Fry 1 to 2 minutes until cumin seeds pop.

2 Tbsp. butter
   OR vegetable oil
1 yellow onion,
   cut in half lengthwise and
   then sliced paper thin

Add butter to pan. Melt butter. Add onion. Stir and fry 5 to 10 minutes until onion is soft and transparent and lightly browned.

2 cups long-grain [preferred]
   brown rice

Add to pan. Stir and fry 3 to 5 minutes until lightly browned and crackling.

4 cups water
1 tsp. sea salt
¼ tsp. black pepper

Add to rice. Mix well. Cover. Bring to boil over high heat. Reduce heat to medium low. Simmer 35 minutes. Remove from heat. Let sit 10 minutes so excess water is absorbed. Turn onto a platter.

¼ to ½ lb. small shrimp

Cook 5 to 8 minutes until pink. If cooked shrimp are used, steam 2 to 3 minutes to heat.

Optional step:
¼ cup fresh parsley,
   chopped
   OR coriander leaves,
      chopped

Sprinkle over rice along with shrimp. Serve hot. Excellent served with a vegetable dish for a dinner meal. Steam to reheat.

VARIATION:

SHRIMP PULAO WITH VEGETABLES [SHRIMP FRIED RICE WITH VEGETABLES] [Serves 4 to 6]
A meal in a bowl!

1 to 2 cups fresh vegetables
   [peas, corn, mushrooms cut
   into ¼ inch slices, carrots
   cut into pea-sized pieces,
   cauliflower broken into
   ½ inch flowerlets, beans
   cut into thin diagonals, etc.]

Follow recipe for Shrimp Pulao. After rice has simmered 20 minutes add one or a combination of vegetables. Mix well. Cover. Simmer an additional 15 minutes over medium low heat. Finish as directed. A quick meal-in-a-bowl. Good served with chutneys or pickles. Steam to reheat.

MEAT PULAO [FRIED RICE WITH MEAT] [Serves 4 to 6]

5 cloves
2 [1 inch] pieces dal chini
  [thick cinnamon stick]
3 to 5 peppercorns
3 Tbsp. vegetable oil

Heat a large cast iron saucepan over medium high heat. Add oil. Heat until a piece of cinnamon added sizzles. Add spices. Stir and fry 1 to 2 minutes.

2 Tbsp. butter
  OR vegetable oil
1 yellow onion,
  cut in half lengthwise and
  then sliced paper thin.
1 chicken breast,
  cut into ¼ inch slices
  OR ¼ to ⅓ lb. meat
    [lamb or beef], cut
    into ¼ inch cubes

Add butter to pan. Melt butter. Add onion. Stir and fry 2 to 3 minutes. Add meat. Stir and fry an additional 5 to 8 minutes until meat is lightly browned.

2 cups long grain [preferred]
  brown rice

Add to pan. Stir and fry 3 to 5 minutes until lightly browned and crackling.

4 cups meat stock
  [chicken, beef or lamb]
  OR water
1½ tsp. sea salt
1 to 2 tsp. garam-masala II

Add to rice. Mix well. Cover. Bring to boil over high heat. Reduce heat to medium low. Simmer 35 to 40 minutes. Remove from heat. Let sit 10 minutes so excess water is absorbed. Turn onto a platter.

Optional step:
¼ cup fresh parsley,
  chopped
  OR coriander leaves,
    chopped

Sprinkle over rice before serving. Serve hot. Excellent served with a vegetable dish and chutney or pickles for dinner. Steam to reheat.

VARIATION:

MEAT PULAO WITH VEGETABLES [FRIED RICE WITH MEAT AND VEGETABLES]
[Serves 4 to 6]
A meal in a bowl!

1 to 2 cups fresh vegetables
  [peas, corn, mushrooms cut into
  ¼ inch slices, carrots cut into
  pea sized pieces, cauliflower
  broken into ½ inch flowerlets,
  beans cut into thin diagonals,
  etc.]

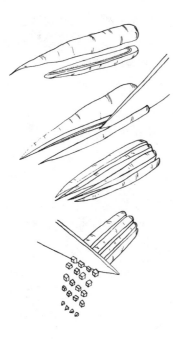

Follow recipe for Meat Pulao. Add one or a combination of vegetables after rice has simmered 20 minutes. Mix well. Cover. Simmer an additional 15 to 20 minutes over medium low heat. Finish as directed. Serve hot. A quick meal-in-a-bowl. Good served with chutneys or pickles. Steam to reheat.

KEDEGREE [RICE AND LENTIL PORRIDGE] [Serves 4 to 6]

6 cups water
1 to 2 tsp. sea salt
1 cup long-grain [preferred]
brown rice
1 cup moong dahl
[mung beans]
OR urad dahl
[see lentil explanation in
Indian Vegetarian Main Dish
section]
OR green lentils

Bring water to boil in a heavy saucepan. Add salt. Add lentils and rice. Cover. Bring to boil over high heat. Reduce heat to medium low. Simmer 30 to 40 minutes until rice and lentils are tender but still porridge like in consistency.

1 Tbsp. butter
1 Tbsp. vegetable oil
1 to 2 tsp. garam-masala I
1 tsp. cumin seed

Heat a small frying pan over medium high heat. Add oil and butter. Melt butter. Add spices. Fry 1 minutes. Remove from heat. Add to cooked lentils and rice. Mix. Serve hot. Excellent dish for children. Good for people recovering from illness if served without oil and spices.

SALADS AND COLD FRUITS

Salads are served with the main meal or with bread and pickles as a lunch. The fruit salads are eaten as snacks or sweet dishes after a meal. Sliced fresh fruit or vegetables sprinkled with lemon juice can take the place of salads at any meal.

CUCUMBERS WITH LEMON DRESSING [Serves 4 to 6]

1 to 2 medium-sized cucumber,
sliced thin

Place in a salad bowl.

Dressing:
2 Tbsp. lemon juice
1 tsp. mild honey
1 tsp. sea salt
¼ tsp. fresh ground black pepper
[optional]

Mix ingredients well. Pour over cucumbers. Serve at once or cucumbers will wilt. Good served with main dish and rice for dinner.

VEGETABLES WITH LEMON DRESSING [Serves 4 to 6]

½ cucumber, sliced thin
1 tomato,
cut in half lengthwise and
sliced thin
1 green pepper,
seeded and sliced thin
2 green onions,
julienned

Place in a salad bowl.

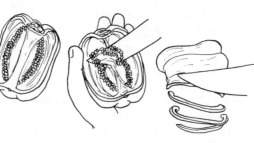

OR IN PLACE OF ABOVE:
Any combination of salad
vegetable you wish except greens

Dressing:
1 tsp. mild honey
2 Tbsp. lemon juice
½ tsp. sea salt
¼ tsp. black pepper

Mix ingredients well. Pour over vegetables. Serve at once or vegetables will wilt. Good served with main dish and rice for dinner. Excellent summer salad.

FRUIT WITH LEMON DRESSING [Serves 4 to 6]

2 cups fresh fruit,
   sliced thin [melons, grapes,
   apples, peaches, pears, etc.]

Place in salad bowl. Use one fruit or a combination of fruits.

Dressing:
1 tsp. mild honey
2 Tbsp. lemon juice
¼ tsp. sea salt

Mix ingredients well. Pour over fruit. Mix well. Chill. Serve cold. Good served with main dish and rice plus chutney for dinner. Excellent summer salad. Good snack or dessert.

PEANUT SALAD [Serves 4 to 6]

Your favorite tossed green
   salad
3 Tbsp. fresh parsley,
   chopped
1 cup bean sprouts

Place salad in large bowl. Add sprouts and parsley. Sprouts add to protein value of salad when served with a grain dish.

1 cup raw peanuts,
   chopped
   OR raw sunflower seeds,
    chopped

Roast in 300° oven 5 to 10 minutes until golden brown. Set aside to add later.

Dressing:
1 tsp. cumin seed
1 tsp. black mustard seed
   OR yellow mustard seed
2 Tbsp. vegetable oil

Heat a small cast iron skillet over high heat. Add oil. Add seeds. Fry 1 minute until seeds crackle. Remove from heat.

½ tsp. sea salt
¼ tsp. fresh ground black pepper
1 Tbsp. mild honey
2 Tbsp. lemon juice

Add salt, pepper and honey to oil. Mix well. Add lemon juice. Mix well. Pour over salad and then add peanuts to salad. Toss salad. Serve at once. Good served with a vegetarian main dish and rice for dinner. Excellent lunch served with bread and pickles.

VARIATION:

CABBAGE PEANUT SALAD
[Serves 4 to 6]

½ head green cabbage, shredded
½ head red cabbage, shredded

OR IN PLACE OF ABOVE
1 head green cabbage, shredded

Follow recipe for Peanut Salad. Use cabbage in place of tossed green salad. Cook as directed. Serve at once. Good served with a vegetarian main dish and rice for dinenr. Excellent lunch served with bread and pickles.

RYTA [YOGHURT SALAD] [Serves 4 to 6]

1 cup fresh vegetables
  cut into thin slices
  [any combination of salad
  vegetables you wish except
  greens — green pepper,
  cucumber, celery, tomatoes,
  radishes, green onions, etc.]

Dressing:
2 cups yoghurt
½ tsp. sea salt
¼ tsp. black pepper
dash ground chili pepper
  [optional]

VARIATION:

MELON RYTA
[MELON YOGHURT SALAD]
[Serves 4 to 6]

2 Tbsp. lemon juice
2 cups melon,
  cut into thin slices
  [cantalope, honeydew, persian,
  musk or combination of any]

Place in bowl. Pour lemon juice over melon pieces. Mix well.

2 Tbsp. mild honey
1 tsp. lemon juice
2 cups yoghurt
¼ tsp. sea salt

Mix honey and lemon juice well. Add yoghurt and salt. Mix gently but well. Pour over melon. Mix gently but well. Chill. Serve cold with dinner. Good snack or dessert.

VARIATION:

KISHMISH RYTA [RAISIN YOGHURT SALAD]
[Serves 4 to 6]

½ cup raisins
1 cup water

Place raisins in a bowl. Pour boiling water over them. Soak 30 minutes to 1 hour. Drain. Chop slightly. Save soaking water to use in making bread.

3 Tbsp. mild honey
1 Tbsp. lemon juice
3 cups yoghurt

Mix honey and lemon juice well. Add yoghurt and raisins. Mix gently but well. Chill. Serve cold. Good with dinner. Excellent snack or dessert.

Place 2 to 3 salad vegetables in a bowl. Mix well.

Mix gently but well. Fold in vegetables. Serve cold. Excellent cooling salad with dinner. Good served with bread and leftovers for lunch.

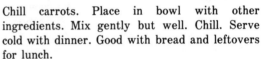

VARIATION:

CARROT RYTA
[CARROT YOGHURT SALAD]
[Serves 4 to 6]

2 cups medium grated carrot,
  steamed 3 minutes
½ tsp. sea salt
¼ tsp. black pepper
dash ground chili pepper
  [optional]
2 cups yoghurt

Chill carrots. Place in bowl with other ingredients. Mix gently but well. Chill. Serve cold with dinner. Good with bread and leftovers for lunch.

VARIATION:

PAKORAS RYTA
[GARBANZO BATTER BITS YOGHURT SALAD]
[Serves 4 to 6]

½ tsp. sea salt
½ tsp. garam-masala I
2 Tbsp. fresh parsley, minced
  OR coriander leaves, chopped
2½ cups yoghurt

Place ingredients in a bowl. Mix gently but well. Chill.

1 cup Pakora Batter Bits
  left over from making Pakoras
  [See Indian Appetizers and
  Snacks]

Save a few bits to sprinkle over top of salad. Add bits to yoghurt. Mix gently but well. Serve at once. Good served with a vegetable curry and a vegetarian main dish and rice or bread. Good served with bread and leftovers for lunch.

VARIATION:

CUCUMBER RYTA
[CUCUMBER YOGHURT SALAD]
[Serves 4 to 6]

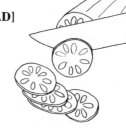

1 cucumber,
  sliced thin
1 tsp. garam-masala I
½ tsp. sea salt
2 cups yoghurt

Place cucumbers in a bowl. Mix gently but well with other ingredients. Chill. Serve cold with dinner. Good with bread and leftovers for lunch.

VARIATION:

BANANA RYTA
[BANANA YOGHURT SALAD]
[Serves 4 to 6]

3 ripe bananas,
  sliced thin

Place in a bowl.

1 tsp. mild honey
1 tsp. lemon juice
2 cups yoghurt

Mix honey and lemon juice well. Add yoghurt. Mix gently but well. Pour over bananas. Mix gently but well. Chill. Serve cold with dinner. Good snack or dessert.

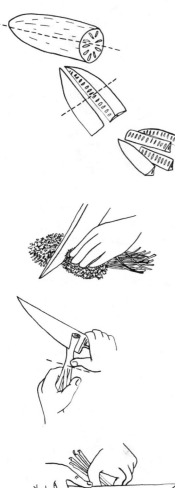

INDIAN POTATO SALAD [Serves 4 to 6]

2 large cooked potatoes,
  cut into ½ inch cubes
2 to 4 cucumbers,
  cut into ¼ inch by 2 inch
  rectangles
2 tomatoes,
  cut into ¼ inch cubes
  [optional]
4 Tbsp. fresh parsley,
  minced
  OR coriander leaves,
    minced
2 green onions,
  minced
  [optional]

Dressing:
1 Tbsp. vegetable oil
1 tsp. mustard seed
1 tsp. cumin seed

1 tsp. sea salt
1 tsp. mild honey
1 Tbsp. lemon juice
¼ tsp. black pepper
  [optional]

Place in salad bowl.

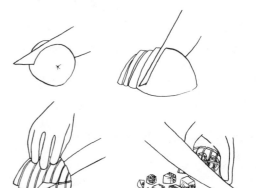

Heat a small cast iron skillet over high heat. Add oil. Add seeds. Fry 1 minute until seeds crackle. Remove from heat.

Add salt, pepper and honey to oil. Mix well. Add lemon juice. Mix well. Pour over salad. Mix well. Chill 30 minutes to 1 hour. Serve cold. Excellent summer dinner meal salad.

VEGETABLE AND FRUIT CURRIES

Vegetable and fruit curries are served with rice, a main dish and chapatis for a simple meal. Curries with yoghurt can be served with an Indian bread or rice dish for a nutritious lunch or simple dinner. Include several vegetable curries in a feast.

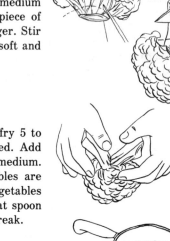

CAULIFLOWER CURRY [Serves 4 to 6]

1 large yellow onion, minced 5 slices fresh ginger root, minced 3 Tbsp. vegetable oil	Heat a heavy saucepan or wok over medium high heat. Add oil. Heat until a small piece of onion added sizzles. Add onions and ginger. Stir and fry 5 to 10 minutes until onions are soft and transparent but not brown.
1 tsp. turmeric ¼ to 1 tsp. ground chili pepper	Add to onions. Mix well.

2 medium potatoes,
   cut into small uniform-sized
   cubes
1 head cauliflower,
   cut and broken into 1 inch
   flowerlets
1 to 1½ tsp. sea salt
	Add potatoes and cauliflower. Stir and fry 5 to 10 minutes until potatoes are half cooked. Add salt. Mix well. Cover. Reduce heat to medium. Simmer 10 to 12 minutes until vegetables are just tender. Stir occasionally to keep vegetables from sticking to bottom of pan. Use a flat spoon and stir gently so cauliflower does not break.

1 to 2 tsp. garam-masala I	Sprinkle over vegetables. Mix well. Cook 1 to 2 minutes. Serve hot with rice, a main dish and bread. Keeps well. Good cold for lunch. Steam to reheat.

VARIATION:

CAULIFLOWER YOGHURT CURRY
[Serves 4 to 6]

½ to 1 cup yoghurt

Follow recipe for Cauliflower Curry. Add yoghurt with garam-masala. Mix gently but well. Simmer 1 to 2 minutes to heat yoghurt. Serve hot. Good with rice and a main dish for dinner. Good cold for lunch. Steam to reheat.

CABBAGE AND CARROT CURRY [Serves 4 to 6]

1 large yellow onion, minced ½ inch fresh ginger root, minced or grated 3 Tbsp. vegetable oil	Heat a heavy saucepan or wok over medium high heat. Add oil. Heat until a small piece of onion added sizzles. Add onions and ginger. Stir and fry 5 to 10 minutes until onions are soft and transparent but not brown.
1 tsp. turmeric ¼ to 1 tsp. ground chili pepper	Add to onions. Mix well.

2 medium potatoes,
   cut into small uniform-sized
   cubes
2 large carrots,
   cut into pea-sized pieces
	Add potatoes and carrots. Stir and fry 5 to 10 minutes until potatoes are half-cooked and lightly browned.

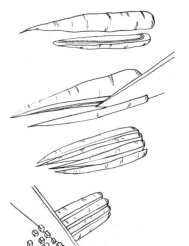

½ **head large cabbage,**
cut in half lengthwise and
then cut into ¼ inch slices

1 tsp. sea salt
1 to 2 tsp. garam-masala I

Add cabbage. Stir and fry 2 to 3 mintues until well mixed with other ingredients. Cover. Simmer over medium heat 5 to 10 minutes until vegetables are just tender.

Sprinkle over vegetables. Mix well. Cook 1 to 2 minutes. Serve hot with rice, a main dish and bread or rice. Keeps well. Good cold for lunch. Steam to reheat.

VARIATION:

GREEN PEA AND CABBAGE CURRY
[Serves 4 to 6]

2 cups green peas

Follow recipe for Cabbage and Carrot Curry. Use peas in place of carrots. Add peas with cabbage. Cook as directed. Serve hot with rice, a main dish and bread or rice, Keeps well. Good cold for lunch. Steam to reheat.

VARIATION:

GREEN BEAN AND POTATO CURRY WITH YOGHURT [Serves 4 to 6]

1 lb. green beans,
cut into 2 inch diagonal slices
½ to 2 cup yoghurt

Follow recipe for Cabbage and Carrot Curry. Use green beans in place of carrots. Add green beans with potatoes. Do not use cabbage. Add yoghurt with garam-masala. Mix gently but well. Simmer 1 to 2 minutes to heat yoghurt. Serve hot. Good with rice or bread and a main dish for dinner. Good cold for lunch. Steam to reheat.

VARIATION:

GREEN PEA AND POTATO CURRY WITH YOGHURT [Serves 4 to 6]

1 lb. green peas
½ to 1 cup yoghurt

Follow recipe for Cabbage and Carrot Curry. Use peas in place of carrots and cabbage. Add peas when potatoes are almost done. Mix well. Cover and simmer 3 to 5 minutes until tender but still bright green. Add yoghurt with garam-masala. Mix gently but well. Simmer 1 to 2 minutes to heat yoghurt. Serve hot. Good with rice or bread and a main dish for dinner. Good cold for lunch. Steam to reheat.

VARIATION:

CABBAGE AND CARROT CURRY WITH YOGHURT [Serves 4 to 6]

½ to 1 cup yoghurt

Follow recipe for Cabbage and Carrot Curry. Add yoghurt with garam-masala. Mix gently but well. Simmer 1 to 2 minutes to heat yoghurt. Serve hot. Good with rice or bread and a main dish for dinner. Good cold for lunch. Steam to reheat.

VARIATION:

GREEN BEAN AND POTATO CURRY
[Serves 4 to 6]

1 lb. green beans, cut into
2 inch diagonal slices

Follow recipe for Cabbage and Carrot Curry. Use green beans in place of carrots. Add green beans with potatoes. Do not use cabbage. Cook as directed. Serve hot with rice, a main dish and bread or rice. Keeps well. Good cold for lunch. Steam to reheat.

VARIATION:

GREEN PEA AND POTATO CURRY
[Serves 4 to 6]

1 lb. green peas

Follow recipe for Cabbage and Carrot Curry. Use peas in place of carrots and cabbage. Add peas when potatoes are almost done. Mix well. Cover and simmer 3 to 5 minutes until tender but still bright green. Finish as directed. Serve hot with rice, a main dish and bread or rice. Good cold for lunch. Keeps well. Steam to reheat.

CAULIFLOWER AND CARROT CURRY [Serves 4 to 6]

1 large yellow onion, minced
½ inch fresh ginger root,
  minced or grated
1 clove garlic,
  crushed and minced or grated
¼ to 1 chili pepper, minced
3 Tbsp. vegetable oil

Mince chilies and onions together so chilies won't scatter. Heat a heavy saucepan or wok over medium high heat. Add oil. Heat until a small piece of onion added sizzles. Add all ingredients. Stir and fry 5 to 10 minutes until onions are soft and transparent but not brown.

1 large tomato,
  cut into ¼ inch cubes
  OR ½ cup stewed tomatoes

Add to onions. Mix well. Simmer 1 to 2 minutes until tomato is broken up and forms a paste with onion mixture.

1 small head cauliflower,
  cut and broken into 1 inch
  flowerlets
3 medium carrots,
  cut into ¼ inch uniform
  diagonal slices

Add to onions and tomatoes. Mix well. Stir and fry 5 to 10 minutes until half done. Cover. Reduce heat to medium low. Simmer 5 to 10 minutes until vegetables are just tender. Stir occasionally to keep vegetables from sticking to bottom of pan. Use a flat spoon and stir gently so cauliflower does not break.

1 tsp. sea salt
1 to 2 tsp. garam-masala I

Sprinkle over vegetables. Mix well. Cook 1 to 2 minutes. Serve hot with rice or bread and a main dish for dinner. Keeps well. Good cold for lunch. Steam to reheat.

VARIATION:

CAULIFLOWER AND CARROT CURRY WITH YOGHURT [Serves 4 to 6]

½ to 1 cup yoghurt

Follow recipe for Cauliflower and Cabbage Curry. Add yoghurt with garam-masala. Mix gently but well. Simmer 1 to 2 minutes to heat yoghurt. Serve hot. Good with rice or bread and a main dish for dinner. Good cold for lunch. Steam to reheat.

VARIATION:

CAULIFLOWER, CARROT AND GREEN BEAN CURRY [Serves 4 to 6]

¼ lb. green beans,
  cut into 2 inch diagonal slices
2 medium carrots,
  cut into ¼ inch uniform
  diagonal slices

Follow recipe for Cauliflower and Carrot Curry. Use green beans in place of 1 carrot and use only 2 carrots. Cook as directed. Serve hot with rice or bread and a main dish for dinner. Keeps well. Good cold for lunch. Steam to reheat.

VARIATION:

CAULIFLOWER, CARROT AND GREEN BEAN CURRY WITH YOGHURT [Serves 4 to 6]

¼ lb. green beans,
  cut into 2 inch diagonal slices
2 medium carrots,
  cut into ¼ inch uniform diagonal
  slices
½ to 1 cup yoghurt

Follow recipe for Cauliflower and Carrot Curry. Use green beans in place of 1 carrot and use only 2 carrots. Cook as directed. Add yoghurt with garam-masala. Mix gently but well. Simmer 1 to 2 minutes to heat yoghurt. Serve hot with rice or bread and a main dish for dinner. Good cold for lunch. Steam to reheat.

GREEN PEA AND CABBAGE CURRY WITH TOMATOES [Serves 4 to 6]

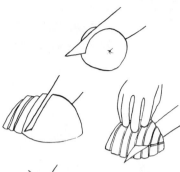

1 large yellow onion, minced
¹/₂ inch fresh ginger root,
**   minced or grated**
1 clove garlic,
**   crushed and minced or grated**
¹/₄ to 1 chili pepper, minced
3 Tbsp. vegetable oil

Mince chilies and onions together so chilies won't scatter. Heat a heavy saucepan or wok over medium heat. Add oil. Heat until a small piece of onion added sizzles. Add all ingredients. Stir and fry 5 to 10 minutes until onions are soft and transparent but not brown.

1 large tomato,
**   cut into ¹/₄ inch cubes**
**   OR ¹/₂ cup stewed tomatoes**

Add to onions. Mix well. Simmer 1 to 2 minutes until tomato is broken up and forms a paste with onion mixture.

¹/₂ large head cabbage,
**   cut in half lengthwise and**
**   then cut into ¹/₄ inch slices**
2 cups green peas

Add to onions and tomatoes. Mix well. Stir and fry 2 to 3 minutes to mix ingredients well. Cover. Reduce heat to medium low. Simmer 5 to 10 minutes until cabbage is just tender.

1 tsp. sea salt
1 to 2 tsp. garam masala I

Sprinkle over vegetables. Mix well. Cook 1 to 2 minutes. Serve hot with rice or bread and a main dish for dinner. Keeps well. Good cold for lunch. Steam to reheat.

VARIATION:

GREEN PEA AND CABBAGE WITH TOMATOES AND YOGHURT
[Serves 4 to 6]

¹/₂ to 1 cup yoghurt

Follow recipe for Green Pea and Cabbage Curry With Tomatoes. Add yoghurt with garam-masala. Mix gently but well. Simmer 1 to 2 minutes to heat yoghurt. Serve hot. Good with rice or bread and a main dish for dinner. Good cold for lunch. steam to reheat.

GREEN PEPPER CURRY [Serves 4 to 6]

1 small hot green pepper,
**   sliced paper thin**
**   OR dried green pepper,**
**   minced**
3 Tbsp. vegetable oil

Heat a heavy saucepan or wok over medium high heat. Add oil. Heat until a small piece of pepper added sizzles. Add pepper. Stir and fry 1 to 2 minutes.

¹/₂ tsp. turmeric
1 tsp. sea salt

Add to peppers. Mix well.

4 to 6 green peppers,
**   seeded and cut into thin strips**
1 large yellow onion
**   cut in half lengthwise and**
**   then sliced paper thin**

Add to hot pepper and oil. Stir and fry 5 to 10 minutes until peppers are just tender. Serve hot. A good dinner dish served with rice and a main dish. A beautiful dish to serve at feasts.

CARROT AND GREEN BEAN CURRY [Serves 4 to 6]

1 large yellow onion,
   minced
½ inch fresh ginger root,
   minced or grated
1 clove garlic,
   crushed and minced
   or grated
3 Tbsp. vegetable oil

Heat a heavy saucepan or wok over medium high heat. Add oil. Heat until a small piece of onion added sizzles. Add all ingredients. Stir and fry 5 to 10 minutes until onions are soft and transparent but not brown.

1 tsp. turmeric
¼ to 1 tsp. ground chili pepper

Add to onion mixture. Mix well.

1 tomato,
   cut into ¼ inch cubes
   OR ½ cup stewed tomatoes

Add to onion mixture. Mix well. Simmer 1 to 2 minutes until tomato is broken up and forms a paste with onion mixture.

3 medium carrots,
   cut into ¼ inch uniform
   diagonal slices
½ lb. green beans,
   cut into uniform 2 inch
   diagonal slices

Add to onions and tomatoes. Mix well. Stir and fry 5 to 10 minutes until carrots and beans are half done. Cover. Reduce heat to medium. Simmer 8 to 10 minutes until vegetables are just tender. Stir occasionally to prevent sticking.

1 tsp. sea salt
1 to 2 tsp. garam-masala I

Sprinkle over vegetables. Mix well. Cook 1 to 2 minutes. Serve hot with rice, a main dish and bread. Keeps well. Good cold for lunch. Steam to reheat.

VARIATION:

CARROT AND BEAN CURRY WITH YOGHURT
[Serves 4 to 6]

½ to 1 cup yoghurt

Follow recipe for Carrot and Green Bean Curry. Add yoghurt with garam-masala. Mix gently but well. Simmer 1 to 2 minutes to heat yoghurt. Serve hot. Good with rice and a main dish for dinner. Good cold for lunch. Steam to reheat.

SUMMER SQUASH [ZUCCHINI, YELLOW CROOKNECK, MARROW] CURRY
[Serves 4 to 6]

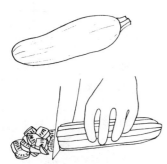

1 large yellow onion,
  minced
¼ to ½ large hot fresh
  red pepper,
  minced
  OR 1 dried chili pepper,
  minced
3 Tbsp. vegetable oil
	Mince chilies and onions together so chilies won't scatter. Heat a heavy saucepan or wok over medium high heat. Add oil. Heat until a small piece of onion added sizzles. Add onions and pepper. Stir and fry 5 to 10 minutes until onions are soft and transparent but not brown.

2 medium potatoes, cut into ¼ to ½ inch cubes	Add to onion mixture. Stir and fry 5 to 10 minutes until half done and lightly browned.
1 tsp. sea salt ½ tsp. turmeric	Add to potatoes. Mix well.

4 cups zucchini,
  cut into ½ inch cubes
  OR 4 cups any summer squash,
  cut into ½ inch cubes
	Add to potatoes. Mix well. Fry 5 to 10 minutes until squash is lightly browned.

1 tomato,
  cut into 1/8 inch cubes
  OR ½ cup stewed tomatoes,
  chopped
	Add to squash. Mix gently. Cover. Reduce heat to medium. Simmer 5 to 10 minutes until squash is tender. Mix occasionally to prevent sticking. Serve hot. Good with main dish and rice or bread for dinner. Good cold for lunch. Keeps well. Steam to reheat.

GREEN BEAN CURRY [Serves 4 to 6]

1 yellow onion,
  minced
½ inch fresh ginger root,
  minced or grated
1 clove garlic,
  crushed and minced
  or grated
3 Tbsp. vegetable oil
	Heat a heavy saucepan or wok over medium high heat. Add oil. Heat until a small piece of onion added sizzles. Add onion, ginger and garlic. Stir and fry 5 to 10 minutes until onions are soft and transparent but not brown.

1 tomato,
  cut into ¼ inch cubes
  OR ½ cup stewed tomatoes
	Add to onions. Mix well. Simmer 1 to 2 minutes until tomatoes are broken up and form paste with onion mixture.

1 lb. green beans,
  cut into uniform 2 inch
  diagonal slices
1 tsp. sea salt
¼ tsp. black pepper
	Add to onions and tomatoes. Mix well. Stir and fry 2 to 3 minutes. Reduce heat to medium. Cover. Simmer 10 to 15 minutes until beans are just tender. Stir occasionally to prevent sticking. Keep cover tight so beans will cook in their own liquid.

1 to 2 tsp. garam-masala I	Sprinkle over vegetables. Mix well. Cook 1 to 2 minutes. Serve hot with rice, a main dish and bread. Keeps well. Good cold for lunch. Steam to reheat.

TOMATO CURRY [Serves 4 to 6]

1 tsp. cumin seed
3 Tbsp. vegetable oil

Heat a heavy skillet or wok over medium high heat. Add oil. Heat until a seed added crackles. Add cumin. Fry 1 to 2 minutes until lightly browned.

1 medium yellow onion,
  minced
1 clove garlic,
  crushed and minced or grated
1 inch fresh ginger root,
  minced or grated

Add to oil. Stir and fry 5 to 10 minutes until onions are soft and transparent but not brown.

2 medium potatoes,
  cut into ¼ inch cubes

Add potatoes. Stir and fry 5 to 10 minutes until half done and lightly browned.

1 cup stewed tomatoes

Add. Simmer 5 minutes until tomatoes and onions form a paste which covers potatoes. Cover. Reduce heat to low. Simmer 10 to 15 minutes until potatoes are tender.

1 tsp. mild honey
1 tsp. sea salt
¼ tsp. black pepper
1 to 2 tsp. garam-masala I
1 lb. tomatoes,
  cut into bite-sized pieces

Add spices and honey first. Mix well. Add raw tomatoes. Mix gently. Simmer 3 to 5 minutes over medium heat until tomatoes are hot but do not lose shape. Excellent summer vegetable dish. Good served with main dish and rice or bread for dinner. Great cold for lunch. Keeps well. Steam to reheat.

EGGPLANT CURRY [Serves 4 to 6]

2 medium eggplant
  OR ½ lb. winter squash

Bake at 350° for 10 to 15 minutes until just slightly tender. Cut into ½ inch cubes. Set aside for later use.

1 tsp. turmeric
½ tsp. cumin seed
½ tsp. black mustard seed
  OR yellow mustard seed
2 Tbsp. fresh parsley,
  minced
  OR coriander leaves,
    minced
¼ to 1 tsp. ground chili pepper
3 Tbsp. vegetable oil

Heat a heavy saucepan or wok over medium high heat. Add oil. Heat until a cumin seed crackles. Add ingredients. Stir and fry 1 to 2 minutes until cumin seeds pop.

3 Tbsp. butter
1 medium yellow onion,
  minced
1 clove garlic,
  crushed and minced or grated

Add butter to herbs. Melt. Add onion and garlic. Stir and fry 5 to 10 minutes until onions are soft and transparent but not brown. Add eggplant cubes. Stir and fry an additional 5 to 10 minutes until eggplant is tender.

1 tsp. sea salt
1 to 2 tsp. garam-masala I
  [optional]

Sprinkle over vegetables. Mix well. Serve hot. Excellent feast dish. Good with a main dish, rice and bread for dinner. Good cold for lunch. Keeps well. Steam to reheat.

MELON CURRY [Serves 4 to 6]

½ **yellow onion,**
   minced
2 **thin slices fresh ginger root,**
   minced
¼ **to 1 chili pepper,**
   minced
2 **Tbsp. vegetable oil**

Mince chilies and onions together so chilies won't scatter. Heat a heavy saucepan or wok over medium high heat. Add oil. Heat until a small piece of onion added sizzles. Add ingredients. Stir and fry 5 to 10 minutes until onions are soft and transparent but not brown.

¼ **tsp. turmeric**
1 **tsp. coriander, ground**
¼ **tsp. cumin, ground**
¼ **tsp. whole cardamom, crushed**
   OR 2 cardamom seeds,
      husked and crushed
¼ **tsp. sea salt**

Add to onions. Stir and fry 1 to 2 minutes until well mixed.

3 **cups melon,**
   cut into ½ inch cubes
   [to be fancy - melon balls]
   use honeydew, casaba, persian
   or cantalope

Add to onions. Mix well. Stir and fry 1 minute. Reduce heat to medium.

juice of 1 lemon
2 **Tbsp. mild honey**

Add to melon mixture. Mix well. Bring to boil over medium heat. Simmer 1 to 2 minutes to heat melon. Serve hot or cold. Excellent summer curry. Good with main dish, rice or bread for dinner. Good cold for lunch on a hot day. Do not reheat.

VARIATION:

MELON CURRY WITH YOGHURT
[Serves 4 to 6]

½ **to 1 cup yoghurt**

Follow recipe for Melon Curry. Chill curry when cooked. Fold in yoghurt before serving. An excellent summer dish. Good as a snack or dessert. Good cold for lunch on a hot day. Do not heat.

VARIATION:

SWEET WINTER SQUASH CURRY
[Serves 4 to 6]

3 **cups winter squash,**
   cut into 1 inch by ¼ inch slices

Follow recipe for Melon Curry. Use winter squash in place of melon. Cook as directed but cover and simmer 10 to 15 minutes until squash is tender. Serve hot or cold. Good winter substitute for Melon Curry. Good with main dish and rice for dinner. Good cold for lunch the next day.

VARIATION:

SWEET WINTER SQUASH CURRY WITH YOGHURT
[Serves 4 to 6]

3 **cups winter squash,**
   cut into 1 inch by ¼ inch slices
½ **to 1 cup yoghurt**

Follow recipe for Melon Curry. Use winter squash in place of melon. Cook as directed but cover and simmer 10 to 15 minutes until squash is tender. Chill. Fold in yoghurt before serving. An excellent winter substitute for Melon Curry with Yoghurt. Good as a snack or dessert. Do not heat.

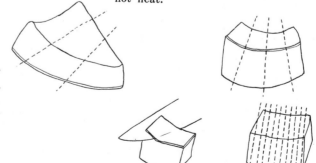

SPINACH WITH HERBS [Serves 4 to 6]

2 Tbsp. fresh parsley,
  minced
  OR coriander leaves,
    minced
1 tsp. cumin seed
1 tsp. black mustard seed
  OR yellow mustard seed
¼ to 2 dried chili peppers,
  minced
2 thin slices fresh ginger root,
  minced
3 Tbsp. vegetable oil

Heat a heavy saucepan or wok over medium high heat. Add oil. Heat until a cumin seed added crackles. Add ingredients. Stir and fry 1 to 2 minutes until seeds pop.

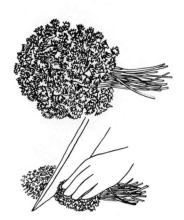

2 lbs. spinach,
  stems removed,
  leaves shredded
½ to 1 tsp. sea salt

Add spinach. Stir and fry 3 to 5 minutes until spinach is soft and well mixed with herbs. Serve hot. Quick vegetable dish for dinner. Good served with a main dish and rice or bread for a dinner meal.

VARIATION:

GREENS WITH HERBS
[Serves 4 to 6]

2 lbs. swiss chard,
  stems removed,
  leaves shredded
  OR mustard greens,
    stems removed,
    leaves shredded
  OR beet greens,
    stems removed,
    leaves shredded
  OR any other cooking green
    stems removed and
    leaves shredded

Follow recipe for Spinach with Herbs. Use other greens in place of spinach. Cook as directed. Serve hot. Quick vegetable dish for dinner. Good served with a main dish and rice or bread for a dinner meal.

VEGETARIAN MAIN DISHES

Vegetarian dishes are the central part of simple Indian meals. Some are used for breakfast or lunches also. Along with these main dishes are served a bread or rice dish or both and one or two vegetable dishes; one of which might be a cooling yoghurt salad. A grain dish must be served with the lentil or bean dishes to get full utilization of the protein. A vegetarian feast should include four or five of these dishes.

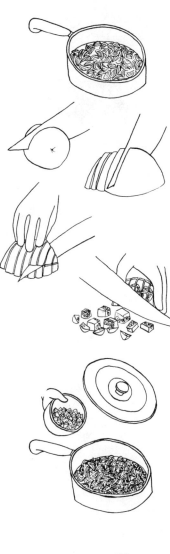

EGG CURRY [Serves 4 to 6]

1 large yellow onion,
   minced
2 to 3 Tbsp. fresh parsley,
   minced
   OR coriander leaves,
     minced
1 clove garlic,
   crushed and minced
   or grated
3 Tbsp. vegetable oil

Heat a heavy cast iron saucepan over medium high heat. Add oil. Heat until a small piece of onion added sizzles. Add ingredients. Stir and fry 5 to 10 minutes until onions are soft and transparent but not brown.

1 Tbsp. dried shredded coconut
1 to 2 tsp. garam-masala I
1½ tsp. sea salt
¼ tsp. black pepper
¼ to 1 tsp. red pepper
   [optional]

Add to onions. Mix well. Simmer 1 to 2 minutes.

4 tomatoes, diced
   OR 2 cups drained
     stewed tomatoes

Add tomatoes to onions. Mix well. Simmer 3 to 5 minutes until tomatoes form a paste with the onions and spices.

¼ cup yoghurt
   [optional]

Add yoghurt. Mix gently but well. Simmer 1 minute.

8 to 12 hard-boiled eggs,
   sliced in half lengthwise

Add eggs yolk side up. Baste with sauce. Simmer 5 to 10 minutes until heated through. Keep covered except to baste eggs. Serve hot. Serve with rice or bread and a vegetable dish. Good cold next day for lunch.

EGG AND POTATO CURRY [Serves 4 to 6]

1 large yellow onion, minced
½ inch fresh ginger root,
  minced or grated
1 large clove garlic,
  crushed and minced
3 Tbsp. vegetable oil

Heat a heavy cast iron saucepan over medium high heat. Add oil. Heat until a small piece of onion added sizzles. Add ingredients. Stir and fry 5 to 10 minutes until onions are soft and transparent but not brown.

2 medium sized potatoes,
  cut into ½ inch cubes

Add to onion mixture. Stir and fry 5 to 10 minutes until half done and lightly brown.

2 tomatoes, diced
  OR 1 cup stewed tomatoes,
    chopped
1 Tbsp. tomato paste
1 to 2 tsp. garam-masala
1 tsp. sea salt
¼ tsp. black pepper
¼ to 2 tsp. chili pepper

Add to onions and potato mixture. Mix well. Stir and fry for 3 to 5 minutes until potatoes are well coated with tomatoes and the tomatoes are broken up.

8 to 12 whole hard-boiled eggs,
  cut in half lengthwise

Add eggs yolk side up. Baste with sauce. Simmer 5 to 10 minutes until eggs heated through. Keep covered except to baste eggs. Serve hot. Serve with rice or bread and a vegetable dish. Good cold for lunch the next day. Keeps up to 1 week in refrigerator.

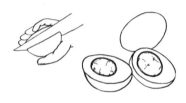

EGG AND PEA CURRY [Serves 4 to 6]

1 inch fresh ginger root,
  minced or grated
1 large clove garlic,
  crushed and minced or grated
1 large yellow onion, minced
½ tsp. turmeric
¼ to 1 tsp. chili powder
3 Tbsp. vegetable oil

Heat a large cast iron skillet over medium high heat. Add oil. Heat until a small piece of onion added sizzles. Add ingredients. Stir and fry 5 to 10 minutes until onions are soft and transparent but not brown.

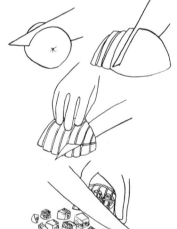

4 fresh tomatoes, diced
  OR 2 cups stewed tomatoes,
    chopped
2 Tbsp. tomato paste
1 tsp. mild honey

Mix well with onions. Simmer 3 to 5 minutes until tomatoes are well mixed and form a paste with other ingredients.

2 cups fresh green peas
1 Tbsp. garam-masala I
3 Tbsp. fresh parsley, chopped
  OR coriander leaves, chopped
1½ tsp. sea salt

Add to tomatoes and onions. Mix well. Simmer 5 minutes until peas are just beginning to get tender.

8 to 12 hard-boiled eggs,
  cut in half lengthwise

Add eggs yolk side up. Baste with sauce. Simmer 5 to 10 minutes until eggs heated through. Keep covered except to baste eggs. Place in serving dish.

Optional step:

**3 Tbsp. fresh parsley, chopped
  OR coriander leaves, chopped**

Sprinkle over dish before serving. Serve hot. Good with rice or bread for a simple dinner. Good cold for lunch the next day. Keeps up to 1 week.

VARIATION:

EGG AND MUSHROOM CURRY
[Serves 4 to 6]

**½ lb. mushrooms,
  cut into ¼ inch slices**

Follow recipe for Egg and Pea Curry. Use mushrooms in place of peas. Cook as directed. Serve hot. Good with rice or bread and a vegetable dish for a simple dinner. Good cold for lunch the next day. Keeps up to 1 week.

EGGS SCRAMBLED INDIAN STYLE [Serves 4]

**5 eggs, beat until well mixed
  but not frothy**
1 tsp. sea salt
1 tsp. garam-masala I
**¼ to ½ tsp. chili pepper
  [optional]**
**2 Tbsp. butter
  OR vegetable oil**

Heat a medium-sized cast iron skillet over medium heat. Add butter and melt. Add eggs. Stir gently so eggs remain in large pieces. Cook 2 to 3 minutes until set but still very moist.

1 tomato, cut into ½ inch cubes
3 green onions, minced
**1 to 2 Tbsp. fresh parsley,
  minced**
** OR coriander leaves, minced**

Add to eggs. Mix gently. Cook 1 minute until tomatoes heated but eggs still moist. Serve hot for breakfast. Also a good quick lunch or serve with rice and vegetables for dinner.

INDIAN EGG OMELET [Serves 4]

5 eggs, beat until frothy
1 tsp. garam-masala I
1 tsp. sea salt
**¼ to ½ tsp. chili pepper
  [optional]**
**2 Tbsp. butter
  OR vegetable oil**

Heat a medium-sized cast iron skillet over medium heat. Add butter. Melt. Add eggs when a small drop added to pan sets. Pour eggs into center of pan. Allow to set 1 minutes. Gently push eggs toward center of pan with spoon. Cook 2 to 3 minutes until eggs set on bottom but still slightly runny.

1 tomato, cut into ½ inch cubes
3 green onions, minced
**1 to 2 Tbsp. coriander leaves,
  minced**
** OR fresh parsley,
    chopped**

Sprinkle over top of eggs. Cover and cook 10 to 12 minutes at medium low until eggs well set. Uncover and loosen edges with a knife. Place plate over top of pan and invert omelet onto plate. Serve hot. Good for breakfast or quick lunch. Makes good dinner dish when served with cooked fried rice and a salad.

DAHL [LENTILS] are an important protein source in India. Lentils should be washed before use since sticks, dirt and small stones often are found with them. The following list contains Dahls which can be obtained in Indian food shops in North America. Those with an (*) asterisk can be obtained in most natural foods stores and in some regular grocery stores.

WHOLE URAD: A small black member of the pea family. Takes 50 to 60 minutes to cook instead of the usual 20 minutes. Good for sprouting for sprout curry.

URAD DAHL: Split whole Urad, hulled or unhulled. Cooks quickly. Used with red lentils or by itself for Varhyas and Dosa.

WHOLE MOONG*: Known as Mung Beans in North America. Takes 50 to 60 minutes to cook instead of the ususal 20 minutes. Good for sprouting for sprout curry or adding to salads.

WHITE MOONG DAHL: Split hulled Mung Beans. Cooks quickly. Used with red lentils or by itself in Dosa and Varhyas.

RED LENTILS*: Common North American red soup lentils. Cook quickly. Used with White Moong Dahl or Urad Dahl in Varhyas and Dosa.

GREEN LENTILS*: Common North American green soup lentils. Cook quickly.

CHANNA DAHL: Small brown garbanzo bean from India. Usually split; in fact yellow split peas* can be substituted for it. Takes 50 to 60 minutes to cook instead of the usual 20 minutes.

TOOR [TUR] DAHL: An oily orange lentil with a pungent flavor. A favorite of many Indians. Cooks quickly.

YAL DAHL: Light yellow lentil similar to green lentils. Cooks quickly.

DAHL I [LENTILS] [Serves 4 to 6]

1 cup white moong dahl plus
1 cup red lentils
  OR 2 cups of any lentil
4 to 5 cups water
1 tsp. turmeric
2 tsp. sea salt

Place ingredients in a heavy saucepan. Cover. Bring to a boil over high heat. Reduce heat to medium low. Simmer 20 to 30 minutes until lentils are tender.

3 Tbsp. vegetable oil
  OR butter
1 large yellow onion,
  minced
1 inch fresh ginger root,
  minced

While lentils are cooking, heat a cast iron skillet over medium high heat. Add oil. Heat until a small piece of onion added sizzles. Add onions and ginger. Stir and fry 5 to 10 minutes until onions are soft and transparent. Remove from heat. Add to lentils when they are tender. Mix well with lentils. Simmer an additional 5 minutes.

2 tsp. garam-masala I
3 Tbsp. fresh parsley, minced
  OR coriander leaves, minced

Mix well with lentils and serve immediately. Good with rice and bread for dinner along with a vegetable dish. Good cold for lunch the next day with bread and chutney. Keeps well.

DAHL II [LENTILS] [Serves 4 to 6]

1 cup white moong dahl plus
1 cup red lentils
  OR 2 cups any lentil
4 to 5 cups water
1 tsp. turmeric
2 tsp. sea salt

Place ingredients in a heavy saucepan. Cover. Bring to a boil over high heat. Reduce heat to medium low. Simmer 20 to 30 minutes until lentils are tender.

4 Tbsp. vegetable oil
2 tsp. cumin seeds

Heat a small cast iron skillet over medium high heat. Add oil. Heat until a cumin seed added jumps. Add seeds. Brown 1 minute. Remove from heat. Add to lentils when tender. Mix well and simmer lentils for an additional 5 minutes.

1 to 2 tsp. garam-masala I
3 Tbsp. fresh parsley, minced
  OR coriander leaves, minced

Mix well with lentils and serve at once. Good with rice and bread for dinner along with a vegetable dish. Good cold for lunch the next day with bread and chutney. Keeps well.

SPLIT URAD DAHL [URAD LENTILS] [Serves 4 to 6]

2 yellow onions, minced
½ inch fresh ginger root,
  crushed and minced or grated
2 Tbsp. fresh parsley, minced
  OR coriander leaves, minced
3 Tbsp. vegetable oil

Heat a heavy cast iron skillet over medium high heat. Add oil. Heat until a small piece of onion added sizzles. Add onion, ginger and herb. Stir and fry 5 to 10 minutes until onions are soft and transparent but not brown.

2 large tomatoes, diced
  OR 1½ cups stewed tomatoes,
    chopped
1 tsp. turmeric
2 tsp. sea salt
¼ to 1 tsp. chili pepper
  [optional]

Add to onions. Mix well. Stir and fry 3 to 5 minutes until tomatoes form a paste with other ingredients.

1½ cups split urad dahl

Soak overnight or a minimum of 6 hours. Drain. Allow to dry for 30 minutes to 1 hour (optional). Add to onion and tomato mixture. Fry 5 minutes until dahl slightly browned.

2½ cups water

Add to dahl and tomato mixture. Cover and bring to boil over high heat. Reduce heat to low and simmer for 20 minutes. Place in an oven at 350° for 10 minutes to finish cooking.

2 tsp. garam-masala I

Add to lentils and mix well. Serve hot. Good with rice and bread for dinner along with a vegetable dish. Good cold for lunch the next day with bread and chutney. Keeps well.

VARIATION:

SPLIT MOONG DAHL [SPLIT MUNG BEANS] [Serves 4 to 6]

1½ cups split moong dahl

Follow recipe for Urad Dahl. Use moong dahl for urad dahl. Cook as directed. Serve hot. Good with rice or bread for dinner along with a vegetable dish. Good cold for lunch the next day with bread and chutney. Keeps well.

WHOLE URAD DAHL [BLACK LENTILS] [Serves 4 to 6]

2 cups black whole urad dahl
6 cups water
1 tsp. turmeric
1½ tsp. sea salt

Place ingredients in a heavy saucepan. Cover. Bring to a boil over high heat. Reduce heat to medium low. Simmer 1 or 1½ hours until beans are tender. Or cook at full pressure for 45 minutes.

½ inch fresh ginger root,
   crushed and minced or grated
2 Tbsp. fresh parsley, minced
   OR coriander leaves, minced
1 large yellow onion, minced
¼ to 1 tsp. chili pepper
2 Tbsp. butter
   OR vegetable oil

Heat a small cast iron skillet over medium high heat. Add butter. Melt. Add other ingredients. Stir and fry 5 to 10 minutes until onions are soft and transparent but not brown. Remove from heat. Add to lentils when they are tender. Mix well with lentils. Simmer an additional 5 minutes.

2 tsp. garam-masala I

Add to dahl and onions. Mix well and serve at once. Good with rice and bread for dinner along with a vegetable dish. Good cold for lunch the next day with bread and chutney. Keeps well.

VARIATION:

WHOLE MOONG DAHL [MUNG BEANS]
[Serves 4 to 6]

2 cups moong dahl

Follow recipe for Whole Urad Dahl. Use whole moong dahl for urad dahl. Cook as directed. Serve hot. Good with rice or bread for dinner along with a vegetable dish. Good cold for lunch the next day with bread and chutney. Keeps well.

CHANNA CURRY [CURRIED GARBANZOS] [Serves 4 to 6]

1 cup garbanzos
4 cups water
   [more if needed to keep
   garbanzos covered]

Cover garbanzos with water and soak overnight. Drain. (optional step) Place garbanzos in heavy saucepan. Add water. Cover. Bring to boil over high heat. Reduce heat to medium low. Simmer 3 to 4 hours until tender (easily mashed with fork). To pressure cook: place garbanzos and water in pressure cooker. Cover. Bring to full pressure. Cook at full pressure 1 hour. Remove from heat and cool. Drain. Reserve stock.

3 Tbsp. vegetable oil
1 large yellow onion,
   minced
1 large clove garlic,
   crushed and minced or grated
½ inch fresh ginger root,
   crushed and minced or grated

Heat a heavy saucepan over medium high heat. Add oil. Heat until a small piece of onion added sizzles. Add onions and remaining ingredients. Stir and fry 5 to 10 minutes until onions soft and transparent but not brown.

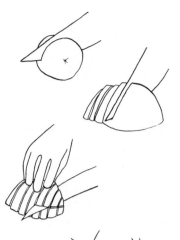

2 medium raw or cooked potatoes,
   cut into ½ inch cubes
1 tomato, diced
   OR ½ cup stewed tomatoes
1 tsp. sea salt
¼ tsp. black pepper

Add to onions. Stir and fry 5 to 10 minutes until potatoes are lightly browned and tomatoes have formed a paste with the other ingredients.

2 cups cooked garbanzos
¼ cup tomato paste
1 cup stewed tomatoes with juice
1 cup garbanzo stock
2 tsp. garam-masala I

Add to onions and potato mixture. Mix well. Cover and bring to boil. Reduce heat to medium low. Simmer 15 to 20 minutes until potatoes are tender; cook only 5 to 10 minutes if potatoes are already cooked. Serve hot. Excellent dinner dish served with rice and a vegetable dish. Good vegetarian feast dish. Good cold for lunch the next day. Mash and serve as a vegetable dip dish or sandwich spread. Keeps well.

VARIATION:

DRIED BEAN CURRY [Serves 4 to 6]

1 cup red kidney beans
   OR 1 cup navy beans
   OR 1 cup pinto beans
   OR 1 cup soybeans
   OR 1 cup fava beans
   OR 1 cup dried beans
      [varieties combined]

Follow recipe for Channa Curry. Use 1 cup of any bean in place of garbanzos. Serve hot with rice and chapatis or good cold. Excellent vegetarian feast dish. Serve with a vegetable dish for dinner. Good cold for lunch the next day. Mash and serve as a vegetable dip dish or sandwich spread. Keeps well.

BEAN SPROUT CURRY [Serves 4 to 6]

1 medium yellow onion, minced
1 clove garlic,
   crushed and minced or grated
½ inch fresh ginger root,
   crushed and minced or grated
3 Tbsp. vegetable oil

Heat a heavy cast iron pan over medium high heat. Add oil. Heat until a small piece of onion added sizzles. Add onions, ginger and garlic. Stir and fry 5 to 10 minutes until onions are soft and transparent but not brown.

2 medium potatoes,
   cut in ½ inch cubes
1 tomato, cubed
   OR ½ cup stewed tomatoes

Add to onions. Stir and fry 15 to 20 minutes until tomatoes are broken down and potatoes are almost done.

1½ tsp. sea salt
¼ tsp. black pepper
1 to 2 tsp. garam-masala I
1 lb. mung bean sprouts,
   sprouted only 3 days
   OR whole urad dahl sprouts,
      sprouted only 3 days
   OR green lentil sprouts,
      sprouted only 3 days
   OR small channa dahl sprouts,
      sprouted only 3 days

Add to potatoes and onions. Mix well. Cover and simmer 2 to 3 minutes until sprouts are just hot. Serve hot. Good with rice or bread and a vegetable dish for dinner. Good cold for lunch the next day.

VARHYA CURRY [LENTIL CAKE CURRY] [Serves 4 to 6]

1 large yellow onion, minced
1 clove garlic,
   crushed and minced or grated
1 inch ginger,
   crushed and minced or grated
3 Tbsp. vegetable oil

Heat a heavy saucepan over medium high heat. Add oil. Heat until a piece of onion added sizzles. Add ingredients. Stir and fry 5 to 10 minutes until onions are soft and transparent but not brown.

15 varhya
   [spicy dried lentil cakes]
   [See Indian Basic Ingredients]

Add to onions. Stir and fry 5 to 10 minutes until lightly browned.

2 large tomatoes, diced
   OR 2 cups stewed tomatoes
¼ cup tomato paste
1 tsp. sea salt
¼ tsp. black pepper
1 to 2 tsp. garam-masala I

Add to onions and varhya. Mix well. Cover. Reduce heat to medium. Simmer 10 to 15 minutes until varhya are tender. Serve hot. Good for dinner served with rice and vegetable dish. Keeps well. Good cold for lunch the next day.

VARIATION:

VARHYA VEGETABLE CURRY [LENTIL CAKE VEGETABLE CURRY] [Serves 4 to 6]

1 cup peas
   OR whole kernel corn
   OR sliced mushrooms
   OR ¼ lb. green beans,
      cut into pea-sized pieces
   OR 2 carrots,
      cut into pea-sized pieces

Follow recipe for Varhya Curry. Add vegetables as follows: beans, carrots and mushrooms with the varhya to be fried with the onions; peas and corn after varhyas have cooked in tomato sauce for 10 minutes. Cook as directed. Serve hot. Good with rice for dinner. Good cold for lunch the next day. A meal-in-a-bowl dish when served with bread. Good dish for camping.

VARIATION:

MONGORHIS CURRY [DEEP FRIED LENTIL CAKE CURRY] [Serves 4 to 6]

15 mongorhis
   [deep fried lentil cakes]
   [See Indian Appetizers and
   Snacks]

Follow recipe for Varhya Curry. Use mongorhis in place of varhya. Cook as directed. Serve hot. Good with rice and vegetable dish for dinner. Good cold for lunch the next day.

VARIATION:

MONGORHIS CURRY WITH VEGETABLES [DEEP FRIED LENTIL CAKE CURRY WITH VEGETABLES] [Serves 4 to 6]

15 mongorhis
   [deep fried lentil cakes]
   [See Indian Appetizers and
   Snacks]
1 cup peas
   OR whole kernel corn
   OR mushrooms, sliced thin
   OR ¼ lb. green beans,
      cut into pea sized pieces
   OR 2 carrots,
      cut into pea-sized pieces

Follow recipe for Varhya Curry. Use mongorhis in place of varhya. Add vegetables as follows: beans, carrots and mushrooms with the mongorhis to be fried with the onions; peas and corn after mongorhis have cooked in tomato sauce for 10 minutes. Cook as directed. Serve hot. Good with rice for dinner. Good cold for lunch the next day. A meal-in-a-bowl served with bread.

UPMA [CRACKED WHEAT WITH VEGETABLES] [Serves 4 to 6]

¼ **cup vegetable oil** ⅓ **cup green lentils**	Heat a large cast iron saucepan over medium high heat. Add oil. Heat until lentil added sizzles. Add lentils. Stir and fry 1 to 2 minutes until lightly browned.
1 large yellow onion **minced** **1 large clove garlic,** **crushed and minced** **or grated** **1 small fresh hot pepper,** **minced**	Add to lentils. Stir and fry 5 to 10 minutes until onions are soft and transparent but not brown.
2 cups bulgur wheat **[fine grind]** **OR regular bulgur,** **cracked in a flour mill** **or blender**	Add to onions and lentils. Stir and fry for 5 minutes until wheat is lightly browned.
1 cup carrots, **cut into pea-sized pieces** ½ **cup green onions,** **sliced thin** **OR leeks, sliced thin** **1 cup green beans,** **cut into pea-sized pieces**	Add. Mix well. Stir and fry 2 to 3 minutes.

2 large tomatoes, diced **OR 1 cup stewed tomatoes,** **drained and chopped**	Add to lentils and vegetables. Mix well. Stir and fry 2 to 3 minutes until tomatoes are well broken up.
5 cups water **2 tsp. sea salt**	Add water and salt. Mix well. Bring to a boil over high heat. Cover. Reduce heat to medium low. Simmer 20 to 30 minutes until lentils tender and water absorbed. Stir occasionally.
3 sprigs parsley, **chopped [optional]** **OR coriander leaves,** **chopped [optional]** **juice of 1 lemon** **2 tsp. garam-masala I**	Add to cooked lentils and vegetables. Mix well and simmer for 2 to 3 minutes. Serve hot. In India Upma is served at breakfast or lunch. Good for a vegetarian dish when served with an egg curry or other vegetarian curry.

GREEN BEAN VARHYA CURRY [LENTIL CAKE AND GREEN BEAN CURRY]
[Serves 4 to 6]

1 large yellow onion, minced ½ inch fresh ginger root, crushed and minced or grated 3 Tbsp. vegetable oil	Heat a heavy saucepan over medium high heat. Add oil. Heat until a small piece of onion added sizzles. Add onions and ginger. Stir and fry 2 to 3 minutes.

15 varhyas
   [spicy dried lentil cakes]
   [See Indian Basic Ingredients]
1 tsp. turmeric
1 tsp. sea salt
¼ to 1 tsp. red pepper [optional]
	Add to onions. Mix well. Stir and fry 5 to 10 minutes over medium heat until onions are soft and transparent.

½ cup water or stock	Add to varhyas. Cover and bring to a boil over high heat. Reduce heat to medium low. Simmer 10 to 15 minutes until varhyas slightly tender.

¾ lb. green beans,
   cut into 2 inch pieces
2 medium potatoes,
   cut into ½ inch cubes
	Add to varhyas. Stir and fry over medium heat 5 to 10 minutes until potatoes are half cooked. Cover and simmer over medium heat 5 to 10 minutes until vegetables are just tender.

1 to 2 tsp. garam-masala I
1 to 2 tsp. fresh parsley,
   minced
   OR coriander leaves,
     minced
	Add to varhyas and vegetables. Mix well. Simmer 1 to 2 minutes. Serve hot. Good for dinner served with rice. A meal-in-a-bowl dish served with bread. Good cold the next day for lunch. Keeps well. An excellent camping dish.

VARIATION:

PEAS AND CABBAGE MONGORHIS CURRY [PEAS AND CABBAGE DEEP FRIED LENTIL CAKE CURRY] [Serves 4 to 6]

10 to 15 mongorhis
   [deep fried lentil cakes]
   [See Indian Appetizers and Snacks]
1 cup peas
½ head cabbage,
   cut into ¼ inch strips

Follow recipe for Green Bean Varhya Curry. Use mongorhis in place of varhya. Add peas and cabbage in place of beans and potatoes. Do not add until mongorhis have cooked. Mix well. Stir and fry 2 to 3 minutes. Cover and cook no more than 8 minutes until cabbage is just tender. Finish as directed for Green Bean and Varhya Curry. Serve hot. Good for dinner served with rice. A meal-in-a-bowl served with bread. Good cold for lunch the next day.

VARIATION:

CABBAGE, CARROT AND MONGORHIS CURRY [CABBAGE, CARROT AND DEEP FRIED LENTIL CAKE CURRY] [Serves 4 to 6]

10 to 15 mongorhis
   [deep fried lentil cakes]
   [See Indian Appetizers and Snacks]
3 medium carrots,
   cut into ¼ inch slices
½ head cabbage,
   cut into ¼ inch strips

Follow recipe for Green Bean and Varhya Curry. Use carrots in place of potatoes. Use mongorhis in place of varhya. Stir and fry carrots 5 to 8 minutes over medium heat until half done. Cover and simmer 5 minutes. Add cabbage. Cover Cook until just tender. Finish as directed for Green Bean and Varhya Curry. Serve hot. Good for dinner with rice or bread. A meal-in-a-bowl served with rice or bread. Good cold for lunch the next day. Keeps well.

VARIATION:

CABBAGE AND MONGORHIS CURRY [CABBAGE AND DEEP FRIED LENTIL CAKE CURRY] [Serves 4 to 6]

10 to 15 mongorhis
  [deep fried lentil cakes]
  [See Indian Appetizers and Snacks]
2 medium potatoes,
  cut into ½ inch cubes
½ head cabbage,
  cut into ¼ inch strips

Follow recipe for Green Bean and Varhya Curry. Use mongorhis in place of varhya. Use potatoes as directed. Stir and fry 5 to 10 minutes until half done. Cover and simmer over medium heat 8 to 10 minutes until potatoes are slightly tender. Uncover. Add cabbage. Stir and fry 2 to 3 minutes. Cover and cook no more than 8 minutes until cabbage is just tender. Finish as directed for Green Bean and Varhya Curry. Serve hot. Good for dinner with rice or bread. A meal-in-a-bowl served with rice or bread. Good cold for lunch the next day. Keeps well.

VARIATION:

CABBAGE, CARROT AND VARHYA CURRY [CABBAGE, CARROT AND LENTIL CAKE CURRY] [Serves 4 to 6]

3 medium carrots,
  cut into ¼ inch slices
½ head cabbage,
  cut into ¼ inch strips

Follow recipe for Green Bean and Varhya Curry. Use carrots in place of potatoes. Stir and fry 5 to 8 minutes over medium heat until half done. Cover and simmer 5 minutes. Add cabbage. Stir and fry 2 to 3 minutes. Cover and cook no more than 8 minutes until cabbage is just tender. Finish as directed for Green Bean and Varhya Curry. Serve hot. Good for dinner with rice or bread. A meal-in-a-bowl served with rice or bread. Good cold for lunch the next day. Keeps well. Good camping dish.

VARIATION:

MONGORHIS AND GREEN BEAN CURRY [DEEP FRIED LENTIL CAKES AND GREEN BEAN CURRY] [Serves 4 to 6]

10 to 15 mongorhis
  [deep fried lentil cakes]
  [See Indian Appetizers and Snacks]

Follow recipe for Green Bean Varhya Curry. Use mongorhis in place of varhya. Cook as directed. Good for dinner served with rice. A meal-in-a-bowl served with bread. Good cold for lunch the next day.

VARIATION:

PEAS AND CABBAGE VARHYA CURRY [PEAS AND CABBAGE LENTIL CAKE CURRY] [Serves 4 to 6]

1 cup peas
½ head cabbage,
  cut into ¼ inch strips

Follow recipe for Green Bean and Varhya Curry. Add peas and cabbage in place of beans and potatoes. Do not add until varhya have cooked. Mix well. Stir and fry 2 to 3 minutes. Cover and cook no more than 8 minutes until cabbage is just tender. Finish as directed for Green Bean and Varhya Curry. Serve hot. Good for dinner served with rice. A meal-in-a-bowl served with bread. Good cold for lunch the next day. Keeps well. An excellent camping dish.

VARIATION:

CABBAGE AND VARHYA CURRY [CABBAGE AND LENTIL CAKE CURRY] [Serves 4 to 6]

2 medium potatoes,
  cut into ½ inch cubes
½ head cabbage,
  cut into ¼ inch strips

Follow recipe for Green Bean and Varhya Curry. Add potatoes as directed. Stir and fry 5 to 10 minutes until half done. Cover and simmer over medium heat 8 to 10 minutes until potatoes are slightly tender. Uncover. Add cabbage. Stir and fry 2 to 3 mintues. Cover and cook no more than 8 minutes until cabbage is just tender. Finish as directed for Green Bean and Varhya Curry. Serve hot. Good for dinner with rice or bread. A meal-in-a-bowl served with rice or bread. Good cold for lunch the next day. Keeps well. Good camping dish.

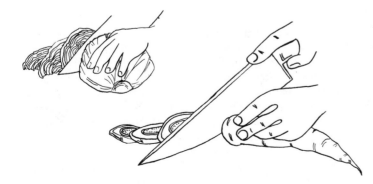

DOSA [LENTIL PANCAKES] [Serves 4 to 6]

1 cup brown rice
½ cup urad dahl
  or white moong dahl
½ cup red dahl

Place in a large bowl. Cover with water. Soak 6 hours or overnight. Place cheesecloth over a collander. Drain lentils and rice. Allow to dry 30 minutes to 1 hour.

1¾ cups water

Place 1 cup lentil mixture in a blender. Add 7 Tbsp. water. Blend 1 to 2 minutes until lentils and rice form a batter and are all ground. Place batter in a bowl. Repeat for 3 remaining cups of soaked lentils and rice.

½ cup yoghurt
  OR 2 eggs well beaten
2 tsp. sea salt
¼ to ½ tsp. chili pepper
  OR black pepper
2 Tbsp. vegetable oil

Add to batter. Mix well. Should be like pancake batter. Heat a cast iron skillet over medium high heat. Brush well with oil using a paper towel or pastry brush. Use only enough oil to prevent sticking. Heat until a small drop of batter added sets. Pour ½ cup batter into pan. Spread thinly. Fry over medium high heat 2 to 3 minutes to a side. Serve hot. These pancakes are served plain for breakfast or as a lunch dish with a yoghurt salad in India. They are also good with syrup or jam and butter. Also they are served with a stuffing as a lunch or dinner dish. To reheat wrap in foil and bake at 350° 3 to 5 minutes until hot.

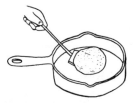

STUFFED DOSA [LENTIL PANCAKES WITH STUFFING] [Serves 4 to 6]

1 recipe Dosa,

Stuffing:
½ cup raw nuts
  [Cashews, peanuts,
  sunflower seeds, etc.]
3 Tbsp. vegetable oil

Heat a heavy saucepan over medium heat. Add oil and heat slightly. Add nuts. Stir and fry 2 to 3 minutes until nuts are golden brown. Remove from pan. Reserve for later use.

½ yellow onion,
  minced
½ inch fresh ginger root,
  crushed and minced
  or grated
1 clove garlic,
  crushed and minced
  or grated
1 to 2 Tbsp. fresh parsley,
  minced
  OR coriander leaves,
  minced

Add to oil. Stir and fry 5 to 10 minutes over medium high heat until onions are soft and transparent but not brown.

2 medium potatoes,
  cut into ¼ inch cubes
2 carrots,
  cut into pea-sized pieces
  OR 1 cup green peas
  OR ¼ lb. green beans,
    cut into pea-sized pieces
½ tsp. sea salt
½ tsp. turmeric

Add to onions. If peas are used do not add until potatoes are half cooked. Stir and fry potatoes and vegetables 5 to 10 minutes over medium heat until half done and potatoes lightly browned. Cover. Cook over medium low heat 10 to 15 minutes until potatoes are just tender.

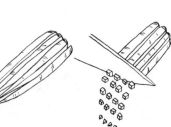

1 cup cabbage,
   shredded
1 to 2 tsp. garam-masala I

Add to potatoes. Mix well. Cover and cook 3 to 5 minutes until just tender. Add garam-masala. Mash ⅔ of potatoes with a fork. Add nuts. Mix well. Spread some of filling on half of a hot fried dosa. Fold other half over stuffing and serve hot. Cut into 2 inch slices. Good for a lunch or light dinner meal. Good cold for lunch the next day.

VARHYA AND POTATO CURRY [LENTIL CAKE AND POTATO CURRY]
[Serves 4 to 6]

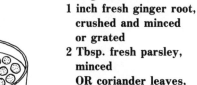

1 large yellow onion,
   minced
1 large clove garlic,
   crushed and minced
   or grated
1 inch fresh ginger root,
   crushed and minced
   or grated
2 Tbsp. fresh parsley,
   minced
   OR coriander leaves,
      minced
3 Tbsp. vegetable oil

Heat a heavy saucepan over medium high heat. Add oil. Heat until a small piece of onion added sizzles. Add ingredients. Stir and fry 5 to 10 minutes until onions are soft and transparent but not brown.

15 varhyas
   [spicy dried lentil cakes]
   [See Indian Basic Ingredients]
2 medium potatoes,
   cut in ½ inch cubes
1 tomato, diced
   OR ½ cup stewed tomatoes

Add to onions. Stir and fry 5 to 10 minutes until potatoes are lightly browned and tomatoes have formed a paste with other ingredients.

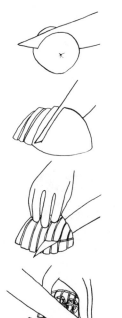

¼ cup tomato paste
1½ cups stewed tomatoes
   with juice
1 to 2 tsp. garam-masala I
1 tsp. sea salt
¼ tsp. black pepper
   [optional]

Add to potatoes. Mix well. Cover. Simmer 10 to 15 minutes over medium heat until potatoes are tender. Serve hot. Good served with rice and a vegetable dish for dinner. Good cold for lunch the next day. Excellent camping dish. Keeps well.

VARIATION:

MONGORHIS AND POTATO CURRY [DEEP FRIED LENTIL CAKE AND POTATO CURRY]
[Serves 4 to 6]

15 mongorhis
   [deep fried lentil cakes]
   [See Indian Appetizers and Sancks]

Follow recipe for Varhya and Potato Curry. Use mongorhis in place of varhya. Cook as directed. Good served with rice and a vegetable dish for dinner. Good cold for lunch the next day. Keeps well.

MEAT MAIN DISHES

Meat dishes are served at the evening or main meal of the day. They are not as common as vegetarian dishes for both religious and monetary reasons. Large festive meals might include both vegetarian and meat dishes.

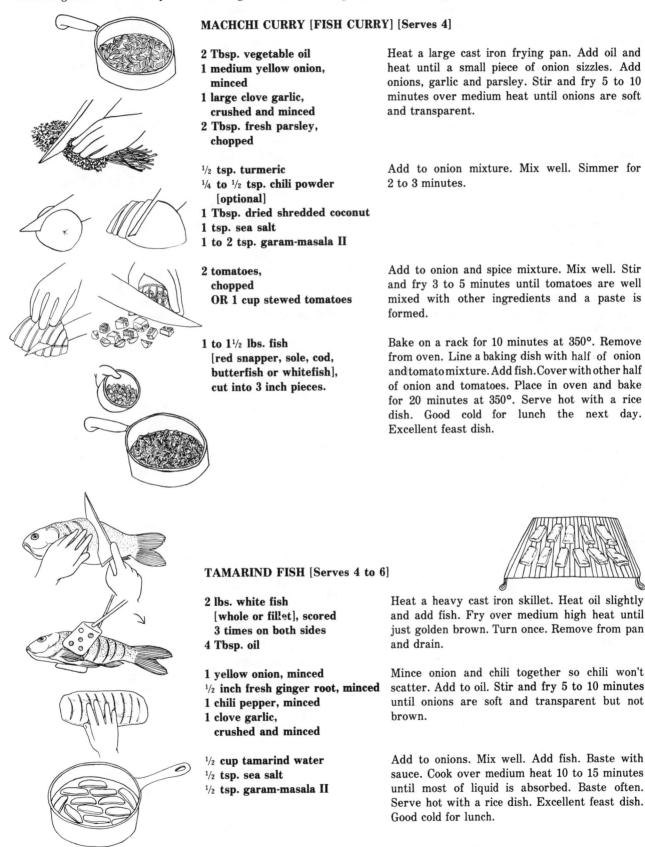

MACHCHI CURRY [FISH CURRY] [Serves 4]

2 Tbsp. vegetable oil
1 medium yellow onion,
  minced
1 large clove garlic,
  crushed and minced
2 Tbsp. fresh parsley,
  chopped

Heat a large cast iron frying pan. Add oil and heat until a small piece of onion sizzles. Add onions, garlic and parsley. Stir and fry 5 to 10 minutes over medium heat until onions are soft and transparent.

½ tsp. turmeric
¼ to ½ tsp. chili powder
  [optional]
1 Tbsp. dried shredded coconut
1 tsp. sea salt
1 to 2 tsp. garam-masala II

Add to onion mixture. Mix well. Simmer for 2 to 3 minutes.

2 tomatoes,
  chopped
  OR 1 cup stewed tomatoes

Add to onion and spice mixture. Mix well. Stir and fry 3 to 5 minutes until tomatoes are well mixed with other ingredients and a paste is formed.

1 to 1½ lbs. fish
  [red snapper, sole, cod,
  butterfish or whitefish],
  cut into 3 inch pieces.

Bake on a rack for 10 minutes at 350°. Remove from oven. Line a baking dish with half of onion and tomato mixture. Add fish. Cover with other half of onion and tomatoes. Place in oven and bake for 20 minutes at 350°. Serve hot with a rice dish. Good cold for lunch the next day. Excellent feast dish.

TAMARIND FISH [Serves 4 to 6]

2 lbs. white fish
  [whole or fillet], scored
  3 times on both sides
4 Tbsp. oil

Heat a heavy cast iron skillet. Heat oil slightly and add fish. Fry over medium high heat until just golden brown. Turn once. Remove from pan and drain.

1 yellow onion, minced
½ inch fresh ginger root, minced
1 chili pepper, minced
1 clove garlic,
  crushed and minced

Mince onion and chili together so chili won't scatter. Add to oil. Stir and fry 5 to 10 minutes until onions are soft and transparent but not brown.

½ cup tamarind water
½ tsp. sea salt
½ tsp. garam-masala II

Add to onions. Mix well. Add fish. Baste with sauce. Cook over medium heat 10 to 15 minutes until most of liquid is absorbed. Baste often. Serve hot with a rice dish. Excellent feast dish. Good cold for lunch.

PRAWN CURRY [Serves 4 to 6]

3 Tbsp. vegetable oil
1 medium yellow onion,
   minced
¼ inch fresh ginger root,
   grated
2 Tbsp. fresh parsley,
   chopped
   OR coriander leaves,
     chopped

Heat a cast iron skillet over medium high heat. Add oil. Heat until a piece of onion added sizzles. Add onion, parsley, and ginger. Stir and and fry 5 to 10 minutes until onions are soft and transparent but not brown.

2 medium potatoes,
   cut in ¼ inch cubes

Add to onions. Stir and fry 5 to 10 minutes until half done.

2 medium tomatoes,
   cut in ¼ inch cubes
   OR 1 cup stewed tomatoes
3 Tbsp. tomato paste
1 tsp. sea salt
¼ tsp. black pepper
1 to 2 tsp. garam-masala II

Add to potatoes. Mix well. Cover. Simmer 5 to 10 minutes until potatoes are almost done.

¼ to ½ lb. prawns,
   shelled, deveined and
   steamed 5 to 10 minutes
   until pink
1 Tbsp. tamarind water
   OR lemon juice

Add to potatoes and tomatoes. Mix well. Cook 3 to 5 minutes until most of liquid is absorbed and prawns are well coated with sauce. Serve hot with a rice dish. Excellent feast dish. Good cold for lunch.

VARIATION:

SHRIMP CURRY [Serves 4 to 6]

1 to 2 cans shrimp
   [pieces, medium or large]
   drained and rinsed
   OR ¼ to ½ lb. small
     fresh shrimp

Follow recipe for Prawn Curry. Use shrimp in place of prawns. Cook as directed. Serve hot with a rice dish. Excellent feast dish. Good cold for lunch.

GOA SHRIMP CURRY [Serves 4 to 6]

1 yellow onion, minced
1 large clove garlic,
   crushed and minced
   or grated
2 Tbsp. fresh coriander leaves,
   minced
   OR fresh parsley,
     minced
½ inch fresh ginger root,
   crushed and minced
   or grated
1 to 2 red peppers,
   minced
3 Tbsp. vegetable oil

Mince onion and chili together so chili won't scatter. Heat a cast iron skillet over medium high heat. Add oil. Heat until a piece of onion added sizzles. Add ingredients. Stir and fry 5 to 10 minutes until onions are soft and transparent but not brown.

½ tsp. turmeric
1 cup stewed tomatoes
   OR 2 medium tomatoes,
     cut into small cubes
½ to 1 tsp. garam masala II

Add to onions. Mix well. Simmer 2 to 3 minutes until tomatoes form a wet paste with other ingredients.

¼ to ½ lb. small
   fresh shrimp
   OR 1 to 2 cans shrimp
     drained and rinsed
     [pieces, medium or
     large]

Add shrimp. Mix well. Coat all shrimp with sauce.

½ cup thick coconut milk
½ tsp. mango powder
   OR 1 tsp. lemon juice

Add mango powder or lemon juice first. Mix well and then add coconut milk. Simmer 3 to 5 minutes until most of liquid is absorbed and a thick moist sauce is formed. Serve hot with a rice dish. Excellent feast dish. Good cold for lunch.

VARIATION:

GOA PRAWN CURRY
[Serves 4 to 6]

½ to 1 lb. prawns,
   shelled, deveined, and
   steamed 5 to 10 minutes
   until pink

Follow recipe for Goa Shrimp Curry. Use prawns in place of shrimp. Cook as directed. Serve hot with a rice and a vegetable dish for a simple dinner. Excellent feast dish. Good cold for lunch.

BAKED FISH WITH SPICES [Serves 4 to 6]

3 to 5 lbs. fish,
  scaled, washed and scored
  3 times on each side
  OR 2 lbs. fish fillet,
    scored 3 times
    on each side
1 tsp. sea salt
¼ tsp. black pepper

Rub fish with salt and pepper inside and out. Set aside for later use.

1½ large yellow onions,
  cut lengthwise and sliced
  into paper-thin slices
3 thin slices fresh ginger root,
  minced
3 Tbsp. vegetable oil

Heat a medium sized skillet over medium high heat. Add oil. Heat until a piece of onion added sizzles. Add onions and ginger. Stir and fry 5 to 10 minutes until onions are soft and transparent but not brown.

2 tsp. coriander seeds,
  ground
1 tsp. cardamom seeds,
  slightly crushed
1 tsp. cumin seeds, ground
½ tsp. fresh ground cinnamon
½ tsp. fresh ground cloves
5 or 6 black peppers,
  parched and crushed
1 tomato,
  cut into small cubes
  OR ½ cup stewed tomatoes

Add spices to onions. Mix well. Add tomatoes. Stir and fry 3 to 5 minutes until a paste is formed with spices. Remove from heat. Place fish on a large piece of foil. Spread spice mix under, over and inside fish. Wrap tightly in foil. Bake at 350° 40 to 50 minutes for whole fish - 30 to 40 for fillets. Serve hot with rice and a vegetable dish for dinner. Excellent feast dish. Good cold for lunch.

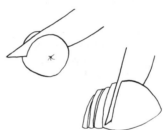

BAKED CHICKEN WITH SPICES [Serves 4 to 6]

1 medium-sized chicken
1 to 2 tsp. salt

Wash chicken well. Rub with salt. Place in a 350° oven for 40 minutes until almost done.

2 yellow onions, grated
3 cloves garlic, grated
1 inch fresh ginger root,
  grated
3 Tbsp. vegetable oil

While chicken is roasting, heat a medium-sized cast iron skillet over medium high heat. Add oil. Heat until a piece of onion added sizzles. Add ingredients. Stir and fry 3 to 5 minutes until mixture just browns.

4 tomatoes,
  minced
  OR 2 cups stewed tomatoes
2 to 3 tsp. garam-masala II

Add to onions. Mix well. Reduce heat to medium. Cover. Simmer 10 to 15 minutes until a paste forms. Baste chicken with spice paste. Return to oven. Cook another 10 to 15 minutes until tender. Baste chicken with drippings. Serve hot. Good with rice and a vegetable dish for dinner. Excellent feast dish. Good cold for lunch the next day.

BAKED CHICKEN WITH SPICES AND STUFFING [Serves 6]

**1 large roasting chicken
OR 1 large chicken cut
into pieces
1 tsp. sea salt
¼ tsp. black pepper**

Wash chicken well. Rub with salt and pepper inside and out.

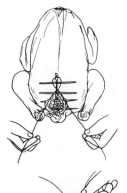

**Stuffing:
3 to 4 cups cooked rice
¼ cup almonds,
chopped fine or slivered
3 Tbsp. butter
¼ cup raisins
½ tsp. coriander,
fresh ground
¼ tsp. cumin,
fresh ground
¼ tsp. cinnamon,
fresh ground
¼ tsp. cardamom,
fresh ground
¼ tsp. saffron
OR ½ tsp. turmeric
¼ tsp. cloves,
fresh ground
¼ tsp. black pepper,
fresh ground
1 Tbsp. honey**

Heat a small cast rion skillet over medium heat. Add butter. Melt. Add almonds. Stir and fry 2 to 3 minutes until almonds are just brown. Remove from heat. Add spices. Mix well. Mix with rice in a large bowl. Stuff chicken with rice. Bind to turn easy. Place on a rack. OR: place stuffing in a baking dish and cover with chicken pieces. Bake at 325° for 20 to 30 minutes until part done.

**Masala:
2 tsp. coriander seeds,
fresh ground
1 tsp. cardamom,
slightly crushed
½ tsp. cumin seeds,
fresh ground
¼ tsp. saffron
½ tsp. cinnamon,
fresh ground
½ tsp. cloves,
fresh ground
4 to 5 whole black peppers,
parched and crushed**

While chicken is roasting, mix spices well. Set aside.

**1 yellow onion, minced
3 thin slices ginger,
minced
4 Tbsp. oil**

Heat a small cast iron skillet over medium high heat. Add oil. Heat until a small piece of onion sizzles. Add onions and ginger. Stir and fry 5 to 10 minutes until just tender. Mix with spices. Spread paste over partly baked chicken. Continue to bake 40 to 50 minutes until done. Baste whole chicken occasionally with drippings. Serve hot. Good with a vegetable dish for a simple dinner. Excellent feast dish. Good cold for lunch the next day.

LAMB CURRY [Serves 4 to 6]

1 large yellow onion, minced
1 to 2 large cloves garlic,
   crushed and minced
   or grated
1/2 inch fresh ginger root,
   crushed and minced
   or grated
3 Tbsp. fresh parsley,
   minced
   OR coriander leaves
     minced
1 tsp. fresh spearmint,
   minced
   [optional]
3 Tbsp. vegetable oil

Heat a heavy cast iron saucepan over medium high heat. Add oil. Heat until a piece of onion added sizzles. Add ingredients. Stir and fry 5 to 10 minutes until onions are soft and transparent but not brown.

1/2 tsp. turmeric
1 to 3 tsp. garam-masala II
1/4 to 1/2 tsp. black pepper
   OR red pepper
     [optional]
1 1/2 tsp. sea salt

Add to onions. Mix well. Cook 1 minute.

1 lb. boneless lamb,
   cut into 1/2 inch cubes

Add to onions and spices. Stir and fry 3 to 5 minutes until meat is lightly browned.

3/4 cup water
   OR meat stock

Add to meat. Mix well. Cover and bring to a boil over high heat. Reduce heat to meidum low. Simmer 30 minutes.

2 medium tomatoes,
   cubed
   OR 1 cup drained stewed
     tomatoes
3 Tbsp. tomato paste

Add tomatoes. Mix well. Cover and bring to a boil over high heat. Reduce heat to medium low and simmer 30 to 40 minutes until meat is tender. Remove cover. Cook until most of liquid is absorbed. Serve hot with a rice dish for dinner. Good warmed up. Excellent feast dish. Good cold for lunch.

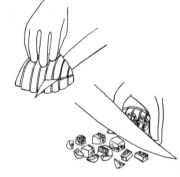

VARIATION:

BEEF CURRY [Serves 4 to 6]

1 lb. boneless beef,
   cut into 1/2 inch cubes

Follow recipe for Lamb Curry. Use beef in place of lamb. Do not use mint. Cook as directed. Serve hot with a rice and a vegetable dish for dinner. Good warmed up. Excellent feast dish. Good cold for lunch.

VARIATION:

LAMB CURRY WITH YOGHURT
[Serves 4 to 6]

1/4 to 1/2 cup yoghurt

Follow recipe for Lamb Curry. Cook as directed. Add yoghurt after meat is tender. Simmer uncovered 2 to 3 minutes over medium heat until yoghurt well heated. Serve hot with a rice and a vegetable dish for dinner. Good warmed up. Excellent feast dish. Good cold for lunch.

VARIATION:

BEEF CURRY WITH YOGHURT
[Serves 4 to 6]

1 lb. boneless beef,
  cut into ¹⁄₂ inch cubes
¹⁄₄ to ¹⁄₂ cup yoghurt

Follow recipe for Lamb Curry. Use beef in place of lamb. Do not use mint. Cook as directed. Add yoghurt after meat is tender. Simmer uncovered 2 to 3 minutes over medium heat until yoghurt is well heated. Serve hot with a rice and vegetable dish for dinner. Good warmed up. Excellent feast dish. Good cold for lunch.

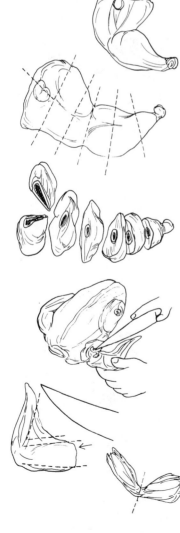

CHICKEN CURRY I [Serves 4 to 6]

3 Tbsp. vegetable oil
1 large yellow onion, minced
1 clove garlic,
  crushed and minced or grated
1 inch fresh ginger root,
  crushed and minced or grated

Heat a heavy saucepan over medium high heat. Add oil. Heat until a small piece of onion added sizzles. Add onion, garlic and ginger. Stir and fry 5 to 10 minutes until onions are soft and transparent but not brown.

3 lb. chicken,
  skinned
  and cut into pieces

Add to onions. Stir and fry for 5 to 8 minutes until lightly browned.

1 fresh tomato, chopped
2 cups stewed tomatoes
2 tsp. garam-masala II
1¹⁄₂ tsp. sea salt

Add toamtoes and spices. Mix well. Cover and bring to a boil over high heat. Reduce heat to medium and simmer for 30 to 40 minutes until chicken is tender. Baste often. Remove cover. Simmer 5 to 10 minutes until most of liquid is absorbed and a moist thick sauce is formed.

3 Tbsp. fresh parsley,
  chopped [optional]
  OR coriander leaves,
    chopped [optional]

Sprinkle over chicken just before serving. Serve hot. Good warmed up. Serve with rice or bread and a vegetable dish for dinner. Excellent feast dish. Good cold for lunch. Keeps well.

VARIATION:

CHICKEN CURRY II [Serves 4 to 6]

¹⁄₄ to ¹⁄₂ cup yoghurt

Follow recipe for Chicken Curry I. Cook as directed. Add yoghurt after chicken is tender. Mix well. Simmer 2 to 3 minutes until heated.

3 Tbsp. fresh parsley,
  chopped
  OR coriander leaves,
  chopped

Place curry on a serving dish. Sprinkle with parsley. Serve hot with a rice and a vegetable dish for dinner. Good warmed up. Excellent feast dish. Good cold for lunch.

CHICKEN LIVER CURRY [Serves 4 to 6]

1 large yellow onion, minced
1 large clove garlic,
    crushed and minced or grated
1 inch ginger root,
    crushed and minced or grated
3 Tbsp. vegetable oil

Heat a medium cast iron skillet over medium high heat. Add oil. Heat until a piece of onion added sizzles. Add onion, garlic and ginger. Stir and fry 5 to 10 minutes until onions are soft and transparent but not brown.

1 lb. tomatoes,
    cut into 1 inch cubes
    OR 2 cups drained
        stewed tomatoes
1 Tbsp. tomato paste
½ to 1 Tbsp. garam-masala II
1 tsp. sea salt
¼ tsp. black pepper

Add to onions. Mix well. Stir and fry 3 to 5 minutes until a paste is formed.

1 lb. chicken livers

Add to tomato-onion paste. Stir and fry 5 minutes until liver is just browned. Cover. Simmer over medium low heat 5 to 10 minutes until liver is just done.

3 Tbsp. fresh parsley,
    chopped
    OR coriander leaves,
        chopped

Sprinkle over the top of the dish before serving. Serve hot or cold. It is good ground up as a pate. Good dinner dish served with rice and a vegetable dish. Excellent feast dish. Great cold for lunch.

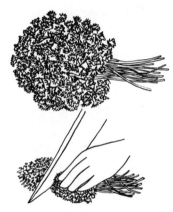

KEMA [FRIED GROUND MEAT CURRY] [Serves 4 to 6]

1 large clove garlic,
    crushed and minced or grated
1 inch fresh ginger root,
    crushed and minced or grated
1 large yellow onion, minced
3 Tbsp. vegetable oil

Heat a cast iron skillet over medium high heat. Add oil. Heat until a small piece of onion added sizzles. Add onion, garlic and ginger. Stir and fry 5 to 10 minutes until onions are soft and transparent but not brown.

1½ lbs. ground beef
    OR ground lamb

Add meat to onion mixture a small portion at a time. Mix well and add more until all is added. Stir and fry 5 to 10 minutes until just browned.

3 Tbsp. tomato paste
1 cup stewed tomatoes
1 to 3 tsp. garam-masala II
1 tsp. sea salt
¼ tsp. black pepper

Add to meat. Mix well. Simmer 2 to 3 minutes.

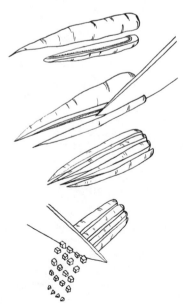

1 cup fresh peas
    OR 1 cup sliced mushrooms
    OR 1 cup corn
    OR 1 cup beans, cut into
        pea sized pieces
    OR 1 cup carrots, cut into
        pea sized pieces

Add vegetable. Bring to a boil. Cover. Simmer over low heat 5 to 10 minutes until vegetable is just tender. Serve hot with a rice dish. Good warmed up. Excellent feast dish. Good cold for lunch.

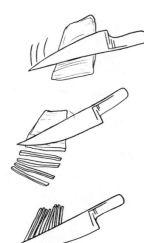

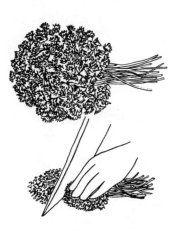

CHICKEN KOFTAS [CHICKEN MEATBALLS IN CURRY SAUCE] [Serves 4 to 6]

½ lb. chicken meat
  [raw or cooked],
  minced
¼ inch fresh ginger root,
  grated
1 to 2 cloves garlic,
  grated
½ small yellow onion,
  grated
1 Tbsp. fresh parsley,
  minced
  OR coriander leaves,
    minced
1 to 2 tsp. garam-masala II
½ tsp. sea salt
½ egg, beaten
3 Tbsp. vegetable oil

Mix ingredients well. Knead and crush mixture 3 to 5 minutes until smooth and doughlike. Form into small ½ inch balls. Heat a heavy skillet over medium high heat. Add oil. Heat until a meatball added sizzles. Add all meatballs. Fry 5 to 10 minutes until golden brown. Remove from pan and drain.

1 yellow onion,
  minced
1 to 2 cloves garlic,
  crushed and minced or grated
¼ inch fresh ginger root,
  crushed and minced or grated
2 Tbsp. fresh parsley,
  minced
  OR coriander leaves,
    minced

Add ingredients to pan meatballs were cooked in. Stir and fry 5 to 10 minutes until onions are soft and transparent but not brown.

½ cup chicken stock
2 cups stewed tomatoes
2 Tbsp. tomato paste
1 to 2 tsp. garam-masala II
1 tsp. sea salt

Add to onions. Mix well. Cover and bring to a boil. Reduce heat to medium low and simmer 10 to 15 minutes. Add koftas and mix well. Simmer 10 minutes. Serve with a rice and a vegetable dish for dinner. Good warmed up. Excellent feast dish. Good cold for lunch.

VARIATION:

CHICKEN KOFTAS WITH YOGHURT [CHICKEN MEATBALLS IN CURRY SAUCE WITH YOGHURT] [Serves 4 to 6]

¼ to ½ cup yoghurt

Follow recipe for Chicken Koftas. Cook as directed. Add yoghurt to curry suace in last 5 minutes of cooking. Mix gently but well. Serve hot with a vegetable and a rice dish for dinner. Good warmed up. Excellent feast dish. Good cold for lunch.

KABABS [GRILLED MARINATED MEAT] [Serves 4 to 6]

1 to 1½ lbs. meat
  [beef or lamb]
  cut into ¼ inch pieces
¼ cup yoghurt
  [optional]
1 to 2 tsp. garam-masala II
1 tsp. sea salt
3 Tbsp. fresh parsley,
  minced
  OR coriander leaves,
    minced
½ Tbsp. mango powder
  OR 1 Tbsp. lemon juice
½ inch fresh ginger root,
  grated
½ yellow onion,
  minced

½ lb. mushrooms,
  cut into thirds

Mix well all ingredients except meat. Add meat and mix. Allow to marinate 30 minutes to 3 hours.

Place 5 or 6 pieces of meat on a skewer then add a mushroom slice. Continue until 5 sections of meat are on one skewer. Assemble meat and mushrooms on skewers until meat is used up. Grill 15 minutes. Turn often to prevent burning. Serve hot with a rice and vegetable dish for dinner. Excellent feast dish. Great for picnics. Good cold for lunch.

SWEETS

Sweets in India are very rich; a small serving goes a long way. Sweets serve as between-meal snacks as well as after-dinner desserts. Sliced fruits are commonly served for the last course in place of these sweetmeats.

GAJAR HALVA [CARROT SWEET] [Serves 6]

4 cups milk
2 cups finely grated carrots

Wash and scrape carrots. Grate fine. Place milk in a stainless steel frying pan. Just bring to a boil over medium heat. Add carrots at once. Cook over medium low heat 50 to 60 minutes until mixture thickens. Stir frequently to prevent sticking.

²/₃ cup mild honey
2 Tbsp. butter, melted

Add to carrot mixture. Mix well. Continue to cook 15 to 20 minutes until all the butter is absorbed and the mixture turns a deep orange red and begins to solidify.

20 to 30 almonds, slivered
OR unsalted pistachio nuts, slivered
¼ tsp. cardamom seeds, ground
OR the seeds of 4 cardamom pods, ground

Butter a flat dish. Spread halva on dish in an even layer. Sprinkle with nuts and cardamom. Cut into ½ inch squares. Serve hot or cold. Excellent snack or dessert.

SHIRA [SEMINOLA PUDDING] [Serves 4 to 6]

7 Tbsp. butter
1 cup semolina
   OR fine ground bulgur wheat

Heat a stainless steel frying pan over medium heat. Add butter. Melt. Add semolina or bulgur. Fry 5 minutes until grain is lightly browned and the butter bubbles up through the wheat.

1 cup water
½ cup mild honey

Bring to a boil in a small saucepan. Simmer 3 to 5 minutes. Add to fried semolina when it has cooked as directed above. Mix well. Simmer 3 to 5 minutes. Stir frequently.

¼ tsp. cardamom seeds,
   ground
   OR the seeds from
      4 cardamom pods,
      ground
6 to 12 almonds,
   blanched and slivered
1 sheet silver leaf
   [optional]

Add to semolina mixture. Reduce heat to medium low. Continue to cook 15 to 20 minutes until the mixture begins to separate and follow the spoon around the pan. Stir often. Remove from heat. Butter a small cup or bowl. Place an almond in the bottom of the bowl and pack tightly with semolina mixture. Invert over a plate. Continue until all mixture is used. Serve hot or cold. In India silver leaf is applied to the outside of these small puddings for special occasions. Good as snacks, for breakfast or as a dessert.

KELA HALVA [BANANA PUDDING] [Serves 4 to 6]

5 firm ripe bananas,
   cut into 1 inch pieces
3 Tbsp. butter

Heat a stainless steel frying pan or a wok over medium high heat. Add butter. Melt. Add bananas. Stir and fry 5 minutes until bananas are slightly browned and soft. Remove pan from heat. Mash bananas with a fork until no large pieces remain.

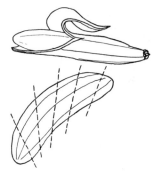

½ cup water
   OR coconut milk
   [See Indonesian Basic
   Ingredients]

Add to bananas. Mix well. Place pan over medium heat. Simmer banana mixture 5 minutes. Stir often.

1 cup water
¼ cup mild honey

Place in a saucepan while bananas are simmering. Bring to a boil. Simmer 2 to 3 minutes. Remove from heat. Pour into banana mixture. Mix well. Simmer over medium heat 10 to 20 minutes until banana mixture thickens and turns gray-green. Stir often to prevent sticking.

½ tsp. rosewater
   OR vanilla
¼ tsp. cardamom seeds,
   ground
   OR the seeds of
      4 cardamom pods,
      ground

Add to banana mixture. Mix well. Continue to cook 5 to 10 minutes over low heat until pudding thickens. Stir often to keep from sticking. Remove from heat. Place in individual serving dishes.

12 almonds, slivered
   OR unsalted pistachio nuts,
     slivered

Sprinkle nuts over individual bowls. Serve warm or cold. Excellent snack or dessert.

COCONUT HALVA [COCONUT SWEETS] [Serves 4 to 6]

1½ cup dried
    unsweetened coconut
    OR finely grated
      fresh coconut
1½ cup milk
    OR coconut milk
    [See Indonesian Basic
    Ingredients]

Place milk and coconut in a saucepan. Bring to a boil over medium heat. Reduce heat to medium low. Simmer 25 to 30 minutes until coconut has almost dissolved. Stir often to prevent burning and sticking.

½ cup mild honey

Add honey. Mix well. Simmer 15 to 20 minutes until pudding thickens.

¼ tsp. cardamom seed,
    ground
    OR the seeds of
      4 cardamom pods,
      ground
10 to 12 almonds,
    slivered
    OR unsalted pistachio nuts,
    slivered

Butter a flat dish. Spread halva on dish in an even layer. Sprinkle with nuts and cardamom. Cut into 2 inch squares or diamonds

½ tsp. rosewater
[optional]

When halva has cooled sprinkle with rosewater. Serve cold. Excellent snack or dessert.

BARPHEE [COCONUT SWEETS WITHOUT MILK] [Serves 4 to 6]

1 cup water
1 cup mild honey

Bring to a boil in a heavy saucepan. Reduce heat to medium. Simmer 10 to 15 minutes until syrup thickens and froth on top of the honey forms large flat-topped bubbles.

4 cups dried unsweetened
    coconut
2 Tbsp. butter

Add coconut and butter to syrup. Cook over medium low heat 8 to 10 minutes until coconut is sticky and when pressed between the fingers stick together. The mixture should be just barely moist. Stir constantly to prevent browning and sticking to the pan.

¼ tsp. cardamom seeds,
    ground
    OR the seeds of
      4 cardamom pods,
      ground
12 almonds,
    slivered
    OR other nuts,
      chopped

Add cardamom and almonds. Mix well. Remove from heat. Cool slightly. Wet hands and press coconut into little round balls about ½ inch in diameter. Do not squeeze balls too hard or they will not hold together. Serve warm or cold. Good for snacks. Excellent dessert.

GALOB JAMIN [SWEET MILK FRITTERS IN SYRUP] [Serves 6 to 8]

2 cups powdered milk
1 cup wholewheat pastry flour
1½ tsp. baking powder
¼ tsp. sea salt
¾ tsp. cardamom seeds,
    ground
    OR the seeds of
        4 cardamom pods,
        ground
½ cup butter

Mix flour, baking powder, salt, cardamom and powdered milk well. Add butter and mix with other ingredients until dough is cornmeal-like in consistency.

¼ cup warm water

Add water to dough. Mix well. Press dough into a ball and cover with a damp cloth. Form dough into small sausage-like balls ½ inch wide by ¾ to 1 inch long. Makes about 3 dozen.

3 to 4 cups vegetable oil

Heat oil in a wok over medium high heat until a piece of dough added falls to the bottom and rises to the surface almost at once. Add 4 to 5 galob jamin. Reduce heat to just above medium and fry galob jamin 5 to 6 minutes until brown on all sides. Remove from oil and drain on absorbent paper. Increase heat of oil until dough added rises almost at once. Add more galob jamin. Repeat until all are fried.

Too Cold

Too Hot

1 cup mild honey
3 cups water
1 to 2 tsp. rosewater
    [optional]

Place in a deep saucepan. Bring to a boil over high heat. Reduce heat to medium and simmer 6 to 8 minutes until slightly thickened. Add galob jamin gently one at a time. Simmer 5 minutes over medium low heat. Remove pan from heat. Pour rosewater over galob jamin. Serve hot or cold. Two or three will be sufficient for one serving. Excellent snack or dessert.

Correct Temperature

SWEET SAVIA [SWEET NOODLES] [Serves 4 to 6]

Reserve syrup from galob jamin
OR

½ cup honey
1 cup water

Place in a small saucepan. Bring to a boil over medium high heat. Reduce heat to medium. Simmer 5 to 10 minutes until syrup slightly thickened. Remove from heat.

2 Tbsp. butter
2 cups broken soy
    OR wholewheat vermicelli

Heat a heavy skillet. Add butter and melt over medium heat. Add noodles. Stir and fry gently over medium heat 5 to 10 minutes until noodles are golden brown. Pour syrup over noodles. Bring to a boil over medium high heat. Boil 3 to 5 minutes. Reduce heat to medium low. Simmer 10 to 15 minutes. Stir gently but often to prevent sticking. Place noodles in 350° oven for 15 to 20 minutes until all liquid is absorbed and noodles are golden brown and no longer soft.

¼ tsp. cardamom seed,
    ground
    OR the seeds of
        4 cardamom pods,
        ground

Sprinkle over hot noodles. Serve hot. Excellent snack or dessert.

SKHIR [RICE PUDDING WITH MILK] [Serves 5 to 6]

6 cups rich milk
½ cup long-grain brown rice

Place milk in a heavy saucepan. Bring to a boil over medium high heat. Add rice. Reduce heat to medium low. Simmer 50 to 60 minutes. Stir frequently to prevent sticking.

½ cup mild honey
¼ cup raisins
¼ cup almonds,
    blanched and slivered
    OR other nuts,
        chopped
¼ tsp. nutmeg
1/8 tsp. cardamom seeds,
    ground
    OR the seeds from
        2 cardamom pods,
        ground

Add to milk and rice pudding. Mix well. Continue to simmer over medium low heat 15 to 20 minutes until pudding thickens slightly. Stir gently but frequently to prevent browning and sticking.

1 Tbsp. rosewater
  [optional]

Remove pudding from heat and cool slightly. Add rosewater. Mix. Serve warm or cold. Good cold for breakfast. Excellent for people recovering from an illness. Good snack or dessert.

SKHIR SUJI [SEMOLINA PUDDING WITH MILK] [Serves 4 to 6]

7 Tbsp. butter
1 cup semolina
  OR fine ground bulgur wheat

Heat a stainless steel frying pan. Add butter. Melt over medium heat. Add semolina or bulgur. Stir and fry 5 minutes until grain is lightly browned and the butter bubbles up through the wheat.

1 cup rich milk
¾ cup mild honey

Bring to a boil in a saucepan over medium heat. Simmer 3 to 5 minutes. Slowly add to fried semolina so no lumps are formed. Mix well. Simmer over medium low heat 50 to 60 minutes until pudding thickens. Stir often to prevent sticking.

¼ cup raisins
¼ cup almonds,
    blanched and slivered
    OR other nuts
        chopped
¼ tsp. cardamom seeds,
    ground
    OR seeds from
        4 cardamom pods,
        ground

Add to pudding. Mix well. Cook 5 more minutes. Pour into individual bowls. Serve hot. Also good cold for breakfast. Excellent snack or dessert.

LADOO BESAN [GARBANZO FLOUR SWEET] [Serves 5 to 6]

1 cup channa
  [garbanzo] flour
½ cup butter

Heat a heavy enamel saucepan. Add butter and melt over medium heat. Add garbanzo flour. Mix well. Reduce heat to medium low. Stir and fry 10 to 15 minutes until butter separates slightly from garbanzo flour and garbanzo flour turns golden.

¾ cup raw sugar
  OR date sugar
¼ tsp. cardamom seeds,
  ground
  OR the seeds of
    4 cardamom pods, ground
12 to 15 almonds, slivered
  OR other nuts, chopped

Add to flour and butter mixture. Continue to simmer 3 to 5 minutes over low heat until sugar is melted and mixture is moist. Remove from heat and cool until tolerable to the hands. Form into ½ inch balls. Chill. Serve cold. Excellent snack or dessert.

VARIATION:

LADOO SUJI [SEMOLINA SWEET]
[Serves 4 to 6]

1 cup semolina
  OR fine ground bulgur wheat
½ cup butter

Follow above recipe except use semolina in place of garbanzo flour. Cook as directed. Stir frequently to prevent the semolina from getting brown. Chill. Serve cold. Excellent snack or dessert.

FRUIT SALAD WITH ORANGE DRESSING [Serves 4 to 6]

1 cup cantalope,
  cut into ½ inch cubes
1 cup watermelon,
  cut into ½ inch cubes
1 cup persian melon,
  cut into ½ inch cubes
1 cup honeydew melon,
  cut into ½ inch cubes
  OR 4 cups of any melon available
    cut into ½ inch cubes
    [preferable at least 2 kinds
    of melon]

  OR 4 cups of any sliced fruit
    such as apples, peaches,
    bananas, grapes,
    strawberries, etc.

Place fruit in a large bowl.

Dressing:
juice of 4 oranges
juice of ½ lemon
3 tsp. mild honey
1 tsp. rosewater
  [optional]

Mix orange juice, lemon juice and honey well. Add rosewater and mix well. Pour over fruit. Mix gently. Chill for a minimum of 30 minutes. Excellent served at the end of a large Indian meal. Also good as a snack on a hot summer day.

CHAPTER FIVE
JAPANESE

INTRODUCTION

Japanese cuisine is highly influenced by Japan's being an island nation with a relatively small land area and a large population. Japan's virtual isolation for hundreds of years has taken these factors and produced a unique cuisine. Numerous sources have been developed for their food: sea farming of fish, shellfish, and seaweed used in everything from soups to vinegared-rice sandwiches and even as gelatin, play an important role in the Japanese diet. Rice and vegetables are predominate in Japanese food while wild plants such as mushrooms, burdock (gobo), watercress and peppergrass flavor or garnish many dishes. Even the springtime cherry blossoms find their way into a delicate soup.

Cooking Japanese means spending more time in preparation and less time actually cooking. Artistic arrangement, natural delicate flavors, and seasonal use of foods are prime concerns. Cutting and slicing becomes a form of sculpture and the finished dishes can have the look of a work of art. If you lack time, however, just the combinations and simple slicing methods can produce beautiful dishes. A good sharp knife is a must with Japanese cooking and again the main pot is the wok but a large stew pot is also necessary and can substitute for the wok as well. The habatchi, originally from Japan, is also a necessity as many foods are grilled on it and it is used to cook community dishes right at the table. A pickle crock is also a must as many of the basic Japanese foodstuffs are pickled for preservation. Steaming, simmering, deep-frying, grilling and pickling are the chief forms of Japanese cooking. These methods take the carefully prepared ingredients and quickly produce a tasty nutritious meal.

Farm wife or Tokyo chef, food is lightly flavored with the ingredients tamari soy sauce, sesame oil or seeds, miso (fermented soy and grain paste), rice wine, rice vinegar, the ubiquitous fish stock, and sugar for which I substitute a mild honey. Rice is the staff of life in Japan but wheat and barley are widely used in noodles, sweets, and bean paste combinations. As in China, bean curd is an important source of protein along with fish and shellfish. Inland, chicken and freshwater fish are frequently used in small amounts to flavor a meal but not overload it with protein. Most vegetables used in Japan are familiar to the Western cook. Those which are not, such as daikon radish or snowpeas, can easily be grown in North America. However these ingredients are combined, the emphasis is on delicacy and natural flavor.

Many Japanese meals consist of one pot meals such as steamed egg custard containing chicken or fish, almonds and vegetables which are served with rice or noodles and the ever present pickles. On cold winter nights a delicious stew called nabemono is served again with rice and pickles for a quick meal. The popular sukiyaki is another example of a simple, fast one pot meal. A rule is small servings - Japanese do not believe in leaving the table with uncomfortably full stomachs. A more elaborate meal would include soup, fish, poultry, hot vegetables, side dishes of cold vegetables in salads and pickles, rice, and a simple sweet. Menus follow to assist you in planning your Japanese meals.

MEAL SUGGESTIONS

1 TO 2 PERSONS
Pickles
Sukiyaki
Rice
Fruit

Yosenabe
Pickles
Rice
Kanten

Gyoden
Pickled Ginger
Fried Rice
Ama-zu

Chicken Teriyaki
Rice
Sunomono

Pickles
Sashimi
Rice
Fruit

Sakana miso-ni
Aemono
Rice

Oyako Domburi
Pickles

Chawan Mushi
Rice
Pickles

Lunch:
Norimaki Sushi
Pickles

3 TO 5 PERSONS
Miso Shiru
Teriyaki
Rice
Sunomono
Ohagi

Pickles
Soup
Miso Dango
Rice
Aemono
Fruit

Pickles
Miso Shiru
Vegetarian Oden
Ama-zu
Rice

Pickled Ginger
Yasai no Kurimi-ae
Tamago Suimono
Beef Yashi Miso-ni
Rice
Yokan

Pickles
Sashimi
Rice
Kakitamajiru
Aemono
Fruit

Suimono
Niwatori Sukiyaki
Rice
Kimi-zu
Yama Imo

Picnic
Sushi
Cold Tatsuta Age
Pickles
Manju

FEASTS

Vegetarian Feast
Pickles
Omeretsu
Tofu Teriyaki
Norimaki Sushi
Sunomono
Miso Shiru
Tempura
Green Beans in Egg Custard
Vegetables with Bean Curd Sauce
Rice
Tempura Fruit

Meat Feast
Nigiri Sushi
Pickles
Nimame
Suimono
Sunomono
Beef Teriyaki
Tempura Dango
Sakana Miso-ni
Rice
Fruit

Mixed Feast
Amai no Ebi
Norimaki Sushi
Pickled Ginger
Tamago Suimono
Squash cooked with Miso
Chicken Cooked with Rice Cakes
Broccoli Ama-zu
Fried Rice
Awayukikan

Mixed Feast
Nigri Sushi
Pickles
Kimi-zu
Miso Shiru
Tatsuta Age
Miso Dango
Niwatori Sukiyaki
Raspberry Kanten

BASIC INGREDIENTS

DASHI [FISH AND SEAWEED STOCK] [Makes 4 cups]

4 cups water
2 inches kombu [kelp]
[optional]

Wash kombu well in cold water to remove excess salt. Drain. Place in a saucepan with water. Cover pan and bring to boil. Remove kombu. Save to use in pickle.

5 Tbsp. katsuobushi
[bonito flakes]

Add to boiling water. Cover pan and remove from heat. Let sit 5 minutes. Strain stock. Will keep in tight container in refrigerator up to 1 week.

KOMBU STOCK [KELP STOCK] [Makes 4 cups]

4 inches kombu
[dried kelp]
4 cups water

Wash kombu well in cold water to remove excess salt. Drain. Place in saucepan with water. Cover and bring to boil. Boil 2 minutes. Remove kombu. Do not cook too long or the stock will taste too strong. Save kombu to use in pickle.

TOGARASHI [HOT PEPPER CONDIMENT] [Makes about ½ cup]

2 Tbsp. mustard seed
4 Tbsp. sesame seed
1 Tbsp. poppy seed
[optional]
1 Tbsp. rape seed
[optional]
15 large dried red peppers
1 tsp. powdered dried
pepper leaf [sansho]
OR powdered dried pepper cress
1 tsp. hemp seed
[if possible to obtain]

Place ingredients in a blender and blend 1 to 2 minutes until almost powdered. If no blender is available grind seeds in a hand mill and pulverize peppers and leaves in a mortar and pestle. Keeps indefinitely in a cool dry place. Sprinkle over rice and noodle dishes plus other cooked foods. Very hot so take it easy.

SESAME SEED OIL [Makes ½ cup]

2 Tbsp. sesame seeds

Parch in a small frying pan over medium high heat 3 to 5 minutes until seeds well browned. Shake pan often to keep seeds from browning only on the bottom.

½ cup vegetable oil

Add to hot seeds. Heat 1 minute. Place in a blender and blend 30 seconds. Allow to sit for 1 to 2 hours. Heat slightly and strain through a fine muslin cloth. Squeeze cloth to get all oil removed from sesame pulp. Use pulp in breads, cookies, etc. Store oil in cool dark place.

RICE FLOUR [Makes ½ cup]

¼ cup short-grain brown rice

Toast rice for 1 minute in a hot skillet. Grind to a fine powder in a food mill or in a blender. Sift with a fine sifter to remove large particles.

AZUKI-AN [SWEET RED BEAN FILLING] [Makes 2½ cups]

1 cup azuki beans
OR kidney beans
3 cups water

Place beans and water in a pressure cooker. Cover and bring to full pressure. Cook at full pressure for 1 hour. If no pressure cooker is available cover beans with cold water and soak overnight. Place in a heavy saucepan with 4 cups water. Cover and bring to a boil over high heat. Reduce heat to medium and simmer 2 to 3 hours until beans are tender. Add more water as needed to keep beans from sticking to bottom of pan. Remove beans from heat. Drain. Save stock for bean soup or to use as a stock in making bread. Press beans through a sieve or food mill to puree beans to a fine paste.

½ cup mild honey
½ tsp. sea salt

Combine with bean paste in a heavy saucepan - enamel cast iron is best. Cook for 30 to 40 minutes over medium low heat until bean paste is thick and smooth. Stir frequently to prevent burning. Paste will keep a long time in the refrigerator. Paste is used in various sweet dishes and in small amounts to accompany a meal such as fish teriyaki.

VARIATION:

SWEET WHITE BEAN PASTE
[Makes about 4 cups]

2 cups small white beans
OR dried lima beans
4 cups water

Follow directions for cooking azuki beans. When beans are tender - mash easily in your fingers - drain. Press a third of the cooked beans through a sieve or foodmill to puree to a fine paste. Return the remaining unpressed beans to a heavy saucepan.

⅔ cup mild honey
½ tsp. sea salt

Add to bean paste. Mix well. Set aside. Cook unmashed beans 20 to 30 minutes until beans are dry. Cook over medium low heat and stir frequently to prevent scorching. Add bean paste. Cook over medium low heat another 28 to 30 minutes until beans are thick and smooth and no longer glossy. A few particles of bean should remain. Stir frequently to prevent scorching. Chill and serve as an accompaniment to broiled or fried chidken or fish dishes. Pureed smooth it is used as a filling for sweet rice cakes. Keeps indefinitely in the refrigerator.

MOCHI [RICE CAKES] [Makes about 3 dozen]

1 cup mochi gumi
  [sweet brown rice]
  OR short grain brown rice
2¼ cups water

OR IN PLACE OF ABOVE
2 cups moist cooked
  short grain brown rice

Place water and rice in a heavy saucepan. Cover and bring to a boil over medium high heat. When steam comes out from under the lid reduce heat to medium low and simmer 25 to 30 minutes until all of water is absorbed. Remove from heat and allow to cool. Turn rice onto a wet chopping board. Chop with a wet sharp knife until most of rice kernels are chopped. Moisten hands and knead rice until glutinous and sticks together. Press rice into an 8 or 9 inch square pan. Let sit 2 or 3 hours or overnight. Loosen edges of rice with a dampened spatula. Cut in pan or turn out on a wet chopping board. Cut into ½ inch squares. Place rice squares on a greased cookie sheet. Leave at least ¼ inch between squares to allow for expansion. Place in oven at least 15 inches below broiler. Grill 10 to 15 minutes in closed oven. Turn when lightly browned on one side and cakes no longer stick to bottom of pan. Grill until lightly browned on second side. Cool on a rack. Store in tight container. Used in special New Year's soup - Zoni - and stewlike dishes. Good as a snack when cut in half and dipped in sesame salt.

GOMA SIO [SESAME SALT] [Makes about ½ cup]

5 Tbsp. sesame seeds

Place seeds in a small heavy cast iron skillet. Cook over high heat 3 to 5 minutes until seeds pop and are golden brown. Mix by shaking pan to move seeds around from top to bottom. Do this frequently to prevent uneven roasting.

1 Tbsp. sea salt

Add to seeds. Roast another minute. Remove from heat. Place in a blender and blend for about 30 seconds. Do not completely pulverize seeds. If no blender is available, grind in a flour mill or in a Japanese mortar and pestle called a suribachi. Store in a tight container. Served on rice, noodles, vegetables or other dishes one would sprinkle salt over.

KAMABOKO [FISH CAKE] [Makes about 4 x 8 inch cake ½ inch wide]

3 inch square of kombu ½ cup water	Wash kombu to remove excess salt. Place in a saucepan with water. Bring to a boil and boil for 2 minutes. Remove from heat. Allow kombu to soak for 5 more minutes. Remove from water. Save for kombu pickle. Cool liquid.
⅓ cup brown rice flour.	Combine with kombu liquid. Mix well.
¾ lb. white fish	Remove all bones from fish. Cut into small pieces. Place on a wet chopping board and chop fine. Puree through a food mill or in a blender until fine and no stringy tissue remains.
1½ tsp. mild honey 1 tsp. sea salt 2 egg whites, slightly beaten 3 Tbsp. sake	Add to bowl with rice flour along with fish puree. Beat until very smooth. Strain through a food mill. Oil a 4 inch by 8 inch bread pan. Place fish puree mixture into pan. Knock pan on counter several times to remove excess air. Place fish cake in a steamer and steam 50 to 60 minutes until fish is firm. Remove from steamer and let sit for 10 minutes.
1 egg yolk, well beaten 1 tsp. sake ½ tsp. mild honey	Mix ingredients well. Brush over top of cooled steamed fish cake. Place under broiler and brown lightly. Brush again with egg yolk mixture. Brown again. Continue until all egg mixture used. Chill. Use in noodle dishes, soups, stews or as Zensai (appetizer). Serve at room temperature when serving by itself.

APPETIZERS AND SNACKS [ZENSAI]

From vinegared rice sandwiches (sushi) to hot fried chestnuts (age-guri), snacks and appetizers are very popular in Japan. Sushi can be a lunch in itself and is very common but dishes such as plum blossom eggs are usually served only at festivals. The rule is small servings.

SUSHI MESHI [VINEGARED SUSHI RICE] [Makes 6 cups]

3½ cups short grain brown rice
4 cups water
6 inch piece kombu [kelp]

Wash rice 1 to 2 hours before cooking. Drain and allow to dry (optional step). Wash kombu to remove excess salt. Place kombu and water in a heavy saucepan. Cover and bring to a boil over high heat. Remove kombu (reserve for kombu pickle). Add rice, stir and cover pan. Bring to a boil over high heat. Reduce heat to medium low and simmer for 30 to 40 minutes until all water is absorbed. Remove from heat and allow to sit 10 minutes. Turn rice out on a large shallow dish or platter.

½ cup rice vinegar
2 Tbsp. mild honey
1½ tsp. sea salt

Heat all ingredients in a small saucepan. Mix well. Do not bring to a boil. Cool until hand is comfortable on bottom of saucepan. After rice is spread on platter pour vinegar mixture evenly over rice in a small steady stream. Fan rice to cool rapidly (an electric fan works really well but a hand fan if vigourously fanned is just as good). Cut in vinegar mixture with a wooden rice paddle while fanning rice to get rice evenly coated with vinegar mixture and to slightly break down rice grains. Cool rice quickly with the fan so it will be slightly dry and glossy. Use to make norimaki, inari, chirashi and nigiri sushi. Store in a tight container to prevent drying. Will keep several days.

VARIATION:

USE LEFTOVER COLD RICE

2 TO 3 CUPS COLD COOKED
  SHORT GRAIN BROWN RICE
4 Tbsp. rice vinegar
1 Tbsp. honey
½ tsp. sea salt

Steam rice 3 to 4 minutes to heat and loosen grains. Place on a platter. Heat vinegar, honey and salt in a small saucepan. Do not bring to a boil. Cool slightly. Pour over rice. Mix well. Use as sushi rice in above recipe. Store in a tight container to prevent drying. Will keep well several days.

NORIMAKI SUSHI [VINEGARED RICE ROLLED IN SEAWEED WITH FILLING] [Serves 4 to 6 or as Appetizer 8 to 10]

½ batch sushi rice
1 sweet thick egg sheet,
  sliced into thin strips
2 vinegared carrots,
  cut into thin strips
6 green onions,
  cut into strips lengthwise

Prepare sushi fillings and have them ready for use when ready to assemble sushi.

OTHER FILLINGS THAT CAN BE USED:

4 sweet mushrooms, chopped
Kamaboko, cut into ¼ inch strips
Sweet pickled shrimp, cut in half
  along back vein [See Amai no ebi
  in Zensai
Raw fish, cut into ¼ inch strips
Sweet canned eel
Fresh parsley, minced

FILLINGS:

SWEET THICK EGG SHEET
4 eggs
2 Tbsp. stock
1 tsp. honey
1 Tbsp. soy sauce

1 Tbsp. vegetable oil

Beat eggs. Add other ingredients and beat or blend well. Heat a medium cast iron skillet over medium heat. Add oil. Heat until a small bit of egg mixture dropped in sets. Pour egg mixture into center of pan. Cover pan. Turn heat to medium low. Cook 10 minutes. Uncover and loosen edges of omelette with a knife. Place plate over skillet. Invert skillet so omelette falls on plate. Brush skillet with oiled pastry brush. Slip omelette into pan. Cook 2 to 3 minutes until eggs firm. Invert onto a plate. Cut into ¼ inch strips for sushi. Good also just by itself cut into ½ inch squares and served on toothpicks with a dipping sauce (See dipping sauces for kamaboko) or just plain.

VINEGARED CARROTS

2 - 8 inch carrots, halved and halves cut in half and then cut lengthwise into ¼ inch to 1/8 inch strips

Steam carrots 3 to 5 minutes until just lost their crispness.

2 Tbsp. rice vinegar
1 Tbsp. soy sauce
1 Tbsp. mild honey

Heat vinegar, soy and honey in a small saucepan. Do not boil. Heat only enough to combine well. Pour over hot carrots. Chill a minimum of 1 hour. Carrots are also good used as a salad.

SWEET MUSHROOMS

4 large mushrooms, chopped coarsely
3 Tbsp. soy sauce
2 Tbsp. mild honey

Place ingredients in a saucepan. Bring to a boil over medium heat. Reduce heat to medium low. Allow to simmer 5 to 10 minutes until sauce thickens and turns mushrooms glossy. Do not cook sauce too long or it will taste slightly burnt.

HOW TO ASSEMBLE AND ROLL NORIMAKI SUSHI:

2 Tbsp. rice vinegar
1 tsp. honey
2 cups cold water
8 sheets nori seaweed

Mix honey and vinegar well. Add to cold water. Place a sheet of nori seaweed on a su (bamboo mat) or bamboo placemat. Spread sushi rice thinly to within 1 inch of the side furtherest from you. Spread rice thinly and evenly and press well on seaweed or sushi will not roll well. Always have hands and utensils wet to prevent rice from sticking to them. Use bowl of water with vinegar and honey it it. Place filling 2 inches from the edge closest to you. Take su in one hand and tuck rice around filling with the other. Like rolling a cigarette. Start to roll sushi away from you, being careful to keep ingredients in place. Pull su with both hands and keep pressure on roll at all times with it. When sushi is rolled squeeze tightly to firm roll. Chill. Cut rolls into ½ inch slices with a wet, sharp knife. Arrange on a tray and serve with soy suace to dip sushi in. Ginger pickle is often served with sushi. Good for snacks. If tightly wrapped and not cut, rolls will keep well for several days and make nice lunches or picnic foods.

INARI SUSHI [DEEP FRIED TOFU STUFFED WITH SUSHI RICE]
[Serves 4 to 6 or 6 to 12 if used as appetizers]

6 cakes age
  [deep fried tofu]
1 cup water

Place age and water in saucepan. Bring to boil. Reduce heat and simmer 2 to 3 minutes until softened. Remove from heat. Drain.

2 Tbsp. stock
1 Tbsp. mild honey
2 Tbsp. tamari soy sauce
2 Tbsp. rice vinegar

Place ingredients in saucepan. Bring to boil. Reduce heat and add boiled age. Simmer 5 minutes. Remove from heat and drain. Cut in half and stuff each age with following mix:

STUFFING:
½ batch sushi rice
2 green onions,
  cut into thin 1 inch strips
Vinegared carrots,
  cut into thin 1 inch strips
  [see Norimaki Sushi]
Sweet egg sheet,
  cut into thin 1 inch strips
  [see Norimaki Sushi]

When age are stuffed, place on a tray and serve cold. Makes a good snack. If tightly wrapped will keep well for several days and make nice lunches or picnic food. Use soy sauce to dip sushi in when served.

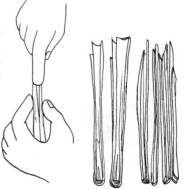

OTHER FILLINGS THAT CAN BE USED:

Sweet mushrooms
  [see Norimaki Sushi]
Sweet pickled shrimp,
  cut into ¼ inch slices
  [see Nigri Sushi]

NIGRI SUSHI [VINEGARED RICE CAKES WITH FISH TOPPING]
[Serves 4 to 6 or 8 to 10 as Appetizer]

1½ Tbsp. washabi powder
  [Japanese horseradish powder]
1 Tbsp. water

Make a paste. Allow to sit for at least 5 minutes

Toppings:
slices of raw tuna
  OR raw clam
  OR salmon
  OR raw abalone
Pickled white fish, sliced
  1 mackerel fillet
    OR red snapper fillet
  1 Tbsp. rice vinegar
  ½ tsp. mild honey
  ½ tsp. sea salt
Pickled shrimp
  8 large raw shrimp,
    shelled and deveined

Use only fresh fish. Never use fish that smells old. Cut fish fillets crosswise to the backline of the fish. Use a wet, very sharp knife. Cut fish at an angle into ¼ inch thick slices.

Marinate fish in vinegar honey sauce for 1 hour before slicing as directed above.

Devein shrimp by making a shallow slit down the back and removing the intestine with a knife tip. String shrimp on a bamboo skewer from head to tail to prevent shrimp from curling when cooked. Place shrimp in boiling water. Cook for 3 to 5 minutes until pink and firm. Leave shrimp on skewers. Remove from water. Cool. Remove from skewers when cool. Cut from the underside almost to the back but do not cut in half. Flatten with a moist knife. Place in a shallow bowl.

2 Tbsp. rice vinegar
½ tsp. sea salt
1 tsp. mild honey

Place ingredients in a small saucepan. Heat until honey dissolves. Remove from heat.

⅓ cup cold stock
   OR water

Add cold stock to vinegar mixture. Pour over shrimp. Marinate for at least 1 hour.

Assembling nigiri sushi:

3 cups sushi rice

Mold rice into small 1 to 1½ inch by ½ inch cakes with moist hands. Press firmly to keep rice together but not so hard that it squeezes between the fingers. Spread a strip of washabi paste down center of each rice cake (very hot so do not use too much). Top with raw fish, clam, abalone, cooked shrimp, etc. Always handle rice with moist hands. Serve as an appetizer or main course. Also very good as a lunch. Serve with soy sauce for dipping sushi in. Ginger pickle is an excellent accompaniment.

VEGETABLE SUSHI WRAPPED IN NORI
[Serves 4 to 6 or — to 10 if used as appetizers]

½ batch sushi rice

SPRINKLE WITH FOLLOWING INGREDIENTS:
Sweet egg sheet, sliced thin
  [see Norimaki Sushi]
Vinegared carrots,
  cut into ½ inch thin strips
  [see Norimaki Sushi]
Green onions,
  cut into 1 inch thin strips
2 inches kombu from stick,
  cut into ½ inch slivers

Mix with rice so ingredients are evenly distributed. Always have hands and utensils wet so rice does not stick to them. Form rice into 1½ inch equal-sided triganles. Press firmly so triangles will hold their shape. Make about ¾ to 1 inch thick.

OTHER FILLINGS THAT CAN BE USED:
Sweet mushrooms
  [see Norimaki Sushi]
Sweet pickled shrimp,
  cut into ¼ inch slices
  [see Nigri Sushi or Amai no Ebi
  in Zensai]

4 sheets nori seaweed,
  cut in quarters

Dampen piece of nori. Wrap around triangles of rice as they are made. Serve at room temperature. Very nice sushi for lunches or picnics. Use soy sauce to dip sushi in when served.

CHIRASHI SUSHI [SUSHI RICE WITH ASSORTED TOPPINGS]
[Serves 4 to 6]

½ batch sushi rice

SPRINKLE TOP OF RICE WITH FOLLOWING INGREDIENTS:
Sweet egg sheet, sliced thin
  [see Norimaki Sushi]
Green onions,
  cut into thin 1 inch strips
  [see Norimaki Sushi]
Vinegared carrots,
  cut into thin 1 inch strips
½ sheet nori seaweed, toasted
    on a grill or broiled until crisp
    and broken into small bits
Steamed snowpeas, chilled and cut
  into thin strips
    OR regular peas, steamed
      2 to 3 minutes and chilled
Sweet pickled shrimp, cut into
  ¼ inch slices [see Nigri Sushi or
  Amai no Ebi in Zensai]

Place rice in a shallow bowl. Use only 3 to 5 ingredients. Sprinkle over top of rice. Serve at lunch or with main meal of the day. Serve with soy sauce to sprinkle over individual servings. Very good served with pickles.

OMERETSU [THICK LAYERED EGG OMELETTE]
[Serves 4 to 6 as a main dish and 8 to 10 as an appetizer]

6 eggs
½ tsp. sea salt
1 tsp. soy sauce
2 tsp. dashi

Beat eggs with other ingredients until well mixed but not frothy.

1 Tbsp. vegetable oil

Heat an 8 inch cast iron skillet or an 8 inch square Japanese omelette pan. Oil with a pastry brush. Keep heat at medium low. Add 3 Tbsp. of egg mixture to pan. Spread evenly by rolling pan. Allow to set 2 to 3 minutes until edges come loose from sides. Lift the egg sheet and reoil under it. Hold up egg sheet and pour 3 more Tbsp. egg mixture under first egg sheet. Roll pan to distribute evenly. Allow to set. Repeat process lifting opposite sides of the egg sheet each time until all the egg mixture is used. Oil between each addition of egg mixture. Place a plate over the pan and invert omelette onto plate. Oil pan and slip back into pan with topside down. Cook 1 to 2 more minutes to firm but not brown top. Remove from pan. Cut into 1 inch diamonds or squares. Serve hot or cold with soy sauce for dipping. Good as a lunch or as a main dish for a small meal.

VARIATION:
**ROLLED OMERETSU [ROLLED THICK
LAYERED EGG OMELETTE] [Serves 4 to 6 as
a main dish and 6 to 8 as appetizer]**

1 thick layered egg omelette
1 sheet nori seaweed

Have all fillings made before making omelette.
Place nori on a su or bamboo mat. Place hot
omelette on seaweed so 1 inch of seaweed
extends at the top.

Fillings:
½ cup crabmeat
   OR 4 sweet pickled shrimp [see Amai no Ebi]
Sweet mushrooms, chopped [see Norimaki Sushi]
2 green onions, cut into thin slivers lengthwise

5 to 6 green beans, cut into long thin slices
¼ cup dashi
3 Tbsp. soy sauce
1 tsp. mild honey

Heat soy, dashi and honey in a saucepan. Add
beans and simmer for 4 to 5 minutes until just
tneder. Drain and chill.

Assembly:
Place 1 to 3 fillings 2 inches from top of egg
omelette on su. Roll hot. Place in refrigerator
while still rolled in su. Chill. Cut into 1 inch
slices when chilled. Serve with soy suace for
dipping. Good as a lunch or picnic food.

BAIKA TAMAGO [PLUM BLOSSOM EGGROLL] [Makes 1 8 to 10 inch roll]
[Serves 4 to 6 or 8 to 10 as an appetizer]

4 large hard boiled eggs	Separate the yolks from the whites. Place in separate bowls.
4 boiled egg whites of above eggs **2 tsp. mild honey** **½ tsp. arrowroot starch** **¼ tsp. sea salt** **few drops of beet juice**	Mix ingredients well. Mash egg whites until a paste is formed with the other ingredients. Blender does this well.
4 egg yolks of above eggs **2 tsp. mild honey** **½ tsp. sea salt**	Mix yolks with other ingredients until a paste is formed. Blender does this well.

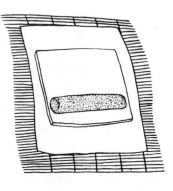

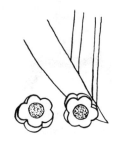

Assembly:

Place a damp muslin cloth (old sheet is good) on a su or bamboo mat. Make a 6 inch by 4 inch rectangle of egg-white mixture on the cloth ¼ inch from the top of the cloth. Make rectangular and an even thickness. Keep hands and tools moist so egg will not stick to tools. Make a sausage of the egg-yolk paste and place 3 inches from the top of egg-white rectangle. Bring cloth over top of egg yolk so white covers yolk evenly on all sides. Tuck in edges of cloth and roll up egg roll in cloth with the su. Press slightly with su to firm roll but not so hard as to squeeze egg from ends of roll. Place 5 even-sized sticks (I use some favorite, even-sized twigs from my apple tree) or chopsticks around outside of roll. Hold tight with rubber bands. Not too tight or again egg will squeeze out ends of roll. Steam roll 20 to 30 minutes until firm. Leave sticks around roll. Chill. Remove sticks and cloth. Slice into ¼ inch slices. Used at New Year's particularly but good as an appetizer any time. Very pretty with red coulored whites and yellow center.

TOFU YAKI [BEAN CURD GRILLED WITH SWEET SAUCE]
[Serves 8 to 10 as an appetizer]

1 cake bean curd	Tightly wrap bean curd in a muslin cloth (an old sheet works well. Place on a board in the sink. Place a small board on top of tofu and weight with rocks or a quart jar full of water. Press for a minimum of 1 hour or overnight.
½ cup vegetable oil	Heat a medium cast iron skillet. Add oil and heat slightly. Add bean curd and fry over medium high heat 5 to 10 minutes until golden brown. Remove from heat. Drain well.

2 Tbsp. sake
  OR dry sherry
  OR dry white wine
2 tsp. arrowroot starch
	Mix ingredients in a medium cast iron skillet.

5 Tbsp. soy sauce
2 Tbsp. mild honey
½ tsp. dark molasses
¼ tsp. washabi powder
  [powdered Japanese
  horseradish]
½ inch fresh ginger root,
  grated
1 clove garlic, grated
	Add to sake and starch. Mix well. Bring to a boil over medium heat. Cook 3 to 5 minutes until mixture thickens. Add fried tofu. Coat bean curd completely in sauce. Place in refrigerator. Chill a minimum of 1 hour. Place on an oiled broiler pan 3 inches from broiler. Grill 1 to 2 minutes to a side. Baste with sauce as broiling. Grill until sauce bubbles. Turn and grill other side. Remove from broiler. Cut into ½ inch cubes.

4 Tbsp. sesame seeds	Parch in a small frying pan 2 to 3 minutes until lightly browned but not scorched. Sprinkle over bean curd cubes. Serve on a small tray with toothpicks to pick up bean curd. Serve hot.

AGE-GURI [HOT FRIED CHESTNUTS WITH PEPPER SPICE] [Serves 5 to 6]

½ lb. chestnuts	Prick the skins with a sharp fork. Steam 15 to 20 minutes until tender. Remove from heat. Cool slightly and peel.
2 Tbsp. vegetable oil	Heat a medium sized skillet over medium high. Add oil and heat slightly. Add chestnuts. Reduce heat to medium. Fry 5 to 10 minutes until chestnuts are a golden brown. Remove from oil. Drain on absorbent paper.
½ tsp. sea salt ½ to 1 tsp. toragashi	Sprinkle over still hot chestnuts. Serve warm. A good snack as well as an appetizer.

KAMABOKO [FISHCAKE]
1 Fishcake will make about 60 servings ¼ inch by 2 inch

1 kamaboko [fish cake]
  cut into ¼ inch by 2 inch
  slices
	Place 3 to 5 pieces of fishcake on small individual plates. Serve with one of the following sauces.

SAUCES:	Plain soy sauce and a small amount of moistened washabi (Japanese horseradish) may be used as a dipping sauce or any dipping sauce in zensai section.

WASHABI SOYU [HORSERADISH SOY DIPPING SAUCE]

2 tsp. washabi powder
  [Japanese horseradish powder]
½ cup soy sauce
1 Tbsp. sake
  OR dry sherry
  OR dry white wine
1 Tbsp. mild honey
1 Tbsp. dashi
	Heat ingredients in a small saucepan just enough to dissolve honey. Cool. Serve at room temperature with fish cake.

DAIKON SOYU [JAPANESE RADISH SOY DIPPING SAUCE]

2 Tbsp. finely grated daikon
  [Japanese radish]
¼ cup soy sauce

Mix ingredients well. Serve at room temperature with fish cake.

SOYU DIPPING SAUCE

1 Tbsp. rice vinegar
3 Tbsp. soy sauce
1 Tbsp. dashi
1 tsp. mild honey

Mix ingredients well in a small saucepan. Heat just enough to dissolve honey. Cool to room temperature. Serve at room temperature with fish cake.

SWEET MUSHROOMS [Serves 4 to 6]

4 large dried mushrooms
1 cup boiling water

OR IN PLACE OF ABOVE:
4 large fresh mushrooms,
  cut into ¼ inch slices

Place dry mushrooms in a shallow bowl. Pour boiling water over mushrooms. Place a weight over mushrooms to keep under water. Allow to soak a minimum of 15 to 20 minutes until soft. Drain and squeeze out excess moisture. Remove tough stems. Cut into ¼ inch slices.

2 Tbsp. mild honey
2 Tbsp. sake
4 Tbsp. soy sauce
1 Tbsp. dashi

Mix ingredients in a medium saucepan. Bring to a boil over high heat. Reduce heat to medium and add mushrooms. Simmer over medium heat 10 to 15 minutes until sauce begins to thicken. Remove from heat. Chill. Serve cold.

NIMAME [SWEET SOYBEANS] [Makes 1 cup]

½ cup black soybeans
  OR any dried soybean
2 cups water

Place water and soybeans in a pressure cooker. Bring to full pressure and cook at full pressure for 1 hour. Allow to cool for 20 minutes. If no pressure cooker is available cover soybeans with water and allow to soak overnight. Drain and wash. Place in a heavy saucepan with 3 to 4 cups of water. Bring to a boil over high heat. Cover and reduce heat to medium low. Simmer 2 to 3 hours until soybeans are tender. Drain. Reserve stock for later use.

3 Tbsp. mild honey
1 Tbsp. molasses
3 Tbsp. soy sauce
½ cup bean stock
  [from soybeans]
½ tsp. sea salt

Place drained soybeans in saucepan with bean stock and other ingredients. Bring to a boil over high heat. Reduce heat to medium and simmer 10 to 15 minutes until sauce just begins to thicken. If cooked too long the beans will get tough. Remove from heat and cool. Serve in small bowls as an appetizer or snack about 1 Tbsp. to a serving.

AMAI NO EBI [SWEET PICKLED SHRIMP] [Serves 8 to 10 as appetizer]

12 to 15 large raw shrimp,
  shelled and deveined
    OR raw prawns,
      shelled and deveined

Devein shrimp by making a shallow slit down the back and removing the intestine with a knife tip. String shrimp on a bamboo skewer from head to tail to prevent shrimp from curling when cooked. Place in boiling water. Cook for 3 to 5 minutes until pink and firm. Remove shrimp from water. Cool. Remove from skewers when cooled. Cut from the underside almost to the back but do not cut in half. Flatten with a moist knife. Place in a shallow bowl.

4 Tbsp. rice vinegar
½ tsp. sea salt
2 Tbsp. sake
2 tsp. mild honey
2 Tbsp. dashi

Mix in a shallow saucepan. Place shrimp in pan and bring to a boil. Cook 2 to 3 minutes. Remove from heat. Chill shrimp. Serve cold. Very good with cold rice or a bowl of Chirashi Sushi for lunch along with some pickles.

KANI NO KINUTA-MAKE [CUCUMBER STUFFED WITH CRAB] [Serves 6 to 8]

2 large cucumbers, unwaxed
2 tsp. sea salt

With a fork score the outside of the cucumbers lightly. Sprinkle with salt. Allow to sit for 15 minutes. Wash off salt. Split cucumbers lengthwise to the seeds. Cut off ends to where the seeds show. Scoop seeds out of cucumber with a small spoon starting with the ends first. Gently open slice and scoop out seeds along opening. Do not push apart too hard or the cucumber will break in half.

FILLINGS:
¼ to ½ cup crabmeat
1 large green onion,
  cut lengthwise into 4 pieces
2 large sprigs of parsley,
  steamed 10 seconds,
  chopped coarsely

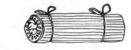

Divide ingredients into 2 equal parts. Place scallions in scooped-out center of cucumber. Next place parsley evenly down center of the cucumber. Last place crab evenly down the center of the cucumber on top of the scallions and parsley. Tie cucumber with string or hold together with rubber bands. Chill. Cut into 1 inch slices. Serve cold with the following sauce. May also be used as a salad.

SAUCE:
2 Tbsp. rice vinegar
2 Tbsp. dashi
1½ tsp. mild honey
2 tsp. soy sauce
1 tsp. lemon juice

Combine all ingredients well. Easiest to mix honey and vinegar first. Chill. Serve with cucumber roll as a dipping sauce. Good appetizer or snack. Excellent main meal salad. Good simple cold supper salad in the summer. Good lunch.

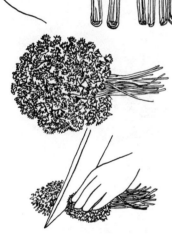

LIVER TSUKUDANI [LIVER IN SWEET SAUCE WITH GREEN ONIONS]
[Serves 4 to 6]

½ lb. chicken livers

Wash liver well. Drain.

1 cup water
3 Tbsp. sake
  OR dry sherry
  OR rice vinegar
2 Tbsp. honey
1 inch fresh ginger root,
  grated
¼ cup soy sauce

Place ingredients in a saucepan. Bring to a boil. Reduce heat to medium. Add chicken liver. Reduce heat to medium low and simmer 15 to 20 minutes until sauce slightly thickens.

4 scallions,
  cut into thin diagonals

Add to liver and sauce. Simmer 5 to 10 minutes until sauce thickens but does not scorch. Stir often. Place liver and sauce on a shallow dish and chill. Slice into ¼ inch slices before serving.

CHICKEN LIVER TERIYAKI [GRILLED CHICKEN LIVERS] [Serves 6 to 8]

½ **lb. chicken liver**

Wash chicken liver well. Drain. Place in a shallow dish.

¼ **cup soy sauce**
3 Tbsp. mild honey
¼ **cup water**

Heat ingredients in a small saucepan just enough to dissolve honey. Remove from heat.

3 Tbsp. sake
  OR rice vinegar
  OR dry sherry
  OR dry white wine

Add to saucepan. Mix well. Pour sauce over chicken livers. Marinate 2 to 3 hours or overnight. Place chicken liver on two bamboo skewers. Oil broiler pan. Place under broiler for 5 to 10 minutes. Baste often with sauce. Grill until livers are coated with a shiny coating of sauce. A hibachi may also be used. Oil hibachi grill. Turn livers often to prevent sauce from scorching. Serve hot. Good as a snack or as a lunch the next day. Excellent appetizer for a feast.

SMALL CHICKEN TERIYAKI [SMALL GRILLED CHICKEN] [Serves 6 to 8]

1 large chicken breast
  skinned and bone removed,
  cut into ½ inch cubes
  OR meat from 2 legs
    and thighs of a chicken
    cut into ½ inch cubes

SAUCE:
¼ **cup sake**
  OR dry sherry
  OR rice vinegar
¼ **cup soy sauce**
1 Tbsp. sesame oil
1 tsp. mild honey
1 clove garlic,
  grated
1 inch fresh ginger root,
  grated

Mix ingredients well in a shallow dish. Place chicken in sauce. Mix well. Marinate 1 to 2 hours or overnight. Place 3 pieces of chicken on a bamboo skewer. Repeat until all chicken is skewered. Oil grill or broiler pan first. Grill under a broiler or over a charcoal fire 5 to 10 minutes until well browned. Baste often with sauce and turn frequently.

4 Tbsp. sesame seeds

Parch in a small saucepan 2 to 3 minutes until lightly browned. Place in a small bowl. Serve with hot chicken teriyaki for a dip. Makes good lunches the next day. Also good picnic food. Take an hibachi along and roast on the spot.

CHICKEN BREAST WITH SAUCE [Serves 6 to 8]

1 large chicken breast,
  skinned and bone removed
½ tsp. sea salt
3 Tbsp. sake
  OR dry sherry
  OR rice vinegar

Rub chicken breast with salt. Prick breast all over with a fork. Place in a shallow dish. Sprinkle with sake. Marinate in sake for 1 to 2 hours. Turn occasionally. Steam breast 15 to 20 minutes until tender and no longer pink inside but still juicy. Remove from steamer. Chill. Cut into ¼ inch slices. Serve with following sauce. Good for lunch also or simple main dish for 2 on a hot summer day.

SAUCE:
¼ cup rice vinegar
2 Tbsp. soy sauce
1 Tbsp. dashi
1 Tbsp. honey
½ tsp. washabi powder
  [powdered Japanese
  horseradish]

Mix ingredients well. Easiest to mix vinegar and honey first. Make sure honey is dissolved. Chill. Serve with chicken as dipping sauce.

SAKANA NO DANGO [FISH BALLS] [Serves 8 to 10]

1 lb. whitefish

Place fish on a wet chopping board. Chop fine with a wet sharp knife. Place in a bowl.

4 green onions,
  minced
¼ inch fresh ginger root,
  grated
1 tsp. sea salt
1 tsp. mild honey
3 Tbsp. arrowroot starch
1 egg white,
  slightly beaten

Mix ingredients well with fish. Allow to sit 20 to 30 minutes.

2 to 3 cups vegetable oil

Heat a wok over high heat. Add oil. Heat until a small piece of fish mixture added sinks to the bottom and then rises to the surface after a slight hesitation. Place 4 to 5 tsp. of fish mixture in hot oil. Fry 3 to 5 minutes until golden brown. Drain on absorbent paper or place on a rack over a bowl of cold water so oil drips into bowl. Keep warm if needed in 200° oven for 5 to 10 minutes. Do not dry out when reheating fish balls. Use any of dips for fish cakes as dipping sauce. Good appetizer. Excellent cold next day for lunch. Great feast dish.

Too Cold

Too Hot   Correct Temperature

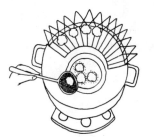

PICKLES [TSUKEMONO]

Every meal in Japan is accompanied by pickles. Pickling is the chief food preserving method used in Japan and everything from seaweed through fish and vegetables are pickled either in brines, miso or vinegar sauces.

SUPAI NO DAIKON [FRESH VINEGARED DAIKON] [Makes about 2 quarts]

3 large daikon

Wash daikon and cut into 1/8 inch slices. Place in a ceramic bowl or in glass jar that can be closed tightly or a pickle crock.

1 cup water
⅓ cup mild honey
½ cup rice vinegar
1½ Tbsp. sea salt
¼ tsp. turmeric

Combine ingredients in a saucepan. Bring to a boil. Pour over daikon. Cover tightly. Cool. Place in refrigerator. Mix once a day for 3 days and then serve. This pickle can be processed in a hot water bath canner for 10 minutes and then stored indefinitely when it seals.

VARIATION:

SUPAI NO KABU [FRESH VINEGARED TURNIP] [Makes 1 quart]

3 large white turnips cut in half and sliced thin

Wash turnips. Place in a ceramic bowl or glass jar that can be closed tightly or pickle crock.

3 Tbsp. mild honey
½ cup water
2 Tbsp. rice vinegar
2 tsp. sea salt

Bring to a boil in a saucepan. Pour over turnips. Cover tightly. Cool. Place in refrigerator. Mix once a day for 3 days and then serve. Keeps up to 1 month.

PICKLED GINGER [Makes ½ cup]

3 Tbsp. rice vinegar
½ Tbsp. mild honey

Place in a small saucepan. Bring to a boil. Remove from heat.

½ cup fresh ginger root, cut into thin slices and julienned

Place in jar with a cover. Pour over hot vinegar and honey. Cover. Let sit 2 to 3 days. Good served with sushi or just as any other pickle. Serve cold.

TENJO KOMBU [PICKLED KELP] [Makes 2 cups]

1 large sheet kombu,
  wash well to remove salt
  OR 3, 8 inch pieces kombu
    leftover from making stock
4 cups water
¼ cup rice vinegar

Combine ingredients in shallow saucepan. Bring to boil. Cover and reduce heat to medium low.

1 cup tamari soy sauce
4 Tbsp. mild honey
2 tsp. fresh ginger root
  grated

Add to kombu and water. Bring to a boil over high heat. Cook over medium high heat 10 minutes uncovered. Cover and reduce heat to medium low and simmer about 1 hour until all liquid is absorbed. Stir frequently but gently to prevent soy from burning and kombu from sticking. Remove from heat and chill. Cut into ¼ inch strips.

1 Tbsp. sesame seeds

Toast in small dry cast iron skillet until seeds pop and brown. Mix with kombu after slicing. Keeps indefinitely in refrigerator. Served as pickle with meals or as a snack.

HAKUSAI NO TSUKEMONO [PICKLED CHINESE CABBAGE] [Makes 1 quart]

1 large Chinese cabbage
sea salt
2 Tbsp. mild honey
2 large chili peppers,
  minced

Separate leaves from stalks. Salt both sides of leaves lightly. Stack thin layer of leaves on bottom of crock or pottery bowl. Sprinkle with small amount of honey and pepper. Stack next layer against the veins of the lower layer. Sprinkle again with honey and peppers. Put each layer crosswise to each other layer and sprinkle each layer with small amount of honey and pepper. Continue until all leaves are used. Place a weight on top of a flat plate or wooden disc covering cabbage. Press overnight or for 3 days maximum. Slice thin and squeeze out excess water. Serve with following sauce or by itself.

SAUCE:
1 Tbsp. lemon juice
1 tsp. mild honey
¼ tsp. grated ginger

Mix ingredients. Serve with pickle. Good with any main dish or rice. Excellent with lunch of leftovers and rice.

YASAI NO TSUKEMONO [PICKLED MIXED VEGETABLES] [makes 2 quarts]

1 large eggplant,
  cut into ¼ inch slices
3 turnips,
  sliced thin
2 carrots,
  cut into thin diagonal slices
2 cucumbers,
  sliced thin
1 daikon,
  sliced thin
1 Tbsp. sea salt

Layer vegetables in a crock. Sprinkle each layer with salt. Place a disc over top of vegetables and weight. Leave 2 to 3 days. Squeeze excess water from vegetables. Cut into thin strips.

SAUCE:
1 Tbsp. soy sauce
1 Tbsp. rice vinegar

Serve vegetables with sauce or just plain soy sauce. Good with any main dish or with soup for lunch or rice and soup for breakfast. Best served cold.

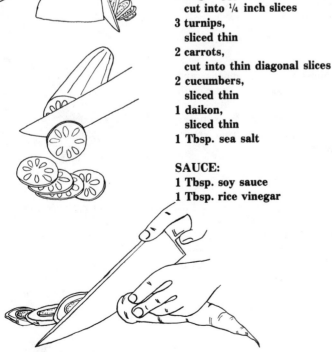

KABU NO TSUKEMONO [PICKLED TURNIPS] [Makes 1 quart]

3 to 4 turnips,
  sliced thin
2 Tbsp. sea salt

Place turnips in a crock. Sprinkle each layer with salt. Place a disc over top of vegetables and weight. Leave 2 to 3 days. Squeeze excess water from vegetables. Cut into thin strips. Place on individual pickle dishes.

SAUCE:
2 Tbsp. rice vinegar
2 Tbsp. mild honey
1 Tbsp. dashi or kombu stock

Mix ingredients well. Pour small amount of sauce over each pickle dish.

TAKUANZUKE [PICKLED DAIKON] [Makes about 2 quarts]

2 large daikon with fresh leaves
  sliced into long, thin strips
  with leaves cut into ¼ to ½
  inch slices
OR 1 lb. turnips with fresh tops
  sliced into thin strips with
  leaves cut into ¼ inch slices
1 Tbsp. sea salt

Sprinkle daikon and leaves with salt. Rub well. Place in a crock. Cover with a disc and weight. Leave 6 hours or overnight. Remove from crock as needed. Press out excess water.

SAUCE:
1 Tbsp. soy sauce
1 Tbsp. rice vinegar

Mix. Serve with pickled daikon. Can also be served with torgarashi or just soy sauce. Excellent with any meal.

HOT CUCUMBER TSUKEMONO [HOT CUCUMBER PICKLE] Makes 1 quart]

3 long cucumbers,
  seeded and cut into ½ inch
  long, thin slices
1 Tbsp. sea salt

Rub cucumbers with sea salt. Let sit for 30 minutes. Rinse. Drain.

1 yellow onion,
  cut into paper-thin rings
2 to 4 cloves garlic,
  crushed and minced
2 to 4 large fresh chili peppers,
  sliced thin
OR 2 to 3 large dried
  chili peppers,
  crushed and minced

Place layers of cucumbers, garlic, onions, and peppers alternately. Sprinkle each layer with salt. Place a disc over top of vegetables and weight. Weight 2 hours or overnight. Squeeze out excess water when removing from crock. Serve with following sauce.

SAUCE:
1 Tbsp. soy sauce
1 Tbsp. rice vinegar

Mix ingredients well. Pour small amount of sauce over pickles arranged in individual dishes. Can be served with plain soy sauce also. Excellent served with any meal.

CUCUMBER TSUKEMONO [CUCUMBER PICKLE] [Makes 1 quart]

3 to 4 pickling cucumbers
1 tsp. sea salt

Seed and slice cucumbers into ½ inch long, thin slices. Rub with sea salt. Place in crock. Cover with a lid and weight for 2 hours. Squeeze out excess water. Drain. Serve with following sauce.

SAUCE:
1 Tbsp. soy sauce
1 Tbsp. rice vinegar

Mix. Serve with cucumber. Can also be served with torgarashi or just soy sauce. Excellent with any meal.

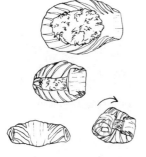

CABBAGE APPLE TSUKEMONO [CABBAGE AND APPLE PICKLE] [Makes 12 to 14 rolls]

½ **Chinese cabbage,**
   separate leaves

Steam leaves 2 to 3 minutes until just limp but still bright colored.

½ to 2 tsp. torgarashi
1 tsp. sea salt
2 tsp. mild honey

Sprinkle each leaf with pepper spice, salt and drop of honey.

3 apples,
   grated fine
1 inch fresh ginger root,
   grated

Mix ingredients well. Sprinkle over each cabbage leaf in a thin layer. Fold over ends of cabbage and then roll from top. Roll tightly. Place roll side down in crock. Cover with a disc and weight 30 minutes to 1 hour or overnight. Remove from crock. Cut into 1 inch slices. Good served cold with a nabe or saucepan food such as sukiyaki. Serve with any dipping sauce in pickle section. Excellent snack.

YASAI NO TSUKEMONO [VEGETABLES PICKLED IN MUSTARD SAUCE] [Makes about 2 to 3 cups]

1 lb. broccoli,
   cut into thin diagonals
   OR 1 lb. green beans,
      cut into thin diagonals
   OR 1 lb. cauliflower, broken
      into small flowerlets
   OR 1 lb. green peppers, seeded
      and cut into thin strips
      [do not steam]

Steam vegetables except green peppers 2 to 3 minutes until hot but still slightly crisp. Remove from heat and cool on a rack or in a cold place. Place in pickle crock or glass dish with a lid.

2 tsp. sea salt

Sprinkle vegetable with sea salt when cool. Mix well. Let sit covered for 30 minutes. Rinse. Drain.

SAUCE:
1 tsp. Japanese powdered mustard
   [washabi]
2 tsp. water
1 Tbsp. stock [dashi or kombu]
3 Tbsp. soy sauce
3 Tbsp. rice vinegar
1½ tsp. mild honey

Mix water and mustard first. Mix honey and vinegar well before adding to other ingredients. Add other ingredients. Mix well. Pour over vegetable. Mix. Cover. Let sit 2 hours or overnight. Good with rice and leftovers for lunch or with miso soup for breakfast. Also served at the main meal. Serve cold.

NASU MISO ZUKE [EGGPLANT PICKLED IN MISO] [Makes about 2 cups]

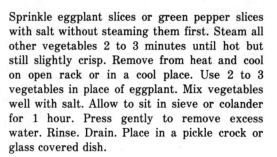

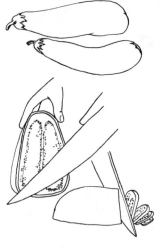

1 medium eggplant,
  cut in half lengthwise and
  then into 1/8 inch slices
  OR 1 lb. Japanese eggplant,
    cut into 1/8 inch slices
  OR 1 lb. carrots,
    cut into 1 inch slices
    and then cut into 1/ inch
    strips
  OR 1 lb. asparagus,
    cut into long thin diagonals
  OR 1 lb. broccoli,
    cut into thin diagonals
  OR 1 lb. brussel sprouts,
    cut in half lengthwise
  OR 1 lb. green beans,
    cut into thin diagonals
  OR 1 lb. cauliflower,
    broken into small flowerlets
  OR 1 lb. green peppers,
    seeded and cut into thin
    slices
2 tsp. sea salt

Sprinkle eggplant slices or green pepper slices with salt without steaming them first. Steam all other vegetables 2 to 3 minutes until hot but still slightly crisp. Remove from heat and cool on open rack or in a cool place. Use 2 to 3 vegetables in place of eggplant. Mix vegetables well with salt. Allow to sit in sieve or colander for 1 hour. Press gently to remove excess water. Rinse. Drain. Place in a pickle crock or glass covered dish.

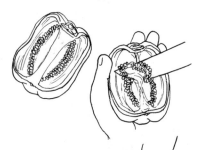

SAUCE:
¼ cup miso
1 Tbsp. stock
  [dashi or kombu]
2 tsp. mild honey
1½ Tbsp. rice vinegar
½ tsp. Japanese powdered
  mustard
  [washabi]

Mix honey and vinegar first. Add other ingredients. Mix well. Pour over vegetables. Chill 1 to 2 hours or overnight. Good as a side dish for a main meal or served with a small bowl of rice for lunch or a snack.

IKA SU MISO [SQUID PICKLED IN MISO SAUCE] [Makes about 2 cups]

1 lb. squid,
  clean, remove beak and ink,
  wash. Cut into ¼ inch slices
2 cups water

Bring water to a boil in a saucepan. Add squid. Stir to keep pieces from sticking to each other. Cook 2 to 3 minutes until just tender and white. Remove from stock. Cool. Save stock for soups.

4 green onions,
  cut into 1 inch slices and
  sliced thin

Steam 30 seconds. Remove from heat. Spread on a rack and cool quickly.

SAUCE:
¼ cup light miso
2 Tbsp. dashi
2 tsp. mild honey
1½ tsp. Japanese powdered
  mustard [washabi]
1½ Tbsp. rice vinegar

Mix honey and miso first. Add remainder of ingredients. Mix well. Pour over squid and onions in a bowl. Mix well. Chill for 30 minutes to 2 hours. Serve cold. Good for lunch with rice or as a side dish for dinner.

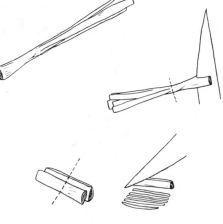

HAMAGARI SU MISO [CLAMS PICKLED IN MISO SAUCE] [Makes about 1 to 2 cups]

½ lb. small fresh clams
  OR 1 8 oz. can baby clams

Scrub clam shells. Place in steamer and steam until shells open. Remove from steamer. Remove from shell. Put in small bowl. For canned clams: Drain, rinse and place in small bowl.

SAUCE:
¼ cup light miso
2 Tbsp. rice vinegar
1 Tbsp. dashi
1 tsp. Japanese powdered
  mustard [washabi]

Mix ingredients well. Pour over clams. Mix. Chill 2 to 3 hours or overnight. Good for side dish with main meal, a small portion with rice for a lunch or snack.

SAKANA-ZU [WHITE FISH PICKLED IN VINEGAR] [Serves 4 to 6]

1 to 1½ lb. mackeral
  or other white fish
  [fillet or whole]
1 Tbsp. sea salt
1 cup rice vinegar

Fillet and debone whole fish. Rub fish with salt. Let sit 2 to 3 hours. Pour over vinegar. Let sit 10 to 20 minutes. Wet knife. Press down on fish with hand and using a very sharp knife slice across the grain into ¼ inch slices. Arrange on a platter.

SAUCE
juice of 1 lemon
½ cup daikon
  [Japanese radish],
    grated fine
  OR ½ cup white turnip,
    grated fine
2 tsp. fresh ginger root,
  grated fine

Mix ingredients well. Serve with fish as a dipping sauce along with soy sauce. Makes a good summer dinner or lunch dish. Also good as a side dish for main meal.

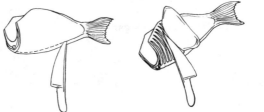

YASAI MISO ZUKE [VEGETABLES PICKLED IN MISO] [Makes about 2 cups]

1 lb. carrots,
  cut into 1 inch slices and
  then cut into 1/8 inch strips
  OR 1 lb. asparagus,
    cut into long thin diagonals
  OR 1 lb. broccoli,
    cut into thin diagonals
  OR 1 lb. green beans,
    cut into thin diagonals
  OR 1 lb. cauliflower,
    broken into small flowerlets
  OR 1 lb. brussel sprouts,
    cut in half lengthwise
  OR 1 cucumber,
    cut into 1 inch slices and
    then cut into long thin strips
  OR 1 daikon radish,
    cut in half lengthwise and
    then cut into thin rounds
  OR 2 large white turnips,
    cut in half lengthwise and
    then cut into thin half rounds
  OR ½ head cabbage,
    cut into thin slices

Steam carrots, asparagus, broccoli, green beans, cauliflower, brussel sprouts 2 to 3 minutes until hot but still slightly crisp. Remove from heat. Place in a bowl. Do not steam cucumber, radish, turnip, or cabbage. Place in a bowl.

SAUCE:
½ cup miso
½ cup cooked short-grain
  brown rice
1 Tbsp. mild honey
1 Tbsp. stock
  [dashi or kombu]

Mix and crush ingredients well in a shirabashi or mortar and pestle. Add to vegetables in a bowl. Mix well but gently. Let soak in sauce overnight, or as long as they last. To serve, wash off rice/miso paste. Good as a snack or light lunch with rice or as a side dish for a main meal.

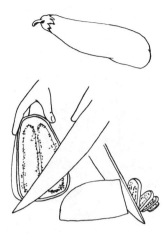

NASU SU ZUKE [EGGPLANT PICKLED WITH SOY, HONEY AND VINEGAR]
[Makes 2 to 3 cups]

1 medium eggplant,
  cut in half lengthwise and
  then into 1/8 inch slices
    OR 1 lb. Japanese eggplant,
      cut into 1/8 inch slices
    OR 1 lb. carrots,
      cut into 1 inch slices and
      then cut into 1/8 inch strips
    OR 1 lb. asparagus,
      cut into long thin diagonals
    OR 1 lb. broccoli,
      cut into thin diagonals
    OR 1 lb. brussel sprouts,
      cut in half lengthwise
    OR 1 lb. green beans,
      cut into thin diagonals
    OR 1 lb. cauliflower,
      broken into small flowerlets
    OR 1 lb. green peppers,
      seeded and cut into thin
      slices
2 tsp. sea salt

Sprinkle eggplant slices or green pepper slices with salt without steaming them first. Steam all other vegetables 2 to 3 minutes until hot but still slightly crisp. Remove from heat and cool on open rack or in a cool place. Use 2 to 3 vegetables in place of eggplant. Mix vegetables well with salt. Allow to sit in sieve or colander for 1 hour. Press gently to remove excess water. Rinse. Drain. Place in a pickle crock or glass covered dish.

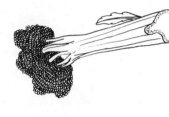

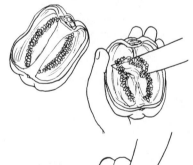

SAUCE:
1 Tbsp. rice vinegar
1½ tsp. mild honey
1 inch fresh ginger root,
  julienned
⅓ cup soy sauce
1 Tbsp. stock
  [dashi or Kombu]

Mix honey and vinegar first. Add other ingredients. Mix well. Pour over vegetables. Mix. Cover. Chill 2 hours or overnight. Good with any meal or as a snack. Serve cold.

HAMAGURI TSUKEMONO [PICKLED CLAMS] [Makes about 1 cup]

1 lb. small fresh clams
  OR 1 8 oz. can baby clams

Scrub clam shells. Place in steamer and steam until shell opens. Remove from steamer. Remove from shell. Put in small bowl. For canned clams: Drain, rinse and place in a small bowl.

SAUCE:
2 Tbsp. soy sauce
2 Tbsp. rice vinegar
¼ cup sake
  OR dry sherry
1 Tbsp. mild honey

Place ingredients in a saucepan. Bring to a boil over medium heat. Simmer 3 to 5 minutes until slightly thickened. Pour over clams. Mix well. Chill 2 to 3 hours or overnight. A good side dish with a main meal, a light lunch or snack served with a small bowl of rice.

IKA TSUKEMONO [PICKLED SQUID] [Makes about 1 to 2 cups]

1 lb. squid,
  cleaned, remove beak and ink,
  wash, cut into ¼ inch slices
2 cups water

Bring water to a boil in a saucepan. Add squid. Stir to keep pieces from sticking to each other. Cook 2 to 3 minutes until just tender. Remove from stock. Save stock for soups.

SAUCE:
2 Tbsp. soy sauce
2 Tbsp. rice vinegar
¼ cup sake
  OR dry sherry
1 Tbsp. mild honey

Place ingredients in a saucepan. Bring to boil over medium heat. Simmer 3 to 5 minutes until slightly thickened. Pour over squid. Mix well. Chill 2 to 3 hours or overnight. A good side dish with a main meal, a light lunch or snack served with a small bowl of rice.

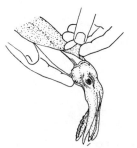
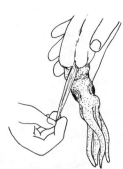

SALADS [AEMONO AND SUNOMONO]

Salads in Japan are small but tasty. Vinegar dressings, miso dressings or ground nut or seed dressings predominate. The vegetables are quite often steamed and chilled before the dressing is added. Japanese have even prefected a mayonnaise-type dressing called kimi-zu only it is made without oil and therefore like most Japanese food very unfattening.

KIMI ZU [THICK EGG DRESSING FOR VEGETABLES] [Serves 4 to 6]
[Or makes 1 cup]

Dressing:
3 egg yolks
¼ cup rice vinegar
1 Tbsp. mild honey
½ tsp. sea salt
1 Tbsp. sake
   OR dry sherry
1 Tbsp. stock
   [dashi or kombu]

Place ingredients in a double boiler. Mix well. Place over boiling water. Mix constantly 3 to 5 minutes until dressing thickens to a mayonnaise like consistency. Chill. Serve with a platter of vegetables or makes a good dressing for potato salad or as a hollandaise sauce for hot vegetables. Keeps in refrigerator for 2 weeks.

Traditional vegetables served with Kimi-zu:
1 to 2 stalks celery,
   cut into 1 inch lengths and
   then sliced paper thin
   lengthwise
1 to 2 cucumbers,
   cut in half lengthwise, seeded,
   then sliced into 1 inch lengths
   and cut paper thin lengthwise
2 to 3 tomatoes,
   cut into 8 wedges and then
   the wedges cut in half
½ cup wakame seaweed,
   soaked in boiling water for
   30 minutes to 1 hour until
   tender, cut into 1 inch slices
   [optional]

Arrange vegetables on a platter with kimi-zu dressing in center. Good served as a side dish for a main meal. Also served with shellfish, cold chicken or fish it makes an excellent summer salad supper. A little bowl of dressing along with some sliced vegetables and rice makes a good lunch.

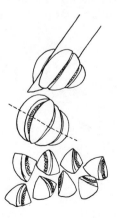

AMA ZU [THICK VINEGAR SOY DRESSING FOR VEGETABLES]
[Makes about 1 cup]

Dressing:
1/3 cup rice vinegar
2 Tbsp. soy sauce
2 Tbsp. mild honey
2 tsp. arrowroot starch
1/4 cup stock [dashi or kombu]
1/4 tsp. sesame oil

Mix ingredients together well in a small saucepan. Bring to boil over medium high heat. Stir to keep from sticking. Cook 1 to 2 minutes until sauce thickens. Remove from heat. Mix with following vegetables while still hot.

Traditional vegetables served with Ama-zu

1 to 2 stalks celery,
  cut into 1 inch lengths and
  then sliced paper thin
  lengthwise
1 to 2 cucumbers,
  cut in half lengthwise, seeded
  then sliced into 1 inch lengths
  and cut paper thin lengthwise

Mix sauce with one or combination of vegetables. Chill 30 minutes to 1 hour. Serve cold. Good served as a side dish for a main meal. With shellfish it makes an excellent summer salad supper. Also good for lunches. Dressing keeps indefinitely if tightly covered and stored in refrigerator. Heat and add a little liquid when reusing. Pour over vegetables hot.

WASHABI-AE [JAPANESE HORSERADISH DRESSING WITH VEGETABLES AND/OR SHELLFISH] [Serves 4 to 6]

Dressing:
2 tsp. washabi
  [Japanese horseradish powder]
1 Tbsp. stock [dashi or kombu]
5 Tbsp. soy sauce

Add liquid slowly to washabi. Mix well. Dressing will keep 2 to 3 weeks in refrigerator.

Traditional vegetables served with Washabi-ae:

1 long thin cucumber,
  sliced paper thin
OR 1 stalk celery,
  sliced paper thin
OR 1 daikon radish,
  cut in half lengthwise and
  sliced paper thin
OR 1 to 2 turnips,
  cut in half lengthwise and
  sliced paper thin
OR 1 small head lettuce,
  shredded
OR 1/2 head cabbage,
  shredded

Arrange vegetables on individual serving dishes or on a large plate. Pour over dressing. Chill. Serve cold. Good served as side dish for main meal or with rice and shellfish for lunch.

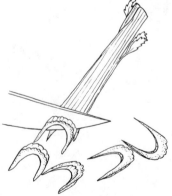

OTHER VEGETABLES THAT CAN BE USED WITH KIMI-ZU, AMA-ZU, OR WASHABI-AE DRESSING:

1 head cauliflower,
  broken into small flowerlets
 OR ½ lb. broccoli,
    cut into thin diagonals
    with heads broken into
    small pieces
 OR ½ lb. carrots,
    cut into 1 inch pieces,
    sliced into paper thin
    pieces lengthwise
 OR ½ lb. green beans,
    cut into long thin diagonals
 OR ½ lb. asparagus,
    ends broken off, cut into
    long thin diagonals
 OR ½ lb. brussel sprouts,
    cut in half lengthwise

OR 2 to 3 green peppers,
  seeded and cut into long
  thin slices

Steam 3 to 5 minutes until hot but still crisp. Remove from steamer.

For Kimi-zu: Chill vegetables and serve on platter with dressing to dip vegetables in.

For Ama-zu: Mix with dressing while still hot. Chill. Serve cold.

For Washabi-ae: Mix with dressing while vegetables still hot. Chill. Serve cold.

Do not steam green pepper. Serve with any of the dressings as directed for each one.

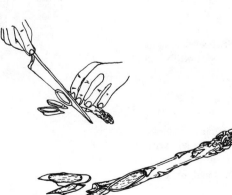

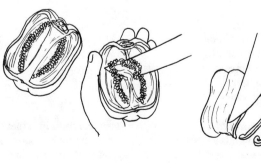

SHELLFISH OR FISH SERVED WITH KIMI-ZU, AMA-ZU, OR WASHABI-AE DRESSING:

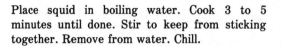

½ lb. small fresh cooked shrimp
   OR 1 small can shrimp,
     rinsed well
   OR ½ lb. squid,
     ink and beak removed
     and sliced into thin slices
   OR 1 can abalone,
     drained, rinsed and
     sliced thin
   OR ½ lb. crab meat

Place squid in boiling water. Cook 3 to 5 minutes until done. Stir to keep from sticking together. Remove from water. Chill.

   OR 6 prawns,
     shelled and deveined
     threaded on a skewer
     along back from head to
     tail to prevent curling
     while cooking

Place prawns in boiling water. Cook 3 to 5 minutes until pink and firm. Remove from skewers. Cut in half along back.

   OR ½ lb. fresh clams,
     scrub shells
   OR 1 small can clams,
     drained and rinsed
   OR any leftover unseasoned
     fish such as baked salmon
     or whitefish

Steam clams 5 to 8 minutes until shells open. Remove from shells. Cool.

Arrange one vegetable or a combination of vegetables along with shellfish or fish as directed in any one of the dressing recipes. Serve cold. Good as lunch or as side dish for main meal. Good summer supper salad.

MOYASHI GOMA-ZU [SPROUTS WITH SESAME SEED VINEGARED DRESSING] [Serves 4 to 6]

Dressing:
2 Tbsp. sesame seeds

Heat a small skillet over high heat. Add seeds Parch 1 to 2 minutes until lightly browned. Shake pan often to evenly brown seeds. Grind in a blender, food mill or shirabashi until well ground.

1 Tbsp. vegetable oil
2 Tbsp. mild honey
¼ cup rice vinegar
½ tsp. sea salt
drop of soy sauce

Add to sesame seeds. Mix well. Store in a tight container. Dressing will keep indefinitely in refrigerator.

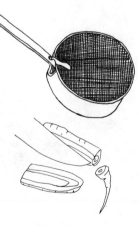

1 lb. fresh sprouts
   [mung, soy, alfalfa, etc.]
1 large carrot,
   cut into 1 inch pieces and
   then sliced paper thin
   lengthwise

Place carrots in steamer 30 seconds. Remove from steamer. Cool. Place in a bowl with sprouts. Add dressing. Toss and serve at once. Good as a side dish for a main meal or good with rice for lunch.

AWABI TO SHITAKI NO GOMA-ZU [ABALONE AND MUSHROOMS WITH VINEGARED SESAME OIL DRESSING[

[Serves 4 to 6]

1 can abalone,
    drained, rinsed and sliced thin
OR ½ lb. crab meat
OR 6 prawns,
    shelled and deveined,
    threaded on a skewer
    along the back from head
    to tail to prevent curling
    while cooking
OR ¼ lb. small fresh cooked
    shrimp

Place prawns in boiling water 3 to 5 minutes until pink and firm. Remove from skewers. Cut in half along the back. Cool.

OR ¼ lb. scallops

Steam scallops 5 to 8 minutes until done. Slice into thin rounds. Cool.

OR ½ lb. fresh clams,
    scrub shells
OR 1 small can clams,
    drained and rinsed
OR any leftover unseasoned
    fish such as baked salmon
    or whitefish

Steam clams until shells open. Remove from shells. Cool.

4 shitaki mushrooms
    [dried Japanese mushrooms]
1 cup boiling water

Place mushrooms in small bowl. Pour over boiling water. Place weight on top of mushrooms to keep them under water. Soak 15 to 30 minutes until tender. Squeeze dry. Cut out stalks. Cut into thin strips.

1 Tbsp. soy sauce
1 Tbsp. mild honey

Place in a pan with mushrooms. Bring to a boil. Simmer 3 to 5 minutes until all liquid is absorbed. Cool. Arrange in individual bowls along with abalone or other shellfish or fish.

Dressing:
3 Tbsp. sesame seeds

Heat a small skillet over high heat. Add seeds. Parch 1 to 2 minutes until lightly browned. Shake pan often to evenly brown seeds. Grind well in a blender, food mill or shirabashi.

1½ Tbsp. mild honey
1½ Tbsp. soy sauce
2 Tbsp. rice vinegar
2 tsp. vegetable oil

Mix honey and vinegar first. Add to ground sesame seeds. Mix well. Pour over mushrooms and shellfish. Marinate 30 minutes to 1 hour. Serve cold. Good served as a side dish for a main meal or with rice and a pickle for lunch.

SUNOMONO [SALAD WITH VINEGAR DRESSING] [Serves 4 to 6]

Dressing:
¼ **cup rice vinegar**
1½ **tsp. mild honey**
¼ **cup stock**
   [dashi or kombu]
½ **tsp. sea salt**
2 **tsp. soy sauce**
1 **tsp. lemon juice**

Combine honey and vinegar first. Add other ingredients. Mix well. Dressing will keep indefinetely in refrigerator.

Traditional vegetable served with Sunomono:
1 **long thin cucumber,**
   sliced paper thin

Arrange cucumber on individual serving dishes or on a large plate. Pour over dressing. Chill.

Traditional shell fish served with Sunomono:
¼ **lb. small fresh cooked shrimp**
   [optional]

Arrange with cucumber on individual serving dishes or on a large plate. Pour over dressing. Chill. Serve cold. Good served as a side dish for a main meal or with rice for lunch. A good cold supper salad for summer.

VARIATION:

SUNOMONO NO SHIRATAKI [SALAD WITH VINEGAR DRESSING AND CLEAR BEAN NOODLES] [Serves 4 to 6]

2 **oz. clear bean noodles**
2 **cups boiling water**

Place bean noodles in a bowl. Pour boiling water over noodles. Cover. Let sit 20 to 30 minutes until soft. OR boil noodles for 5 minutes. Drain. Cool.

Use along with cucumber and shrimp with sunomono dressing. Arrange cucumber, noodles and shellfish in 4 to 6 individual bowls. Pour dressing over ingredients. Chill. Serve cold. Good served as a side dish for a main meal. With shellfish it makes an excellent summer salad supper. Also good for lunches.

GOMA-ZU [SALAD WITH VINEGARED SESAME OIL DRESSING] [Serves 4 to 6]

Dressing:
2 **Tbsp. rice vinegar**
1 **tsp. mild honey**
1 **Tbsp. soy sauce**
1 **tsp. sesame oil**

Combine honey and vinegar first. Add other ingredients. Mix well. Dressing will keep indefinitely in refrigerator.

Traditional vegetable served with Goma-zu:
1 **cucumber,**
   cut in half lengthwise, seeded
   cut into 1½ inch lengths and
   then cut paper thin lengthwise
4 **green onions,**
   cut into 1½ inch lengths and
   then cut paper thin lengthwise

Arrange on individual serving dishes or on a large plate. Pour dressing over vegetables. Marinate 30 minutes to 1 hour. Mix genltly 3 or 4 times. Good as a side dish for a main meal or served with rice and leftovers for lunch.

OTHER VEGETABLES THAT CAN BE SERVED WITH SUNOMONO AND GOMA-ZU DRESSING:

1 long stalk celery,
   sliced paper thin
OR 1 daikon radish,
   cut in half lengthwise
   and sliced paper thin
OR 1 to 2 turnips,
   cut in half lengthwise and
   sliced paper thin

OR 1 large carrot,
   cut into 1 inch pieces and
   then sliced into paper thin
   lengths
OR ½ lb. green beans,
   cut into long thin diagonals
OR ½ lb. asparagus,
   break off ends, cut into long,
   thin diagonals
OR ½ lb. brussel sprouts,
   cut in half lengthwise
OR ½ lb. broccoli,
   cut into long, thin diagonals
   with heads broken into small
   pieces
OR 1 small cauliflower,
   broken into small flowerlets

Arrange on individual serving dishes or on a large plate. Pour over sunomono or goma-zu dressing. Serve as directed. Good served as side dish for main meal or with rice and shellfish for lunch.

Steam 3 to 5 minutes until hot but still crisp and bright-colored. Remove from steamer. Arrange on individual dishes or on a large plate. Pour dressing over vegetables. Chill. Serve cold. Serve as directed. Good served as side dish for main meal or with rice and shellfish for lunch.

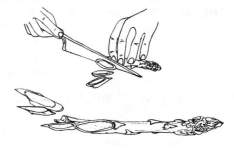

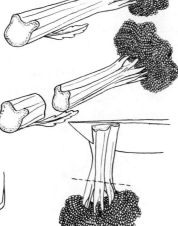

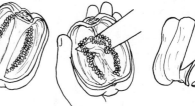

OTHER FISH AND SHELLFISH THAT CAN BE SERVED WITH SUNOMONO AND GOMA-ZU DRESSING:

½ lb. crab meat
  OR 6 prawns,
    shelled and deveined,
    threaded on a skewer
    from heat to tail
    to prevent curling while
    cooking
  OR ¼ lb. scallops

  OR ½ lb. fresh clams,
    scrub shells
  OR 1 small can clams,
    drained and rinsed
  OR 1 can abalone,
    drained, rinsed and
    sliced thin
  OR any leftover unseasoned
    fish such as baked salmon
    or white fish

Place prawns in boiling water 3 to 5 minutes until pink and firm. Remove from skewers and cut in half along the back. Cool.

Steam scallops 5 to 8 minutes until tender. Slice into thin rounds. Cool.
Steam clams until shells open. Remove from shells. Cool.

Arrange one type of fish or shellfish along with one kind of vegetable or a combination of vegetables in individual dishes or on a large plate. Pour over dressing. Chill. Serve as directed. Good as a main meal side dish or as a lunch when served with shellfish/fish and rice. Good light summer salad supper.

OROSHI-AE [SHELLFISH IN VINEGAR SAUCE WITH DAIKON] [Serves 4 to 6]

½ lb. fresh clams, scrub shells
  OR 1 small can clams,
    drained and rinsed
  OR 1 can abalone,
    drained and rinsed and
    sliced thin
  OR ¼ lb. fresh cooked small
    shrimp
  OR 6 prawns,
    shelled and deveined,
    threaded on a skewer
    along the back from head
    to tail to prevent curling
    while cooking
  OR any leftover unseasoned fish
    such as salmon or white fish

Steam until shells open. Remove from shells.

Place prawns in boiling water 3 to 5 minutes until pink and firm. Remove from skewers and cut in half along the back.

Dressing:
3 Tbsp. rice vinegar
1 Tbsp. soy sauce
1 tsp. lemon juice
½ tsp. mild honey

Place in a small saucepan. Heat enough to melt honey. Do not bring to a boil. Remove from heat. Place shellfish in hot dressing. Marinate in dressing 1 to 2 hours until cold. Drain.

1 large daikon,
  grated fine
  OR 2 large white turnips
    grated fine
  OR ½ head green cabbage,
    shredded fine

Place on a towel and gently squeeze out excess liquid. Place on individual serving dishes. Place marinated shellfish on top. Good as a side dish for a main meal. Especially good with a tempura dinner.

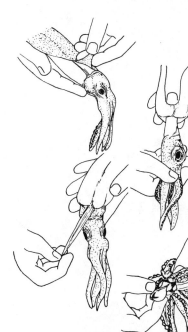

IKA SU MISO NO YAMA-UDO [SQUID WITH ASPARAGUS PICKLED IN MISO SAUCE] [Serves 4 to 6]

1 lb. squid,
  clean, remove beak and ink,
  wash. Cut into ¼ inch slices
2 cups water

Bring water to a boil in a saucepan. Add squid. Stir to keep pieces from sticking to each other. Cook 2 to 3 minutes until just tender and white. Remove from stock. Cool. Save stock for soups.

1 lb. asparagus,
  break off ends, cut into long,
  thin diagonals

Steam 3 to 5 minutes until just tender. Cool on open rack. Arrange asparagus and squid on a plate in an attractive pattern.

Sauce:
¼ cup light miso
1½ Tbsp. rice vinegar
1 Tbsp. mild honey
2 Tbsp. sesame seeds

Roast sesame seeds in a dry hot pan for 1 to 2 minutes until lightly browned. Shake pan often to evenly brown seeds. Grind slightly in a mortar and pestle, blender or shirabashi. Add rest of ingredients. Mix well. Pour over squid and asparagus. Chill. Can be served as a side dish for a main meal or a main dish for a simple meal or salad supper in the summer. Good for lunch with rice also.

HAMAGURI SU-MISO [CLAM AND GREEN ONIONS WITH VINEGARED MISO DRESSING] [Serves 4 to 6]

½ lb. fresh clams,
  scrub shells
  Or 1 small can clams,
    drained and rinsed
  OR ½ lb. crab meat
  OR 6 prawns, shelled and
    deveined, threaded on a
    skewer along the back
    from head to tail to
    prevent curling while
    cooking
  OR ¼ lb. small fresh
    cooked shrimp
  OR ¼ lb. scallops
  OR any leftover unseasoned
    fish such as baked slamon
    or whitefish

Steam fresh clams until shells open. Remove from shells.

Place prawns in boiling water 3 to 5 minutes until pink and firm. Remove from skewers. Cut in half along the back.

Steam 5 to 8 minutes until done. Slice into thin rounds. Cool.

6 green onions, cut into
  1½ inch pieces and sliced
  paper thin lengthwise

Place in a bowl with clams. Mix well. Can be arranged on individual plates also.

Dressing:
⅓ cup miso
  [strained through a fine
  sieve]
2½ Tbsp. dashi
1½ Tbsp. sake
  OR dry sherry
1½ Tbsp. mild honey

Place in a saucepan. Bring to boil over medium heat. Stir often to prevent burning. Cook 1 to 2 minutes to mix well. Remove from heat.

2 Tbsp. rice vinegar

Add to miso mixture. Chill. Pour over individual servings. Good as a side dish for a main meal or served with rice for lunch.

KURIMI-AE [WALNUT DRESSING] [Serves 4 to 6]

Dressing:

¼ cup walnuts
2½ Tbsp. mild honey
3 Tbsp. soy sauce
3 Tbsp. rice vinegar

Crush walnuts in mortar and pestle, blender or shirabashi. Add other ingredients. Mix well.

Traditional vegetable served with Kurimi-ae:

1 lb. asparagus

Break tough ends off asparagus. Steam 5 to 10 minutes until just tender and still bright green. Chill. Arrange asparagus on individual serving dishes or on a large plate. Pour dressing over asparagus. Chill. Serve cold.

Fresh ground black pepper
  [optional]

Sprinkle fresh ground pepper over each dish. Good served as a side dish for a main meal or as a light lunch along with rice.

AEMONO [NON-VINEGARED SESAME SEED DRESSING] [Serves 4 to 6]

Dressing:

3 Tbsp. sesame seeds

Heat a small skillet over high heat. Add seeds. Parch 1 to 2 minutes until lightly browned. Shake pan often to evenly brown seeds. Grind in a blender, food mill or shirabashi until well ground.

1 Tbsp. soy sauce
1 Tbsp. stock
  [dombu or dashi]
2 tsp. mild honey

Add to sesame seeds. Mix well. Dressing will keep indefinitely in refrigerator.

Traditional vegetable served with Aemono:

1 lb. spinach

Steam 1 to 2 minutes until no longer crisp but still bright green. Cool. Roll each leaf into individual rolls and cut into 1 inch pieces or bunch a few leaves together and then cut into 1 inch bundles. Arrange on individual serving dishes or on a large plate. Pour dressing over spinach. Chill. Serve cold. Good served as a side dish for a main meal or with rice for lunch.

GOMA-AE [SESAME SEED VINEGAR DRESSING] [Serves 4 to 6]

Dressing:

3 Tbsp. sesame seeds

Heat a small skillet over high heat. Add seeds. Parch 1 to 2 minutes until lightly browned. Shake pan often to evenly brown seeds. Grind in a blender, food mill or shirabashi until well ground.

2 Tbsp. stock
  [kombu or dashi]
2½ Tbsp. rice vinegar
1 Tbsp. mild honey
1 tsp. lemon juice
2 tsp. soy sauce

Add to ground sesame seeds. Mix well. Store in tight container. Will keep indefinitely in refrigerator.

Traditional vegetable served with Goma-ae:

1 long thin cucumber,
  sliced paper thin

Arrange cucumber on individual serving dishes or on a large plate. Pour over dressing. Chill. Serve cold. Good served as a side dish for a main meal or with rice for lunch.

OTHER VEGETABLES THAT CAN BE SERVED WITH KURIMI-AE, AEMONO AND GOMA-AE DRESSING:

1 long stalk celery,
    sliced into 1 inch lengths and
    then sliced paper thin lengthwise
OR 2 green peppers,
    seeded and cut into long,
    thin slices
OR 1 daikon radish,
    cut in half lengthwise and
    then sliced paper thin
OR 1 to 2 turnips,
    cut in half lengthwise and
    then sliced paper thin

OR 1 large carrot,
    cut into 1 inch pieces
    and then sliced paper thin
OR ½ lb. green beans,
    cut into long thin diagonals
OR ½ lb. snowpeas,
    each cut into 3 long,
    diagonal pieces
OR ½ lb. asparagus,
    break off ends, cut into long,
    thin diagonals
OR ½ lb. brussel sprouts,
    cut in half lengthwise
OR ½ lb. broccoli,
    cut into long thin diagonals
OR 1 small cauliflower,
    broken into small flowerlets

OR 1 lb. spinach
OR 1 lb. swiss chard
OR 1 lb. any cooking green

Arrange vegetables on individual serving dishes or a large plate. Pour over dressing. Chill. Serve cold. Good served as a side dish for a main meal or with rice for lunch.

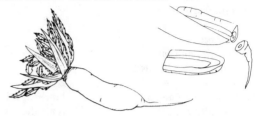

Steam 3 to 5 minutes until hot but still crisp and bright colored. Remove from steamer. Cool. Arrange on individual serving dishes or a large plate. Pour over dressing. Chill. Serve cold. Good served as a side dish for a main meal or with rice for lunch.

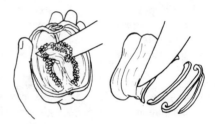

Steam 1 to 2 minutes until no longer crisp but still bright green. Cool. Roll each leaf into individual rolls and cut into 1 inch bundles or bunch a few leaves and then cut into 1 inch bundles. Arrange on a platter or on individual serving dishes. Pour over dressing. Chill. Serve cold. Good served as a side dish for a main meal or with rice for lunch.

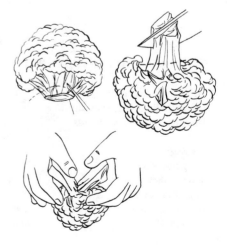

NASU NO SHOGA [EGGPLANT WITH GINGER DRESSING] [Makes 1 quart]

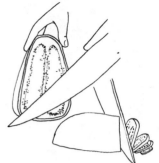

1 medium eggplant,
  cut in half lengthwise and
  then cut into thin slices
  OR ½ lb. Japanese eggplant,
    cut into thin slices
¼ tsp. sea salt

Sprinkle salt over eggplant. Place in a sieve or colander. Let sit for 15 to 20 minutes. Squeeze lightly in a towel to remove excess moisture. Place in a bowl.

Dressing:
1 inch ginger root,
  peeled and julienned
¼ cup soy sauce
1 Tbsp. rice vinegar
1 tsp. mild honey

Mix soy sauce, vinegar and honey well. Add ginger. Pour over eggplant. Mix well. Marinate 2 to 3 hours or overnight. Good served with lunches, miso soup or with rice and a main dish for a dinner. Good served with tempura or other fried foods to aid digestion and clear the mouth. Keeps 1 to 2 weeks in refrigerator.

YASAI NO SHOGA [VEGETABLES WITH GINGER DRESSING]
[Makes about 1 quart]

1 lb. green beans,
  cut into long thin diagonals
  OR 1 lb. snowpeas,
    cut into 3 diagonal slices
  OR 1 lb. zucchini,
    cut into thin slices

Steam 3 to 5 minutes until vegetables are hot but still crisp and bright colored. Remove from steamer. Place in a covered glass or ceramic bowl.

Dressing:
1 inch fresh ginger root,
  peeled and julienned
¼ cup soy sauce
1 Tbsp. rice vinegar
1 tsp. mild honey

Mix soy sauce, vinegar and honey well. Add ginger. Pour over vegetables. Mix well. Marinate 2 to 3 hours or overnight. Good with lunches, miso soup, or with rice and a main dish for dinner. Good served with tempura or other fried foods to aid digestion and clear the mouth. Keeps 1 to 2 weeks in the refrigerator.

SHOGA SUNOMONO [GINGER WITH VINEGAR SOY DRESSING]
[Makes about ½ cup]

2 inches fresh ginger root,
  peeled and sliced paper thin

Place in a small covered dish.

Sauce:
1½ Tbsp. rice vinegar
1½ tsp. soy sauce
1½ tsp. mild honey

Place ingredients in a small saucepan. Heat enough to melt honey and mix well. Pour over ginger slices while hot. Mix. Cover and let cool. Chill 1 hour or overnight. Excellent served with sushi or as a snack with rice. Also good served as a side dish for a main meal.

SOYU NO DAIKON [DAIKON WITH SOY DRESSING] Makes about 1 quart

1 large daikon radish,
  cut in half lengthwise and
  then cut into thin rounds

Place in a large china or glass bowl.

Dressing:
½ cup soy sauce
1 Tbsp. stock
  [dashi or kombu]
1 tsp. lemon juice
  [optional]

Mix ingredients well. Pour over daikon in bowl. Cover. Allow to sit overnight. Keeps well for 2 to 3 days. Good served with rice and a main dish for dinner or with rice and leftovers for lunch. Also good with sushi for lunch or a picnic.

VARIATION:

SOYU NO KABU [TURNIPS WITH SOY DRESSING] [Makes about 1 quart]

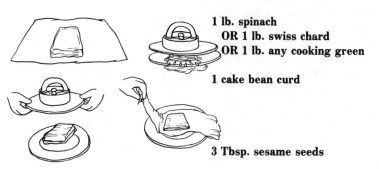

2 to 3 turnips,
  cut in half lengthwise and then
  cut into thin rounds

Place in a large china or glass bowl.

Dressing:
½ **cup soy sauce**
1 Tbsp. stock
  [dashi or kombu]
1 tsp. mild honey
1 tsp. lemon juice

Mix ingredients well. Pour over turnips in bowl. Cover. Allow to sit overnight. Keeps well for 2 to 3 days. Good served with rice and a main dish for dinner or with rice and leftovers for lunch. Also good with sushi for lunch or a picnic.

SPINACH AND BEAN CURD WITH SESAME SEEDS [Serves 4 to 6]

1 lb. spinach
  OR 1 lb. swiss chard
  OR 1 lb. any cooking green

Steam 2 to 3 minutes until vegetables no longer crisp but still bright green. Remove from steamer. Cool. Cut into ¼ inch strips.

1 cake bean curd

Wrap in a cloth. Press for 1 to 2 hours or overnight until quite firm. Break up with a fork or fingers into small grain-sized pieces. Place in bowl with spinach.

3 Tbsp. sesame seeds

Heat a small skillet over high heat. Add seeds. Parch 1 to 2 minutes until lightly browned. Shake pan often to evenly brown seeds. Grind in a blender, food mill or shirabashi until well ground. Sprinkle over spinach and bean curd. Toss. Serve cold.

2 Tbsp. soy sauce

Serve salad with soy sauce to sprinkle over salad for each person. Good as a lunch dish with rice or as a main meal salad. Also good as a light salad supper with a soup.

SPINACH AND BEAN CURD WITH SESAME SEED/MISO DRESSING
[Serves 4 to 6]

Dressing:

3 Tbsp. sesame seeds

Heat a small skillet over high heat. Add seeds and parch 1 to 2 minutes until lightly browned. Shake pan often to evenly brown seeds. Grind well in a blender, food mill or shirabashi.

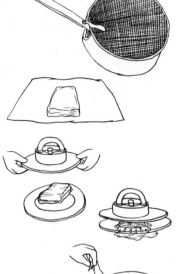

1 tsp. soy sauce
2 Tbsp. miso
1 Tbsp. mild honey
2 tsp. stock
 [dashi or kombu]
1 tsp. rice vinegar

Add to ground sesame seeds. Mix well.

1 lb. spinach
 OR 1 lb. swiss chard
 OR 1 lb. any cooking green

Steam 2 to 3 minutes until vegetable is no longer crisp but still bright green in color. Remove from steamer. Cool. Cut into ¼ inch slices.

1 block bean curd

Wrap in a cloth. Press 1 to 2 hours or overnight until quite firm. Break up with a fork or fingers into small grain-sized pieces. Place in a bowl with spinach. Pour dressing over top and toss.
     Serve cold. Good as a lunch dish with rice or as a side dish for a main meal. Also good as a light salad supper along with rice and a soup.

OTHER VEGETABLES THAT CAN BE SERVED WITH BEAN CURD AND SESAME SEEDS OR SESAME SEED/MISO DRESSING:

1 lb. green beans,
 cut into long thin diagonals
 OR ½ lb. carrots,
  cut into 1 inch pieces and
  then cut into paper thin
  pieces lengthwise
 OR ½ lb. broccoli,
  cut into long thin diagonals
  with heads broken into
  small pieces
 OR 1 small cauliflower,
  broken into small flowerlets
 OR ½ lb. brussel sprouts,
  cut in half lengthwise
 OR 1 lb. water cress,
  cleaned and cut into ¼ inch
  slices [do not steam]

Steam vegetables 3 to 5 minutes until hot but still crisp and bright colored. Remove from steamer. Cool. Follow recipe for Spinach and Bean Curd with Sesame Seed/Miso Dressing. Use one or combination of vegetables in place of spinach. Cook as directed. Serve salad with soy sauce to sprinkle over salad for each person. Good as a lunch dish with rice or as a main meal salad. Also good as a light salad supper along with soup.

VEGETABLES WITH AZUKI BEANS AND BEAN CURD WITH SWEET SOY DRESSING [Serves 4 to 6]

½ **cup azuki beans**
OR kidney beans
OR pinto beans
2 to 3 cups water

Soak overnight in warm water. (Optional step.) Place beans in a heavy saucepan. Add water. Cover and bring to a boil over high heat. Reduce heat to medium low and simmer 2 to 3 hours until beans are tender. Add just enough liquid to keep beans just covered. To pressure cook: Add water and beans to pressure cooker. Cook at full pressure for 45 to 50 minutes until beans are tender. When beans are cooked, drain. Reserve stock to use in soups or in bread.

½ **tsp. sea salt**
¼ **cup bean stock**
½ **cup stock**
[dashi or kombu]
1 Tbsp. soy sauce
2 Tbsp. plus 1 tsp. mild honey

Place in a saucepan along with beans. Bring to a boil. Reduce heat to medium and cook 3 to 5 minutes to flavor beans.

½ **lb. carrots,**
cut into 1 inch pieces and then cut into paper thin pieces lengthwise
OR ½ **lb. broccoli,**
cut into long, thin diagonals with heads broken into small pieces
OR 1 small cauliflower,
broken into small flowerlets
OR ½ **lb. brussel sprouts,**
cut in half lengthwise
OR ½ **lb. green beans,**
cut into long, thin diagonals
OR ½ **lb. asparagus,**
break off ends, cut into long, thin diagonals
OR ½ **lb. snowpeas,**
each cut into 3 long diagonals

Add one vegetable or a combination to the beans and sauce. Cook 3 to 5 minutes until vegetables are just tender. Remove from heat. Cool.

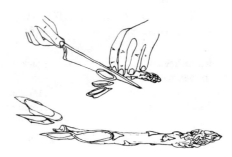

4 Tbsp. sesame seeds

Heat a small skillet. Add seeds. Parch 1 to 2 minutes until lightly browned. Shake pan often to evenly brown seeds. Remove from heat. Grind coarsely in a blender, food mill or shirabashi. Add to bean and vegetable mixture. Mix well.

1 block bean curd
cut into ½ **inch cubes**

Steam 2 to 3 minutes. Remove from heat. Press lightly in a tea towel to remove excess water. Add bean curd to bean, vegetable and sesame seed mixture. Mix gently to prevent bean curd from breaking into smaller pieces. Chill. Serve cold. Good as a lunch with or without rice or even as a main dish for a vegetarian dinner along with rice and a pickle or soup. Also good as a side dish for a main meal.

TOFU NO SHITAKI [BEAN CURD AND MUSHROOM SALAD] [Serves 4 to 6]

2 blocks bean curd,
  cut into 1 inch cubes

Arrange in individual bowls.

4 shitaki mushrooms
  [Japanese dried mushrooms]
1 cup boiling water

Place mushrooms in small bowl. Pour boiling water over them. Place weight on top of mushrooms to keep under water. Soak 15 to 30 minutes until tender. Drain. Save stock. Squeeze out moisture. Cut out tough stalks. Cut into ¼ inch slivers. Arrange with bean curd in individual bowls.

Dressing:
2 Tbsp. lemon juice
1 Tbsp. stock [dashi or kombu]
1 tsp. soy sauce
2 tsp. rice vinegar
½ tsp. mild honey

Mix honey and vinegar first. Add other ingredients. Mix well. Pour over individual bowls. Marinate 1 hour. Serve cold.

Garnish:
2 green onions, minced
  OR 2 large sprigs parsley,
    minced
  OR 2 Tbsp. watercress,
    minced

Sprinkle over each bowl of mushrooms and bean curd. Serve at once. Good as a lunch with rice or as a side dish for a main meal. Also good as a vegetarian main dish along with rice.

TORI TO KYURI NO KARASHIZU-AE [CHICKEN, CUCUMBER WITH MUSTARD DRESSING [Serves 4 to 6]

1 chicken breast
¼ tsp. sea salt
1 Tbsp. sake
  OR dry sherry

Prick chicken breast with a fork and rub with salt. Place in a dish and sprinkle over sake. Marinate for 1 hour. Turn often. Place in a steamer. Steam 10 to 15 minutes until tender and white but still moist. Cool. Cut into thin strips.

1 cucumber,
  cut in half lengthwise, seeded
  and sliced paper thin
  OR 1 large stalk celery,
    cut into 1 inch pieces and
    then sliced into paper thin
    lengths
  OR 1 daikon radish,
    grated fine, excess moisture
    squeezed out in absorbent
    towel

Arrange vegetable with sliced chicken breast on individual serving dishes or on a large plate. Place chicken on top of daikon if that is used.

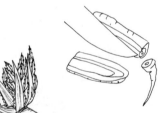

  OR ½ lb. snowpeas,
    each cut into 2 long, thin
    diagonals
  OR 1 to 2 carrots,
    cut into 2 inch pieces and
    then sliced into paper thin
    lengths
  OR ½ lb. green beans,
    cut into long, thin diagonals

Steam 3 to 5 minutes until hot but still crisp and bright colored. Remove from steamer. Cool. Place one vegetable or a combination of them on individual serving dishes or on a large plate. Arrange chicken breast with vegetables.

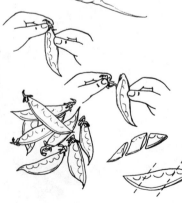

Dressing:
1 egg yolk,
  well beaten but not foamy
1 tsp. Japanese horseradish
  powder [washabi]
2 Tbsp. rice vinegar
1 tsp. mild honey

Mix honey and vinegar first. Add liquid slowly to horseradish powder. Mix well. Pour over chicken breast and vegetable. Mix well. Place on 4 to 6 individual serving dishes.

1 Tbsp. pickled ginger
  [optional]

Decorate each dish with pickled ginger. Serve cold. Good as a side dish for a main meal or with rice for a lunch.

EBI NO DAIKON [SHRIMP AND DAIKON SALAD] [Serves 4 to 6]

¼ lb. small fresh cooked
  shrimp
OR ½ lb. crab meat
OR 6 prawns,
  shelled and deveined
  threaded on a skewer
  along the back from head to
  tail to prevent curling while
  cooking

Place prawns in boiling water 3 to 5 minutes until pink and firm. Remove from skewers. Cut in half along the back.

OR ¼ lb. scallops
OR 1 small can clams,
  drained and rinsed

Steam 5 to 8 minutes until done. Slice into thin rounds. Cool.

OR ½ lb. fresh clams,
  scrub shells
OR 1 can abalone,
  drained, rinsed and sliced
  thin

Steam until shells open. Remove from shells. Cool.

1 medium daikon,
  grated fine
OR 2 turnips,
  grated fine

Squeeze out excess water lightly in an absorbent towel.

2 tsp. mild honey
¼ tsp. sea salt.
2½ Tbsp. rice vinegar
2 tsp. fresh grated ginger root
2 tsp. fresh grated horseradish
  OR 1 tsp. Japanese horseradish
    powder mixed with 1 tsp.
    water

Mix ingredients well. Add to daikon. Mix well. Add shellfish and mix well. Marinate for 1 hour.

2 cups shredded greens
  [lettuce, cabbage, spinach,
  swiss chard, watercress, etc.]

Place on 4 to 6 individual plates. Mound shellfish and daikon mixture on top of each. Serve cold. Good served as side dish for main meal or with rice for lunch.

INGEN NO AMA-ZU [GREEN BEANS, GREEN ONIONS AND EGGS WITH THICK VINEGARED DRESSING] [Serves 4 to 6]

4 hard boiled eggs
  cut into ¼ to ½ inch rounds

½ lb. green beans,
  cut into long, thin diagonals

Steam 3 to 5 minutes until hot but still crisp and bright colored. Remove from steamer. Cool.

4 green onions,
  cut into 1½ inch pieces and then sliced into paper thin lengths

Layer green beans, eggs, and green onions in individual layers in a bowl. Have several layers of each.

Dressing:
⅓ **cup rice vinegar**
2 **Tbsp. soy sauce**
⅓ **cup stock**
1 **tsp. sesame oil**
2 **tsp. arrowroot starch**
½ **tsp. mild honey**

Mix ingredients well. Place in a small saucepan and bring to boil over medium high heat. Cook 1 to 2 minutes until dressing thickens slightly. Pour over layered vegetables. Chill. Serve cold. Good for lunch or as a side dish for a main meal. Also good for a vegetarian main dish or a light salad supper along with soup and rice on a hot summer day.

VARIATION:

INGEN TO HAMAGURI NO AMA-ZU [GREEN BEANS, GREEN ONIONS, EGGS, CLAMS WITH THICK VINEGARED DRESSING] [Serves 4 to 6]

4 hard boiled eggs,
  cut into ¼ to ½ inch rounds

½ lb. green beans
  cut into long thin diagonals

Steam 3 to 5 minutes until hot but still crisp and bright colored. Remove from steamer. Cool.

½ lb. fresh clams, scrub shells
  OR 1 small can clams,
    drained and rinsed

Steam until shells open. Remove from shells. Cool.

  OR 1 can abalone, drained,
    rinsed and sliced thin
  OR ½ lb. crab meat
  OR 6 prawns, shelled and
    deveined, threaded on a
    skewer along the back from
    head to tail to prevent
    curling while cooking

Place prawns in boiling water 3 to 5 minutes until pink and firm. Remove from skewers. Cut in half along the back.

OR ¼ lb. fresh cooked shrimp
OR ¼ lb. scallops

Steam scallops 5 to 8 minutes until done. Slice into thin rounds. Cool.

OR any leftover unseasoned fish
such as baked salmon or
whitefish

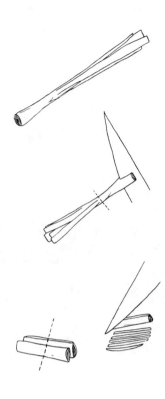

4 green onions,
cut into 1½ inch pieces and
then sliced into paper thin
lengths

Layer green beans, eggs and green onions in individual layers in a bowl. Have several layers of each.

Dressing:
⅓ cup rice vinegar
2 Tbsp. soy sauce
⅓ cup stock
1 tsp. sesame oil
2 tsp. arrowroot starch
½ tsp. mild honey

Mix ingredients well. Place in a small saucepan and bring to boil over medium high heat. Cook 1 to 2 minutes until dressing thickens slightly. Pour over layered vegetables. Chill. Serve cold. Good for lunch or as a side dish for a main meal. Also good for a vegetarian main dish or as a light salad supper along with soup and rice on a hot summer day.

HOT DRESSED VEGETABLES

Meals-in-a-bowl or just simple lemon dressed spinach, Japanese hot vegetables are lightly cooked with sauces which emphasize the taste of the vegetables. Stuffed pumpkin (Kabocha Mushi) can be a whole meal served with pickles and rice but most hot cooked vegetables serve as side dishes at a main meal or make an excellent lunch on a cold day.

VEGETABLES WITH BEAN CURD SAUCE [Serves 4 to 6]

Sauce:

2 tsp. sesame seeds

Heat a small cast iron skillet over high heat. Add sesame seeds. Parch 1 to 2 minutes until just browned. Shake pan often to evenly brown seeds. Grind in a blender, food mill or shirabashi until finely ground.

1 cake bean curd, wrap tightly in a muslin cloth, place a weight on top and press 2 to 3 hours or overnight until very dry
2 Tbsp. miso
1 Tbsp. mild honey
2 tsp. stock [dashi or kombu]
¼ tsp. sea salt

Break up pressed bean curd with a fork until crumbled into small grain sized pieces. Mix miso with honey and dashi until no lumps remain. Add to tofu. Mix well. Add salt and sesmae seed paste. Mix well.

VEGETABLES WITH MISO SAUCE [Serves 4 to 6]

Sauce:

2 Tbsp. sesame seeds

Heat a small cast iron skillet over high heat. Add sesame seeds. Parch 1 to 2 mintues until just browned. Shake pan often to evenly brown seeds. Grind in a blender, food mill or shirabashi until finely ground.

¼ cup miso
½ inch fresh ginger root, grated
1½ Tbsp. mild honey
1½ Tbsp. stock [dashi or kombu]
1½ Tbsp. rice vinegar

Add miso and honey to sesame seeds. Mix well. Slowly add other ingredients. Mix between each addition so sauce is not lumpy

VEGETABLES WITH SESAME SEED SAUCE [Serves 4 to 6]

Sauce:

2 Tbsp. sesame seeds

Heat a small cast iron skillet over high heat. Add sesame seeds. Parch 1 to 2 minutes until just browned. Shake pan often to evenly brown seeds. Grind in a blender, food mill or shirabashi until finely ground.

2 tsp. stock [dashi or kombu]
1 Tbsp. mild honey
2 Tbsp. soy sauce

Add to ground sesame seeds. Mix well.

VEGETABLES WITH MISO HORSERADISH SAUCE [Serves 4 to 6]

Sauce:

¼ cup light miso
1½ Tbsp. rice vinegar
1½ Tbsp. mild honey
2 tsp. stock [dashi or kombu]
1 tsp. Japanese horseradish powder [washabi]
OR dried yellow mustard

Mix stock and mustard into a paste. Add miso and mix well. Slowly add other ingredients so sauce is not lumpy. Pour into a small saucepan. Heat over medium heat 2 to 3 minutes until well mixed. Do not boil. Keep hot.

HOT DRESSED VEGETABLES

VEGETABLES TO BE SERVED WITH BEAN CURD, MISO, SESAME SEED OR MISO HORSERADISH SAUCE:

1 eggplant, cut in half and
  then cut into ¼ inch slices
OR 1 small cauliflower,
  broken into flowerlets
OR ½ to 1 lb. pumpkin,
  cut into thin slices
OR ½ to 1 lb. winter squash,
  cut into thin slices
OR ½ to 1 lb. asparagus,
  break off tough ends and
  cut into long, thin diagonals
OR ½ to 1 lb. green beans,
  cut into long, thin diagonals
OR ½ to 1 lb. carrots,
  cut into long, thin diagonals
OR ½ to 1 lb. broccoli,
  cut into thin diagonals with
  heads broken into small
  pieces
OR ½ to 1 lb. summer squash,
  cut into thin slices
OR ½ to 1 lb. brussel sprouts,
  cut in half lengthwise
OR ½ head cabbage,
  cut into ¼ inch slices
OR 1 small head Chinese
  cabbage, cut into 1 inch
  cubes

OR 1 lb. spinach
OR 1 lb. swiss chard
OR 1 lb. any cooking green
OR 1 lb. watercress

Steam 5 to 10 minutes until vegetables are tender but still bright colored. Arrange on a serving dish or on individual serving dishes. Pour sauce over hot vegetables. Serve at once. Good as a lunch dish with rice or as a side dish for a main meal. When served with a miso soup or bean curd dish and rice it can serve as a main dish for a vegetarian meal.

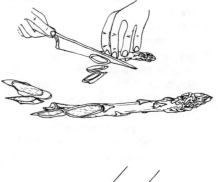

Place in a steamer. Steam 3 to 5 minutes until tender but still bright green. place on a serving dish or on individual plate. Pour sauce over hot vegetables. Serve hot. Good as a lunch dish with rice or as a side dish for a main meal. When served with a miso soup or a bean curd dish and rice it can serve as a main dish for a vegetarian meal.

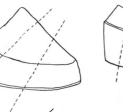

VEGETABLES WITH LEMON SAUCE [Serves 4 to 6]

Sauce:
3 Tbsp. soy sauce
2 Tbsp. lemon juice
2 tsp. mild honey
1 Tbsp. sake
  OR dry sherry
  OR rice vinegar
1 Tbsp. stock [dashi or kombu]

Place in a saucepan. Heat over medium heat 2 to 3 minutes until honey is melted and sauce is hot. Do not bring to a full boil.

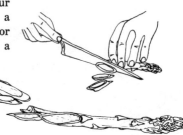

Vegetables to be served with lemon sauce:
1½ lb. spinach
  OR watercress
  OR swiss chard
  OR any cooking green
  OR ½ head green cabbage, shredded
  OR 1½ lb. Chinese cabbage, shredded
  OR 1 lb. asparagus, tough ends broken off and then cut into thin diagonals

Steam 3 to 5 minutes until tender but still bright green. Place in a serving dish and pour hot sauce over vegetables. Good to serve as a side dish for a main meal such as Tempura or other deep fried dishes. Do not serve with a saucepan food such as Yoshenabe or Sukiyaki.

TERINIMONO [VEGETABLES WITH BEAN CURD COOKED IN SOY, HONEY AND SAKE] [Serves 4 to 6]

½ lb. fresh mushrooms, cut into ¼ inch slices
  OR 4 to 6 large dry mushrooms and 1 cup boiling water
  OR ½ lb. carrots, cut into thin diagonals
  OR 1½ cup bamboo shoots, cut into thin slices
  OR combination of ¼ lb. mushrooms, sliced thin, ¼ lb. carrots, cut into thin diagonals and ½ cup bamboo shoots, cut into thin slices

Place one or a combination of vegetables in a saucepan.
Place dry mushrooms in a small bowl. Pour boiling water over them. Place weight on top to keep under water. Soak 15 to 30 minutes. Squeeze out moisture. Cut out tough stalks. Cut into ¼ inch slices. Save stock.

1 cup stock
[dashi or kombu]

Pour over vegetables. Cover. Bring to a boil over medium heat. Reduce heat to medium low and simmer 5 minutes.

2 Tbsp. sake
  OR dry sherry
1½ Tbsp. mild honey
1½ Tbsp. soy sauce

Add to vegetables. Cover and simmer another 3 to 5 minutes until just tender.

1 block bean curd, cut into 1 inch cubes [optional]

Add to vegetables. Cook 1 minute until bean curd hot. Serve hot with rice and leftovers for lunch, good as a main dish for a vegetarian meal if tofu is used. Also good as a side dish for a main meal if no bean curd is used.

TSUKENIMONO [VEGETABLES COOKED IN SEASONED STOCK]
[Serves 4 to 6]

Sauce:
½ **cup stock [dashi or kombu]**
2 **tsp. mild honey**
1 **tsp. soy sauce**

Mix well. Place in a saucepan.

Vegetables to be cooked in sauce:
1 **eggplant, cut in half and**
   then cut into ¼ inch slices
   OR 1 small cauliflower, broken
      into small flowerlets
   OR ½ to 1 lb. pumpkin,
      cut into thin slices
   OR ½ to 1 lb. winter squash,
      cut into thin slices
   OR ½ to 1 lb. asparagus, break
      off tough ends and cut into
      long, thin diagonals
   OR ½ to 1 lb. green beans,
      cut into long, thin diagonals
   OR ½ to 1 lb. carrots, cut into
      long, thin diagonals
   OR ½ to 1 lb. broccoli, cut
      into thin diagonals with
      heads broken into small
      pieces
   OR ½ to 1 lb. summer squash,
      cut into thin diagonals
   OR ½ to 1 lb. brussel sprouts,
      cut in half lengthwise

Place in a saucepan with sauce and daikon. Cover and bring to a boil over medium heat. Cook 5 to 10 minutes until vegetables are just tender but still bright colored. Good with rice and leftover fish or egg dish for lunch. Also good served as a main meal side dish.

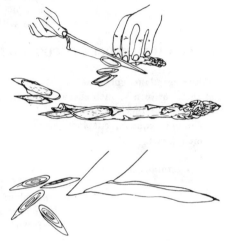

   OR 1 lb. spinach
   OR swiss chard
   OR any cooking green
   OR watercress
   OR ½ head cabbage, shredded
   OR 1 small head Chinese
      cabbage, cut into 1 inch
      cubes

Place greens in saucepan with sauce and daikon. Cover. Cook 3 to 5 minutes until greens are just tender but still bright green. Good with rice and leftover fish or egg dish for lunch. Also good served as a main meal side dish.

1 **large daikon,**
   cut into ¼ inch slices
   OR 2 large turnips,
      cut in half lengthwise and
      then cut into ¼ inch slices
   OR 2 to 3 parsnips,
      cut into thin diagonals
      steamed 5 minutes

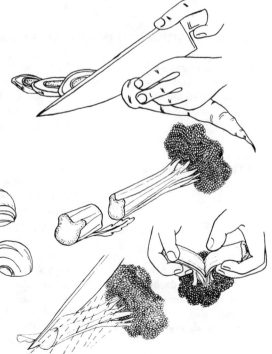

KABOCHA TUSKENI [PUMPKIN OR WINTER SQUASH SIMMERED IN SAUCE] [Serves 4 to 6]

1 small pumpkin,
  cut into ½ inch cubes
  OR 1½ lb. winter squash,
    cut into ½ inch cubes
  OR 1½ lb. piece of large pumpkin,
    cut into ½ inch cubes

Place in a saucepan.

1½ cup stock [dashi or kombu]
3 Tbsp. mild honey
2 Tbsp. soy sauce
1 tsp. sea salt

Place in saucepan with pumpkin. Cover leaving slight crack for liquid to escape. Bring to a boil over high heat. Reduce heat to medium low and simmer 15 to 20 minutes until pumpkin is tender and most liquid is absorbed. Serve with rice, pickles and a main dish for a dinner meal. Good with rice and pickles for a lunch.

NASU NO SAKE [EGGPLANT COOKED IN SAKE] [Serves 4 to 6]

1 medium eggplant, cut in half
  and then cut into ¼ inch slices
  OR 1 medium zucchini or other
    summer squash, cut into ¼
    inch slices

Steam 2 to 3 minutes. Remove from steamer. Cool slightly.

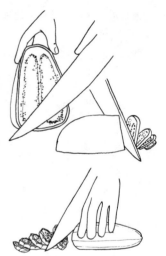

¼ cup vegetable oil

Heat a large, heavy frying pan. Add oil and heat until a piece of eggplant added sizzles. Add eggplant. Stir and fry 3 to 5 minutes over medium high heat until slightly browned. Pour off 2 Tbsp. of oil.

2 Tbsp. soy sauce
1½ Tbsp. mild honey
1 Tbsp. stock [dashi or kombu]
5 Tbsp. sake
  OR dry sherry

Pour over eggplant. Cover. Bring to boil over medium high heat. Reduce heat to medium low and simmer 10 to 15 minutes until eggplant is tender and sauce is slightly thickened. Serve hot with rice and a non-sweet main dish for dinner. Good cold with rice for lunch the next day.

EGGPLANT SIMMERED IN MISO SAUCE [Serves 4 to 6]

2 medium eggplant,
  cut into 1 inch cubes
¼ cup vegetable oil
1 Tbsp. sesame oil

Heat a wok over high heat. Add oil. Heat until eggplant cube added sizzles. Stir and fry 3 to 5 minutes until lightly browned. Reduce heat to medium. Cover. Cook 5 to 10 minutes until tender. Drain off excess oil.

Sauce:
2 Tbsp. sesame seeds

Heat a small cast iron skillet over high heat. Add sesame seeds. Parch 1 to 2 minutes until just browned. Shake pan often to evenly brown seeds. Grind in a blender, food mill or shirabashi until finely ground.

⅓ cup miso
1½ Tbsp. mild honey
2 Tbsp. stock [dashi or kombu]
1 Tbsp. soy sauce
2 Tbsp. sake
  OR dry sherry

Mix miso with sesame paste. Add other ingredients slowly to prevent sauce from being lumpy. Pour over eggplant. Mix gently. Bring to a boil. Cook 1 to 2 minutes. Remove from heat. Good served with rice as a side dish for a main meal. For a vegetarian meal this is very good served with rice and a plain tofu dish. Good the next day cold with rice and pickles for lunch.

WINTER SQUASH COOKED IN MISO SAUCE [Serves 4 to 6]

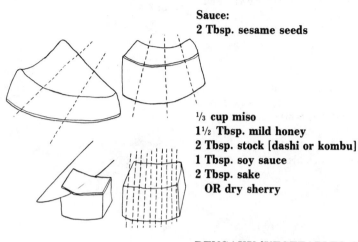

1½ lbs. winter squash cut into
   1 inch cubes
1 tsp. sesame oil

Pour oil over squash. Mix well. Place in steamer. Steam 10 to 15 minutes until just tender. Remove from steamer and place in a saucepan.

Sauce:
2 Tbsp. sesame seeds

Heat a small cast iron skillet over high heat. Add sesame seeds. Parch 1 to 2 minutes until just browned. Shake pan often to evenly brown seeds. Grind in a blender, food mill or shirabashi until finely ground.

⅓ cup miso
1½ Tbsp. mild honey
2 Tbsp. stock [dashi or kombu]
1 Tbsp. soy sauce
2 Tbsp. sake
   OR dry sherry

Mix miso with sesame paste. Add other ingredients slowly to prevent sauce from being lumpy. Pour over squash. Mix gently. Cook 3 to 5 minutes until sauce slightly thickens. Serve hot with rice as a main dish for a vegetarian meal along with a soup and pickles. Also good as a side dish for a main meal or cold the next day with rice and pickles for lunch.

DENGAKU [VEGETABLES GRILLED WITH MISO SAUCE] [Serves 4 to 6]

1 lb. yams, cut in half lengthwise
   OR 1 lb. sweet potatoes, cut
      in half lengthwise
   OR 1 lb. taro, cut in half
      lengthwise
   OR 1 lb. pumpkin, cut into
      4 to 6 pieces
   OR 1 lb. winter squash, cut
      into 4 to 6 pieces

Steam 15 to 20 minutes until just tender. Peel yams, sweet potatoes or toro when cooked. Place on a well oiled broiler pan.

Sauce:
⅓ cup light miso
1 Tbsp. mild honey
1 Tbsp. sake
   OR dry sherry
1 tsp. stock [dashi or kombu]

Press miso through a sieve. Add other ingredients and mix well. Brush over vegetables. Broil 3 to 5 minutes until lightly browned. Serve hot. Good with rice for lunch or as a side dish for a main meal.

YAKI MO [GRILLED YAMS] [Serves 4 to 6]

1 lb. yams, cut in half lengthwise
   OR 1 lb. sweet potatoes,
      cut in half lengthwise

Steam 10 to 15 minutes until still slightly firm. Remove from heat and cool.

1 tsp. sesame oil
¼ tsp. soy sauce
¼ tsp. sea salt
¼ tsp. mild honey [optional]

Mix ingredients well. Place yams in 350° oven 10 to 20 minutes until tender and bright orange with a crusty top. Remove from oven. Cut an X pattern in top of each yam and brush with sauce. Serve hot. A good snack. Also good served with rice and pickles for lunch. One can use leftover cooked yams or sweet potatoes and then just bake them as directed above and get the same results.

GRILLED FRESH WILD MUSHROOMS [Serves 4]

½ lb. fresh wild mushrooms
  morels or fairy ring
  mushrooms best
  OR 6 to 8 large dried
    mushrooms and
    1 cup boiling water

Place mushrooms on 4 skewers. Place over a charcoal grill 2 to 3 minutes until heated but not browned. Turn several times while heating.
Place dry mushrooms in a small bowl. Pour boiling water over them. Place weight on top to keep under water. Soak 15 to 30 minutes. Drain. Cut out tough stalks. Squeeze dry. Use like wild mushrooms.

2 tsp. soy sauce
½ tsp. sesame oil
¼ tsp. mild honey

Mix well. Dip pastry brush in sauce and baste mushrooms with sauce. Continue to cook 1 to 2 more minutes basting constantly until sauce is all used. A great spring treat to do with rice and a grilled dish such as fish teriyaki for a main meal. Good as a snack also.

VEGETABLES SIMMERED IN SAUCE AND COOKED IN EGG CUSTARD
[Serves 4 to 6]

½ cup stock [dashi or kombu]
2 Tbsp. soy sauce
1 Tbsp. mild honey
1 lb. green beans,
  cut into long, thin diagonals
  OR carrots, cut into long,
    thin diagonals
  OR broccoli, cut into thin
    diagonals with heads broken
    into small pieces
  OR asparagus, tough ends
    broken off, cut into long, thin
    diagonals
  OR 1 small cauliflower, broken
    into small flowerlets
  OR brussel sprouts,
    cut in half lengthwise

Place ingredients in saucepan. Cover and bring to a boil over medium high heat. Reduce heat to low and simmer 3 to 5 minutes until vegetables are still crispy and brightly colored but slightly tender. Remove from heat and cool liquid until lukewarm by placing pan in cold water. Keep covered.

4 eggs
¼ tsp. sea salt

Beat eggs and salt until well mixed but not frothy. Use chopsticks for best results as eggs will not become so frothy when beaten with them. Place beans and broth in a bowl. Add eggs. Mix well. Cover bowl and place in a steamer. Steam 15 to 20 minutes until eggs are just set. Serve hot with rice for a hearty lunch or as a main dish for a vegetarian dinner. Good cold the next day with pickles and cold rice for lunch.

STUFFINGS FOR NASU MUSHI AND KABOCHA MUSHI

Chicken or shellfish stuffing:
4 to 6 dried mushrooms
1 cup boiling water

Place mushrooms in small bowl. Pour boiling water over them. Place weight on top to keep under water. Soak 15 to 30 minutes. Drain. Cut out tough stalks. Cut into thirds. Save stock for soup or sauce bases.

2 medium carrots,
  cut into thin diagonals
1 cup cooked chicken,
  sliced thin
  OR cooked turkey or duck,
    sliced thin
  OR 1 cup fresh cooked small
    shrimp
  OR 1 cup crab meat
  OR 1 cup cooked unseasoned
    fish, flaked
½ cup snowpeas,
  cut into 3 long diagonal slices
  OR ½ cup peas
3 eggs,
  beaten until well mixed but
  not frothy
1 tsp. mild honey
1 tsp. sea salt
1 tsp. stock
  [dashi or kombu]

Combine honey and stock first. Add other ingredients. Mix well.

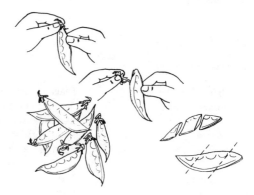

STUFFINGS FOR NASU MUSHI AND KABOCHA MUSHI

Meat stuffing:

1 chicken breast,
  cut into thin slices and
  then minced [easiest done if
  chicken frozen]
1 cup minced vegetable
  [eggplant center, winter squash
  or pumpkin]
½ inch fresh ginger root,
  grated
½ tsp. sea salt
¼ tsp. black pepper
1 tsp. arrowroot starch

Mix ingredients well. Allow to soak 15 to 30 minutes. Place in saucepan.

2 Tbsp. sake
  OR dry sherry
2 Tbsp. dashi stock
1 tsp. mild honey

Pour over chicken mixture. Bring to a boil over medium heat. Simmer 5 minutes. Stir often to separate pieces of chickens.

3 Tbsp. miso
2 tsp. mild honey
3 Tbsp. dashi stock
½ tsp. sea salt

Mix ingredients in a small bowl well to remove all lumps from miso. Add to chicken mixture. Simmer 3 to 5 minutes until sauce thickens and meat is tender.

Vegetarian stuffing:

4 to 6 dried mushrooms
1 cup boiling water

Place mushrooms in small bowl. Pour boiling water over them. Place weight on top to keep under water. Soak 15 to 30 minutes. Drain. Cut out tough stalks. Cut into strips. Save stock for soup or sauce bases.

2 medium carrots,
  cut into thin diagonals
1 block bean curd,
  wrap in tight cloth, weight
  1 to 2 hours to press out excess
  liquid, mash fine with fork
1 to 2 cakes Age
  [deep fried bean curd] cut into
  ¼ inch strips [optional]
½ cup snowpeas,
  cut into 3 long diagonal slices
  OR ½ cup peas
3 eggs,
  beaten until well mixed but
  not frothy
1 tsp. mild honey
1 tsp. sea salt
1 tsp. stock
  [dashi or kombu]

Mix stock and honey first. Add other ingredients. Mix well. Add mushrooms. Mix well.

NASU MUSHI [STUFFED EGGPLANT] [Serves 4 to 6]

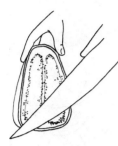

2 medium eggplant, cut in half lengthwise	Scoop out center of eggplant with a teaspoon. Leave a shell ½ inch thick. Save center for filling.
4 Tbsp. vegetable oil	Heat a large, heavy frying pan. Add oil and heat until a piece of eggplant added sizzles. Add eggplant hollow side down. Cook covered over medium heat 3 to 5 minutes until lightly browned. Uncover and turn.
1 batch meat, vegetarian, chicken or shellfish stuffing [see page 333-334]	Pour stuffing into eggplant hollows. Cover. Cook 5 to 10 minutes until eggplant tender. Good served with rice as a side dish for a main meal or a main dish. Good cold the next day with rice and pickles for lunch.

KABOCHA MUSHI [PUMPKIN STUFFED] [Serves 4 to 6]

1 small pumpkin [1½ to 2 lbs.] OR 1 small winter squash [1½ to 2 lbs.]	Cut off top like a jack-o-lantern, seed, scrape out loose fiber on the inside. Peel in strips from top to bottom having alternate sections of peel and unpeeled around the pumpkin.
2 tsp. sea salt	Rub inside and outside of pumpkin with salt. Place on a strong cloth along with top in a steamer and steam for 5 minutes. Remove from heat.
¼ cup sake OR dry sherry	Sprinkle over hot pumpkin. Steam another 5 to 10 minutes until almost tender.
1 batch of vegetarian, meat, chicken or shellfish stuffing [see page 333-334]	Pour stuffing into hot pumpkin. Place lid of jack-o-lantern on pumpkin. Steam another 20 to 25 minutes until stuffing is set and pumpkin is tender. Remove steamer from heat and lift out of steamer with steamer cloth. Slide gently onto a platter.
Sauce: 1 cup stock [dashi or kombu] 2 tsp. soy sauce 2 tsp. mild honey 1 Tbsp. sake OR dry sherry	Place in a saucepan and bring to a boil over high heat. Reduce heat to medium.
2 tsp. arrowroot starch 2 Tbsp. water	Mix well. Add to sauce. Stir 1 to 2 minutes until sauce thickens and clears. Pour over pumpkin on platter. Cut into 6 pie-shaped wedges and serve with hot rice. An excellent main dish. Also good served cold with rice and pickles for lunch.

KABOCHA NO TORI [PUMPKIN OR WINTER SQUASH WITH CHICKEN]
[Serves 4 to 6]

¾ to 1 lb. pumpkin,
   peel in strips but leave parts
   of peel on. Cut into ½ x 1 inch
   rectangles
   OR ¾ to 1 lb. winter squash,
      peel in strips but leave
      parts of peel on. Cut
      into ½ x 1 inch rectangels
   OR ¾ to 1 lb. piece of
      large pumpkin,
      peel in strips but leave
      parts of peel on. Cut
      into ½ x 1 inch rectangles

1½ cup stock
   [dashi or kombu]
2 Tbsp. mild honey
2 Tbsp. soy sauce
1 Tbsp. sake
   OR dry sherry

1 cup minced cooked chicken
½ cup dashi stock
2 tsp. soy sauce
1 tsp. mild honey

2 tsp. arrowroot starch
2 Tbsp. sauce from chicken
   marinade

Place ingredients in a saucepan. Cover and bring to a boil over high heat. Reduce heat to medium. Simmer 15 to 20 minutes until pumpkin is tender.

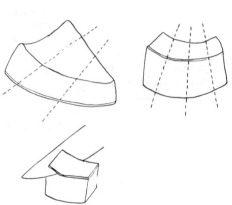

Place chicken in a bowl with other ingredients. Marinate while squash is cooking 15 to 20 minutes.

Mix sauce with starch. Add chicken and non-thickened sauce to pumpkin. Mix well. Add thickening with remainder of sauce. Stir 1 to 2 minutes until sauce thickens. Serve hot with rice. Good as a lunch along with cold rice and pickles. Also good as a main dish with rice and a cold vegetable for dinner.

Garnish: [optional]
½ cup watercress,
   chopped coarsely
3 green onions,
   cut into 1 inch pieces and
   then sliced paper thin lengthwise

Sprinkle over dish before serving.

UMANI [CHICKEN WITH VEGETABLES] [Serves 4 to 6]

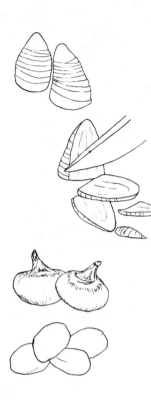

**Meat from legs and thighs
  of 1 chicken, deboned and
  sliced thin
  OR 1 chicken breast,
    sliced thin
1 cup bamboo shoots,
  cut into ¼ inch slices
  [optional]
5 to 6 water chestnuts,
  peeled and cut into
  ¼ inch slices
  [optional]
  OR ½ cup Jerusalem artichokes,
    cut into ¼ inch slices
½ lb. taro,
  peeled and rolled in salt and
  then steamed for 5 minutes.
  Washed and then cut into
  ¼ inch cubes
  OR ½ lb. potatoes,
    peeled and cut into
    ½ inch cubes
2 medium carrots,
  cut into ¼ inch thick diagonals
1 small can gingo nuts,
  drained [optional] and threaded
  on 3 bamboo skewers
¼ lb. mushrooms,
  cut into ¼ inch slices
4 cups dashi stock
⅓ cup soy sauce
3 Tbsp. mild honey
1 tsp. sea salt**

**¼ lb. green beans,
  cut into thin diagonals
4 green onions,
  cut into 1 inch pieces and
  then sliced paper thin
  lengthwise**

Place all ingredients in a large pot. Cover and bring to a boil over high heat. Reduce heat to medium. Simmer 10 to 15 minutes until vegetables are just tender.

Add to vegetables and sauce. Mix. Cook 3 to 5 minutes until beans are just tender. Serve hot with rice as a main dish. Also good with rice the next day as a lunch.

BEAN CURD WITH VEGETABLES [Serves 4 to 6]

1 cup bamboo shoots,
  cut into ¼ inch slices
  [optional]

5 to 6 water chestnuts,
  peeled and cut into
  ¼ inch slices
  [optional]
  OR ½ cup Jerusalem artichokes,
    cut into ¼ inch slices

½ lb. taro,
  peeled and rolled in salt
  and then steamed for
  5 minutes. Washed and
  then cut into ½ inch
  cubes
  OR ½ lb. potatoes,
    peeled and cut into
    ½ inch cubes

2 medium carrots,
  cut into ¼ inch thick
  diagonals

1 small can gingo nuts,
  drained [optional] and
  threaded on 3 bamboo
  skewers

¼ lb. mushrooms,
  cut into ¼ inch slices

4 cups dashi stock

⅓ cup soy sauce

3 Tbsp. mild honey

1 tsp. sea salt

¼ lb. green beans,
  cut into thin diagonals

4 green onions,
  cut into 1 inch pieces and
  then sliced paper thin
  lengthwise

1 to 2 cakes bean curd,
  cut into 1 inch cubes

Place all ingredients in a large pot. Cover and bring to a boil over high heat. Reduce heat to medium and simmer 10 to 15 minutes until vegetables are just tender.

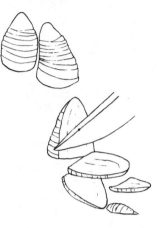

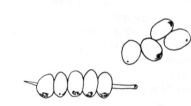

Add green onions and beans first. Mix with other vegetables. Cook 3 to 5 minutes until beans just tender. Add bean curd. Mix gently so bean curd does not break up into small pieces. Cook 1 more minutes until bean curd hot. Serve hot as a vegetarian main dish. Good served cold the next day with rice for lunch.

FUROFUKI [VEGETABLES IN SESAME MISO SAUCE]
[Serves 4 to 6]

1 lb. daikon,
  cut into ½ inch
cubes
  OR turnips,
    cut into ½ inch
    cubes
  OR pumpkin,
    cut into ½ inch
    cubes
  OR winter melon,
    cut into ½ inch
    cubes
  OR winter squash,
    cut into ½ inch
    cubes

Steam 10 to 15 minutes until vegetable is just tender but still bright colored.

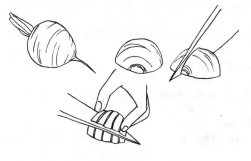

3 Tbsp. black or unhulled sesame seeds

Heat a small cast iron skillet over high heat. Add sesame seeds. Parch 1 to 2 minutes until just browned. Shake pan often to evenly brown seeds. Grind in a blender, food mill or shirabashi until finely ground.

½ cup miso
1½ Tbsp. mild honey
1½ Tbsp. sake
  OR dry sherry
1 Tbsp. stock
  [dashi or kombu]

Place miso in a saucepan. Slowly add other ingredients to miso so sauce will not be lumpy. Mix well. Bring to a boil over medium heat. Immediately remove from heat. Pour into bowl with sesame paste. Mix well. Place hot vegetables on top of miso-sesame sauce.

Garnish:
2 green onions,
  cut into 1 inch slices
  and then sliced lengthwise
into paper thin slices
  OR ¼ cup parsley,
    minced
  OR ¼ cup peppercress,
    minced
  OR ¼ cup watercress,
    minced

Sprinkle over top of vegetables. Serve hot with rice as a side dish for a main meal. Very good with rice for lunch.

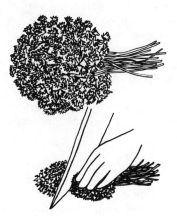

SOUPS

Japanese soups vary from meals-in-a-bowl such as miso shiru with noodles, meat and vegetables to very elegant appetizers such as suimono, a clear fish stock soup with just small pieces of lemon peel cut to resemble pine needles and perhaps carrots cut into flower shapes or small pieces of fish or chicken. Suimono is served with larger meals and miso shiru is served with smaller meals or even at breakfast.

MISO SHIRU [SOYBEAN/GRAIN PASTE SOUP] [Serves 4 to 6]

½ cup light miso
  OR ⅓ cup dark miso
1 to 2 tsp. mild honey

Combine in a bowl. Mix well.

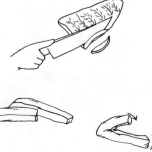

4 cups stock
  [dashi or kombu]

Add ¼ cup of stock to miso-honey paste. Mix well. Remove all lumps. Add another ¼ cup of stock and mix well. Add remaining stock. Mix well. If a blender is available combine all ingredients in blender and blend 20 to 30 seconds until ingredients well mixed and no lumps of miso remain. Pour into saucepan.

¼ to ½ cake bean curd,
  cut into ¼ inch cubes
  OR ¼ lb. white fish,
    cut into thin slices and tied
    in small knots

Add to stock. Bring soup to boil. Remove from heat immediately.

4 green onions,
  chopped
  OR 4 to 5 sprigs parsley,
    chopped
  OR 1 leek, chopped
  OR 2 Tbsp. chives, chopped
1 cake age [deep fried bean curd],
  slivered [optional]

Sprinkle greens into 4 to 6 individual soup bowls. Add age. Pour soup over ingredients. Serve at once. Good for breakfast along with rice and a cold vegetable dish. Also a hearty lunch or dinner soup.

VARIATION:

FISH MISO SHIRU [FISH WITH SOYBEAN/ GRAIN PASTE SOUP] [Serves 4 to 6]

¼ to ½ lb. leftover broiled fish
  without sauce

Follow recipe for Miso Shiru. Use fish in place of bean curd. Cook as directed. Good for breakfast along with rice and a cold vegetable dish. Also a hearty lunch or dinner soup.

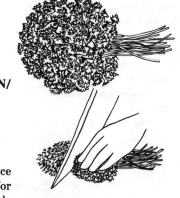

KAKI MISO SHIRU [OYSTER SOYBEAN/GRAIN PASTE SOUP] [Serves 4 to 6]

¼ to ½ lb. small shucked
  oysters
4 cups dashi stock

Place oysters and dashi in a saucepan. Bring to a boil. Boil 2 to 3 minutes until done.

½ cup light miso
  OR ⅓ cup dark miso
1 to 2 tsp. mild honey
½ to 1 dried pepper, crushed
  and pulverized in a mortar and
  pestle or blender

Take ½ cup of dashi and mix with miso and honey. Mix until no lumps remain in miso. Add to oysters and dashi. Bring to a boil again. Add red pepper. Mix. Remove from heat.

arnish:
green onions, chopped
OR 4 to 5 sprigs parsley,
   chopped
OR 1 leek, chopped
OR 2 Tbsp. chives, chopped

Place in individual soup bowls. Pour soup over garnish. Serve hot. Good for lunch or dinner.

IISO SHIRU WITH MEAT, FISH OR EGGS AND VEGETABLES SOYBEAN/GRAIN PASTE SOUP WITH MEAT, FISH OR EGGS AND EGETABLES] [Serves 4 to 6]

4 to ½ chicken breast,
   sliced into thin strips and
   tied in knots
OR 1 can clams,
   drained and rinsed
OR ¼ lb. small fresh cooked
   shrimp
OR ¼ fish cake, cut into
   ¼ inch cubes
OR 1 egg custard, cut into
   ¼ inch cubes

Make basic miso soup. Use any of these ingredients in place of bean curd. Cook just long enough to cook meat or heat pre-cooked items. Do not use too many ingredients as this is supposed to be a simple soup. Usually three and a garnish are enough.

OR fish/chicken/or shrimp
   balls [see **Dango Suimono**]
   2 cups dashi stock

Cook fish balls in dashi 5 to 10 minutes then add to soup.

Vegetables:
3 or 4 dried mushrooms
1 cup boiling water

Place mushrooms in a small bowl. Pour boiling water over them. Place weight on top to keep under water. Soak 15 to 30 minutes. Drain. Cut out tough stalks. Cut into ¼ inch strips. Save stock.

¼ large cucumber, cut
   into 1/8 inch slices
OR 3 to 4 fresh mushrooms,
   cut into 1/8 inch slices
OR leftover greens,
   cut into ¼ inch slices
OR ½ daikon, cut into
   1/8 inch slices
OR ½ short medium carrot,
   cut into 2 inch pieces, cut
   5 v's into outside of carrot
   at even intervals and then
   slice into thin rounds
   resembling flowers or cut
   carrot into thin rounds

Place 2 or 3 vegetables in soup, along with mushrooms.

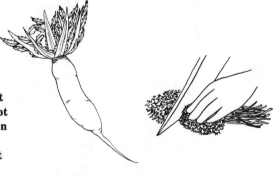

Garnish:
4 green onions, chopped
  OR 4 to 5 sprigs parsley,
    chopped
  OR 1 leek, chopped
  OR 2 Tbsp. chives, chopped

Place 1 garnish in soup bowls. Pour soup over garnish. Serve hot. Good for breakfast, lunch or dinner. When served with rice and pickles or cold vegetables makes a nice lunch.

MISO SHIRU WITH MEAT, VEGETABLES AND NOODLES [SOYBEAN/GRAIN PASTE SOUP WITH MEAT, VEGETABLES AND NOODLES] [Serves 4 to 6]

5 cups dashi stock
½ yellow onion,
   cut in half lengthwise
   and sliced thin
½ daikon,
   cut into 1/8 inch
   sliced
   OR 1 large turnip,
     cut in half lengthwise
     and sliced thin
1 chicken breast,
  sliced thin
  OR ¼ lb. meat
    [pork, beef or lamb],
    sliced thin

Heat stock. Add meat and vegetables. Bring to a boil. Reduce heat to medium low and simmer 2 minutes until meat is done and vegetables are just tender.

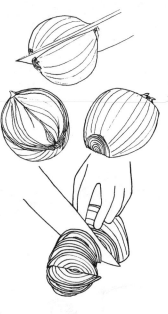

1 small bunch spinach
  OR ¼ lb. swiss chard,
    cut into 1 inch strips
  OR ¼ lb. watercress
  OR ¼ lb. any green,
    cut into 1 inch strips

Add to soup. Cook 1 minute.

½ tsp. sea salt
⅓ cup red miso
  OR ½ cup light miso
1 to 2 tsp. mild honey
½ to 1 red pepper,
  crushed and pulverized
  [optional]
  OR ½ to 1 tsp. torgarashi
  [optional]

Mix ingredients well. Add ½ cup stock from soup. Mix well until all lumps removed from miso. Add to soup. Bring to a boil. Remove from heat.

2 cups cooked whole wheat
  or buckwheat vermicelli

Place in 6 individual soup bowls. Pour soup over noodles. Serve hot. Makes a hearty lunch or can serve as a main dish for dinner.

SUIMONO [CLEAR SOUP WITH FEW INGREDIENTS] [Serves 6]

Ingredients for soup:

¼ inch strips raw fish,
   tied into loose knots
¼ inch strips raw chicken,
   tied into loose knots
18 small dried fish
   OR 6 larger dried fish
6 prawns, shelled, deveined,
   skewered from heat to tail
18 small fresh cooked shrimp
6 large cooked clams,
   cut into thirds
6 cooked scallops, sliced thin
18 thin strips of abalone
18 thin cucumber slices
6 thin slices daikon
6 thin slices turnip, cut in half
½ block bean curd, cut into
   18 pieces
6 to 12 snowpeas, strings removed
2 inch slice of carrot with 5 v's
   cut into the outside at even
   intervals and then sliced into
   thin slices to resemble flowers
6 slices of kamaboko [fish cake]
6 omelette strips
   [see Omeretsu in Appetizers
   and Snacks]
leftover or pre-steamed greens,
   cut into 6 one inch slices
1 cake age, cut into 18 thin
   slices

Garnishes for soup:

6 small sprigs parsley
18 thin slices of lemon peel,
   cut into slices to resemble
   pine needles.
1 large green onion, cut into
   1 inch slices and then julienned
   into thin slices
18 thin slivers fresh ginger root,
   cut to resemble pine needles
1 leek, cut into 1 inch slices
   and then julienned into thin
   strips

Soup:

4 cups stock [dashi or kombu]
½ tsp. sea salt
2 tsp. tamari soy sauce
1 tsp. lemon juice

Attractively arrange equal amounts of 1 to 3 ingredients in the bottom of 6 bowls.

Boil 3 to 5 minutes until pink and firm. Remove from skewers. Cut in half along back.

Attractively arrange equal amounts of 1 to 2 garnishes in the bottom of 6 bowls along with the other ingredients.

Place dashi stock in a saucepan. Bring to a boil. Add salt, soy and lemon juice. Remove from heat. Pour over a selection of garnishes and ingredients placed in individual soup bowls. Do not use too many ingredients as this is a simple soup. Good dinner soup.

KAKITAMAJIRU SUIMONO [CLEAR EGG SOUP] [Serves 6]

5 cups stock
  [dashi or kombu]
1 tsp. sea salt
1 tsp. tamari soy sauce

Bring broth to a boil. Add salt and soy sauce.

4 tsp. arrowroot starch
3 Tbsp. slightly cooled
  soup broth

Add broth to starch. Pour into rest of soup slowly. Mix well.

2 eggs, slightly beaten
18 snowpeas, snipped and
  strings removed
  OR 6 to 8 sprigs parsley

Add eggs and peas or parsley together. Mix gently. Cook 2 to 3 minutes until eggs are set. Serve at once.

TOFU, MEAT AND VEGETABLE SOUP [Serves 6]

¼ to ½ lb. meat
  [pork or beef],
  cut into thin slices
  OR 1 chicken breast,
    cut into thin slices
5 cups chicken stock
1 yellow onion, cut into
  8 pieces and individual layers
  separated

Bring stock to a boil. Add meat and onions. Cover and reduce heat to medium. Simmer 10 to 15 minutes until meat is done (pork takes longer than chicken).

½ small bok choy head,
  each stalk cut into 3 or 4
  long, thin pieces
  OR ½ lb. spinach, cut
    leaves into 3 or 4 pieces
  OR ½ lb. swiss chard, each
    leaf cut into 3 to 4 long,
    thin pieces
  OR ½ lb. Chinese cabbage,
    each leaf cut into 2 to 3
    long, thin pieces
¼ to ½ lb. mushrooms,
  cut into thin slices

Add to soup. Cover and simmer 3 to 5 minutes until greens are just tender.

2 Tbsp. soy sauce
1 to 2 cakes bean curd,
  cut into ½ inch cubes

Add to soup. Mix gently. Cook 1 to 2 more minutes to heat bean curd. Serve at once. Good hardy meal soup. Excellent lunch. A meal-in-a-bowl served with rice and pickles.

TAMAGO SUIMONO [CLEAR SOUP WITH EGG CUSTARD] [Serves 6]

4 eggs
1 cup stock
   [dashi or kombu]
1 tsp. soy sauce
½ tsp. sea salt
½ tsp. mild honey

Mix until well combined but not frothy. Pour into bowl so egg ½ inch deep.

8 to 10 fresh
   cooked shrimp
   OR ¼ lb. salmon,
      cut into ¼ inch by 1 inch
      strips
   OR ½ cup clams
6 to 8 sprigs parsley
   OR ¼ lb. spinach
      cut into 1 inch pieces
   OR ¼ lb. swiss chard,
      cut into 1 inch pieces
   OR ¼ lb. watercress,
      washed and cut into
      2 to 3 inch pieces

Add 1 or 2 ingredients to eggs. Mix lightly. Cover bowl. Place in steamer and steam 10 to 15 minutes until well set. Loosen edges. Invert custard over plate and cut into 1 inch squares. Place 3 squares in each soup bowl.

Garnish:
3 to 4 spinach leaves,
   steamed 1 minute,
   cut into 1 inch strips
   OR 6 sprigs parsley,
      steamed 1 minute
   OR swiss chard leaves,
      steamed 1 minute and
      cut into 1 inch strips
   OR 6 sprigs watercress,
      steamed 30 seconds
2 inch piece lemon peel,
   cut into thin strips to
   resemble pine needles

If no greens are used in custard, arrange one green garnish and lemon peel on bottom of soup bowl along with egg custard squares.

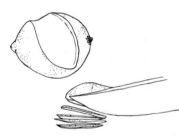

5 cups stock
   [dashi or kombu]
1½ Tbsp. sake
   OR dry sherry
1 tsp. sea salt
1 tsp. soy sauce
dash lemon juice

Bring to a boil. Pour over egg squares in soup bowls. Serve hot. Excellent with a tempura meal.

TORI ZONI [NEW YEAR'S RICE CAKE SOUP] [Serves 6]

1 chicken breast 1 Tbsp. arrowroot starch	Dust chicken breast on both sides with arrowroot starch. Pound thin with back of a cleaver. Cut into thin strips. Steam 5 to 7 minutes until done.

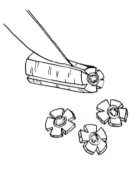

½ fish cake, cut into ¼ inch strips	
1 medium short thick carrot	Cut into 2 inch pieces, make 5 v cuts at even intervals on the outside of each carrot piece. Slice into 1/8 inch rounds to resemble flowers. Steam 3 to 5 minutes until tender.

3 taro, peeled and sliced
   lengthwise into ¼ inch slices
   OR 1 medium potato, peeled,
      sliced in half lengthwise and
      then cut into ¼ inch slices
	Steam 5 to 10 minutes until tender.

½ tsp. sea salt ½ tsp. soy sauce 1 Tbsp. dashi	Mix. Sprinkle over carrots and taro when they are removed from the steamer. Allow to sit. Mix gently.

½ lb. spinach
   OR swiss chard
   OR New Zealand spinach
	Steam 2 to 3 minutes until just tender but still bright green. Cut on diagonal into 1 inch slices.

1 by 2 inch lemon peel,
   cut into thin strips to
   resemble pine needles	

12 mochi [rice cakes]	Toast until soft and just brown on edges in 300° oven.
6 cups stock [dashi or kombu] 1½ tsp. sea salt 1 Tbsp. soy sauce dash lemon juice	Bring to a boil. Place above ingredients equally into 6 large soup bowls. Pour stock over ingredients. Serve hot. This soup can be a meal-in-a-bowl when served with a little rice and pickles. A New Year's festival soup.

SAKANA DANGO SUIMONO [FISH BALL SOUP] [Serves 4 to 6]

½ lb. white fish, minced
1 green onion, minced
2 thin slices fresh ginger root,
   minced
2 Tbsp. whole wheat pastry flour
2 Tbsp. arrowroot starch
1 egg plus 1 egg yolk,
   slightly beaten
½ tsp. sea salt
	Mix ingredients well. Let sit for 20 to 30 minutes. Mix again.

5 cups dashi stock
2 Tbsp. soy sauce

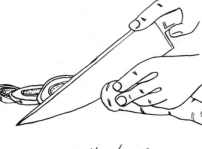

1 medium carrot, cut into
1/8 inch diagonal slices
4 to 5 mushrooms,
cut into ¼ inch slices
OR 4 to 5 dried mushrooms,
soaked for 15 minutes in
boiling water, drained and
sliced into ¼ inch strips

2 to 3 green onions, cut into
thin diagonal slices
OR 3 to 4 sprigs parsley,
chopped
OR 5 to 6 sprigs watercress

Bring stock to a boil. Add ½ tsp. of fish mixture at a time, until all is used. Boil 5 to 10 minutes until fish balls are firm and done all the way through.

Add to soup. Bring to boil. Pour into individual soup bowls.

Garnish each soup bowl with one of greens. Serve hot. Good lunch or hearty dinner soup. Can be a meal-in-a-bowl served with rice and pickles.

VARIATION:

EBI DANGO SUIMONO
[SHRIMP BALL SOUP] [Serves 6]

½ lb. raw shrimp, minced
1 green onion, minced
3 thin slices fresh ginger root,
minced
1 Tbsp. whole wheat pastry flour
2 Tbsp. arrowroot starch
1 egg plus 1 egg yolk,
slightly mixed
½ tsp. sea salt

Mix ingredients well. Allow to sit 20 to 30 minutes. Mix again. Follow recipe for Sakana Dango Suimono. Use same vegetables and garnishes. Cook as directed. Serve hot. Good lunch or hearty dinner soup. Can be a meal-in-a-bowl served with rice and pickles.

VARIATION:

TORI DANGO SUIMONO
[CHICKEN BALL SOUP] [Serves 6]

1 chicken breast, minced
2 green onions, minced
3 thin slices fresh ginger root,
minced
¼ tsp. black pepper
2 Tbsp. whole wheat pastry flour
2 Tbsp. arrowroot starch
2 eggs, slightly mixed
1 tsp. sea salt

Mix ingredients well. Allow to sit 20 to 30 minutes. Mix again. Follow recipe for Sakana Dango Suimono. Use same vegetables and garnishes. Cook chicken balls longer than fish or shrimp balls. Cook as directed. Serve hot. Good lunch or hearty dinner soup. Can be a meal-in-a-bowl served with rice and pickles.

VARIATION:

NIKU DANGO SUIMONO
[MEAT BALLS SOUP] [Serves 6]

½ lb. ground meat
[beef, pork, or lamb]
2 green onions, minced
1 tsp. fresh ginger root, grated
¼ tsp. black pepper
1 Tbsp. whole wheat pastry flour
1 Tbsp. arrowroot starch
1 egg, slightly mixed
1 tsp. sea salt

Mix ingredients well. Allow to sit 20 to 30 minutes. Mix again. Follow recipe for Sakana Dango Suimono. Use same vegetables and garnishes. Cook meatballs 10 to 15 minutes. Skim off foam on top of soup as meatballs cook. Cook as directed. Serve hot. Good lunch or hearty dinner soup. Can be a meal-in-a-bowl served with rice and pickles.

ZOSUI [THICK RICE SOUP WITH VEGETABLES] [Serves 6 to 8]

8 cups stock
   [dashi or chicken]
1 cup short grain brown rice
½ tsp. sea salt
3 thin slices fresh ginger root,
   julienned
1 Tbsp. soy sauce

Bring stock to a boil in a heavy saucepan. Add rice, ginger, salt and soy. Cover and cook over low heat 40 to 50 minutes until rice very tender. Take out 2 cups of cooked rice with stock. Blend until smooth. Add back to soup.

½ cup fresh peas
   OR 1 carrot, cut into
      pea sized pieces
   OR 1 cup snow peas, ends
      removed and strings
      removed, cut into thirds
1 sheet nori seaweed, shredded

Add to rice soup. Cover. Simmer 2 to 3 minutes.

2 eggs, slightly beaten

Slowly add to soup. Stir soup slowly with chopsticks in a circular motion while adding eggs. Cover and simmer 3 to 5 minutes until eggs are set and vegetables are just tender.

Garnish:
2 green onions, minced
   OR 4 to 5 sprigs parsley,
      minced
   OR 1 leek, minced
   OR ¼ cup watercress,
      cut into small pieces

Place garnish in bottom of 8 soup bowls. Ladle soup over it. Serve hot. Good lunch or dinner soup.

TORI ZOSUI [CHICKEN RICE CHOWDER] [Serves 4 to 6]

5 cups chicken stock
4 cups leftover cooked rice
2 Tbsp. sake
   OR dry sherry
¼ inch fresh ginger root,
   grated
2 Tbsp. soy sauce
1 tsp. sea salt

Place in a saucepan. Bring to a boil over high heat. Cover. Reduce heat to medium. Simmer 15 to 20 minutes until rice is very tender. Blend in a blender until smooth or beat with an egg beater until rice grains are broken up and a thick creamy soup is formed.

1 to 2 cups shredded, cooked
   chicken meat [tear meat into
   small shreds with fingers]

Add to rice. Simmer 3 to 5 minutes until chicken is hot.

3 green onions, cut into 1 inch
   strips and julienned

Add to soup. Mix.

3 eggs, beaten until well mixed
   but not frothy

Add to soup. Mix slightly. Cover. Remove from heat. Let sit 3 to 5 minutes until eggs are set. Serve hot. Can be a one-pot meal when served with a salad or pickle.

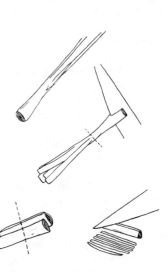

FISH SOUP [Serves 6]

½ lb. white fish fillet,
   cut into ½ inch slices
4 cups kombu stock
   OR water

Bring stock to a boil over high heat. Add fish. Reduce heat to medium. Mix gently. Cover. Simmer 5 to 10 minutes until fish tender and flakey.

½ lb. spinach,
   cut into 1 inch strips
   OR swiss chard,
     cut into 1 inch strips
   OR bok choy,
     each stalk cut into 2 to 4
     long, thin pieces
   OR watercress,
     cut into 1 inch pieces
4 to 5 dry mushrooms,
   soaked in 1 cup boiling water for
   15 minutes until soft, cut into
   thin pieces, discard stems
   OR 4 to 5 large fresh mushrooms
     cut into ¼ inch slices
1 Tbsp. soy sauce
1½ tsp. sea salt
1 tsp. lemon juice

Add vegetables, soy sauce and salt to soup. Simmer 2 to 3 minutes until greens just tender but still bright green. Add lemon juice. Mix. Serve hot. Good soup with fried or rich foods.

CLAM OR SHRIMP SOUP [Serves 6]

¼ lb. fresh cooked clams
   OR ¼ lb. fresh cooked small
     shrimp
12 small spinach leaves
   OR 3 swiss chard leaves,
     each cut into 4 pieces
   OR 3 bok choy leaves,
     cut into 4 pieces
   OR 12 pieces of watercress,
     cut into 2 inch pieces
2 fresh mushrooms,
   cut into 18 slices

Arrange ingredients in 6 soup bowls.

4 cups dashi stock
1 tsp. sea salt
2 tsp. soy sauce
½ tsp. lemon juice

Bring ingredients to a boil in a saucepan. Pour into soup bowls. Serve hot. Good with fried food dishes such as tempura or tasuta age.

1 red pepper,
   ground fine
   OR 1 tsp. torgarshi

Sprinkle over clam soup.

RICE AND NOODLES

Plain rice, rice cooked with seasonings, fried rice or rice topped with an omlette or leftover tempura and sauce for a meal-in-a-bowl: rice occurs at every meal. Noodles are served both hot and cold as snacks, lunches, or again as meals-in-a-bowl. Noodles even turn into salad-type dishes in Japan and are good served this way on a hot summer day.

GOHAN [RICE] [Serves 4 to 6]

2 cups short grain brown rice
4 cups water

Place rice and water in a heavy saucepan with a tight fitting lid. Bring to a boil over high heat. When steam escapes from lid reduce heat to medium and simmer 30 to 35 minutes until all water is absorbed. Remove from heat and allow to sit for 10 minutes to let rice fluff and absorb all water. Plain rice is served with most main dishes or by itself with a few leftovers for lunch. Leftover rice can be used in rice cakes, puddings, fried rice or sushi. Cooked rice will keep 3 to 4 days in the refrigerator.

KAKI-MESHI [OYSTERS COOKED WITH RICE] [Serves 4 to 6]

2 cups short grain brown rice
3 Tbsp. sake
  OR dry sherry
3 Tbsp. soy sauce
¼ cup stock [dashi]
3 cups water

Place rice and other ingredients in a heavy saucepan with a tight fitting lid. Bring to a boil over high heat. When steam excapes from lid reduce heat to medium and simmer 20 minutes.

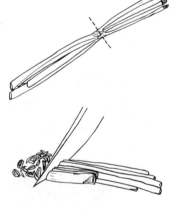

1 lb. small shucked oysters, well washed, and cut into thirds
  OR 1 pt. oysters, drained and cut into thirds.

Add to rice. Mix gently. Cover. Cook 10 more minutes until all water is absorbed and oysters are tender. Remove from heat. Let sit for 10 minutes for rice to fluff and remainder of liquid to be absorbed.

Garnish:
4 green onions, chopped
  OR ¼ cup watercress, chopped
  OR 4 to 6 large sprigs parsley, chopped
  OR 4 leaves spinach, slivered
  OR 1 sheet nori seaweed brushed with ¼ tsp. soy sauce and ¼ tsp. sesame oil, grilled 1 minute under broiler until crisp, crumble

Serve individual bowls of oyster rice. Sprinkle one of garnishes over rice and serve hot. Makes a complete dinner when served with a vegetable dish. Also good for lunch hot or cold.

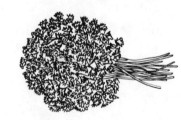

HIRAME-MESHI [HALIBUT COOKED WITH RICE] [Serves 4 to 6]

2 cups short grain brown rice
3 cups water
3 Tbsp. sake
   OR dry sherry
1 Tbsp. mild honey
1 tsp. sea salt
¼ cup stock [dashi]

Place rice and other ingredients in a heavy saucepan with a tight fitting lid. Bring to a boil over high heat. When steam escapes from lid reduce heat to medium and simmer 25 minutes.

4 to 6 dried mushrooms
½ cup boiling water

Place mushrooms in a small bowl. Pour boiling water over them. Place weight on top to keep under water. Let sit 15 to 30 minutes until soft. Remove from water. Squeeze dry. Cut out tough stems. Cut into ¼ inch strips. Reserve mushroom stock for other uses.

6 to 8 oz. of halibut,
   cut into ¼ inch strips
   OR other white fish
     [red snapper, turbot, sole,
     cod, etc.], cut into ¼ inch
     strips

Add to rice along with mushrooms. Mix gently. Cover. Cook 10 more minutes until all water is absorbed and halibut or other fish is tender. Remove from heat. Let sit for 10 minutes for rice to fluff and remainder of liquid to be absorbed.

½ lb. spinach
   OR swiss chard
   OR watercress
   OR other cooking green

Steam 2 to 3 minutes until tender but still bright green. Remove from steamer. Gather into long bundles and cut into 1 inch pieces. Mix with rice. Place rice in individual bowls.

Garnishes:
4 green onions, chopped
   OR ¼ cup watercress,
     chopped
   OR 4 to 6 large sprigs parsley,
     chopped
   OR 4 leaves spinach,
     slivered
   OR 1 sheet nori seaweed,
     brushed with ¼ tsp. soy
     sauce and ¼ tsp. sesame oil,
     grilled 1 minute under
     broiler until crisp, crumble

Sprinkle one of garnishes over rice. Serve hot. Makes a complete dinner-in-a-bowl. Good served with pickles also. Good cold for lunch the next day served with pickles.

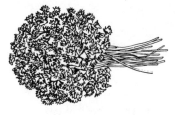

MATSUDAKI MESHI [RICE COOKED WITH SEASONINGS AND VEGETABLES] [Serves 4 to 6]

2 cups short grain brown rice
4 cups water
2 Tbsp. soy sauce
1 Tbsp. sake
   OR dry sherry
   OR rice vinegar
1 tsp. sea salt
1 tsp. mild honey

Place rice and other ingredients in a heavy saucepan with a tight fitting lid. Bring to a boil over high heat. When steam escapes from lid reduce heat to medium and simmer 20 minutes.

4 to 6 dried mushrooms
½ cup boiling water

Place mushrooms in a small bowl. Pour boiling water over them. Place a weight on top to keep under water. Let sit 15 to 30 minutes until soft. Remove from water. Squeeze dry. Cut out tough stems. Cut into ¼ inch strips. Reserve mushroom stock for other uses.

18 to 20 snowpeas,
   each sliced into 6 thin
   diagonals
   OR green beans, cut into
      long, thin diagonals

Add to rice along with mushrooms. Mix gently. Cover. Cook 10 more minutes until all water is absorbed and vegetables are tender. Remove from heat. Let sit for 10 minutes for rice to fluff and remainder of liquid to be absorbed.

Garnishes:
4 green onions, chopped
   OR 4 to 6 large sprigs parsley,
      chopped
   OR ¼ cup watercress, chopped
   OR 4 leaves spinach, slivered
   OR 1 sheet nori seaweed brushed
      with ¼ tsp. soy sauce and
      ½ tsp. sesame oil, grilled
      1 minute under broiler until
      crisp, crumble

Serve individual bowls of flavored rice. Sprinkle one of garnishes over each bowl of rice. Good with a main dish for dinner along with pickles. Also good cold for lunch.

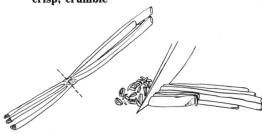

CHA-MESHI [RICE COOKED IN GREEN TEA WITH SOYBEANS AND CHESTNUTS] [Serves 4 to 6]

2 Tbsp. green tea
4 cups boiling water
   OR 4 cups leftover green tea

Make pot of tea. Steep 3 to 5 minutes and then strain. Cool.

2 cups short grain brown rice
2 Tbsp. sake
   OR dry sherry
½ tsp. sea salt
½ tsp. honey

Place rice, other ingredients, and tea in a heavy saucepan with a tight fitting lid. Bring to a boil over high heat. When steam escapes from lid reduce heat to medium and simmer 30 to 35 minutes until all water is absorbed. Remove from heat and allow to sit for 10 minutes to let rice fluff and absorb all water.

1 cup cooked soybeans

Steam 3 to 5 minutes to heat.

| ¼ lb. chestnuts
   OR Jerusalem artichokes | Prick chestnut skin with a sharp fork. Steam 15 to 20 minutes until tender. Remove from heat. Cool slightly. Peel. Cut into 4 to 5 pieces. |

2 Tbsp. vegetable oil — Heat a medium sized skillet. Add oil and heat slightly. Add chestnuts. Fry over medium heat 5 to 10 minutes until chestnuts are golden brown. Remove from oil.

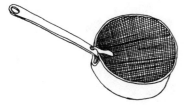

½ tsp. sea salt
1 tsp. soy sauce
½ tsp. red pepper
   or toragashi

Add beans and fried chestnuts to rice. Add salt, soy sauce and red pepper. Mix well. Serve hot with a main dish and vegetables for a main meal. This can be served as a vegetarian main dish along with a salad or pickles for dinner. Good cold for lunch with pickles.

VARIATION:

Cook rice with green tea but do not add soybeans and chestnuts.

AZUKI MESHI [RED BEANS COOKED WITH RICE] [Serves 4 to 6]

1 cup azuki beans
   OR 1 cup red kidney beans
   OR 1 cup pinto beans
4 cups water
1 tsp. sea salt

Place beans in large cast iron dutch oven with water and salt. Cover and bring to a boil over high heat. Reduce heat to medium low and simmer 2 to 3 hours until beans are just tender. Add more water as necessary to keep water level with beans. Cool. Reserve stock. To pressure cook: place beans, water and salt in pressure cooker. Bring to full pressure. Cook at full pressure 45 to 50 minutes. Cool. Reserve stock.

2 cups short grain brown rice
2 cups water
1½ cups bean stock
1 tsp. sea salt

Place rice, beans, water, bean stock and salt in a heavy saucepan with a tight fitting lid. Bring to a boil over high heat. When steam escapes from lid reduce heat to medium and simmer 20 to 25 minutes.

2 Tbsp. sake
1 Tbsp. soy sauce

Add to rice. Mix. Cover. Cook 5 to 10 minutes until all water is absorbed. Remove from heat. Let sit 10 minutes.

4 Tbsp. sesame seeds
¼ tsp. sea salt

Heat a small skillet over high heat. Add seeds and salt. Parch 1 to 2 minutes until lightly browned. Shake pan often to evenly brown seeds. Remove from heat. Grind coarsely in a blender, food mill or shirabashi. Sprinkle over rice in individual bowls. Usually served in Japan as a festival dish but an excellent vegetarian main dish with pickles and a side dish of vegetables or soup. Also good for lunch cold the next day served with pickles.

NA-MESHI [GREENS COOKED WITH RICE] [Serves 4 to 6]

2 cups short grain brown rice
3¾ cups water
2 Tbsp. sake
  OR dry sherry
1 tsp. sea salt
2 Tbsp. stock [dashi or kombu]

Place ingredients in a heavy saucepan with a tight fitting lid. Bring to a boil over high heat. When steam escapes from lid reduce heat to medium. Simmer 25 to 30 minutes until all water is absorbed.

1 lb. spinach, cut into thin slices
  OR swiss chard, cut into thin slices
  OR ½ lb. watercress, coarsely chopped
  OR 1 lb. any cooking green, cut into thin slices

Add to rice. Mix gently. Cover and cook 3 to 5 more minutes. Remove from heat. Let sit 10 minutes so vegetables are tender but still bright green and all water is absorbed in rice.

4 Tbsp. sesame seeds
¼ tsp. sea salt

Heat a small skillet over high heat. Add seeds and salt. Parch 1 to 2 minutes until lightly browned. Shake pan often to evenly brown seeds. Remove from heat. Grind coarsely in blender, food mill, or shirabashi. Sprinkle over top of rice. Good as a combined vegetable and rice dish with a main dish for a dinner meal. Good cold with leftovers and pickles for lunch.

TORI CHA HAN [CHICKEN FRIED RICE] [Serves 4 to 6]

1 cup cooked leftover chicken, cut into long, thin strips
  OR ½ breast chicken, cut into long thin strips
  OR 1 cup roast beef or pork, cut into long, thin strips
  OR 1 cup turkey, cut into long, thin strips
  OR 1 cup duck, cut into long, thin strips
  OR 1 cup rabbit, cut into long, thin strips
  OR ¼ lb. small shrimp
2 Tbsp. vegetable oil

Heat a wok over high heat. Add oil. Heat until a piece of chicken added sizzles. Add meat. Stir and fry 2 to 3 minutes until browned lightly. Remove from pan.

¼ lb. snowpeas, each cut into 6 to 7 long, thin diagonals
  OR 1 cup frozen or fresh peas
  OR ¼ lb. green beans, cut into long, thin diagonals
  OR ¼ head green cabbage, shredded
  OR 1 medium carrot, cut into long, thin diagonals
  OR a combination of these vegetables

Steam vegetable 1 to 2 minutes to heat but not so long they are limp. Remove from steamer.

2 Tbsp. vegetable oil
4 to 6 green onions, minced

Add oil to wok after meat is removed. Add green onions and vegetables. Fry 2 to 3 minutes until slightly browned.

4 cups cooked short grain brown rice

Add to vegetables 1 cup at a time. Mix well to remove lumps between each cup. Stir and fry 3 to 5 minutes to heat through.

1 Tbsp. soy sauce
2 Tbsp. stock [dashi]
¼ tsp. honey
1 tsp. sea salt

Add to rice. Mix. Add chicken. Cook 1 to 2 minutes to heat. Serve hot with a main dish and salad or pickles for a dinner meal. Can serve as main dish by itself or very good with a soup or vegetable dish. Good cold for lunch the next day.

VEGETARIAN CHA HAN [VEGETARIAN FRIED RICE] [Serves 4 to 6]

6 to 8 egg sheets

Egg sheets:
3 eggs
1 tsp. soy sauce
½ tsp. honey
2 tsp. kombu stock

Mix ingredients until well mixed but not frothy.

1 tsp. vegetable oil

Heat a medium sized cast iron skillet over medium heat. Brush with oil. Heat until a small bit of egg mixture added sets. Add 3 Tbsp. of egg mixture. Roll pan to evenly cover bottom of pan with egg mixture. Cook 1 to 2 minutes until edges of egg sheet are brown. Loosen edges with a knife and flip egg sheet. Cook 30 seconds to 1 minute on bottom side. Remove from pan. Brush pan with oil again. Repeat process until all egg mixture is used. Cut egg sheets in half and then cut halves into toothpick thin strips.

½ to 1 cup sesame seeds
  OR ½ to 1 cup sunflower seeds
  OR ½ to 1 cup raw peanuts, chopped
  OR 2 cakes age [deep fried bean curd], cut into long, thin strips

Roast nuts or seeds in 300° oven 5 to 10 minutes until golden brown.

¼ lb. snowpeas, each cut into 6 to 7 long, thin diagonals
  OR 1 cup frozen or fresh peas
  OR ¼ lb. green beans, cut into long, thin diagonals
  OR ¼ head green cabbage, shredded
  OR 1 medium carrot, cut into long, thin diagonals
  OR combination of any of these vegetables

Steam vegetables 1 to 2 minutes to heat but not so long they are limp. Remove from steamer.

2 Tbsp. vegetable oil
4 to 6 green onions, minced

Heat a wok over high heat. Add oil. Add green onions and vegetables. Fry 2 to 3 minutes until slightly browned.

4 cups cooked short grain brown rice

Add to vegetables 1 cup at a time. Mix well to remove lumps between each cup. Stir and fry 3 to 5 minutes to heat through.

1 Tbsp. soy sauce
2 Tbsp. stock [dashi]
½ tsp. honey
1 tsp. sea salt

Add to rice. Mix. Add seeds, nuts, egg sheets or age. Mix. Cook 1 to 2 minutes to heat. Serve hot with a main dish or by itself as a main dish. Good for lunch the next day with pickles.

CHA HAN SHOYU [CREAMY SOY FRIED RICE] [Serves 4 to 6]

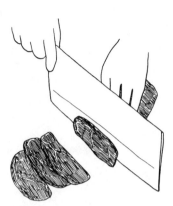

1 cup cooked leftover chicken
  cut into long, thin strips
  OR ½ breast chicken,
    cut into long, thin strips
  OR 1 cup roast beef
    or pork, cut into long, thin
    strips
  OR 1 cup duck,
    cut into long, thin strips
  OR 1 cup rabbit,
    cut into long, thin strips
  OR ¼ lb. small shrimp
2 Tbsp. vegetable oil

Heat a wok over high heat. Add oil and heat until a piece of chicken added sizzles. Add meat. Stir and fry 2 to 3 minutes until browned lightly. Remove from pan.

2 eggs,
  lightly beaten but not frothy
4 green onions,
  minced
2 Tbsp. vegetable oil

Heat a wok over medium heat. Add oil and heat until a small amount of egg added sets. Add eggs and onions. Scramble 1 to 2 minutes until partly congealed but still very moist.

¼ lb. snowpeas,
  each cut into 6 to 7 long,
  thin diagonals
  OR 1 cup frozen or fresh peas
  OR ¼ lb. green beans,
    cut into long, thin
    diagonals
  OR ¼ head green cabbage,
    shredded
  OR 1 medium carrot,
    cut into long, thin
    diagonals
  OR a combination of these
    vegetables

Steam vegetables 1 to 2 minutes to heat but not so long that they are limp. Remove from steamer.

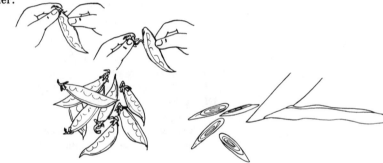

4 cups cooked short grain
  brown rice

Add rice and vegetables to egg mixture. Mix well. Cook 1 to 2 minutes.

1 Tbsp. soy sauce
2 Tbsp. stock
  [dashi or kombu]
¼ tsp. mild honey
1 tsp. sea salt

Add to rice along with meat. Mix. Cover. Cook over medium heat 3 to 5 minutes until eggs are all set. Serve as a main dish, one-pot meal, or with a main dish and pickels for a larger meal. Good cold for lunch the next day.

VEGETARIAN CHA HAN SHOYU [VEGETARIAN SOY FRIED RICE]
[Serves 4 to 6]

6 to 8 egg sheets

Egg sheets:
3 eggs
1 tsp. soy sauce
½ tsp. honey
2 tsp. kombu stock

Mix ingredients until well mixed but not frothy.

1 tsp. vegetable oil

Heat a medium sized cast iron skillet over medium heat. Brush with oil. Heat until a small bit of egg mixture added sets. Add 3 Tbsp. of egg mixture. Roll pan to evenly cover bottom of pan with egg mixture. Cook 1 to 2 minutes until edges of egg sheet are brown. Loosen edges with a knife and flip egg sheet. Cook 30 seconds to 1 minute on bottom side. Remove from pan. Brush pan with oil again. Repeat process until all egg mixture is used. Cut egg sheets in half and then cut halves into toothpick thin strips.

OR ½ to 1 cup sesame seeds
OR ½ to 1 cup sunflower seeds
OR ½ to 1 cup raw peanuts, chopped
OR 2 cakes age [deep fried bean curd], cut into long, thin strips

Roast in 300° oven 5 to 10 minutes until golden brown.

2 eggs,
lightly beaten but not frothy
4 green onions, minced
2 Tbsp. vegetable oil

Heat a wok over medium heat. Add oil and heat until a small amount of egg added sets. Add egg and onions. Scramble 1 to 2 minutes until partly congealed but still very moist.

¼ lb. snowpeas, each cut into 6 to 7 long thin diagonals
OR 1 cup frozen or fresh peas
OR ¼ lb. green beans, cut into long, thin diagonals
OR ¼ head green cabbage, shredded
OR 1 medium carrot, cut into long, thin diagonals
OR combination of any of these vegetables

Steam vegetables 1 to 2 minutes to heat but not so long they are limp. Remove from steamer.

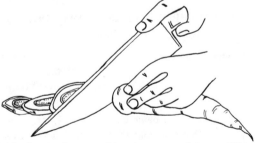

4 cups cooked short grain brown rice

Add rice and vegetables to egg mixture. Mix well. Cook 1 to 2 minutes.

1 Tbsp. soy sauce
2 Tbsp. stock [dashi or kombu]
½ tsp. mild honey
1 tsp. sea salt

Add to rice along with egg sheets, nuts, seeds or age. Mix. Cover. Cook over medium heat 3 to 5 minutes until eggs are set. Serve as a main dish, one-pot meal or with a main dish and pickles for a larger meal. Good cold for lunch the next day.

DOMBURI SOBORO [EGG, GROUND MEAT TOPPING FOR HOT RICE]
[Serves 4 to 6]

½ to 1 cup snowpeas, cut into long, thin diagonal slices
  OR ½ to 1 cup peas
  OR ½ to 1 cup green beans cut into long, thin diagonal slices
2 medium carrots, grated
3 to 4 green onions, cut into thin diagonals
5 to 6 large sprigs parsley, chopped
2 Tbsp. vegetable oil

Heat a medium sized cast iron skillet over medium high heat. Add oil. Heat until a piece of onion added sizzles. Add vegetables. Stir and fry 1 to 2 minutes just to heat.

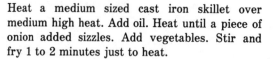

½ lb. ground meat [beef or pork or lamb]

Add meat to vegetables. Stir and fry 3 to 5 minutes until meat is no longer pink.

½ tsp. sea salt
4 Tbsp. soy sauce
1 Tbsp. mild honey
1 Tbsp. sake
  OR dry sherry
  OR rice vinegar
3 to 5 Tbsp. stock [dashi or mushroom]

Add to meat and vegetables. Cover and simmer over medium heat 2 to 3 minutes.

3 eggs, beaten until well mixed but not frothy

Add to meat and vegetables. Mix. Cover. Let sit 3 minutes. Remove lid. Stir like scrambled eggs. Do not mix too much. Cook 2 to 3 minutes until eggs are set.

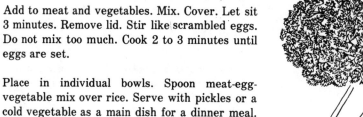

4 to 6 cups hot cooked short grain brown rice

Place in individual bowls. Spoon meat-egg-vegetable mix over rice. Serve with pickles or a cold vegetable as a main dish for a dinner meal. A good meal-in-a-bowl dish. Good cold for lunch the next day.

TOFU DOMBURI [BEAN CURD COOKED WITH VEGETABLES AND EGGS OVER RICE] [Serves 4 to 6]

2 cakes bean curd

Wrap tightly in muslin cloth. Place weight on top. Press 1 to 2 hours to remove most of liquid. Cut into ¼ x ½ inch pieces.

½ to 1 cup snowpeas, cut into long, thin diagonal slices
  OR ½ to 1 cup peas
  OR ½ to 1 cup green beans cut into long, thin diagonal slices
2 medium carrots, grated
3 to 4 green onions, cut into thin diagonals
5 to 6 large sprigs parsley, chopped
2 Tbsp. vegetable oil

Heat a medium sized cast iron skillet over medium high heat. Add oil. Heat until a piece of onion added sizzles. Add vegetables. Stir and fry 1 to 2 minutes just to heat. Add bean curd to vegetables. Mix gently. Cook 3 to 5 minutes until lightly browned.

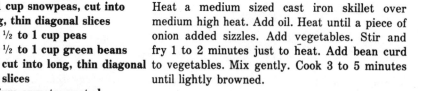

4 Tbsp soy sauce
1 Tbsp. mild honey
1 Tbsp. sake
  OR dry sherry
  OR rice vinegar
½ tsp. sea salt
3 Tbsp. stock [kombu]
	Add to bean curd and vegetables. Cover. Simmer over medium heat 3 to 5 minutes until bean curd is well flavored.

3 eggs, beaten until well mixed but not frothy	Add to bean curd and vegetables. Cover. Cook 3 minutes. Remove lid. Stir like scrambled eggs. Do not mix too much. Cook 3 to 5 minutes until eggs are set.
4 to 6 cups hot cooked short grain brown rice	Place in individual bowls. Spoon bean curd-egg-vegetable mix over rice. Serve with pickles or a cold vegetable as a main dish for a dinner meal. A good meal-in-a-bowl. Good cold for lunch the next day also.

OYAKO DOMBURI [RICE WITH EGG AND SAUCE TOPPING] [Serves 4 to 6]

½ chicken breast, cut into
  thin strips
1½ cups stock [dashi or chicken]
¼ cup soy sauce
1½ Tbsp. mild honey
¼ cup sake
  OR dry sherry
  OR rice vinegar
	Place in a saucepan. Bring to a boil over medium high heat. Stir chicken often so pieces do not stick together. Cook 3 to 5 minutes until chicken done.

2 to 4 large dried mushrooms ½ cup boiling water	Place mushrooms in a small bowl. Pour over boiling water. Place weight on top to keep under water. Let sit 15 to 30 minutes until mushrooms soft. Remove from water. Squeeze dry. Cut out tough stems. Reserve stock for other use. Cut each mushroom into 5 pieces.

8 to 16 slices fish cake [kamaboko]
3 green onions, cut into thin,
  diagonals
1 cup snowpeas, cut into three
  thin diagonals
  OR 1 carrot, cut into thin
    diagonals
  OR 1 cup peas
  OR 1 cup green beans, cut into
    thin diagonals
  OR 1 cup broccoli, cut into
    thin diagonals
½ lb. spinach, cut into 1 inch
  strips [optional]
	Add to stock along with mushrooms. Bring stock to a boil again. Let simmer 1 to 2 minutes until vegetables are heated.

5 eggs, beaten until well mixed but not frothy	Add to stock all at once. Cook 3 to 5 minutes until eggs are well congealed.
4 to 6 cups hot cooked short grain brown rice	Place in individual bowls. Spoon mixture with sauce over each bowl. Place cover on bowls and serve at once. Good meal-in-a-bowl. Can be accompanied by pickles or cold vegetables for a dinner meal. Good cold for lunch the next day also.

VARIATION:

Beef or pork can be used for chicken.

TOFU YASHI DOMBURI [RICE WITH BEAN CURD VEGETABLE EGG SAUCE TOPPING] [Serves 4 to 6]

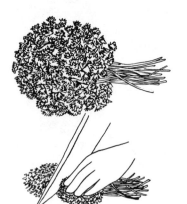

2 cakes bean curd

Wrap tightly in muslin cloth. Place a weight on it. Press 1 to 2 hours to remove most of liquid. Break up with a fork until well crumbled.

1 carrot,
  grated fine
2 to 4 green onions,
  cut into thin, diagonal pieces
5 to 6 sprigs parsley, chopped
  OR ½ cup packed watercress,
    chopped
10 to 12 snowpeas,
  each cut into three diagonal
  slices
    OR 10 to 12 green beans,
      cut into thin diagonals
    OR 1 cup broccoli,
      cut into thin diagonals
4 to 5 fresh mushrooms,
  sliced thin
2 Tbsp. vegetable oil

Heat a medium sized saucepan over medium high heat. Add oil. Heat until a piece of onion added sizzles. Add vegetables. Stir and fry 2 to 3 minutes until heated through but not limp.

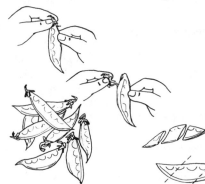

1½ cups stock
  [kombu or mushroom]
¼ cup soy sauce
1½ Tbsp. mild honey
¼ cup sake
  OR dry sherry
  OR rice vinegar

Add to vegetables along with bean curd. Bring to a boil.

5 eggs,
  beaten until well mixed but
  not frothy

Add to stock all at once. Cook 3 to 5 minutes until eggs are well congealed.

4 to 6 cups hot cooked short
  grain brown rice

Place in individual bowls. Spoon mixture with sauce over each bowl. Place cover on bowls and serve at once. Good meal-in-a-bowl. Can be accompanied with pickles or cold vegetable dish for a dinner meal. Good cold for lunch the next day also.

AGE DOMBURI [DEEP FRIED BEAN CURD, VEGETABLE AND EGG TOPPING FOR HOT RICE] [Serves 4 to 6]

4 large dried mushrooms
½ cup boiling water

Place mushrooms in a small bowl. Pour over boiling water. Place weight on top to keep under water. Let sit 15 to 30 minutes until mushrooms are soft. Remove from water. Squeeze dry. Cut out tough stems. Reserve stock for adding to kombu stock. Cut each mushroom into 5 pieces.

2 to 3 cakes age
[deep fried bean curd],
sliced thin
1 cup stock [kombu]
½ cup mushroom stock
¼ cup soy sauce
¼ cup sake
OR dry sherry
OR rice vinegar
1½ Tbsp. mild honey

Place in a saucepan with mushrooms. Bring to a boil over medium high heat. Simmer 3 to 5 minutes until age is tender.

2 to 4 green onions,
cut into thin, diagonals
4 to 6 sprigs parsley,
chopped
OR ¼ cup watercress,
chopped
10 to 12 snowpeas,
each cut into 3 diagonals
OR ½ cup peas
OR 10 to 12 green beans,
cut into long, thin diagonals
OR 1 carrot,
cut into thin diagonals
OR 1 cup broccoli,
cut into thin diagonals

Add to stock. Bring to a boil over medium high heat. Let simmer 1 to 2 minutes until vegetables are heated.

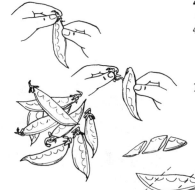

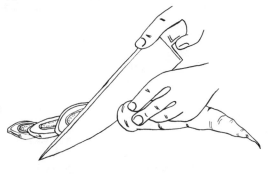

5 eggs,
beaten until well mixed but
not frothy

Add to stock all at once. Cook 3 to 5 minutes until eggs are well congealed.

4 to 6 cups hot cooked short
grain brown rice

Place in individual bowls. Spoon mixture with sauce over rice in each bowl. Place cover on bowls and serve at once. Good meal-in-a-bowl. Can be accompanied with pickles or cold vegetable dish for a dinner meal. Good cold next day for lunch.

TORI YASHI DOMBURI [RICE WITH EGG OMELETTE, CHICKEN AND VEGETABLE TOPPING]
[Serves 4 to 6]

6 to 8 fresh mushrooms,
 sliced thin
½ cup snowpeas,
 cut into thin diagonals
 OR ½ cup green beans,
 cut into thin diagonals
3 to 4 green onions,
 cut into thin diagonals
2 Tbsp. vegetable oil

Heat a cast iron skillet over medium high heat. Add oil. Heat until a small piece of onion added sizzles. Add vegetables. Stir and fry 1 to 2 minutes until heated.

½ chicken breast,
 cut into thin slices
 OR ¼ lb. turkey meat,
 cut into thin slices
 OR ¼ lb. duck,
 cut into thin slices
 OR ¼ lb. rabbit,
 cut into thin slices

Add to vegetables. Stir and fry 2 to 3 minutes until lightly browned.

½ cup stock
 [chicken, kombu or dashi]
3 Tbsp. sake
 OR dry sherry
1 Tbsp. mild honey
3 Tbsp. soy sauce
½ inch fresh ginger root,
 grated fine

Add to chicken and vegetables. Cook 5 to 10 minutes over medium heat until sauce is reduced by half.

5 eggs,
 beaten until well mixed but
 not frothy

Reduce heat to low. Slowly add eggs to sauce. Pour eggs so they cover all ingredients. Cover and cook 3 to 5 minutes until eggs set.

4 to 6 cups hot cooked
 short-grain brown rice

Place in individual bowls. Top with egg mixture and sauce.

Garnish:
4 green onions, chopped
 OR 4 to 6 large sprigs parsley,
 chopped
 OR ¼ cup watercress,
 chopped
 OR 4 leaves spinach, slivered
 OR 1 sheet nori seaweed,
 brushed with ¼ tsp. soy
 sauce and ½ tsp. sesame oil,
 grilled 1 minute under
 broiler until crisp, crumble

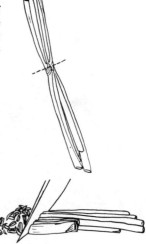

Sprinkle one of garnishes over rice and egg mixture. Serve hot. Good meal-in-a-bowl. Can be accompanied with pickles or cold vegetable dish for a larger dinner meal. Good cold next day for lunch.

AGE YASHI DOMBURI [DEEP FRIED BEAN CURD STRIPS, VEGETABLES AND EGG TOPPING FOR RICE]
[Serves 4 to 6]

6 to 8 fresh mushrooms,
   sliced thin
½ cup snowpeas,
   cut into thin diagonal slices
   OR ½ cup green beans,
      cut into thin diagonal slices
3 to 4 green onions,
   cut into thin diagonal slices
2 Tbsp. vegetable oil

Heat a cast iron skillet over medium high heat. Add oil. Heat until a small piece of onion added sizzles. Add vegetables. Stir and fry 1 to 2 minutes until heated.

2 cakes age
   [deep fried bean curd],
   cut into thin slivers

Add to vegetables. Stir and fry 1 to 2 minutes to heat.

½ cup stock
   [kombu or mushroom]
3 Tbsp. sake
   OR dry sherry
1 Tbsp. mild honey
3 Tbsp. soy sauce
½ inch fresh ginger root,
   grated fine

Add to age and vegetables. Cook 5 to 10 minutes over medium high heat until sauce is reduced by half.

5 eggs,
   beaten until well mixed but
   not frothy

Reduce heat to low. Slowly add eggs to sauce. Pour eggs so they cover all ingredients. Cover and cook 3 to 5 minutes until eggs set.

4 to 6 cups hot cooked
   short-grain brown rice

Place in individual bowls. Top with egg mixture and sauce.

Garnish:
4 green onions, chopped
   OR ¼ cup watercress, chopped
   OR 4 to 6 large sprigs parsley,
      chopped
   OR 4 leaves spinach, slivered
   OR 1 sheet nori seaweed,
      brushed with ¼ tsp. soy
      sauce and ½ tsp. sesame oil,
      grilled 1 minute under
      broiler until crisp, crumble

Sprinkle one of garnishes over rice and egg mixture. Serve hot. Good meal-in-a-bowl. Can be accompanied with pickles or cold vegetable dish for a larger dinner meal. Good cold next day for lunch.

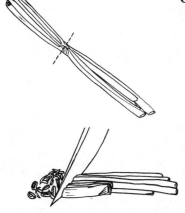

GROUND MEAT AND PEA DOMBURI [GROUND MEAT AND PEA EGG TOPPING FOR HOT RICE] [Serves 4 to 6]

4 to 6 green onions,
  cut into thin diagonals
2 Tbsp. vegetable oil

Heat a cast iron skillet over medium high heat. Add oil. Heat until a small piece of onion added sizzles. Stir and fry 1 minute.

1 cup snowpeas,
  cut into thin diagonals
  OR 1 cup frozen peas
  OR 1 cup green beans,
    cut into thin diagonals

Add to onions. Stir and fry 1 minute until peas are hot.

½ lb. ground meat
  [beef, pork or lamb]

Add to onions and peas. Stir and fry 2 to 3 minutes until meat no longer pink.

½ cup stock [beef, chicken,
  kombu or dashi]
3 Tbsp. sake
  OR dry sherry
1 Tbsp. mild honey
3 Tbsp. soy sauce

Add to meat and peas. Cook 5 to 10 minutes until sauce is reduced by half.

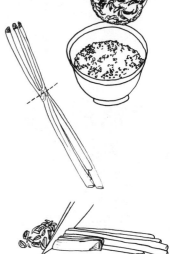

5 eggs,
  beaten until well mixed but
  not frothy

Reduce heat to low and slowly add eggs to sauce. Pour eggs so they cover all ingredients. Cover and cook 3 to 5 minutes until eggs set.

4 to 6 cups hot cooked
  short grain brown rice

Place in individual bowls. Top with egg-meat mixture.

Garnishes:
4 green onions, chopped
  OR ¼ cup watercress, chopped
  OR 4 to 6 large sprigs parsley,
  OR 4 leaves spinach, slivered
  OR 1 sheet nori seaweed,
    brushed with ¼ tsp. soy
    sauce and ½ tsp. sesame oil,
    grilled 1 minute under
    broiler until crisp, crumble

Sprinkle one of garnishes over rice and egg mixture. Serve hot. Good meal-in-a-bowl. Can be accompanied with pickles or cold vegetable dish for a larger dinner meal. Good cold next day for lunch.

TOFU YASHI DOMBURI [BEAN CURD, VEGETABLE AND EGG TOPPING FOR HOT RICE] [Serves 4 to 6]

2 cakes bean curd

Wrap tightly in muslin cloth. Place a weight on it. Press 1 to 2 hours to remove most of liquid. Crumble with a fork. Set aside to add later.

4 to 6 green onions,
  cut into thin, diagonals
2 Tbsp. vegetable oil

Heat a cast iron skillet over medium high heat. Add oil. Heat until a small piece of onion added sizzles. Stir and fry 1 minute.

1 cup snowpeas,
  cut into thin diagonals
  OR 1 cup peas
  OR 1 cup green beans,
    cut into thin diagonals

Add to onions. Stir and fry 1 minute until peas are hot.

1 Tbsp. sesame oil

Add to vegetables. Heat. Add crumbled bean curd (tofu). Stir and fry 2 to 3 minutes until lightly browned.

½ cup stock [kombu]	Add to bean curd and peas. Cook 5 to 10 minutes until sauce is reduced by half.
3 Tbsp. sake OR dry sherry	
1 Tbsp. mild honey	
3 Tbsp. soy sauce	
5 eggs, beaten until well mixed but not frothy	Reduce heat to low. Slowly add eggs to sauce. Pour eggs so they cover all ingredients. Cover and cook 3 to 5 minutes until eggs set.
4 to 6 cups hot cooked short-grain brown rice	Place in individual bowls. Top with egg-meat mixture.

Garnishes:
4 green onions, chopped
  OR 4 to 6 large sprigs parsley, chopped
  OR 4 leaves spinach, slivered
  OR 1 sheet nori seaweed, brushed with ¼ tsp. soy sauce and ½ tsp. sesame oil, grilled 1 minute under broiler until crisp, crumble

Sprinkle one of garnishes over rice and egg mixture. Serve hot. Good meal-in-a-bowl. Can be accompanied with pickles or cold vegetable dish for a larger dinner meal. Good cold next day for lunch.

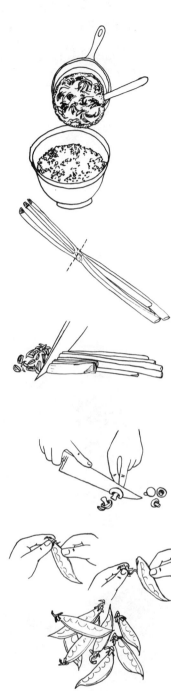

MEAT STRIPS WITH CARROT DOMBURI [MEAT STRIPS, CARROTS AND EGG TOPPING FOR HOT RICE] [Serves 4 to 6]

6 to 8 fresh mushrooms, sliced thin	Heat a cast iron skillet over medium high heat. Add oil. Heat until a small piece of carrot added sizzles. Add vegetables and garlic. Stir and fry 1 to 2 minutes until heated.
½ cup snowpeas, cut into thin diagonals	
½ small carrot, grated fine	
1 clove garlic, grated	
2 Tbsp. vegetable oil	
6 oz. boneless meat [pork, beef lamb], cut into thin strips	Add to vegetables. Stir and fry 2 to 3 minutes until meat is no longer pink but not brown.
½ cup stock [chicken, kombu, beef or dashi]	Add to meat and peas. Cook 5 to 10 minutes until sauce is reduced by half.
3 Tbsp. sake OR dry sherry	
1 Tbsp. mild honey	
3 Tbsp. soy sauce	
5 eggs, beaten until well mixed but not frothy	Reduce heat to low. Slowly add eggs to sauce. Pour eggs so they cover all ingredients. Cover and cook 3 to 5 minutes until eggs set.
4 to 6 cups hot cooked short grain brown rice	Place in individual bowls. Top with egg mixture and sauce.

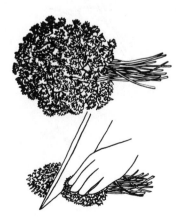

Garnishes:
4 green onions, chopped
  OR ¼ cup watercress, chopped
  OR 4 to 6 large sprigs parsley, chopped
  OR 4 leaves spinach, slivered
  OR 1 sheet nori seaweed, brushed with ¼ tsp. soy sauce and ½ tsp. sesame oil, grilled 1 minute under broiler until crisp, crumble

Sprinkle one of garnishes over rice and egg mixture. Serve hot. Good meal-in-a-bowl. Can be accompanied with pickles or cold vegetable dish for a larger dinner meal. Good cold next day for lunch.

SHELLFISH YASHI DOMBURI [SHELLFISH, VEGETABLE AND EGG FOR HOT RICE]
[Serves 4 to 6]

1 cup snowpeas,
  cut into long diagonals
  OR 1 cup peas
  OR 1 cup green beans,
    cut into long, thin diagonals
4 to 6 green onions,
  cut into thin diagonals
2 Tbsp. vegetable oil

Heat a cast iron skillet over medium high heat. Add oil. Heat until a small piece of onion added sizzles. Add onion and peas. Stir and fry 1 to 2 minutes until heated.

½ cup stock [dashi]
3 Tbsp. sake
  OR dry sherry
½ Tbsp. mild honey
1 tsp. soy sauce
½ tsp. sea salt

Add to vegetables. Cook 5 to 10 minutes over medium heat until sauce is reduced by half.

¼ lb. crab meat
  OR ¼ lb. small shrimp
  OR ¼ lb. small clams

Add to vegetables and sauce. Stir and fry only 30 seconds to 1 minute. Just enough to heat.

5 eggs,
  beaten until well mixed but not frothy

Reduce heat to low. Slowly add eggs to sauce. Pour eggs so they cover all ingredients. Cover and cook 3 to 5 minutes until eggs set.

4 to 6 cups hot cooked
  short-grain brown rice

Place in individual bowls. Top with egg mixture and sauce.

Garnish:
4 green onions, chopped
  OR ¼ cup watercress, chopped
  OR 4 to 6 large sprigs parsley,
    chopped
  OR 4 leaves spinach, slivered
  OR 1 sheet nori seaweed,
    brushed with ¼ tsp. soy
    sauce and ½ tsp. sesame oil,
    grilled 1 minute under
    broiler until crisp, crumble

Sprinkle one of garnishes over rice and egg mixture. Serve hot. Good meal-in-a-bowl. Can be accompanied with pickles or cold vegetable dish for a larger dinner meal. Good cold next day for lunch.

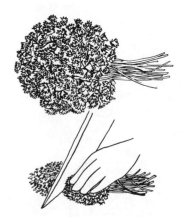

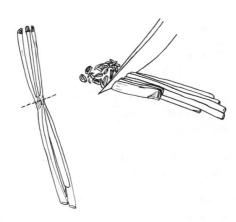

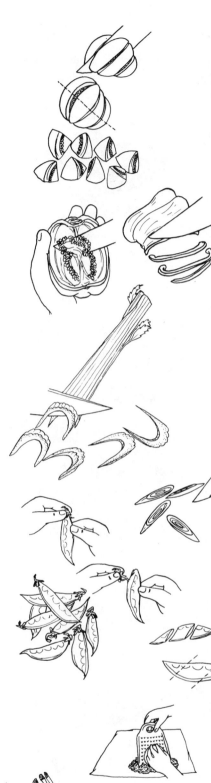

HIYA-MUGI [COLD NOODLES WITH SAUCE AND VEGETABLES]
[Serves 4 to 6]

1 lb. thin whole-wheat vermicelli
  OR 1 lb. spinach vermicelli
  OR 1 lb. tomato vermicelli
  OR 1 lb. soy vermicelli
6 cups boiling water
½ tsp. sea salt

Bring water to a boil in a large saucepan over high heat. Add noodles. Bring to boil. To prevent noodles from boiling over have cup of cold water handy and add a few tsp. of cold water if pot looks like it is going to boil over. Add salt. Reduce heat to medium. Cook 8 to 10 minutes until noodles are just tender but not soft. Drain. Rinse well in cold water. Place in a shallow bowl. Cover. Chill 2 to 3 hours.

2 tomatoes, cut into 8 wedges, then wedges cut in half
  OR 1 green pepper, seeded and cut into ¼ inch thin rounds
  OR 1 stalk celery, cut into paper thin diagonals
  OR 12 to 16 snowpeas, each cut into 3 diagonals

Steam 1 minute. Chill.

  OR 1 stalk broccoli, cut into long, thin diagonals

Steam 2 to 3 minutes. Chill.

  OR 12 to 16 green beans, cut into long, thin diagonals

Steam 2 to 3 minutes. Chill.

  OR ½ lb. asparagus, tough ends broken off, cut into long, thin diagonals

Steam 2 to 3 minutes. Chill.

Assembly:

Place noodles in 4 to 6 individual bowls. Place one of above vegetables in bowl with noodles.

Sauces:

I

1½ cups stock [dashi or kombu]
⅓ cup soy sauce
3 Tbsp. sake
  OR dry sherry
  OR rice vinegar
2 tsp. mild honey

Place in a saucepan. Bring to a boil over high heat. Reduce heat to medium and simmer 2 to 3 minutes.

II

¾ cup stock [dashi or kombu]
2 tsp. soy sauce
1 tsp. mild honey

Place in a saucepan. Bring to boil over high heat. Remove from heat.

½ daikon radish, grated
2 green onions, minced
1 sheet nori seaweed, brushed with ¼ tsp. sesame oil and ½ tsp. soy sauce, grilled 1 minute under broiler until crisp, crumble

Add to soy sauce and stock. Mix. Chill 2 to 3 hours until very cold. Dip vegetables and noodles into sauce as you are eating them. This is an excellent lunch on a hot day served along with a cold leftover main dish like deep-fried ginger chicken (tatsuta-age) or good served as a side dish for a main meal like tempura.

HIYASHI-SOBA [COLD NOODLES WITH MUSHROOMS, EGG STRIPS, CUCUMBERS AND CHICKEN]
[Serves 4 to 6]

½ lb. Japanese buckwheat
   noodles
   OR ½ lb. whole-wheat noodles
3 cups boiling water
½ tsp. sea salt

Bring water to a boil in a large saucepan over high heat. Add noodles. Bring to a boil. To prevent noodles from boiling over have a cup of cold water handy and add a few tsp. of cold water if pot looks like it is going to boil over. Add salt. Reduce heat to medium. Cook 8 to 10 minutes until noodles are just tender but not soft. Drain. Rinse well in cold water. Place in a shallow bowl.

1 chicken breast
   [optional step]
1 Tbsp. sake
   OR dry sherry
   OR rice vinegar
½ tsp. sea salt

Rub chicken breast with salt. Prick with a meat fork until well pierced with tiny holes. Sprinkle with sake. Soak 30 minutes to 1 hour. Place in a steamer. Steam 10 to 15 minutes until white all through but still moist. Chill 1 to 2 hours. With a very sharp knife slice paper thin.

Sauce:
¼ cup rice vinegar
   OR sake
   OR dry sherry
¼ cup soy sauce
¼ cup stock
   [dashi or kombu]
1 tsp. mild honey

Place in a small saucepan. Heat over medium heat 3 to 5 minutes. Pour over noodles. Chill 2 to 3 hours until very cold.

3 to 4 dried mushrooms
½ cup boiling water
   OR 4 fresh mushrooms,
     sliced paper thin

Place mushrooms in a small bowl. Pour boiling water over them. Place a weight on top to keep under water. Let sit 15 to 30 minutes until mushrooms are soft. Remove from water. Squeeze dry. Reserve stock. Cut out tough stems. Cut into paper-thin slices.

2 Tbsp. stock
2 tsp. soy sauce
2 tsp. mild honey
   [dashi or kombu]

Place in a saucepan. Add mushrooms. Bring to a boil over medium heat. Simmer 1 to 3 minutes. Remove from heat. Drain mushrooms. Chill.

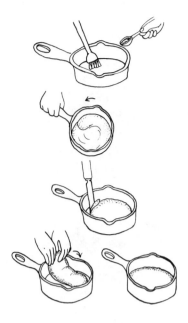

Sweet egg strips:

2 eggs,
   beaten until well mixed but
   not frothy
½ tsp. mild honey
¼ tsp. soy sauce
¼ tsp. sake
   OR dry sherry
   OR rice vinegar
¼ tsp. sea salt
1 tsp. kombu stock

Mix ingredients until well mixed but not frothy.

1 tsp. vegetable oil

Heat a medium sized cast iron skillet over medium heat. Brush with oil. Heat until a small bit of egg mixture added sets. Add 3 Tbsp. of egg mixture. Roll pan with egg mixture. Cook 1 to 2 minutes until edges of egg sheet are brown. Loosen edges with a knife and flip egg sheet. Cook 30 seconds to 1 minute on bottom side. Remove from pan. Brush pan with oil again. Repeat process until all egg mixture is used. Cut egg sheets in half and then cut halves into toothpick-thin strips.

1 cucumber,
   sliced paper thin

Arrange cucumbers with noodles, chicken breast, mushrooms, and egg sheets on a platter. Chill 1 hour or until cold. Good as a main dish on a hot summer day. Makes an excellent lunch. Can be served as a side dish for a main meal or a main dish with a hot soup or vegetables and pickles.

HIYA SOMEN [COLD NOODLES WITH SAUCE] [Serves 4 to 6]

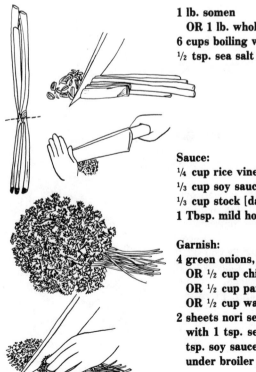

1 lb. somen
   OR 1 lb. whole-wheat vermicelli
6 cups boiling water
½ tsp. sea salt

Bring water to a boil in a large saucepan over high heat. Add noodles. Bring to a boil. To prevent noodles from boiling over have a cup of cold water handy and add a few tsp. of cold water if pot looks like it is going to boil over. Add salt. Reduce heat to medium. Cook 8 to 10 minutes until noodles are just tender but not soft. Drain. Rinse well in cold water. Place in a shallow bowl. Cover. Chill 2 to 3 hours. OR: If cold day keep noodles hot - do not chill.

Sauce:
¼ cup rice vinegar
⅓ cup soy sauce
⅓ cup stock [dashi or kombu]
1 Tbsp. mild honey

Place in a saucepan. Bring to boil over high heat. Immediately remove from heat. Chill 2 to 3 hours until ice cold. OR: If cold day in winter pour hot sauce over noodles and serve hot.

Garnish:
4 green onions, minced
   OR ½ cup chives, minced
   OR ½ cup parsley, minced
   OR ½ cup watercress, minced
2 sheets nori seaweed, brushed
   with 1 tsp. sesame oil and ½
   tsp. soy sauce, grilled 1 minute
   under broiler until crisp, crumble

Place green onions or other sharp green in one small sauce bowl and toasted seaweed in another. Serve with noodles. Place noodles in individual serving dishes. Each person tops noodles with amount of green and seaweed that they want. Good served with leftover main dish for a lunch or as a side dish for a main meal.

369

HIYA SOBA [COLD NOODLES WITH SAUCE] [Serves 4 to 6]

1 lb. soba noodles
  OR 1 lb. whole-wheat vermicelli
6 cups boiling water
½ tsp. sea salt

Bring water to a boil in a large saucepan over high heat. Add noodles. Bring to a boil. To prevent noodles from boiling over have a cup of cold water handy and add a few tsp. of cold water if pot looks like it is going to boil over. Add salt. Reduce heat to medium. Cook 8 to 10 minutes until noodles are just tender but not soft. Drain. Rinse well in cold water. Place in a shallow bowl. Cover. Chill 2 to 3 hours.

Sauce:
½ cup stock [dashi or kombu]
1 Tbsp. sake
  OR dry sherry
  OR rice vinegar
1½ tsp. honey
1 Tbsp. soy sauce

Place in a saucepan. Heat over medium heat until honey is melted and alcohol is evaporated. Cook 2 to 5 minutes but do not bring to a boil. Remove from heat. Chill 2 to 3 hours until cold. Pour over noodles. Mix gently. Cover. Chill 1 hour.

1 Tbsp. Japanese horseradish powder [washabi]
3 Tbsp. hot stock [dashi or kombu]

Add stock slowly to horseradish powder. Mix well. Let sit for 1 hour. Place in a small sauce bowl to serve with noodles as a dipping sauce.

Garnish:
4 green onions, minced
  OR ½ cup chives, minced
  OR ½ cup parsley, minced
  OR ½ cup watercress, minced
2 sheets nori seaweed, brushed with 1 tsp. sesame oil and ½ tsp. soy sauce, grilled 1 minute under broiler until crisp, crumble

Place green onions or other sharp green in one small sauce bowl and toasted seaweed in another. Serve with noodles. Place noodles in individual serving dishes. Each person tops noodles with amount of green and seaweed that they want. Good served with leftover main dish for a lunch or as a side dish for a main meal.

GOSHIKI SOMEN [MIXED NOODLES WITH MUSHROOMS, SWEET EGG STRIPS AND GREEN ONION]
[Serves 4 to 6]

¼ lb. whole-wheat vermicelli
  OR whole-wheat spaghetti
¼ lb. whole-wheat tomato vermicelli
¼ lb. whole-wheat egg vermicelli
¼ lb. soy vermicelli
¼ lb. whole-wheat spinach vermicelli
  OR IN PLACE OF ABOVE:
  1¼ lb. any above vermicelli
6 cups boiling water
½ tsp. sea salt

Bring water to a boil in a large saucepan over high heat. Add noodles. Bring to a boil. To prevent noodles from boiling over have cup of cold water handy and add a few tsp. of cold water if pot looks like it is going to boil over. Add salt. Reduce heat to medium. Cook 8 to 10 minutes until noodles are just tender but not soft. Drain. Rinse well in cold water. Place in a shallow bowl. Cover. Chill 2 to 3 hours.

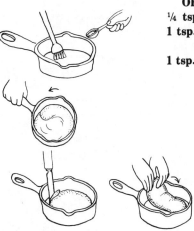

3 to 4 dried mushrooms
½ cup boiling water
   OR 4 fresh mushrooms,
     sliced paper thin

Place dried mushrooms in a small bowl. Pour boiling water over them. Place a weight on top to keep under water. Let sit 15 to 30 minutes until mushrooms are soft. Remove from water. Squeeze dry. Reserve stock. Cut out tough stems. Cut into paper thin slices.

2 Tbsp. stock [dashi or kombu]
2 tsp. soy sauce
2 tsp. mild honey

Place in a saucepan. Add mushrooms. Bring to a boil over medium heat. Simmer 1 to 2 minutes. Drain mushrooms. Chill. Remove from heat.

Sweet egg strips:
2 eggs, beaten until well mixed
  but not frothy
½ tsp. mild honey
¼ tsp. soy sauce
¼ tsp. sake
  OR dry sherry
  OR rice vinegar
¼ tsp. sea salt
1 tsp. kombu stock

Mix ingredients until well mixed but not frothy.

1 tsp. vegetable oil

Heat a medium sized cast iron skillet over medium heat. Brush with oil. Heat until a small bit of egg mixture added sets. Add 3 Tbsp. of egg mixture. Roll pan to evenly cover bottom of pan with egg mixture. Cook 1 to 2 minutes until edges of egg sheet are brown. Loosen edges with a knife and flip egg sheet. Cook 30 seconds to 1 minute on bottom side. Remove from pan. Brush pan with oil again. Repeat process until all egg mixture is used. Cut egg sheets in half and then cut halves into toothpick thin strips.

4 green onions,
  cut into thin diagonals

Arrange noodles in a bowl with mushrooms, egg sheets and green onions.

Sauces:

I

1½ cups stock [dashi or kombu]
⅓ cup soy sauce
3 Tbsp. sake
  OR dry sherry
  OR rice vinegar
2 tsp. mild honey

Place in a saucepan. Bring to a boil over high heat. Reduce heat to medium and simmer 2 to 3 minutes. Chill 2 to 3 hours until very cold. Dip vegetables and noodles in sauce as you are eating them. This is an excellent lunch on a hot day or served as a side dish for a main meal. Very colorful dish with many colored noodles.

II

¾ cup stock [dashi or kombu]
2 tsp. soy sauce
1 tsp. mild honey

Place in a saucepan. Bring to boil over high heat. Remove from heat.

½ daikon radish, grated
2 green onions, minced
1 sheet nori seaweed, brushed
  with ¼ tsp. sesame oil and
  ½ tsp. soy sauce, grilled
  1 minute under broiler until
crisp, crumble

Add to soy sauce and stock. Mix. Chill 2 to 3 hours until very cold. Dip vegetables and noodles into sauce as you are eating them. This is an excellent lunch on a hot day or served as a main dish for a dinner meal along with a hot soup or vegetable dish. Very colorful dish with many colored noodles.

KAKE UDON [HOT NOODLES IN BROTH WITH GREEN ONIONS, SEAWEED AND TEMPURA BITS]
[Serves 4 to 6]

1 lb. udon
OR 1 lb. whole-wheat noodles
OR 1 lb. whole-wheat spaghetti
6 cups boiling water
½ tsp. sea salt

Bring water to a boil in a large saucepan over high heat. Add noodles. Bring to a boil. To prevent noodles from boiling over have a cup of cold water handy and add a few tsp. of cold water is pot looks like it is going to boil over. Reduce heat to medium. Add salt. Cook 8 to 10 minutes until noodles are just tender but not soft. Drain. Rinse in hot water.

Stock:
4 cups stock
[dashi or kombu]
4 Tbsp. soy sauce
2 tsp. mild honey

Place in a saucepan. Bring to a boil over medium heat. Simmer 2 to 3 minutes. Add noodles.

2 to 3 dried mushrooms
½ cup boiling water
OR 4 fresh mushrooms,
cut into thin slices

Place mushrooms in a small bowl. Pour boiling water over them. Place a weight on top to keep under water. Let sit 15 to 20 minutes until mushrooms are soft. Remove from water. Squeeze dry. Reserve stock. Cut out tough stems. Cut into thin strips. Place in saucepan along with noodles and stock.

3 to 4 green onions,
cut into thin, diagonal slices
2 sheets nori seaweed,
brushed with 1 tsp. sesame
oil and ½ tsp. soy sauce,
grilled 1 minute under broiler
until crisp, crumble
½ to 1 cup tenkasu
[leftover tempura batter bits]

Add to noodles and stock. Simmer 2 to 3 minutes. Serve hot for lunch or as a side dish for a main meal along with a vegetarian main dish or meat main dish and a pickle.

OKAME SOBA [HOT NOODLES IN BROTH WITH VARIOUS INGREDIENTS]
[Serves 4 to 6]

1 lb. soba noodles
OR whole-wheat vermicelli
OR tomato vermicelli
OR spinach vermicelli
OR soy vermicelli
6 cups boiling water
½ tsp. sea salt

Bring water to a boil in a large saucepan over high heat. Add noodles. Bring to a boil. To prevent noodles from boiling over have a cup of cold water handy and add a few tsp. of cold water if pot looks like it is going to boil over. Reduce heat to medium. Add salt. Cook 8 to 10 minutes until noodles are just tender but not soft. Drain. Rinse in hot water.

Stock:
4 cups stock [dashi or kombu]
4 Tbsp. soy sauce
2 tsp. mild honey

Place in a saucepan. Bring to a boil over medium heat. Simmer 2 to 3 minutes. Add noodles.

2 to 3 dried mushrooms
½ cup boiling water
**   OR 4 fresh mushrooms,**
**   cut into thin slices**

Place mushrooms in a small bowl. Pour boiling water over them. Place a weight on top to keep under water. Let sit 15 to 20 minutes until mushrooms are soft. Remove from water. Squeeze dry. Reserve stock. Cut out tough stems. Cut into thin strips. Place in saucepan along with noodles and stock.

Other ingredients that may be added to stock:
8 to 16 slices kamaboko fish
**   cake**
**   OR ¼ lb. fish,**
**   cut into thin strips**
**   OR ¼ lb. fresh cooked shrimp**
**   OR ½ chicken breast,**
**   cut into thin strips**
**   OR ¼ lb. meat [beef or pork],**
**   cut into thin strips**
**   OR 2 to 3 hard boiled eggs,**
**   cut into ¼ inch slices**
2 bamboo shoots, sliced thin
4 large spinach leaves,
**   cut into 1 inch strips**
**   OR swiss chard leaves,**
**   cut into 1 inch strips**
**   OR ½ cup watercress**
**   coarsely chopped**
**   OR ½ cup parsley,**
**   coarsely chopped**
**   OR 4 large leaves any cooking**
**   green, cut into 2 inch strips**
**   OR 1 stalk broccoli,**
**   cut into thin diagonals**
**   OR 1 to 2 carrots,**
**   cut into thin diagonal slices**
**   OR ¼ head cauliflower,**
**   broken into small flowerlets**
**   OR 6 asparagus, tough**
**   ends broken off, cut into**
**   thin diagonals**

Add one protein food such as fish cake, fish or eggs to stock along with a selection of vegetables. Heat 3 to 5 minutes until greens are just tender. Good as a lunch or as a main dish for a dinner meal served along with a hot vegetable and pickles.

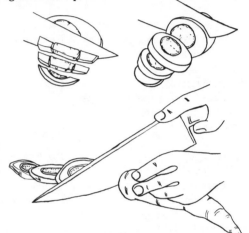

Steam 2 to 3 mintues until just tender.

Steam 2 to 3 minutes until just tender.

Steam 2 to 3 minutes until just tender.

Steam 2 to 3 minutes until just tender.

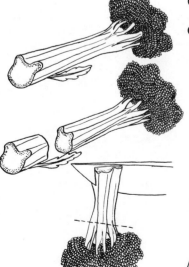

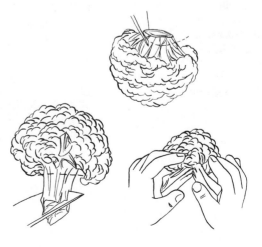

TORI NO KAKI UDON [HOT NOODLES WITH CHICKEN, AGE, DAIKON AND VEGETABLES WITH SAUCE]
[Serves 4 to 6]

1 lb. udon noodles
  OR 1 lb. whole-wheat spaghetti
  OR 1 lb. whole-wheat noodles
6 cups water
½ tsp. sea salt

Bring water to a boil in a large saucepan over high heat. Add noodles. Bring to a boil. To prevent noodles from boiling over have a cup of cold water handy and add a few tsp. of cold water if pot looks like it is going to boil over. Reduce heat to medium. Add salt. Cook 8 to 10 minutes until noodles are just tender but not soft. Drain. Rinse in hot water.

2 thighs and legs from 1 chicken
  OR 2 thighs and legs from
    1 rabbit
  OR 2 thighs and legs from
    1 duck
  OR 1 turkey leg and thigh
5 cups water

Place in a saucepan. Bring to a boil over high heat. Reduce heat to medium and cover. Simmer 45 to 50 minutes until meat very tender. Remove from heat. Reserve stock for later use. Remove meat from bones and cut into bite sized pieces.

⅓ large daikon, cut into half
  lengthwise, then into ½ inch
  half circles

Steam 10 to 15 minutes until just tender. Remove from heat.

½ pint oysters,
  drained and washed
  OR ½ lb. oysters,
    shucked and washed

Set aside to use later.

4 cakes age
  [deep fried bean curd] cut
  in thirds
¾ cup dashi
1 Tbsp. soy sauce
1 tsp. mild honey

Place in a saucepan. Bring to a boil over high heat. Reduce heat to medium and simmer 10 to 15 minutes until age is softened. Drain. Set aside for later use.

¼ cup celery leaves
  OR peppercress leaves
  OR watercress

Set aside to add later.

5 cups stock
  [chicken stock from cooking
  chicken legs plus kombu stock
  to make up difference]
¼ cup soy sauce
2 Tbsp. sake
  OR dry sherry
  OR rice vinegar
1 Tbsp. mild honey
½ tsp. sea salt

Place ingredients in a large saucepan. Bring to a boil over high heat. Reduce heat to medium. Add all other ingredients, i.e., noodles, chicken, daikon, oysters, age and green leaves. Arrange in an attractive manner. Heat 4 to 5 minutes. Serve hot.

juice of 2 lemons

Served with ingredients to dip in as eaten. A good meal-in-a-bowl, this hearty stew is an excellent winter meal. Also good heated for lunch the next day.

CURRIED UDON [NOODLES IN CURRY SAUCE] [Serves 4 to 6]

1 lb. whole-wheat spaghetti
  OR 1 lb. whole-wheat noodles
  OR 1 lb. udon noodles
6 cups boiling water
¼ tsp. sea salt

Bring water to a boil in a large saucepan over high heat. Add noodles. Bring to a boil. To prevent noodles from boiling over have a cup of cold water handy and add a few tsp. of cold water if pot looks like it is going to boil over. Reduce heat to medium. Add salt. Cook 8 to 10 minutes until noodles are just tender but not soft. Drain. Rinse in hot water. Place noodles on large platter.

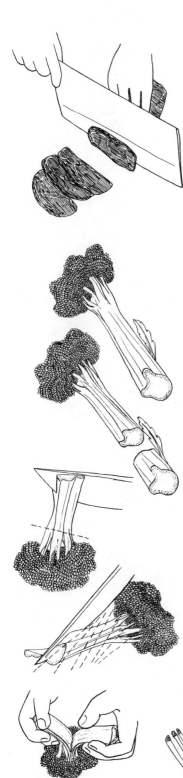

½ lb. meat [pork, beef, chicken, turkey, duck or rabbit] sliced thin
  OR ½ lb. shellfish
  OR ½ lb. fish, sliced thin
  OR ½ lb. ground meat
½ large yellow onion, minced
2 Tbsp. vegetable oil

Heat a heavy cast iron skillet over high heat. Add oil and heat until a piece of meat added sizzles. Add onions and meat. Stir and fry 3 to 5 minutes until lightly browned.

1 large carrot
  cut into thin diagonals
  OR ¼ lb. beans, cut into thin diagonals
  OR 1 stalk broccoli, cut into thin diagonals with heads broken into small pieces
  OR 1 cup peas

Steam 2 to 3 minutes. Add to meat and onions. Stir and fry 1 to 2 minutes to heat.

3 cups stock
  [chicken, dashi, kombu]
2 tsp. mild honey
1 Tbsp. soy sauce
1 to 2 tsp. garam masala [see Indian Special Ingredients]
½ tsp. Japanese horseradish powder [washabi powder]

Mix ingredients well. Add to meat. Cover. Reduce heat to medium and simmer 5 minutes until meat tender.

1½ Tbsp. arrowroot starch
4 Tbsp. water

Mix starch well. Add to sauce. Mix well. Cook 1 to 2 minutes until sauce thickens. Pour sauce over noodles on platter.

Garnish:
4 green onions, chopped
  OR 4 to 6 large sprigs parsley, chopped
  OR ¼ cup watercress, chopped
  OR 4 spinach leaves, slivered
  OR 1 sheet nori seaweed brushed with ¼ tsp. soy sauce and ½ tsp. sesame oil, grilled 1 minute under broiler until crisp, crumble

Sprinkle one of garnishes over platter of curried udon. Serve at once. A good meal-in-a-bowl. Good cold for lunch the next day.

KITSUNE-UDON [SIMMERED DEEP FRIED BEAN CURD WITH NOODLES IN SAUCE] [Serves 4 to 6]

1 lb. udon
  OR 1 lb. whole-wheat noodles
  OR 1 lb. whole-wheat spaghetti
6 cups boiling water
½ tsp. sea salt

Bring water to a boil in a large saucepan over high heat. Add noodles. Bring to a boil. To prevent noodles from boiling over have a cup of cold water handy and add a few tsp. of cold water if pot looks like it is going to boil over. Reduce heat to medium. Add salt. Cook 8 to 10 minutes until noodles are just tender but not soft. Drain. Rinse in hot water.

Stock:
4 cups stock [dashi or kombu]
4 Tbsp. soy sauce
2 tsp. mild honey

Place in a saucepan. Bring to a boil over medium heat. Simmer 2 to 3 minutes. Add noodles.

4 to 6 cakes age
  [deep fried bean curd]
2 Tbsp. soy sauce
½ cup stock [dashi or kombu]
1½ Tbsp. mild honey

Place in a saucepan. Bring to a boil over medium heat. Simmer 10 to 15 minutes until age is tender. Drain. Cut age in half.

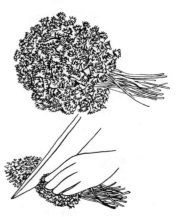

Garnish:
4 green onions,
  cut into long, thin diagonals
  OR ½ cup watercress, chopped
  OR ½ cup parsley, chopped
2 sheets nori seaweed, brushed
  with ½ tsp. sesame oil and
  ¼ tsp. soy sauce, grilled
  1 minute under broiler until
  crisp, crumble

Place noodles in individual serving bowls. Top with simmered age and one of the garnishes. Serve hot as a vegetarian main dish along with a hot vegetable and pickle. Makes a good lunch dish served with a pickle.

AGE UDON [FRIED NOODLES] [Serves 4 to 6]

1 lb. whole-wheat noodles
  OR 1 lb. whole-wheat spaghetti
  OR 1 lb. udon noodles
6 cups boiling water
½ tsp. sea salt

  OR IN PLACE OF ABOVE:
  4 cups leftover cooked noodles

Bring water to a boil in a large saucepan over high heat. Add noodles. Bring to a boil. To prevent noodles from boiling over have a cup of cold water handy and add a few tsp. of cold water if pot looks like it is going to boil over. Reduce heat to medium. Add salt. Cook 8 to 10 minutes until noodles are just tender but not soft. Drain. Rinse well in cold water. Let sit 1 hour to dry (optional).

½ head Chinese cabbage,
  cut into 1 inch pieces
  OR ½ head green cabbage,
    cut into 1 inch pieces
3 Tbsp. vegetable oil

Heat a wok over high heat. Add oil. Heat until a piece of cabbage added sizzles. Add cabbage. Stir and fry 1 to 2 minutes to heat. Add cold noodles. Mix well. Stir and fry 2 to 3 minutes to heat.

4 Tbsp. soy sauce
1 Tbsp. stock
½ tsp. mild honey
¼ tsp. torgarashi
  OR red pepper [optional]

Add to noodles. Mix well. Stir and fry 1 to 2 minutes to mix well and heat through.

Garnish:

4 green onions, chopped
  OR ¼ cup watercress, chopped
  OR 4 to 6 large sprigs parsley,
    chopped
  OR 4 leaves spinach, slivered
  OR 1 sheet nori seaweed,
    brushed with ¼ tsp. soy
    sauce and ½ tsp. sesame oil,
    grilled 1 minute under
    broiler until crisp, crumble

Place noodles in individual bowls. Sprinkle one of garnishes over noodles and serve hot. A good meal-in-a-bowl when served with a cold or hot vegetable dish and pickles. Good cold the next day for lunch.

TORI AGE UDON [CHICKEN FRIED NOODLES] [Serves 4 to 6]

1 lb. whole wheat noodles
  OR whole wheat spaghetti
  OR udon noodles
  OR whole wheat vermicelli
6 cups boiling water
½ tsp. sea salt

OR IN PLACE OF ABOVE:

4 cups leftover cooked noodles

Bring water to boil in a large saucepan over high heat. Add noodles. Bring to boil. To prevent noodles from boiling over have a cup of cold water handy and add a few tsp. of cold water if pot looks like it is going to boil over. Add salt. Reduce heat to medium. Cook 8 to 10 minutes until noodles are just tender but not soft. Drain. Rinse in hot water.

½ inch fresh ginger root,
  grated fine
1 medium carrot, grated
12 to 16 snowpeas, cut into
  long, thin diagonals
  OR ½ cup green peas
4 fresh mushrooms, sliced thin
  [optional]
3 Tbsp. vegetable oil

Heat a wok over high heat. Add oil. Heat until a carrot added sizzles. Add ginger. Stir and fry 30 seconds. Add vegetables. Stir and fry 1 to 2 minutes until heated but not completely cooked.

1 cup leftover cooked chicken
  meat, sliced thin
  OR ½ chicken breast,
    sliced thin
  OR 1 cup any leftover meat
    or fish, sliced thin
  OR 1 cup of any shellfish
  OR 2 cakes age [deep fried bean
    curd], sliced thin

Add to vegetables. Stir and fry 2 to 3 minutes until meat or age slightly browned. Add noodles. Stir and fry 2 to 3 minutes until noodles are hot.

4 Tbsp. soy sauce
1 Tbsp. stock [dashi or kombu]
½ tsp. mild honey
¼ tsp. torgarashi [optional]
  OR red pepper [optional]

Add to noodles. Mix well. Stir and fry 1 to 2 minutes.

Garnishes:

4 green onions, chopped
  OR 4 to 6 large sprigs parsley,
    chopped
  OR ¼ cup watercress, chopped
  OR 4 spinach leaves, slivered
  OR 1 sheet nori seaweed,
    brushed with ¼ tsp. soy
    sauce and ½ tsp. sesame oil,
    grilled 1 minute under
    broiler until crisp, crumble

Place noodles in individual bowls. Sprinkle one of garnishes over noodles. Serve hot. A good meal-in-a-bowl when served with a cold or hot vegetable dish and pickels. Good cold for lunch the next day.

MAIN DISHES

Japanese main dish servings are smaller than those of the West and most involve fish in some way. Raw fish (Sashimi) is very popular. Foods are deep-fried as in Tempura or Tantsuta-Age (Agemono), simmered at the table as in Sukiyaki or served in stews or community cooked foods (Nabemono), grilled with various basting sauces (Yakimono), steamed (Mushimono) or simmered in flavored sauces (Nimono). Another method is baking items in casseroles lined with river pebbles. These dishes are served with rice or noodles and a vegetable dish and pickles. Many of them are one-pot meals when served with rice - Nabemono and Nimono are good examples. See soups and rice and noodle dishes for other main dishes.

SASHIMI [RAW FISH WITH DIPPING SAUCE] [Serves 4 to 6]

Many people object to eating raw fish because of its fishy taste. If the fish has an odor or taste of fish it should never be used for sashimi. Only the freshest fish is used and it has a unique flavor and texture all its own which I find extremely delicious.

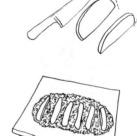

1 to 2 lbs. tuna, salmon, sword fish, sea bass, or similar fish [use sea fish only -- fresh water fish has the danger of parasites]

Use only fresh fish with no "fishy odor." Skin fish. Remove dark parts of fish. Use very sharp wet knife to cut fish. Cut into ¼ by 2 inch diagonal slices. Chill.

1 large daikon radish, grated fine
OR 2 large carrots, grated fine
OR 2 cucumbers, seeded, cut into 1 inch slices and then sliced into paper thin lengths
OR ½ head cabbage, shredded fine
OR 1 small head lettuce, shredded
OR combination of daikon and carrot
OR combination of carrot and cabbage
OR combination of carrot and lettuce

Arrange vegetable on individual plates. Place equal portions of fish on each plate on bed of vegetables. Serve with dipping sauce to dip fish in as it is eaten. Served with a cold vegetable dish and rice for an excellent and refreshing meal. Good for lunch or dinner.

Sauces;

I

1 tsp. Japanese horseradish powder [washabi]
1 Tbsp. hot stock [dashi]

Mix wasabi and dashi well.

¾ cup soy sauce

Add to dashi and wasabi. Mix well. Chill. Serve as dipping sauce with raw fish.

II

½ inch fresh ginger root, grated
¾ cup soy sauce

Mix ingredients well. Chill. Serve as dipping sauce with raw fish.

MACKERAL OR RED SNAPPER SASHIMI [RAW PICKLED FISH WITH DIPPING SAUCE [Serves 4]

1 lb. mackeral or red snapper fillet

Place fish in a shallow dish. Prick with a fork.

1 Tbsp. rice vinegar
1 tsp. mild honey
1 tsp. soy sauce
½ tsp. sea salt

Mix ingredients well. Pour over fish. Marinate fish in sauce for 1 to 3 hours. Turn occasionally. Cut fish fillets crosswise to the backline of the fish. Use a wet, very sharp knife. Cut fish at an angle into ¼ inch thick slices. Drain and chill.

1 large daikon radish, grated fine
   OR 2 large carrots, grated fine
   OR 2 cucumbers, seeded, cut into 1 inch slices and then sliced into paper thin lengths
   OR ½ head cabbage, shredded fine
   OR ½ head Chinese cabbage, shredded fine
   OR 1 small head lettuce, shredded fine
   OR combination of daikon and carrot
   OR combination of carrot and lettuce

Arrange vegetable on individual plates. Place equal portions of fish on each plate on bed of vegetables. Serve with dipping sauce to dip fish in as it is eaten. Served with a cold vegetable dish and rice for an excellent and refreshing meal. Good for lunch or dinner.

Sauce:

I

1 tsp. Japanese horseradish powder [washabi]
1 Tbsp. hot stock [dashi]

Mix wasabi and dashi well.

¾ cup soy sauce

Add to dashi and wasabi. Mix well. Chill. Serve as dipping sauce with raw fish.

II

½ inch fresh ginger root, grated
¾ cup soy sauce

Mix ingredients well. Chill. Serve as dipping sauce with raw fish.

VARIATION:

TORI SASHIMI [RAW CHICKEN WITH DIPPING SAUCE] [Serves 4]

1 chicken breast, boned and cut into 2 inch long, paper thin slices [easiest to do if chicken frozen]

Place on a rack or in a sieve so not too thickly layered. Dip into boiling water. Hold 30 seconds. Remove from water. Place on large plate so all slices are in one layer. Chill 1 to 2 hours until very cold.

Follow recipe for Sashimi. Use chicken in place of raw fish. Serve with dipping sauce to dip chicken in as it is eaten. Served with a cold vegetable dish and rice for an excellent and refreshing summer meal. Good for lunch or dinner.

TEMPURA [DEEP FRIED FISH, SHELLFISH AND VEGETABLE FRITTERS]
[Serves 4 to 6]

Batter:

¾ cup whole wheat pastry flour 6 Tbsp. arrowroot starch	Combine in a bowl. Mix well. Premix, otherwise batter will be lumpy.
1 tsp. mild honey 1 egg yolk 1 to 1½ cups ice water	Mix yolk and honey well. Add water slowly. Mix well. Slowly add flour and starch to liquid. Mix well with chopsticks or wire whisk but do not beat. Do not overmix. Batter can be slightly lumpy.
1 egg white	Beat until egg whites hold a stiff peak. Fold gently into batter. Keep batter cold while using it for best results. I keep it in a bowl of ice as I am dipping in vegetables to fry.

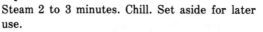

Vegetables that can be used for Tempura:

1 carrot, cut in half and then halves cut into 1/8 inch strips	Steam 2 to 3 minutes. Chill. Set aside for later use.
½ eggplant, cut in half lengthwise and then cut into ¼ inch half-circles	Sprinkle eggplant with salt. Let sit 10 minutes. Steam 2 to 3 minutes. Chill. set aside for later use.
¼ lb. mushrooms, cut into ¼ inch slices	Set aside for later use.
1 small summer squash, cut into ¼ inch slices	Sprinkle squash with salt.
¼ lb. broccoli, cut into long, thin diagonals	Steam 2 to 3 minutes. Chill. Set aside for later use.
½ lb. asparagus, tough ends broken off and cut in half lengthwise	Steam 2 to 3 minutes. Chill. Set aside for later use.
2 green peppers, seeded and cut into 4 to 6 pieces	Set aside for later use.
½ lb. green beans, ends snipped and washed	Steam 2 to 3 minutes. Chill. Set aside for later use.
1 medium yellow onion, cut in half lengthwise and then the halves cut into ¼ inch slices	Secure each slice with a toothpick through the middle so onion holds together in oil. Chill. Set aside for later use.
1 sweet potato, cut into ¼ inch slices	Steam 2 to 3 minutes. Chill. Set aside for later use.
½ small cauliflower, broken into 1 inch flowerlets	Steam 2 to 3 minutes. Chill. Set aside for later use.

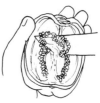

Use any three of these vegetables. Do not fry vast amounts for one person as all Japanese servings are smaller than those served traditionally in the West.

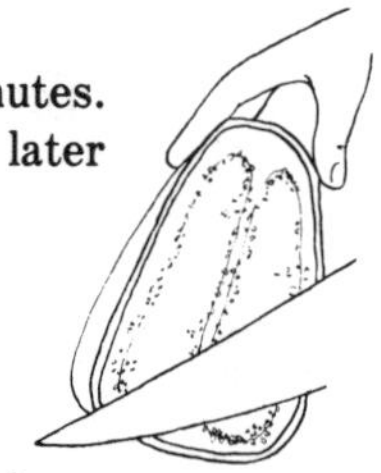

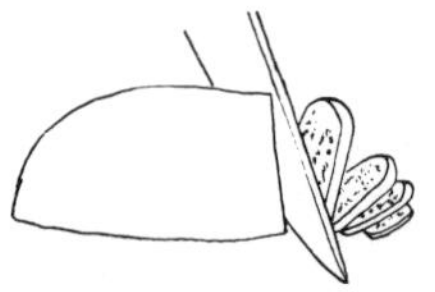

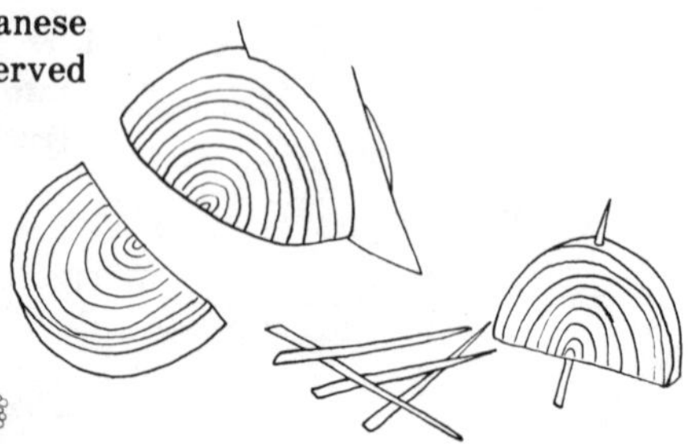

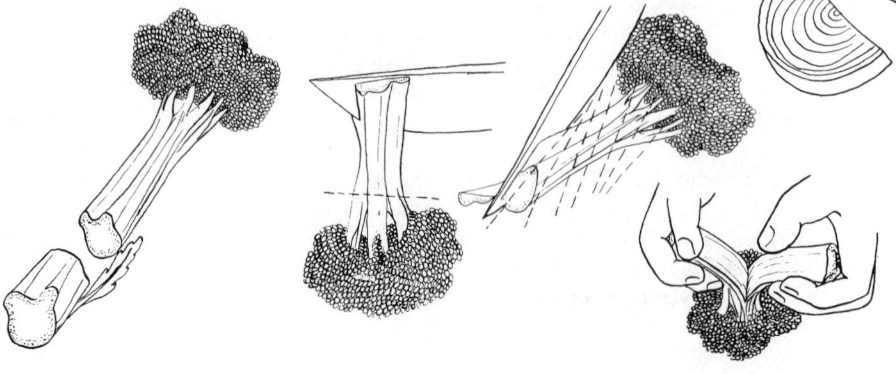

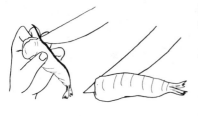

Fish, meat or bean curd that can be used for Tempura:
4 to 6 large raw shrimp or
    prawns, shelled and deveined
OR ½ to 1 lb. fish fillets
    red snapper, sole, cod,
    butterfish, salmon, etc.],
    cut into 2 inch slices
OR ½ lb. whole small raw fish
OR 1 chicken breast, cut into
    8 to 16 pieces
OR 2 cakes bean curd

Remove shell. Cut a narrow slit along back and remove intestine with tip of knife. Cut shrimp open by cutting lengthwise from belly almost through to the back. Flatten shrimp out into a butterfly shape with a wet knife. Cut an "X" design on shrimp to prevent it from curling when it is fried. Chill. Set aside for later use.

Wrap tightly in muslin cloth. Place weight on top. Press 1 to 2 hours to remove excess liquid. Cut each cake into three equal pieces. Arrange fish, shellfish, chicken or bean curd on platter along with selected vegetables.

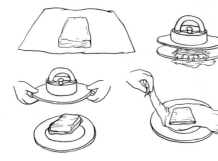

Cooking Method:
3 cups vegetable oil
¼ to ½ cup sesame oil
    [optional]

Heat a wok. Add oil. Sesame oil gives tempura a more fragrant flavor. Combine oil in wok and heat to 350°. If no thermometer is available test oil by dropping a small amount of batter into oil. If batter sits on bottom oil is too cold. If batter stays on top sizzling, oil is too hot. If batter goes to bottom and then rises almost at once, oil is right for frying. Dip shrimp, fish, chicken or bean curd in batter one at a time. Place in oil. Fry 4 to 6 pieces at a time. Do not fry too much as oil temperature will drop too much and food will not cook well but absorb too much oil. Fry 3 to 5 minutes until golden brown. Turn once to brown both sides evenly. When shrimp are fried, remove from oil and drain on wire rack or brown paper to remove excess oil. Test oil again for heat and then dip vegetable you have selected in batter and fry 3 to 5 minutes until golden brown. Remove from oil and drain on wire rack or brown paper to remove excell oil. Keep hot or serve each person individually as the tempura is cooked. An excellent way to cook this dish is to have a selection of ingredients ready for each person and let each one cook their own batch.

Tentsuyu sauce [dipping sauce]:
1 cup stock [kombu or dashi]
5 Tbsp. soy sauce
⅓ cup sake
    OR dry sherry
    OR rice vinegar
1 Tbsp. mild honey

Combine in saucepan. Bring to a boil. Reduce heat to low and simmer 2 to 3 minutes. Serve hot in individual bowls to dip tempura in as it is eaten. This helps cut the oil of fried foods and also gives the tempura a salty taste since there is no salt in the batter.

Garnishes:
½ cup grated daikon
    [said to aid digestion]
2 Tbsp. fresh ginger root,
    grated

Serve in small dishes alongside tentsuyu sauce and plate with tempura. This makes an excellent meal when served with rice, miso soup and a pickle or cold, vinegar-dressed vegetable.

Too Cold

Too Hot

Correct Temperature

TENDON [DEEP FRIED FISH OR SHELLFISH AND VEGETABLE FRITTERS ON HOT RICE WITH SAUCE] [Serves 4 to 6]

4 to 6 large raw shrimp or prawns
OR 2 cakes bean curd, wrapped tightly in muslin cloth, weighted and pressed 1 to 2 hours to remove excess liquid, cut into 3 pieces each

Remove shell. Cut a narrow slit along back and remove intestine with tip of knife. Cut shrimp open by cutting lengthwise from belly almost through to the back. Flatten shrimp out into a butterfly shape with a wet knife. Cut an X design on shrimp to prevent it from curling when it is fried. Chill. Set aside for later use.

Vegetables to be used for Tendon:

1 carrot, cut in half and then halves cut into 1/8 inch strips

Steam 2 to 3 minutes. Chill. Set aside for later use.

OR ½ eggplant, cut in half lengthwise and then cut into ¼ inch half-circles

Sprinkle eggplant with salt. Let sit 10 minutes. Steam 2 to 3 minutes. Chill. Set aside for later use.

OR 1 small summer squash, cut into ¼ inch slices

Sprinkle squash with salt. Set aside for later use.

OR ¼ lb. mushrooms, cut into ¼ inch slices

Set aside for later use.

OR ¼ lb. broccoli, cut into long, thin diagonals

Steam 2 to 3 minutes. Chill. Set aside for later use.

OR ½ lb. asparagus, tough ends broken off and cut in half lengthwise

Steam 2 to 3 minutes. Chill. Set aside for later use.

Use any three of these vegetables. Do not fry fry vast amounts for one person as all Japanese servings are smaller than those traditionally served in the West.

1 batch Tempura batter

Make as directed for Tempura.

Cooking Method:

3 cups vegetable oil
¼ to ½ cup sesame oil [optional]

Heat a wok. Add oil. Sesame oil gives tempura a more fragrant flavor when fried in it. Combine oil in wok and heat to 350°. If no thermometer is available test oil by dropping a small amount of batter into oil. If batter sits on bottom oil is too cold. If batter stays on top sizzling, oil is too hot. If batter goes to bottom and then rises almost at once, oil is right for frying. Dip shrimp in batter one at a time. Place in oil. Fry 4 to 6 pieces at a time. Do not fry too much as oil temperature will drop too much and food will not cook well but absorb too much oil. Fry 3 to 5 minutes until golden brown. Turn once to brown both sides evenly. When shrimp are fried, remove from oil and drain on wire rack or brown paper to remove excess oil. Test oil again for heat and then dip vegetable you have selected in batter and fry 3 to 5 minutes until golden brown. Remove from oil and drain on wire rack or brown paper to remove excess oil.

Too Cold

Too Hot

Correct Temperature

4 to 6 cups hot cooked short grain brown rice

Place in individual bowls. Place a tempura fried shrimp and some vegetables on top of each bowl of rice.

1 cup stock [dashi or kombu]
1 Tbsp. mild honey
4 Tbsp. soy sauce
2 Tbsp. sake OR dry sherry

Place in saucepan. Heat over medium high heat until sauce is well mixed and hot but not boiling Reduce heat to low and keep hot until tempura shrimps and vegetables are cooked.

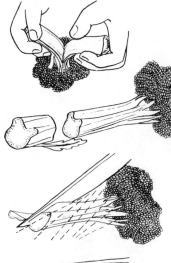

2 inches daikon, grated
½ inch fresh ginger root, grated

Mix. Add to sauce. Pour over bowls of tempura-topped rice.

Garnishes:
4 green onions, chopped
OR ¼ packed cup watercress,
    chopped
OR 4 to 6 large sprigs parsley,
    chopped
OR 4 leaves spinach, slivered
OR 1 sheet nori seaweed,
    brushed with ¼ tsp. soy
    sauce and ½ tsp. sesame oil,
    grilled 1 minute under
    broiler until crisp, crumble

Sprinkle one of garnishes over rice and tempura. Serve hot. Good meal-in-a-bowl dish or can be accompanied with pickles or cold vegetable dish for a larger dinner meal.

VARIATION:

TEMPURA UDON OR SOBA [DEEP-FRIED FISH, SHELLFISH OR BEAN CURD AND VEGETABLE FRITTERS ON HOT NOODLES WITH SAUCE] [Serves 4 to 6]

1 lb. udon noodles
OR soba noodles
OR whole-wheat vermicelli
OR whole-wheat spaghetti
OR whole-wheat soy vermicelli
OR whole-wheat tomato noodles
OR whole-wheat spinach noodles
6 cups boiling water
½ tsp. sea salt

Bring water to a boil in a large saucepan over high heat. Add noodles. Bring to boil. To prevent noodles from boiling over have a cup of cold water handy and add a few tsp. of cold water if pot looks like it is going to boil over. Reduce heat to medium. Add salt. Cook 8 to 10 minutes until noodles are just tender but not soft. Drain. Rinse in hot water. Follow recipe for Tendon. Use noodles in place of rice. Use stock recipe below. Cook as directed.

Stock:
4 cups stock [dahi or kombu]
4 Tbsp. soy sauce
2 tsp. mild honey

Place in a saucepan. Bring to a boil over medium heat. Simmer 2 to 3 minutes. Place noodles in individual serving bowls. Top with tempura fried shrimp or bean curd and some vegetables on each bowl. Pour over stock. Good meal-in-a-bowl dish or can be accompanied by pickles or cold vegetable dish for a larger dinner meal. Good hearty lunch if made with leftover tempura with hot stock poured over it.

KAKI AGE [TEMPURA PANCAKES WITH FISH OR SHELLFISH] [Serves 4 to 6]

1 medium carrot, grated
1 turnip, grated
  OR ½ daikon radish, grated
½ inch fresh ginger root, grated
½ cup green peas
  OR ½ cup green beans, cut into thin diagonal slices
  OR ½ cup snowpeas, cut into thin diagonal slices
6 oz. shrimp, chop into ¼ inch pieces
  OR 6 oz. scallops, chop into ¼ inch pieces
  OR 6 oz. white fish, chop into small pieces
  OR ½ chicken breast, cut into small pieces
  OR 6 oz. baby clams

Place vegetables and fish in a bowl. Mix well. Chill.

1 cup tempura batter
2 to 3 Tbsp. whole-wheat flour

Add tempura batter to cold vegetables. Mix gently but well. Sprinkle with flour. Fold in gently to vegetables and batter. Place in refrigerator and chill 10 to 15 minutes. Keep cold at all times -- best to set bowl of mixture in a larger bowl of ice to keep it cold while using it.

3 cups vegetable oil
¼ to ½ cup sesame oil [optional]

Heat a wok. Add oil. Sesame oil gives tempura a more fragrant flavor. Combine oil in wok and heat to 350° to 375°. If no thermometer is available test oil by dropping a small amount of batter into oil. If batter sits on bottom oil is too cold. If batter stays on top sizzling, oil is too hot. If batter goes to bottom and then rises almost at once, oil is right for frying. Place 2 Tbsp. of vegetable mixture on a wooden rice paddle or spoon. Flatten with a spatula and push into oil with chopsticks. Fry 2 to 3 minutes until lightly browned. Turn once to brown both sides evenly.

Too Cold

Fry only 4 to 5 at a time so the oil temperature is not reduced too much and the patties start absorbing too much oil. Test oil temperature between each batch. Drain on absorbent paper or in a wicker basket. Keep hot in 200° oven or serve each person individually as tempura cakes are cooked. An excellent way to serve this dish is to allow each person to fry their own portions.

Too Hot

Correct Temperature

Tentsuyu sauce [dipping sauce]:
1 cup stock
   [kombu or dashi]
5 Tbsp. soy sauce
¹/₃ cup sake
   OR dry sherry
   OR rice vinegar
1 Tbsp. mild honey

Combine in a saucepan. Bring to a boil. Reduce heat to low and simmer 2 to 3 minutes. Serve hot in individual bowls to dip kaki age in as it is eaten. This helps cut the oil of fried foods and also gives the kaki age a salty taste since there is no salt in the batter.

Garnishes:
¹/₂ cup grated daikon
   [said to aid digestion]
2 Tbsp. fresh ginger root,
   grated

Serve in small dishes alongside tentsuyu sauce and plate with kaki age. This makes an excellent meal when served with rice, miso soup and a pickle or cold, vinegar-dressed vegetable. Good cold for lunch the next day. Use in Nabe cooking.

VARIATION:

TEMPURA DANGO [TEMPURA PANCAKES]
[Serves 4 to 6]

1 cake bean curd, wrapped tightly
   in muslin cloth, weight,
   press 1 to 2 hours to remove
   excess liquid, brake into small
   pieces
   OR 2 cakes age, [Deep-fried bean
      curd] cut into ¹/₄ inch cubes

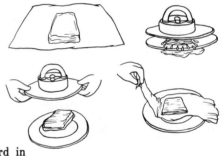

Follow recipe for Kaki Age. Use bean curd in place of shrimp. Cook as directed. Serve hot with Tentsuyu sauce and garnish. Makes an excellent meal served with rice, miso soup and pickles or cold vinegar-dressed vegetable. Excellent cold for lunch the next day. Use in Nabe cooking.

TATSUTA-AGE [CHICKEN MARINATED IN GINGER SOY AND DEEP FRIED]
[Serves 4 to 6]

½ **chicken, skinned and cut
  into 2 to 3 inch pieces**
2 **Tbsp. soy sauce**
2 **Tbsp. mild honey**
1 **Tbsp. sake
  OR dry sherry
  OR rice vinegar**
1 **inch fresh ginger root, grated**

Place chicken in a large bowl. Add other ingredients. Mix well. Place a plate over the chicken and weight with a rock or other heavy object. Marinate for 30 minutes to 3 hours. Drain well on a rack.

¼ **cup arrowroot starch**

Dust each piece of marinated chicken with arrowroot starch. Place on rack again.

3 **to 4 cups vegetable oil**
¼ **to ½ cup sesame oil
  [optional]**

Heat a wok. Add oil. Sesame oil gives chicken a more fragrant flavor. Combine oil in wok and heat to 350° to 375°. If no thermometer is available test oil by dropping a small amount of chicken into oil. If chicken sits on bottom oil is too cold. If chicken stays on top sizzling oil is too hot. If chicken goes to the bottom and then rises almost at once. oil is right for frying. Place 5 to 6 pieces of chicken in hot oil. Fry 5 to 8 minutes until well browned and chicken cooked through. Remove from oil. Clean oil to remove pieces of chicken before adding another batch. Drain chicken well. Serve hot with rice for an excellent main dish for dinner. Best served with a vinegar dressed cold vegetable. One of the best dishes for cold leftover lunch the next day.

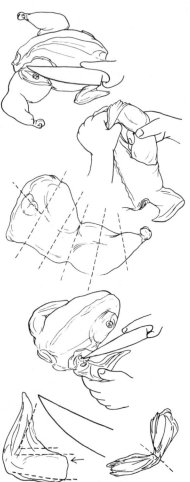

Too Cold   Too Hot   Correct Temperature

VARIATION:

[FISH MARINATED IN GINGER SOY AND DEEP FRIED] [Serves 4 to 6]

1 **lb. firm white fish fillet
  [red snapper, sea bass, swordfish,
  etc.], cut into 3 inch pieces
  OR salmon, cut into 3 inch pieces**

Follow recipe for Tatsuta-age. Use fish in place of chicken. Do not weight fish when marinating. Cook as directed. Serve hot with rice for an excellent main dish for dinner. Best served with a vinegar dressed cold vegetable. One of the best dishes for cold leftover lunch the next day.

VARIATION:

EGI-AGE [SHRIMP MARINATED IN GINGER SOY AND DEEP FRIED] [Serves 4 to 6]

12 **to 18 large shrimp or prawns,
  shelled and deveined, flattened
  as for tempura into butterfly
  shape**

Follow recipe for Tatsuta-age. Use shrimp in place of chicken. Cook as directed. Serve hot with rice for an excellent main dish for dinner. Best served with a vinegar-dressed cold vegetable. One of the best dishes for cold leftover lunch the next day.

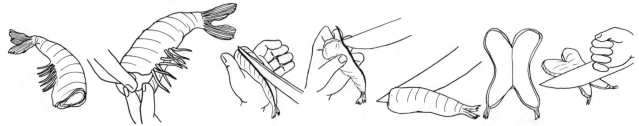

TOFU DANGO [BEAN CURD EGG PATTIES] [Serves 4 to 6]

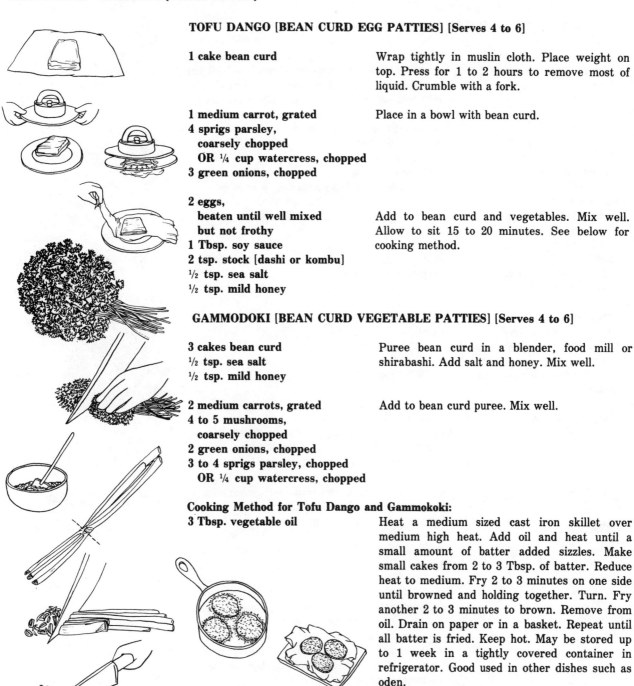

1 cake bean curd	Wrap tightly in muslin cloth. Place weight on top. Press for 1 to 2 hours to remove most of liquid. Crumble with a fork.

1 medium carrot, grated
4 sprigs parsley,
  coarsely chopped
  OR ¼ cup watercress, chopped
3 green onions, chopped
	Place in a bowl with bean curd.

2 eggs,
  beaten until well mixed
  but not frothy
1 Tbsp. soy sauce
2 tsp. stock [dashi or kombu]
½ tsp. sea salt
½ tsp. mild honey
	Add to bean curd and vegetables. Mix well. Allow to sit 15 to 20 minutes. See below for cooking method.

GAMMODOKI [BEAN CURD VEGETABLE PATTIES] [Serves 4 to 6]

3 cakes bean curd ½ tsp. sea salt ½ tsp. mild honey	Puree bean curd in a blender, food mill or shirabashi. Add salt and honey. Mix well.

2 medium carrots, grated
4 to 5 mushrooms,
  coarsely chopped
2 green onions, chopped
3 to 4 sprigs parsley, chopped
  OR ¼ cup watercress, chopped
	Add to bean curd puree. Mix well.

Cooking Method for Tofu Dango and Gammokoki:

3 Tbsp. vegetable oil	Heat a medium sized cast iron skillet over medium high heat. Add oil and heat until a small amount of batter added sizzles. Make small cakes from 2 to 3 Tbsp. of batter. Reduce heat to medium. Fry 2 to 3 minutes on one side until browned and holding together. Turn. Fry another 2 to 3 minutes to brown. Remove from oil. Drain on paper or in a basket. Repeat until all batter is fried. Keep hot. May be stored up to 1 week in a tightly covered container in refrigerator. Good used in other dishes such as oden.

Dipping sauce for Tofu Dango or Gammodoki:

1 Tbsp. stock [dashi or kombu]
2 tsp. Japanese horseradish
  powder [washabi]
  OR dried mustard
3 Tbsp. soy sauce
	Mix stock and horseradish powder. Add soy sauce. Mix well. Serve with hot patties to dip patties in while eating. Good served with tempura vegetables, rice and pickles. Good cold for lunch when dipped in soy sauce.

MISO DANGO [MISO AND RICE PATTIES] [Serves 4 to 6]

2 cups cold, moist, cooked short-grain brown rice

Turn out rice on wet chopping board. Chop with a wet knife until all kernels of rice are well cut and rice starts to stick together. Knead rice with wet hands on a wet board 3 to 5 minutes until rice forms a paste - very important. Keep all utensils, hands and board wet so rice does not stick to them.

1 tsp. mild honey
¼ cup miso
1 tsp. sea salt
1 Tbsp. whole-wheat flour
1 Tbsp. arrowroot starch

Add miso and other ingredients to rice. Mix well. Easiest to mix by kneading with hands.

3 eggs, beaten until well mixed but not frothy

Add to miso and rice mixture. Mix well with chopstick or a spoon.

4 green onions, minced
4 sprigs parsley, minced OR ¼ cup watercress, minced
1 cup vegetables, minced or grated [carrot, beans, peas, cauliflower, broccoli, etc.]

Add to miso and rice mixture. Mix well. Allow to sit 15 to 20 minutes.

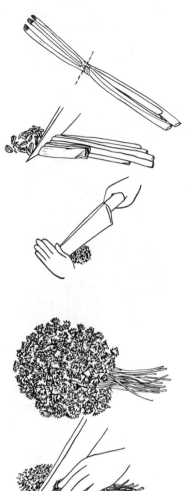

¼ cup vegetable oil

Heat a medium sized cast iron skillet over medium high heat. Add 2 Tbsp. of oil and heat until a small amount of batter added sizzles. Reduce heat to medium. Make small cakes from 2 to 3 Tbsp. of batter. Fry 2 to 3 minutes on one side until browned and holding together. Turn. Fry on other side 2 to 3 minutes until brown. Remove from oil. Drain on paper or in a basket. Repeat until all batter is fried. Add more oil as needed. Keep dango hot while others are cooking. Good served with tempura vegetables, rice and pickles or a cold vegetable dish. Good served as a main dish with rice or noodles and a hot vegetable such as spinach in lemon sauce. Can be used in vegetarian nabemono also. Good the next day for lunch cold. Also good used in other dishes such as Oden. Use Tempura tentsuyu sauce or Gammodoki dipping sauce when serving hot.

VARIATION:

TORI MISO DANGO [CHICKEN, MISO AND RICE PATTIES] [Serves 4 to 6]

½ cup cooked chicken, minced
   OR ½ cup cooked meat [beef,
     lamb, pork], minced
   OR ½ cup cooked fish, minced
   OR ½ cup shellfish, minced

Follow recipe for Miso Dango. Use meat in addition to vegetables. Cook as directed. Serve hot. Good served with tempura vegetables, rice and pickles or a cold vegetable dish with rice or noodles and a hot vegetable dish. Good served as a main dish with rice or noodles and a hot vegetable such as spinach in lemon sauce. Good the next day cold for lunch. Also good used in other dishes such as Oden. Use Tempura tentsuyu sauce or Gammodoki dipping sauce when serving hot.

TOFU TAMAGO YAKI [EGG OMELETTE WITH BEAN CURD] [Serves 4 to 6]

4 to 5 dried mushrooms
½ cup boiling water

Place mushrooms in a small bowl. Pour boiling water over them. Place a weight on top to keep under water. Let sit 15 to 30 minutes until soft. Remove from water. Squeeze dry. Cut out tough stems. Cut mushrooms into thin strips.

2 Tbsp. vegetable oil
1 Tbsp. sesame oil [optional]
3 to 4 green onions, cut into
   thin diagonal slices
2 to 3 sprigs parsley, chopped

Heat a medium sized cast iron skillet over medium heat. Add oil and heat until onion added sizzles. Add onions and parsley. Stir and fry 1 minute until just tender.

1 tsp. mild honey
2 Tbsp. soy sauce
1 Tbsp. stock [dashi or kombu]

Add to vegetables. Cook 1 to 2 minutes. Just bring sauce to a gentle bubble.

1 cake bean curd, cut into
  ½ inch cubes

Add to sauce and vegetables. Add mushrooms. Gently stir and fry 1 to 2 minutes to heat but do not brown. Baste with sauce while frying.

5 eggs,
  beaten until well mixed
  but not frothy

Add to pan of bean curd and vegetables. Let sit 1 minutes. Mix slightly. Cover. Cook just below medium heat 10 to 12 minutes until eggs firm. Loosen edges with a knife. Invert over large plate. Slide omelette back into pan. Cook 1 to 2 more minutes to brown and set top of omelette. Invert onto a plate. Cut into 1 inch cubes or diamonds. Serve hot with soy dipping sauce.

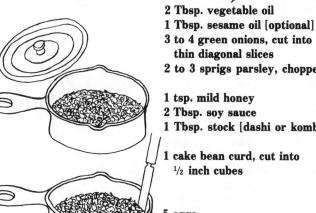

Dipping sauce:
2 Tbsp. soy sauce
½ tsp. mild honey
1 Tbsp. stock [dashi or kombu]

Mix sauce well. Serve with egg squares for dipping sauce. Serve hot with rice and pickles for a light meal or with a hot vegetable dish and soup for a larger meal. Good cold the next day for lunch.

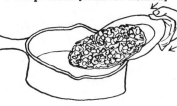

HORENSO TAMAGO YAKI [LAYERED SPINACH EGG OMELETTE SQUARES]
Serves 4 to 6]

½ lb. spinach

Steam 2 to 3 minutes until tender but still bright green.

2 Tbsp. sesame seeds
¼ tsp. sea salt

Heat a small skillet over high heat. Add seeds. Parch 1 to 2 minutes until seeds lightly browned. Shake pan often to evenly brown seeds. Coarsely grind in a blender, food mill or shirabashi. Mix ground seeds with salt. Sprinkle over spinach.

6 eggs, beaten until well
  mixed but not frothy
1 Tbsp. mild honey
1 Tbsp. sake
  OR dry sherry
  OR rice vinegar
½ tsp. sea salt
2 tsp. soy sauce

Mix ingredients except for eggs well. Add eggs. Mix well, but do not make eggs frothy.

1 Tbsp. sesame oil
  OR vegetable oil

Heat a medium sized cast iron skillet on medium heat. Add oil and heat until a piece of egg added sets. Add ⅓ of egg mix. Let sit 1 minute. Scramble 1 to 2 minutes until firm but still very moist. Add another third of egg mixture. Scramble 1 to 2 minutes until firm but still very moist. Add last third of egg mixture. Cover. Reduce heat to medium low and cook 8 to 10 minutes until eggs firm. Remove lid. Loosen edges of omelette with knife. Invert omelette over large plate. Slide omelette back into pan. Cook 1 to 2 more minutes to brown top side. Invert onto a plate.

1 sheet nori seaweed,
  cut into ¼ inch strips

Cut into two equal layers. Place spinach in center like a filling for a cake. Top with other layer of egg. Cut into 1 x 3 inch rectangles or diamonds. Wrap each egg diamond with nori seaweed strip around the center. Serve hot with rice and pickles for a light meal or add a hot vegetable for a more substantial meal. Dip in soy sauce when eating. Good cold the next day for lunch.

TAKARA YAKI [EGG AND VEGETABLE SQUARES] [Serves 4 to 6]

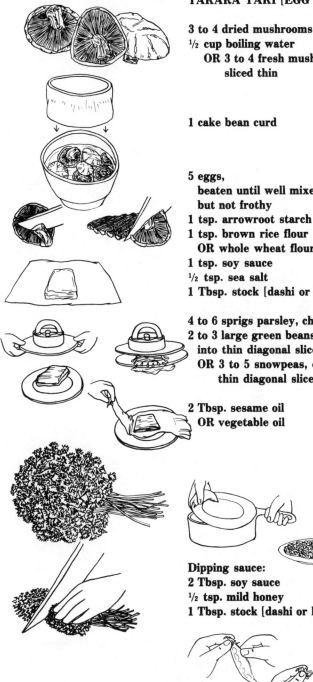

3 to 4 dried mushrooms
½ cup boiling water
  OR 3 to 4 fresh mushrooms,
    sliced thin

Place dried mushrooms in a small bowl. Pour boiling water over them. Place a weight on top of mushrooms to keep them under water. Let sit 15 to 30 minutes until soft. Remove from water. Squeeze dry. Remove tough stems. Cut into thin slices.

1 cake bean curd

Wrap tightly in muslin cloth. Place weight on top. Press for 1 to 2 hours to remove most of liquid. Crumble with a fork.

5 eggs,
  beaten until well mixed
  but not frothy
1 tsp. arrowroot starch
1 tsp. brown rice flour
  OR whole wheat flour
1 tsp. soy sauce
½ tsp. sea salt
1 Tbsp. stock [dashi or kombu]

Mix flour and starch well. Add all ingredients except eggs. Mix well. Add mixture to eggs. Mix well.

4 to 6 sprigs parsley, chopped
2 to 3 large green beans, cut
  into thin diagonal slices
  OR 3 to 5 snowpeas, cut into
    thin diagonal slices

Add vegetables to egg mixture along with mushrooms and bean curd. Mix well.

2 Tbsp. sesame oil
  OR vegetable oil

Heat a medium sized cast iron skillet. Add oil and heat until a small drop of egg mixture sets. Add egg mixture. Let sit 1 minute. Mix slightly. Cover. Cook just below medium heat 10 to 12 minutes until eggs firm. Loosen edges with a knife. Invert over large plate. Slide omelette back into pan. Cook 1 to 2 more minutes to brown and set top of omelette. Invert onto a plate. Cut into 1 inch cubes or diamonds. Serve hot with soy dipping sauce.

Dipping sauce:
2 Tbsp. soy sauce
½ tsp. mild honey
1 Tbsp. stock [dashi or kombu]

Mix sauce well. Serve with egg squares for dipping sauce. Serve hot with rice and pickles for a light meal or with a hot vegetable dish and soup for a larger meal. Good cold the next day for lunch.

JAPANESE GRILL [VEGETABLES, MEAT AND TOFU GRILLED WITH DIPPING SAUCES] [Serves 4 to 6]

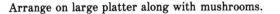

4 to 6 dried mushrooms
½ cup boiling water
   OR ¼ lb. fresh mushrooms,
     cut into thirds

Place dried mushrooms in a small bowl. Pour boiling water over them. Place a weight on top to keep under water. Let sit 15 to 30 minutes until soft. Remove from water. Squeeze dry. Remove tough stems. Place on a large platter.

Arrange on large platter along with mushrooms.

3 cakes bean curd,
   each cut into 4 cubes
2 leeks, cut into 1 inch lengths
   and then cut in half lengthwise
   OR 4 large green onions, cut into
      1 inch lengths and then cut
      in half lengthwise
4 green peppers, seeded, cut
   into 4 to 6 pieces
½ lb. bean sprouts
¼ lb. green beans, cut into long,
   ¼ inch diagonals
12 to 18 snowpeas [optional],
   ends snipped
4 to 6 slices yellow onion,
   cut into ¼ inch thick slices

½ lb. boneless beef [stew meat,
   steak, roast] cut into ¼ by 2
   inch strips 1 inch wide
   [optional]
   OR 1 large chicken breast cut
      into ¼ inch by 2 inch strips
      [optional]

Place on platter along with mushrooms and vegetables.

2 Tbsp. vegetable oil

Heat a grill, Ghenghiskhan charcoal grill, or electric frying pan on high heat. A pancake griddle on top heat may also be used. Reduce heat to medium. Brush with oil. Each person should add a selection of the above ingredients to the grill and fry their own meal 2 to 3 minutes to a side on the meat until it is just browned and just enough to heat the vegetables through and make them tender. Turn once to grill both sides. Dip in the following sauces as the ingredients are eaten.

Sauces:

I

¼ cup miso
¼ cup peanut butter
½ cup stock [dashi or kombu]
1 tsp. mild honey

Slowly mix peanut butter and miso until no lumps remain. Add honey. Mix well. Slowly add stock to miso sauce so no lumps are formed in sauce. If blender is available place all ingredients in blender and blend until smooth. Place in a small bowl to serve with grilled vegetables and tofu. This is a good meal-in-a-bowl dish when served along with rice and pickles.

II

½ cup soy sauce
¼ cup rice vinegar
1 tsp. mild honey
1 garlic clove, minced fine
¼ to ½ tsp. red pepper

Mix ingredients well. Serve as one of three dipping sauces with mixed grill.

III

½ cup soy sauce
2 Tbsp. tomato paste
1 tsp. mild honey
¼ tsp. Chinese Five Spices mix
2 Tbsp. lemon juice
2 Tbsp. grated onion
2 Tbsp. grated green pepper
½ tsp. sea salt

Mix ingredients well. Serve as one of three dipping sauces for the mixed grill. Just one of the dipping sauces may be used but it gives the dinner a more exciting taste when all three are prepared and used.

TOFU YAKI [BEAN CURD FRIED IN EGGS AND BROWN RICE FLOUR]
[Serves 4 to 6]

2 eggs, beaten until well mixed but not frothy

Place in a bowl and set aside for later use.

¼ cup brown rice

Place in a saucepan over medium heat. Shake pan frequently to prevent rice from burning. Cook 4 to 8 minutes until rice is toasted - it will lose its translucency and be slightly browned. Remove from heat. Blend 2 Tbsp. at a time in a blender until a fine flour is formed or grind into rice flour in a food mill. Put through twice.

3 cakes bean curd

Wrap tightly in a muslin cloth. Place a weight on top. Press 1 to 2 hours to remove excess liquid. Cut into ½ x 2 inch rectangles.

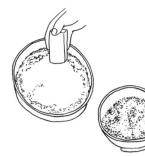

½ cup vegetable oil
1 Tbsp. sesame oil [optional]

Heat a medium sized frying pan over medium high heat. Add oil. Heat until a piece of bean curd added sizzles. Dip bean curd in egg and then bread in flour. Place in frying pan. Fry 5 to 10 minutes until golden brown. Turn once to brown both sides. Drain on absorbent paper or in a wicker basket. Serve hot with the following sauce.

Sauce:
1 cup stock [dashi or kombu]
1 tsp. soy sauce
½ tsp. sea salt
2 tsp. mild honey
1 tsp. arrowroot starch

Place ingredients in a small saucepan. Mix well. Bring to a boil over high heat. Cook 30 seconds to 1 minute until sauce thickens..

½ inch fresh ginger root, grated

Add to sauce. Serve with fried bean curd. A good main dish when served with rice and a hot vegetable dish and pickles. Good cold dipped in soy sauce.

SHABU-SHABU [MEAT COOKED IN BROTH WITH DIPPING SAUCES]
[Serves 4 to 6]

½ to 1 lb. boneless beef, cut into
    paper thin, 1 inch by 3 inch
    strips [roast, stew meat,
    or steak]
1 cake bean curd, cut into
    1 by 2 inch cubes
4 green onions, cut into long,
    thin diagonal slices
4 to 6 large leaves Chinese
    cabbage cut into 1 by 2 inch
    slices with the white stalks
    cut into thin 2 inch matchstick
    like pieces

Partly frozen beef is easiest to slice into thin slices. When meat is sliced arrange on 4 to 6 individual serving dishes.

Arrange along with beef on individual plates.

4 oz. bean noodles
2 cups boiling water

Place noodles in a bowl. Pour boiling water over them. Allow to soak 15 to 30 minutes until tender. Drain. Arrange along with beef and vegetables on individual plates.

Sauce:
4 cups chicken stock
½ tsp. sea salt
1 Tbsp. sake
    OR dry sherry
½ tsp. mild honey

Place sauce ingredients in a pan that can be heated at the table like an electric frying pan, a charcoal heated hot pot or a deep pan on a small electric or gas burner. Bring stock to a boil over high heat. Reduce heat to medium low - just enough to keep broth simmering. Each person dips one piece of meat at a time into the simmering broth. Cook about 30 seconds to 1 minute until no longer red but not completely cooked - still having traces of pink. Each person dips meat in the following sauces.

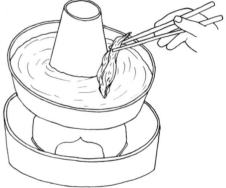

Dipping Sauces:
I
⅓ cup rice vinegar
3 Tbsp. soy sauce
1 Tbsp. stock [dashi]
¼ tsp. Japanese horseradish
    powder [wasabi]

Mix horseradish powder with small amount of soy sauce first. Add to rest of ingredients and mix well.

2 Tbsp. sesame seeds
¼ tsp. sea salt

Heat a small skillet over high heat. Add seeds and salt. Parch 1 to 2 minutes until seeds are lightly browned. Shake pan often to evenly brown seeds. Remove from heat. Grind seeds well in a blender, food mill or shirabashi. Add to dipping sauce. Mix well. Serve in individual bowls for each person to dip their cooked meat into before they eat it.

II
juice of 1 lemon
2 Tbsp. soy sauce
1 Tbsp. stock [dashi]

Mix ingredients well. Serve in individual bowls for each person to dip meat in after cooking it.

III
juice of one large orange
2 Tbsp. rice vinegar
1 Tbsp. soy sauce.

Mix ingredients well. Serve in individual bowls for each person to dip meat in after cooking it.

½ tsp. sea salt
¼ tsp. black pepper

Add to broth when all meat is cooked. Add bean curd and vegetables when meat is cooked. Cook 2 to 3 minutes until bean curd heated and vegetables just tender. Remove from stock. Place in bowls. Sprinkle one of dipping sauces over vegetables and bean curd. Eat at once. Now place noodles in simmering stock. Cook 1 to 2 minutes to heat through. Place in bowls. Serve hot as a soup. When served with rice and pickles this dish makes a complete meal. Shabu-Shabu is very good to serve for small gatherings of 4 to 6 people but not good for large groups.

HAMANABE [OYSTERS AND VEGETABLE SAUCEPAN FOOD] [Serves 4]

½ cup sweet white bean paste
  [see Japanese Basic
  Ingredients]
2 Tbsp. soy sauce
1 Tbsp. sake
  OR dry sherry
1 tsp. mild honey
½ tsp. sea salt
1 inch fresh ginger, grated fine

Mix ingredients well. Place in a dutch oven or deep frying pan. Arrange in center of pot.

1 pint oysters,
  drained and rinsed
  OR 16 to 18 small oysters,
    shucked and rinsed
½ lb. spinach
6 to 8 sprigs parsley,
  coarsely chopped
  OR ¼ cup watercress,
    coarsely chopped
1 cake bean curd, cut into
  1 inch cubes
4 green onions, cut into
  paper thin slices

Arrange around bean paste, each in a separate section of the pan. Place over high heat.

Sauce:
1 cup stock [dashi]
2 Tbsp. soy sauce
1 tsp. mild honey

Mix ingredients well. Pour over ingredients in pan. Cook over high heat. Gently mix bean paste with vegetables and other ingredients with chopsticks. Bring to a boil. Reduce heat to medium low. Cover. Simmer 3 to 5 minutes until edges of oysters just curl. Serve hot with rice. A good one-pot meal served with pickles and rice. Good cold the next day for lunch.

SUKIYAKI [MEAT AND VEGETABLE SAUCEPAN FOOD] [Serves 4 to 6]

1 lb. boneless beef
  [steak, roast, stew meat]
  cut into 1 inch by 3 inch paper
  thin strips

Partly frozen beef is easiest to slice into thin slices. When meat is sliced arrange on a platter.

4 to 8 dried mushrooms
½ cup boiling water
  OR ¼ lb. fresh mushrooms,
    cut into ¼ inch slices

Place dried mushrooms in a small bowl. Pour boiling water over them. Place a weight on top to keep under water. Let sit 15 to 30 minutes until soft. Remove from water. Squeeze dry. Cut out tough stems. Place on platter with meat.

[optional]
1 oz. shirataki
  OR dry bean noodles and
    2 cups boiling water

Place bean noodles in a bowl. Pour boiling water over them. Allow to soak 15 to 30 minutes until soft. Drain. Place on platter with mushrooms and meat.

6 to 12 green onions, cut into
  thin diagonal slices
1 small yellow onion, cut in half
  lengthwise and then sliced
  paper thin
1 cake bean curd, cut into 1 inch
  cubes [optional]
½ lb. fresh spinach
  OR 1 bunch parsley, minced
1 small can bamboo shoots, cut into
  thin slices [optional]
  OR 1 carrot, cut into thin
    diagonals

Arrange on platter with mushrooms, noodles and meat.

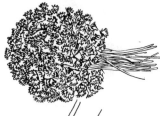

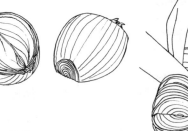

Sauce:
½ cup stock [dashi]
¼ cup soy sauce
¼ cup sake
  OR dry sherry
2 to 3 Tbsp. mild honey

Place in a small bowl. Mix well.

2 oz. beef suet
  OR 2 Tbsp. vegetable oil

Cooking Method:
1. Place a sukiyaki pan or large frying pan on a charcoal, electric, or gas burner on the table. Can be cooked at stove and served immediately. Heat over high heat. Add beef suet. Cook 1 to 2 minutes until 1 to 2 Tbsp. of oil has been rendered from the suet. Move suet around the pan while cooking to distribute oil evenly - also pressing suet with chopsticks helps oil to come out of it. Remove suet from pan when oil is rendered.

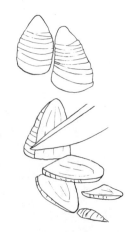

2. Add meat. Stir and fry over high heat 1 to 2 minutes until just lightly browned but still slightly pink.

3. Pour sauce over meat. Let sauce just come to a boil - about 30 seconds.

4. Add green onions, mushrooms and yellow onions in separate areas of the pan.　cook 1 minute to heat.

5. Add tofu, noodles and bamboo shoots. Keep in separate groups.　　1 minute to heat.

6. Add spinach. Cover. Cook 3 to 5 minutes to heat through and until spinach is just tender. Serve at once with hot rice. A good meal-in-a-dish for a small party of friends. Excellent with miso soup and pickles.

TOFU NABEMONO [BEAN CURD AND VEGETABLE STEW] [Serves 4 to 6] [Vegetarian Sukiyaki]

¼ lb. bean noodles
2 cups boiling water
　OR shirataki

2 cakes bean curd, cut into
　1 x 2 inch rectangles
4 to 6 mushrooms, cut into
　thin slices
2 small carrots, cut into thin,
　diagonal slices and steamed
　2 to 3 minutes
2 small stalks celery with tops,
　cut into thin, diagonal slices
　OR 6 large sprigs parsley,
　coarsely chopped
　OR ½ cup watercress,
　　chopped
½ lb. spinach, cut into
　2 to 3 inch strips
1 cup bean sprouts

Sauce:
⅔ cup stock [dashi or kombu]
¼ cup soy sauce
2 Tbsp. sake
　OR dry sherry
　OR rice vinegar
1 Tbsp. mild honey

Place noodles in bowl. Pour over boiling water. Soak 15 to 30 minutes until noodles tender. Drain. Set aside to use later.

Attractively arrange ingredients along with bean noodles in a large sukiyaki pan, deep frying pan or electric frying pan. Place on high heat.

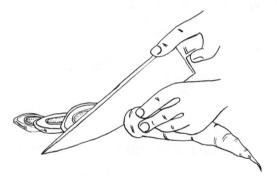

Mix ingredients well. Heat in a small saucepan. Pour over ingredients in frying pan. Bring to a boil quickly over high heat. Cover. Reduce heat to low and simmer 3 to 5 minutes until spinach is just tender but still bright green. Serve hot with rice and a cold dressed vegetable dish and pickles.

NIWATORI SUKIYAKI [CHICKEN AND VEGETABLE SAUCEPAN FOOD]
[Serves 4]

This dish can be cooked like sukiyaki at the table or on the stove. I usually cook it on the stove and serve it immediately.

1 to 2 chicken breasts
   [or leg or thigh meat]
   boned and sliced thin
2 Tbsp. vegetable oil

Heat a large skillet over high heat. Add oil and heat until a piece of chicken added sizzles. Reduce heat to medium. Stir and fry chicken 3 to 5 minutes until lightly browned.

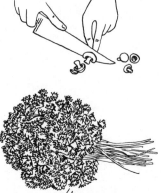

Sauce:
½ cup chicken stock
3 Tbsp. soy sauce
2 tsp. mild honey
1 Tbsp. sake
   OR dry sherry
2 Tbsp. stock [dashi]

Place in a small saucepan. Heat until honey is well mixed. Pour over cooked chicken meat. Simmer 1 to 2 minutes.

6 green onions, cut into thin
   diagonal slices
6 fresh mushrooms, sliced thin
½ lb. spinach, cut into
   3 inch slices
   OR 10 to 12 sprigs parsley,
   coarsely chopped
2 small carrots, cut into
   paper thin diagonal slices
2 small stalks celery with tops,
   sliced into paper thin diagonal
   slices

Place in pan with chicken and sauce. Keep each ingredient separate. Cover. Simmer 3 to 5 minutes until spinach is just tender. Serve at once with rice and pickles. Also good accompanied by miso soup. Makes a good simple meal.

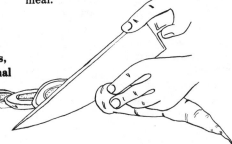

YOSENABE [VEGETABLES AND TOFU SIMMERED IN KOMBU STOCK]
[Serves 4 to 6]

5 cups stock [kombu]
¼ cups soy sauce
1 Tbsp. sake
   OR dry sherry
2 tsp. mild honey
1 tsp. sea salt

Combine ingredients in heavy saucepan. Bring to boil over high heat.

2 oz. bean noodles, soak in hot
   water 30 minutes, drain
1 carrot, cut into thin diagonals
3 green onions, cut into 1 inch
   pieces and sliced thin

Add to boiling stock. Reduce heat. Simmer 3 to 5 minutes until vegetables just losing crispness.

2 to 3 cakes bean curd, cut into
   1 inch cubes
¼ heat Chinese cabbage cut
   into 2 inch cubes
1 large sprig parsley, torn
   in small pieces

Place in large pottery bowl. Pour hot stock and vegetables over ingredients in bowl. Serve at once with following dipping sauce:

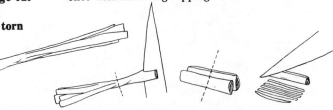

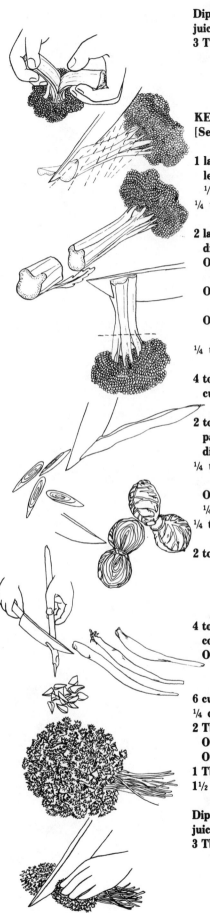

Dipping sauce:
juice of 1 lemon
3 Tbsp. soy sauce

Combine in bowl and serve with Yosenabe. Good one-pot meal when served with rice or noodles. Pickles or cold dressed vegetable dishes are also good with Yosenabe.

KENCHAN-JIRU [MASHED BEAN CURD AND VEGETABLE STEW]
[Serves 4 to 6]

1 large daikon, cut in half
   lengthwise and then cut into
   ½ inch half circles
¼ tsp. sea salt

Sprinkle daikon with salt. Steam 10 to 15 minutes until just tender. Set aside to use later.

2 large carrots, cut into ¼ inch
   diagonal slices
   OR 1 large stalk broccoli, cut
      into thick diagonal slices
   OR ½ lb. green beans, cut into
      ¼ inch diagonals
   OR ½ lb. brussel sprouts, cut
      in half lengthwise
¼ tsp. sea salt

Sprinkle vegetable with sea salt. Steam 5 to 10 minutes until vegetables are just tender. Set aside to use later.

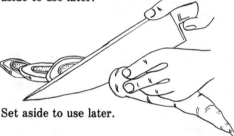

4 to 6 large mushrooms,
   cut into thirds

Set aside to use later.

2 to 3 burdock [gobo]
   pared and cut into thin,
   diagonal slices
¼ tsp. sea salt

Soak burdock in hot water for 30 minutes. Squeeze dry. Sprinkle with salt. Steam 10 to 20 minutes until tender. Set aside for later use.

   OR 2 parsnips, cut into
      ¼ inch diagonal slices
¼ tsp. sea salt

Sprinkle parsnips with salt. Steam 5 to 10 minutes until just tender. Set aside for later use.

2 to 3 cakes bean curd

Wrap tightly in a muslin cloth. Place weight on top. Press for 1 to 2 hours to remove most of liquid. Mash coarsely with a fork. Set aside for later use.

4 to 6 large sprigs parsley,
   coarsely chopped
   OR ¼ cup watercress,
      coarsely chopped

Set aside for later use.

6 cups stock [dashi or kombu]
¼ cup soy sauce
2 Tbsp. sake
   OR dry sherry
   OR rice vinegar
1 Tbsp. mild honey
1½ tsp. sea salt

Place in a large saucepan. Bring to a boil over high heat. Add all ingredients above. Arrange in an attractive manner in broth. Reduce heat to medium. Cook on low heat 2 to 3 minutes just to heat all ingredients. Serve hot with rice or noodles.

Dipping sauce:
juice of 1 lemon
3 Tbsp. soy sauce

Combine in bowl and serve with Kenchan-jiru. Good one-pot meal when served with rice or noodles. Pickles or cold dressed vegetable are also good with Kenchan-Jiru.

NI YASAIMONO [BOILED VEGETABLE STEW WITH TOFU] [Serves 4 to 6]

2 carrots,
  cut into ¼ inch diagonal slices
  OR 2 parsnips,
    cut into ¼ inch
    diagonal slices
  OR ½ lb. green beans, cut into
    ¼ inch diagonal slices
4 small new potatoes,
  cut into halves
  OR 1 large potato, pared and cut
    into 1 inch cubes
4 cakes age [deep fried bean curd],
  cut into 3 inch pieces
1 large daikon radish, cut in
  half lengthwise and then cut
  into ½ inch half circles
5 cups stock [dashi or kombu]
¼ cup soy sauce
2 Tbsp. mild honey
½ tsp. sea salt

Place all ingredients in a large saucepan. Cover and bring to a boil over high heat. Reduce heat at once to just below medium and simmer 10 to 15 minutes until vegetables are just tender.

4 to 6 gammokoki [optional]
½ cup very hot water

Dip gammokoki in hot water to remove excess oil. Add to stew pot.

½ lb. spinach,
  cut into 2 inch strips
  OR ½ lb. any other cooking
    green, cut into 2 inch strips

Add to stew. Cover and cook another 2 to 3 minutes until spinach is just tender.

Dipping sauce:
3 Tbsp. grated daikon radish
¼ cup stock [dashi or kombu]
1 tsp. mild honey
½ cup soy sauce
½ cup orange juice

Mix all ingredients except daikon well. Add daikon. Mix. Use as a dipping sauce for ingredients as stew is being eaten. Serve with rice and pickles for a simple one-pot meal.

NAMASHOYU DOFU [BEAN CURD IN SOY] [Serves 4 to 6]

2 cups water
4 inch square kombu,
　washed to remove excess salt
½ cup tamari soy sauce

Place all ingredients in saucepan. Bring to boil. Remove kombu (save for pickle).

4 cakes bean curd, cut into
　1 inch x ¾ inch rectangles

Add bean curd to stock. Simmer 1 to 2 minutes to heat bean curd.

juice of ½ lemon
1 tsp. fresh ginger root, grated
1 lemon, cut into thin slices

Add to bean curd and stock. Bring to boil again. Take off heat. Serve hot with lemon slices for each bowl. Good served with a rice or noodle dish and a pickle or vegetable dish for a simple main meal.

SAKANA OR TORI NABE [FISH OR CHICKEN STEW WITH VEGETABLES AND RICE CAKES] [Serves 4]

1 cup stock [dashi]
⅓ cup soy sauce
¼ cup sake
　OR dry sherry
1½ Tbsp. mild honey

Place in a large frying pan. Bring to a boil over high heat. Reduce heat to medium and simmer 2 minutes.

1 chicken breast, cut into
　paper thin slices
　OR ½ lb. fresh fish fillet,
　　cut into thin strips

Add to stock in one part of pan.

4 to 6 fresh mushrooms,
　sliced thin
6 green onions, cut into
　paper thin diagonal slices
　OR 1 small yellow onion,
　　cut in half lengthwise and
　　then sliced paper thin
4 to 5 large sprigs parsley,
　coarsely chopped

Add each ingredient to pan in its own separate area. Cook 3 to 5 minutes until chicken is tender.

12 to 16 mochi, toasted
　[see Basic Ingredients section]

Add to chicken and vegetable mixture in its own separate area. Cook 2 to 3 minutes until rice cakes are heated. Serve hot with rice and pickles. A good one-pot meal. Also I like it cold for lunch the next day.

ODEN [FISH AND VEGETABLE STEW] [Serves 4 to 6]

1 daikon radish, cut in half
  lengthwise and then cut into
  ½ inch half circles
  OR 2 large turnips, cut in
     quarters lengthwise and then
     cut into ½ inch pieces
¼ tsp. sea salt

Sprinkle daikon with salt. Place in a steamer.
Steam 10 to 15 minutes until just tender. Set
aside to use later.

4 to 6 small new potatoes,
  with skins left on, cut in half
  OR 1 large potato, cut into
     1 inch cubes
¼ tsp. sea salt

Sprinkle potatoes with salt. Place in a steamer.
Steam 10 to 15 minutes until just tender. Set
aside to use later.

2 large carrots, cut into
  ¼ inch diagonals
  OR 1 large stalk broccoli,
     cut into thick diagonals
  OR ½ lb. green beans,
     cut into ¼ inch diagonals
  OR ½ lb. brussel sprouts,
     cut in half lengthwise

Sprinkle vegetable with sea salt. Place in a
steamer. Steam 5 to 10 minutes until vegetables
just tender. Set aside to use later.

Set aside to use later.

4 hard boiled eggs,
  peeled and cut in half across
  the center

6 gammokoki cakes
  OR tofu dango
  OR miso dango
  OR 3 cakes age [deep fried
     bean curd], cut into thirds

Dip in hot water to remove excess oil. Set aside
to use later.

1 to 2 cakes bean curd, cut
  into 2 inch cubes

Set aside to use later.

4 to 6 large shrimp, shelled
  and deveined
½ lb. white fish, cut into
  2 to 3 inch pieces
¼ tsp. sea salt

Sprinkle fish with salt. Mix well. Place on plate
with shrimp.

4 to 6 large clams

Scrub shells. Place on plate with fish and
shrimp.

8 cups stock [dashi]
1½ tsp. sea salt
¼ cup soy sauce
¼ cup sake
   OR dry sherry
   OR rice vinegar
2 Tbsp. mild honey

Place in a large saucepan. Bring to a boil over high heat. Add all ingredients above. Arrange in an attractive manner in broth. Reduce heat to medium. Cook on low heat 2 to 3 minutes just to heat all ingredients. Serve hot with rice or noodles and dipping sauce.

Dipping sauces:

I

3 Tbsp. daikon radish,
   grated fine
¼ cup dashi stock
1 tsp. mild honey
½ cup fresh orange juice
½ cup soy sauce

Mix honey and dashi well. Add other ingredients. Serve at room temperature to dip ingredients from Oden in as they are taken from the pot by each diner. A good one-pot meal.

II

½ cup soy sauce
juice of 1 lemon
2 Tbsp. dashi stock

Mix ingredients well. Serve at room temperature to dip ingredients from Oden in as they are taken from the pot by each diner.

III

3 Tbsp. stock [kombu or dashi]
1½ tsp. Japanese horseradish
   powder [washabi]

Slowly add stock to horseradish powder. Mix well. Let sit 15 to 30 minutes. Dip Oden ingredients in sauce before eating. This is a good one-pot meal when served with rice or noodles. Pickles or cold dressed vegetable dishes are also good with Oden.

VARIATION:

VEGETARIAN ODEN [VEGETARIAN JAPANESE STEW] [Serves 4 to 6]

8 cups stock [kombu]

Follow recipe for Oden. Omit all fish and shellfish. Use kombu stock in place of dashi stock. Cook as directed. Serve hot with rice or noodles. Use Oden dipping sauces to dip ingredients in as they are eaten. A good one-pot meal served with rice or noodles. Pickles or cold dressed vegetable dishes are also good with Oden.

NABEMONO [FISH STEW WITH VEGETABLES] [Serves 4 to 6]

4 to 6 large shrimp, shelled and deveined	Set on a large plate.
½ lb. white fish, cut into 2 to 3 inch pieces ¼ tsp. sea salt	Sprinkle fish with salt. Mix well. Place on plate with shrimp.

4 to 6 large fresh mushrooms	Make an "X" design on top of the mushrooms by cutting a shallow "X" on top of the mushrooms and pulling back the skin on top. Set on plate with fish and shrimp.
4 to 6 large clams	Scrub shells. Place on plate with fish and shrimp.

2 large carrots, cut into ¼ inch diagonal slices OR 1 large parsnip, cut into ¼ inch diagonal slices OR ½ lb. green beans, cut into long thin diagonals	Steam 5 to 10 minutes until just tender. Place on plate with fish, shrimp and other ingredients.

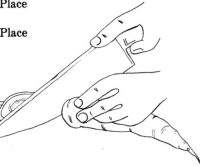

4 medium sized new potatoes, cut into 1 inch cubes	Steam 10 to 15 minutes until just tender. Place on plate with other ingredients.
1 large daikon, cut into ½ inch cubes	Steam 10 to 15 minutes until just tender. Place on plate with other ingredients.
½ cup celery leaves OR parsley OR watercress OR peppercress OR spinach	Place on plate with other ingredients.
1 cake bean curd [optional], cut into 1 inch cubes	Place on plate with other ingredients.

5 cups dashi stock ¼ cup soy sauce 2 Tbsp. mild honey ½ tsp. sea salt	Place in a large pot. Bring to a boil over high heat. Add ingredients on plate in separate areas of the pot. Reduce heat to medium. Cook 3 to 5 minutes until clams open and greens are tender. Serve hot with rice and the following dipping sauces in which the ingredients are dipped before eating.

Sauces:

I

3 Tbsp. daikon radish, grated fine ¼ cup dashi stock 1 tsp. mild honey ½ cup soy sauce ½ cup fresh orange juice	Mix honey and dashi well. Add other ingredients. Serve at room temperature to dip ingredients from Nabemono in as they are taken from the pot by each diner. A good one-pot meal.

II

½ cup soy sauce juice of 1 lemon 2 Tbsp. dashi stock	Mix ingredients well. Serve at room temperature to dip ingredients from Nabemono in as they are taken from the pot by each diner.

TORI NABEMONO [CHICKEN STEW WITH VEGETABLES] [Serves 4 to 6]

1 chicken breast, cut into
  1 by 2 inch pieces
¼ tsp. sea salt
1 tsp. sake
  OR dry sherry
  OR rice vinegar
	Sprinkle chicken breast with salt and sake. Place on a large plate.

4 to 6 large fresh mushrooms	Make an "X" design on top of the mushrooms by cutting a shallow "X" on top of the mushrooms and pulling back the skin on top. Set on plate with chicken.

2 large carrots, cut into
  ¼ inch diagonal slices
  OR 1 large parsnip, cut into
    ¼ inch diagonal slices
  OR ½ lb. green beans, cut into
    long thin diagonals
	Steam 5 to 10 minutes until just tender. Place on plate with chicken and other ingredients.

4 medium sized new potatoes, cut into 1 inch cubes	Steam 10 to 15 minutes until just tender. Place on plate with other ingredients.
1 large daikon, cut into ½ inch cubes	Steam 10 to 15 minutes until just tender. Place on plate with other ingredients.

½ cup celery leaves
  OR parsley
  OR watercress
  OR peppercress
  OR spinach
	Place on plate with other ingredients.

½ lb. bean sprouts	Place on plate with chicken and vegetables.
1 cake bean curd [optional], cut into 1 inch cubes	Place on plate with chicken and vegetables.

5 cups chicken stock
3 Tbsp. sake
  OR dry sherry
  OR rice vinegar
3 Tbsp. soy sauce
1 tsp. mild honey
¼ cup stock [dashi]
	Place in a large pot. Bring to a boil over high heat. Add ingredients on plate in separate areas of the pot. Reduce heat to medium. Cook 3 to 5 minutes until chicken is just tender. Serve hot with rice and following dipping sauces in which ingredients are dipped before eating.

Sauces:

I

3 Tbsp. daikon radish, grated fine ¼ cup dashi stock 1 tsp. mild honey ½ cup soy sauce ½ cup fresh orange juice	Mix honey and dashi well. Add other ingredients. Serve at room temperature to dip ingredients from Nabemono in as they are taken from the pot by each diner. A good one-pot meal.

II

½ cup soy sauce juice of 1 lemon 2 Tbsp. dashi stock	Mix ingredients well. Serve at room temperature to dip ingredients from Nabemono in as they are taken from the pot by each diner.

TOMATO NABEMONO [FISH OR CHICKEN AND TOMATO STEW]
[Serves 4 to 6]

1 lb. fish fillet
 [cod, sole, mackeral, salmon,
 etc.] cut into ¼ by 2 inch pieces
 OR 1 large chicken breast,
  bone removed and cut into
   ¼ by 2 inch pieces
½ tsp. sea salt
1 Tbsp. sake
 OR dry sherry
 OR rice vinegar

Place fish or chicken in a shallow bowl. Sprinkle fish or chicken with salt and wine. Marinate for 30 minutes to 1 hour. Turn occasionally.

2 Tbsp. sesame oil
 OR vegetable oil

Heat a wok on high heat. Add oil. Heat until a small piece of chicken or fish added sizzles. Fry 2 to 3 minutes until just lightly browned. Remove from pan. Drain.

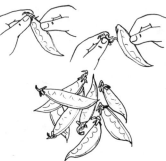

4 green onions, cut into
 thin diagonal slices
5 thin slices fresh ginger root,
 cut into long, paper thin lengths

Add to oil. Fry 30 seconds. Reduce heat to medium.

1 cup stock [dashi or chicken]
1 Tbsp. sake
 OR dry sherry
 OR rice vinegar
2 tsp. soy sauce
½ tsp. mild honey
1 tsp. sea salt

Add to onions and ginger in wok. Cover and bring to a boil.

20 to 24 snow peas, ends
 snipped and strings removed
 OR 20 to 24 green beans, cut
  into long thin diagonal slices

Steam 2 to 3 minutes. Add to wok.

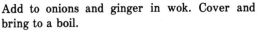

2 large tomatoes, cut into
 8 wedges and then each
 wedge cut in half

Add to stock along with chicken or fish. Cover and bring to a boil again. Allow to simmer 1 to 2 minutes until snowpeas are just tender, but tomatoes are not broken up into pieces.

2 tsp. arrowroot starch
2 Tbsp. water

Push vegetables and fish to one side of pan. Add thickening to sauce. Cook 1 to 2 minutes until sauce thickens and clears. Serve with rice. A good one-pot meal. Also good cold the next day for lunch.

TOFU SHITAKI MUSHI [BEAN CURD STEAMED WITH MUSHROOMS AND SAUCE]
[Serves 4 to 6]

2 cakes bean curd,
  cut in half

Place in a large casserole.

2 green onions,
  cut into thin diagonal slices
1 inch fresh ginger root,
  grated

Sprinkle over bean curd in casserole.

4 to 6 dried mushrooms
½ cup boiling water

Place mushrooms in a small bowl. Pour boiling water over them. Place a weight on top of mushrooms to keep them under water. Let sit 15 to 30 minutes until soft. Remove from water. Squeeze dry. Remove tough stems. Cut into thin slices, then mince. Sprinkle over bean curd in casserole.

¼ cup soy sauce
¼ cup sake
  OR dry sherry
  OR rice vinegar
1 tsp. sesame seed oil
½ cup stock [dashi or kombu]
2 tsp. mild honey

Mix ingredients well. Pour over bean curd in casserole. Place in a steamer and steam 10 minutes.

2 tsp. arrowroot starch
2 Tbsp. cold water

Mix starch and water well. Remove casserole from steamer and add thickening to sauce. Mix gently. Place back in steamer and steam 3 to 5 minutes until sauce thickens. Serve hot with sauce. Good with rice and a vegetable dish and pickles.

VARIATION:

Vegetables such as carrots, cauliflower, broccoli, asparagus, snowpeas, beans, etc., may be added to casserole and then the dish becomes a meal.

YU DOFU [STEAMED BEAN CURD WITH SOY DAIKON DIPPING SAUCE]
[Serves 4 to 6]

4 cakes bean curd
  cut into ½ inch cubes
1 cup boiling water

Place water and bean curd in pottery bowl. Place in steamer and steam 3 to 5 minutes.

Sauce:
¼ cup grated daikon radish
¼ cup stock [dashi or kombu]
3 to 4 Tbsp. soy sauce
1 tsp. lemon juice [optional]

Mix sauce and place in small bowl. Dip hot bean curd in sauce when eating. Good served with fried rice or noodles and pickles for a simple main meal.

CHAWAN MUSHI [STEAMED EGG CUSTARD] [Serves 4 to 6]

4 dried mushrooms
½ cup boiling water
  OR 4 fresh mushrooms,
    cut into thirds

Place mushrooms in a small bowl. Pour boiling water over them. Place a weight on top of mushrooms to keep them under water. Let stand 15 to 30 minutes until soft. Remove from water. Squeeze dry. Remove tough stems. Cut each into three pieces. Place mushrooms in individual bowls or in large casserole.

8 to 10 almonds
½ cup boiling water

Place almonds in small bowl. Pour boiling water over them. Allow to soak 3 to 5 minutes until skins are loose. Remove skins. Arrange with mushrooms in individual bowls or in large casserole.

Vegetables that can be used in Chawan Mushi:

½ large carrot, cut into
  long thin diagonals
  OR 3 to 4 leaves of cooking
    greens [spinach, swiss
    chard, collards, watercress,
    etc.], cut into 1 inch strips
  OR 8 to 10 snowpeas, each cut
    into 3 diagonal slices
  OR 8 to 10 green beans, cut
    into long thin diagonals
  OR 4 asparagus, break off
    tough ends, cut into long
    thin diagonals
  OR 1 large stalk broccoli, cut
    into long, thin diagonals
  OR 10 to 12 brussel sprouts,
    cut in half lengthwise
  OR 1 turnip, cut in half
    lengthwise and then cut into
    thin slices
  OR 1 daikon radish, cut into
    thin slices
  OR ½ head cauliflower, broken
    into small flowerlets

Arrange 3 to 4 vegetables of different colors along with mushrooms and almonds in individual bowls or in a large casserole.

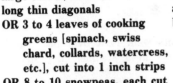

Fish, shellfish, meat or bean curd that can be used in Chawan Mushi:

8 slices kamaboko fish cake
  OR 1 cup cooked chicken
    cut into thin strips
  OR 1 cup cooked meat [pork,
    beef, lamb], cut into
    thin strips
  OR 1 cup cold cooked fish, cut
    into ¼ inch strips
  OR ¼ lb. fresh small shrimp
  OR 2 cakes age [deep fried
    bean curd], cut into
    ¼ inch strips
  OR 1 cake bean curd, cut into
    1 by ¼ inch rectangles and
    fried 2 to 3 minutes to a side
    in hot oil until light brown,
    drained
  OR 4 to 6 gammokoki
  OR 4 to 6 tofu dango
  OR 4 to 6 miso dango

Arrange one of these ingredients along with vegetables, mushrooms and almonds in individual bowls or a large casserole.

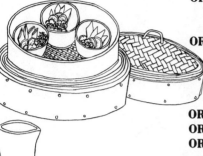

4 cups stock [dashi or kombu],
  chilled
5 eggs, beaten until well mixed
  but not frothy
2 tsp. soy sauce
½ tsp. sea salt
1 Tbsp. sake
  OR dry sherry
  OR rice vinegar
1 tsp. mild honey

Combine all ingredients in a bowl, except eggs. Mix well. Add eggs. Mix gently so eggs do not get frothy. Pour over arrangement of various vegetables and meat or fish in individual bowls so bowls are ¾ full. If using a casserole pour in all liquid.

Garnish:
¼ cup celery leaves
4 sprigs parsley
  OR ¼ cup watercress
4 to 6 lemon wedges

Top each individual bowl with green garnish or top casserole with green garnish. Cover. Steam 15 to 20 minutes until eggs are well set and knife comes out clean when inserted in custard. Serve with lemon wedges. A good meal when served with rice and a cold vegetable dish or pickles. Good the next day cold for lunch.

VARIATION:

ODAMAKI MUSHI [STEAMED EGG CUSTARD WITH NOODLES]
[Serves 4 to 6]

2 cups cooked whole-wheat noodles
  OR whole-wheat spaghetti
  OR whole-wheat vermicelli
  OR any other noodles or vermicelli

Follow recipe for Chawan Mushi. Use noodles in addition to other ingredients. Cook as directed. Serve hot with lemon wedges. A good meal-in-a-bowl. Makes a larger meal when served with a soup and pickles or cold vegetable dish. Excellent cold for lunch.

KENCHI-MUSHI [STEAMED EGG LOAF] [Serves 4 to 6]

6 eggs, beaten until well mixed but not frothy
⅓ cup stock [dashi or kombu]
1 tsp. sea salt
1 Tbsp. mild honey

Mix ingredients well.

1 cake bean curd

Wrap tightly in muslin cloth. Place weight on top. Press for 1 to 2 hours to remove most of liquid. Crumble with a fork. Add to eggs. Mix well.

1 large carrot, grated

Add carrots to eggs and bean curd. Mix well.

3 to 4 dried mushrooms
½ cup boiling water
  OR 3 to 4 fresh mushrooms, cut into thin slices

Place dried mushrooms in a small bowl. Pour boiling water over them. Place a weight on top to keep under water. Let sit 15 to 30 minutes until soft. Remove from water. Squeeze dry. Cut out tough stems. Cut mushroom into thin strips. Add to egg mixture.

2 Tbsp. sesame oil
  OR vegetable oil

Heat a medium sized cast iron skillet over high heat. Add oil and heat until a drop of egg mixture sets. Add egg mixture. Reduce heat to medium. Let sit 1 minute. Scramble 1 to 2 minutes to just barely set the egg mixture but still quite runny.

1 cup snowpeas, cut into long, thin diagonal slices
  OR 1 cup peas

Add peas to egg mixture. Mix. Pour mixture into an oiled loaf pan. Steam 10 to 15 minutes. Cool. Loosen edges with a knife. Invert over a plate or chopping board. Slice into ½ x 2 inch slices. Good served with rice and a hot vegetable for a dinner meal. Also very good for a snack or lunch. Can be dipped in soy sauce when eaten.

CHICKEN TERIYAKI [CHICKEN GRILLED WITH A SWEET SOY SAUCE DRESSING] [Serves 4 to 6]

½ chicken, cut into 2 to 3 inch pieces

Take a whole chicken and cut off legs and wings. Place chicken on back. Cut to ribs. Cut along cartilage joint of rib cage to top of back. Pull front from back. Slice at wing joints. Skin each piece. Fillet breast and save for other dishes. Cut other pieces small with meat cleaver. Place 5 to 6 pieces on one skewer. Place on a grill and grill 3 to 5 minutes until meat turns white. OR place on an oiled broiler pan and grill 3 to 5 minutes until meat is just white.

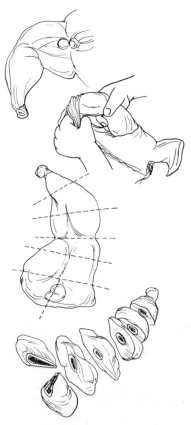

Sauce:
⅓ cup soy suace
1 Tbsp. sake
  OR dry sherry
  OR rice vinegar
⅓ cup water
3 Tbsp. mild honey
2 tsp. arrowroot starch

Combine ingredients in a saucepan. Bring to a boil over medium heat. Cook 1 to 2 minutes until sauce thickens and clears. Remove from heat. Baste whitened chicken meat with sauce - a spoon or pastry brush are the best method of basting. Baste each piece 3 to 4 times and cook 2 to 3 minutes between bastings. Turn often. Cook 10 to 15 minutes until meat is well coated with browned sauce and well done. Serve hot with rice, miso soup and a cold dressed vegetable or pickle. Also good the next day for lunch.

VARIATION:

EBI TERIYAKI [PRAWNS GRILLED WITH SWEET SOY SAUCE DRESSING]
[Serves 4 to 6]

12 to 18 large shrimp or prawns,
shelled and deveined

Slit shrimp along center back. Score with knife in "X" pattern. Flatten with knife. Place on grill. Grill 2 to 3 minutes until shrimp turns pink or place on oiled broiler pan and grill 2 to 3 minutes until shrimp turns pink. Follow recipe for Chicken Teriyaki. Use shrimp in place of chicken. Cook as directed. Serve hot with rice, miso soup and a cold dressed vegetable or pickle. Good cold for lunch.

VARIATION:

FISH TERIYAKI [FISH GRILLED WITH A SWEET SOY SAUCE DRESSING]
[Serves 4 to 6]

1 lb. white fish fillet
OR 1 whole fish, skewered
and scored on both sides

Cut fish into 4 to 6 pieces. Skewer each piece with three skewers through the long way of the piece of fish. Score with a knife down to the skewers on each side. Place on a grill and grill 2 to 3 minutes until fish turns white. OR place on an oiled broiler pan and grill 2 to 3 minutes to a side until fish turns white. Follow recipe for Chicken Teriyaki. Use fish in place of chicken. Cook as directed. Serve hot with rice, soup and a cold dressed vegetable or pickle. Good cold for lunch.

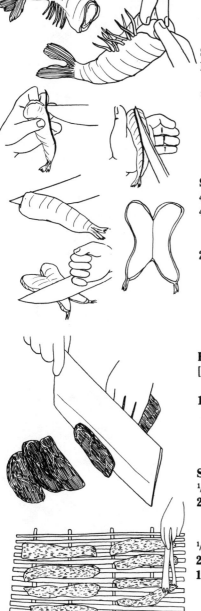

SALMON TERIYAKI [SALMON GRILLED WITH A SWEET SOY SAUCE DRESSING] [Serves 4 to 6]

½ to 1 lb. salmon fillet or
steaks cut into
2 by 3 inch pieces

Skewer each piece of salmon with two skewers. Score salmon down to skewers on each side. Place on a charcoal grill and grill 2 to 3 minutes to a side. OR place on an oiled broiler pan and broil 2 to 3 minutes to a side.

Sauce:
4 Tbsp. soy sauce
4 Tbsp. sake
OR dry sherry
OR rice vinegar
2 Tbsp. mild honey

Place ingredients in a saucepan. Heat 1 to 2 minutes over medium heat until well mixed. Set aside to cool. Dip fish in sauce after it has cooked on both sides. Heat on grill and then dip in sauce again. Repeat 3 to 4 times until all sauce is used and fish is well glazed. Turn several times to glaze both sides. Serve with rice and a cold dressed vegetable such as Sunomono or vegetables with Ama-zu dressing. Good next day cold for lunch.

BEEF TERIYAKI [BEEF GRILLED WITH SWEET SOY SAUCE DRESSING]
[Serves 4 to 6]

1 lb. boneless beef [steak,
roast or stew meat], cut into
1/8 inch thin slices
1 inch in width

It is easiest to cut meat into thin slices when it is partially frozen. A very sharp knife is a necessity for cutting meat thin.

Sauce:
⅓ cup soy sauce
2 Tbsp. sake
OR dry sherry
OR rice vinegar
⅓ cup stock [dashi or beef]
2 Tbsp. mild honey
1 tsp. arrowroot starch

Combine ingredients in a saucepan. Bring to a boil over medium heat. Cook 1 to 2 minutes until sauce thickens and clears. Remove from heat. Cool. Place meat in sauce and marinate 1 to 2 hours. Remove from sauce and grill over charcoal 2 to 3 minutes until crisp. OR Place on an oiled broiler pan and grill 1 to 2 minutes until crisp. Serve with hot rice and vinegar, cold dressed vegetables. Good next day cold for lunch with rice and pickles.

BEEF SHOYU YAKI [GRILLED BEEF MARINATED IN SOY SAUCE AND GARLIC] [Serves 4 to 6]

1 lb. boneless beef
  [steak, roast or stew meat],
  cut into 1/8 inch thin slices
  1 inch in width
1 to 2 large cloves garlic,
  grated
¼ cup soy sauce
1 Tbsp. sake
  OR dry sherry
  OR rice vinegar
1 tsp. mild honey

Mix meat with other ingredients. Allow to marinate 30 minutes to 1 hour. Mix occasionally. Remove from sauce and drain on a rack over a pan so sauce is caught in pan as it drains. Place beef strips on a charcoal grill and grill 1 minute until brown. Dip in sauce and grill other side 1 minute. OR place beef strips on a well oiled broiler pan and broil 1 minute to a side.

½ large daikon, grated
juice of 1 lemon

Mix ingredients well. Sprinkle over hot grilled beef as it is being served. Serve with rice and a cold, dressed vegetable dish. Good next day cold for lunch along with cold rice and pickles.

HAMAGURI YAKI [CLAMS GRILLED WITH SWEET SOY SAUCE DRESSING] [Serves 4 to 6]

1 lb. large clams [razor clams
  are very good for this dish]

Wash clams. Place on bamboo skewers.

Sauce:
⅓ cup sake
  OR dry sherry
  OR rice vinegar
3 Tbsp. mild honey
⅓ cup soy sauce
2 Tbsp. miso
1 Tbsp. stock
1 tsp. arrowroot starch

Mix miso and stock. Add honey. Mix well. Add sake slowly so sauce is smooth. Add other ingredients and mix well. Place in a saucepan. Bring to a boil over medium heat. Cook 1 to 2 minutes until sauce thickens. Place clams on a charcoal grill. Cook 1 to 2 minutes to a side. Dip clams in sauce several times as they are being cooked. OR place on a well oiled broiler pan and grill 1 to 2 minutes. Serve hot with rice and cold, dressed vegetables. Good next day cold for lunch with rice and pickles.

GYODEN [SMALL FISH GRILLED WITH MISO SAUCE BASTE] [Serves 4 to 6]

1 lb. smelt, trout or other
  small fish, cleaned but heads
  kept on fish, skewer smelt

Place fish on a charcoal grill or oiled broiler pan. Grill 1 to 2 minutes to a side until just white.

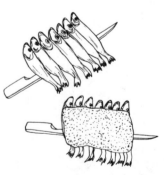

Sauce:
⅓ cup light miso
2 Tbsp. lemon juice
1 Tbsp. dashi stock

Mix ingredients well so no lumps remain. Baste partly cooked fish with sauce. Turn and baste again. Continue cooking 5 to 8 minutes until fish are tender and sauce is lightly browned. Serve with hot rice and a vegetable dish, either hot or cold. Like most Japanese main dishes this is good the next day served cold for lunch with rice and pickles.

VARIATION:

SAKANA MISO YAKI [FISH GRILLED WITH MISO SAUCE BASTE] [Serves 4 to 6]

1 lb. whitefish fillet, cut into 3 inch pieces
  OR 1 whole fish, skewered and
    scored on both sides

Cut fish into 4 to 6 pieces. Skewer each piece with three skewers through the long way of the piece of fish. Score with a knife down to the skewers on each side. Place on a grill and grill 2 to 3 minutes until fish turns white OR place on an oiled broiler pan and grill 2 to 3 minutes to a side until fish turns white.

Sauce:
1/3 cup light miso
2 Tbsp. lemon juice
1 Tbsp. dashi stock

Mix ingredients well so no lumps remain. Baste partly cooked fish with sauce. Turn and baste again. Continue cooking 5 to 8 minutes until fish is tender and sauce is lightly browned. Serve with hot rice and a vegetable dish, either hot or cold. Like most Japanese main dishes this is good the next day served cold for lunch with rice and pickles.

VARIATION:

TORI MISO YAKI I [CHICKEN GRILLED WITH MISO SAUCE] [Serves 4 to 6]

1/2 chicken, cut into 1 to 2 inch pieces

Skin chicken. Cut with a cleaver into small pieces. Place on 4 to 6 skewers. Place on a charcoal grill or oiled broiler pan and grill 2 to 3 minutes, turning often until meat whitens. Follow recipe for Sakana Miso Yaki. Use chicken in place of fish. Cook as directed. Serve with hot rice and a hot or cold vegetable dish. Good cold for lunch the next day with rice and pickles.

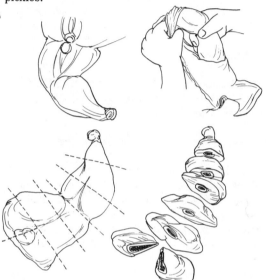

SALMON MISO YAKI [SALMON MARINATED IN MISO SAUCE AND GRILLED] [Serves 4 to 6]

1 lb. salmon fillets,
  cut into 3 inch pieces
  OR 1 lb. salmon steaks with
    2 skewers in each steak
  OR 1 lb. white fish fillet, cut
    into 3 inch pieces and then
    each piece skewered with
    2 skewers

Sauce:
1/3 cup light miso
1 Tbsp. soy sauce
1 1/2 tsp. mild honey
1 tsp. sake
  OR dry sherry
1 Tbsp. dashi

Place salmon in a shallow bowl with cover.

Slowly add liquid ingredients to miso. Mix well. Make sure all lumps are removed from miso. Pour sauce over salmon. Cover all parts. Marinate salmon in miso sauce 3 to 6 hours or overnight. Remove from sauce. Scrape excess marinade off salmon. Place on a charcoal grill. Grill 2 to 3 minutes to a side until just done. OR place on an oiled broiler pan and grill 2 to 3 minutes to a side. Serve hot with rice and a cold, dressed vegetable. Good next day cold for lunch.

413

MISO YAKI [MEAT MARINATED IN MISO SAUCE AND GRILLED]
[Serves 4 to 6]

1 lb. boneless beef
  [roast, stew meat or steak], cut
  into 1/8 inch thin slices
  1 inch in width

Place in a shallow bowl with a cover.

⅓ cup dark miso
2 Tbsp. sake
  OR dry sherry
  OR rice vinegar
2 Tbsp. mild honey
1 Tbsp. stock [dashi]

Slowly add liquid ingredients to miso. Mix well. Make sure all lumps are removed from miso. Pour sauce over beef. Cover all parts of meat. Marinate 3 to 6 hours or overnight. Scrape excess marinade off meat. Place on a charcoal grill and grill 1 minute on each side until just done. OR place on an oiled broiler pan and grill 1 minute to each side. Serve hot with rice and a cold, dressed vegetable. Also good the next day for lunch.

VARIATION:

TORI MISO YAKI II [CHICKEN MARINATED IN MISO SAUCE AND GRILLED]
[Serves 4 to 6]

½ chicken, cut into 1 to 2 inch pieces

Cut chicken with a cleaver into small pieces. Place in a shallow bowl with a cover. Follow recipe for Miso Yaki. Use chicken in place of meat. Cook as directed. Serve hot. Serve with rice and a cold, dressed vegetable. Good for lunch the next day.

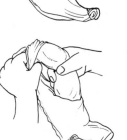

GOMA YAKI [SESAME SEED BASTE FOR GRILLED FOOD] [Serves 4 to 6]

1 lb. boneless meat
  [stew meat, roast, steak], cut
  into 1/8 inch thin strips
  1 inch in width

It is easiest to cut meat into thin slices when it is partially frozen. A very sharp knife is a necessity for cutting meat thin.

Sauce:
¼ cup sesame seeds

Heat a small skillet over high heat. Add seeds. Parch 1 to 2 minutes until lightly browned. Shake pan often to keep seeds from browning unevenly. Remove from heat. Grind in a food mill, blender or shirabashi until well ground.

¼ cup vegetable oil
1 Tbsp. lemon juice
1 tsp. stock [dashi]
1½ tsp. soy sauce
¼ tsp. red pepper [optional]

Mix ingredients well with ground sesame seeds. Dip meat in sauce and then place on a grill for 30 seconds. Dip in sauce again and grill other side. Repeat for each side until meat browned. Serve hot with rice and pickles or a cold, dressed vegetable. Good cold the next day for lunch.

VARIATION:

SAKANA GOMA YAKI [SESAME SEED BASTE WITH GRILLED FISH]]serves 4 to 6]

1 lb. smelt, trout or other small fish, cleaned but heads kept on fish
   OR 1 lb. white fish fillet, cut into 3 inch pieces and then skewered with 3 skewers
   OR 1 whole fish, skewered and scored on both sides

Place fish on a charcoal grill or oiled broiler pan. Grill 1 to 2 minutes to a side until just white. Follow recipe for Gamo Yaki. Use fish in place of meat. Cook as directed. Serve hot with rice and pickles or a cold, dressed vegetable. Good cold for lunch the next day.

VARIATION:

TORI GOMA YAKI [SESAME SEED BASTE WITH GRILLED CHICKEN] [Serves 4 to 6]

½ chicken, cut into 1 to 2 inch pieces

Skin chicken. Cut with a cleaver into small pieces. Place on 4 to 6 skewers. Place on a charcoal grill or oiled broiler pan and grill 2 to 3 minutes, turning often until meat whitens. Follow recipe for Goma Yaki. Use chicken in place of meat. Cook as directed. Serve hot with rice and pickles or a cold vegetable. Good cold for lunch the next day.

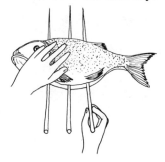

KUSHI YAKI [MARINATED FISH OR MEAT GRILLED WITH VEGETABLES]
[Serves 4 to 6]

1 small chicken, skinned and cut into 1 to 2 inch pieces
   OR 1 lb. boneless beef [roast, stew meat, steak], cut into ½ inch cubes
   OR 1 lb. fish fillet, cut into 1 inch cubes

Skin chicken. Cut with a cleaver into small pieces. Place in a large bowl.
Place meat in bowl.

Place fish in bowl.

Sauce:
½ cup soy sauce
3 Tbsp. mild honey
½ cup sake
   OR dry sherry
   OR rice vinegar
1 inch fresh ginger root, grated
1 tsp. sesame oil
   OR vegetable oil

Pour ingredients over meat or fish. Place a cover over meat or fish that fits inside bowl and covers all the meat or fish. Weight with a rock or other heavy object and let sit for 1 to 4 hours.

3 green peppers, seeded and cut into 1 inch pieces
4 to 6 green onions, cut into 1 inch lengths
½ lb. fresh mushrooms, stems removed

Place green onions and mushrooms in marinade sauce and allow to soak for 15 to 30 minutes. Skewer meat or fish alternately with peppers, green onions and mushrooms. Place on a charcoal grill or a well oiled broiler pan. Grill 1 to 2 minutes until meat turns white. Dip in sauce and grill another 1 to 2 minutes. Repeat process until meat is well browned and all sauce is used. Good served with hot rice and a cold, dressed vegetable dish or pickles. Good cold the next day with rice and pickles for lunch.

VARIATION:

Use any of the meats or fish mentioned but leave out the vegetables. Also sometimes fresh pineapple is used instead of mushrooms.

GRILLED CHICKEN GIBLETS [Serves 4 to 6]

8 to 12 chicken gizzards,
  cut into 4 pieces
  OR 8 to 12 chicken hearts
1 cup water

Place in a pressure cooker. Bring to full pressure for 5 minutes. Cool. OR place in a small saucepan and simmer 10 to 15 minutes until tender. When gizzards or hearts are cool, drain and place in a small bowl. Do not cook liver. Place in a small bowl.

OR IN PLACE OF ABOVE:
½ lb. chicken liver, cut into
  2 inch pieces

Sauce:
¼ cup soy sauce
2 Tbsp. honey
3 Tbsp. sake
  OR dry sherry
  OR rice vinegar
½ inch fresh ginger root, grated

Pour ingredients over giblets. Marinate for 3 to 4 hours or overnight.

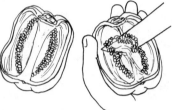

3 green peppers, seeded and
  cut into 1 inch pieces
4 to 6 green onions, cut into
  1 inch lengths
½ lb. fresh mushrooms,
  stems removed

Place green onions and mushrooms in marinade sauce and allow to soak for 15 to 30 minutes. Skewer giblets alternately with peppers, green onions and mushrooms. Place on a charcoal grill or a well oiled broiler pan. Grill 1 to 2 minutes. Dip in sauce and grill another 1 to 2 minutes. Repeat process until giblets are well browned and all sauce is used. Good served with hot rice and a cold, dressed vegetable dish or pickles. Good cold the next day with rice and pickles for lunch.

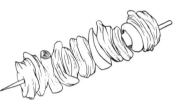

KOGANE-YAKE [BAKED FISH WITH STUFFING] [Serves 4 to 6]

2 large fish fillets
  OR 1 - 5 lb. salmon or trout
1 tsp. sea salt

If whole fish is used leave on head. Scale and wash well. Rub with salt inside and outside. Place on a large piece of foil.

Stuffing:
3 eggs
1 tsp. soy sauce
½ tsp. salt

Mix eggs until well mixed but not frothy. Add salt and soy sauce. Mix well.

5 to 6 fresh mushrooms,
  sliced thin
¼ lb. snowpeas, cut in half
  diagonally

Add to eggs.

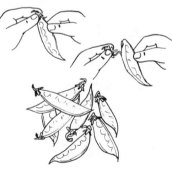

2 tsp. sesame oil

Heat a medium cast iron skillet over medium heat. Add oil. Heat until a small drop of egg added sets. Add egg mixture. Scramble 1 to 2 minutes until eggs are just set but still very moist. Stuff fish with egg mixture. If fillets are used place egg mixture between layers of fish. Wrap tightly with foil. Bake at 350° for 45 minutes to 1 hour until fish is flaky. Serve hot with rice and a cold vegetable dish. Good next day cold for lunch.

TOBAN-YAKI [CHICKEN, SHRIMP AND VEGETABLES BAKED ON TOP OF ROCKS AND PINE NEEDLES] [Serves 4 to 6]

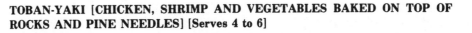

½ chicken,
 skinned and bones removed
½ tsp. sea salt

Rub chicken with sea salt. Let sit 20 to 30 minutes. Place on a plate.

8 large shrimp
 OR ¼ to ½ lb. white fish
  fillet, cut into 3 inch pieces
 OR salmon steak, cut into
  3 inch pieces

Remove shell. Devein shrimp by making a shallow slit down the back of the shrimp with a sharp knife. Remove intestine with the tip of the knife. Place on plate with chicken.

10 large dried mushrooms
1 cup boiling water
 OR ½ lb. fresh wild mushrooms
¼ tsp. sea salt

Place dried mushrooms in a bowl. Pour boiling water over them. Place a weight on top of mushrooms to keep them under water. Let sit 15 to 30 minutes until soft. Remove from water. Squeeze dry. Cut out tough stems. Sprinkle with salt. Place on plate with chicken and shrimp.

10 to 15 water chestnuts,
 peeled
 OR 2 turnips, cut into
  ½ inch cubes
 OR 2 medium carrots, cut into
  ½ inch cubes
 OR 1 daikon, cut into
  ½ inch cubes
 OR 2 parsnips, cut into
  ½ inch cubes
 OR 1 large potato, cut into
  ½ inch cubes
¼ tsp. sea salt

Sprinkle vegetables with sea salt. Steam 3 to 5 minutes. Cool. Place on platter with chicken, shrimp and mushrooms.

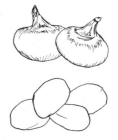

20 pine needles

Line the bottom of a crockery dish with clean stream-washed pebbles. Lay a thin bed of pine needles over pebbles. Arrange chicken, shrimp, mushrooms and vegetable on stones. Cover and bake at 425° for 15 minutes or place over charcoal grill and bake for 10 to 15 minutes.

juice of 1 lemon
3 Tbsp. soy sauce

Mix ingredients well. Serve with baked chicken, shrimp, mushrooms and vegetables as a dipping sauce. Serve dish with hot rice and pickles. An excellent meal for fall or when fresh mushrooms are in season.

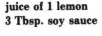

TORI MISO-NI [CHICKEN COOKED IN MISO SAUCE] [Serves 4 to 6]

½ **cup light miso**
   OR ⅓ cup dark miso
¼ **cup sake**
   OR dry sherry
   OR rice vinegar
3 **Tbsp. mild honey**
2 **tsp. fresh ginger root, grated**

Slowly add sake and honey to miso. Mix well so miso is not lumpy. Add ginger. Mix well. Place in a large saucepan.

1 **cup stock [dashi or chicken]**

Slowly add to sauce. Add ¼ cup at a time so stock gets well mixed with ingredients and sauce is not lumpy. Bring to a boil over medium heat. Stir constantly to prevent burning.

½ **chicken,**
   skinned and cut into small
   1 to 2 inch pieces
   with a cleaver

Add chicken. Mix well. Cook 2 to 3 minutes uncovered. Cover. Reduce heat to medium low. Simmer 20 to 30 minutes until chicken is tender and lightly browned. Stir occasionally to prevent sauce from burning. Serve hot with rice and a cold, dressed vegetable dish or pickles. Good cold next day for lunch.

VARIATION:

BEEF MISO-NI [BEEF COOKED IN MISO SAUCE] [Serves 4 to 6]

1 **cup stock [dashi or beef]**
½ **lb. boneless beef, cut into ¼ inch by**
   2 inch rectangles

Follow recipe for Tori Miso-ni. Use beef and beef broth in place of chicken. Cook as directed. Serve hot with rice and a cold vegetable dish or pickle. Good cold next day for lunch.

VARIATION:

SAKANA MISO-NI [FISH COOKED IN MISO SAUCE] [Serves 4 to 6]

1 **lb. fish fillet [cod, butterfish,**
   red snapper, salmon, etc.], cut into
   3 inch pieces

Follow recipe for Tori Miso-ni. Use fish in place of chicken. Cook as directed except simmer only 15 to 20 minutes until fish is tender and lightly browned. Serve hot with rice and a cold vegetable dish or pickle. Good cold for lunch the next day.

VARIATION:

BUTA MISO-NI [PORK COOKED IN MISO SAUCE] [Serves 4 to 6]

1 **cup stock [dashi or pork]**
½ **lb. boneless pork, cut into ¼ inch by**
   2 inch rectangles 1 inch in width

Follow recipe for Tori Miso-ni. Use pork and pork stock in place of chicken. Cook as directed. Serve hot with rice and a cold vegetable dish or pickle. Good cold next day for lunch.

YASHI MISO-NI [VEGETABLES, BEAN CURD AND MEAT COOKED IN MISO SAUCE] [Serves 4 to 6]

½ **cup light miso**
   OR ⅓ **cup dark miso**
¼ **cup sake**
   OR dry sherry
   OR rice vinegar
3 **Tbsp. mild honey**
2 **tsp. fresh ginger root, grated**

Slowly add sake and honey to miso. Mix well so miso is not lumpy. Add ginger. Mix well. Place in a large saucepan.

1 **cup stock**
   [dashi, kombu, chicken, beef or pork]

Slowly add to sauce. Add ¼ cup at a time so stock gets well mixed with ingredients and sauce is not lumpy. Bring to a boil over medium heat. Stir constantly to prevent burning.

4 **to 6 dried mushrooms**
½ **cup boiling water**
   OR 4 to 6 large fresh mushrooms, cut into ¼ inch slices

Place dried mushrooms in a small bowl. Pour boiling water over them. Place a weight on top of mushrooms to keep them under water. Let sit 15 to 30 minutes until soft. Remove from water. Squeeze dry. Remove tough stem. Cut each mushroom into thirds.

1 **lb. fish fillet,**
   cut into 3 inch pieces
   OR ½ lb. boneless meat [beef or pork], cut into ¼ by 2 inch rectangles
   OR ½ chicken skinned and cut into 1 to 2 inch pieces with a cleaver

Add fish, meat or chicken and mushrooms. Mix well. Cook 2 to 3 minutes uncovered. Cover and reduce heat to medium low. Simmer 20 to 30 minutes until fish, meat or chicken is tender and lightly browned. Stir occasionally to prevent sauce from burning.

2 **large carrots, cut into ¼ inch diagonal slices**
   OR ½ lb. broccoli, cut into ¼ inch slices
   OR ½ lb. green beans, cut into long thin diagonals

Steam 5 to 8 minutes until just tender.

1 **cake bean curd, cut into 1 inch cubes**

Add to fish, meat or chicken along with vegetables. Mix gently. Heat 2 to 3 minutes to heat bean curd. Serve hot with rice. This dish can be a one-dish meal or is good served with a cold, dressed vegetable or pickle. Good cold the next day for lunch.

VARIATION:

VEGETARIAN YASHI MISO-NI TOFU [VEGETABLES AND BEAN CURD COOKED IN MISO SAUCE] [Serves 4 to 6]

1 **cup kombu stock**
2 **cakes bean curd, cut into 1 inch cubes**

Follow recipe for Yashi Miso-ni. Do not use meat, chicken or fish. Use kombu stock in place of meat or fish stock. Simmer sauce 10 minutes before adding bean curd and vegetables. Cook as directed. Serve hot with rice. A one-dish meal served with vegetables or pickles. Good cold for lunch the next day.

419

TOFU DENGAKU [BEAN CURD GRILLED WITH MISO SAUCE TOPPING]
[Serves 4 to 6]

3 to 6 cakes bean curd, cut into 4 equal pieces

Wrap tightly in a muslin cloth. Place weight on top. Press for 1 to 2 hours to remove most of liquid.

4 to 8 Tbsp. oil

Heat a large heavy skillet over medium high heat. Add oil and heat until a small piece of bean curd added sizzles. Add bean curd. Fry 3 to 5 minutes a side until just brown. Drain. Place 2 broad skewers through each fried bean curd slice. Keep warm.

Broiling sauces:

I

¼ cup red miso
2 Tbsp. mild honey
1 Tbsp. sake
3 Tbsp. stock [dashi or kombu]

Mix honey and sake with miso. Slowly add stock to prevent miso from being lumpy. Place in a small saucepan. Bring to a boil over medium heat. Stir constantly and simmer 3 to 5 minutes until sauce is thickened. Set aside to use later.

II

¼ cup light miso
2 Tbsp. mild honey
1 Tbsp. sake
OR dry sherry
OR rice vinegar
3 Tbsp. stock [dashi or kombu]

Mix honey and sake with miso. Slowly add stock to prevent miso from being lumpy. Place in a small saucepan. Bring to a boil over medium heat. Stir constantly and simmer 3 to 5 minutes until sauce is thickened. Set aside to use later.

III

2 to 3 large spinach leaves

Steam 4 to 5 minutes until soft but still bright green. Blend to puree or press through a food mill.

¼ cup light miso
2 Tbsp. mild honey
1 Tbsp. sake
OR dry sherry
OR rice vinegar
2 Tbsp. stock [dashi or kombu]

Mix honey and sake with miso. Slowly add spinach. Slowly add stock to prevent miso from being lumpy. Place in a small saucepan. Bring to a boil over medium heat. Stir constantly and simmer 3 to 5 minutes until sauce is thickened. Set aside to use later.

1 tsp. vegetable oil

Brush a broiler pan with oil. Place skewered curd blocks on pan. Brush ⅓ of them with red sauce, ⅓ of them with light sauce, and ⅓ of them with green spinach sauce. Place under broiler and grill 3 to 5 minutes until light sauce is just turning golden brown. Remove from grill. Place three on each plate.

Garnishes:
¼ cup watercress, chopped
OR 4 sprigs parsley, chopped
2 Tbsp. sesame seeds, parched

Heat a small skillet over high heat. Add seeds. Parch 1 to 2 minutes until lightly browned. Shake pan often to evenly brown seeds. Remove from heat. Use sesame seeds to sprinkle over spinach sauce, bean curd squares and green garnish to sprinkle over light and red squares. Serve with rice and pickles for a small meal. Also good with tempura vegetables and a hot vegetable dish.

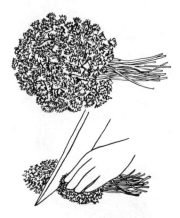

SQUID COOKED IN SOY SAUCE [Serves 4]

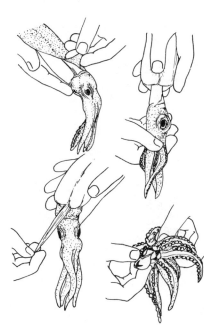

1 lb. squid

Clean squid by pulling off head and removing insides. Wash well. Cut off tentacles from head and remove beak. Remove ink sack. Cut body into ¼ inch rings.

⅓ cup sake
   OR dry sherry
   OR rice vinegar
2 Tbsp. mild honey
3 Tbsp. soy sauce
½ inch fresh ginger root, grated

Combine ingredients in a heavy saucepan. Bring to a boil over medium heat. Add squid. Reduce heat to medium low and cook 20 to 30 minutes until liquid thickens. Serve hot with rice and a cold vegetable dish for dinner. This dish is also good served cold as an appetizer or with cold rice and pickles makes a good lunch.

EBI SHOYU [SHRIMP COOKED IN SOY SAUCE] [Serves 4 to 6]

⅓ cup sake
   OR dry sherry
   OR rice vinegar
2 Tbsp. mild honey
3 Tbsp. soy sauce
½ inch fresh ginger root, grated

Combine all ingredients except shrimp in a heavy saucepan. Bring to a boil over medium heat. Reduce heat to medium low and simmer 15 minutes.

1 lb. small shrimp

Add shrimp to simmering sauce. Mix well. Let simmer 5 to 10 minutes until sauce thickens. Serve hot with rice and a cold or hot vegetable dish for a dinner meal. This dish is also good served cold as an appetizer or with cold rice and pickles makes a good lunch.

HAMANABI SHOYU [SMALL CLAMS COOKED IN SWEET SOY SAUCE] [Serves 4 to 6]

1 lb. small clams
⅓ cup sake
   OR dry sherry
   OR rice vinegar
2 Tbsp. mild honey
3 Tbsp. soy sauce
½ inch fresh ginger root, grated

Combine all ingredients in a heavy saucepan. Bring to a boil over medium heat. Reduce heat to medium low and simmer 20 to 30 minutes until sauce thickens. Serve hot with rice and a cold or hot vegetable dish for a dinner meal. This dish is also good served cold as an appetizer or with cold rice and pickles makes a good lunch.

NAMBAN-ZUKE [SMALL FISH COOKED IN HOT SAUCE] [Serve 4]

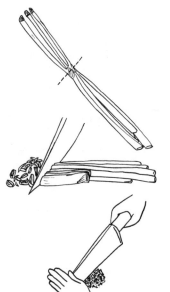

½ lb. herring, trout, smelt or small fish, cleaned but heads left on

Place on a charcoal grill or well oiled broiler pan and grill 3 to 5 minutes until fish is lightly browned and flaky. Turn once so both sides are browned. Remove from grill. Place in a bowl.

4 Tbsp. stock [dashi]
1 tsp. sea salt
⅓ cup soy sauce
⅔ cup rice vinegar
1½ Tbsp. mild honey
¼ inch fresh ginger root, grated
2 to 3 red peppers, minced
3 green onions, minced

Place in a small saucepan. Heat 1 to 2 minutes over high heat until honey is melted and onion is just tender. Pour over fish in bowl. Marinate 6 hours or overnight. An ideal picnic food when served with a bowl of rice and a cold vegetable dish. Also good for lunch with rice and pickles.

OCTOPUS COOKED IN SOY SAUCE [Serves 4 to 6]

5 lbs. octopus legs

Place in a large pot. Cover with water and bring to a boil. Cover and simmer for 3 to 5 hours. OR pressure cook at full pressure for 1 hour. Cool until octopus can be easily handled. Remove outer skin, it should peel right off. Cut legs into ¼ inch slices and then pound into thin rounds with a wooden mallet.

½ cup sake
  OR dry sherry
  OR rice vinegar
¼ cup soy sauce
3 Tbsp. mild honey
¼ cup water
½ inch fresh ginger root, grated

Combine ingredients in a heavy saucepan. Bring to a boil. Add octopus. Reduce heat to medium low and simmer 30 to 40 minutes.

1 Tbsp. arrowroot starch
2 Tbsp. water

Mix starch and water well. Add to sauce and mix. Cook 1 to 2 minutes until sauce thickens and clears. Serve hot with rice and a hot or cold vegetable dish for a dinner meal. Good cold as an appetizer or for lunch the next day with rice and pickles.

SWEETS

The ususal Japanese dessert is a piece of fresh fruit of the season served fresh or deep-fried in a batter coating. Other sweets used as after-dinner desserts are fruit gelatins and sweet steamed eggs. The rice cakes and buns are usually served as snacks with tea during the day.

OHAGI [SWEET RICE BALLS WITH FILLING] [Makes approximately 4 dozen]

2 cups sweet brown rice
3½ cups water
   OR 4 cups leftover cooked
      short grain brown rice

Place rice and water in a heavy saucepan. Cover and bring to a boil over high heat. Reduce heat to medium and simmer 20 minutes. Reduce heat to medium low and cook another 15 minutes. Remove from heat and allow to sit 10 minutes. Turn rice out on a moist platter and spread out to cool. Allow to cool 30 minutes to 1 hour until rice is cool to the touch.

3 Tbsp. mild honey
dash sea salt

Turn rice out on a wet chopping board. Chop rice with a sharp wet knife or cleaver until rice grains are cut fine. Add honey and salt. Knead rice with wet hands until rice is smooth and glutinous. Divide rice into three equal portions. Chopping board, knife and hands are kept wet so rice will not stick to them.

RED OHAGI [SWEET RICE BALLS WITH RED BEAN PASTE]
[Makes approximately 1½ dozen]

⅓ of sweet rice mixture

With moist hands form ½ to 1 tsp. of sweet rice mixture into a small ½ inch diameter round ball. First compress the rice in one hand, then toss the ball from hand to hand to form it into rounds. Roll occasionally between your hands to make the ball round. Set on a plate.

½ batch Azuki-an
  [Sweet Red Bean Paste]
  [See Basic Japanese
  Ingredients]

Take 1½ to 2 tsp. of bean paste and form into 3/8 inch thick round flat cake. Place rice ball in center of cake. Bring sides of bean paste round up and encase rice ball in paste. Mould with fingers until smooth. Place on a plate. Can be served as a snack with tea. Good in a lunch for a sweet. Also one or two per person can be served at the end of a meal for dessert.

WHITE OHAGI [SWEET RICE BALLS WITH WHITE BEAN PASTE]
[Makes approximately 1½ dozen]

⅓ of sweet rice mixture

With moist hands form ½ to 1 tsp. of sweet rice mixture into a small ½ inch diameter round ball. First compress the rice in one hand then toss the ball from hand to hand to form it into rounds. Roll occasionally between your hands to make the ball round. Set on a plate.

⅓ batch Sweet White Bean Paste
  [See Basic Japanese
  Ingredients]

Take 1½ to 2 tsp. of bean paste and form into 3/8 inch thick round flat cake. Place rice ball in center of cake. Bring sides of bean paste round up and encase rice ball in paste. Mould with fingers until smooth. Place on a plate. Can be served as a snack with tea. Good in a lunch for a sweet. Also one or two per person, can be served at the end of a meal for dessert.

BLACK OHAGI [SWEET RICE BALLS WITH BLACK SESAME SEED COVERING] [Makes approximately 1½ dozen]

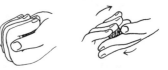

¼ cup black sesame seeds, toasted
OR unhulled sesame seeds, toasted

Roast sesame seeds for 3 to 5 minutes at 300° until lightly browned. Remove from heat. Allow to cool.

¼ batch Azuki-an [Sweet Red Bean Paste] [See Basic Japanese Ingredients]
¼ batch sweet white bean paste [See Basic Japanese Ingredients]

With moist hands form ½ to 1 tsp. sweet bean paste or red bean paste into small ½ inch diameter round balls. First compress paste in one hand and then toss the ball from hand to hand to form it into round balls. Roll occasionally between your hands to make the ball round. Set on a plate.

⅓ of sweet rice mixture

With moist hands take 1 Tbsp. sweet rice mixture and form into 3/8 inch thick round flat cake. Place bean ball in center of cake. Bring sides of rice cake up and encase bean ball in rice cake. Mould with moist fingers until smooth. Roll each ball in black sesame seeds until covered and then place on a plate. Can be served as a snack with tea. Good for a lunch sweet. Also one or two per person can be served at the end of a meal for a dessert.

YAMA IMO [SWEET GLAZED YAMS WITH SESAME SEEDS] [Serves 4 to 6]

1 lb. yams, cut into random 1/8 inch diagonal slices [pencil sharpen a yam]
OR 1 lb. sweet potatoes, cut into random 1/8 inch diagonal slices [pencil sharpen a potato]
½ cup vegetable oil

Heat a heavy saucepan or wok over medium high heat. Add oil. Heat until a piece of yam added sizzles. Add half of yams. Stir and fry 5 to 8 minutes until golden brown. Remove from pan and drain on absorbent paper on a rack. Keep warm while frying the remainder. When all yams are fried pour oil out of pan (can be saved for other frying).

3 Tbsp. mild honey
2 Tbsp. soy sauce
2 Tbsp. water

Add to wok. Reduce heat to medium and simmer 3 to 5 minutes until sauce is simmering well and slightly thickened. Add yams to sauce. Mix well with sauce. Stir and fry 3 to 5 minutes until sauce thickens and yams are well coated. Remove from heat.

2 Tbsp. sesame seeds

Heat a small skillet over high heat. Add seeds. Parch 1 to 2 minutes until lightly browned. Shake pan often to evenly brown seeds. Remove from heat. Sprinkle over yams. Mix. Place yams in individual serving dishes. Good as a dessert after a shabu-shabu or nabemono dinner. Also good as a snack. Serve either warm or cold.

NISHIKI TAMAGO [STEAMED SWEET LAYERED EGGS] [Serves 4 to 6]

4 hard boiled eggs, peeled

Separate yolks from whites. Mash each separately and press through a food mill or fine sieve. Place yolks and whites in separate containers.

1 tsp. arrowroot starch
1 Tbsp. mild honey
1 Tbsp. orange juice
   OR water

Add starch to egg yolks. Mix well. Add other ingredients and mix well. Lightly oil a small loaf pan. Spread egg-yolk mixture over bottom of pan. Tap pan on counter to remove air bubbles.

1 tsp. arrowroot starch
1 Tbsp. mild honey
1 drop almond concentrate
   [optional]

Add starch to egg whites. Mix well. Add other ingredients. Mix well. Spread egg white mixture evenly over egg yolk mixture in loaf pan. Press lightly. Tap pan gently on counter to remove all air bubbles. Cover top of pan and steam 20 to 30 minutes until egg loaf is firm. Cool 10 to 20 minutes. Loosen edges with a knife and remove from pan. Chill. Cut into ¼ to ½ inch pieces. Good served as a snack for lunch or a few slices per person can be served as an after dinner dessert.

YOKAN [RED BEAN PASTE FLAVORED SEAWEED GELATIN] [Serves 4 to 6]

¾ cake agar-agar [katen]
2 cups water

Shred agar-agar with a knife OR place in a blender with water and blend fine. Place in water in pan. Soak 10 minutes. Bring to boil over medium high heat. Stir until gelatin melts.

½ cup mild honey

Add and mix well. Reduce heat to medium. Simmer 5 minutes.

⅓ cup Azuki-an
   [Sweet Red Bean Paste]
   [See Basic Japanese
   Ingredients]

Slowly add ⅓ cup of liquid to bean paste and mix well until all lumps are removed. Add another ⅓ cup of liquid to bean paste mixture. Mix well. Add bean paste liquid to pan. Mix well. Cook 2 to 3 minutes until well mixed and all heated. Pour into a shallow pan. Chill 1 to 2 hours until set. Cut into 1 by 1½ inch rectangles. Serve cold. Good as an after dinner dessert or just as a snack. A very traditional Japanese dessert.

KANTEN [SWEET SEAWEED GELATIN] [Serves 4 to 6]

⅓ to ½ long cake agar-agar [kanten] 2 cups water	Shred agar-agar with a knife OR place in a blender with water and blend fine. Place in water in saucepan. Soak 10 minutes. Bring to a boil over medium high heat. Stir until gelatin melts.
½ cup mild honey	Add and mix well. Reduce heat to medium. Simmer 5 minutes.

1 Tbsp. lemon juice
1 cup fresh orange juice
  OR juice of 2 oranges
  OR 1 cup blended or mashed strawberries, raspberries, cherries, melons, etc.
  OR 1 cup pink grapefruit juice
  OR 1 cup tangerines, blended
	Add juice to pan. Continue to simmer 1 minute. Remove from heat. Strain through a fine sieve (optional) and pour into a shallow dish. Chill 1 to 2 hours until set. Cut into 1 inch by 1½ inch rectangles. Serve cold. Usually only 1 or 2 pieces are served per person. Good as an after dinner dessert or just as a snack. Melts in your mouth. Japan's superb answer to Jello.

AWAYUKIKAN [SEAWEED GELATIN WITH EGG WHITE AND FRUIT] [Serves 4 to 6]

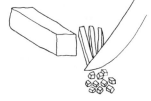

¾ cake agar-agar [katen] 2 cups water	Shred agar-agar with a knife OR place in blender with water and blend fine. Place in water in pan. Soak 10 minutes. Bring to boil over medium heat. Stir until gelatin melts.
½ cup mild honey	Add and mix well. Reduce heat to medium. Simmer 5 minutes.

1 Tbsp. lemon juice
1 cup fresh orange juice
  OR 1 cup blended or mashed strawberries, raspberries, cherries, melons, etc.
  OR 1 cup pink grapefruit juice
  OR 1 cup tangerines blended
	Add juice to pan. Continue to simmer 1 minute. Remove from heat. Strain through a fine sieve (optional). Chill 20 to 30 minutes until cool but not set.

Optional garnish:
1 tangerine, sectioned and each section halved
  OR 1 orange, sectioned and each section halved
  OR 6 strawberries, cut in half lengthwise
  OR ½ cup firm raspberries
  OR ½ cup cherries, pitted and cut in half lengthwise
  OR 6 orange slices, cut in half
  OR 6 thin lemon slices, cut in half
	Place sliced fruit on bottom of a shallow pan. Pour a small amount of gelatin in pan and chill immediately to set fruit in place.

1 egg white	Warm egg to room temperature. Beat egg white until stiff peaks are formed. Slowly fold egg whites into cooled gelatin mixture. Pour into shallow pan with fruit set in bottom. Chill 2 to 3 hours until gelatin firm. Cut into 1 to 2 inch diamonds. Serve cold. An excellent dessert for a hot summer day. Also good as a snack.

LAYERED AWAYUKIKAN [FLAVORED SEAWEED GELATIN WITH EGG WHITE LAYER]
[Serves 4 to 6]

¾ cake agar-agar [katen]
2 cups water

Shred agar-agar with a knife OR place in a blender with water and blend fine. Place in water in pan. Soak 10 minutes. Bring to a boil over medium high heat. Stir until gelatin melts.

½ cup mild honey

Add and mix well. Reduce heat to medium. Simmer 5 minutes.

1 Tbsp. lemon juice
1 cup fresh orange juice
  OR 1 cup blended or mashed
      strawberries, raspberries,
      cherries, melons, etc.
  OR 1 cup pink grapefruit juice
  OR 1 cup tangerines blended

Add juice to pan. Continue to simmer 1 to 2 minutes. Remove from heat. Strain through a fine sieve (optional). Set one cup of mixture aside. Pour remainder of liquid into a loaf pan with garnish. Chill until set. Cool 1 cup of liquid for 20 to 30 minutes until almost set.

Optional garnish:
1 tangerine, sectioned and each
    section halved
  OR 1 orange, sectioned and
      each section halved
  OR 6 strawberries, cut in
      half lengthwise
  OR ½ cup firm raspberries
  OR ½ cup cherries, pitted and
      cut in half lengthwise
  OR 6 orange slices, cut in half
  OR 6 thin lemon slices,
      cut in half

Place sliced fruit on bottom of the loaf pan. Pour a small amount of gelatin in pan and chill immediately to set fruit in place.

1 egg white

Beat egg white until stiff peaks are formed. Slowly fold 1 cup of cooled gelatin mixture into egg whites. Pour over gelatin in loaf pan. Chill 1 to 2 hours or overnight until firm. Cut into ½ inch thick slices. Serve on side.

TEMPURA FRUIT [DEEP-FRIED BATTER-COATED FRUIT WITH SWEET DIPPING SAUCE] [Serves 4 to 6]

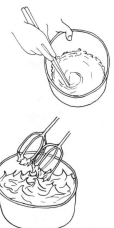

Batter:
¾ cup whole-wheat pastry flour
6 Tbsp. arrowroot starch

Combine in a bowl. Mix well.

1 tsp. mild honey
1 egg yolk
1 to 1½ cups ice water

Mix yolk and honey well. Add water slowly. Mix well. Slowly add flour and starch to liquid. Mix well with chopsticks or with whisk but do not beat. Do not overmix. Batter can be slightly lumpy.

1 egg white

Beat until egg white holds a stiff peak. Fold gently into batter. Keep batter in the refrigerator until ready for use. Keep batter cold while using it for best results. I keep it in a bowl of ice as I am dipping in vegetables or fruits to fry.

2 to 4 apples, cored and cut
into ¼ inch slices
OR 2 to 4 bananas cut into
2 inch diagonal slices
OR 2 to 4 ripe firm pears,
cored and cut into
¼ inch slices
OR 4 to 6 slices pineapple,
fresh or canned, cut into
1 to 3 inch slices
juice of 1 lemon

Slice fruit and sprinkle with lemon juice to prevent browning. Chill.

3 cups vegetable oil
¼ to ½ cup sesame oil
[optional]

Heat a wok. Add oil. Sesame oil gives tempura a more fragrant flavor. Combine oil in wok and heat to 350° to 375°. If no thermometer is available test oil by dropping a small amount of batter into oil. If batter sits on bottom oil is too cold. If batter stays on top sizzling, oil is too hot. If batter goes to bottom and then rises almost at once, oil is right for frying. Dip fruit in batter one at a time. Place in oil. Fry 4 to 6 pieces at a time. Do not fry too much since oil temperature will drop and food will not cook well and absorb too much oil. Fry 3 to 5 minutes until golden brown. Turn once to brown both sides evenly. When fruit is fried, remove from oil and drain on wire rack or brown paper to remove excess oil. Test oil again for heat and then dip next batch until all fruit is fried.

Dipping sauce:
½ cup mild honey
2 Tbsp. lemon juice
¼ cup fruit juice

Heat honey over medium heat 3 to 5 minutes. Add juice. Mix well. Simmer 30 seconds to heat. Serve with batter-fried fruit. Dip fruit in sauce when eating it. Good to use leftover tempura batter with at end of tempura dinner. Good snack also.

Too Cold

Too Hot

Correct Temperature

MANJU [STEAMED BUNS WITH SWEET BEAN OR FRUIT FILLING]
[Serves 4 to 6]

1 cup Azuki-an [Sweet Bean Paste] [See Basic Japanese Ingredients]
OR 2 apples, cut into 20 ½ inch cubes
OR 2 pears, cut into 20 ½ inch cubes
OR 2 to 4 slices pineapple, cut into 20 ½ inch pieces

Make sweet bean paste into 20 round ½ inch diameter balls. Set on a plate for later use.

Dough:
2 cups whole-wheat pastry flour
1 Tbsp. arrowroot starch
¼ tsp. sea salt
1 tsp. baking powder

Mix well so pastry will not be lumpy.

⅓ cup plus 1 Tbsp. water
3 Tbsp. mild honey

Mix well. Add to flour. Mix well. Beat until smooth. Flour hands. Divide dough into 20 portions and form into round balls. Flatten into rounds 3/8 inch thick. Place bean filling in center and encase in dough. Smooth ball by rolling between hands. Place in a steamer and steam 15 to 20 minutes until smooth and firm. Cover with a towel while steaming. A good after-dinner dessert served one or two per person on individual small plates. Also an excellent snack.

HIKISHAMANJU [STEAMED BUNS WITH FILLING AND GREEN-TEA CRUST]
[Serves 4 to 6]

1 cup Azuki-an [Sweet Bean Paste] [See Basic Japanese Ingredients]
OR 2 apples, cut into 20 ½ inch cubes
OR 2 pears, cut into 20 ½ inch cubes
OR 2 to 4 slices pineapple, cut into 20 ½ inch pieces

Make sweet bean paste into 20 round ½ inch diameter balls. Set on a plate for later use.

Dough:
2 cups whole-wheat pastry flour
1 Tbsp. arrowroot starch
¼ tsp. sea salt
1 tsp. baking powder
1 tsp. powdered green tea

Mix well so pastry will not be lumpy.

⅓ cup plus 1 Tbsp. water
3 Tbsp. mild honey

Mix well. Add to flour. Mix well. Beat until smooth. Flour hands. Divide dough into 20 portions and form into round balls. Flatten into rounds 3/8 inch thick. Place bean filling in center and encase in dough. Smooth ball by rolling between hands. Place in a steamer and steam 15 to 20 minutes until smooth and firm. Cover with a towel while steaming. A good after-dinner dessert served one or two per person on individual small plates. Also an excellent snack.

GLOSSARY

AGAR-AGAR—An edible tasteless seaweed used to make jelled salads, main dishes and desserts in the Orient. Agar-agar is a good source of minerals. It has a much softer jell than animal product gelatin, it melts in your mouth and is preferred in the Orient. Foods jelled with agar-agar are very easy to digest, in fact almond curd made from almond milk and agar-agar is used as a convalescent food in China as well as a dessert. Will jell in warm as well as cool temperatures. Found in white or red cakes in Japanese and Chinese shops—the red ones have food coloring in them, so do not buy them. Found in flakes or powder in natural and health food stores. 1 cake = about ⅔ cup flakes, 2 Tbsp. flakes = 1 Tbsp. powder.

AGE—Short for abura age.   See *Bean Curd, Deep Fried* for further explanation.

AJINOMONTO—Japanese for MSG. See *Monosodium Glutamate* and DON'T USE IT.

ALMOND—A nut of high mineral content with comparatively low fat content. The aristocrat of nuts in the Orient, prized for its distinct rich flavor. Used with vegetables, meats, rices, and in sweet dishes. Cashews or peanuts can be substituted for almonds in many dishes, but almonds are preferred by all cuisines except the Indonesians, which favor the peanut.

ALLSPICE—A dried berry of a tropical bush, allspice gets its name from mimicking the flavors of a combination of cinnamon, nutmeg and cloves. A favorite of the Middle East, allspice is used in salads, soups, hot vegetables, meat and vegetarian dishes as well as sweets. Best to buy whole berries and grind them yourself.

ANCHOR POWDER—Indian for mango powder. See *Mango Powder* for further explanation.

ANCHOVY PASTE—Used in place of trassi or blanchan in Indonesian cooking. Anchovy paste is a fishy smelling paste made from pulverized anchovies. Found in Western specialty food shops and Italian markets. See *Trassi* or *Blanchan* for further explanation.

ANISEED—See *Star Aniseed*.

ARAB OLIVES—Same as Greek olives. See *Greek Olives* for further explanation.

ARROWROOT STARCH—A powder of the tropical American tuber arrowroot, high in minerals and calcium ash. This starch is easily digested and thickens to a clear non-starchy tasting sauce when mixed with water and heated. Use in place of refined cornstarch, which has little nutritive value and gives sauces a starchy flavor. Kuzu, the Oriental arrowroot, can be used but is very expensive. Found in natural and health food stores. Store in an airtight container.

AZUKI BEAN—A small, strongly flavored red bean grown in Japan. Cooked with rice (Azuke meshi, *page 353*), but most often used as a base for sweet bean paste used in desserts in both China and Japan. Found in Chinese, Japanese and natural food stores. Kidney beans can be substituted for azuki beans.

AZUKI-AN—Japanese word for a sweet red bean paste used as a filling for Ohagi or rice cakes. Made from azuki beans, honey and sea salt. Do not buy ready made, since the ready-made bean paste is made with refined sugar.

BAJRE—Indian for millet flour. Used in breads and to make tasty dumplings that are cooked in a spicy tomato, yoghurt or coconut-milk sauce. Find in Indian shops or grind your own from whole millet.

BAMBOO SHOOTS—Young tender shoots of an edible tropical bamboo plant used in China and Japan as a vegetable. The two varieties sprout in the spring and winter. Winter shoots are smaller and smoother textured but more expensive. Found canned in Chinese and Japanese markets and some Western grocery stores. Drain and rinse before using. Store in refrigerator in cold water.

BEAN CURD— Used by the Orient in many dishes or eaten plain. Used in place of meat as a protein source in the Orient but valued for its own light texture and taste as well. It contains all the essential amino acids, is high in phosphorus, potassium and vitamins and is low in fat. Found in either firm or soft cakes. The firmer cakes are best for dishes where the bean curd will be stirred (e.g., stir-fries) while the soft cakes are good in soups, savory dishes, steamed dishes and desserts. Keep in fresh water in the refrigerator. Change water daily to keep fresh. Can be stored up to 3 weeks. Found in Chinese, Japanese and many Western markets plus natural and health food stores. Easy to make at home from the recipe on *pages 6-7*.

BEAN CURD, DEEP FRIED—A light-brown cake of deep fried bean curd found in Japanese markets. Used by the Chinese and Japanese in many dishes. May be done at home by deep frying your own pressed bean curd. Can be frozen and stored up to 6 months in the freezer.

BEAN CURD, PRESSED—Bean curd that is wrapped in a muslin cloth and then pressed several hours to overnight to remove most of the water from it. Done to make the curd firmer.

BEAN SPROUTS—See *Sprouts*.

BESAN—Indian name for flour made from chick peas. See *Channa Flour* for further explanation.

BLACHAN—A cake of rotted dried pulverized shrimp with a strong fishy smell. Never use raw. Roast in tightly wrapped foil package and then mince if used in uncooked dishes. Cheaper than trassi, it can be found in Indonesian and Philippine shops. Usually comes canned. Keep refrigerated in an airtight container once blachan is open.

BLACK BEANS, SALTED—Small black beans that have been fermented and then preserved with salt. Strong flavored and moist, these beans are used to make the pungent black bean sauce dishes. Usually garlic and ginger are used with the black beans for a pungent, highly flavored dish. Mash or crush before using. Store in an airtight container. Found in Chinese stores.

BLACK FUNGUS, DRIED—See *Mushrooms, Clouds Ears*.

BULGUR WHEAT—Parboiled or steamed whole wheat berry that is cracked and then dried again. A whole food having all the nutritional value of whole wheat (see *Whole Wheat Flour*). Developed by the fuel short peoples of the Persian uplands because it takes little cooking time. A favorite of the Middle East in salads, pilafs, fillings and desserts. Found in Middle Eastern, natural and health food stores as well as some Western grocery stores. Keep in dry, airtight container.

BURDOCK, JAPANESE EDIBLE—see *Gobo*.

CARDAMOM—The dried seed pod of a tropical plant grown in India. There are two kinds, the large white podded dark brown seeds and the small green pods. The latter are chewed in India for a breath freshener. Either type may be used. Best removed from the seed pods and ground fresh, since the spice quickly loses its flavor when ground.

CARROTS, INDIAN—Carrots in India are reddish in color, so use a small beet in Indian carrot dishes to get the right color.

CASHEWS—A nut from a tropical tree which sits like cupped fingers at the top of the blossom of the tree. The nut until roasted contains a poison, so even "raw" cashews have been roasted enough to drive off this poison. Used in all Oriental cuisines. Can be used in place of Macadamia nuts in Indonesian cooking.

CHANNA—Indian for garbanzo. See *Garbanzo* for further explanation.

CHANNA DAHL—Small form of garbanzo used in India.

CHANNA FLOUR—Ground garbanzo beans made into a flour used in Indian and Middle Eastern dishes. Should be kept refrigerated; it will go rancid when left at room temperature. Recipe for how to make your own flour on *page 213*. May be purchased in Indian and Middle Eastern shops.

CHICK PEA—English for garbanzo. See *Garbanzo* for further explanation.

CHILIS—Although these plants of the Capsicum family are native to North America they were quickly adopted by the Orient for their preserving qualities and their superior ability to impart heat to a dish. There are many types of red and green chilis but all of them have the most heat value in the seeds. When handling either dried or fresh chilis, always wash your hands before touching either your eyes or mouth, as the oils will make your eyes and mouth sting. Chilis lose heat with age, so be sure to use fresh dried or fresh chilis. When using dried chilis, to keep them from scattering when chopping, place them with onions or other ingredients and mince them in the middle of the onions. Sambal olek, a mixture of chilis and vinegar used by the Indonesians, may be used in place of chilis in many

recipes. May be found in Indian, Indonesian, Chinese, Japanese and Middle Eastern spice shops. Different varieties of chilis have different heats, so test before using large amounts. Chilis flavor and heat in a geometric progression, so do not double the chili content when doubling the recipe.

CHINESE GREENS—There are many types of greens used by the Chinese, but three are easily obtained in the West. These are Sou Choy or Chinese cabbage, a tightly packed 10- to 14-inch oblong head of light green, tender cabbage with a tender white stalk. The leaves are cut from the stalk and cooked after the stalk in stir-fries so they do not get overcooked. Bok choy or Chinese chard is shaped like celery with a long white stalk and dark green leaves—one of the Chinese favorites. Stalks are fried first in stir-fries so the leaves will not be overcooked. A favorite in soups and stir-fries, especially the tender center stalks and flower buds. Gai Choy or Chinese mustard greens are less bitter than the American variety. The dark green leaves are used in soups and stir-fries. Found in Chinese, Japanese or Western markets.

CHINESE PARSLEY—See *Coriander*.

CHIVES—An herb member of the onion family, chives are a green shoot that emerges early in the spring. Used in salads, soups and as a garnish. Easy to grow in North American gardens or in a pot in your kitchen. Found frozen or dried in many Western grocery stores and dried in spice and herb shops. Easy to freeze yourself. Just wrap in foil and put into freezer.

CHUTNEY, COOKED—A thick mixture of fruits, vegetables, spices, herbs, vinegar, a sweetener and garlic. A slowly simmered sauce which thickens and blends all these flavors into a condiment sauce which is used to accompany most Indian meals. Cooked chutney is also used in the preparation of Chinese Plum Sauce. Recipes for cooked chutneys are found on *page 217*.

CHUTNEY, RAW—A combination of herbs or nuts or seeds ground and mixed with coconut, chilis or onions and spices into a condiment sauce. Served with Indian meals. Make in small amounts and use immediately for best flavor.

CINNAMON, GROUND—The ground bark of a tropical tree found throughout Southeast Asia and India. Used by all cuisines except Japanese. The Chinese use it in Five and Ten Spices mix, while India, Indonesia and the Middle East use it in their spice mixes and also in sweets, savory meat dishes and vegetarian main dishes. Store in tight container away from heat so spice does not lose flavor. Found in Western grocery stores as well as specialty shops of India, Indonesia and the Middle East.

CINNAMON, STICK—Small pieces of dried bark from a tropical tree found throughout Southeast Asia and India. Used mainly by the Indian and Middle Eastern cuisines. Store in tight container away from heat. May be used to grind cinnamon for ground cinnamon, since the flavor is stronger and more aromatic. Used to flavor stocks and meat dishes. Also used to flavor rice dishes such as Pulao and Chicken Pilaf. May be found in Western grocery stores or spice shops, but the heavy Indian bark known as Dal Chini is found only in Indian specialty shops.

CITRUS LEAVES—Lemon or lime leaves used in Indonesian cooking. Found dried in Dutch and Indonesian shops. Easy to dry your own if you have a small lemon or lime tree.

CLEAR BEAN NOODLES—Clear thin noodles made from mung beans used in Japanese and Chinese cooking. Can be substituted for shiratake, clear noodles made from devil's tongue plant. Soak in hot water before using. Found in Chinese and Japanese shops.

CLOUDS EARS—See *Mushrooms, Clouds Ears*.

CLOVES—Dried, pungent-tasting unopened bud of the tropical tree *Caryophyllus aromaticus* which grows in India and Southeast Asia. A favorite spice of India, used in garam-masala spice mix, rice dishes and sweet dishes. Also used in the Middle East in meat and sweet dishes and in Indonesia. Found in Western grocery stores and spice shops. Best kept whole and ground as needed. Store in cool dry airtight container.

COCONUT—A large, 1- to 3-lb. brown nut of the coconut palm with a soft, sweet white nutmeat. Fresh coconuts have lots of water inside; without liquid, a moldy or wet eye means don't buy. To open a coconut, drain liquid by puncturing two of the eyes with a nail and draining the liquid—drinkable water with a slight coconut flavor but not "coconut milk." Knock the shell with a cleaver or hammer to loosen the nut inside, then cleave open and remove the white meat from the shell. Can be eaten fresh as a snack or dessert, but most often used to make coconut milk or grated to form parts of other dishes. Used mostly by the Indians and Indonesians. Found in Western grocery stores. Much easier to use dried coconut than the fresh coconut. Coconut is high in saturated fats.

COCONUT CREAM OR BUTTER—A concentrated form of coconut milk that comes in a bar or cake. Melted with water, it makes coconut milk. Must be kept refrigerated. Found in Indonesian and Indian shops.

COCONUT, DRIED SHREDDED—*Unsweetened* dried coconut used in making coconut milk and as a substitute for fresh coconut when soaked in hot water. Used extensively in Indian and Indonesian food for appetizers, sauce bases and in sweets.

COCONUT MILK—A white liquid made from grated fresh coconut or dried unsweetened coconut soaked in hot water and then mashed and squeezed to remove the coconut-flavored liquid. Recipe *page 153*. Spoils quickly, so excess milk should be frozen into ice cubes and stored in plastic bags in the freezer for easy use.

COCONUT MILK POWDER, DRIED—A dried form of coconut milk that is reconstituted with boiling water. 3 Tbsp. should be used for each cup. 5 Tbsp. should be used for thick coconut milk. Found in Indonesian, Indian and specialty food shops. Does not need to be refrigerated.

COOKING GREENS—See *North American Cooking Greens*.

CORIANDER—A flavorful herb of the parsley family. The green leaves of the plant are used in Chinese and Indian dishes in place of parsley. They are commonly known as Chinese parsley. It can be grown cheaply in North American gardens from seeds purchased in a spice shop. The dried seed, ground or whole, is used in Indian, Middle Eastern and Indonesian cooking. The spice mixes Ras el Hanout and garam-masala both contain coriander. A favorite of the Indonesians and Indians for meat, vegetable and sweet dishes. Store in tight container away from heat and light. Best kept whole and ground as needed, for it loses flavor quickly when ground. Found in Indian, Middle Eastern and Indonesian shops as well as Western spice shops and grocery stores.

CORNSTARCH—A pure form of starch made from corn, but with all germ and bulk matter removed so there is little nutritive value. Gives sauces a starchy flavor.

CUCUMBERS—If purchased from a large food store, always test to see if covered with wax. Scrape with your fingernail, and if the wax peels off, peel the cucumber before using.

CUMIN—An herb seed which is a member of the parsley family; it can be grown in North American gardens. The seed sets sparingly, so sew thickly. A pungent herb used in spice mixes in China, India and the Middle East, and also found in Indonesian cooking. Used to flavor meat and vegetable dishes, but rarely found in sweets. Best purchased as whole seeds and then ground as needed. The Indians fry the whole seeds to flavor rice dishes and for salad dressings and lentil dishes, so it is necessary to have whole seeds available. Store in airtight container in a cool, dry place. Can be purchased in Indian, Arab, Indonesian and Western shops.

CURRY—A spicy Indian stew-like dish with tomato, coconut milk or yoghurt as a base. Curry is started with a basic masala of onions, garlic and fresh ginger; then spices and the sauce base are added, along with vegetables or meat to complete the dish. Western curries are usually made with a flour cream sauce base and commercial curry powder and do not have nearly the flavor of authentic Indian curries.

CURRY LEAVES—See *Indonesian Laurel Leaf*.

CUTTING TECHNIQUES—The most important thing to remember in preparing vegetables and meats for Oriental cooking is to cut all items evenly so that they will cook at a uniform rate. Most items are cut thinly so that they will cook quickly and not lose flavor or color. Condiments are minced or julienned so the flavors blend in with other ingredients well without standing out themselves.

CLEAVERS, HOW TO USE—When cutting chicken into bite-sized pieces or any large, soft-boned piece of meat or fish, it is easiest to use a cleaver. A wrist-like Karate chop is the correct way to use a cleaver—much more force is given to the cleaver with a quick flick of the wrist than bearing down with the whole arm straight down on the object to be butchered.

CUT INTO PEA-SIZED PIECES—Vegetables, usually beans or carrots, cut into cubes about the size of a pea. Cut evenly so vegetable will cook evenly.

CUT INTO THIN DIAGONAL SLICES—Done to show off the colors of the vegetable well and so they are easy to pick up with chopsticks. Always slice evenly.

GARLIC, CRUSHED AND MINCED—The easiest way to peel garlic is to crush it with a knife and then pull off the skin. It is easy to mince garlic once it is crushed.

JULIENNE—A cooking term meaning to slice into paper-thin matchstick-like pieces.

MINCE—Chop into extremely fine pieces. Done usually for condiments or ingredients in spice pastes so the flavors will blend well and not cover the flavor of the main ingredients of the dish.

SCORE—Shallow, ½- to 1-inch cuts made on the surface of meat, fish or vegetables to allow sauces or marinades to flavor the interior. Usually done with fish which are marinated and then cooked quickly in a sauce.

SHREDDING—Cutting—cabbage or greens, usually—with a very sharp knife into thin slices. To shred meat means to pull cooked meat (or chicken) apart into long thread-like pieces rather than cut it.

THIN SLICES—Remember to always cut the vegetables uniformly. Appearance and texture are important in Oriental cuisine, and these should be uniform for each item. Uniform slicing is important so that all items will cook at the same speed.

DAIKON RADISH—A long, white radish from 10 to 18 inches long and 1 to 2 inches thick. Crisp, white, firm interior with a biting taste. A favorite of the Japanese for pickles, salads or as an accompaniment for raw fish. Easy to grow in North American gardens. Plant after the middle of July and harvest in the fall. Bolts to seed in hot weather. Found in Chinese and Japanese markets as well as Western grocery stores.

DAL CHINI—Thick bark of the cinnamon tree. Used in India to flavor rice dishes and for the spice mixture garam-masala. See *Cinnamon, Stick* for further explanation.

DASHI—Japanese soup stock made from bonito shavings (katsuobushi) or kelp (kombu). Used in many dishes as a stock base. Dashi was traditionally used instead of MSG by the Japanese as a flavor enhancer.

DOMBURI—Large Japanese deep porcelain bowl with lid used to serve rice snacks. These dishes have come to be called domburi from the bowl in which they are served.

EELS, SWEET CANNED—Small Japanese eels, smoked and cooked in sweet soy sauce. Used as an appetizer or as filling in norimaki sushi. Watch out for MSG if buying canned.

EGGPLANT—A large, dark purple, pear-shaped vegetable, *Solanum melongena*, which has a mild oyster-like flavor when fried. A favorite of the Middle East and India, it is used in many vegetarian dishes and even pickled. When frying eggplant use sufficient oil to saturate the vegetable, otherwise it will be tough when cooked later in a sauce. Easy to grow in North American gardens. Like tomatoes, it is frost sensitive and likes heat. Can be frozen if fried first and then placed in airtight containers.

EGGPLANT, JAPANESE—A smaller, long, thin variety of eggplant grown in Japan. Has a slightly tarter flavor than regular eggplant. Used in pickles, salads, and as a cooked vegetable by the Japanese. A more hardy plant than the Middle Eastern type, can be grown in colder climates but still is frost sensitive. Found in Japanese markets and some Western grocery stores. Regular eggplant can be substituted for it, but should be cut into four long, lengthwise wedges to have the same shape as Japanese eggplant before being prepared as the recipes direct.

EPSOM SALTS—Used to curd soy milk when making bean curd (Tofu) recipe, *pages 6-7*. Magnesium chloride, commonly known as epsom salts, is found in drug stores. Store in an airtight, dry container.

FALAFEL—Jewish word for tamia. More commonly known in North America. See *Tamia* for further explanation. Recipe *pages 94-95*.

FAVA BEAN—Known as broad beans in the English-speaking world, favas are a favorite of the Middle East. Can be grown in cool climates and will take frost, so very good for all areas of North America either as a summer or winter vegetable. Found dried in Middle Eastern, Italian and some Western grocery stores.

FAVA BEAN FLOUR—Flour made from ground fava beans. Should be kept refrigerated. Used in making tamia. Found in Middle eastern markets.

FETA CHEESE—A sour, soft white cheese made from sheep's or goat's milk. Found in Greek shops and some Western grocery stores.

FILO—A thin pastry used by the Middle East to make main dishes and sweets. Found in Greek and Middle Eastern stores. Can be kept up to 6 months in the freezer.

FISH, SMALL DRIED—1- to 2-inch paper-thin, small dried fish found in Chinese, Japanese and Indonesian shops. Used in Indonesian cooking. Keep indefinitely in tightly covered container. Trassi, anchovy paste, blachan or pulverized dried shrimp can be substituted for dried fish.

FIVE SPICES MIX—Equal amounts of star aniseed, dried orange peel, licorice root, cardamom and cinnamon: a fragrant mix used in savory liver and meat sauces. Best mixed as needed so that spices will not lose flavor. Recipe on *page 3*.

FOOD MILL—Round pan with sieve bottom and interior masher with handle used for pureeing or mashing food without destroying the texture. Use it for mashing garbanzo for hummus b'tahini to save your blender. Found in Western hardware and kitchen shops.

FUNGUS, DRIED—Either small blackish gray fungus or larger dark brown. See *Mushrooms, Clouds Ear* or *Woods Ear Fungus*.

GARAM-MASALA—A mixture of spices used by the Indians to flavor vegetables and lentil and meat dishes. Commonly known as curry powder in the West, this spice mix should be mixed fresh in small amounts so that the spices do not lose flavor from storage. The garam-masala mixes in this book are from the North Indian State of Punjab and are mild compared to the hotter mixes of Southern and Eastern India. Recipe on *page 213*.

GARBANZO—The light, cream-brown, irregularly round-shaped legume *Circer arietinum* grows wild around the Mediterranean and farther East. Dried, it is used as a dahl in India and also ground into flour. A favorite in the Middle East, it is pureed to form the base of hummus b'tahini, a lemon, garlic-flavored paste, used in salads and casseroles. A good source of calcium, iron, potassium, B vitamins and complete protein when used in conjunction with grains.

GHEE—Clarified butter made by boiling butter and skimming off all the solids. Ghee is used in Indian cooking but is extremely high in saturated fats, and makes food taste rather heavy, so cold-pressed vegetable oils are used in place of it in *Feast*. See *Vegetable Oil, Cold Pressed* for further explanation.

GINGER, DRIED GROUND—The dried ground powder of ginger. Used in spice mixes of China and the Middle East. Also used to flavor meat and sweet dishes. Has a slightly bitter flavor, so fresh ginger is better to use if it can be obtained.

GINGER ROOT, FRESH—A tropical rhizome similar in appearance to an iris root which grows throughout Southeast Asia, India and parts of China and Japan. Can be grown in North America in sandy soils in non-frost areas from fresh sprouted roots found in the spring. Also grows well in sandy-soiled tubs in a sunny window.

GINKGO NUTS—Seeds about the size and shape of a small olive. The seeds of the ginkgo tree are used in Japanese cooking as a vegetable. Found canned in Japanese markets.

GOBO—Edible Japanese burdock. Long dark-brown, thin roots are seen in Japanese markets. Can be grown in North America, but make sure that it doesn't spread and become a weed, which it can easily do. Prepared by peeling the root, paring it thin, soaking it in hot water, and then squeezing it dry before using.

GRAPE LEAVES—The tender first spring leaves of the grape vine are best used as wrappers for a stuffed vine-leaf dish called dolmeh. Can be purchased fresh or canned at Middle Eastern shops. If you have a grape plant it is easy to can or freeze the leaves yourself. When freezing, first steam and then treat like spinach. Swiss chard or green cabbage can be used in place of grape leaves.

GRATER, GINGER—Metal form of porcelain grater. See *Grater, Porcelain,* for further explanation.

GRATER, PORCELAIN—A fine grater made of porcelain with fine porcelain serrations which is excellent for grating fresh ginger, garlic and daikon radish very fine. Found in Japanese markets. Excellent for grating any herb or spice small, so use for Chinese, Indian or Indonesian cooking also.

GREEK OLIVES—Dark, slightly dried, sour-tasting olive found in Greek, Middle Eastern and Western grocery stores as well as some delicatessens. Also sold in bulk, never found canned. Black olives may be used in place of Greek olives.

GREENS—See *North American Cooking Greens*.

HONEY, MILD—Use a mild honey in all recipes calling for honey in this book so that it does not cover the flavor of the other ingredients. Some mild honeys are fireweed, fruit blossom, clover, alfalfa and lima bean honeys. Eucalyptus, buckwheat, dandelion and wildflower honeys are too strongly flavored and cover all other ingredients when used in these recipes. Honey is used in place of refined sugar to help avoid the detrimental effects that eating white sugar has on the body. It is easy to digest and contains some minerals and vitamins. Unprocessed honey contains no artificial additives (processed honey contains added glucose and has been heated so that all the vitamins are removed and most of the minerals, to make it again conform to manufacturers' standards). Some tips for easy use: when a recipe calls for both oil and honey, measure the oil first and then add the honey to the measuring cup—it comes out easier; when using honey and vinegar, dissolve the honey in the vinegar or lemon juice first before adding the other ingredients; grease measuring spoons or cups before using and the honey will come out easier.

HOT GREEN PEPPERS—See *Chilis*.

INDONESIAN LAUREL LEAF—Leaf from an Oriental tropical tree in the same family as the bay tree. Has a cinnamon-like flavor. Also called curry leaves. Found in Indian and Indonesian shops. European bay leaf can be substituted.

INDONESIAN SOY SAUCE—A sauce made from tamari or dark Chinese soy sauce, honey and molasses. In Indonesia, palm sugar is used to make this sweet, thick soy sauce, but this is too difficult to obtain in North America. Raw sugar from Indian or Mexican stores may be used in place of the honey and molasses to make this soy sauce. Recipe on *page 153*. A ready-made product can be purchased in Indonesian specialty shops, but is very expensive, and Indonesian soy sauce is very easy to make at home.

IODIZED SALT—Refined salt to which iodine has been added to prevent goiter. See *Sea Salt* for further explanation.

JERUSALEM ARTICHOKE—A native North American perennial tuber shaped somewhat like a ginger root which has a sweet, crisp, nutlike flavor. It is easy to grow in North America. It is used in place of water chestnuts in Oriental cooking. Found in Western grocery stores. No relative of the green or globe artichoke which is in the thistle family.

KAMABOKO—Japanese fish cake made from pounded fish, rice flour or arrowroot starch and eggs. Most commercial brands contain MSG, so make your own from recipe on *page 284*.

KANTEN—Japanese word for long cakes or agar-agar gelatin. See *Agar-Agar* for further explanation.

KARCHI—Long-handled slotted spoon used in India to remove food from deep frying oil.

KARHAI—Indian wok-type pan with rounded handles used for frying foods. Made of tin-lined brass in India; the ones found in North America are made of steel since we do not have tinsmiths to retin the brass pots every month. Found in Indian markets.

KATSUOBUSHI—Japanese for dried bonita shavings used to make dashi. Found in Japanese markets.

KETJAP MANIS—Sweet Indonesian soy sauce made from dark soy sauce, honey and molasses or dark palm sugar. Recipe *page 153*. The word ketjap, meaning a sauce added to food for extra flavor, was brought by the Portuguese from the Spice Islands nearly 500 years ago. Our word catsup is derived from this, meaning a sweet tomato-based sauce added to food for extra flavor. See *Indonesian Soy Sauce* for further explanation.

KHOYA—Whole milk that is simmered for hours and then mixed and kneaded into a smooth texture to use in Galob jamin. Indians also use the short-cut of making Khoya from *whole* powdered milk mixed with a small amount of water.

KLEAN-RAW SUGAR—See *Sugar, Refined*.

KOMBU—Japanese for kelp. Comes as a dried seaweed. Kombu is high in iodine and other minerals. Used in Japan for soup stock (recipe *page 281*) and to make an excellent pickle (recipe *page 298*). Wash off white salt deposits before using. Found in Japanese and natural foods stores.

KRUPUCK—Shrimp puffs made from tapioca flour and pulverized shrimp. Found in Chinese, Indonesian and Philippine shops. Be sure to get undyed puffs. Deep fried they expand to 3 to 4 times their dried shape.

KUZU—A powder of the Oriental arrowroot tuber used both medicinally and as a thickener for sauces and gravies. Kuzu is high in minerals. It can be used in place of American arrowroot starch but is much more expensive. Found in Japanese markets, natural foods and health food stores.

LAOS—A member of the ginger family, laos is a tuber that grows in Southeast Asia. Laos has a ginger-like flavor but is sweeter and does not have the slightly bitter taste of dried ginger. Found in powdered form in Indonesian shops. Ginger with a touch of cinnamon can be substituted for laos.

LAVENDER—An English herb with a bright lavender flower and aromatic scent. Used by the Middle East in the spice mix ras el hanout. (Middle Eastern cuisine uses the flavors of many flowers.) Found in herb and spice shops and Middle Eastern shops. Use the dried flowers. Easy to grow in your own garden. Makes an excellent tea just steeped in hot water.

LEBAN—Arabic for yoghurt. Often cut with cold water and mixed with a little salt to make a refreshing Middle Eastern drink. See *Yoghurt* for further explanation.

LEBNA—Yoghurt cheese made by the Middle East with salted yoghurt that is placed in a cheese cloth bag and allowed to drain overnight. The resulting dry curd is rolled into small balls and then stored by dropping into olive oil. Sprinkled with paprika or oregano, this is a favorite Arab snack. May be used in place of feta cheese.

LEEKS—A member of the onion family which looks like a large green onion. Leeks have a mild and sweeter flavor than most onions, and are favored by the Middle East, Indonesians and Japanese. Found in Western grocery stores.

LEMON—A yellow citrus fruit high in Vitamin C used extensively in Middle Eastern cooking. To free the juice first, roll the lemon on a counter to break down the fibers inside; the lemon squeezes much more easily this way.

LEMON GRASS—A lemon-flavored tropical grass used to flavor many dishes in Indonesia. Can be grown as a house plant or outside in frost-free areas of North America. Found dried in Indonesian stores either as a grass or powdered. Also found in natural food stores and herb shops, where it is used as an herb tea.

LEMON PEEL—Used in cooking to bring out the lemon flavor of a dish. Buy organic lemons because others are died and have fungicides on the skin as well as being sprayed with insecticides.

LENTILS—Dried members of the legume family which are a good source of minerals, B vitamins and complete proteins when served with grains. There are many types of lentils; the Middle East prefer the small Egyptian red lentil and the common green lentil. Called dahl in India, lentils are an important source of protein there. Some of the more common Indian lentils are whole urad, urad dahl, white moong dahl, mansoor dahl, channa dahl, toor dahl and yal dahl. A mainstay in the vegetarian cooking of India, dahl is prepared in numerous varieties. Explanation of dahls on *page 252*. Found in Indian, Middle Eastern, Italian, Spanish and natural food stores. The more common ones such as red and green lentils are found in Western grocery stores.

LICORICE ROOT—Dried root of the licorice plant, a member of the pea family. Ground and used in Chinese spice mixes and soup stocks. Can be kept indefinitely in the dried root. Found in Chinese shops.

LIME LEAVES—Dried leaves of the lime tree used in Indonesian cooking. If you have a lime tree, dry your own. Found dried in Indonesian shops.

435

LIMES—A green, lemon-like fruit with a distinct sour flavor. Preferred by the Indonesians, especially for sweet dishes. Lemon Juice can be substituted.

MACADAMIA NUT—A hard-shelled nut from a tropical tree. Used in Indonesian cooking. Best to purchase shelled since they are very difficult to shell. Can be found in most stores.

MACE—The inner membrane of the husk surrounding the nutmeg. Used in spice mixes in the Middle East and for sweet dishes. May be purchased whole or ground but best whole as spices lose much flavor when ground and allowed to sit. Store in a tight container away from heat. Can be purchased in Western grocery stores or spice shops.

MACROBURGER—A tasty mixture of grains, soybeans, vegetables, oils, herbs and spices that makes a complete protein substitute for ground meat. Vegetarians can use it for any recipe calling for ground meat. Recipe for how to make Macroburger on *page 88*.

MAKKI—Indian for corn flour. Finely ground corn flour, not to be confused with corn meal, is found in Indian and Italian shops. Store in cool, dry place.

MANGO POWDER—Dried, pulverized mango used in Indian cooking. Has a slightly lemon-like flavor. Found in Indian shops. A sprinkle of lemon juice or dried, pulverized lemon peel can be substituted.

MARINADE—A flavored liquid sauce used for marinating meat or vegetables.

MARINATE—Verb meaning to soak in seasoned liquid to flavor and tenderize meat or vegetables.

MASALA—Mixture of spices, herbs, onions, garlic and fresh ginger root which are finely minced, ground, blended or pounded to form the base for Indian curry dishes. Yoghurt, tomatoes or coconut milk are added to this sauce to make a wet masala for egg, fish and meat curries.

MATSUDAKI—Type of Japanese dried mushroom. Not as available as the shiitake mushroom. Found in Japanese markets. See *Mushrooms, Dried (Japanese)* for further explanation.

MEXICAN CHILI POWDER—A pungent mixture of various chilis ground to a powder. Used in Macroburger. Found in Mexican, spice and herb shops as well as natural food stores and Western grocery stores. Store in airtight container away from heat and light.

MILLET—A grain used extensively in China, Japan, India and Africa. A good source of protein when used in conjunction with beans or peas. Also high in calcium. May be substituted for rice in grain dishes and desserts. Found in natural food stores.

MILLET FLOUR—See *Bajre*.

MINT—There are numerous varieties of mint, but the true mint, *Mentha viridis*, is the best one to use in Middle Eastern cooking. Spearmint may be used in place of true mint, but do not use peppermint, since the flavor is too strong. Used in salads, meat dishes and desserts in the Middle East. Fresh mint is best and easy to grow in North American gardens, so start your own mint patch growing if you like Middle Eastern food.

MISO—A basic Japanese food made from fermented soybeans, malt and salt, and sometimes grain. Like yoghurt, it aids digestion, because the proteins are predigested by bacteria which are beneficial to the human digestive tract. Do not overcook miso or the bacteria will be killed. This is especially true of the soup miso shiru (miso soup), the traditional Japanese breakfast. There are many varieties of miso, but the most common are:

Kome miso—rice miso made from rice, soybeans and salt. Can be red or white depending on where it comes from.

Hatcho miso—made from soybeans alone.

Mugi miso—strong-tasting miso made from barley, soybeans and salt. Usually dark brown in color.

Miso is high in protein, minerals (especially calcium) and Vitamin B_2. When using miso, use less of the dark misos because they are stronger in flavor. Used in soups, to make pickles, as a sauce base and in salad dressings by the Japanese. Also used by the Chinese and Indonesians. Found in Japanese, Chinese and natural food shops and some Western grocery stores. Since it is a fermented product that is aged, miso keeps well with or without refrigeration.

MOCHI—Japanese rice cakes made from cooked glutinous sweet rice called mochi gumi. Can be purchased in Japanese shops, but these are made from white rice. Make your own from brown rice.

MOCHI GUMI—See *Rice, Brown (Sweet)*.

MOLASSES, BLACKSTRAP—The final residue of the sugar refining process. Has a strong, bitter flavor and should not be used in cooking foods with a delicate flavor. Blackstrap molasses is not used in *Feast*.

MOLASSES, SULPHURED—A residue of the sugar refining process. It picks up its sulphur flavor from the sulphur gases used in refining white sugar. Do not use, for its flavor will overwhelm other foods used with it.

MOLASSES, UNSULPHURED—Made from sun-ripened sugar cane which is pressed and the juice boiled down to a sweet, unbitter syrup. Used in all recipes in *Feast*. Found in natural and health food stores and Western grocery stores.

MONOSODIUM GLUTAMATE—Also known as MSG, is not used in this book. It has been found to cause mild to severe diarrhea in humans and has also been linked with birth defects and genetic damage in infants. The use of natural ingredients that have not had the flavor removed and good stocks obviate the use of this dangerous food additive.

MUNG BEAN—A small, dried green legume used mainly for growing sprouts. The Indians use it as a lentil in lentil stews. See sprouts and lentils for further explanation.

MUSHROOMS, CLOUDS EARS—A small, dried, gray-brown fungus which expands to 4 to 5 times its size when soaked in boiling water. Remove tough stems before using. Have a more delicate flavor than winter mushrooms, with a crisp texture. May be used in place of dried mushrooms in

Chinese dishes. Found in Chinese markets. Often sold under the name of dried black fungus.

MUSHROOMS, DRIED (JAPANESE)—The large, dark-brown mushroom (*Cortinellus shiitake*) grown in Japan on the dead bark of oak trees. Very fragrant, pungent, smoky flavor used in many Japanese soups and simmered saucepan dishes. Soak in boiling water 15 minutes to 1 hour before using. Chinese dried mushrooms ("winter mushrooms") can be substituted for shiitake mushrooms. Store in an airtight, dry container. Found in Japanese markets.

MUSHROOMS, DRIED (WINTER MUSHROOMS)—A medium-sized, dark-brown, dried mushroom from the Orient. They have a pungent, smoky flavor and meaty texture which adds flavor to many Chinese and Japanese dishes. Soak in boiling water 15 minutes to 1 hour before using. See recipe *page 4*. They are used as a condiment by themselves as well as to flavor stir-fries, stews, savory and steamed dishes. Store in an airtight, dry container. Found in Chinese and Japanese stores.

MUSTARD, DRY—A dry powder of the ground yellow mustard seed. Pungent flavored, so use lightly. Used by the Chinese to make mustard sauce.

MUSTARD SEED, BLACK—A black seed of the mustard plant used by the Indians. Black mustard seed is much hotter and more aromatic than yellow mustard seed. It is fried in oil along with cumin seeds for a salad dressing. Store in an airtight container away from heat and light. Found in Indian specialty shops. Yellow mustard seed may be substituted for them with the addition of a little black pepper.

MUSTARD SEED, YELLOW—A yellow seed of the mustard plant used by the Chinese for hot mustard sauce in which meat is dipped. Store in an airtight container away from heat and light. Grind seeds to fine powder before use. Found in Western grocery stores. Recipe on *page 3*.

NIGIRI—Sodium chloride made from drippings of rock salt suspended in a burlap bag in a damp room. Used by the Japanese to curd soy milk when making bean curd (tofu), recipe *pages 6-7*. Found in natural and health food stores. Store in an airtight dry container.

NORI—Dried purple laver, *Porphyra tenera*, is collected on rope nets in cold tidal waters and spread on matting to sun dry. The best variety comes from the cold coastal waters off Korea.

NORTH AMERICAN COOKING GREENS—Spinach, collards, mustard greens, Swiss chard, or the wild greens dandelion, nettle or lambs' quarters. Used in place of Chinese greens. See *Chinese Greens* for further explanation.

NUTMEG—Fruit of the tropical tree *Myristica fragrans* which grows throughout Southeast Asia and India. The sun-dried fruit is husked and the inner nut is used whole or ground in meat and sweet dishes as well as spice mixes. The membrane surrounding the nut is called mace and has a similar flavor and is used in spice mixes and sweets. Grinding the whole nut gives a much fresher and stronger flavor, so get a nutmeg grater at a spice or kitchen shop. Store whole nuts indefinitely in a tight container away from heat. Can be found in Western grocery stores.

OCTOPUS—Used by the Japanese. Very tough, so must be cooked for a long period, peeled and then pounded to tenderize it.

ORANGE BLOSSOM WATER—An aromatic fluid made from distilled fresh orange blossoms. Used in Middle Eastern sweet dishes. Smells like an orange orchard in full bloom. Very strong, so only use a few drops. Found in Middle Eastern shops.

ORANGE PEEL, DRIED—See tangerine peel.

ORANGES, COOKING—When cooking oranges, be sure to remove all white membrane, inner skin and seeds from the orange first. When cooked, these will make the orange bitter. Peel the orange with a knife below the inner skin, then remove the wedges with a knife so that no skin is on them. Only cook the succulent, sweet centers.

OREGANO—*Marjoram vulgaris* or wild marjoram is a green herb of the mint family which grows wild in the Mediterranean region. Often confused with the milder-tasting sweet marjoram, oregano is favored by the Greeks, Italians and Middle Eastern cuisines for its hearty flavor in salads, vegetables, rice and meat dishes. Can be grown in North American gardens, but be sure you are getting oregano and not one of the other *marjorams*—there are over 30 varieties of which oregano is only one. Found in spice, herb, natural foods, Italian, Greek and Middle Eastern stores as well as Western grocery stores. Store in airtight container away from heat and light.

OROSHI-KI—Japanese grater used for grating ginger, garlic, turnip and daikon radish. See *Grater, Porcelain*, for further explanation.

PAPADUMS—Indian snack made from lentil or tapioca flour and spices or herbs. Papadums expand 3 to 4 times their size when fried in hot oil. There are numerous varieties of papadums, ranging from little round rice puffs to the hot chili lentil papadums. Found dried in Indian shops. Keep in a cool place.

PAPRIKA—A mild, sweet-tasting member of the Capsicum family (chili), high in Vitamins A and C. Add toward the end of cooking or use in salads, since the flavor quickly deteriorates with heat. Used extensively in Middle Eastern cuisine, especially in cold foods. Found in spice shops, Middle Eastern shops and Western grocery stores.

PARAFFIN WAX—See *Wax As a Preservative*.

PEANUTS, RAW—Uncooked peanuts. Store in a cool place away from heat or light. Found in natural or health food stores. Called the poor man's almond in India.

PEARS, WINTER—Hard variety of pear that stores well in winter. Wrap separately and do not bruise when storing. Found in Western grocery stores in winter. Used in place of vegetable pears in Indonesian dishes. See *Vegetable Pear* for further explanation.

PEAS, EDIBLE POD—See *Snow Peas*.

PEPPER, BLACK—A berry from the old-world tropical plant *Piper nigrum*. Prized by all cultures of the world for its flavor and heat-imparting characteristics; it was even used as a medium of exchange in medieval Western countries. Black pepper comes from the unripe berry which is picked green, and then shrivels into a small black ball. It is hotter than white pepper, which is the fully ripe berry. Pepper is used mainly in meat and vegetable dishes and rarely in sweet dishes. It is found in most spice mixes such as the Chinese Ten Spice Mix, the Indian garam-masala, and the Middle Eastern Ras el Hanout. Best purchased whole and ground as needed. Pepper loses heat and aroma when stored too long or exposed to heat or light.

PEPPER, WHITE—The fully ripe berry of the *Piper nigrum* plant. White pepper is milder in flavor than black pepper and not as hot. Used in the Middle Eastern spice mix Ras el Hanout. Store in dry, airtight container away from heat or light. Best purchased whole and ground as needed.

PEPPERCORNS—Whole black pepper. See *Peppers, Black*, for further explanation.

PEPPERCRESS—Also known as garden cress or pepper grass, this salad herb is used as a garnish for soups, salads and noodle dishes by the Japanese. Cress is easy to grow in North American gardens.

PEPPERS, RED—See *Chilis*.

PEPPERS, SWEET RED—Fully ripe "green" peppers with a mild, sweet flavor. Found in Western grocery stores in season. Easily grown in North America, and can be frozen for later use. Best to grow your own, since market peppers are usually coated with wax to prolong shelf life.

PILAF—A savory grain dish made from either rice or bulgar wheat fried in olive oil or butter with onions and herbs and then cooked in stock.

PISTACHIOS—A favorite nut of the Middle East; about the size of a filbert with a soft shell. Often the shells are dyed red, but the best ones are purchased undyed. Has a soft, green-white nutmeat with a very rich taste. Found in Middle Eastern and natural food stores as well as some Western grocery stores.

PITA—Often called pocket bread, this bread of the Middle East accompanies most meals. Made of white flour in the cities, in the back country it is still made of nutritious whole wheat flour, which is what the recipe in *Feast* calls for on *page 92*. When baking, the bread rises quickly to form a hollow center, and that is why the name of pocket bread.

PLUM SAUCE—A thick, dark-red sauce made from plums, peaches or apricots, chili, rice vinegar chutney and sugar or honey. Spicy and thick, it is used as a condiment to dip meat into or with other sauce ingredients to baste roast chicken or duck. Also used as a dip sauce for egg rolls. Sold in Chinese shops, but best made yourself with whole, natural ingredients and no sugar.

POMEGRANATE—A fruit of a shrub-like tree which is a favorite of the Middle East. The outer red husk is peeled and the seeds of the fruit are eaten. Also used as a red dye. Eaten by itself for its sweet, tangy flavor, or used to decorate Balouza. Found in Middle Eastern stores and Western grocery stores in season.

PUMPKIN—A small, sweet pumpkin called a sugar pumpkin is used in *Feast*. A small standard pumpkin, or pieces of a larger pumpkin can be substituted. Sugar pumpkins are easy to grow in North American gardens, and are quick maturers because they are so small. Found in Japanese and Middle Eastern markets. Good winter storer. Firm, yellow winter squash can be substituted for pumpkin.

RAISINS—Most common raisins are the dried *vinifera* grapes. The best are sun-dried, unsulphured, seedless Thompson raisins which can be purchased in natural, health food and some Western grocery stores. These dark, succulent raisins are used in all recipes in *Feast*. Raisins are a good source of iron and other minerals. Currants can be substituted for raisins.

RAS EL HANOUT—Arabic meaning head of the household and referring to a spice mix. Each spice shop has its own mix, and the number of spices going into Ras el Hanout can vary from the simple one in this book to 50 different spices and herbs. An aromatic mix which can be used in place of the cinnamon, nutmeg, allspice mixtures given in many of the Middle Eastern recipes.

RAW SUGAR—See *Sugar, Refined*.

RED PEPPER—See *Chilis*.

RICE, BROWN—Unpolished, unprocessed whole grain of the Asiatic cereal plant, *Oryza sativa*, cultivated by the Chinese for over 4,000 years. Used throughout the Orient as the chief cereal grain. Good source of trace minerals, Vitamin E and the B complex vitamins, plus unsaturated fatty acids. Also adds to the necessary bulk with its bran to keep your digestion in good working order. Used in place of white rice in *Feast*. See *Rice, White*, for further explanation.

RICE, BROWN (LONG GRAIN)—A rice variety with a long, narrow cereal head. Cooks to dry fluffy rice. Preferred by the Chinese, Indian, Indonesian and Middle Eastern cuisines.

RICE, BROWN (SHORT GRAIN)—A shorter-grain rice which is quite starchy. Preferred by the Japanese and the macrobiotic method of cooking. Short-grain rice is starchier than the long-grain varieties and is slightly sticky when cooked.

RICE, BROWN (SWEET)—A short, fat, golden-brown rice with a high sugar and starch content. Used in the Orient for sweet dishes such as rice cakes and puddings for its starch-sweet qualities. Found in natural and health food stores. Short-grain brown rice may be substituted for sweet brown rice.

RICE FLOUR, BROWN—Always use short-grain brown rice to make rice flour. Long-grain rice is not as absorbent, and flour made from it tends to harden when steamed. Recipe *page 283*. Found in natural foods stores.

RICE, WHITE—Rice with the bran removed, called polished rice. Even if "enriched," a nutritionally inadequate food with only 3 B vitamins and iron partially restored. It is coated with alum to help keep grain pests from eating it. Mainly starch, white rice is a principle ingredient in laundry starch and dusting powders.

RICE VINEGAR—A sweet-flavored vinegar made from rice, which has a much milder flavor than most vinegars because the acetic acid level is lower. Used in all recipes calling for vinegar in this book. A favorite of the Orient which can be found in Chinese and Japanese shops. If it cannot be found, use white vinegar cut in half with water in place of rice vinegar and add a little more sweetener.

RICE WINE—See *Sake*.

RICOTTA CHEESE—A sour, curded cheese made by the Italians. Similar to uncreamed cottage cheese. May be used in place of feta cheese.

ROSEWATER—A liquid distilled from freshly gathered rose petals. Used both as a fragrance for perfume and to flavor foods. The Middle East adds it to its spice mixture Ras el Hanout (I generally do not add it until ready to use the spice mix because its moisture will cause the mix to mold in storage). It is a favorite in dessert dishes in both the Middle East and India. Found in drug stores or in Middle Eastern, Indian and specialty spice shops.

SAFFRON—The bright orange stigmas of the Fall or Saffron crocus are dried and ground into the most expensive spice obtainable. Can be purchased either in threads or powdered form. It is used sparingly; a little goes a long way to add color and to impart its delicate, bitter-sweet flavor. Used by the Middle Eastern and Indian cuisines in meat, rice and dessert dishes. The best saffron is Spanish saffron. Found in spice shops.

SAKE—A dry, white wine made from fermented rice. Used in all recipes calling for rice wine in *Feast*. It is also drunk before Japanese meals, but not with the meal. Usually it is heated to near boiling before being served in a small carafe and then poured into small sake cups. Found in most liquor stores.

SALT, REFINED—Either sea salt or salt mined inland that has been refined to remove "impurities," i.e., trace minerals useful to our bodies' health. Other ingredients are added once the salt has been stripped to make the final product conform to the manufacturer's, and not the body's, specifications. See *Sea Salt* for further explanation.

SALTED BLACK BEANS—See *Black Beans, Salted*.

SAMBAL OLEK—An Indonesian chili sauce made from coarsely ground chili peppers, salt and water. Sambal olek is very hot. Found in Dutch and Indonesian shops.

SANSHO—Japanese pepper leaf plant. Used for garnish and in togarashi. Found dried in Japanese markets. Peppercress can be substituted.

SEA SALT—An unrefined, sun-dried salt that contains iodine naturally along with many other trace minerals which have been removed from processed table salt. Refined salt, because of its manufacturing process, is slow to dissolve and difficult to digest as a result. It also contains additives such as calcium bicarbonate or aluminum salts to keep it dry and pourable, iodine (which has been removed in manufacturing) to prevent goiter, dextrose to keep the iodine stable, and other ingredients to keep the salt white. Sea salt has no additives, and nothing is removed from it in processing, so it adds many trace minerals to our diet, even though used in small quantities.

SEED POPPER—Small round pan with screened top used by the Japanese to roast seeds. Excellent for roasting any seeds which pop when heated, such as sesame or mustard seeds. Found in Japanese markets and hardware stores.

SEMOLINA—A coarsely ground wheat similar to cream-of-wheat cereal. Made from whole wheat berries with all the same nutrition. Fine bulgur or cream-of-wheat cereal may be substituted for semolina. Found in Indian and Western grocery stores. See *Whole Wheat Flour* for nutritional information. Store in cool, dry place.

SESAME OIL, CHINESE OR JAPANESE—A golden to dark-brown oil made from toasted sesame seeds. A pungently flavored oil used mainly as a flavoring. Also used by the Chinese to flavor stir-fries. Found in Chinese or Japanese stores. Recipe for how to make on *page 281*.

SESAME SEEDS—The seeds of the plant *Sesamun oriental*, cultivated by the Chinese for centuries as a source of oil and for its aromatic seeds which they use in desserts. The Japanese and Middle Eastern cuisines also use large amounts of sesame seeds, the former in dressings for salads, hot vegetables and meats and the latter for the ubiquitous tahini, a sauce made from sesame seeds and oil which is used on salads, meats and cooked vegetables as well as going into the desert Halva. The seeds are high in calcium and Vitamin C and a good source of essential amino acids when used with grains. Found in bulk, unhulled, in natural and health food stores.

SESAME SEEDS, HULLED—A pale, creamy-colored seed which has been processed to remove the outer covering of the seed. Not as nutritious as unhulled sesame seeds. See *Sesame Seeds* for further explanation.

SESAME SEEDS, UNHULLED—A light-brown colored seed without the hull removed. An unprocessed product which contains all the vitamins and minerals of the sesame seed. See *Sesame Seeds* for further explanation.

SHIRATAKE—Japanese thin clear vermicelli like noodles made from gelatinous starch of the devil's tongue plant (konnyaku). Used in sukiyaki and salads. Found in Japanese markets, fresh or canned. Clear bean noodles can be substituted.

SHITAKI—Dried Japanese mushrooms. See *Mushrooms, Dried Japanese*, for further explanation.

SHRIMP, DRIED—Small, ¼- to ½-inch, salty, dried shrimp.

SMALL SQUARE SKILLET, JAPANESE—Used in making layered egg omelettes in Japan. Found in Japanese markets.

SMELT—Small fish, either freshwater or salt, often used in Japanese cooking.

SNOW PEAS—Edible pod peas picked before the pea has matured. Used in Japanese, Chinese and Indonesian cooking. Easy to grow in North America, and will bear most of the summer in cool climates. Found in Chinese, Japanese and even Western grocery stores.

SOBA—Thin Japanese buckwheat noodle. Found in Japanese and natural food stores.

SOMEN—Thin Japanese wheat vermicelli. Use soy vermicelli or whole wheat vermicelli in place of somen. Found in Japanese markets.

SORREL—Green herb similar to lettuce with a slightly sour taste. A perennial that grows well in North American gardens.

SOURDOUGH STARTER—A wild yeast mix made from soured flour and water and natural yeasts. Used to start or assist in making breads in the Middle East. Get a starter from a friend or purchase in natural foods and specialty food stores.

SOY POWDER FOR MILK—Dehydrated soy milk that has already been cooked so it can be used at once instead of being cooked for 40 minutes. Do not confuse this with soymilk powder, which often is a combination of dehydrated soy milk and dried milk powder. Can be obtained in natural and health food stores.

SOY SAUCE—A sauce made from wheat, soybeans, water and salt that is naturally fermented. Many commercial soy sauces are chemically aged to speed up the fermentation process, and have sugar, MSG and preservatives added to them, so they taste bitter and do not have the flavor of naturally aged soy sauces. Tamari soy sauce, obtained in natural or health food stores, is used for all recipes calling for soy sauce in *Feast* because it is naturally aged and has an excellent flavor. A dark Chinese soy sauce, if it contains no sugar or other additives, may be substituted for tamari. Found in Chinese or Japanese markets. Read the label before buying, since many soy sauces contain additives which detract from the flavor.

SOY SAUCE, THICK RED—A dark, sweet soy sauce made from soy sauce and thick, high-molasses-content sugar. Found in Chinese shops. Molasses and soy sauce mixed can be used in place of thick red soy sauce.

SOY VERMICELLI—Thin noodles made from soy flour. Found in natural foods stores. Can be used in place of Japanese somen.

SOYMILK POWDER—A combination of milk and soy milk powder for milk. Be careful when you are purchasing soy milk powder for making bean curd that you buy the product without milk powder in it. Can be purchased at natural or health food stores. See *Soy Powder for Milk*.

SPEARMINT—A mild mint native to North America which can be used in place of *Mentha viridis*, the true European mint.

SPICES—Spices, like people, tend to grow old, but they have an accelerated scale and should be replaced once a year. Spices are the aromatic roots, seeds, bark and berries of tropical plants (as opposed to herbs, which are temperate zone plants). The flavor from spices comes from essential oils which are destroyed by heat, light and age, so the older the spice the less aroma it has. It is best to purchase small quantities and preferably whole spices, since these tend to lose flavor at a much slower rate. Do not overcook spices or they will lose most of their flavor qualities and only the heat will remain. Store in cool, dry, airtight containers away from heat or light.

SPINACH VERMICELLI—Thin noodles made from soy flour and spinach. Found in natural foods stores.

SPRING ROLLS—*Egg Rolls, Deep Fried*.

SPROUTS—Three- to four-day-old sprouts from soaked lentils, beans, seeds and grains. Used by the Chinese, Indonesians, Japanese and Indians, both raw and cooked. Sprout recipes on *pages 3 and 214*. May be purchased fresh in Chinese and Japanese markets, but otherwise it is best to sprout your own.

STAR ANISEED—A small evergreen tree similar to a laurel with a fruit shaped like a star. Best cultivated in warm frost-free climates. Will ripen in one season, seed should be left on the plant to dry, then flower stalks picked and the seeds threshed. The brown licorice-flavored spice is used in Chinese spice mixes and to flavor poultry dishes. Spice keeps well if stored in a tight container away from heat. Found in Chinese shops or spice shops.

STOCK—A base for soups and sauces made from chicken bones, meat bones, bean sprouts, soybeans, fish, shrimp, fish flakes or seaweed. If a good stock is made no MSG need be added to any dish to enhance the flavor because the stock does this. The Chinese use stocks for all dishes in their cuisine except sweets. The Japanese use mainly fish-flake and seaweed stocks. The Indonesians use shrimp and meat stocks but mainly use coconut milk as a base for their cuisine. The Arabs make a lovely stock from chicken and cinnamon stick and a meat stock. These recipes are found on *pages 4, 5, 87, 155 and 281*. An easy way to store stock for future use is to freeze it in ice-cube trays and then store the cubes in plastic bags so any amount can be used as needed. Make your own stocks for best results.

SUDARE—A thin bamboo mat used by the Japanese to make sushi and other rolled dishes. Found in Japanese markets. A bamboo place mat can be substituted for the sudare.

SUGAR PEAS—See *Snow Peas*.

SUGAR, RAW—True unprocessed, unrefined raw sugar may be obtained in North America only in Mexico and Canada. A good source of raw sugar is sold in East Indian markets in Canada in the form of large blocks of sticky brown cakes of sugar which have none of the minerals, vitamins or other nutrients removed.

440

SUGAR, REFINED—White sugar is so refined that all it has left is calories in the form of sucrose. True raw sugar, which is against the law to sell in the United States, is high in minerals, especially calcium, and the B vitamin complex. In refining sugar all these are removed to produce a "pure" form of sucrose. To digest this "pure" food the body steals from its own supply the minerals, calcium and B complex vitamins which have been removed in processing. White sugar, the so-called energy food, gives the body an energy spurt known as the "sugar-rush" but because it contains no backup nutrition and is often mixed with other processed foods which have little nutritional value, the body has a net loss from ingesting it. The developed countries' diseases of hypoglycemia (low blood sugar levels due to an overproduction of insulin from too fast an injection of pure sucrose into the bloodstream), diabetes and heart disease have been linked to the excessive use of this "pure" food. The average North American consumes the excessive amount of up to and over 100 lbs. of this "pure" food a year. Sugar is considered a culprit in heart disease because excess amounts are converted by the liver into fatty acids which are stored in the body as fats. Sugar is also a leading contributor to tooth decay. Brown sugar and "klean-raw" sugar are just white sugar that has had a certain amount of molasses sprayed back into it, but not a significant amount for nutritional value.

SUKIYAKI BEEF—Thinly sliced, extremely tender beef used by the Japanese for making sukiyaki. The best beef comes from cattle that are fed beer and given a massage every day to make sure that the meat is tender. Thinly sliced steak may be used in place of sukiyaki beef, which is very expensive.

SUMMER SQUASH—Zucchini, yellow crookneck or small turban-shaped green squash with thin skins. Marrow can also be used as a summer squash, although its flavor is not as rich as the others.

SURIBACHI—Japanese pottery bowl with serrated interior used to grind sesame seeds. Found in Japanese and natural food stores.

SWEET RED PEPPER—See *Peppers, Sweet Red*.

TAHINI—A thick paste of crushed or ground sesame seeds and oil that is high in minerals and Vitamin E. Its nutlike flavor is a favorite of the Middle East. Tahini is used in sauces, salad dressings, and with meat and fish dishes. A recipe for how to make your own tahini is on *page 87*—it is much easier and cheaper to make your own. Keeps indefinitely in refrigerator but will become rancid if kept in hot place. Found in natural foods stores.

TAMARI SOY SAUCE—A naturally aged soy sauce with no sugar or other additives. Used in this book for all recipes calling for soy sauce. See *Soy Sauce* for further explanation.

TAMARIND—A sour/sweet fruit that is used in Indonesian and Indian cooking. Tamarind comes in dried bars that look like bars of dried dates. It has the same acidic quality as lemon. Found in Chinese, Indian and Indonesian shops. The dried bar keeps indefinitely. Used in cooking as tamarind water.

TAMARIND WATER—Made from soaking dried tamarind in boiling water. See *page 155*.

TANGERINE PEEL, DRIED—Dried orange-brown peel of the tangerine (make sure to use organic undyed peel if drying your own). Used as a flavoring by the Chinese. Soak in hot water to soften, and scrape off any white membrane before using. Also ground in the dry state and used in Five and Ten Spices Mix. Used to flavor soup stocks and congee and especially good in poultry dishes using duck. The older the skin the better and mellower the flavor, but you can dry your own and use it.

TARO—A starchy tuber similar to a potato, used in Japan. Should be peeled and rolled in salt and steamed before using. Potatoes can be substituted for taro.

TEMPURA RACK—Rack which fits the top of a wok; used to drain deep fried food, particularly tempura. Very inexpensive but handy kitchen tool found in Japanese and kitchen specialty shops. Useful for all deep frying.

TEMPURA SPOON—Large round spoon-like oil skimmer with a wire mesh bottom used by the Japanese to lift food from frying oil and to clean oil of debris so that it does not burn and flavor the oil. Great for all deep fat frying. Found in Japanese markets. Very inexpensive and useful tool.

TEN SPICES MIX—A mixture of ten spices mixed in equal amounts used to make plum sauce and flavor savory meat dishes. Recipe on *page 3*. May be purchased ready mixed in Chinese shops.

TENKASU—Fried bits of batter left over from making tempura. Japanese equivalent of croutons.

THICK RED SOY SAUCE—See *Soy Sauce, Thick Red*.

THYME—A member of the mint family, this herb iis easy to grow in North American gardens. The dried leaves are a favorite in North American cooking. It is used in making Macroburger.

TOFU—See *Bean Curd*.

TOMATO PASTE—A thick tomato mixture made from tomatoes that have been skinned and seeded and then almost all the liquid removed either in partial vacuum or by boiling for long periods. To make at home, first cook the tomatoes for a few minutes, then puree in a blender. Pass through a food mill to remove skin and seeds and then allow liquid to sit for 1 night so liquid will rise to top. Skim off top liquid—use for juice—and simmer paste at bottom on low heat two to three hours until it thickens. Place in hot jars and process in a boiling water bath for 25 minutes. Can be cut with water to make tomato sauce.

TOMATO SAUCE—A sauce about the thickness of thin gravy made of tomatoes. Do not confuse with tomato paste, which is much thicker and more concentrated. Can be used in place of stewed tomatoes in a pinch.

TOMATO VERMICELLI—Thin noodles made from soy flour and tomatoes. Found in natural food stores.

TOMATOES, STEWED—Canned tomatoes. Home-canned are best because they are usually ripe when processed, and the skins are removed.

TRASSI—A cake or bar made from dried salt shrimp that are pulverized and then rotted and formed into cakes and baked. A flavoring used throughout Southeast Asia, trassi has a very strong fishy odor, so keep in a tight container. Because it is baked it may be used uncooked. Mince and use to flavor Indonesian food. Blachan, dried shrimp or anchovy paste can be substituted for trassi. Found in Indonesian and Philippine shops. Blachan, which is similar but uncooked, is much cheaper.

TURMERIC—Often called poor man's saffron for its yellow coloring qualities and cheapness, turmeric is an Indian tuber similar in appearance to an iris root. *Curcuma longa*, the plant, is native to the tropical regions of India where it is dried and ground to use in foods and as a dye. A must in Indian kitchens, turmeric is also used in the Middle East, Indonesia and as far away as Japan. A slightly bitter, oily spice used with vegetables, pickles and rices for color and taste. Turmeric is a strong-flavored spice—a little goes a long way—so when doubling recipes do not double the turmeric. In Southern India turmeric is also used in garammasala, but the Punjab prefers to use it only in vegetables, pickles and rice dishes. Found in spice shops, Indian, Middle Eastern and Western grocery stores. Store in airtight container away from heat and light.

UDON—Thick Japanese noodles made from wheat or corn flour. Use whole-wheat noodles as a substitute. Found in Japanese stores.

VEGETABLE OIL, COLD PRESSED—Unrefined oil that still contains its own natural preservatives, nutrients and flavor. Natural oils provide a rich source of Vitamins A, E and K as well as lecithin, which breaks down cholesterol. These oils have not been exposed to heat or chemical sin processing. I recommend safflower, sesame, peanut or olive oil be used. Unrefined soy or corn oil have so strong a flavor that they should not be used or they will cover other food flavors. The Chinese and Indonesians prefer peanut oil, while the Middle East prefers olive oil. Found in natural or health food stores as well as regular grocery stores. Many oils will say "cold-pressed," but only those which are dark, thick and have the flavor of the produce from which they were derived are truly cold-pressed, unrefined oils.

VEGETABLE OIL FOR DEEP FRYING—Peanut, sesame, safflower or soy oil are good to use for deep frying. Olive oil tends to break down under heat faster than these oils, so should not be used. Vegetable oil can be reused for deep frying several times if strained and kept refrigerated after each use. If the oil is heated past 400° it should not be reused.

VEGETABLE OIL, REFINED—A "pure" refined product of light color usually containing preservatives. "Pure" refined oil is obtained from seeds or grains by high temperatures, addition of solvents, straining and bleaching. The refined product is both nutritionless and utterly tasteless. I recommend using cold-pressed vegetable oil for all recipes in *Feast*. See *Vegetable Oil, Cold Pressed*, for further explanation.

VEGETABLE PEAR—Tropical squash used in Indonesian dishes. Has a firm, crisp flesh with a slightly fruity flavor. Found in Chinese vegetable markets. Summer squash may be substituted for it. Also, winter pears may be used in place of vegetable pears because they remain fairly firm when cooked.

VERMICELLI—See *Whole-Wheat Vermicelli*.

WASHABI POWDER—Hot green powder of the fried Japanese horseradish, *Eutrema washabi*. Makes a very hot paste when mixed with water. Used in Japanese sauces, dips, as a salad dressing and for sashimi (raw fish) and nigiri sushi (raw fish sushi). Found canned in Japanese stores. Keeps indefinitely in dry state.

WATER CHESTNUTS—The bulb of an Oriental marsh plant about the size of a walnut. Peel before using. Has a white, sweet, crisp interior which is cut into thin slices before cooking. Found fresh or canned in Chinese markets or canned in Western grocery stores. The white variety of the Jerusalem artichoke may be substituted for water chestnuts.

WATERCRESS—A member of the mustard family which grows in slowly flowing water. Watercress is high in Vitamin C, iron and iodine. It is used by the Japanese as a garnish and in some vegetable dishes. May be substituted for Chinese greens in stir-fries or salads. Has a slightly peppery flavor. Can be found in Western grocery stores and grows wild in many areas of North America.

WAX AS A PRESERVATIVE—Paraffin wax, a petroleum-based product toxic to the human body, is used as a preservative agent on many vegetables and fruits. Apples, cucumbers, green peppers, winter squash and turnips are among these that are dipped or sprayed with wax to retard water loss and thus increase shelf life. If using these vegetables or fruits in winter always peel them to remove the wax.

WHITE BEANS—Small, dried, white beans often called navy beans. Cooked and used in salads in the Middle East. Can take the place of garbanzos in Indian bean curry. Good source of minerals and whole proteins when served with grains.

WHOLE-WHEAT FLOUR—Flour made from the whole grain of wheat. Used originally by the Indian culture and many others, but white flour has come to be a status food in many Eastern cultures and has been substituted for the dark flour. *Feast* reverses the processes and uses only whole-grain flour. Usually ground from hard winter wheat, it contains both the bran and germ of the wheat berry, which are high in Vitamins E and the B complex, plus minerals and trace elements. When these are removed in white flour the remaining flour is mainly starch with little nutrition besides the few B vitamins and iron added back to "enrich" it. Whole-wheat flour also provides the body with needed roughage to aid digestion. Whole-wheat flour loses some of its nutrients with age, so should not be purchased in large quantities; better yet it should be freshly ground at home for use as needed. Store in cool, airtight container away from heat and light. Found in natural and health food stores.

WHOLE-WHEAT NOODLES—Noodles made from high-gluten, hard durum-wheat flour. Contain all the nutrients of whole-wheat flour (see *Whole-Wheat Flour* for further explanation).

WHOLE-WHEAT PASTRY FLOUR—Flour made from the whole grain of soft wheat. Low in gluten, this flour makes light pastry and doughs. Similar to white flour in action, this flour still contains all the vitamins and minerals of whole-wheat flour. See *Whole-Wheat Flour* for further explanation. Store in an airtight, cool container away from heat and light. Found in natural and health food stores.

WHOLE-WHEAT SPAGHETTI—Spaghetti noodle made from high-gluten, hard, durum-wheat flour with all the nutrients of whole grain. See *Whole-Wheat Flour* for further explanation.

WHOLE-WHEAT VERMICELLI—A thin form of whole-wheat spaghetti. Contains all the nutrients of whole-wheat flour. See *Whole-Wheat Flour* for further explanation. Used in place of thin Chinese and Indonesian noodles in *Feast*.

WINTER MELON—A large, green winter squash of melon shape with a frosty-white dust on the skin. Scrub off white powder before using and remove seeds and white pulp from the inside. Delicate soft, white interior that is almost translucent when cooked. Can be stir-fried or used in soups. Found in Chinese markets whole or in pieces.

WINTER SAVORY—A green, perennial herb easy to grow in North American gardens. Has a distinct, pungent flavor used in soups, salads and meat dishes.

WINTER SQUASH—Hubbard, banana, butternut and acorn squash all have hard skins, so keep well in the winter—thus the name. Used in place of melons and summer squash as well as pumpkin.

WOK—Concave-shaped pan used to cook all types of food in the Orient. Especially adapted to low-fuel cooking because it spreads the heat evenly over its surface. Excellent for frying quickly, simmering, steaming or deep frying. Uses very little oil because of its shape, which gives a much greater frying surface for volume of oil, so it's great for deep frying. When deep frying, simmering or steaming with a wok, always use the wok stand with it so that the wok does not tip.

WOK SPOON—Special spoon used for woks since they are shaped to fit the rounded sides and bottom of a wok. Found in Chinese, Japanese, natural foods and specialty kitchenware shops.

WOODS EAR FUNGUS—Brown, thin fungus similar to clouds ear mushrooms but larger and tougher. Have a stronger flavor than clouds ear, so if using in place of clouds ear mushrooms, do not use as much. Always soak in boiling water, wash before using and remove tough ends. Also called dried fungus in Chinese markets. Found in Chinese markets.

YELLOW BEAN SAUCE—Thick, pungent sauce made from yellow beans, salt and water. Used by Chinese and Indonesians as a flavoring. Found in Indonesian and Chinese shops. Sold in cans. Can be kept refrigerated 2 to 3 months when opened.

YOGHURT—The easiest to digest of all dairy products because the proteins have been predigested by the beneficial bacteria *Lactobacillus bulgaricus* into a thick, creamy curd. In fact yoghurt aids digestion and helps the body assimilate B vitamins as well as producing some B vitamins in the intestines. A favorite of the Middle East and India, yoghurt is used in soups, salads, sauces for meat and vegetarian main dishes and desserts. Make your own; it is easy and better for you than the commercial yoghurts, which have thickeners and preservatives added. Recipe on *pages 88-89*. If you must purchase it, go to a natural foods store to avoid additives and get really fresh yoghurt. Store in refrigerator.

NATURAL FOODS PROVISIONERS

A list of natural foods stores in North America would make a book in itself, so only mail order businesses are included in this list. The use of natural foods has become so widespread that even large supermarkets are now carrying some products and most towns have a natural foods store. I recommend as much as possible that local sources be used. To find a natural foods store in your area you might consult the following books:

Goldstein, J., and Goldman, M.C., eds., Guide to Organic Food Shopping and Organic Lining, Emmaus Pa., Rodale Books 1971.

Farmilant, Eunice, The Natural Foods Sweet-Tooth Cookbook, Doubleday and Company, Garden City, New York 1973

MAIL ORDER BUSINESSES:

UNITED STATES

Shilo Farms
Box 97
Sulphur Springs, Arizona 72768

Spiral Foods
P. O. Box 1004
Chico, California 95927

Erewhon Trading Company
8454 Steller Drive
Culver City, California 90230

Better Foods Foundation, Inc.
200 North Washington Street
Greencastle, Pennsylvania 17225

Walnut Acres
Rural Delivery
Penns Creek, Pennsylvania 17862

Janus Natural Foods
1523 Airport Way South
Seattle, Washington 98134

Basic Needs
114 West Main
Grand Prairie, Texas
(Bulk Items Only)

Arrowhead Mills
Box OG-866
Hereford, Texas 79045

ORIENTAL FOODS PROVISIONERS

An extensive list of oriental food provisioners who deal in mail orders is being included for your convenience and to show that oriental foods can be obtained throughout North America. Many of the businesses are concentrated on the West and East coasts but there are numerous ones in other parts of the continent. Many more stores are listed in telephone books available at local libraries. All of these businesses will take mail orders. Some require a minimum order and will charge a set fee for handling and shipping. If you cannot find a specific shop in your area the following types of shops will carry certain oriental items: Greek and Italian will carry Middle Eastern and Indian items; Philippine will carry some Chinese, Japanese and Indonesian; Dutch shops will carry Indonesian items; Chinese and Japanese shope will carry items that can be used in both cuisines. If you have local stores which carry oriental items use them as half the fun of cooking oriental foods is the shopping experience. Also, the cost will be less.

UNITED STATES

ALABAMA

Daleville
Toni's Oriental Grocery
Rural Route No. 2, Box 259, 36322
Japanese, Chinese

CALIFORNIA

Bellflower
Holland American Market
10343 East Artesia Boulevard, 90406
Oriental

Berkeley
Bazaar of India
1331 University Avenue, 94702
Indian, Middle Eastern

Fresno
Manukian's Basturma and Soujouk Company
International Foods
1720 South Orange Avenue, 93702
Middle Eastern, Indian

Los Angeles
Bezjian Grocery
4725 Santa Monica Boulevard, 90029
Indian

Curl's Fancy Grocery
Stall 430, Farmer's Market
Third and Fairfax, 90036
Indian

Enbun Company
248 East First Street, 90012
Japanese

Europa Grocery Company
321 South Spring, 90013
Middle Eastern

Greek Importing Company
2801 West Pico Boulevard, 90006
Middle Eastern

Ida Company
339 East First Street, 90012
Japanese

India Bazaar
10651 Pico Boulevard, 90064
Indian

Modern Food Market
318 East Second Street, 90012
Japanese

Rafu Bussan Company
344 East First Street, 90012
Japanese

Sam Ward Company, Inc.
957-961 North Hill Street, 90015
Chinese

Wing Chong Lung Company
922 South San Pedro Street, 90015
Chinese

Yee Sing Chong Company
960-961 North Hill Street, 90015
Chinese

Monterey
Three Star Market
245 Washington Street, 93940
Japanese

Oakland
G.B. Ratto and Company
International Grocers
821 Washington Street, 94607
Arabic, Indian, Indonesian

San Francisco
American Fish Market
1836 Buchanan Street, 94115
Japanese

Freed, Teller, Freed
1326 Polk Street, 94109
Middle Eastern

Haig's Delicacies
642 Clement, 94118
Indian, Indonesian, Middle Eastern

House of Coffee
1847 Irving Street, 94122
Middle Eastern

Istanbul Pastries and Imported Grocers
900 North Point, 94109
Middle Eastern

Kenson Trading Company
434 Clement Street, 94118
Oriental

Manley Produce
1101 Grant Avenue, 94133
Chinese

Oh's Fine Food
2651 Mission Street, 94110
Indian, Indonesian, Middle Eastern

Phil-Oriental Foods
738 Clement, 94118
Indonesian, Indian, Middle Eastern

Sa Kai Company
1656 Post Street, 94115
Japanese

Sang Wo and Company
867 Grant Avenue, 94108
Oriental

Shing Chong and Company
800 Grant Avenue, 94108
Chinese

Superior Trading Company
867 Washington Street, 94108
Chinese

Ti Hang Lung and Company
846 Grant Avenue, 94108
Chinese

Uoki
1656 Post Street, 94115
Japanese

Yee 0--10
725 Douglas, 94114
Chinese

San Jose
Dobashi
240 East Jackson Street
Japanese   95112

Nishioka Fish Market
665 North Sixth Street, 95112
Japanese

San Mateo
Takahashi Company
221 South Claremont Avenue, 94401
Japanese

Temple City
The Hollinda Company
9544 Las Tunas Drive, 91780
Indonesian

COLORADO

Denver
American Tea, Coffee and Spice Company
1511 Champa Street, 80202
Indian

Granada Fish Market
1919 Lawrence Street, 80202
Oriental

Pacific Mercantile Company
1946 Larimie Street, 80202
Japanese

**DISTRICT OF COLUMBIA,
WASHINGTON**

House of Nanna
1468 'T' Street Northwest, 20009
Japanese

Mee Wah Lung Company
608 'H' Street Northwest, 20001
Chinese

Mikado
4709 Wisconsin Avenue, Northwest, 20016
Japanese

FLORIDA

Miami
Greek American Grocery Company
2690 Coral Way, 33145
Middle Eastern, some Indian

Tropi Pac Food Products
3664 North West 48th Street, 33142
Japanese

Orlando
Oriental Imports
54 North Orange Avenue, 32801
Japanese

Tampa
Schiller's Delicatessen
3411 South Manhattan Avenue, 33609
Japanese

GEORGIA

Columbus
Sachi's Japanese Restaurant Market
3838 Cusseta Road, 31903
Japanese

ILLINOIS

Berwyn
Holland Dutch
6911 West Roosevelt Road, 60402
Indonesian

Champaign
Ginza and Company
315 East University, 61820
Japanese

Chicago
Franklin Food Store
1309 East 53rd Street, 60615
Japanese

Kam Shing Company
2246 South Wentworth Street, 60616
Chinese

Red and Blue Company
2247 Wentworth Avenue, 60616
Chinese

Shiroma
1058 West Argyle, 60640
Oriental

Star Market
3349 North Clark Street, 60657
Chinese

Toguri Mercantile Company
5358 North Clark Street, 60640
Japanese

S. Y I Grocery
1058 West Argyle Street, 60640
Japanese

York Super Foods
3240 North Clark Street, 60657
Japanese

Peoria
World Foods and Drug
312 Adams Street, 61602
Japanese

Waukegan
White Hen Pantry
150 Gold Road, 60085
Japanese

INDIANA

Elkhart
Wilt's Food Center
100 Easy Shopping Center, 46514
Japanese

Kokomo
Fuji Oriental Food and Gift
1401 East Markland Avenue, 46901
Japanese

West Lafayette
Smitty's Foodliner
1812 Northwestern Avenue, 47906
Japanese

KANSAS

Junction City
Jade East Store
1030 Grant Avenue, 66441
Japanese

Wichita
Imported Foods
1038 McCormick, 67213
Japanese

LOUISIANA

Metairie
Oriental Trading Company
2636 Edenborn Avenue 70002
Japanese

New Orleans
Central Grocery
923 Decatur, 70116
Indian

Chinese American Company
719 Royal Street, 70116
Oriental

Progress Grocery
915 Decatur, 70116
Indian, Middle Eastern

MASSACHUSETTS

Boston
S. S. Pierce
133 Brookline Avenue, 02215
Indian

Wing Wing Imported Groceries
79 Harrison Avenue, 02111
Chinese

Cambridge
Cambridge Coffee, Tea and Spice House
1765 Massachusets Avenue, 02140
Oriental, Indian

Cardullo Gourmet Shop
6 Brattle Street, 02138
Oriental, Middle Eastern, Indian

Legal Sea Foods Market
237 Hampshire Street, 02139
Chinese

Sage's Market
60 Church Street, 02138
Indian

Yoshinoya
36 Prospect Street, 02139
Japanese

MICHIGAN

Birmingham
Kado's Oriental Imports
251 Merrill, 48011
Japanese

Detroit
Delmar and Company
501 Monroe Avenue, 48226
Indian

Gabriel Importing Company
2461 Russell Street, 48207
Indian

Kuwahara Trading Post
3126 Cass Avenue, 48201
Japanese

Wah Lee Company
3409 Cass Avenue, 48201
Oriental and Indonesian

East Lansing
Goodrich's Spartan Shop
940 Trowbridge Road, 48823
Japanese

Southfield
Mt. Fuji Oriental Foods
22040 West 10 Mile Road, 48075
Japanese

American Oriental Grocery
2076 Lahser Road, 48075
Middle Eastern, Indian

MINNESOTA

Minneapolis
International House
712 Washington Avenue, South East, 55414
Japanese

MISSOURI

Kansas City
Aloha Enterprises
1741 Swope Parkway, 63110
Japanese

St. Louis
Asia Food Products
1509 Delmar Boulevard, 63103
Oriental and Indonesian

Italo-American Importing Company
512 Franklin Avenue, 63101
Middle Eastern

Maruyama's
100 North 18th Street, 63103
Japanese

NEBRASKA

Omaha
Oriental Trading Company
1115 Farnam Street, 68102
Japanese

NEVADA

Reno
Terry's Oriental Gift Shop
and Imports
120 West Second Street, 89501
Japanese

NEW JERSEY

Browns Mills
Haruko's Oriental Bazaar
Route No. 3, Box 3143, 08015
Japanese

West New York
Mr. Jack Wittkamp
320 West 50th Street, 07093
Indonesian

NEW YORK

Brooklyn
George Malko
185 Atlantic Avenue, 11201
Indian

Sahadi Importing Company, Inc.
187 Atlantic Avenue, 11201
Indian, Arabic

Chatham
Pacific Trader
12037
Chinese

Jamaica
Nippon Do
82-69 Parsons Boulevard, 11432
Japanese

New York City
Eastern Trading Company
2801 Broadway, 10025
Chinese

Japanese Foodland
2620 Broadway, 10023
Japanese

Japan Mart, Incorporated
239 West 105th Street, 10025
Japanese

Kalustyan Orient Export Trading
Corporation
123 Lexington Avneue, 10016
Middle Eastern, Indian

Katagiri Company
224 East 59th Street, 10022
Japanese

M. Kehayan
380 Third Avenue, 10016
Indian

Oriental Food Shop
1302 Amsterdam Avenue, 10027
Chinese

Tanaka and Company
326 Amsterdam Avenue, 10023
Japanese

Toko Garuda
997 First Avenue, 10022
Indonesian

Trinacria Importing Company
415 Third Avenue, 10016
Oriental, Middle Eastern, Indian

Yuet Hing Market Inc.
23 Pell Street, 10013
Chinese

NORTH CAROLINA

Jacksonville
Oriental Market
307 Marine Boulevard, 28540
Japanese

Spring Lake
Oriental Food Shop
P. O. Box 202 (North Main Street)
Japanese   28390

OHIO

Cincinnati
Soya Food Products
2356 Wyoming Street, 45214
Japanese

Cleveland
Omura Japanese Food and Gift Shop
3811 Payne Avenue, 44114
Japanese

Columbus
Ida Oriental Foods and Gift
614 Yearling Road, 43213
Japanese

Dayton
Dayton Oriental Food
812 Xenia Avenue, 45410
Japanese

OKLAHOMA

Lawton
Takara Oriental Foods
2012 Cache Road, 73501
Japanese

Tulsa
Antone's
2606 Sheridan, 74129
Indian

OREGON

Ontario
Soy Bean Products
P. O. Box 568 (336 South West 5th Street)
97914
Japanese

Portland
Anzen Importers
736 North East Union Avenue, 97232
Japanese

PENNSYLVANIA

Bangor
Mrs. De Wildt
245A Fox Gap Road, 18013
Indonesian

SOUTH DAKOTA

Rapid City
Black Hills Staple and Spice Company
Old Time Food Market
601 Mt. Rushmore Road, 57701
Middle Eastern and Indian

TEXAS

El Paso
Plaza Grocery
425 South El Paso, 79901
Oriental

Tachibana's
4886 Hercules, 79904
Japanese, Indonesian, Indian, Middle Eastern

Houston
Antone's
Box 3352, 77001
Oriental, Middle Eastern, Indian

Chinese Food Products Company
1119 Jackson Street 77003
Oriental

India Foods Inc.
3820 South Shepherd Drive, 77098
Indian, Middle Eastern

Jamail's
3114 Kirby Drive, 77006
Indian

Oriental Import-Export Company
2009 Polk Street, 77002
Chinese

Oversea Import Company
1103 Chartres, 77003
Chinese, Japanese

Samperi's
430 Almeda Mall
430 Northwest Mall, 77017
Indian

San Antonio
Arirang Oriental Foods and Gifts
2150 Austin Highway, 78218
Japanese, Indonesian

Paletta's Imported Foods
202 Recoleta, 78216
Middle Eastern, Indian

UTAH

Ogden
Yamaguchi and Company
260 25th Street, 84401
Japanese

Salt Lake City
Sage Farm Market
52 West First Street South, 84101
Japanese

WASHINGTON

Seattle
Angelo Merlino and Sons
816 Sixth Avenue South, 98134
Middle Eastern

House of Rice
4112 University Way North East, 98105
Japanese, Indian, Indonesian, Arabic,
Chinese, Middle Eastern

Uwajimaya Inc.
422 South Main Street, 98104
Japanese

Wah Young Company
717 King Street, 98104
Oriental

Spokane
North Coast Supply
West 27 Main Street, 99201
Japanese, Chinese

R and R Market
Ninth and Hatch, 99202
Chinese, Japanese

WISCONSIN

Madison
Indian Grocery and Spices
4807 West North Avenue, 53713
Indian

Topitzes, James W. and Sons
Foods of All Nations
4401 West Lisbon Avenue
Chinese, Japanese, Indian, Indonesian
Middle Eastern

Milwaukee
Oriental Grocery and Gifts
821 North 27th Street, 53208
Japanese